PEOPLE IN ORGANIZATIONS UNDERSTANDING THEIR BEHAVIOR

McGraw-Hill Series in Management

Keith Davis and Fred Luthans, Consulting Editors

Allen Management and Organization

Allen The Management Profession

Argyris Management and Organizational Development: The Path from XA to YB

Beckett Management Dynamics: The New Synthesis

Benton Supervision and Management

Bergen and Haney Organizational Relations and Management Action

Blough International Business: Environment and Adaptation

Bowman Management: Organization and Planning

Brown Judgment in Administration

Buchele The Management of Business and Public Organizations

Campbell, Dunnette, Lawler, and Weick Managerial Behavior, Performance, and Effectiveness

Cleland and King Management: A Systems Approach

Cleland and King Systems Analysis and Project Management

Cleland and King Systems, Organizations, Analysis, Management: A Book of Readings

Dale Management: Theory and Practice

Dale Readings in Management: Landmarks and New Frontiers

Davis Human Behavior at Work: Organizational Behavior

Davis Organizational Behavior: A Book of Readings

Davis and Blomstrom Business and Society: Environment and Responsibility

DeGreen Systems Psychology

Dunn and Rachel Wage and Salary Administration: Total Compensation Systems

Dunn and Stephens Management of Personnel: Manpower Management and Organizational Behavior

Edmunds and Letey Environmental Administration

Fiedler A Theory of Leadership Effectiveness

Finch, Jones, and Litterer Managing for Organizational Effectiveness: An Experiential Approach

Flippo Principles of Personnel Management

Glueck Business Policy: Strategy Formation and Management Action

Glueck Readings in Business Policy from *Business Week*

Hampton Contemporary Management

Hicks and Gullett The Management of Organizations

Hicks and Gullett Modern Business Management: A Systems and Environmental Approach

Hicks and Gullett Organizations: Theory and Behavior

Johnson, Kast, and Rosenzweig The Theory and Management of Systems

Kast and Rosenzweig Experiential Exercises and Cases in Management

Kast and Rosenzweig Organization and Management: A Systems Approach

Knudson, Woodworth, and Bell Management: An Experiential Approach

Koontz Toward a Unified Theory of Management

Koontz and O'Donnell Essentials of Management

Koontz and O'Donnell Management: A Book of Readings

Koontz and O'Donnell Management: A Systems and Contingency Analysis of Managerial Functions

Lee and Dobler Purchasing and Materials Management: Text and Cases

Levin, McLaughlin, Lamone, and Kottas Production/Operations Management: Contemporary Policy for Managing Operating Systems

Luthans Contemporary Readings in Organizational Behavior

Luthans Introduction to Management: A Contingency Approach

Luthans Organizational Behavior

McNichols Policymaking and Executive Action

Maier Problem-solving Discussions and Conferences: Leadership Methods and Skills

Margulies and Raia Conceptual Foundations of Organizational Development

Margulies and Raia Organizational Development: Values, Process, and Technology

Mayer Production and Operations Management

Miles Theories of Management: Implications for Organizational Behavior and Development

Miles and Snow Organizational Strategy: Structure and Process

Mills Labor-Management Relations

Mitchell People in Organizations: Understanding Their Behavior

Monks Operations Management: Theory and Problems

Mundel A Conceptual Framework for the Management Sciences

Newstrom, Reif, and Monczka A Contingency Approach to Management: Readings

Petit The Moral Crisis in Management

Petrof, Carusone, and McDavid Small Business Management: Concepts and Techniques for Improving Decisions

Porter, Lawler, and Hackman Behavior in Organizations

Prasow and Peters Arbitration and Collective Bargaining: Conflict Resolution in Labor Relations

Ready The Administrator's Job

Reddin Managerial Effectiveness

Richman and Copen International Management and Economic Development

Sartain and Baker The Supervisor and the Job

Schrieber, Johnson, Meier, Fischer, and Newell Cases in Manufacturing Management

Shore Operations Management

Shull, Delbecq, and Cummings Organizational Decision Making

Steers and Porter Motivation and Work Behavior

Sutermeister People and Productivity

Tannenbaum, Weschler, and Massarik Leadership and Organization

Wofford, Gerloff, and Cummins Organizational Communications: The Keystone to Managerial Effectiveness

McGraw-Hill Book Company

New York   St. Louis   San Francisco   Auckland   Bogotá   Düsseldorf
Johannesburg   London   Madrid   Mexico   Montreal   New Delhi
Panama   Paris   São Paulo   Singapore   Sydney   Tokyo   Toronto

PEOPLE IN ORGANIZATIONS
UNDERSTANDING THEIR BEHAVIOR

TERENCE R. MITCHELL
Professor of Management and Organization
and Professor of Psychology
University of Washington

People in Organizations: Understanding Their Behavior

1234567890   VHVH   78321098

This book was set in Times Roman by University Graphics, Inc.
The editors were William J. Kane and Anne T. Vinnicombe; the designer
was Hermann Strohbach; the production supervisor was Dominick Petrellese.
The drawings were done by J & R Services, Inc. The cartoons were
drawn by Christina A. Romano.
Von Hoffmann Press, Inc., was printer and binder.

Library of Congress Cataloging in Publication Data

Mitchell, Terence R
    People in organizations.

    (McGraw-Hill series in management)
    Includes bibliographies and index.
    1. Management. 2. Organization. 3. Organizational
behavior. 4. Industrial relations. I. Title.
HD31.M478   658.3   77-24756
ISBN 0-07-042530-2

To the three ladies of my life
and the laughing gull.

CONTENTS

Preface   xiii

PART ONE
FOUNDATIONS

Chapter 1
Introduction   3

The field of organizational behavior   3
Format of the text   4
Underlying philosophy   5
Content and outline   6

Chapter 2
Organization theory   9

Organizations and rationality   9
Background   14
Classical theory   16
Human-relations approach   20
Systems theory   24
Contingency approaches   27
Summary   33
Implications for practice   34
Discussion questions   34
Case: Starting a new division   35
Additional readings   36   **ix**

Chapter 3
Understanding human behavior   38

The uniqueness of human beings   39
The continuity of growth   43
Internal versus external determinants
    of behavior   45
Human limitations   48
Understanding behavior: Learning   49
Learning in the social setting   52
Summary   54
Implications for practice   55
Discussion questions   56
Case: Learning about booze   56
Additional readings   57

Chapter 4
Research foundations   59

Conceptual research issues   60
The scientific method   61
Types of research   66
Research design   70
Participation in an experiment   79
Summary   85
Implications for practice   85
Discussion questions   86
Case: Did the training work?   86
Additional readings   87

PART TWO
INDIVIDUAL CHARACTERISTICS

Chapter 5
Perception and personality   91

Perception   91
Person perception   95
Personality   105
Personality and behavior   108
Summary   113
Implications for practice   114
Discussion questions   115
Case: The main manipulator   115
Additional readings   116

Chapter 6
Attitudes   118

Definition   118
Background   119
Attitude organization and dynamics   125
Attitude change   131

Attitudes and the world of work   136
Summary   143
Implications for practice   144
Discussion questions   145
Case: Morale and malaise   146
Additional readings   146

Chapter 7
Motivation   148

Basic background   149
Motivation in organizations   151
Theories of motivational arousal   153
Theories of motivated choice   160
Summary   169
Implications for practice   170
Discussion questions   171
Case: Pushing papers can be fun   171
Additional readings   172

PART THREE
SOCIAL PROCESSES

Chapter 8
Group dynamics   175

What is the small group   175
Individuals and groups   176
An overview of group variables   180
Group inputs: Personal characteristics   183
Group inputs: Situational variables   183
Group inputs: Group structure   190
Summary   200
Implications for practice   201
Discussion questions   202
Case: The holdout   202
Additional readings   203

Chapter 9
Communication   205

A communication model   206
Blocks to effective communication   216
The external environment   219
Some remedies for poor
    communication   223
Summary   224
Implications for practice   225
Discussion questions   225
Case: On being informed and being well
    informed   226
Additional readings   227

Chapter 10
Roles, norms, and status   228

Role relationships   230
Norms   237
Status   242
Summary   249
Implications for practice   249
Discussion questions   250
Case: From the diaries and letters of
    President Truman   250
Additional readings   252

PART FOUR
ACCOMPLISHING ORGANIZATIONAL OBJECTS

Chapter 11
Decision making   255

The decision-making process   255
Individual decision making   258
Decision making in groups   268
Summary   275
Implications for practice   276
Discussion questions   278
Case: To go or to stay—that is the
    question   278
Additional readings   279

Chapter 12
Power and control   280

Social power   281
Power in use   284
Control systems   292
Summary   302
Implications for practice   303
Discussion questions   304
Case: Obedient Betty   304
Additional readings   305

Chapter 13
Leadership   306

Definitions of leadership   306
Leadership emergence   307
Trait approach   309
Behavior approach   311
Functional approach   313
Contingency approaches   314
Summary   321
Implications for practice   322
Discussion questions   322
Case: Will the leader please stand up   323
Additional readings   324

PART FIVE
INDIVIDUAL AND ORGANIZATIONAL EFFECTIVENESS

Chapter 14
Employee performance   327

Determinants of performance   327
Selection   331
Performance appraisal   340
System of rewards   347
Summary   351
Implications for practice   352
Discussion questions   352
Case: Affirmative action in action   352
Additional readings   354

Chapter 15
Training and development   355

Training defined   356
Training programs   361
Evaluation   373
Summary   378
Implications for practice   379
Discussion questions   380
Case: The popular panacea   380
Additional readings   380

Chapter 16
Organizational change   382

Perspectives on change   383
The change process   386
Organization development   390
Organizational change techniques   394
Problems in changing organizations   406
Summary   409
Implications for practice   410
Discussion questions   411
Case: Implementing change   411
Additional readings   412

PART SIX
CURRENT TOPICS

Chapter 17
Political support   417

Rationality   417
The distribution of power   421
Some determinants of due process:
    Differentiation and integration,
    political concerns   430
Governance models   434

Summary 439
Implications for practice 439
Discussion questions 440
Case: The end of the line 440
Additional readings 441

Chapter 18
Organizational outlook 442

Areas of change 443
Current problems 454

Some possible solutions 459
General reassessment 462
Summary 463
Implications for practice
Discussion questions 464
Case: Knowledge as fuel 464
Additional readings 466

Indexes 467
  Name Index
  Subject Index

PREFACE

Upon completion of a textbook such as this, there is a great sense of both accomplishment and relief. It is a good feeling to be *done.*

Besides these very personal feelings, there are a couple of professional conclusions as well. First, after reviewing all the material that went into the book (or was screened out), one cannot help but learn some new things and gain new perspectives. In that sense, it has truly been a learning experience for me.

A second conclusion that reflects professional issues has to do with the productivity of our field. The sheer amount of literature is immense, and most of it is of high quality. People in the field of organizational behavior should be proud of their accomplishments. We have come a long way.

I have also been struck by the amount of joint activity that went into the production of the book. People have helped me in all stages of preparation and production of the manuscript. At a very broad level, I would like to thank those people who have been particularly helpful and stimulating throughout my career. Fred Fiedler, Bill Scott, and Lee Beach at the University of Washington; Harry Triandis, Don Dulany, and Martin Fishbein at the University of Illinois; and Uriel Foa at Temple University have all helped to shape my thinking about our field. With respect to the preparation of the book, I am particularly indebted to Fred Luthans at the University of Nebraska and his critical reviews of the manuscript. David Van Fleet at Texas A&M, Larry Michaelson at the University of Oklahoma, Lincoln Deihl at Eastern Michigan University, and Dennis Moberg at the University of Santa Clara also provided helpful comments. Christina A. Romano drew the cartoons, and Sandra Goodman, Mabel Vassey, Shirley Yackey, and Wendy Day helped on the typing of the manuscript. Their assistance is greatly appreciated. Finally, I would like to thank my wife Sandra, who managed in the last 18 months to finish her own Ph.D., have a baby, sell a house, move three times, sell a car, buy a car, type substantial portions of the book, and still be a loving and supportive wife and mother.

Terence R. Mitchell

ONE

FOUNDATIONS

A central theme of this book is that individuals' behavior is jointly caused by their own personal characteristics and the setting in which they find themselves. Since our interest is in the area of organizational behavior, we will focus upon the organizational setting. Empirical research has uncovered some general rules or relationships that predict this behavior, and we will review these findings.

However, before we can begin any sort of thorough coverage of these topics, we must lay the foundation for the rest of the book. In order to understand people's behavior in organizations, we must know more about (1) organizations—how they are formed, persist, and are designed; (2) people—what is known about the nature of human beings; and (3) research methods—how we can go about discovering rules and relationships in the organizational setting. That is, in order to fully comprehend the principles of organizational behavior, we must know more about the process by which these principles were discovered (research methods) and the two components that constitute the principles (people and organizations). Part 1 is designed to cover these issues.

The introduction (Chapter 1) is meant to give you some insight into my biases and goals. In short, the purpose of this book is not so much to provide answers but to learn how to ask the right questions. The first chapter also provides the rationale for the structure of the book. The philosophical and structural foundations help to set the scene for the substantive topics which follow.

Chapter 2 provides a survey of organization theory. The reasons for organizing and the common characteristics of most organizations are described. Some of the problems of current organizations, such as size and complexity, are discussed. An historical summary of the development of organizations and their role in society comes next. Finally, the major approaches to how organizations should be designed are presented and evaluated.

Chapter 3 turns its attention to the basic principles of human nature. We start out by discussing some important philosophical and empirical questions such as: Are humans a unique species? What is our capacity for change? To what extent is our behavior externally caused (e.g., our behavior is regulated by the situation) or internally caused (e.g., our behavior is regulated by internal processes such as instincts or personality traits). In general, we conclude that people are unique, are capable of great change, and are clearly influenced by their environment. We then discuss in some detail the major mechanism of change: learning. Particular emphasis is placed on learning in the organizational setting.

Chapter 4 provides an overview of some important research principles. The process by which research is done is described. Emphasis is placed on the empirical and impartial nature of this process. Some poor research designs are criticized and some good ones presented as alternatives. The major goal of a good research design is to unambiguously answer the question under investigation. The chapter closes with a discussion of the ethical conduct of researchers in organizations.

1
Introduction

---

*Knowledge is the only instrument of production
that is not subject to diminishing returns.*   J. M. Clark

Before proceeding into the more substantive content of this text, the reader should be aware of the book's educational objectives, its structure, and its philosophical underpinnings. *People in Organizations* was written with four major goals in mind. First, it is meant to be a review book. It provides an overview or survey of the field. Second, it is designed to be easy and enjoyable to read. Both the language and format emphasize this goal. Third, the underlying philosophy is optimistic. Organizations can be productive and satisfying places for people to work. And fourth, the content is meaningfully organized. Later chapters build on the material presented in earlier chapters. The purpose of this first chapter is to discuss these four goals in more detail. It provides the foundation for the rest of the book.

The field of organizational behavior

Historically, most universities, colleges, and junior colleges had only one introductory business course with a behavioral emphasis. This course might include some theory, research, and management principles. In recent years, however, these content areas have become more distinct, and many schools may have separate courses for principles of management, personnel, organization theory, and organizational behavior.

This last topic (called OB) has begun to develop a clear identity. In general, the field of organizational behavior covers two main substantive areas: (1) the causes of human behavior (alone and in groups) and (2) how this knowledge can be used to help people be more productive and satisfied in the organizational setting. The focus is on individuals and groups, the principles are usually based upon empirical research, and there is a definite applied orientation.

3

There seems to be increasing agreement about the above definition. This agreement is partly reflected in the content of the professional journals, the training of people in the professional associations, and the courses being offered in business schools and psychology departments.

Some examples might help. For many years, *The Academy of Management Journal* published papers covering the broad spectrum of management thought. Research and theory papers were included on topics that were quite varied in their emphasis. However, in 1975 the *Journal* split into two publications: *The Academy of Management Review* and *The Academy of Management Journal*. The *Review* publishes theoretical papers, review papers, or "think pieces." The new *Journal* publishes empirical research only. Most of these empirical pieces deal with individual and group behavior and would be included in our definition of OB.

This increased emphasis on research-based behavioral material is partly attributable to the kinds of people teaching OB courses and practicing OB in the field. Over the last 15 years, the field of psychology, which is very research oriented, has played an important role in this regard. The fields of social and industrial psychology have become more applied in their orientation and broader in their concerns. For example, Division 14 of the American Psychological Association used to be called the Division of Industrial Psychology. Industrial psychology traditionally meant the topics covered in the areas of personnel: selection, placement, training, and performance appraisal. In the last few years, however, Division 14 has changed its name to the Division of Industrial and Organizational Psychology. This change was meant to reflect and encourage broader interests in the field.

Also, because of the recession and changing interests, psychologists sought out and were eagerly received by business schools. Apparently this movement has been satisfying to both parties. Many professionals in the management area have found the material from psychology to be useful to their teaching, research, and practice. And the psychologists seem to have thrived as well. Many of the leaders in the OB field have had some training in psychology.

The result of this type of cross fertilization is that OB has (1) maintained its organizational and applied orientation from its management roots and (2) increased its emphasis on empirical behavioral research as a reflection of the infusion of psychologists and their ideas.

However, many of the textbooks in the field of organizational behavior do not reflect these changes. They still put under the heading of OB many of the traditional principles of management or organization-theory literature. *People in Organizations* was written to avoid this problem. It is an *empirically based review* of what we know about *individual* and *group behavior* in organizational settings and how this knowledge can be *applied* to increase the *effectiveness* and *satisfaction* of organizational participants.

Format of the text

A second goal in writing the book was to produce a text that students could enjoy and learn from at the same time. The book is designed to be a learning tool. It is not a review of the author's research, a treatise supporting one orientation or another, or an attempt to change or modify the direction of the field.

With this goal in mind, the following things were done. First, the writing style is short, concise, and to the point. There has been a systematic attempt to remove jargon. While there is heavy emphasis on being precise about what we mean when we use certain terms, this precision is not gained by adding new confusing words to your vocabulary.

Another indication of this orientation is the absence of lots of names, references, and specific studies in the body of the text. The memorization of names has little to do with the understanding of ideas. It is ideas and principles that one should take away from this book.

But one should not think that because these names and studies are missing that the content is based on speculation or that it is easy to assimilate. The ideas and principles discussed in many cases will require considerable effort by the reader to understand. The book, while written simply, is meant to be challenging intellectually.

Almost all the ideas are based upon summaries of empirical research. The research is cited in footnotes and at the end of each chapter in an "Additional Readings" section. Those who are interested in pursuing some topic in more detail or verifying the basis for statements made in the chapters can easily do so using the references provided.

Finally, besides these attempts to emphasize ideas over jargon and substance over detail, there is an attempt to make the text pleasant to read and applicable to the student's experience. Numerous stories or episodes that illustrate a point are provided. There is a "Case" at the end of each chapter which serves a similar purpose. And there are cartoons, quotations, photographs, and advertisements which recognize or capture a point through the use of another media or perspective.

To help in the learning process, there are summaries at the end of each chapter which cover the major points discussed. Along with these summaries are some discussion questions to direct your thinking about the topic and a section on how these ideas could be applied in the organizational setting. In short, everything has been done to make the text a pleasant experience for the reader without sacrificing the integrity of the material.

Underlying philosophy

No textbook can be written without some of the author's biases being present. Some material is selected to be included and some is not; some people or theories are discussed and some are not. *People in Organizations* is no different in this regard.

However, in the following paragraphs some of these biases are openly discussed. In this way the student or professor can be aware of the philosophical premise on which the text is based. This knowledge allows the reader to place the material in its proper perspective.

One initial issue to discuss is the author's perception of the responsibilities of the textbook writer. As alluded to earlier, this book is not seen as an attempt to reflect the author's ideas or research orientation. Rather, it is an attempt to integrate and organize existing material. Where the author's experience or research is discussed, it is because this experience illustrates well a particular point. But in general, the author's role is as reviewer and organizer, not innovator.

A second underlying bias is the optimistic tone of the text. In Chapter 4, "Understanding Human Behavior," and in other discussions throughout the text, the point is made that humans have a great capacity for change. Some of our behavior is under our own control and some is influenced by the environment. Thus, both individuals and the social institutions in which they work can change behavior.

The obvious conclusion of such optimism is that organizations can be more enriching and satisfying places to work than they are currently. The responsibility for such changes is joint. Both individuals and organizations must work to raise the quality of life at work.

The final point to make about the general orientation of the book is with regard to its practical implications. This text is not designed to give the reader answers or solutions to specific organizational problems. Its purpose is to describe how one might go about trying to solve the problems which arise. The emphasis is on telling you how to properly *diagnose* situations.

If you are faced with a problem of low employee morale or poor leadership performance, the answer is not to give everyone a raise or to send all your leaders to some type of training. First you must discover more about the problem. What is it that people find dissatisfying? Are technical or communication problems the cause of the poor performance? If you understand the problem *and* you understand the basic principles of human behavior, then you can begin to think about solutions. Once the real problem is known, the solution is usually available.

Content and outline

It is often difficult for students to figure out why chapters appear in a text where they do. The particular order of the material is often a mystery. The rationale presented below is designed to at least inform you of the logical basis used for structuring *People in Organizations*.

First the assumption was made that if one wants to understand human behavior in organizations, one must be exposed to some information about (1) human behavior, (2) the organizational environment, and (3) the process by which this knowledge is gained. The first section of the book reviews these topics. Chapter 2 discusses the ways in which organizations have been designed and the underlying assumptions made about human behavior inherent in these designs. Chapter 3 discusses some principles of human behavior—why humans are a unique and changeable species. Chapter 4 presents some information about the research process. Understanding how good research is done can help the reader to critically evaluate and understand much of what follows.

The second set of chapters (Part 2) is designed to investigate *individual* behavior in more detail. What does the human being bring to the organization? What is unique about that person? Chapter 5 discusses the topics of perception and personality and Chapter 6 discusses attitudes. Chapter 7, on motivation, is in many ways the foundation for the rest of the book. Its focus is on why people choose to do what they do—what motivates them.

Part 3 switches its focus to the *social environment*. The emphasis is on how the individual behaves when dealing with others. Chapter 8 provides an overview of groups—how they form and develop and their strong and weak points. Chapter 9 discusses the communication process and how it can be more effective. Chapter 10 focuses on three ways in which an individual learns what behavior is expected and rewarded in the social setting, that is, through norms, roles, and status differences.

Once we have a firm understanding about why people behave the way they do, alone and in groups, we can begin to discuss how to use this knowledge to change people's behavior and increase effectiveness. We can discuss how we *get things done* in the organizational setting. Part 4 covers this topic. Chapter 11 describes the decision-making process and ways it can be done effectively. Chapters 12 and 13 focus on ways to change peoples' behavior through the use of power and control or through the use of leadership.

Part 5 also emphasizes change but from a somewhat different perspective. While Part 4 covers change as a result of individual or interpersonal action, Part 5 discusses ways in which an organization through its personnel policies and general approach to institutional change can *increase organizational effectiveness*. Chapter 14 deals with the classical functions of personnel—selection, placement, performance appraisal, and rewards—while Chapter 15 discusses training and development. Chapter 16 presents a number of general strategies of organizational change designed to increase effectiveness.

Thus Parts 1 through 3 really provide background and understanding while

Figure 1-1. Outline of the text.

Parts 4 and 5 focus on ways to change behavior and increase effectiveness. Finally, Part 6 is meant to look forward, to anticipate *future perspectives and problems*. Chapter 17 takes the position that organizations are more and more becoming political arenas. The implications of such changes may have a profound impact on our definition of the effective organization. The last chapter (Chapter 18) discusses the general political, social, and economic conditions that are causing problems in today's organizations (e.g., strikes, drug abuse, theft) and makes some projections about the future.

A summary of the outline of the book is presented in Figure 1-1. Part 1 gives an overview, Parts 2 and 3 describe the causes of behavior, Parts 4 and 5 focus on behavioral and organizational change, and Part 6 predicts the future. The topics are arranged from an individual analysis to an aggregate analysis and from static understanding to introducing change. The materials in later sections utilize principles discussed earlier in the text. While other progressions or structures are obviously possible, this one seemed logical and easy to understand. It is hoped that it will help to increase your understanding of behavior in organizations.

2

Organization theory

A formal organization is a system of coordinated
activities of a group of people working cooperatively
toward a common goal under authority and leadership.   W. G. Scott

While the focus of this book is meant to be the individual's behavior, it is
necessary to understand the organizational setting in which that behavior occurs.
The purpose of this early chapter is to provide a general overview of theoretical
positions that apply to the total organization and how it should be designed. More
specifically, we are interested in the basic underlying philosophies about why
organizations exist, why they are supported, and how they can be effective. To
comprehend these broad views, we must first discuss some basic definitional
issues and describe the historical perspective in which these approaches evolved.

Organizations and rationality

Our society is an organizational society. The activities that surround our birth,
education, work, leisure, spiritual growth, and death are frequently regulated or
influenced by an organizational environment. The hospital, school, workplace,
church, and gym may be the locations where most of us spend a considerable
portion of our lives. In order to understand why people behave the way they do
within these settings, we must understand more about the settings themselves.
    Probably the first question that one would ask is why do organizations exist at
all. How did they come to be? Why have they grown in size and number? The
answers to most of these questions can be expressed in economic and rational
terms. In most cases, people bound together and joined forces in order to gain
some sort of physical, personal, or economic advantage. Historically, the specific reasons for organizing have varied widely from military might or safety to
reasons of affiliation, trade, or agricultural bounty. The underlying premise,

however, was the same: People organized because they believed it was the most successful way to reach their goals.

Thus, most organizational theorists ascribe to the *principle of rationality:* Organizations are designed and exist to facilitate the attainment of objectives. The major components of this principle are (1) the process of organizing, (2) the identification of goals, (3) the proper management of resources to reach these goals, and (4) the value orientation that goal attainment is a good thing. We discuss these elements below.

Organization

The term *organization* implies a number of things. For example, it is often seen as synonymous with words such as "structured" or "directed." There is also the implication that organization is somehow the opposite of chaos.

Observation of most organizations would support these interpretations. There are rules and regulations. There are goals and objectives. There are charts which describe who talks to whom, and lines of command are clearly described. There are people doing different tasks that are coordinated and integrated. To be organized is to be directed. It should be made clear that in the process of organizing, people are usually asked to relinquish some individual flexibility and freedom in order to attain other sorts of benefits for themselves, society, or some other aggregate of people. The central aspects of successful organizing are goals and management.

Getting organized is a central principle for any group.

Goals and goal setting

You will recall that part of the definition of an organization was people working together toward a common goal. These goals are typically defined as the aspirations of the organizational participants. In earlier times, when organizations were somewhat smaller and less complex, it was fairly easy to find out what these goals were. In many cases, today, these goals may be more difficult to define. They still serve, however, to bind people together.

Besides the function of serving as a common bond, goals may also serve as a standard of evaluation. In many cases, organizational effectiveness is defined as the extent to which goals have been attained. And at the individual level there is a whole body of research that uses personal goal attainment as a method of performance appraisal. So, goals can be seen as both a unifying force and a standard for effective performance.

Management

The process of management involves the coordination of human and material resources toward the accomplishment of certain objectives or goals. Since almost every organization has a division of labor, we are faced with situations where different people are doing different jobs. They need different physical and informational resources at different times to accomplish their tasks. The responsibility of the manager is to coordinate, regulate, and integrate all these activities so that the goal is accomplished efficiently and on time.

For example, let us look at the job of a manager of a shipping company. In the process of moving freight from one place to another there are numerous operations. Packages must be taken in, they must be packed, and they must be shipped. Time schedules have to be established, and clerical help is needed to keep the records straight. Truck drivers are needed as well as a maintenance staff to take care of the trucks. Phone operators, receptionists, filing clerks, and numerous other types of jobs need to be filled. Somehow, the manager has to keep track of all these operations and know who the people are on whom he or she can depend.

Thus, the manager must know both technical aspects and behavioral aspects of the job. Coordination is done through people, and it requires a firm knowledge of what motivates people to behave in a particular way. It is only within the last hundred years, in fact, that we have formally recognized management as a special role in and of itself. As organizations have become more complex, the role of the manager has become increasingly vital to organizational success.

Values

All the elements discussed above (e.g., rationality, organization, goals, and management) reflect a rational means-ends *value* orientation. The efficiency imperative suggests that we minimize inputs and maximize outputs. We are exhorted to higher levels of performance. The central value is technical efficiency, and it is held by almost all political or economic systems. Organizations should be run so that resources, science, and technology will expand the wealth, might, and well-being of a nation.

This value orientation of our particular society also has become a state of mind. How many times have you heard someone say, "If our country could send a man to the moon, it can certainly solve the energy crisis. All we need to do is get organized." Americans believe in rationality. They believe in the economic and intellectual potential of the collective. While many people today may be critical of organizations, it is the particular way they are run, not the concept of organizing, which is frequently under attack. The rational value system still prevails. One can see this perspective by reviewing current organizational problems.

Current issues

Part of why this book is being written is because of a crisis in understanding organizations. We are running out of many critical natural resources. There is growing concern about the state of our surrounding physical and social environment. And there is a feeling that somehow organizations may not be able to cope with our problems. Before we proceed to discuss the different philosophical explanations of how organizations can be most effective, we must understand the problems which they currently face.[1]

Complexity. Organizations have become more complex. With the development of different disciplines and areas of expertise (e.g., management, marketing, and research and development), we find increasing division of labor and specialization. We have more complicated units and problems. We have lots of different kinds of people doing different kinds of jobs.

What this does is to put stress on the two factors that hold organizations together: goals and management. Organizational participants have different goals rather than similar goals, and therefore the "purpose" of the organization becomes more difficult to define. Some people think organizations should be responsible for social problems; others do not. There are people who suggest an organization's main concern should be the satisfaction, well-being, and intellectual growth of the participants, while others think productivity should be the only concern. The result of these different opinions and goals is that complex organizations are frequently faced with internal conflict. These disagreements obviously cause problems in terms of decisions about how a particular organization should proceed. Without agreement about goals it is hard to make decisions about the proper means to attain the goals.

Complexity also causes difficulty for managers. Coordination and integration are more difficult. Central to this problem is the issue of control and conformity. With different types of people holding different values and goals, it becomes increasingly difficult to encourage joint, agreed-upon action. We become paralyzed by the attempt to agree upon the goals. For example, should we build cars that pollute the air and save gas or should we build cars that use more gas but pollute less? The point is that management is being required to increase efficiency, and at the same time the task is becoming increasingly difficult to accomplish because of conflicting goals caused by organizational complexity.

[1]For more detail see W. G. Scott & T. R. Mitchell. *Organization theory: A structural and behavioral analysis.* Homewood, Ill.: Irwin-Dorsey, 1976, 1–48.

Size. Another issue is simply the size of organizations today. It has been pointed out that a hundred years ago (1) the average college enrolled fewer than 100 students and had a faculty of 10, (2) there were fewer corporations with $5 million in annual sales than there are with $50 million in sales today, (3) the total revenue of the federal government was less than the sales of any of the 300 largest private companies in 1972, and (4) fewer people lived in cities such as White Plains, New York, than currently work there for single corporations such as IBM or General Foods.[2]

With this increase in size has come problems. People no longer know what is being done in other parts of the company. They have less identification with the organization and its goals. And they do not know most of the people with whom they work. Again, both the process of setting agreed-upon goals and the process of managing the ongoing activities have become more difficult.

The sheer size of many organizations has vastly increased. Some big universities now graduate almost 10,000 students a year. (*By permission of University of Washington* Daily.)

Science and technology. The final issue is that science and technology have begun to play an increasingly important role in organizations. Disciplines such as psychology, management science, and human engineering focus on scientific and technical ways that people can be more productive. There are decision-making models, man-machine systems, time and motion studies, and selection tests. All

[2]H. J. Leavitt, W. R. Dill, & H. B. Eyring. *The organizational world.* New York: Harcourt, Brace, 1973.

these techniques require highly skilled professionals to develop, implement, and evaluate them. Again, the complexity and diversity of the organization is affected.

At the core of most of these issues is the process of change. We are living in a world where the speed of change has dramatically increased. Obsolescence is planned. The time lag between discovery and implementation is reduced. For example, the goal of the automobile industry was to produce big, fast, flashy, powerful cars in the 1960s. In the 1970s we are starting to see small, slow, conservative, gas-saving vehicles. Basic production and management strategies have had to undergo major modifications.

In summary, the problem of having efficient organizations has become more central to most people's life-styles. We all participate in organizations and most of us are struck by their complexity, size, and technology. Through the years there have been a number of writers and researchers suggesting ways in which organizations should be run and designed. We turn now to a review of those approaches.

Background

Throughout the history of Western society the view of organizations in general and business organizations in particular has varied quite a bit. Sometimes they have been highly valued, while at other times they have been criticized and neglected. To understand fully the positions of today's organization theorists, we must examine those philosophical positions that have dominated our past.

Historical summary

From the time of the early Greeks up through the Middle Ages, the organizations that dominated society were the church and the government. The Greeks and Romans engaged in some trade, but there was general mistrust of business. In the medieval period there were regulations and restraints against business activities. Charging interest, for example, was considered to be a sin. It was not until the Reformation that these attitudes began to change. The Protestant ethic emphasized individual enterprise, thrift, and hard work. Trade and business activities were encouraged. The eighteenth- and nineteenth-century arguments of Adam Smith (an economist) and Charles Darwin, respectively, also suggested that self-interest and competition would ensure the maximization of social benefits for all.

All these forces led to the industrial revolution. There was an increased dependence on science and technology. People lived in large cities; their economic activity was encouraged and free of control. The church was no longer the dominant organization. Industrial capitalism was on the rise.

For a short period of time (1850 to 1900), the large business organizations dominated and controlled much of society. Great power and wealth were accumulated by those who ran large organizations. After the turn of the century, however, both unions and government regulation limited the freedom of big business. And then came the Great Depression. All the predictions of endless

Table 2-1. Historical View of Business Organizations

Time	Events	View of Business	Dominant Organization
2000 B.C.	Greeks and Romans have some trade	Mistrust of business	Church and government
Medieval period	Regulations and restraints	Negative—usury is a sin	Church
Early modern period	Reformation	Protestant ethic— frugality and industry	Government and church
1900–1920	Industrial revolution	Positive support without control	Big business
1930–1940	Great Depression	Negative—business must be controlled	Government
Today	Technological and scientific impact	Role of business in society increases	Government and business

prosperity meant little to the unemployed. The system had failed, and the businessman was the scapegoat. Increased government control and regulation was the result. Table 2-1 reviews these historical developments.

Value orientation

One final point generated by our historical survey needs to be emphasized. It is obvious from our overview that organizations rise and fall in power as a function of changes in values, technology, social movements, or philosophical positions. What is revered today may be scorned tomorrow.

One of the most basic causes of this variability in values is our view of the basic nature of human beings. When the church was dominant in the Middle Ages, the prevailing view was that humans were fallen creatures, prone to base and sinful activity. Control and regulation were needed. The later ideas of competition and survival of the fittest were somewhat more neutral and less negative. However, people were still seen as being dominated by economic self-gain. More recently the argument has been made that people are basically good and that we are concerned about the growth and development of ourselves and our fellow creatures.

Thus, the view of mankind has ranged from very negative to neutral to positive. Those who postulate a negative view suggest that people need to be controlled, that they are basically lazy and not to be trusted. We will find that much of *classical* organization theory held this view. A more neutral position saw the influence of the environment. Most of our behavior was attributed to learning. By changing the environment we could change the individual. This position is the basis for the "behaviorist" point of view frequently cited in today's literature on psychology and education. Finally, the positive position suggested we were striving for perfection in our natural state. People were kind, generous, caring, and worthy of trust and development. The human-resources

Table 2-2. View of Human Nature

Position	Historical Background	Current Representative*
Negative	Max Weber	Goal setting
	Administrative design theory	Human engineering
Neutral	Learning theory	Behaviorism
	Mayo's early work	Contingency theory
Positive	Human relations	Industrial humanism
		Organization development

*Some of the current representatives are logical progressions of their background, but they may not make explicit statements about their view of human nature. Also, many of the terms in this column such as *contingency theory* or *organization development* are new to the reader. They will be defined and fully discussed in the following sections.

and industrial-humanist movements reflect these values today. Table 2-2 summarizes these views and the approaches which we will discuss.

Before proceeding to a discussion of these different approaches, we should mention that all three of these *orientations* are alive and well in today's organizations. There is much research which we will cover throughout the book which suggests that goal setting, behaviorism, and humanistic approaches can have positive effects on organizational participants. So, just because some of these approaches are older and somewhat dated does not mean that their modern counterparts should be dismissed.

Classical theory

> This new development (automation) has
> unbounded possibilities for good and for evil.   Norbert Wiener

We have already described the organizational environment at the turn of the century. There was a great increase in industrialization and the use of science and technology. The great movements to the city created large mass markets and a new urban proletariat. With these changes came accumulated tensions due to inequality which were easily noticed. There was also a wave of nationalistic sentiment.

It was during this time that the first formal statements appeared in Europe about how organizations should be designed and administered in order to be maximally effective. Max Weber (1864 to 1920) wrote a number of well-known papers which dealt with the issues of organizational structure, leadership, and rationality. The overall picture described by Weber was known as the bureaucratic model, and it spelled out explicitly those aspects on which the *classical* approach was based.

We should initially point out that bureaucracy as defined by Weber did not refer to the red-tape or inefficiency aspects of organizations. It referred instead to what Weber believed was an ideal design for organizational effectiveness. The underlying structural principles were based on means-to-ends rationality and are listed below.

1 Rules and regulations are explicit. They are needed to provide order and continuity. Through rules and regulations we can standardize how things are done and treat everyone equally.
2 There should be specific spheres of competence. People should have a well-defined job and the authority to carry out the job. Thus, the principle of the division of labor was an integral aspect of the design.
3 The root of authority is technical training, competence, and expertise. There should be objective standards for who is qualified or promoted to specific jobs.
4 Members of the administrative staff should be completely separated from ownership of the means of production. Ownership was separated from leadership in an attempt to make decision making rational and objective.
5 The principle of hierarchy suggests that each lower office is under the direct control and supervision of a higher office. Lines of communication are vertical rather than horizontal.
6 Acts, decisions, and rules are recorded and kept in writing. The ongoing functioning of the organization is part of the public record.

These structural principles implied a number of important points. First, work was not necessarily designed to be pleasant. It was designed to be unemotional and efficient and to have a minimum of conflicts of interest. Second, everything was meant to be explicit and public. Positions were clearly defined, and people were essentially interchangeable. There was a marked emphasis on the structural and administrative aspects of organizations but very little attention to the human aspects of life on the job.

Besides the structural principles there were process principles. At the root of the bureaucratic model was the concept of authority and legitimate control. Positions within the organization carried with them rights and responsibilities. If you accepted the job, you accepted the premise that people had legitimate authority over you and you might in turn have authority over others.

In his analysis of how people acquired legitimacy, Weber described three possibilities: traditional, charismatic, and bureaucratic. The traditional authority might be represented by a monarch, someone who assumed a position simply because it was the way things were done. The charismatic leader gained authority through personal magnetism. The personality of the leader compelled others to follow. Finally, the bureaucratic leader was accorded responsibility because of expertise and legally defined qualifications. It is this bureaucratic type of leader that Weber argued should be in command.

One must remember that Weber's model was just that—a model. It was a description of what he believed would be an ideal type of design. Obviously, in the real world there are not any organizations that exactly fit the ideal type. However, to the degree that an organization approximated the bureaucratic type, it should be approaching its maximum efficiency according to Weber.

There were also a number of Europeans who elaborated and augmented the classical approach. Instead of building an ideal typology, however, they attempted to classify and describe those aspects of successful organizations which they had actually observed. Henri Fayol (1841 to 1925) was a French industrialist who developed a theory which focused on the five functions of the manager and fourteen principles of management. The functions of the manager were (1) planning, (2) organization, (3) command, (4) coordination, and (5) control. These functions still appear today in most textbooks concerned with management.

The fourteen administrative management principles generated by Fayol are similar to those of Weber and they are briefly listed below.

1 *Division of work.* The principle of specialization of labor in order to concentrate activities for more efficiency.
2 *Authority and responsibility.* Authority is the right to give orders and the power to exact obedience.
3 *Discipline.* Discipline is absolutely essential for the smooth running of business, and without discipline no enterprise could prosper.
4 *Unity of command.* An employee should receive orders from one superior only.
5 *Unity of direction.* There should be one head and one plan for a group of activities having the same objectives.
6 *Subordination of individual interests to general interests.* The interest of one employee or group should not prevail over that of the organization.
7 *Remuneration of personnel.* Compensation should be fair and, as far as possible, afford satisfaction both to personnel and the firm.
8 *Centralization.* Centralization is essential to the organization and is a natural consequence of organizing.
9 *Scalar chain.* The scalar chain is the chain of superiors ranging from the ultimate authority to the lowest rank.
10 *Order.* The organization should provide an orderly place for every individual. A place for everyone and everyone in their place.
11 *Equity.* Equity and a sense of justice pervades the organization.
12 *Stability of tenure of personnel.* Time is needed for the employee to adapt to his or her work and to perform it effectively.
13 *Initiative.* At all levels of the organizational ladder, zeal and energy are augmented by initiative.
14 *Esprit de corps.* This principle emphasized the need for teamwork and the maintenance of interpersonal relationships.

Notice that seven of these principles deal with the chain of command and the allocation of authority. There are also two principles concerned with the equity of the system and two with stability and order. Weber also recognized the importance of these factors.

But also note that there are some points that are new. There is a concern for initiative and esprit de corps. This was the initial recognition that the human element needed to be considered. Also of importance was the discussion of centralization. Fayol seemed to suggest that centralization was not necessarily good in all circumstances and that latitude and decentralization are a question of balance to be determined by each organization. Thus the traditional bureaucratic model was broadened in scope.

In the United States the classical approach was best expressed by the work of Frederick W. Taylor (1856 to 1915). Taylor worked in the production area of an organization as an executive and as a consultant. He believed that the interests of management and nonmanagement employees could be brought together through the principles of self-interest. By making the company maximally efficient, the increased benefits would be distributed to everyone.

At the heart of Taylor's ideas was the notion that there was one best way to do a job. By intensive study people could determine where they should stand or sit, how they should orient their bodies, where tools or supplies should be placed, the order in which activities should be completed, and so on. Once one determined all these aspects of the job, then Taylor would argue that the job should be done that way on every occasion—the ultimate in standardization.

Taylor's work combined a number of trends in management thought. First, there was the idea that work could be analyzed scientifically. Detailed *time and motion studies,* as they were called, would tell us the best way to do a job. Second, through standardization, the processes of selection, placement, and training could be made somewhat easier. The time and motion studies described what skills were needed for a particular job. Finally, it was an important step toward the engineering, man-machine–systems philosophy. People were seen as interchangeable and adaptable to the mechanical environment.

The example typically cited about Taylor's work concerned a laborer named Schmidt whose job it was to load pig iron. Taylor focused on the most effective way that the pig iron could be moved between two points and the proper body placement, movement, rest periods, and amount to be carried each time. At the end of the study, Taylor reported that Schmidt had increased his productivity from 12 to 15 long tons a day to 47.5 tons a day. This was a dramatic result and was widely publicized. It was one of the best representations of Taylor's approach, which came to be described as scientific management.

To summarize, the classical approach focused on division of labor, proper lines of command, legitimate power and authority, standardization, and explicit rules and procedures. It was a highly rational approach that assumed a maximum of control over the individual worker. The list below shows, for example, the rules and regulations of employees at Carson, Pirie, Scott (a department store) in Chicago around the turn of the century.

1 Store must be open from 6 A.M. to 9 P.M.
2 Store must be swept; counters and base shelves dusted; lamps trimmed, filled, and chimneys cleaned; a pail of water, also a bucket of coal brought in before breakfast; and attend to customers who will call.
3 Store must not be open on the Sabbath day unless necessary and then only for a few minutes.
4 The employee who is in the habit of smoking Spanish cigars, being shaved at the barber shop, and going to dances and other places of amusement will surely give his employer reason to be suspicious of his honesty and integrity.

Many hands and feet make light the work.

Through division of labor we have greatly increased our productive capacity.

5 Each employee must not pay less than $5 per year to the church and must attend Sunday school regularly.
6 Men employees are given one evening a week for courting and two if they go to prayer meeting.
7 After 14 hours of work in the store, the leisure time should be spent mostly in reading.

Dress, habits, church, and social life were all fair game.

These ideas illustrate what we earlier called a fairly pessimistic or negative view of human nature. People were seen as motivated only by economic self-interest. They were also believed to be basically lazy, which prompted the emphasis on control: unless they were told how to behave properly they would by definition behave inappropriately. Frivolity and excess had to be regulated. Pay was the only important motivator. It was not long before this system was highly criticized as dehumanizing, biased, and simply wrong.

The human-relations approach

A number of things were happening in the United States in the 1920s and 1930s. Organizations were growing in size and in their dependence upon technology. People were receiving training which was more and more specialized. Social groups were breaking down. And then came the Depression—an upheaval that was so climactic that our Constitution and mode of government were severely shaken.

The combination of all these external factors with the growing dissatisfaction with paced, mechanized, highly standardized work led to changes in two major directions. Management science developed as a technical discipline concerned with the establishment of efficiency models of managerial and organizational behavior. Quantitative techniques were developed to help decision makers be more effective. The emphasis was on mathematical and technical solutions to complex problems. We will trace the development of this discipline later in the chapter.

The other perspective was initiated by the work of Elton Mayo at the Hawthorne Plant of Western Electric from 1927 to 1932. Since this early work serves as both the foundation of the human-relations approach and as one of the first good examples of social-science research, we will discuss it in some detail.

The research can be easily divided up into four phases. In the first phase, a study examined the effect of environmental conditions on worker productivity. A small group of women was involved in making telephone assemblies. While they were working, the researchers would change the amount of illumination and observe the resultant change, if any, in productivity.

The results were puzzling to the investigators. It appeared that no matter what type of change occurred, productivity increased. They found that as they increased the illumination, productivity went up. However, when they reached a point where the illumination by objective standards was too bright, they continued to observe increases in productivity. So, they started to decrease the illumination—productivity still went up. Obviously, there was something other than the level of illumination that was influencing the work habits of the women.

At this point Mayo and then Roethlisberger and Whitehead joined the research effort.[3] They set up the relay-room experiments which investigated the effects of various factors (e.g., rest pauses, method of payment) on the productivity of a small group of six women. Again, the results were the same. Increases in productivity seemed to occur independent of the actual changes being made. However, on this occasion the researchers actively consulted with the experimental participants. They asked them a number of questions about why they were working harder, and the results were of major importance. The women reported six reasons in the following order of preference:

1 Small group
2 Type of supervision
3 Earnings
4 Novelty of the situation
5 Interest in the experiment
6 Attention received in the test room

These last three elements are usually described as the Hawthorne effect. More

[3]E. Mayo. *The human problems of an industrial civilization.* New York: Macmillan, 1933; T. N. Whitehead. *The industrial worker.* Cambridge, Mass.: Harvard, 1938; F. J. Roethlisberger & W. V. Dickson. *Management and the worker.* Cambridge, Mass.: Harvard, 1939.

specifically, it looked as if just being in an experiment and getting special attention was a major reason why productivity increased.

It was also true that the experimenters, by putting together this separate small team, had changed some variables that they had not realized they had changed. The size of the work group had decreased, and apparently the supervision was also more flexible and tolerant in the small experimental group. All these facts led the investigators to believe that motivation and productivity on the job were far more complex than the simple economic-man principles present in the prevailing classical approach. Other human factors were involved.

The third phase of the research was an extensive interview of 20,000 employees. The interviews at first were very structured but later on were flexible and open-ended—employees were encouraged to speak freely and honestly about their jobs. They could choose their topics and could talk in as much depth as they wished. Some of the general sorts of findings are described below.

1 People very often will not initially tell you what the real problem is. They will tell you what they think you want to hear.
2 People view their job in terms of its social meaning. Their satisfaction is related to who they work with and for.
3 One's status on the job is important for determining many aspects of their social environment.
4 The groups themselves have norms and values that may be different from company policy.

Thus, there was a recognition that many individual and social factors were influencing behavior on the job. In retrospect this seems rather obvious, but at the time these were revolutionary ideas.

The final phase of the research was called the bank-wiring-room experiment. Here, fourteen men were wiring telephone switchboards (called banks), and the work required both individual and team effort. This phase differed from the relay-room work in some significant ways. First, there were no experimental changes made. The men were put in a separate room and interviewed and observed but nothing else was changed. Second, the conditions were designed to be as similar as possible to the ongoing wiring department's regular work conditions.

The results were dramatically different from the relay-room findings. Productivity did not increase, and in fact it slightly decreased. It was hard to pinpoint the cause of these differences because of the many alternative answers that were plausible (e.g., the sex of the participants, the fact that no changes were implemented, or the fact that as little special attention was given as possible). However, the observational data and some interviews provided some insights into what was happening.

One major finding was that the group set an informal norm of what was a satisfactory day's work. While the time-and-motion specialists had determined that 2½ banks could be done, the group decided that 2 banks was about right. Thus, employee and management expectations were different by 20 percent. A second related result was that the group put pressure on its members to complete the standard—not much more and not much less. Those who shirked their responsibility were called "chiselers" and those who exceeded it were described as "speed kings" or "rate-busters." This latter group was subjected to social and physical pressure to slow down. When they didn't respond, they were occasionally "binged" on the arm by their other group members.

All these studies led to a number of rather startling conclusions:

1 The organization was more than just a set of individual man-machine systems. It was a social organization where people had friends, enemies, hopes, fears, and desires that were unaccounted for by the system.
2 The level of productivity was not determined by some norm set by management but rather by some set of social norms and standards set by the group.
3 As a direct corollary, it was obvious that in many cases noneconomic rewards were as important as the economic ones. One's friends and interpersonal interactions were an important part of the job.
4 Workers do not always respond as individuals acting alone. Groups, in fact, make decisions, and these groups and subgroups may not be recognized as part of the formal organization.
5 Research methods could be used to study the work environment. Social scientists could make important contributions to our understanding of people's behavior in the organizational setting.

These principles challenged the underlying philosophy of the classical approach. There was an informal structure as well as a formal one. People communicated to one another in ways which were not prescribed formally. The division of labor made less sense if people were not in fact independent. How was this group action to be taken into account? Horizontal relationships might be as important as vertical ones.

In terms of management practice the human-relations approach required a radical change in thinking. Managers had to be aware of the fact that group norms existed. Output was not just a simple function of each individual working up to capacity. In fact, people might work at rates less than full capacity because of group pressure—even if this pressure was contrary to individual self-interest in economic terms. The solution to the problem would not be to take a few slow individuals aside and criticize them or fire them. New people would soon adjust to the norm as well. The answer had to come from an understanding of the group as a unit and the complex interpersonal pressures and relationships that made up that unit. The manager had to have a much broader and thorough grasp of interpersonal behavior and motivation than had been previously required.

And most important, this new position challenged the assumptions about the nature of human beings. The human relationists illustrated that humans were motivated by other aspects of their work besides money. The social setting, the style of leadership, and the attention they got from their friends and supervisor were also important. Much of this work was later developed into a general concern about the welfare and working conditions of the employee. The research of people such as Likert and McGregor (sometimes labeled the human-resources approach) will be discussed in detail further on in the book. It is important to point out, however, that these more current authors believed that employees under the proper conditions could and would work very hard without close supervision or obvious economic rewards. There was the suggestion that people might even like their work if it were made more interesting, challenging, and rewarding.

In summary, the human relationists focused more attention on the individual employees, their reactions to the work situation, and the people around them as well as the informal aspects of working in a group. This interest in the individual was developed into a more general "humanistic" concern by later researchers.

But there were critics of the human-relations approach and its advocates. Some people felt the human relationists had gone too far. Formal aspects of the organizational structure were important, as were economic incentives. Specialization and standardization had dramatically increased our standard of living. They were reluctant to scrap the whole philosophy of scientific management. Our observation of the current scene suggests that elements of both scientific management and the human-relations approach are prominent still today. That is, both schools of thought suggested important principles for management that are major elements of current organizational practice. We will discuss these trends at the end of the chapter.

In the middle of this controversy arose some supposedly value-free ways of looking at organizations and their potential for effective functioning. *Systems approaches* and *contingency models* became hot topics. These approaches were concerned with an understanding of the complexity and interrelationships of organizational units without reference to a "one best way" to organize. We turn now to an examination of these ideas.

Systems theory

> In one way or another, we are forced to deal with complexities, with "wholes" or "systems" in all fields of knowledge. This implies a basic re-orientation of scientific thinking.
> Ludwig von Bertalanffy

The emphasis of the classical approach had been on the formal structure of the organization. The human-relations advocates had switched the focus to interpersonal relationships. However, neither of these groups had emphasized the relationships, both formal and informal, among and between subgroups within the organization. This was the contribution of the systems approach.

The basic idea of systems theory is that the whole is more than the sum of the parts. Organizations should be seen as an assemblage or combination of subunits or parts and an analysis of just the parts does not provide a complete picture. We must look at the relationships between these parts.

This idea, while not new, does require a major shift in scientific thinking. First, it is antireductionist. Most areas of scientific inquiry have moved toward a more detailed and refined analysis of subunits. A reductionist tries to analyze a phenomenon in terms of its individual parts. One must understand the component parts in order to understand the whole. In the area of human behavior, for example, many people argued that ultimately we will have to understand the biological, chemical, and electrical processes of the brain and central nervous system in order to understand behavior. Another illustration comes from physics. Many physicists believed that we had to understand the molecule to understand matter; then we had to understand the atom, then the proton and neutrons, and then the subatomic particles, and so on. The emphasis was on constantly shifting the level of analysis to smaller parts or subunits in order to understand the whole. A systems approach challenged this line of thought by arguing that it is the whole, the combination and interrelationship of parts, that will provide the greatest insights. They suggested that it was the *interaction between* the brain and the physiological state that caused behavior, or that it was the *relationship between* subatomic particles, atoms, and molecules that would help us to understand matter. From an organizational perspective, a systems approach suggested that we look at how different units interacted with each other in order to form an overall whole rather than breaking down our analysis into smaller parts.

The second shift concerns the view of human beings and their underlying motivation. While the classicists were pessimists and the followers of the human relationists were optimists, the systems theorist took a more neutral position. People and systems were seen as adaptive. They interacted with their environment and much of their behavior was learned. Thus the basis for an effective organization was not the positive or negative nature of humans but the proper match between the human being and the environment.

The major principles of the systems approach are presented next.

Subsystems of components. A system by definition is composed of interrelated parts or elements. This is true for all systems—mechanical, biological, and social. Every system has at least two elements, and these elements are interconnected.

Holism, synergism, organicism, and gestalt. The whole is not just the sum of the parts; the system itself can be explained only as a totality. Holism is the opposite of elementarism, which views the total as the sum of its individual parts.

Open-system view. Systems can be considered in two ways: (1) closed or (2) open. Open systems exchange information, energy, or material with their environments. Openness is seen as a dimension; that is, systems are relatively open or relatively closed.

Input-transformation-output model. The open system can be viewed as a transformation model. It receives various inputs, transforms these inputs in some way, and exports outputs.

System boundaries. It follows that systems have boundaries which separate them from their environments. The concept of boundaries helps us understand the distinction between open and closed systems. The relatively closed system has rigid impenetrable boundaries, whereas the open system has permeable boundaries between itself and a broader suprasystem. Boundaries are relatively easily defined in physical and biological systems but are very difficult to delineate in social systems, such as organizations.

Entropy. Closed physical systems are subject to the force of entropy which increases until eventually the entire system fails. The tendency toward maximum entropy is a movement to disorder, complete lack of resource transformation, and death. In a closed system, entropy must always increase; however, in open biological or social systems, entropy can be stopped and may even be reversed into a process of more complete organization and ability to transform resources—because the system imports resources from its environment.

Internal elaboration. Closed systems move toward entropy and disorganization. In contrast, open systems appear to move in the direction of greater differentiation, elaboration, and a higher level of organization.

Steady state, dynamic equilibrium, and homeostasis. The concept of steady state is closely related to that of entropy. A closed system eventually must die. However, an open system may attain a state where the system remains in dynamic equilibrium through the continuous inflow of materials, energy, and information.

Feedback. The concept of feedback is important in understanding how a system maintains a steady state. Information concerning the outputs or the process of the system is fed back as an input into the system, perhaps leading to changes in the transformation process and/or future outputs.

Hierarchy. A basic concept in systems thinking is that of hierarchical relationships between systems. A system is composed of subsystems of a lower order and is also part of a suprasystem. Thus, there is a hierarchy of the components of the system.

One can see first that many of these ideas are built on the findings of biological research. Living organisms have inputs (e.g., oxygen, food) which they transform and process and which results in outputs (e.g., energy, waste). For life to continue a complex system of adaptation and interrelationship between the organism and the environment is required. There are certain mechanisms which tell us when things are wrong and there are self-correcting mechanisms available to deal with such problems. The strived-for state is one of homeostasis: the organism exists in harmony with its environment.

These principles are supposedly applicable to organizations as well as other nonliving systems (e.g., astronomy). Organizations have informational and human inputs as well as material ones. These inputs may be transformed in one way or another and result in outputs. And for an organization to be effective, it must be able to adapt to its environment. The effective design of an organization is dependent upon the match between the environment and the organization's internal structure and the interrelationships between the two. Thus, *there is no one best structure:* it depends upon the environment and the inherent characteristics of the organization itself.

Let us take an example. The university or college is constantly taking in a new group of students (inputs). These people attend a variety of classes and engage in other educational activities (process) and most of them eventually graduate (outputs). Large sums of money may come in for research (input) which is carried out (process) and written up as books, journal articles, or technical reports (output). To survive in the education business it is obvious that inputs are needed, and the successful educational institutions are able to obtain them. Others are not. In the last 10 years a number of colleges have had to close down simply because they could not attract enough students and money to support the ongoing operations of the system. A systems theorist's approach to this problem would not automatically have been to "follow the classical structure" or to "get better interpersonal communication." Instead, the analysis would focus on the kind of environment in which universities exist (e.g., is it predictable? does it change?) and the type of structure and interrelationships that would be best suited to that environment.

A first question would simply be, "What are the parts of the systems?" Obviously, there are individuals, subgroups, and the composite whole. These subgroups might consist of a production or technical subsystem (e.g., teaching); some supportive subsystems (e.g., selection, placement); maintenance subsystems that reward, socialize, and sanction the behavior of participants; adaptive or future-oriented subsystems such as research and development activities; and, finally, the managerial subsystem for planning, coordinating, and controlling (e.g., the administration).

Next, the systems analyst would want to know how the subsystems are related to one another. Are they independent or interdependent? Do they communicate directly or indirectly, formally or informally? Finally, what does the environment look like? What are the demands made on the organization? How much time does it have to respond? How much change is there?

The results of this type of analysis will supposedly tell us the best type of structure for that type of situation—a kind of contingency approach. The best type of structure is contingent upon the type of environment. In some cases an open, informal, flexible structure may be best, while in others a formal, inflexible structure will do the job. Some organizations may require a rigid structure in one part of the organization (e.g., production) and a flexible structure in some other part (e.g., research and development). Or a structure which is somewhat in between the two extremes may be most appropriate. Effectiveness is seen as *contingent* upon the right match of internal structure with the external environment. A number of researchers have tried to specify contingency theories of organizations, and we will turn to their work next.

Contingency approaches

There is much empirical work which supports systems and contingency ideas. One comprehensive review of all the research examining the relationships between structural variables and organizational criteria was presented by Porter and Lawler.[4] They looked at the variables listed on the next page.

Some of the results were as expected. In general people at upper levels of an organization enjoyed their jobs more than people at lower levels, and people in small groups seemed more satisfied than people in large groups. But besides these two generalizations there was little to add. The startling point was that few principles seemed to hold across all settings. In some cases a large span of control was effective, in other cases a small span of control. Sometimes the flat, decentralized structure did best, and at other times a tall, centralized structure

[4]L. W. Porter & E. E. Lawler. Properties of organization structure in relation to job attitudes and job behavior. *Psychological Bulletin,* 1965, **64,** 23–51.

Structure	**Criteria**
SUBORGANIZATIONAL PROPERTIES	JOB ATTITUDES
1 Organizational levels	1 Satisfaction
2 Line and staff hierarchies	2 Need fulfillment
3 Span of control	3 Role perceptions
4 Size: subunits	4 Leader attitudes
TOTAL—ORGANIZATIONAL PROPERTIES	JOB BEHAVIOR
5 Size: total organization	5 Absenteeism
6 Shape: tall or flat	6 Turnover
7 Shape: centralized or decentralized	7 Output
	8 Accidents
	9 Grievances

was most effective. The overwhelming conclusion was that there was no one best structure. Effectiveness depended upon the interaction of the particular structure with its task and environment.

The focus of much of the recent research on organizational structure reflects this change in emphasis. Investigators began to analyze the type of task in which the organization was engaged. Of particular interest were those attempts to develop classification systems of organizational tasks so that we could identify the critical similarities and differences among them. How, for example, is a nursing home different from an insurance agency? How is a pencil manufacturer different from a gas station? What are the dimensions that distinguish and characterize types of organizations? Once these dimensions were discovered, we could have a better idea about how to design an organization.

The initial research in this area focused on the task to be done. What sort of good or service was being produced? How was it being produced? For example, some organizations provide services for many different parties and they serve as an intermediary (e.g., real estate agencies), and in other cases the individual provides a service directly to the client (e.g., a hotel or a hospital). Some goods are produced by assembly lines and others are done individually. These different ways to provide goods or services are often described as *technologies,* and this term is used in many of the classification systems that were developed.

Some of these classification systems were quite effective in pointing out differences in technology. Thompson, for example, distinguished among long-linked, mediating, and intensive technologies.[5] Figure 2-1 represents this typology. The long-linked technology represents the assembly-line situation, while the mediating technology describes organizations providing services to two or more clients (sort of a go-between). Finally, the intensive technology represents a situation where the organization can provide multiple services for the client. Thus, organizations could be classified according to their technology—the means by which they accomplished their goals.

But a number of researchers have carried this idea even further. They have argued that a classification system of technologies will allow us to suggest what type of structure and process will exist and, in some cases, the structure and

[5]J. D. Thompson. *Organizations in action.* New York: McGraw-Hill, 1967.

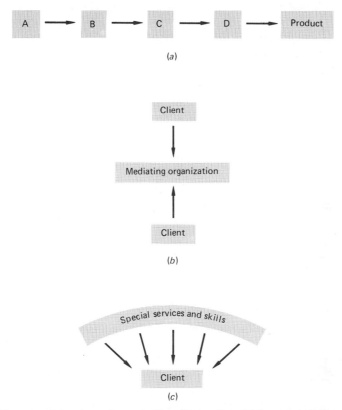

Figure 2-1. Thompson's typology of organizational technology. (*a*) *Long-linked:* These are based on serial interdependence. One step must be completed before advancing to the next phase. Many mass-producing assembly-line operations would fit here. (*b*) *Mediating:* The organization mediates between two parties, providing services for both. Examples might be banks, advertising companies, or freight companies. (*c*) *Intensive:* A wide variety of services are performed by the organization. An example might be a hospital or private research and consulting firm.

process that should exist for maximum effectiveness. There are only a few really good examples of this type of research, mostly because it is particularly difficult research to conduct. One must have a large number of different types of organizations participating in the research and gather a lot of data within each one. It is a monumental job. However, there are some good examples around, and we will describe the ones that have had the greatest impact on our current thinking.

Technology and structure

Some researchers have argued that the technology of the organization in fact determines its structure. Perrow, for example, has looked at two major dimensions of technology: the degree to which the task is variable and the degree to which the technology is analyzable. The variability simply refers to the number of exceptional cases. For example, a company that produces custom-made products would have a large number of exceptional cases, while a mass-production industry might have very few exceptions. The analyzability dimension refers to the degree to which the task and technology are broken down and well specified. Combining these two dimensions provides the following matrix:

Technology	Exceptional Cases	
	Few	Many
Unanalyzable	Craft	Nonroutine
Analyzable	Routine	Engineering

An example of a routine technology would be a highly mechanized mass-production industry such as automobile manufacturing. The task is broken down and well specified as well as having few exceptional cases. An example of a nonroutine technology might be the psychiatric care provided in a mental hospital. Every psychiatrist has his or her own approach, and each problem is unique. Craft industries are self-explanatory—the individual makes the whole product but probably in the same way each time—while engineering technologies are those where the task may be analyzable, but a large number of exceptional cases may exist. A good example would be a research consulting firm that might have many different types of contracts but the scientific method was applicable to all of them.

The argument made by Perrow is that if we classify organizations according to their technology we should be able to predict the structure of those firms that are most effective. Some data exists to support this hypothesis. Magnusen classified fourteen medium-sized manufacturing firms according to Perrow's system and then looked at the organizational structure, goals, and processes.[6] His results supported Perrow's analysis. He found, for example, that companies that dealt with many exceptional cases had to have more flexibility, greater decentralization, and less hierarchical control in order to be successful. Also, the more analyzable the task, the more control and close supervision was possible. In highly routine situations a more classical approach might be appropriate, while a more flexible structure might be needed in a nonroutine setting. Thus, the technology of an organization can be seen as having a major impact on its structure.

One of the most well-known classification systems for technology was developed by Joan Woodward in England.[7] She was interested only in industrial firms and she classified them into three types:

1 *Process production.* Continuous manufacturing industries with highly standardized goods. Production is done in anticipation of demand with long production runs and large lot sizes. Labor costs are low.

[6]K. O. Magnusen. *Perspectives on organizational design and development.* Research paper No. 21, Columbia University, Graduate School of Business, New York, May 1973. Also see C. Perrow. A framework for the comparative analysis of organizations. *American Sociological Review,* April 1967, 199–208.

[7]J. Woodward. *Industrial organization: Theory and practice.* London: Oxford, 1965.

2 *Unit or small batch production.* This is job-order manufacturing of custom-ized products. Production is done according to demand in small runs and lots. Labor costs are high.

3 *Large-batch production.* A technology somewhere between the two above. There is some custom manufacturing and some in anticipation of demand. Medium-sized lots and runs are the rule.

In analyzing these different types of technologies, Woodward found many differences in the structure and the ongoing process of the organization. For example, much of the decision making was done by high-level policy committees in process industries. The chief executive acted as a committee chairperson rather than a unilateral decision maker. The complex mechanical technology of the process industries also demanded the greatest number of managerial levels, while unit manufacturing had the least. Therefore, the unit manufacturers had rather flat organizations with large spans of control while process industries had tall organizations with narrow spans of control. The ratio of management to nonmanagement personal was 1:8 in process industries and 1:23 in unit industries.

While Woodward's analysis is narrower in scope than the Perrow analysis, there are some striking similarities. Both theorists believe that the degree to which the task can be broken down into component parts is an important determinant of organization structure and process. Also important is the degree to which the environment is predictable. In Perrow's case we are dealing with exceptional cases, while Woodward talks about reaction to an anticipation of demand. Thus, predictability and analyzability are important aspects of both approaches.

Using very similar ideas, Burns and Stalker attempted to classify managerial systems according to their ability to deal with unpredictable and unanalyzable situations.[8] They studied a number of stable manufacturing firms moving into a new, highly changeable industry (electronics). Those organizations that had a managerial system that was rigidly prescribed with well-defined tasks and hierar-chical arrangements were called "mechanistic." Those managerial structures that were flexible with more horizontal communication and latitudes of power were described as being "organic." The data they gathered seemed to strongly suggest that the organic management structure was more likely to survive and perform well because it was a better *match* with the changing environment than the mechanistic structure. Neither system was described as inherently good or bad. Effectiveness was dependent upon having the organizational design be a good fit for the technology and environment within which the industry must operate.

The research by Lawrence and Lorsch also attempts to describe the proper match between the organization and its environment.[9] These authors look at the degree to which an organization is facing a turbulent (changing, unpredictable) or a stable (static, predictable) environment. Their analysis of the internal structure

[8]T. Burns & G. M. Stalker. *The management of innovation.* London: Tavistock, 1961.

[9]P. R. Lawrence & J. W. Lorsch. *Organization and environment: Managing differentiation and integration.* Boston: Harvard Business School, Division of Research, 1967.

utilized two concepts: differentiation (the degree to which differences in structure and people exist) and integration (the way in which the organization dealt with these differences). Differentiation implies heterogeneity. A highly differentiated organization will be composed of many different types of people doing different types of jobs in departments with different goals and missions. With this type of diversity, some sort of integration is necessary for effective cooperation and communication. Committees, flowcharts for communication, and liaison positions may serve this function.

Based on research with some industrial organizations, these authors suggest a contingency principle for matching the amount of differentiation with the turbulence of the environment. They found that the effective organizations in highly turbulent environments used greater differentiation than the effective organizations in stable environments. The more changing and unpredictable the environment, the more differentiated the structure should be in order to cope effectively with external pressure and demands.

In summary, the systems and contingency approaches tried to analyze organizational effectiveness in terms of the fit and relationships between an organiza-

There are even "contingency" theories of what socks to wear. *(By permission of Hanes-Mills Sales Corporation.)*

tion and its environment. This approach suggests to a manager that there is not one best way to organize, design, or manage an organization. Rather, it suggests that the best style is dependent upon the demands of the situation. It demands a more complex understanding of the relationships between and among the structure of the organization, its various interrelated parts, and the external environment.

Finally, we should emphasize that contingency approaches have a neutral position with respect to the nature of human-motivation questions. The use of tall or flat, centralized or decentralized, autocratic or participative structures is dependent upon the situation and the technology. The underlying assumption is that humans are malleable and adaptable. They can learn to like and appreciate different types of organizational environments. Effectiveness is contingent upon the proper match between environments, technologies, structures, and people.

Summary

This chapter was meant to serve as an introduction to the major theoretical approaches of organizational effectiveness. We have argued that each of these approaches makes certain assumptions about the nature of human motivation and that these assumptions are reflected in their approaches. The major points to remember are as follows:

1 Throughout history the approach to organizational design and the assumptions about human behavior have varied extensively.
2 Today we are confronted with a much more "organizational society." This condition has increased the demand for better understanding of organizational effectiveness.
3 The classical approach to organizations emphasized a fairly rigid, formal, autocratic, highly rational, regulated environment. People needed to be controlled.
4 The human-relations approach pointed out the informal structures, interpersonal relationships, and norms that existed in groups. Social-science research techniques were utilized, and the emphasis shifted to the positive aspects of human motivation.
5 The system approach suggested that we look at more than subunits or individuals acting in isolation. We must analyze the interdependencies and interrelationships among the parts in order to gain an accurate view of the whole.
6 Contingency theories were built on a systems philosophy. They pointed out the complex interaction between the environment, technology, structure, and human motivation. They argued that there was no best way to design an organization, and their view of human motivation was essentially neutral.

Where does that leave us? Well, throughout the book we will try to point out how these different positions are reflected in current approaches to understanding human behavior. For example, much of the work in goal setting and human engineering still includes a scientific-management point of view. The attempts to increase interpersonal effectiveness through sensitivity training and many of the interventions used in what is called organization development are direct descendants of the human-relations approach. So is the basic philosophy of human-resource development. The emphasis is on people, and their aspirations, development, and interpersonal competence. Finally, behaviorist positions and a variety of contingency theories of motivation, leadership, and training are fairly neutral in their orientation. They emphasize the adaptability of human beings. Thus, the present chapter serves as a foundation for much of what is going to come.

Implications for practice

There are some practical points we should emphasize again. The overwhelming conclusion that one must draw from the type of historical survey presented above is that *there is no one best way to design an organization*. Simplistic formulas such as "listen to your employees" or "decentralize the decision process" just do not work all the time. Effectiveness and efficiency come from the *proper match* between the organization and its environment. What this means is that being a good-listener manager may be good in some situations but not in others. The question is not *whether to use it* but *when to use it*.

A related point is that *what is thought to be effective today may not be effective tomorrow*. Values change, people change, and so do task environments. Technological advances occur. New competitors appear on the scene. The founder or president of the organization dies or changes jobs. These fluctuations mean that the manager must be constantly aware of changes and whether the changes are serious enough to demand a change in style or procedure.

So, not only is it hard to define one best way, it is apparent that any specific best way in a specific situation may lose its effectiveness over time. The implication for managers is to stay flexible and constantly monitor the fit between the organization and its environment. Obvious signs of discontent, such as grievances, turnover, and absenteeism, will occur when problems exist. They are indications of a poor match between the organizational design (e.g., its policies and structure), the employees, and the outside world. The best approach is to try to understand where the poor fit exists and make the appropriate modifications. It is hoped that, as we proceed through the text, what is appropriate will become more clear.

Discussion questions

1 What is an organization? How do terms such as *management, values, rationality,* and *goals* fit into this definition?
2 What were the important substantive and methodological findings of the Hawthorne studies?

3 What are the different views of the nature of humans and how are these positions represented in modern organization theory? Which position do you advocate?

Case: Starting a new division*

"After working 10 years for a large ($500 million sales) multidivisional, multiproduct firm, you have been assigned the task of starting up a new division to produce and distribute recreational equipment. This is a new line of business for your company, so the management recognizes the need to provide you with enough independence and authority to get geared up and start operating effectively. To underscore this need and their support for you, while also making clear that the full responsibility for the success of this new venture is yours, the management has indicated that you will be designated as president of the recreational equipment division.

One of the first tasks that you will be concerned with is organizing your division for action. The parent company will help you staff your operation from its present managerial ranks and will help recruit any additional managerial or sales personnel you may need. But before you start considering the structural possibilities or the relationships between your managers and departments, you make the following assessments of your new organization's situation:

Because of the type of equipment that you plan to produce, the demand is likely to be very inelastic, that is, slight changes in your products' prices will have little effect on sales volume. Therefore, it will be relatively easy for you to secure distributors. In fact, one distributor has been willing to agree to a 3-year sales contract for your equipment. The rationale underlying this position is that since no other firm produces similar equipment, there will be little competition for sales. Additionally, consumers are likely to perceive your equipment as being of a unique quality, so that viable alternatives will be unavailable. Besides, patent protection for your type of product is virtually guaranteed.

In relation to production, you doubt that there will be many problems. On the one hand, your production process includes readily available materials, and there are many possible suppliers. Thus, it may be possible for you to contract with your suppliers for a 3-year period at a constant price. Also, the production equipment required will necessitate little negotiation on your part, since such equipment is usually in stock and the cost is reasonable.

The current market for the type of labor that is needed can be characterized as open. Recent graduations from local trade schools have left the market with many available craftsmen. Additionally, it is unlikely that a union will enter the picture with this type of personnel. Recent attempts by the local AFL-CIO organizer to unionize the recreational-equipment workers have been met with opposition. But even if unionization occurs, it is unlikely that there would be much disruption in the industry, since this particular branch of the AFL-CIO has not been excessively aggressive in other industries.

Another significant factor for your operations relates to government regulation. Up to this point the government has been fairly flexible with the industry, and it is likely that that position will be maintained. Governmental regulation has been increasing in all industries, but at this stage, regulation of the recreational-equipment industry is considered to be still inappropriate by most legislators. Consumer advocates seem to be less concerned with the social, economic, or political impact of the industry, thus little public scrutiny is likely. The public attitude is unlikely to be reflected in future financing of the operations, since strong financial backing has already been secured.

A final area of possible concern is future technological change. In the past the recreational-equipment industry has been characterized by frequent product improvements and new-product introductions. Your products, however, are unlikely to be subject to this volatility. Your products will employ the most current technology and materials, and the industry is expected to stabilize. The industry has innovated on the magnitude of about fifty new changes per year for the last decade; indications at a recent trade show, however, signal a change rate of around ten innovations or less per year for the foreseeable future.''

Questions about the case

1 Would you describe the environment as stable or turbulent? Is it risky or predictable? Can you control what is going on?
2 How much change is there likely to be? How certain are you about what the future will look like?
3 To what extent do you think procedures should be written down and clearly specified? Should there be a policy manual containing the rules?
4 What about communication processes? Should everything be kept in writing? Should people communicate mainly through the chain of command?
5 Will you encourage people to be able to handle a variety of tasks, or should everyone have a fairly distinct and clearly specified job of their own?

Additional readings

Bennis, W. G. *Changing organizations.* New York: McGraw-Hill, 1966.
** Carzo, R. J., & Yanouzas, J. N. *Formal organizations.* Homewood, Ill. Dorsey-Irwin, 1967.
* Cleland, D. I. Understanding project authority. *Business Horizons,* Spring 1967, 63–70.
** Ellul, J. *The technological society.* New York: Knopf, 1965.
Fayol, H. *General and industrial administration.* London: Sir Isaac Pitman & Sons, 1949.
* Hickson, D. J., Pugh, D. S, & Pheysey, D. C. Organization structure: Is technology the key? *Personnel Management,* 1970, **2,** 21–26.
* Hunt, R. G. Technology and organization. *Academy of Management Journal,* September 1970, 235–252.
* Kast, F. E., & Rosenzweig, J. E. General systems theory: Applications for organization and management. *Academy of Management Journal,* December 1972, 447–465.
Longenecker, J. G. Systems, semantics and significance. *S. A. M. Advanced Management Journal,* April 1970, 63–67.
* Perrow, C. The short and glorious history of organization theory. *Organizational Dynamics,* AMACOM, a division of American Management Association, Summer 1973.
* Ross, J. E., & Murdick, R. G. People, productivity and organizational structure. *Personnel,* September–October 1973, 9–18.
* Scott, W. G. Organization theory: A reassessment. *Academy of Management Journal,* June 1974, 242–254.

* Stieglitz, H. What's not on the organization chart. *The Conference Board Record,* November 1964, 7–10.
* Thompson, J. D., & Bates, F. L. Technology, organization and administration. *Administrative Science Quarterly,* December 1957, 325–342.
* Weber, M. The essentials of bureaucratic organization: An ideal-type construction. In R. K. Merton *et al.* (Eds.), *A Reader in Bureaucracy.* Glencoe, Ill. Free Press, 1952, 18–27.

*Possible reading for students

**Review of literature or comprehensive source material

3

Understanding human behavior

Knowledge about what man has been and is
can protect the future.

Margaret Mead

In the preceding chapter we discussed some broad theories about how organizations should be viewed, designed, and administered. Almost all these approaches had an implicit or explicit view of human nature. They made certain assumptions about what motivates organizational members, and these assumptions were reflected in their prescriptions about rewards, leadership, motivation, power, and numerous other topics. The first part of Chapter 3 will attempt to describe the current thinking of most social scientists with respect to some basic questions about human nature.

Our earlier discussion focused on whether people were viewed as naturally lazy or self-serving; neutral; or positive and self-motivated. Proponents of the first position argue that people are rather lazy and need to be pushed and controlled and under surveillance, never to be trusted to put in a good day's work by themselves. Many of the early classical approaches made these types of assumptions. Economic rewards were the only ones considered, and close, autocratic supervision was suggested.

A more neutral position was held by the systems and contingency theorists. They saw people as adaptable and felt therefore that much of behavior was learned and not attributable to predispositions to be negative or positive. Different types of people were needed for different types of environments: the goal was the proper match between people and settings. In some cases an autocrat might work best, in other cases a more democratic approach would be successful. Finally, people such as Likert and McGregor and Bennis, who developed and extended the findings of the human-relations theorists, had a positive view of human nature. People were seen as striving for personal and social well-being. If left alone, they would work hard for the intrinsic satisfaction of a job well done. The emphasis was on democratic decision making and leadership. Jobs were to be challenging and allow the individual employee to be creative.

A closer inspection of the positive-neutral-negative trichotomy seemed to raise more questions than it answered. The terms "positive" and "negative" were obviously value-laden. Other issues which related to human nature seemed to be less emotionally charged and more relevant for decisions about organizational design. For example, one would like to know how flexible or changeable people actually are. Is their nature fixed or malleable? To what extent can training be used to modify one's behavior? Can we really change people once they join the organization? An equally important topic that was frequently debated by social scientists was whether the causes of behavior are internal or external events. Those that argued for external events tended to see the environment and immediate situational variables as causes of behavior. Those that believed in internal causes used instincts and personality traits as their explanations. To the degree that internal explanations were true, the organizational processes of selection and placement would become crucial. It would be very important to initially select the right type of person and place them in the right type of job, since there would be little chance of changing them later. If external events were the major cause of behavior, then the proper organizational environment could produce those behaviors deemed to be appropriate.

A related issue dealt with the uniqueness of human beings. Were we clearly different from our animal ancestors or were we guided by and subject to the same urges as animals? Also important was the question of uniqueness among human beings. Just how different are we from each other? If we are all very different and if much of our behavior cannot be predicted from simple observations of animal behavior, then an organization must build in flexibility to handle our complex unique characteristics. However, if we are all the same basically, then we can treat everyone alike (a boon for designers of any system).

The debates over these questions are far from over. They raise some profound philosophical and practical issues. There is, however, some consensus among most social scientists on these topics, and we will briefly review the evidence that led to these position. We will be concerned with the following questions.

1 Are humans unique?
2 How much and what kind of change can occur in people?
3 Are we controlled by internal or external processes?
4 Is our capacity for learning and change unlimited?

The conclusions we will draw from these discussions will point up two central facts: (1) learning is the central mechanism for changing people's behavior and (2) most people are capable of large amounts of change. The second part of the chapter discusses the basic concepts of learning theory and their importance for organizational practice.

The uniqueness of human beings

> Man is a predator whose natural instinct
> is to kill with a weapon.
>
> Robert Ardrey

For most of recorded history, human beings have been seen as unique, as holding a set of characteristics above and apart from those held by animals. Religious thought helped to support this interpretation. Humans had souls and had a special relationship to God.

One hundred years ago Charles Darwin published his revolutionary works *The Origin of Species* (1859) and *The Descent of Man* (1871). Darwin argued that human beings evolved just like other animals and that similar laws of selection and evolution were applicable for man and animals. In 1871 Darwin went even further with the claim that there was no fundamental difference in the higher mental processes of man and animals. Animals had intelligence and memory and learning and problem-solving abilities. The differences were relative and quantitative rather than qualitative.

This position essentially argues that human beings are not unique, that by studying animal behavior we can learn much about human behavior. It has continued to gain supporters, and in fact, today, there is a group of scientists called ethologists who hold strongly to these views. Many of these writers have published very successful and frequently cited books such as Konrad Lorenz' *On Aggression,* Robert Ardrey's *African Genesis* and *The Territorial Imperative,* or Desmond Morris' *The Naked Ape.*

In most cases those ethologists who take this position believe that (1) humans are animals and (2) any behavior pattern that seems to be generally true for most animals is probably true for humans. Each species evolves a set of behaviors that

A question of major importance is the degree to which human beings are different from their animal ancestors. (*By permission of University of Washington* Daily.)

have proved helpful for adaptation and survival. When these behaviors seem to be similar for most animal species, it seems natural that they should be important for humans as well.

Let us take an example. Ardrey and others have observed that most animals seem to have systems of dominance. Some animals within a particular species have more power and prestige than others, and this rank is known and recognized by others (e.g., the pecking order). Each animal knows to whom it must defer and whom it can dominate. Ardrey goes so far as to say: "Every organized animal society has its system of dominance. Whether it be a school of fish or a flock or birds or a herd of grazing wildebeest, there exists within that society some kind of status order in which individuals are ranked."[1] He provides numerous observational examples of such hierarchies.

The second element of the argument is that these behaviors have survival value for the species. In our example, Ardrey argues that systems of dominance make it likely that the strongest members of the species (highest rank) will have access to the best mate, the best living space, and the most food. Therefore, the species will continue to survive and evolve.

The final part of the argument is the analogy drawn between animals and humans. Since the pattern is present in most animals and has survival value, it is argued that it must be present in humans and it also has survival value. Similar analogies have been made to suggest that humans (1) are naturally aggressive, (2) have a drive to gain and defend territory, and (3) will naturally form closed social units which (4) will have a hierarchy or order of dominance. Thus, calls for social equity and peaceful international and social relationships are perhaps beyond our natural capabilities.

This is a provocative analysis. It suggests that the human race will continue to have wars, injustice, greed, and aggression due to our basic urges. We are not unique. We are nothing more than highly evolved apes.

The reaction to the current popularity of the ethological point of view has been mixed. Some writers find it unduly pessimistic and others criticize many of its basic positions. Still others have provided data which support the uniqueness of mankind. We should present their arguments as well.

The critics point out what they think is a logical fallacy in the ethologist's arguments. Just because certain behaviors seem to be similar across species does not necessarily mean that the motivation for that behavior or its consequences are also similar across species. Just because we use similar words or labels to describe the behavior (e.g., status) does not mean that the explanations are the same. We need additional information which shows that the behaviors have the same underlying cause and biological function.

There are also some areas of human behavior which seem to be unique to our species. First, and most obvious, is language development. Our ability to use linguistic symbols is not found elsewhere. While it is probably true that many animals communicate with one another, there is little evidence that they can make known anything more than very simple emotional reactions.

Recently there has been some research which has shown that chimpanzees can

---

[1]R. Ardrey. *African genesis*. New York: Dell, 1961.

By the way, whose territorial waters are we swimming in now?

The drive to defend territory has been described by some ethologists as an inborn characteristic.

learn a rudimentary form of sign language. These chimps, if continuously trained from an early age, can learn around 100 different signs and can string them together in sentencelike sequences. However, the sort of language sophistication reached by the best of these apes is little beyond what we expect from a 3-year-old child. We can conclude that while language development may not be completely unique, it is many magnitudes more sophisticated than that illustrated by the best animals.

There are also some differences in the way that mankind adjusts to its environment. Human beings clearly control and manipulate their environments in ways that facilitate adaptation. For most species an inhospitable environment meant a change in the species or death. Humans, on the other hand, will change the environment to suit their needs. This is a basic difference which in many respects can be seen as the reason we have survived and prospered as a species. Again, while there is evidence that some animals can use rudimentary tools (e.g., chimpanzees), the difference between humans and animals on this dimension is great.

Where does this leave us with respect to the uniqueness of the human race? Well, as usual, a position somewhere in between the two extremes seems to be most widely held. While it is true that our animal ancestry may have more to do with our current behavior than was previously believed, it is also true that there are certain dimensions which clearly differentiate our species from others. It is these dimensions of language, control, and adaptability which compound our complexity. An understanding of animal behavior will not be sufficient to understand human behavior.

These conclusions also help us to answer the second uniqueness question pertaining to the variability within the human species. Since we are not all governed by some easily describable set of behavior patterns, it is argued that humans are also not all alike. Individuals are not only unique with respect to other species but also with respect to their own species. We have all observed that people are different physically, emotionally, and intellectually. The questions of interest are, "How do they become that way?" and "What are the common elements of the human experience?" There are differences—but there are also similarities. To understand how this uniqueness occurs and the extent to which it overshadows similarities, we must understand how people develop and change.

The continuity of growth

One often hears the old saw "You can't teach an old dog new tricks" with reference to human beings. The essence of this statement is that with age we become more rigid, more fixed in our behavior patterns and habits. It becomes increasingly difficult to learn new skills and behaviors.

The implications for organizations are obvious. Most organizations need and desire some degree of flexibility, especially in our current complex, rapidly changing environment. Yet, there is some reason to believe that our older, more senior, people (who probably hold more responsible positions) are less flexible than other younger employees. If this is true, we may be placing the people with the least flexibility in those positions where flexibility is needed most. The homily about old dogs and new tricks needs to be thoroughly examined.

There is evidence from a number of sources that suggests we do in fact become more rigid with age. Some of this evidence discusses characteristics of people which makes it difficult to change, while other sources discuss aspects of the environment. We will review both these positions.

Personal characteristics

One set of personal characteristics that inhibit change would be personality traits. These traits are defined as enduring behavior patterns that seem to persist across situations. An individual is described as shy or extroverted or ambitious. These labels suggest that the person will behave in a certain way and will do so consistently. The traits develop very early in our life and are supposedly fixed by late adolescence.

A second source of the idea of personal constancy comes from social-psychological theories of attitudes and attitude change. These approaches are described as consistency theories, and their basic tenet is that humans strive for cognitive consistency or balance. We try to hold beliefs and attitudes that do not contradict one another. When a contradiction does occur, we are uncomfortable and feel motivated to reduce or eliminate the contradiction. We build up over time a very complex, interrelated structure of beliefs and attitudes that are supportive of our behavior. This structure is hard to change bit by bit, since the individual is more likely to reject the one new item of information than to change the whole cognitive structure.

Finally, there is some evidence that we selectively expose ourselves to information and people that already support our views. Very seldom do people seek out discrepant information or attitudes. Very seldom do people seek out other people that are very different from themselves. Thus, our personality traits and cognitive structures are constantly being bolstered and supported by the information and people to which we are exposed. This process reduces the possibilities for change.

Environmental characteristics

There are also some aspects of the *situation* which reduce the likelihood of change. First, the interpersonal environment stays fairly constant for most of us. Our friends, relatives, neighbors, and acquaintances tend to stay the same. While this circle may incorporate new people occasionally and discard others, there is more constancy than change.

This is also true of the groups to which we belong. Our church, social clubs, and recreational groups provide another source of stability. These social groups add some additional dimensions: norms and roles. Within most social settings, including the work environment, there are some fairly well-known rules about how people should behave in general (norms), and specifically how people in particular positions should behave (roles). There is a lot of pressure on all of us not to deviate from these norms or unwritten rules. To do so would encourage a reprimand or rejection by other group members. No one wants to be a social outcast.

At a somewhat larger level of analysis is our cultural environment. There are certain expectations about interpersonal behavior that exist in the United States but not in other countries. For example, Americans are very time-oriented, and punctuality is seen as a good characteristic. The same type of behavior in some other cultures might be seen as rude and insulting. These general cultural expectations also reduce the individual's ability to change.

In summary, the evidence seems to suggest that it may in fact be hard to teach an old dog new tricks. There are both personal and environmental pressures that reduce change and increase constancy. But before we despair, we should examine these issues further. What in fact can the organization do? Well, it is unlikely that most organizations will be able to change the basic personality structure of their employees. On the other hand, management does have some control over the organizational environment. Rules, regulations, policies, rewards, chains of command, and other formal aspects of the organization's structure can be modified. Communication lines can be influenced as well as the types of people who are selected to join the organization. Some social aspects of the situation can be controlled.

The crucial question then becomes, "Which is the *most important* determinant of behavior, the internal personal characteristics of the individual or the outside environment?" If our answer is personal characteristics, then there probably is little that can be done in organizations where people do not even enter the situation until their late teens or early twenties. If our answer is the environment, however, there is a lot we can do. The next section examines this debate in more detail.

Internal versus external determinants of behavior

Men's natures are like, it is their habits
that carry them far apart.   Confucius

The controversy over internal versus external determinants of behavior exists in many forms and is relevant for many other topics on human behavior. The environmentalists, at one extreme, believe that almost everything is learned and can therefore be attributed to the environment. If we can control the environment, we can control the individual. This is the external position. Those opposed to this view (e.g., ethologists, cognitive psychologists) have suggested a number of internal mechanisms as causes of behavior, such as instincts, personality traits, or beliefs and thought processes. We will briefly review three internal arguments and attempt to arrive at some sort of conclusion with respect to this issue.

Instincts versus the environment

Earlier in this century, much of human social behavior was described as instinctive. Instinct was defined as an *internally* generated drive to activity. These drives were hereditary and genetically programmed. There were instincts for aggression, shyness, and cleanliness. There were instincts for just about anything, including the liking for apples. What started out as a scientific explanation of behavior soon turned into a word game. To describe some behavior as caused by instincts did little to help our understanding of why the behavior occurred.

The reaction of many American social scientists was to go to the opposite extreme. They argued that almost all behavior was learned and environmentally (externally) determined. John Watson, who was the founder of this position (called *behaviorism*), went so far as to say that if you gave him a healthy infant, he could train the child to be any type of specialist one might select—doctor, lawyer, beggarman, or thief. However, as we will discuss more fully in a moment, behaviorism rejected too much.

The current evidence suggests that perhaps a few neural patterns are instinctual and that specific behaviors do occur in response to specific stimuli. For example, there is some evidence that infants have instinctual preferences for certain types of visual stimuli. Also, the work of Piaget suggests that intelligence and cognitive development pass through a series of genetically regulated stages.

Finally, there are numerous linguists that believe language development is greatly influenced by inborn determinants. But these examples are of minor importance to the richness of our behavior. The prevailing view is that most behavior is learned rather than instinctual.

Personality versus the environment

A somewhat different internal explanation of behavior refers to personality traits. The debate here focuses on whether behavior is caused by enduring personal characteristics or by external environmental events. It is different from our instinct argument because most personality theorists believe that one's personality is partly learned (i.e., not due to instincts). The differences with the external environmental position are twofold. First, most personality theorists believe that personality is formed at a fairly early age. They argue, therefore, that it is long-forgotten past environmental events that determine behavior. The environmentalist position holds that more immediate and current external events cause behavior. Second, the personality theorists believe that traits are fairly enduring and consistent. Therefore, a person who is shy in one situation should be shy in all situations. The environmentalist says, on the other hand, that someone can be shy in one setting and extroverted in another; it all depends on the demands of the situation.

Recently there have been some summaries of lots of studies that examine both positions. These papers review research where both personality variables and situational variables are simultaneously measured and observed as determinants of behavior. The results support both positions but are more supportive of the environmentalist point of view. While personality traits do seem to be useful for predicting behavior across settings, the situational variables do about twice as well. The obvious conclusion is that both personality and situational variables must be taken into account in order to explain an individual's behavior.

Cognitions versus the environment

The third and final internal versus external argument is between behaviorist and cognitive points of view. The strict behaviorist believes in environmental determinism: All noninstinctual behavior is caused by past and present environmental events. To understand one's behavior all we have to know is the individual's past responses to similar stimulus situations and the rewards or punishments that followed that response. There is no reference to internal cognitive events such as attitudes, beliefs, or values as causes of behavior.

The cognitive viewpoint says that, yes, the environment is important as are past rewards and punishments, but it is our cognitive interpretations (e.g., our evaluations, our memories, our expectations) that actually cause our behavior. The behaviorist model might best be represented as a stimulus-response model (S-R model), and the cognitive model, by a stimulus-organism-response model (S-O-R model). Both approaches see learning and the environment as having a major impact on behavior. However, the cognitive position says that there is an intermediate step between the external environmental stimulus and the response.

This intermediate step is the cognitive processing and evaluation of the environment. While both approaches might make similar *predictions* about how an individual would behave, their *explanation* for the behavior would be very different.

Again, we find that the position held by most social scientists is not the extreme point of view. Most of them would reject the idea that behavior can be completely explained by external environmental events and contingencies. There is ample evidence that in some cases cognitive events are better predictors of behavior.

To summarize, most social scientists have moved a long way toward, but not all the way to, a position that suggests an environmental determination of behavior. Instincts are infrequently seen as determinants of behavior. Personality traits are important but less so than the environment. But the movement in the environmental direction stops there. Few social scientists have gone all the way to the position of environmental determinism, the belief that all behavior can be explained by past external events. There is still the strong belief that human beings are cognitively active processors and evaluators of the environment and

What do you think is the problem with me, Mom? Is it heredity or the environment?

Both heredity and environment help to shape our behavior with a somewhat greater contribution made by the latter than the former.

that this cognitive activity influences their behavior. Our final question deals with the limitations of these cognitive activities.

Human limitations

An analysis of the internal-versus-external-causes-of-behavior question posed another problem. If we were guided completely or mostly by instincts and our genetic composition, then somehow the amount of change that would be possible for each individual would be severely limited. On the other hand, if behavior was completely determined by the environment, then the capacity of the human being was almost unlimited. We could become anything we wanted.

Well, as we mentioned before, most people seem to feel that the "true" answer to this question lies somewhere between the two extremes—our capacity is determined by both internal genetic factors and external environmental ones with a much greater emphasis on the latter than the former.

The social implications of this type of position were of extreme importance. It meant that large numbers of people who previously were classified as disadvantaged because of their genetic background were not seen as disadvantaged anymore. Their poor performance in school, on the job, and in other areas of social competence could be attributed to an impoverished environment. It meant that organizations could have a powerful impact on the behavior of their members through education and training. It meant that a society could allocate resources to increase the skills and abilities of its disadvantaged members. Much of the social and political reform of the 1960s reflected this type of thinking.

In retrospect we were perhaps too ambitious. There were incredible practical, financial, and ethical problems with attempts to consistently control and manipulate the environment. But there were also some scientific problems. That is, we learned that even in areas of functioning that could not be attributed to genetic factors, human beings were limited. There were points beyond which more training or education were irrelevant. People as *individuals* had physical and psychological limits.

Some examples might help. In the areas of processing of information and perception, we find that the human being is limited. People are only able to deal with a few (5 ± 2) dimensions of information at a time. More complex inputs cause confusion and overload. Similarly, there are limits to what we can store and remember. Our memory does not have an unlimited capacity. Finally, the research in decision making shows that humans make some systematic errors in processing information. They are cautious in their reevaluation of data, they do not use all of the information available, and that which they do use often has less of an impact than some mathematical model (which could generate an optimal solution) says that it should. While some change is possible, we will never be able to remove human error and limitations.

Review

An examination of all of the questions raised above shows that certain positions seem to cluster together. Some people believe that behavior is mostly caused by instincts and personality traits that are formed at an early age. They think that change is very difficult for the individual and that one's capacity is severely limited. Some schools of thought still hold these views today. The opposite position is that our behavior is mostly learned through our interactions with the environment, that current events rather than past events are important, and that even though there are some limitations on our capacities we are capable of great amounts of change.

While these issues are far from settled, one thing is clear. There is an overwhelming consensus that the environment has a much greater effect on our behavior than we used to believe. The implications for organizations are important. It means that large areas of human behavior are modifiable. Organizational design, training, and development can have a profound impact on the behavior of the members of an organization. Thus, it becomes imperative that we understand the basic processes of individual and social learning—the ways in which these changes come about.

Understanding behavior: Learning

> One thorn of experience is worth
> a whole wilderness of warning.　　　James Russell Lowell

Much of our behavior in organizations is learned behavior. We learn various skills and interpersonal techniques that help us to function successfully in that setting. These are frequently skills and behaviors that we did not have before we entered the particular setting (e.g., running a lathe or giving orders to subordinates). Learning implies a basic change in our behavior. We are able to do something we could not do before.

In the next few pages we will attempt to define and describe some of the basic concepts of learning. Many new terms will be introduced and it may be difficult at first to remember all of them. However, most of the terms and concepts discussed will appear again in other chapters (e.g., motivation, training) and you should soon be familiar with them.

One preliminary point is worth mentioning. In an earlier section we emphasized that each human being is unique, but that there were some common elements to the human experience. Learning is one of those processes which is basically similar for most people. *What* we learn may be drastically different due to our different environments, but *how* we learn is pretty much the same. It is a process common to the human condition.

A definition of learning

The research on learning has been extensive over the last 60 years. Numerous definitions of learning exist which differ in a variety of ways. However, some agreement is apparent, and it suggests the following.

First, learning involves change. It has to do with the acquisition of new knowledge or skills. Second, learning is a process. It involves some sort of opportunity to repeat or practice the skills. This process typically involves some sort of feedback from the outside (e.g., teacher, trainer) about what is being done well or poorly. This information facilitates the learning process. Finally, in most cases we see learning as a fairly permanent change. However, as we shall see, unless someone has the opportunity to illustrate the behavior and to receive feedback every once in a while, the learning may eventually disappear.

Instrumental learning

While a variety of types of learning are discussed in the literature (e.g., classical conditioning, escape-avoidance learning), by far the most frequently studied process is described as *instrumental* learning. The focus is on some past behavior or response and three elements associated with the response:

1 The stimulus situation in which the response occurs
2 The response itself
3 The action of the environment on the individual after the response has been made

The emphasis of most of the principles of learning is on the interrelationships of these three elements: the stimulus situation, the response, and the consequences (action of the environment) of the response. The first and most basic of these principles is described as reinforcement.

When the consequences of a particular behavior are positive, that is, pleasant or desirable to the individual, we would expect that when the same stimulus conditions occur that the same response would occur. Consequences or environmental actions that *increase* the frequency of a response are called *positive reinforcers*. Food positively reinforces those behaviors that are related to eating. If the termination or removal of a negative outcome or consequence results in an *increase* in behavior, this outcome is described as a *negative reinforcer*. If, for example, you have your finger on a hot stove, removing your finger from the stove results in the reduction of pain. The hot stove would be a negative reinforcer. Finally, if the consequences seem to *decrease* the frequency of a behavior, we would describe those consequences as punishments. If every time you come to work early your boss says, "You're being a little overeager, aren't you?" you may stop coming early. Thus, reinforcement has to do with the effect of the consequences of a response on whether the response will increase or decrease in frequency.

One has to choose words carefully in a discussion such as this. You will recall that a basic conflict which still exists today is between the cognitive theorist and the behaviorist who believes that only external environmental events cause behavior. The cognitive theorist believes that reinforcement—the action taken by the environment—affects cognitive events. If as a consequence of my behavior (I show up to work on time) something happens to me that I like (I get a $2 bonus), I will be more likely to show up on time the next day because I *expect* to get a bonus, and the bonus is *attractive* to me.

The behaviorist would not refer to these cognitive events such as liking or expecting, but would simply say that if the consequence of the behavior increases the likelihood of the behavior, then positive reinforcement has occurred. If the frequency of the behavior decreases, then punishment has occurred. While these differences in explanation are important from a philosophical viewpoint (and we will discuss them more fully in the chapter on motivation), they are less important from a practical viewpoint. That is, both theorists might make highly similar predictions of behavior even though the underlying explanation for that behavior was different. With these differences in mind, we will continue the discussion of learning.

Some important distinctions

A number of different classification systems exist for the type of reinforcement used or the way it is administered. One fairly common distinction is made between intrinsic and extrinsic reinforcement. Intrinsic factors are seen as coming from the job itself. Things such as responsibility, achievement, and recognition are often described as intrinsic. Extrinsic factors typically come from the organization or from outside the individual. Some examples are pay, working conditions, and job security. For example, let us look at the consequences of a builder completing the construction of a house. The completion of the task will result in some external or extrinsic rewards that may bear no direct relationship to the building behavior itself (it is not a natural consequence of it). Such rewards might include great financial benefits. However, there is also some reward in just completing the job itself. This reward would be described as intrinsic because it is a natural consequence of the behavior itself. A job finished is a pleasant experience. Much of the research on organizational reward systems, as we shall see, divides up rewards into these extrinsic and intrinsic categories (e.g., a financial bonus versus more autonomy on the job).

Another distinction that is related to reinforcement is between primary and secondary reinforcers. Primary reinforcers are those rewards which are innately satisfying to the individual in terms of the reduction of basic physiological drives. Food for a hungry individual is a good example. However, secondary reinforcers are consequences which are satisfying because they were initially paired or related to primary reinforcers. It is a learned reward (as opposed to being innately satisfying), and most of the rewards in the organizational setting are described as secondary reinforcers. For instance, a hungry child begins to associate food with the warm cuddling it receives from its mother. Later, the warm cuddling becomes satisfying in itself. Rewards such as affection and approval may later become important secondary reinforcers in an organizational setting.

One other issue that should be mentioned is the difference between reinforcement and punishment. Punishment can be described as *either* the withholding of a positive reward (e.g., no bonus) or the introduction of a noxious stimulus (e.g., a reprimand). The research that investigates whether positive/negative reinforcement or punishment is more effective has produced conflicting results. It seems as if punishment is most effective when (1) it is severe, (2) it forces the person to produce the desired behavior which can be positively reinforced, and (3) it is administered immediately after the undesirable response. When these conditions do not occur, people often do not know what they are being punished for. Also, punishment demands that you are able to monitor or observe what the individual is doing (a person is sure to tell you when something good has happened but not when something bad has happened). It is therefore often difficult to actually administer punishment consistently and appropriately. For these reasons most learning theorists suggest that one use positive reinforcers for desired behaviors and ignore rather than punish undesirable behaviors.

The timing and administration of rewards brings up the discussion of schedules of reinforcement and learning curves. In organizations, we may be able to control both the amount and the occasion when a reward is administered. Going back to our example of receiving a bonus for showing up at work on time may be helpful. The organization can control how much of a bonus I receive (e.g., $2 or $5) and when I receive it (e.g., every occasion I arrive on time or every other occasion). The differences in amount and frequency produce different learning processes. In general, the more frequent and more positive the reward, the more quickly the behavior is learned. We will discuss some specific schedules of reinforcement with regard to organizational behavior in the chapter on motivation.

Finally, there are some concepts which are also important for understanding the complexity of the learning process. One obvious point is that if after learning a behavior (e.g., coming to work on time) the reward is removed or not administered, *extinction* may occur. The individual may stop being punctual. Another principle is called *generalization*. What frequently happens is that when an individual learns a specific response to a specific situation (e.g., coming to work on time), he or she may after a while illustrate the same behavior in other stimulus conditions which are similar but not exactly the same as those conditions where the initial learning took place. Our employee may start showing up to all meetings on time as well. The opposite of generalization is called *discrimination*. At the point where two stimulus situations (similar in some respects, different in others) produce two different behaviors, we say that discrimination has occurred. If we find that our employee comes to work on time but not to meetings on time, we must assume that there are major differences between the two stimulus settings.

So, in general, we can change people's behavior through the learning process. This requires that we understand how to administrer various types of rewards and that we observe the responses to these rewards. Since the organization has at its disposal a wide variety of rewards, it can have a powerful impact on the learning that takes place.

Learning in the social setting

Much of what we learn occurs in social situations. Since our interest is the causes of behavior in organizational settings, these social aspects of learning are of primary importance. The following discussion of these topics will be brief, but the issues raised will be discussed in detail in later sections of the text.

Roles

What happens when we join an organization? Well, usually we are given a title of some sort, such as novice, secretary, research analyst, or administrative assistant. This title usually reflects the fact that we hold some sort of position in the organization. Each position carries with it a number of duties, responsibilities, rules, regulations, and generally expected behavior patterns. This set of expected behaviors for a given position is defined as a role. The term *role* is used to reflect the fact that all persons (regardless of their unique personal characteristics) are supposed to behave a certain way if they occupy this specific position. The role, therefore, is impersonal.

If we recall our basic principles of learning, we can readily see what is provided by the role. Whether the expectations are written down or to be observed, they still serve the function of making contingencies known to the role occupant. More specifically, the person learns what behaviors are rewarded (positively reinforced) and not rewarded. Let us take an example. You join a large advertising agency as a secretary. You notice on your first day of work that all the secretaries address their supervisor as Mr. or Ms. However, on your last job you addressed people by their first name and you continue to do so. What will happen? Well, perhaps after a day or two one of the other secretaries may alert you to the fact that you are being too personal with the supervisor, or even worse the supervisor may say something to you about not showing the proper respect. In any case you would quickly learn what was appropriate—what was rewarded and what was not.

Some roles are easier to learn than others. Obviously, the clearer the role the better. If expectations are explicit and agreed upon, people can see them, read them, verbalize them, and practice them. However, in some cases there are internal inconsistencies or aspects of the job that are unclear (e.g., one supervisor likes to be addressed as Ms. while another likes to be addressed by her first name). To the degree to which these ambiguities exist, it will be more difficult for the individual to learn what behavior is appropriate.

Role models

Another important way that people learn to behave appropriately in social settings is through the use of human models. Even if role expectations are unclear or not explicitly written down (e.g., as a job description), one can observe the behavior of another person in a similar position. Through these observations one can learn the prevailing environmental contingencies. You can see what gets rewarded and what does not.

There are some aspects of the modeling process which make it more likely to be effective. First, the model should be readily observable and attractive. It helps if the learner *wants* to be like the model. It is also important that the learner has the capacity to do what the model does and that opportunities exist to try out what is learned from observing the model. Practice facilitates learning.

Finally, an important aspect of both role and model learning is that the person receive feedback (positive or negative reinforcement). In many cases this feed-

This will teach you not to fight and hit people.

People learn from models and they often "do what you do" rather than "do what you say."

back is readily available in the external environment. Systems of evaluation, financial rewards, and interactions with peers and supervisors all provide feedback information. In some cases the feedback is built into the job itself (e.g., a secretary knows when two typewriter keys have been hit at the same time). In other situations feedback is very hard to come by.

One of the most prevalent feedback mechanisms is internal, and it is part of what we describe as the social comparison process. No one may tell us that we are doing something wrong, but it may be obvious to us that our peers are getting many rewards (praise, bonuses) and we are not. We immediately ask ourselves "What am I doing wrong?" or "What are they doing right?" As we shall see later, this social comparison process is the basis of an important theory of motivation.

So, the learning process in social settings is very complex. We are positively and negatively reinforced by many different sources and aspects of the job. However, a number of things are clear: The more explicit the contingency, the more frequently it is expressed, the more obvious the feedback, and the more important the reward, the more likely it is to be learned. These principles will appear frequently throughout the text.

Summary

The focus of this chapter was to increase our understanding of the causes of human behavior. If we know what causes behavior we will be better able to (1) realize our limitations and (2) realize our capabilities. We should have a better idea of what is changeable and how it is changeable. Let us review some of the most important points.

1 The human race and individual persons are unique. While our genetic makeup may broadly influence our behavior, the most important contribution comes from what we learn.
2 The external environment is being recognized as an increasingly important determinant of behavior. Instincts and personality traits as internal causes of behavior are being deemphasized.
3 The individual has a great capacity for change. While with increasing age it becomes increasingly difficult to change people's behavior, this does not mean that the person is not capable of change. It often means that we cannot control many of the environmental aspects that would produce this change.
4 The major mechanism through which change occurs is learning. Learning involves the fairly permanent acquisition of new knowledge or skills.
5 The most important aspects of learning are the stimulus, the response, and the consequences of the response. These consequences, or reinforcers, tend to strengthen or weaken the relationship between the stimulus situation and the behavioral response.
6 The organization can formally have a great influence on the reinforcements provided. Systems of financial rewards, bonuses, praise, and training can change the behavior or organizational members.
7 Finally, the social environment composed of role expectations, models, and social comparisons also influences learning. The organization can have a significant effect on these aspects of the learning process.

Implications for practice

There are some important conclusions of practical value that should be strongly emphasized. The first point is that people are *changeable*. While increasing age may slightly decrease the ease with which change is brought about, it by no means should be seen as a serious limitation. We are always capable of learning new behavior.

The second point is that the *external environment makes an important contribution to what we learn and how we behave.* Learning occurs as a function of the relationship between the environment, organizational rewards, and our cognitive processing of this information. Combining the two points suggests that an organization can have a very powerful impact on the behavior of its participants.

So what happens when you have a "people" problem; some employee continually fails to meet deadlines or some manager is particularly hard to get hold of. The traditional view is to refer to internal states as the cause of behavior: "He does that because he's ornery or lazy." What we are arguing is that you try out other interpretations. Look at the environment surrounding the individual. See if there are situational explanations for the person's behavior. Perhaps he fails to meet deadlines because he is overloaded with work.

If, in fact, we can see various situational explanations for the behavior, then it is hoped that we can do something short of firing the person. Asking a person to leave the organization is very expensive and time-consuming. A new person must be interviewed, selected, and trained. Also, if the cause is in fact situational, the new employee will soon have the same problem.

Since the organization has a large amount of control over environmental contingencies, you should be able to change the situation in such a way that the desired behaviors can be learned. Training can be used, tasks can be changed, and rewards administered. What was originally a people problem becomes an organizational puzzle, a problem that may be solved through the learning process.

Discussion questions

1 Is behavior caused by our environment or by internal mechanisms such as instincts, personality traits, or cognitions? What are the implications of your answer for social policy and organizational design?
2 Describe the learning process. What are the major elements involved?
3 What are the ways we learn in an organization? Are there ways to facilitate this process?

Case: Learning about booze

Through much of his college career and graduate school, Alan Daily was known as a conscientious and personable young man. He worked hard to get his master's degree in urban planning. Upon graduation he took a job with the Department of Housing and Urban Development as a technical analyst. He was excited about the job and looked forward to being involved with the policy issues focusing on urban housing.

Because of his rather easy social manner, Alan fit in on the job immediately. He made friends with everyone and was soon considered to be "one of the group." Most of his four or five professional peers had similar training and similar interests, so Alan enjoyed his interactions with them immensely. One of the times he liked best was the lunch break. Almost everyone went outside to one of the nearby restaurants to eat, and it was a good time to exchange ideas. Alan had been used to bringing a bag lunch in graduate school or eating at the university cafeteria, so eating out every day was a real treat.

Alan noticed that almost everyone had an alcoholic drink before lunch, sometimes two. At first he declined to have a drink but eventually he decided to join in. He had had drinks before—plenty when he was in college—but drinking at lunch was new. However, he soon found that the drink seemed to make the lunch hour just a little bit more pleasant, and it didn't seem to disturb his effectiveness on the job. In fact, it seemed to relax him a little.

Over the next few years the newness of the job began to wear off. Alan was less excited about what he did—much of the job turned out to be paper pushing, and he felt that most decisions were being made based on political issues rather than technical knowledge. He began to look forward more and more to lunch and his two drinks beforehand. He also had a drink—sometimes two—before dinner. When he came home, he wanted to forget about the job, and alcohol seemed to help.

Before long, Alan knew he had a problem. He was drinking too much. He was ineffective most of the afternoon and he found himself coming in late and then leaving early for lunch (''I'll go get a table''). He decided to seek out professional help.

One group in town was well known for its work with people with a drinking problem, so he signed up for a set of sessions designed to stop someone from drinking. At the first session, Alan was placed in a room that was very similar to a restaurant or tavern. There was a bar, other people, the lights were low, and there were plenty of tables and chairs. Alan was asked to order a drink and he did—a dry double martini on the rocks—lots of olives. The drink had a slightly funny taste, and after he finished it he felt violently ill. He ran to the nearest bathroom and threw up. Once again he was told to have a drink—again he threw up and he was allowed to go home.

The sessions continued this way, and Alan soon found that the thought of a drink was very aversive. Every time he thought of alcohol he thought about being sick. His discussions with the medical director of the program confirmed his beliefs about was was happening—they were drugging his drinks to make him sick. He was told that in some cases of early alcohol dependency this sort of treatment could be effective. Alan was convinced. Just the thought of a bar and a drink made him ill. He started bringing his lunch to work and, although he missed the lively discussions at lunchtime, he felt he had learned a valuable lesson about himself.

Questions about the case

1 What was the valuable lesson that Alan learned?
2 Would Alan have developed a drinking problem if he had been on some other type of job?
3 What was the *cause* of Alan's drinking problem? Was it Alan's personality or was it the job? Or his friends?
4 What was the process by which Alan gave up alcohol?
5 Do you think he will stay off the booze?

Additional readings

* Allee, W. C., Nissen, H. W., & Nimkoff, M. F. A reexamination of the concept of instinct. *Psychological Review*, 1953, **60**, 287–297.
* Ardrey, R. *The territorial imperative*. New York: Atheneum, 1966.
** Bandura, A. *Social learning theory*. New York: General Learning Press, 1971.
   Beach, L. R. *Psychology: Core concepts and special topics*. New York: Holt, 1973.
* Berger, S. M. Observer practice and learning during exposure to a model. *Journal of Personality and Social Psychology*, 1966, **3**, 696–701.
   Freedman, J. L., & Sears, D. O. Selective exposure. In M. L. Berkowitz (Ed.), *Advances in Experimental Social Psychology*. New York: Academic, 1965, **2**, 57–97.

** Gagne, R. M. *The conditions of learning*. New York: Holt, 1970.

 * Gardner, R. A., & Gardner, B. T. Teaching sign language to a chimpanzee. *Science,* 1969, **165,** 664–672.

** Hebb, D. O., & Thompson, W. R. The social significance of animal studies. In G. Lindzey & E. Aronson (Eds.), *Handbook of Social Psychology*. Reading, Mass.: Addison-Wesley, 1968, **2,** 729– 774.

** Hilgard, E. R., & Bower, G. H. *Theories of learning*. New York: Appleton, 1966.

** Hill, W. F. *Learning: A survey of psychological interpretations*. Scranton, Pa.: Chandler, 1971.

     Lorenz, K. *On aggression*. Translated by Marjorie Wilson. New York: Harcourt, Brace, 1966.

** Montagu, M. F. A. (Ed.). *Men and aggression*. New York: Oxford, 1973.

 * Taylor, F. V. Four basic ideas in engineering psychology. *American Psychologist,* 1960, **15,** 643– 649.

 * Watson, G. What do we know about learning. *NEA Journal,* March 1963, 20–22.

*Possible reading for students

**Review of literature or comprehensive source material

4

Research foundations

No action, whether foul or fair, is ever done
but it leaves somewhere a record.   Longfellow

The last chapter in this section discusses research issues. In order to understand human behavior in organizations we need to know (1) something about humans, (2) something about organizations, and (3) something about the process by which we can acquire this knowledge. Chapters 2 and 3 covered some principles of human nature and the organizational environment. Chapter 4 provides an overview of the research process. As a package these three chapters should supply the background material that is necessary to understand subsequent sections of the book.

An understanding of the research process is of central importance to anyone working in an organizational environment. This is true for a number of reasons. First, people in responsible positions in organizations are constantly in need of good, reliable *information*. Decisions have to be made, and better decisions are made when the information is correct. Suppose you are asked by your boss to come up with a plan to increase morale and decrease absenteeism. What do you need to know? How would you do it? Well, at a very general level you would want to know (1) are people really dissatisfied, (2) does low morale cause absenteeism, (3) what causes dissatisfaction, (4) what causes satisfaction—what can I do to turn the situation around? All these questions require reliable, empirically based answers. In order to acquire these answers and obtain unambiguous information, high-quality research is needed.

Besides those situations where research can be used to help the manager to make decisions, there are numerous other situations where understanding the research process is important for effective organizational or personal performance. The most obvious of these is the situation where information from a completed research project has to be *evaluated*.

We are constantly being bombarded by the results of this or that survey, both on the job and at home. The advertisements on television and radio provide excellent examples. Is the statement that "95 percent of the doctors surveyed that recommend chewing gum, recommend sugarless gum" a believable testimonial about the positive effects of chewing gum? Before answering that question, one needs to know who was sampled and how; what was the number of respondents; and most crucially what percent of doctors actually recommend that people chew gum at all. Ninety-five percent of, let us say, the five percent who make such recommendations is not very many doctors.

In order to evaluate research we have to understand how it is done and some basic rules which separate good research from poor research. When a research report comes across your desk, you should be able to evaluate the way it was done. You may not be familiar with the technical content or the statistical procedures, but if you can discriminate a good study from a poor one, you can make a fairly good estimate about how confident one should be with the conclusions.

Finally, we are constantly being asked to be *participants* in research. At home, there are surveys by mail and by phone. At the office there are always different studies going on, especially in large organizations. Your time is a valuable resource and it should not be wasted on frivolous research. There are also some ethical questions about one's right to privacy, who is sponsoring the research, and whether consent is voluntary.

In summary, research is increasingly impinging on our everyday lives. In some cases we need to sponsor it in order to acquire information or we have to evaluate it once it is done. In other cases, we are the participants. In all these situations a better understanding of the research process should increase our ability to cope successfully with our personal and organizational environment.

Conceptual research issues

The behavioral sciences are valuable for management on at least three levels. First, they formulate abstract concepts and explanations about human behavior. This is the conceptual contribution to management. Second, they provide a way of gathering data and thinking about these relationships. This is the methodological contribution. Third, they contribute to administrative policy decisions with respect to change. This is the action contribution. All three of these levels also have ethical implications both for the people doing the research and those participating in the research. It is the conceptual issues with which we will concern ourselves in this section.

The scientific approach

Scientific activity is designed to generate rules or laws which help us to understand the relationship among current events and to predict future events. Science attempts to simplify into general laws the processes which govern the external objects of sense perception. It does this by setting forth a set of general strategies for making inferences about observations. These strategies or characteristics of scientific inquiry reflect a certain spirit as to how we pursue knowledge and how we evaluate it. There are a number of elements that make up this process.

First, it is important to point out that when a scientist is doing research, he or she is *systematically planning* in an *unbiased* way how a particular question will be answered. Second, one usually gathers some sort of record of one's observations. These records are one's *data* and although they may be gathered in a variety of ways—questionnaires, observation, interviews, and so on—they emphasize the empirical nature of the process. Third, these data are usually subjected to some sort of *unbiased analysis* which addresses itself to the kinds of inferences that can be made. That is, how much confidence can one have in the results? Fourth, the findings are usually *public* in the sense that they are communicated to others through various media (journals, speeches, and so forth) and can therefore be replicated or extended if necessary. Fifth, because of its systematic and public nature, the knowledge can be *cumulative*. One can build on what others have done.

How does this process differ from common-sense procedures for gaining knowledge? There are a number of important differences worth mentioning. Scientists are more *systematic* and less selective in the ways that they gather information. Hopefully, *both positive and negative support* for one's ideas or theories are recorded. It is also true that scientists often *actively pursue* certain relationships. That is, they actually set up situations to test their ideas. By setting up these situations, they are also *establishing some control* over the setting which is often missing in our everyday experiences. Finally, scientists usually attempt to *rule out metaphysical (not testable) explanations* of observed phenomena. An example of this last point comes from the early work on leadership where observational studies were made of successful leaders or managers. The behavior of these individuals was often attributed to instincts or inherited characteristics. The list of instincts became so long that the approach did little to further our understanding or prediction of successful leaders because of the nontestable nature of the explanation.

The scientific process, therefore, requires a method of inquiry that actively seeks out information, both supportive and nonsupportive, in a systematic and unbiased manner and reports this information in a way that can be used by others. It should also be mentioned that although the process of inquiry may indeed lead to great increases in knowledge, it is not the only route to knowledge, nor is it always done well. A poorly run experiment contributes very little more to our knowledge than any other person's personal assumptions about behavior. Because it is "scientific" does not necessarily make it good or right.

The scientific method

The scientific way of thinking usually proceeds through a regular progression of logical steps. There is some time spent in formulating ideas and stating hypotheses. This is a problem identification and clarification stage. There is a period during which the actual experiment is carried out. This is the data-

The first part of any research effort or problem-solving activity is the clear recognition of the problem or issue itself. (*By permission of University of Washington* Daily.)

gathering and analysis phase. And there is some final work which involves the conclusions that can be drawn and their public presentations. This is the inference phase. We will discuss these steps in more detail.

Generating ideas

> Theories are attempts at explaining the inner workings of a watch
> whose mechanisms are not accessible to direct observation. Albert Einstein

Usually the first step in the process of scientific investigation is to state explicitly some question for which the scientist wants an answer (e.g., what makes an organization effective?). To provide possible suggestions may require intuition, reference to some sort of model, or the development of an elaborate theory. To communicate these suggestions requires the clear usage of language and agreed-upon usage of terms.

Terms. The whole problem of definition centers around the meaning which we ascribe to a given term. The words in a theory may refer to observable objects (e.g., number of people present in the organization) or unobservable states (e.g., the level of morale of the managers). It is fairly clear what one means by the first variable (i.e., number of people), because people agree on such things as how to count and everyone can observe the objects of study.

The issue is not as clear for the second variable of interest. Different people may not agree on what they mean by morale. It is definitely true that we cannot see it. Therefore, the two things that make the first term clear—that it can be seen and that there is agreement on how it should be measured—are not available for the second term. We remedy this problem by developing theories or by the use of models.

Theories. There are numerous definitions of what is meant by theory. In general theories are sets of statements which make predictions about empirical events. There are three critical elements of this definition.

First, a theory is an understandable set of statements. This means that it is communicable and public. Other people can read it, test it, or discard it. With a theory, the crucial thing is that others can see how and why you did what you did. They may not agree with your theory, but then, the answer to that problem is a matter of empirical support.

Second, theories make predictions. That is, they are to some extent anticipation systems. They may also interpret or unify established laws or enable one to fit unanticipated data into their formulation. Anticipation does not necessarily mean that the theory must be used for future events but simply that it correctly accounts for events that have been, are, or would be unaccountable for without the theory.

Both theory and practice are important for advances in any field.

Finally, theories deal with empirical events. At some point every theory must be tied to events and objects with some sort of observable referent about which people agree. If one has a theory about how a manager's anxiety is related to performance, then at some point he or she must specify what would happen if the relationship existed. For example, one might suggest that a small amount of anxiety increased output, whereas large amounts hindered output. If the measurement of anxiety (some questionnaire, for example) is related to actual productivity measures in the way that the theory predicts, then the manager has increased our confidence in his or her conceptualization of anxiety and in the theory as a whole.

Models. In conceptualizing an area of interest more clearly, it may be helpful to use a model of some sort. Models are systems which represent an area of interest in terms of the structure but not of the content. Comparing the behavior of a human being with that of a machine is an example that is often used. Supposedly, whenever a relationship exists between two elements of one system, a corresponding one exists between elements of the other system.

There are different kinds of models. Some of them might present a physical representation of one's interests. Simulations such as those seen on space flights are good examples. Business games also attempt to simulate the actual setting. One may have symbolic or conceptual analogies such as the analogy between people and machines or ideal structures similar to Weber's early work on organizations. There are also models of and for theories which show how theories should look as a structure of uninterpreted symbols.

Models are therefore guides in the process of formulating and understanding a problem. They may help to organize our thoughts, show us gaps in our knowledge, or guide us in what to look for in relationships and how to look for relationships.

One must be careful, however, of the possible shortcomings of models. Occasionally an overemphasis is put on either the symbols or the form of a model. Because a model is elegant does not mean it is correct. Another problem with models is that they may be oversimplified or narrow people's perspective in ways which cause them to overlook critical issues related to their theory or observations. In general, then, it must be remembered that models are analogies and that analogies are not expected to be completely accurate.

Data gathering

Suppose that one has developed a theory of organizational effectiveness and wishes to test it. He or she wants some empirical support for the predictions that have been made. To obtain the answers one must address oneself to two major issues: methodology and practical problems.

Methods. There are many different ways to gather data. We can use questionnaires, observations, interviews, archives, movies, and other procedures. The method we use will determine the kind of information we gather, and each method has strong and weak points. The more objective measures such as archival records and behavioral observations may be "hard" in some sense, but they also may be narrow in focus. Archival records (e.g., turnover and absenteeism) were probably not recorded with research in mind. On the other hand, more subjective measures generated by questionnaires and interviews tend to be very rich sources of information. However, since they are self-reports, they may also include some systematic bias. People may tell you what they think you want to hear rather than what they actually feel.

The conclusions that one reaches with regard to methods are twofold. First, no one procedure is "best." The data can be gathered many different ways, and it is probably better to use a technique that is best suited to the theory and situation at hand. Second, do not get caught by method fads. Just because some other company or group was successful using their pet questionnaire does not mean it will work for you. Methods are meant to be functional—they are simply tools to help us answer our research questions.

Practical problems. Hand in hand with methodological problems is a set of practical issues that must be resolved. Decisions must be made in terms of how much money can be spent. The elegance of design, number of subjects tested, and the type of analyses performed are often determined by the amount of money or time available. Different methods require different amounts of resources. But good research does not have to be expensive research. The way in which it is done is more important than its cost.

Explanation

After generating a theory and conducting an experimental test of this theory, one must attempt to make some statements about the experiment that will describe what has been found. Suppose it has been observed that certain managers are more effective than others and we ask for an *explanation* of that phenomena. What we want is to be able to fit this particular finding into some set of statements which are broader in scope. We hope our theory will present these statements.

The problems of explanation, however, are twofold. First, one must ascertain the degree to which his or her observations have indeed been supportive of the theory. This process involves both the ruling out of alternative hypotheses and some indication of the strength of the support provided. The elimination of other interpretations can be partially handled by the way in which the study is designed, and this will be discussed later in detail. The strength of the support is typically inferred through the use of statistics. That is, mathematical tools provide us with probabilistic estimates of support. The analyses essentially ask, "How probable is it that we should find this relationship (e.g., that very anxious managers had low productivity) if in reality these two factors are unrelated (anxiety and productivity)?" More specifically, statistics help one to determine the likelihood that information has just been gathered from an unrepresentative group. If this likelihood is small, one puts more confidence in the findings and therefore in the theory. This confidence is always probabilistic, never absolute. Support is always *more* or *less* strong.

The second problem deals with the generality of the findings. Are the findings just applicable to the kinds of managers with whom the experiment was conducted or are they applicable to all managers? To answer this latter question may require numerous experiments in numerous settings, using various observation techniques. The final acceptance of a theory as an explanation probably stops when our curiosity rests and the new law is in some sense coherent with the rest of the research in areas relevant to our theory (e.g., leadership, anxiety, and so on).

In summary, scientific research is a way of thinking. It involves an unbiased planning, data-gathering, and analysis phase. It is systematic, and there are general rules about what is appropriate and inappropriate. The following section discusses some different types of research in more detail.

Types of research

There are many different dimensions that can be used to categorize the wide variety of research projects that are conducted. Some of these dimensions describe what the investigator is doing, where it is being done, and the goals of the research. Understanding these distinctions helps us to select the appropriate type of research and to be aware of its strengths and limitations.

Correlational versus experimental research

One of the primary ways to classify research studies is based on the type of inference that the design allows. In those cases where the researcher wishes to make an inference about what causes what, *experimental* research should be used. In other cases the investigator simply wants to know the extent to which two variables co-vary or "go together." This is called correlational research. *Correlational* research is designed to investigate the relationship between two or more variables. The question being asked is whether *increases* in the values of variable A occur with *increases* in the values of variable B. If the answer is yes, you have a *positive* correlation. If *increases* in A occur with *decreases* in B, you have a *negative* correlation. If *increases* in A are *unrelated* to the values of B, you have a *zero* correlation.

Suppose you were interested in the relationship between an individual's satisfaction with a job and the degree to which everyone liked one another in the group. You give out a questionnaire to the people in your organization and you measure (1) how satisfied they are with their job and (2) how much they like their coworkers. Using a statistical formula you can generate a numerical index called the *correlation coefficient* (represented by the symbol r) which will describe the direction and strength of the relationship between these two variables. The value you obtain for r will range from -1.00 (a perfect negative relationship) to 0.00 (no relationship) to $+1.00$ (a perfect positive relationship).

So, you've gathered your data on job satisfaction (let us say on a scale from 1 to 10) and attraction to coworkers (on a similar scale). You have a score for each of these variables for each person. By computing the correlation coefficient you can determine whether people who have relatively high job satisfaction scores also have relatively high or low attraction to coworker scores. If you get a positive correlation (e.g., +0.60) it suggests that satisfied people like their coworkers while dissatisfied people dislike their coworkers. If the correlation is negative (e.g., −0.60) it suggests that satisfied people dislike their coworkers while dissatisfied people like their coworkers. If the correlation is zero or very near zero, it means that there is no relationship between the two variables. The closer the coefficient is to either +1.00 or −1.00, the stronger the relationship.

The real purpose of correlational research is to give the investigator some idea of the current state of affairs. It helps to know what goes with what. It gives the researcher a picture of existing relationships. What it does not do, however, is tell you anything about *causality*. You have no idea which variables are the causes of the relationships you uncover.

Let us go back to our example. Let us say the correlation coefficient between job satisfaction and attraction for coworkers was positive (+0.60): satisfied people like their coworkers and dissatisfied people do not. This may be helpful information but it does not imply that high job satisfaction *causes* high attraction to coworkers nor does it suggest that liking one's coworkers causes high job satisfaction. The relationship could go in either direction or it could be caused by some third variable. For example, having an effective supervisor might cause both high satisfaction and attraction to coworkers.

The point is that correlational research is a good technique for gathering large amounts of descriptive data. It is also helpful in situations where experimental research is not possible. However, if the researcher is interested in uncovering causal relationships, then *experimental* research should be used.

The attempt to discover cause-and-effect relationships by systematically introducing some factor into a stiuation and observing the effect is the concern of experimental research. The variable that is introduced is called the *independent variable* and the observed effect is called the *dependent variable*. If different degrees of the independent variable are followed by different degrees of the dependent variable, then the former is presumed to cause the latter.

Let us consider the situation where you believe that setting a specific difficult goal leads to higher performance than a nonspecific difficult goal. You take your group of thirty managers and draw the names of fifteen of them out of a hat. For these fifteen managers you set specific difficult performance goals for the next 3 months. You tell the other fifteen managers to "do their best." After 3 months you compare the performance of the two groups and find that the group with a specific goal did substantially better than the "do-your-best" group. In this case, the specificity of the goal is the independent variable, performance is the dependent variable, and degree of goal specificity seems to cause different degrees of performance.

Experimental research has the major advantage of telling you something about causality. As a manager or practitioner this type of information is very helpful. It tells you what to change in order to get some desired effect. The major problem with experimental research is that it is often difficult in ongoing organizations to control the environment in the necessary fashion. That is, the investigator has to be able to actually introduce some change, control who gets exposed to that change, and assess the impact of the change; and this is difficult. We might also point out that most experimental studies focus on a narrow range of variables.

In summary, experimental research generates evidence about causality but is usually narrow in focus and is hard to conduct in ongoing organizations. Correlational studies provide information about relationships (not causality), can be wide in scope, and can be fairly easily conducted. No one type is best; it depends upon what the researcher needs to know and the conditions under which the research is to be done.

Different research settings

Another way to classify research studies is to look at the setting in which they were conducted. At least four main categories are used: field studies, field experiments, laboratory experiments, and computer simulations.

Field studies. Investigations that fall under this heading are distinguished by the fact that the research is carried out in the natural or "real-life" setting, with a minimum of disturbance of that setting. These investigations would include case studies or systematic and extensive observational studies. They might also include broad surveys where questionnaires or interviews are used. They do not, however, include studies that actively attempt to change the environment or people involved. They are correlational rather than experimental.

Field experiments. In this type of study the investigator is still working in the field or natural setting but introduces a change in this setting by way of manipulating or controlling some variables. The introduction of a goal-setting program would be a good example. The program could be introduced for one group and not for another. Comparisons of performance could be taken later to determine if the goal setting had any effect. We will report a number of studies that have followed this type of format.

Laboratory experiments. The fundamental characteristic of the laboratory experiment is that the environment in which the subject works is created by the investigator. The situation is typically one where the researcher is interested in refining and studying in detail various aspects of a theory. One of the better presentations of this approach with reference to organizations would be the studies on attitude change. Because attitude change is not dependent on any particular situation—that is, it can happen anywhere—it is a particularly good phenomenon to study in the laboratory.

One might also include in this category studies which are often called experimental simulations. These investigations are really partway between field and laboratory experiments. More specifically, these simulations attempt to represent the environment as closely as possible, which is not necessarily a major concern of laboratory investigations. This representation, however, is a created one and is different in major ways from the actual environment. People are participants in these studies as subjects, not as people going about their everyday jobs. Also, events that are represented in these simulations are often compressed in time (i.e., what might happen in a year happens in an hour). We have recently conducted some studies where we simulate an ongoing work environment and hire people to do part-time work. For the participants this setting is both research and a part-time job, yet it allows the researcher to control a number of variables (e.g., pay, supervision, the task demands). We will report in more detail about these types of studies later in the book.

Computer simulations. This final type of study is sometimes called a mathematical model. Human participants are no longer necessary. Variables representing the inputs, process, and outputs are programmed into the computer along with their relationships and the varying probabilities of these relationships. A run through the simulation will generate data according to preprogrammed information. Various types of economic and operation systems models use this approach.

Basic versus applied research

A third way to classify research is as to whether it is basic or applied. The motivation for doing pure or *basic* research is essentially one of curiosity. The scientist is interested in understanding some phenomenon without particular reference or thought as to how the findings could or should be used. Research which would be termed *applied* is typically concerned with not only the explanation of observations but also the use of these explanations. The popular image of science is that applied sciences use and adapt the abstractions, laws, and generalizations of the pure sciences to solve concrete problems. While this may be true in the case of engineering and physics, and this is not altogether certain, it is not applicable to the behavioral sciences. The exchange of ideas in the behavioral sciences goes both ways. Indeed, if the applied branches of the behavioral sciences stood in dependent and subsidiary relation to pure science, administration would derive little of value from them. However, because of the strong emphasis on doing functional or usable research (which is part of the Protestant-ethic tradition), the applied areas have flourished and will continue to do so.

The applications of behavioral science to organizational behavior cover almost the whole range of organizational concerns. The organization is composed of some people, some technology (machines, supplies, etc.), and, to some extent, an output or product of its endeavors.

Research from industrial psychology has been concerned with topics such as selection, management training, job satisfaction and morale, and job performance. Some of the findings from psychology, anthropology, and social psychology have been concerned with the areas of personality, perception, and motivation; the specialized interests of attitude change and persuasion are important for marketing both the organization's image and product.

Other disciplines, such as sociology and anthropology, have looked at organizational structure as it is related to effectiveness. Engineering psychology has produced research on the optimal fit between human and machine.

Problems of bargaining, legislation, budgets, grievances, and leadership are of interest to economists, sociologists, lawyers, and political scientists. Other areas, such as consulting and mental-health research, are also applicable. Thus, the interests of behavioral scientists cover rather comprehensively the problems with which managers and organizations are concerned, both from a theoretical and applied perspective.

In summary, the research process can be divided up or classified many different ways. However, some of these categories generally go together. Field studies tend to be correlational and applied, while laboratory studies are usually experimental and concerned with basic research questions. None of these strategies are inherently better than any other. What is important is how the research is designed.

Research design

When a behavioral scientist is reviewing or criticizing a research study, there are two basic questions that he or she asks. First, he will examine the study to see if there are alternative suggestions as to why the results turned out the way they did. If there are no equally likely interpretations of the results other than the one reported, the study is said to have *internal validity*. The inferences made by the original investigator seem to be warranted for the study in question.

But there is a second set of questions. Would the results have been the same if different people had participated, or would another method of observing the behavior in question produced similar findings? More specifically, if the results seem to be generalizable—that is, applicable to a wide range of people and situations—then the study or studies are said to have *external validity*. The inferences are not only applicable for the specific study but for a wider range of phenomena.

To assure that a study has both internal and external validity requires that the investigator have some knowledge of research design. Since the applications of the necessary principles are somewhat clearer for experimental settings, our discussion will begin there and then move to the relevant issues for correlational research.

Experimental design: Internal validity

Campbell and Stanley[1] state, "Internal validity is the basic minimum without which any experiment is uninterpretable: Did in fact, the experimental treatments make a difference in this specific instance?"[2] To understand the answer to this question more fully, we will present the example of a human-relations course being presented to a group of first-line supervisors. The objective of the investigator is to assess the degree to which the course influenced the productivity of these supervisors. Certain symbols will be used, and their meaning is as follows:

S = Subjects, the people participating in the experiment
O = Our observation techniques, the measurement device
X = The experimental treatment, the manipulated variable
R = The process of randomization

[1]Much of this section comes from D. T. Campbell & J. C. Stanley. *Experimental and quasi-experimental designs for research*. Chicago: Rand McNally, 1963.
[2]Ibid, p. 5.

Table 4-1. Some Types of Research Designs

Type	Characteristics
1. The one-shot design: $X\ O$	Subject to error due to history, maturation, testing, instrument decay, selection
2. One-group pretest-posttest design: $O_1\ X\ O_2$	Subject to error due to history, maturation, testing, instrument decay, regression
3. Static group comparison: $\dfrac{X\quad O_1}{\quad O_2}$	Subject to error due to selection, regression, mortality
4. Pretest-posttest control group design: $R\begin{cases} O_1\ X\ O_2 \\[2pt] O_3\quad\ O_4 \end{cases}$	Subject to error due to interaction of testing and X
5. Posttest only control group design: $R\begin{cases} X\ O_1 \\ \ O_2 \end{cases}$	Controls for but does not measure effects of history, maturation
6. Solomon four-group design: $R\begin{cases} O_1\ X\ O_2 \\ O_3\quad\ O_4 \\ \ X\ O_5 \\ \quad\ O_6 \end{cases}$	Combines features of designs 4 and 5 Controls for and also measures effects of history, maturation, and testing

Three poor designs will be described and their problems pointed out. Three good designs will be presented that remedy these problems. A summary of these designs is presented in Table 4-1. Finally, some quasi-experimental designs will be discussed for situations where the proper controls are not available to the investigator.

Poor designs. Suppose that a personnel manager gives a human-relations training course to *all* supervisors and 3 months later observes their performance. How would he or she evaluate it? The manager could not compare their performance scores to earlier performance scores (before training) nor could they be compared against a group that did not receive the training. This is called a *one-shot* design and is diagrammed below.

$X\ O$

Here, X stands for the treatment, the training course, and O for the observation, the performance measure. The investigator has no way of knowing whether the performance scores are good or bad and if the training influenced these scores. This type of design is rarely used because of its obvious weaknesses.

Perhaps our manager was aware of some of these problems and used the following design.

$O_1\ X\ O_2$

The manager gathered performance measures on the supervisors, gave them the training course, and then remeasured their performance and found O_2 was higher than O_1. This design is called a *one-group pretest-posttest* design. A pretest is given, then the treatment, a posttest administered, and differences between averages on the pretest and the posttest are attributed to the treatment.

There are numerous problems with this design. What if, at the same time that the course was given, completely new machinery was installed in the organization? Would it not be an equally plausible explanation to say that the new machinery caused the changes in performance? This type of alternative hypothesis is called a *history* factor. Definitions of this type of confound along with seven others are presented in the following list.

SOME CLASSES OF FACTORS WHICH CONFOUND EXPERIMENTAL RESULTS

History: Events other than the experimental treatment (X) which occurred between premeasurement and postmeasurement.

Maturation: Changes in the subject population which occur with the passage of time and which are independent of the experimental treatment (X).

Testing: Changes in subject performance which occur because previous measurement of performance sensitized the person regarding that area.

Instrument decay: Changes in measures of subject performance that arise because of changes in the measurement instruments or conditions—such as wear of parts for physical instruments or learning, boredom, or fatigue for human observers.

Selection: If subject assignment to different groups (i.e., experimental and control groups) in the design is on any basis other than random assignment from a common pool, those other bases of selection will represent *systematic* biases making for differences between groups which are unrelated to effects of experimental treatment X—or which may interact with X.

Mortality: If some subjects who initially start the experiment drop out before its completion, the experimental and control groups may not be comparable at the end even though they were in the beginning.

Interactive effects: Any of several of the above factors may *interact* with the experimental treatment (X) making for confounding effects. For example, pretesting may only sensitize the subject when it is followed by X. Or, the types of subjects who drop out of a study (mortality) may differ for the group receiving X (experimental) and the group not getting X (control).

Maturation might also be a confound in that the supervisors are 3 months older and more familiar with their surroundings. This familiarity with people and environment might have produced increased performance regardless of training.

One might also argue that the first performance measure made the supervisors aware of the fact that some type of evaluation of their performance was being made and most of them decided to work extra hard over the next 6 months in case they were being monitored for one reason or another. This type of confound would be due to *testing*.

Perhaps the first performance observations were recorded in the afternoon when the observers were somewhat tired and the second evaluations were done in the morning when they were more alert. Differences in the two observations due to changes in the measurement device are called *instrument decay*. All four of the possible confounds discussed above would provide alternative explanations to the suggestion that the training course had made the supervisors more effective.

The third poor design is called a static group comparison and it is diagrammed as follows:

$$-\,-\,\frac{\text{X}}{}\,-\,\frac{O_1}{O_2}$$

In this case one group of managers receives the training (called the *experimental group*) and another group receives no training (called the *comparison* or *control group*), and the assignment to the two groups is made on a nonrandom basis (indicated by the broken line between groups). Random assignment requires that people are assigned to the two groups by some chance method such as drawing names out of a hat or some sort of lottery. An example of nonrandom assignment would occur if the managers from the production department get the training and those in sales do not. Or perhaps you choose the first 20 (out of 40) that sign up on a sheet that is passed around. After the training you measure the performance of both groups, and if O_1 is greater than O_2, you say that the training had its intended effect.

There are two major types of confounds in this design, selection and mortality. A selection error occurs when people are assigned to experimental and comparison groups on a nonrandom basis. Perhaps the production managers are better than the sales managers to start with, or perhaps the first 20 to sign up are more motivated than the 20 who initially passed the opportunity by. The point is that the two groups may have been different to start with, and the static group comparison does not control for this confound.

What if the course is a very difficult one and some of the supervisors who have signed up find it frustrating and quit their job? Not only would you have only highly motivated supervisors but you would also now have only the brightest ones taking the training. When there are systematically different dropout rates for the experimental and control groups, differences between the two groups may be attributable to errors of *mortality*.

Three good designs

The first good design simply adds a control group to the one-group pretest-posttest design and randomly assigns individuals to the two groups. It is called a *pretest-posttest control group* design.

$$R \begin{array}{l} \diagup O_1 \quad \text{X} \quad O_2 \\ \diagdown O_3 \qquad\;\; O_4 \end{array}$$

The comparison made is one of change scores. That is, were the changes from O_1 to O_2 greater than the changes from O_3 to O_4? Change scores are used because the investigator can then rule out alternative interpretations due to history, testing, maturation, and so forth. More specifically, anything that happens to the experimental group should also happen to the control group, so that any difference in the *degree of change* should be attributed to X, the treatment. By randomly assigning people to the two groups, there should be no initial bias as to why an individual ends up in a given group. The only possible error is the interactive one suggested in the list on page 72. Perhaps being observed the first time makes everyone work a little harder, but the experimental group also works hard at doing well in the training program. The differences in change scores may indeed be due in part to the training course but only when the individuals know that it is partially related to their performance ratings. The people in the experimental group are in some sense more receptive to the training because of the pretest. This is a relatively minor problem and can be corrected with a design called a *posttest-only control group* design.

$$R \begin{cases} X & O_1 \\ & O_2 \end{cases}$$

In this design, people are randomly assigned to the two groups, the treatment administered and scores on posttests compared. It remedies the minor problem with the previous design by not administering a pretest. However, this omission also means that the investigator does not have a group which receives a pretest and a posttest without the treatment. This can be a useful group because it provides information on the effects of history, maturation, instrument decay, and so on.

Occasionally, an investigator will combine the last two designs to form a *Solomon 4-group* design.

$$R \begin{cases} O_1 & X & O_2 \\ O_3 & & O_4 \\ & X & O_5 \\ & & O_6 \end{cases}$$

The supervisors would be randomly assigned to four groups, two of which would receive the training course (one with a pretest, one without) and two of which would not. This design provides the investigator with much information. One can examine history effects (O_3 to O_4), testing effects (O_4 to O_6), the interaction of testing and the treatment (O_2 to O_5), and so on. However, in some cases this type of design requires the use of more experimenters, more subjects, and therefore, more money. The added information must be weighed against the cost.

In summary, then, investigators want to *conduct* a study with a design that will allow them to answer the questions they wish to ask. By ruling out alternative interpretations of their results, they can produce an internally valid study. The two most important components of the good designs discussed are that a comparison group is needed (one that does not get the treatment or one that receives some other treatment) and the random assignment of subjects to the two groups so that theoretically no initial differences will exist for the two groups. The differences that are found can then be attributed to the independent variable, the experimental treatment.

Experimental design: External validity

The three components of experimental research are the subjects, the treatment, and the observation techniques. When the results of a study are tied to the specific people, the treatment or measurement device, or the situation which produced the results, then the study lacks *external validity*.

Subjects. People come to or serve in experiments for different reasons. Some volunteer, some are paid. College students often are asked to serve as part of an introductory psychology course, and much of the research in psychology has consequently been performed on the American college sophomore. It can and has been argued that this is not a representative group. The results generated with the subjects may tell us a lot about college sophomores but very little about other groups. Investigators should use subjects from the larger group of people to whom they wish to generalize their findings. This may require that an experiment be repeated a number of times with different types of people participating for varied reasons, but it must be done if one is to argue that the findings are general in nature.

Treatments. In certain cases the experimenter makes broader generalizations about his or her treatment than is justified. For example, certain types of human-relations training are probably good for certain types of people, but to argue that all group experiences are good is not justified based on the results of one experiment. Another example would be helpful. Suppose that some employees on the shop floor of an industrial plant thought that music would be nice to listen to while they work, and an industrial psychologist tries out two levels of loudness of the music to see which is most conducive to hard work. The psychologist obtains the following results:

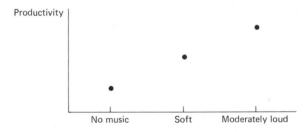

Having randomly assigned employees to the three conditions, the psychologist concludes that the results represent the following relationship: Increases in loudness increase productivity.

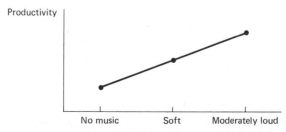

The investigator therefore recommends that the music be played at the loudest possible level, and the employees suffer ear damage as a consequence. The problem arises because the experimenter attempted to generalize the results to loudness levels other than those that had been tested. A more logical guess might have produced the following curve:

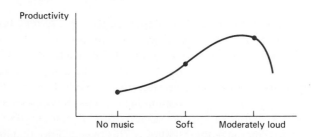

Again, the remedy for generalization is to try out a wider range and different presentations of the manipulated variable. If the results still hold, one has more confidence in the generalizability of the findings.

Observations. Occasionally results can be attributed to the specific measurement procedure. For example, subjects respond differently on multiple-choice tests where guessing is allowed than when it is penalized.[3] An attempt should be made to try out various procedures such as questionnaires, interviews, and observers. If the findings are still replicated, the results are more externally valid.

Reactive effects. Particular situational characteristics (the specific experimenter, the room in which people worked, the time of day, and so on) that might explain the results are called *reactive effects*. By conducting the experiment at different times in various places with different experimenters, the results again become more generalizable.

To be externally valid, therefore, a research result must be generalizable to other people, occasions, and observational and treatment techniques. Three strategies can be helpful in this regard: (1) take a broad sample which represents the population to which you wish to generalize, (2) try introducing the treatment in various ways and at different intensities, and (3) use multiple observation techniques. If the finding still holds up, it is probably externally valid.

Quasi-experimental designs

In some settings the investigator is not able to obtain a control group or randomly place the subjects into one condition or another. Although there are a variety of ways one can deal with these problems, only one representative example for each will be presented. Modifications of these examples are available if one wishes to pursue the topic.

[3]L. Cronbach. Response sets and test validity. *Education and Psychological Measurement,* 1946, **6,** 475–494.

Time series. In the case where a control group is not available the investigator is mostly concerned about changes that occur between a pretest and posttest that might confound the results (history, maturation, instrument decay). One possible solution to the problem is to use a time-series design where multiple pretests and posttests are used.

$$O_1 \quad O_2 \quad O_3 \quad O_4 \quad O_5 \quad X \quad O_6 \quad O_7 \quad O_8 \quad O_9 \quad O_{10}$$

If there are no differences between O_1 and O_2 or O_2 and O_3 or O_7 and O_8, and so forth, and there is a large difference between O_5 and O_6, the investigator may have some confidence that the treatment made some difference. For example, the manager might monitor performance ratings before and after some training program and then examine the relationship over time. If something like what is plotted below occurred, then the manager might have some support for use of the program (especially if he or she is relatively sure that nothing dramatic, like installation of new machinery, occurred at the same time as the training).

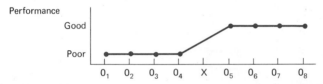

Nonequivalent control group. When investigators cannot randomly assign people to experimental and control groups, they can still have some control over selection or mortality errors. The design below calls for two groups, one that receives the treatment and one that does not. Both groups receive a pretest.

$$O_1 \quad X \quad O_2$$
$$\overline{ \; - \; - \; - \;}$$
$$O_3 \qquad O_4$$

Randomization is an attempt to get rid of systematic bias between the experimental and control group. If it cannot be done, then having information (pretests) on the variables which would be critical if a difference existed is available. Statistical techniques would allow the proper comparison to be made (adjustments can be made for original differences). Also, if people dropped out of one group or another, similar people could be chosen to be dropped from the other group in order to maintain their comparability. The central point is that pretests give you information about the similarity of the groups *before* the experiment. When they are dissimilar, corrections can be made for the original differences. When they become dissimilar (people drop out), adjustments in the other group can again be made. Since one cannot measure everything, you are never sure if they are completely comparable, but it is better than not having the information. Without the pretests the design would be a static group comparison which has serious problems.

Correlational design: Internal and external validity

The other type of research, where we are simply interested in whether variables are related, is called *correlational*. In correlational studies, the results are in the form of correlation coefficients, and the question of internal validity has to do with alternative explanations of the implied inference. If one found a high correlation for students between weight and reading ability, one might suggest that a possible confound—age—was responsible for the relationship. Ruling out the possibility that a correlation between two variables is due to their relationship to a third is both an intuitive process and a process that can be systematically introduced into the design. Some fairly elaborate statistical procedures are available to help answer this question.

Other alternative interpretations can mostly be ruled out by having confidence in one's *measures*. By making sure that they are both reliable and valid, the investigator may be relatively sure that the relationship found did indeed exist for the group that was tested. A reliable measure is one that has little error in it which can be attributed to the measurement process. A valid measure assesses what we think it should be assessing (e.g., do intelligence tests really measure intelligence?). Most books on measurement and research design discuss these topics in some detail.

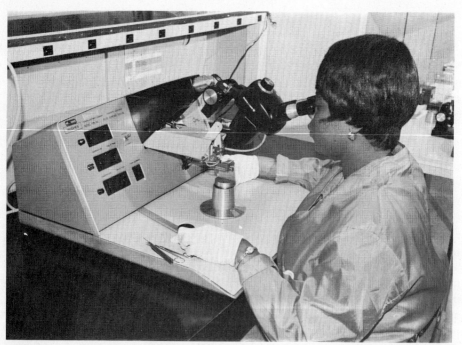

Reliable measurement tools increase our confidence in our findings. *(By permission of the Boeing Company.)*

The problems of external validity are largely the same as for experimental studies. The investigator must ascertain whether the relationship exists for other groups of people, under other conditions, with the use of alternative observation techniques. If so, we can be confident of the generalizability of the results.

Participation in an experiment

The purpose of almost all scientific inquiry in the behavioral sciences involves the observation of human beings. These observations may be unobtrusive measures such as personnel or attendance records or they may simply be observations recorded in the fashion of a diary. More frequently they involve questionnaires, interviews, or other intrusions into the lives of those people participating, and this intrusion raises two major questions.

First, do individuals behave differently because they are in an experiment? Most scientists believe that in the process of studying anything we change it. This is certainly true for behavioral sciences, and only lately have attempts been made to deal adequately with the problem.

Also, what rights does the subject or investigator have in the process of experimentation? What sorts of questions can be asked? It is the objective of this final section to examine these questions and their implications for research conducted on organizational behavior.

In conducting an experiment there are two aspects of the situation which might produce data that was not representative of how one would behave in "real life." First, there is the situation. That is, the degree to which the experimental *setting* causes the individual to behave differently. These possible confounds are called *demand characteristics.*

A second problem is caused by the experimenter. In some cases he or she may unwittingly convey expectations about the experiment to the participants. For example, interviewees for jobs often try very hard to say what they think the interviewer wants to hear. These confounds are called *experimenter-bias*[4] effects. The effects of both these errors on organizational research are potentially very great and will be discussed in more detail.

Demand characteristics

You will recall from Chapter 2 that the original intent of the Hawthorne studies was to examine the effects of various physical characteristics of the work environment on the workers' output. In one study, a group of women were selected to work together under various lighting intensities. The investigators soon discovered, however, that the output produced by this group was not related to the lighting conditions. The situation has been described as follows: "The girls felt 'it was fun' and, even though the number of observers was greater and their attention higher in the test situation than in the ordinary work environment, the girls felt no sense of anxiety because of tight control."[5] They became highly motivated to work hard and developed warm relationships with each other

[4]R. Rosenthal. *Experimenter effects in behavioral research.* New York: Appleton-Century-Crofts, 1966.

[5]E. Mayo. *Social problems of an industrial civilization.* Cambridge, Mass.: Harvard University Press, 1945.

and their supervisors. In short, the setting and attention changed their behavior, not the experimental variable of interest (illumination in this case).

Even with this auspicious beginning, social scientists continued to believe that the individual that participated in an experiment was a passive responder. Subjects were treated as if they were behaving in exactly the same way that they would outside of the experiment. This idea has recently been challenged by Martin Orne, who has presented data to support his contentions.[6] Orne cites one experiment (the most tedious and boring task that he could imagine) where participants were asked to do 224 simple additions from each of a large stack of printed papers, record their answers on another sheet and then tear up this answer into 32 pieces. This task was to be repeated for 2000 sheets: clearly a task that few individuals would ever undertake in a "real-life" setting. In one case, Orne reports that a subject continued work for 5½ hours and then the experimenter gave up!

Possible confounds. The possible demands of an experimental setting are numerous. The one aspect they have in common, however, is that the participant behaves differently *because he or she is in an experiment*.

1 *Looking good.* An example of this type of problem has already been mentioned: the interviewee. It is clearly important to "look good" to a prospective employer in habits, dress, appearance, and background. How many job applicants say, "Oh yes, I drink a lot on the job and I'll probably be absent once a week"?

2 *Helping science.* In certain settings participants may feel that they are furthering the cause of social science and try very hard to do a good job. The Hawthorne studies can be partially viewed in this light. That is, the women knew they were being observed and wished to do well both for themselves (looking good) and for the observers.

3 *Problem solving.* Many experimental studies of leadership utilize tasks specifically set up for an experiment. Subjects may approach these tasks with a bent at problem solving or gaming rather than perceiving them as tests of their leadership skills.

4 *Unknown effects.* Imagine a setting where employees know they are being observed. Then, one day, new guidelines for doing a job are established and more observations take place. Orne states that even the dullest person is aware that change is expected after a pretest, treatment, posttest sequence. The subject may choose to help or hinder the experimenter or he or she may choose to do something else. The point is that investigators are usually not sure about the motivational incentives under which their subjects are operating.

Possible solutions. Since the investigator is by definition changing the situation

---

[6]M. T. Orne. On the social psychology of the psychological experiment: With particular reference to demand characteristics and their implications. *American Psychologist,* 1962, **17**, 776–783.

through experimentation, the problem cannot be solved altogether. There are, however, a few strategies which can be suggested:

1 *Unobtrusive measures.* One possible solution is to make the experiment as unnoticeable as possible. Webb suggests the use of records already available, either printed, published, or filed, or of physical indications of behavior.[7] He cites an example of a situation where an owner of a museum was interested in which displays were viewed the most. Rather than place an observer to watch people as they watched the displays, he measured the wear of the tile in front of the displays. In many cases, some of the data which are needed are on file or can be gathered with a minimum of intrusion.

2 *Ask participants.* If the investigator must carry out the study with questionnaires, experimental tasks, or other methods of direct contact with subjects, he or she might ask them about their behavior when the experiment is completed. If it turns out that most of the subjects respond by saying that they behaved in a way that was not representative of their everyday actions, then the investigator should question the generality of the findings.

3 *Dry-run the experiment.* A third strategy is to simulate the experiment with some volunteers. More specifically, the investigator could present a group of individuals with exactly what is going to be done. The investigator would then ask them: "If you were to serve in this experiment, what would you think was going on? How naturally would you behave?" This method has the advantage of giving the investigator information before the study actually has been completed. Again there is no solution, but there are certainly some ways in which the effects of demand characteristics can be measured or minimized.

Experimenter bias

Not only is an experimental subject often placed in an unrepresentative setting, he or she may also interact with an investigator that influences his or her behavior. When subjects behave differently than they ordinarily would because of contact with the experimenter, it is an example of what is termed experimenter bias. One author points out that "while we have traditionally recognized that the characteristics of an experimenter may indeed influence behavior, it is important to observe that we have not seriously attempted to study him as an independent variable."[8]

There are a number of ways that experimenter effects may operate. In studies with only one investigator, the experimenter may convey expectations to the experimental group. That is, the experimenter may behave toward one group differently from another, and differences between an experimental and control

---

[7]E. Webb, D. Campbell, R. Schwartz, & L. Sechrest. *Unobtrusive measures: Non reactive research in the social sciences.* Chicago: Rand McNally, 1966.

[8]F. J. McGuigan. The experimenter: A neglected stimulus object. *Psychological Bulletin,* 1963, **60,** 421–435.

group could be attributed to the interaction with the experimenter and not the variables of interest. In cases of multiple data collectors, one investigator may gather data from the experimental group and one from the control group. Once again, the differences between groups may be because of their differential treatment by the investigators.

Another set of similar problems may be traced to the experimenters making systematic mistakes in favor of their hypothesis. More specifically, in situations which require the judgment of the investigator (observations, interpretations of answers) mistakes may be recorded that favor the support of one's theory. Although in most cases these errors are not done on purpose, it is worth noting that checks for this type of problem are often not reported.

Possible bias. Numerous studies have been conducted which show the effects of experimenter bias, and reviews of this literature are available.[9] Some of the most important variables effecting this bias are listed below:

1 *Personality.* A variety of personality characteristics of experimenters may influence the behavior of subjects. Research has been reported showing that subjects behave differently for experimenters with different anxiety levels, neuroticism levels, and other personality traits.

2 *Person characteristics.* Information about the experimenter's religion, sex, or research experience may also produce systematically different data. One survey report indicated that Christian experimenters when interviewing subjects found that 50 percent of the participants believed that Jewish people had too much influence. Jewish interviewers working with a similar sample reported that only 22 percent of their subjects felt that way.

3 *Expectations.* Rosenthal has presented a number of striking findings which illuminate the importance of experimenter expectations. He has reported data indicating that teachers' expectations as to the amount of potential held by their students influences the students' actual performance. More specifically, teachers were told that some students would improve markedly while others would not. In reality, the students were randomly placed into these two groups. However, at the end of the year, Rosenthal reports that the students for whom the teachers held high expectations did indeed show improvement in comparison to the other group.

Clearly, the important question is how these expectations get translated into systematically different treatment for the experimental and control groups, without the investigator's active attempts to do so. Rosenthal suggests a number of possibilities: tone of voice, facial expressions, unintentional verbal reinforcement, misjudgment of responses, and so forth. Although there have been some legitimate criticisms raised about both the generality of his findings and the ways in which certain studies were conducted, it is still true that this type of bias does exist and may influence the empirical results.

[9]See B. L. Kintz, D. J. Delprato, D. R. Mettee, C. E. Persons, & R. H. Shappe. The experimenter effect. *Psychological Bulletin,* 1965, **63**, 223–33; or Robert Rosenthal. Experimenter outcome, orientation and the results of the psychological experiment. *Psychological Bulletin,* 1964, **61**, 405–412.

Organizational settings. There are a number of settings in organizational research where these types of bias may be operating:

1 *Selection.* Both selection interviews and personality tests put the interviewee in a situation where he or she wishes to please a possible employer. Clearly it is to a person's advantage to not only ascertain what is expected but to meet these expectations as well. This is one of the reasons that many of these tests or interviews have very little relationship to how the individual eventually behaves in the organization.

2 *Guidance.* On a more positive note, some investigators have reported that clinical psychologists or vocational-guidance experts find positive expectations to be a powerful determinant of eventual mental health. However, the opposite would also be true; those expected to fail often do.

3 *Experimental research.* Some reports of managerial training have the following design: Managers' attitudes about a set of issues are assessed as pretest material, the company spends $1000 to send an employee away for two weeks of training, the employee returns and is asked "Did it change your attitudes? Did it do you any good?" The expectations of the investigator are rather explicit. The argument as to whether real effects indeed occurred is not at issue here. The problem is that bias was built into the investigation.

4 *Survey research.* Much of the research on consumer behavior has involved elaborate surveys of public opinion. As pointed out earlier, the experimenter's sex or religion may influence the responses received. It has also been found that contingent questions or open-ended questions on surveys increase the likelihood of error. The greater the flexibility allowed in the questions, the greater the probability of bias.

Possible remedies. In experimental settings where there are experimental and control groups, there are three major ways to correct for experimenter bias. First, experimenters can be run blind. More specifically, experimenters can be assigned to collect data without knowing to which group the subject belongs. A second, similar strategy is to randomly assign individuals to experimenters so that conditions and experimenters are mixed. Finally, in situations where different experimenters are carefully assigned to different groups, questions may be asked or analyses conducted to see if any bias did indeed occur. Although far from satisfactory, this last alternative should be taken whenever multiple investigators are involved.

In interview or survey settings there are also a couple of possible ways to control experimenter bias. One important strategy is to structure interviews or surveys so that relatively few decisions or judgments are left up to the investigator. This procedure minimizes error. A second technique is to interview your interviewers; that is, find out what characteristics might bias a given study (the Christian-Jewish example) and eliminate certain investigators from collecting data in that setting.

In summary, both demand characteristics and experimenter bias will always exist. It should be clear, however, that these effects in some cases can be measured or controlled and that these procedures should be used if possible. These precautions will increase our confidence in the investigators' results.

Ethical considerations

In designing and planning research that involves human subjects, the investigator must be concerned not only with issues pertinent to experimental design, but with questions of ethics. The most important topics for research on organizational behavior are those of deception and testing.

Deception. It is frequently the case that the purpose of the research is disguised from the subject. This is done because the researcher is afraid the subject will catch on to what is wanted and respond either to please or discourage the investigator. As a response to this problem, rather elaborate deception may be used to get what is needed: long surveys may really include only a few items of real interest to the investigator, or laboratory experiments may use lengthy cover stories to establish credibility.

The result of all this deception has been a heated debate in the literature about what procedures are ethically permissible. The question revolves around the scientist's need to know and the public's right to be tested honestly. While the issue is far from resolved, some guidelines have appeared. First, participation in *any* research should be truly voluntary. The use of coercion is unacceptable. Second, whenever possible, especially if there will be any physical or psychological discomfort, the subject should be informed of the nature of the study and its potential harms or benefits. Finally, after the study the subject should be thoroughly debriefed about the research and any deception that took place. The general rule of thumb is that a subject should not leave a research study more uncomfortable or less happy than he was when he arrived.

Testing. A second area of concern is the use of psychological tests as screening devices for jobs. There are two issues of an ethical nature. The first focuses on the use of tests as devices for intentional and unintentional discrimination. We will discuss this topic fully in Chapter 14, "Employee Performance."

The second issue deals with the subject's right to privacy. Prospective job candidates are often subjected to extensive test batteries including a number of personality measures. These latter techniques often include items that probe highly sensitive and personal areas. These questions may arouse anxiety and defensiveness in the candidate.

Again, the resolution to this problem is far from settled. In general, however, most professionals agree on two things. First, the test should be valid. That is, scores on the test should have a substantial relationship with actual on-the-job performance. Second, those people who take the tests should be informed of their use and confidentiality. Some researchers even argue that a candidate who is uncomfortable with this information should have the right to refuse to respond without prejudice (i.e., without automatically being rejected for the position). Highly personal information is highly sensitive information. It should be treated as such.

One final comment: Research is meant to be a helpful tool. It is one route to knowledge, not the only one. It is not an end in itself. As an organizational participant you may be involved as a researcher or a subject; as a user of research, a planner of research, or an evaluator of research. The point to keep in mind is that research with the proper concern for design and ethical considerations can produce valuable information. And this information can help you and those around you to be more effective.

Summary

We covered some fairly difficult material in this chapter. Conceptually, it is probably the most difficult in the whole book. However, a good grasp of the major points should help to understand the remaining chapters. The most important points are as follows:

1 The scientific approach is one way to acquire knowledge. It is a process that involves planned, unbiased, and public analysis of empirical data.
2 The research process incorporates a number of distinct steps: problem identification, data gathering, analysis, and explanation.
3 Research can be classified in many different ways: correlational versus experimental; field versus laboratory; or applied versus basic. Different types of research answer different types of questions.
4 A well-designed study is internally valid if it rules out alternative hypotheses and externally valid if the results can be generalized to other situations, people, or occasions.
5 Both demand characteristics (e.g., the Hawthorne effect) and experimenter bias can invalidate one's conclusions.
6 There are ethical constraints as to how research should be conducted. In general, participants should be volunteers and thoroughly briefed.

Implications for practice

The central issue is how one uses all this information about research. If you are in a situation where you have to initiate or evaluate research, what should you do? Here are some simple questions you should ask:

1 First, what is the problem that needs to be investigated? Do you need to know causal information or will information about relationships be sufficient? Write the research problem down in a sentence or two and then analyze the question in terms of the type of information you will need.
2 Can the suggested research design answer the question? For questions of causality, experimental research designs will be most appropriate. Surveys and correlational research can tell you how variables are interrelated but not causally related.
3 Is the research design internally and externally valid? For experimental studies the best designs will include a control group and random assignment

to conditions. For correlational studies you should be provided with information about the reliability and validity of the *measures.*

4 Is the conduct of the study unbiased? Are there ways in which the investigator's hypotheses and expectations could influence the results? Will the participants be acting naturally or will they be responding to the demands of the research setting?

5 Will the participants be asked to release confidential information or experience psychological or physical discomfort? If so, will consent be voluntary, information kept confidential, and initial briefing and postexperimental debriefing employed?

6 Given that the answers to the above questions are favorable, how can the research results be used? Will the information *really* be helpful in the decision process, or are we just going through the motions?

Research is an expensive, time-consuming, and often disruptive process. If it is going to be done, it might as well be done correctly.

Discussion questions

1 Think of the types of jobs you might have when you graduate. How would knowledge of research methods be helpful to you?

2 Suppose a new accounting system was being introduced which included some behavior controls (e.g., objectives). How would you evaluate its effectiveness?

3 Do you think managers should be forced to attend a training program? What do you do if they refuse?

Case: Did the training work?

As the head of the personnel department of a large Midwestern hospital, Tom Jackson was responsible for the hiring, placement, training, and professional development of the hospital's staff. One of the new innovations that he had tried to introduce was some sort of management training for the physicians. He had found that most doctors were unaware of some of the basic ideas of management. Besides that, they were frequently difficult to teach—they thought that management training was unrelated to their job and they just told the nurses, lab technicians, or orderlies what needed to be done and it was done.

So, over the years, Tom began to introduce a series of short seminars. He discussed some basic principles of motivation, leadership, decision making, and issues related to management planning and administration. The participants in the classes were volunteers—doctors who thought that such techniques might be of some use to them. While the number of doctors who came was rather small, the response was enthusiastic. Whenever he got feedback, it seemed to be positive. Some of the doctors even wrote him letters of congratulations. The doctors liked the material and thought it was helpful, and the number of volunteers seemed to be increasing.

However, Tom's immediate boss, Dr. Ruth Spich (a member of the board of directors) was unenthusiastic. She did not think the program was doing anything beneficial. During the early 1970s, in the midst of the economic downturn, Dr. Spich went to Tom and laid it on the line. She said that she thought the program was frivolous and time-consuming. And time was money—which was in short supply. However, she was willing to give Tom a chance to prove its worth. If he could show clear, unambiguous data that such a program was useful, she would support it. Otherwise it had to go. Tom had 6 months to put together his report.

Questions about the case

1 Do you think the evidence that Tom currently has is good support for the program?
2 What are the weak points about the support? How would you criticize a report based on Tom's present evidence?
3 What would you do in Tom's place? How could you set up a program that would provide the evidence Dr. Spich is looking for?

Additional readings

* Becker, S. W. The parable of the pill. *Administrative Science Quarterly,* 1970, **15,** 94–96.
* Case, P. B. How to catch interviewing errors. *Journal of Advertising Research,* 1971, **11,** 39–43.
   Cronbach, L. J. The two disciplines of scientific psychology. *American Psychologist,* 1957, **12,** 671–684.
* Dean, L. R. Interaction, reported and observed: The case of one local union. *Human Organization,* 1958, **17,** 36–44.
** Helmstadter, G. G. *Research concepts in human behavior.* New York: Appleton-Century-Crofts, 1970.
* Hovland, C. I. Reconciling conflicting results derived from experimental and survey studies of attitude change. *American Psychologist,* 1959, **15,** 8–17.
   Kaplan, A. *The conduct of inquiry.* Scranton, Pa.: Chandler, 1964.
* Kelman, H. C. Human use of human subjects: The problem of deception in sociological experiments. *Psychological Bulletin,* 1967, **67,** 1–11.
   Kerlinger, F. N. *Foundations of behavioral research.* New York: Holt, 1973.
** Runkel, P. J., & McGrath, J. E. *Research on human behavior: A systematic guide to method.* New York: Holt, 1972.
* Seaman, J. Deception in psychological research. *American Psychologist,* 1969, **24,** 1025–1028.
** See the following three papers in M. D. Dunnette (Ed.), *Handbook of industrial and organizational Psychology,* New York: Rand McNally, 1976.
      1 Cook, T. D., & Campbell, D. T. The design and conduct of quasi-experiments and true experiments in field settings, 223–326.
      2 Bouchard, T. J., Jr. Field research methods: Interviewing, questionnaires, participant observation, systematic observation, unobtrusive measures, 363–414.
      3 Fromkin, H. L., & Streufert, S. Laboratory experimentation, 415–466.

*Possible reading for students
**Review of literature or comprehensive source material

TWO
INDIVIDUAL
CHARACTERISTICS

The second part of the book discusses the individual in more detail. The material presented in the Chapter 2, "Understanding Human Behavior," provides the framework for this section. The focus is on those basic human processes and characteristics that the individual brings to the organizational setting.

Chapter 5 discusses perception and personality. A definition of perception is presented and the way in which it affects our behavior is described. Much of what we report that we perceive is actually a biased interpretation of the real world (e.g., we hear what we *want* to hear). These biases often influence important organizational decisions (e.g., selection, evaluation), and some examples of how to remedy these problems are discussed.

The personality section of Chapter 5 defines personality and discusses in detail the controversy over whether personality is stable and enduring or more transitory in nature. We conclude that while personality may be one cause of how we behave, it is a minor cause. The situation and environment seem to be more important. The implications of this point are explored in some detail.

Chapter 6, "Attitudes," emphasizes the central role that attitudes have played in social science. People have attitudes about just about everything. We define attitudes and discuss how they are developed and changed. Much of the discussion focuses on job attitudes—how can we ensure that people are more satisfied with their working environment. A number of suggestions are presented.

Chapter 7 might be described as the heart of the book. While perception concerns how we process information and attitudes concern how we evaluate it, motivation tells us what we *do* about it. That is, why do we behave the way we do? Once we know what motivates people *and* if the causes of the motivation are under our control, then we can have a direct impact on their behavior.

We initially divide the motivation topic into two questions: (1) what activates us, what gets us started, and (2) what do we choose to do about it. Most of the theories that deal with the first question seem to focus on needs. Need deprivation is described as the mechanism that arouses the individual to action. Maslow, McGregor, and Herzberg are all famous for their theories on how human needs operate in organizations. The answer to the second question, choice of behavior, focuses on the process by which we make that choice. Learning, reinforcement, expectations, and goal setting are presented as alternative explanations of behavioral choice.

What we have at the end of Part 2 is a better understanding of what the individual brings to the organizational setting. You should have a fairly good idea of the basic processes that regulate human behavior—how we perceive things, how we evaluate them, and what we do about it.

5
Perception and personality

One of the most common observations of any manager or person working in an organizational setting is that people are different. They differ in terms of physical characteristics such as size, weight, age, and sex; background characteristics such as training and education; and personality traits such as extroversion or aggressiveness. The major consequences of such differences are twofold. First, people need to be treated as individuals. Different types of people will want different kinds of organizational rewards and probably work best in different kinds of settings. Second, every individual will not see things in the same way. There will be differences of opinion and evaluation on almost every topic.

In order to understand why people behave the way they do in organizational settings we must understand what makes them unique. People differ in their reactions to similar situations, and the explanations given for such divergence frequently refer to some underlying processes which result in individual differences. Two such processes are *perception* and *personality development*. The rest of this chapter will define and discuss these processes in light of their relationship to organizational behavior.

Perception

All of us are constantly being bombarded by sensory stimulation. There are noises, sights, smells, tastes, and tactile sensations. Yet somehow we manage to process this information without too much confusion. This process is known as perception. It is defined as those factors that shape and produce what we actually experience. It is a process that includes both a selection and an organizing mechanism.

There are two basic components of this definition. First, perception is a system of *selection* or screening. Some information is processed, some is not. Think of the times, for example, that you were disturbed by the ticking of a clock just before you went to sleep. The noise made by the clock is not typically selected. That is, you notice it only for a brief time and only occasionally. The noise itself, however, is constant. This screening helps us to avoid processing irrelevant or disruptive information.

The second component is *organization*. The information that is processed must be ordered and categorized in some fashion that allows us to ascribe meaning to the stimulus information. The stimulus provides certain cues as to its nature. An orange has color, texture, shape, and size, all of which help in the categorization process. These categories may be more or less elaborate, but their central function is the reduction of complex information into simpler categories. However, to say that perception is a process of selection and categorization begs

We are often overwhelmed by the stimuli bombarding our senses. (*By permission of University of Washington* Daily.)

the question. How exactly does one choose to select what one does and categorize this information in their own unique fashion?

Factors influencing perception

There are numerous general factors which are related to what one perceives. The first factor is called *response disposition:* People tend to perceive familiar stimuli more quickly than unfamiliar ones. Research has shown, for example, that when words are flashed on a screen at high speeds, subjects tend to recognize words that are frequently used more readily than ones that have infrequent usage.

A second factor is one's *feelings* toward the objects in question. There is considerable evidence that those things for which we hold strong feelings are also recognized more quickly than neutral stimuli. In general, it appears that we select things about which we hold positive feelings, but in some cases we recognize negative stimuli, especially where recognition would lead to the avoidance of a highly negative situation. It should be pointed out that frequency and evaluation are not independent of one another. It appears that the more frequently one is exposed to something, the greater the likelihood that it will be positively evaluated. Those in advertising would recognize the "repetition is recognition" principle here. The current debates over the presentation of violence and sex in the mass media are also tied to this relationship. Many people believe that seeing lots of sex and violence will cause us to view these activities more favorably and will therefore result in greater levels of sexual permissiveness and violent behavior.

A third factor is called *response salience.* Salience refers to the contemporary aspects of the situation which may influence our experience. Particular instructions, current needs, or actions that immediately precede a situation may influence our perceptions. If you are hungry, for example, you might easily pick out advertisements for food as you are driving down the street. Or if someone warned you to look out for glass on the road, you might be more attentive to the road surface than usual. So, both historical variables, such as past exposure and evaluation, as well as contemporary factors, such as needs and expectations, influence what we perceive.

Besides these more "internal" factors there are some external conditions which increase the likelihood that something will be perceived. One obvious condition is the intensity of the stimulus. We will tend to notice bright lights, pungent odors, and loud noises. Many advertisements utilize this idea by presenting their product in attention-getting ways. They use bright distinctive colors, and frequently advertisements on radio and television are slightly louder than the program being interrupted. In examining our own personal behavior we can probably remember times when we raised our voice in a discussion to gain someone else's attention. This happens in the workplace as well. For example, bright danger signs may be placed where they will be noticed, or loud buzzers or bells may be used to signify the beginning or end of work or rest periods.

Another factor that frequently prompts attention is motion. Thus, moving objects tend to be more readily perceived than stationary objects. Again in advertising we can notice the utilization of this principle. Lights on signs come on

Advertisements are frequently loud and obtrusive in an attempt to capture your attention.

sequentially or intermittently to give the appearance of motion. Store displays frequently have moving parts. Many of the studies in engineering psychology concentrate on the optimal man-machine match and therefore attempt to design display panels such that distracting motions are reduced while important motions are accentuated.

A third external factor is simply the size of the object. Large obtrusive objects tend to be perceived more easily than small ones. This may result in differential treatment for people or for physical objects such as machines. Basketball players are frequently recipients of rather inept jokes about their size—and, of course, it is rather hard for them to hide in a crowd. But there is also research which suggests that size is related to attention and goodness. That is, we tend to pay attention to larger things, and, somehow, bigness has a goodness quality to it.

A final set of variables are those that represent the physical environment. Research has shown that living in certain types of settings (e.g., big urban areas versus plains or forests) influences our perceptions. For example, one study has shown that people living in situations or cultures called "carpentered" (numerous structures with right angles) tend to have different perceptions of two-dimensional representations of three-dimensional objects than those who live in noncarpentered environments.[1] More specifically, they are able to look at a

[1]M. H. Segall, D. T. Campbell, & J. J. Herskovits. *The influence of culture on visual perception.* Indianapolis, Ind. Bobbs-Merrill, 1966.

picture (which is two dimensional) and respond to it as if it were three dimensional. The authors also present data supporting the idea that people who live on plains have different perceptions about the representation of vertical lines than do people living in environments where views of distant territory are absent. In summary, what one perceives is a function of both past experiences and the immediate environment. To some extent the specific content of these experiences and environments are determined by one's culture, but the underlying processes or major contributing factors are the same. The next section discusses how these and other factors are related to our perceptions of people.

Person perception

Almost everyone spends part of each day interacting with other people, and in general, this interaction progresses rather smoothly. Most of our relationships are harmonious and pleasant. Yet to maintain these relationships requires a knowledge of social behavior which we seldom verbalize. That is, we are constantly making judgments about other people's needs, emotions, and thoughts, and we do this rather automatically. The crucial point is that these judgments are very important for individual and organizational effectiveness.

Some examples might help. Listed below are a number of situations where the accurate perception and evaluation of other people's feelings and intentions could influence the success of the organization.

1 Evaluation of job candidates based on a short personal interview.
2 Decisions about how to proceed in a labor-management bargaining session.
3 Personnel judgments on which salary and promotional decisions are based.
4 Encounters with someone new from the "front office."
5 The initial exchange between a salesperson and a prospective buyer of a product.

In examining the process of how we perceive and evaluate others, there seems to be two stages of development. The first stage is one of first impressions. At this point the perceiver tends to make inferences and evaluations based on rather simple information about the other person. These evaluations also seem to be biased by the perceiver's own habits and beliefs and some situational characteristics.

When the interpersonal exchange is longer in duration, the process becomes more complex. The perceiver has the opportunity to observe the other person's behavior over a series of occasions and situations. At this point the perceiver is likely to form a more complex description and evaluation focusing on what are believed to be enduring personality traits. We will discuss both this first impression stage and the later ongoing interaction stage in more detail.

Forming impressions of others

We are frequently faced with situations where we meet new people, and in many cases how we evaluate the person will have important implications for the future.

Research has shown that there are three sets of characteristics which influence these perceptions.

The person perceived. In an interpersonal situation, one's evaluation and behavior toward the other is partly influenced by the characteristics of the individual with whom one is interacting. These characteristics fall under four headings: physical, social, historical, and personal.

Some of the more important *physical* ones are gestures, posture, facial expressions, and pigmentation. An example of how gestures can influence our judgments might be illustrated by a recent picture of Vice-President Rockefeller raising his middle finger to a group of hecklers at a political rally. Since few of us have a close personal relationship with the Vice President, we must form our impressions based upon his public behavior. For many people this gesture represents a somewhat vulgar public response and probably influenced many people's evaluations.

One's posture also is important. One often attributes laziness or lack of motivation to someone who slouches. Also, in many foreign countries one's importance is judged according to how tall he or she stands in relation to others. For example, a Thai who is interacting with a countryman of higher status will try not to have his head be higher than that of his companion even when this companion is physically shorter. Facial expressions and features may influence our feelings about others as well. Smiling is related to positive attitudes, for example, and people with eyes that are small and close together are often judged to be shifty or dishonest. Finally, and perhaps most important, is the fact that in many cultures darker skin pigmentation is associated with negative attributes. Research has shown that darkness is related to hostility, dishonesty, unfriendliness, slyness, and other variables which one might classify as negative, while blondness and light skin are most frequently associated with heroes and positive characteristics.

The *social* characteristics which appear to be important are voice qualities and appearance. In many cases one's education, place of residence, and status can be tied to his or her manner of speech. It is also clear that one's clothes and grooming are used by others in their evaluation. A few years ago it was the fashion to call anyone with long hair and casual attire a hippie, which implied judgments about the person's political, social, and moral values.

Certain *historical* factors or attributes have a large effect on our evaluation of others. One's sex, age, occupation, religion, and, most importantly, race, contribute to others' evaluation of that person. For example, research has shown that the racial characteristic is often as important as occupation, religion, or nationality in determining whether another individual will be accepted into an American's social group (called social distance).[2] People from other countries tend to emphasize other characteristics such as religion (Greeks) or occupation (Germans) as most important.

To summarize, it appears as if a wide variety of cues given off by another

[2]H. C. Triandis, & L. M. Triandis. Some studies of social distance. In I. Steiner and M. Fishbein (Eds.), *Current studies in social psychology.* New York: Holt, 1965, 207–216.

*I'd like to remind your honor once again, that I am
not the defendant, I am the defendant's counsel.*

We often use clothes and appearance as a general way of initially categorizing people.

person help in our evaluation of them. Some of these cues may give us accurate information and some may be inaccurate. The particular way in which these cues are used is partially dependent upon one's culture and values; that is, the characteristics of the perceiver are also important for understanding how first impressions are formed.

The perceiver. In general there appear to be two sets of variables about the perceiver that are important in understanding one's perceptions of others. First, one's own social and personality characteristics make a difference. In one study mentioned above, people who were more secure, more independent, and had a high tolerance for ambiguity were more accepting of others who were different from themselves. People who were high on a scale reflecting the social sophistication or breadth of perspective of the subject were more accepting than those who had low scores on this scale. The implications for selection in multiracial or national organizations that desire an accepting attitude is clear: Choose people to work overseas who are independent, have a high tolerance for ambiguity, and are accepting of others.

A large body of related research seems to suggest that one's knowledge and confidence in one's self influences one's perceptions of others. In general, people with accurate perceptions of what they are really like are more accurate in perceiving the characteristics of others. Also, as we would suspect, the more optimistically and confidently people see themselves, the more positively they evaluate others.

A second set of variables of importance refer to the complexity with which we describe others. Some people tend to use rather simple physical labels to describe someone (e.g., tall, dark, and handsome) while others might refer to personality traits that were all consistent and dependent upon only one central trait (e.g., sly, tricky, and untrustworthy). A third level of complexity would include a wide variety of traits such as friendly, aggressive, and honest, while a fourth description might include both favorable and unfavorable characteristics: sly, honest, passive, and charming. This latter constellation of traits is a more complex mode of perceiving than that which uses traits which are all very similar or physical characteristics. Some research in the area of leadership has shown that the leader's complexity of perceiving his or her coworkers is significantly related to the group's performance, depending upon the situation in which they are working. We will discuss this research in Chapter 13, "Leadership."[3]

The situation. The final set of circumstances which is related to one's perceptions of others is the situation in which one finds oneself. This is particularly true where first impressions are being formed. Since there are few behavioral cues, one must often rely on situational variables such as where you meet (a bar or the executive lunchroom), who the target person is with (a respected colleague or a disliked subordinate), and the occasion for the meeting (an office party or a long-range planning session).

We are constantly meeting new people and forming impressions of them. These evaluations are often based on rather unreliable factors such as appearance and dress and our own personality. The interesting point is that even though these impressions may be inaccurate, the process by which we make them is fairly consistent. And, of course, first impressions change over time. As we come to observe the person more frequently, a somewhat different process begins to operate. The following section discusses this process more fully.

Ongoing interaction: The use of attributions

Once we have the opportunity to interact with someone and to observe their behavior, we begin to form a richer picture of what the individual is *really* like. We make inferences about the person's motives, personality, feelings, and attitudes. While we can never know for sure what another person is thinking, the observation of their behavior is usually treated as a more reliable cue than their dress or the way they comb their hair.

This inference process—the attempt to accurately assess and evaluate people based upon their behavior—is called the attribution process. An attribution is simply an inference that an individual makes about his or her own internal states or someone else's internal states based upon overt behavior. This line of inquiry has become one of the most active areas of research in social psychology over the last ten years and has produced a number of findings that are important for understanding people's behavior in organizational settings.

Theorizing about attributions began with the work of Heider who was interested in how people made judgments about causal relationships in their environ-

---

[3]F. E. Fiedler. *A theory of leadership effectiveness.* New York: McGraw-Hill, 1967.

ment.[4] Heider believed that people like to figure out what causes what, and that these relationships were particularly relevant for how we treat other people. We see the action of most nonliving objects as behaving in accordance with physical laws: rocks fall because of gravity, the planets move around the sun because of similar forces, and the blowing of the wind, the movement of the tides, and the running of our automobiles can be explained by physical relationships. Humans, on the other hand, have intentions, motives, and goals. We tend to see the behavior of others as intentional: they do things because they want to. Therefore, when people do something which we observe, we automatically try to figure out why they did it.

The study of the attribution process has shown that people are remarkably consistent in how they evaluate others. The first and perhaps the most important judgment that we make is one of internal or external causation. A person is perceived as either acting from free will or as forced by the situation to the action. If an employee leaves a job, is it because the person did not work hard or was not smart enough (internal attributions), or is it because the boss was difficult to work with or the job was boring and unexciting (external attributions)? If a subordinate is late with a financial report, is it because of laziness (internal) or overwork (external)? Our judgments of the individuals involved will differ dramatically depending upon whether an internal or an external explanation is accepted.

Factors involved in making attributions. The work of Harold Kelley has been particularly helpful in describing those factors that determine whether an internal or external attribution is chosen.[5] He suggests that we use three criteria: (1) distinctiveness, (2) consensus, and (3) consistency. We will elaborate on these three criteria using the example of a student who fails a midterm exam in a particular course.

Obviously we can make numerous inferences about why the student failed. Was it because the student did not work hard or is not very smart? These are internal attributions. Or was it because the professor is a poor lecturer or the test was unfair (it did not cover the assigned material)? These are external attributions. The *distinctiveness* criterion would suggest that we would want to know whether this individual failed midterms in other courses or just this one. In other words, how distinctive or different was this action? If the student got low grades or failed most of the other tests, we are more likely to make an internal attribution than if the student got A's on the other tests and an F in only this one course. The *consensus* criteria would tell us whether most students in the class had trouble with the test or whether our student of interest was the only one with a low grade. That is, consensus tells us whether everyone responded in the same way to the situation. If consensus is high, we would expect an external attribution, and the reverse would be true if consensus was low.

Finally, the *consistency* criterion would have us examine whether our student fails the final exam as well. If the student fails the midterm but aces the final, we

[4]F. Heider. *The psychology of interpersonal relations.* New York: John Wiley, 1958.

[5]H. H. Kelley. *Attribution in social interaction.* Morristown, N.J.: General Learning Press, 1971.

Table 5-1. The Use of Distinctiveness, Consensus, and Consistency as Criteria for Making Internal or External Attributions

	Distinctiveness	Consensus	Consistency
Internal attribution	Student fails all midterms	Student is the only one with a failing grade	Student fails the final exam too
External attribution	Student gets A's on other midterms	All the students in the class get low grades	Student gets a good grade on the final exam

are more likely to think that the initial failure was externally caused rather than attributing it to a stable enduring personality or motivational characteristic. Table 5-1 summarizes these factors.

Related research findings. Using the model developed by Kelley, a number of interesting research results have been reported. One finding is that when one perceives that situational demands are strong for an individual to behave in a certain fashion, yet he or she deviates from this expected course of action, the inference of an internal attribution is more likely.

Suppose a series of debates are set up in class where two students are assigned different points of view on particular issues. You know you are to be graded on how well you criticize your opponent's presentation. After a series of these debates if you were asked whether all these people were normally as critical of others as they sounded, you would probably reply negatively. It is likely that they were being critical because the situation demanded it. But what about a student who failed to point out any of the shortcomings of the opponent's presentation? What would you think of this person? You would probably infer that he or she was particularly reluctant to criticize others. In other words, a behavior that differs from situational demands will probably result in more extreme and confident attributions about the person's internal traits and states than will an action that complies with the situational pressures.

Finally, a further refinement of particular interest to organizational settings is the application of Kelley's principles to the evaluation of one's performance on a task.[6] The extension in this case includes not only the question of whether a behavior is internally or externally caused, but also whether the cause was due to a stable or an unstable factor.

For example, a new salesperson in the insurance business brings in a contract from a large corporation worth over a $1 million to the company. You are this person's supervisor and you have to figure out how this happened. Your first question is whether to attribute the success to internal or external causes. Using our distinctiveness, consensus, and consistency criteria would help in this regard. For example, if this was a hard account to get (others had failed before), you would probably make an internal attribution. If, on the other hand, you knew this particular corporation was highly interested in what you had to offer and it

[6]B. Weiner, I. Freize, A. Kukla, L. Reed, B. Rest, & R. M. Rosenbaum. *Perceiving the causes of success and failure.* Morristown, N.J.: General Learning Press, 1971.

was just a matter of time before they signed a contract, you might make an external attribution.

The question of the stability of the cause of behavior would be an important factor as well. If you decided that, in fact, this salesperson was the cause of the good performance, you would want to know if it was due to his or her ability (a stable trait) or just the fact that they worked superhard—exerted a lot of effort—to get this particular contract (unstable trait). If the behavior is seen as externally caused, is it due to the task being easy (stable characteristic) or because of luck (unstable characteristic)? Table 5-2 summarizes these possible interpretations.

Table 5-2. Classification Scheme for the Causal Attributions Made about Successful or Unsuccessful Performance

| | Attribution | |
Cause of Behavior	Internal	External
Stable	Ability	Task difficulty
Unstable	Effort	Luck

If we believe that ability is involved, we are much more likely to rate our new salesperson favorably than if we think the performance was attributable to effort, luck, or an easy task. Both the stability of the cause and its internal/external control are important factors for how we evaluate the behavior.

Implications for organizational participants

The perceptual world obviously intrudes on much of our behavior. It shapes what we see, how we evaluate it, and the ways we behave toward it. This is true for both our observations of objects and of people. There are, however, a number of systematic errors that people are inclined to make because of the perceptual process. You will recall that perception entails a simplified categorization process and that our past experience, present needs, and aspects of the environment all tend to shape this sorting and labeling activity. Described below are a number of ways that this process generates inaccurate or unrepresentative information.

Stereotyping. We are frequently confronted with situations where we know very little about a person except some prominent characteristic such as age, race, or occupation. Given just this one bit of information, we tend to make a classification which attributes a whole set of characteristics to the person. This categorization process is called stereotyping, and it serves the function of reducing the complexity of the interpersonal world. Instead of dealing with people in terms of their unique individuality, we frequently deal with them as representatives of a class or category.

In some cases this process may be helpful. Stereotyping reduces ambiguity and enables one to classify people quickly and easily. In other situations it may provide too simplistic an evaluation and lead to errors of judgment. A number of studies have helped to clarify our understanding of the stereotyping process.

The interesting fact is that there is some consensus among people as to what attributes are most descriptive of a given group. One study asked 100 Princeton students to indicate which attributes from a list of 84 were most applicable to 10 ethnic groups.[7] If traits were assigned at random, one would expect about 6 percent of the students to pick any given characteristic for any given group. However, for almost every ethnic group at least three traits were selected by over 20 percent of the students and at least one attribute by over 50 percent of the students. For example, Americans were seen as materialistic (67 percent), English as conservative (53 percent), and Germans as industrious (59 percent). Thus, there appears to be some agreement about the attributes that belong with a given classification.

Some researchers argue that the reason for this consensus is that there may be a kernel of truth in the stereotyping process. They suggest that people make judgments of other groups compared to their own group. If Germans on the average are seen as slightly more industrious than Americans, then that characteristic will be part of the stereotype, even though the average difference may be very small. A good example recently appeared in the literature with respect to the stereotype that people have about older workers. One study showed that older people were rated as harder to change, less creative, more cautious, and have less physical capacity even when their performance records were as good as those of younger employees.[8] The results were used as evidence that a stereotype for older employees exists in many organizations. On the other hand, another study done a few years earlier actually examined the decision-making styles of managers of different ages and found that, in fact, older managers were somewhat less risky (more cautious) than younger managers.[9] These data suggest that perhaps there is some truth to the existing stereotype. The problem is that the stereotype is used to make judgments about individuals rather than groups.

In recent years there have been a number of studies that have investigated the effects of stereotyping in the workplace. A particular emphasis has been placed on the organizational implications of stereotypes with regard to sex, race, or age. The research strategy employed typically asks people to look at films or read dossiers or engage in some managerial simulation in which some personnel decision is to be made about the people involved (e.g., hired, evaluated, assigned to jobs, etc.). For example, one study had people engage in a managerial simulation in which a number of decisions about hiring and placement were involved. Some of the dossiers were prepared with male names while others were labeled as females. The substantive content of the dossier, however, was exactly the same.[10] Other studies use a similar strategy for testing the effects of different ages or races on personnel decisions.

[7]M. Karlins, T. L. Coffman, & G. Walters. On the fading of social stereotypes: Studies in three generations of college students. *Journal of Personality and Social Psychology,* 1969, **13,** 1–16.

[8]B. Rosen & T. H. Jerdee. The influence of age stereotypes on managerial decisions. *Journal of Applied Psychology,* 1976, **61,** 428–432.

[9]V. H. Vroom, & B. Pahl. Relationship between age and risk taking among managers. *Journal of Applied Psychology,* 1971, **55,** 399–405.

[10]J. R. Terborg & D. R. Ilgen. A theoretical approach to sex discrimination in traditionally masculine occupations. *Organizational Behavior and Human Performance,* 1975, **13,** 352–376.

The findings from these studies are what we would expect. Females, minority-group members, and older employees are often the victims of negative stereotypes. Women, for example, are offered lower salaries, assigned more routine jobs, and are expected to be followers rather than leaders. Older employees are given less challenging jobs.

The use of such stereotyping has moral, legal, and economic drawbacks. First, it is just plain wrong to use race, sex, age, religion, national origin, or any other similar category to judge people. There is plenty of evidence that people of every age, sex, race, or religion are highly competent, effective members of society. Second, it is now legally prohibited to discriminate against people based on these categories. Litigation may be the result. Finally, the use of discrimination based on stereotypes is a potential loss of major human resources for the organization involved. Everyone should have the opportunity to contribute up to their capacity. Their race, age, or sex should not be a limiting factor.

Halo effects. Another bias in evaluating others is the halo effect. Here we are referring to the process where one's impression (either favorable or unfavorable) of a person in one area tends to influence his or her judgment about other areas. The reason for halo effects can be explained by attribution theory. We have mentioned that people tend to attribute personality traits to others based upon the behavior they observe. These attributions tend to be consistent and persistent. That is, we tend to believe that a person who we think is an extrovert on the job is an extrovert off the job, and that he or she has been an extrovert for a long time and will continue to behave that way.

The idea is that we generalize what we think about someone based on our limited observations to other settings and times. We also find that people use what might be described as "implicit personality theories." We believe that certain personality traits go with other personality traits. Extroverts are warm, jolly, and generous, while introverts are cold, serious, and miserly. We use limited information to form an overall picture of the individual. Not only do we generalize a person's specific traits, we tend to generalize our overall impression of them.

In organizations, halo effects may have a serious impact on performance ratings. In most cases a supervisor only observes a small sample of an employee's actual behavior. If for some reason or another the supervisor samples an area where the employee does well (e.g., in meetings or on an interpersonal skill level), the supervisor may judge the individual's performance to be excellent in other areas about which he has little information. The reverse is also true—if you mess up once or in one area, your boss may think you are making mistakes elsewhere. The result of this latter bias is that many employees may be more concerned with *not* making a noticeable mistake than with excellent performance.

In terms of interpersonal behavior and halo effects, we often find that supervisors tend to rate subordinates higher that have similar values or personality characteristics. A number of research studies show that the closer the match between the values of the manager and the subordinate, the more competent the subordinate is rated. Clearly, then, these halo effects have an important impact on various areas of organizational behavior.

Projection. This term has assumed a number of different meanings. Its original usage suggested that people relieve feelings of guilt about themselves by projecting the blame onto someone else. More recently the term has come to mean any situation where one attributes to others the same feelings that he or she is having. There is also evidence that people will attribute to others those characteristics which one feels represent negative aspects of his or her own personality. For example, some research shows that people high on traits such as stinginess, obstinacy, or disorderliness see others in a similar light.

This process serves an important role in maintaining a positive self-concept. We can justify our own aggressiveness, pettiness, or greed by saying that others are worse. However, these types of misperceptions are critical for a number of organizational situations. What frequently occurs is that we may make inferences about the causes of people's behavior based on what we would do in the same situation. If we want a raise, we think others want the same thing; if we constantly butter up the boss, we are suspicious of the motives of subordinates. What we are saying is that our attributions of others are often based upon what we would do under similar circumstances. If we see someone behave in a particular way (e.g., ask for a raise), we assume that the motivation for the behavior is similar to what we would feel if we behaved in the same way (e.g., he or she needs the money and feels that a raise is deserved).

In many instances these attributions are incorrect. Perhaps the subordinate wants the raise because of the status attached to getting more money. Or perhaps the subordinate butters up the boss because he or she actually likes the boss. Like stereotypes and halo effects, projection can lead to systematic biases which will affect numerous organizational decisions such as hiring, firing, rewarding, and job assignments.

Selective perception

Such are promises, all lies and jest.
Still a man hears what he wants to hear
and disregards the rest.   Simon and Garfunkel

A final perceptual process which leads to inaccuracies is called selective perception. We have already discussed the fact that our current needs and past experience partly determine what we attend to and what we perceive. It is also true that the more ambiguous the external situation, the more we rely on these internal cues.

In a good research example of the selective perception process twenty-three executives read a long (10,000 words) and factual case study about a steel company.[11] Each of the executives was placed in one of four groups depending upon their departmental affiliation. There were six from sales, five from production, four from accounting, and eight miscellaneous (research and development, public relations, etc.).

---

[11]D. C. Dearborn & H. A. Simon. Selective perception: A note on the departmental identification of executives. *Sociometry*, 1958, **21**, 140–144.

Table 5-3. Selective Perception of Managers

Department	Total Number of Executives	Number Who Mentioned:		
		Sales	"Clarify Organization"	Human Relations
Sales	6	5	1	0
Production	5	1	4	0
Accounting	4	3	0	0
Miscellaneous	8	1	3	3
Totals	23	10	8	3

SOURCE: D. C. Dearborn & H. A. Simon. Selective perception: A note on the departmental identifications of executives. *Sociometry,* 1958, **21,** 143.

Each of these executives were asked to list what they thought was the major problem that a new president of the steel company should deal with first. Table 5-3 presents these data. It is clear from this table that people tended to see problems in those areas of major interest to themselves. Accountants and sales executives were concerned with financial sales problems. Production people were anxious about clarifying various production issues. Two executives in public relations and industrial relations saw human relations as the problem. These executives attended to those aspects of the situation which were directly relevant to their own goals and concerns.

At a somewhat broader level, selective perception has a major impact on the communication and decision processes. We hear what we want to hear and screen out other information. We overestimate the importance of past trends or circumstances. We simplify rather complex relations to fit an already determined pattern.

To summarize, we make many perceptual mistakes. To overcome these problems we must consciously develop a number of "checking" mechanisms to aid us in situations where these errors are the most dangerous. We must attempt to use only accurate, observable, reliable information about others. We should become better aware of our own biases and learn to truly take *the role of the other.* Finally, in many organizations people are depending upon technological aids. Computers can store, record, and generate data on a variety of issues. It is hoped that all these processes can reduce inaccuracies and in many cases inequities that occur because of perceptual errors.

The aggregate of all our perceptual biases and experiences is part of what makes each of us unique. This uniqueness is typically described as one's personality. We turn now to an analysis of this concept.

Personality

> Men acquire a particular quality by constantly acting in a particular way.
>
> Aristotle

For many years the matter of individual uniqueness was the domain of the personality theorists. Personality was defined as the individual's internal organization of psychological processes and behavioral tendencies. It was assumed that through the process of development we acquired fairly well-established ways of dealing with our environment. These internal constellations were seen as consistent over situations and circumstances. The personality was the integrated whole, the self, the total set of intrapsychic forces that established us as unique and served as the cause of our behavior.

This traditional view prompted research on numerous personality *traits*. People were described as shy, lazy, melancholy, ambitious, aggressive, and so on. Groups of these traits were then aggregated to form personality *types*. The introvert/extrovert distinction is one such typology. These traits and typologies were then used as descriptive labels for counseling, clinical judgments, and personnel activities.

In the last 10 years, however, there has been extensive criticism of this traditional view.[12] Walter Mischel and others have argued that we have carried the trait and type approach too far. They suggest that, in fact, people behave very differently across settings, circumstances, and time. The most appropriate topics for study should not be human consistency but rather the causes of inconsistency.

Let us take an example. According to the Boy Scout creed, each scout should possess a whole series of laudable personality traits (e.g., loyalty, honesty, trustworthiness, etc.). The research on these traits is rather interesting. In a number of studies it has been shown that honesty and trustworthiness are dependent upon the situation. Almost everyone is honest under certain circumstances and dishonest under others. Mischel's argument is that we should pay more attention to these circumstances which cause changes in behavior rather than focusing on behavioral consistency.

The controversy has resulted in a great number of papers discussing the issue of which is the most important cause of behavior: personality traits or the environment? You will remember that we reviewed this topic in Chapter 3, "Understanding Human Behavior." Briefly summarized, we found that while both personality characteristics and the environment are jointly found as causes of behavior, the environment seems to be somewhat more important than the traits.[13]

The implications of these findings are important. They suggest that personality traits, as we have traditionally viewed them, are probably too rigid and inflexible. It is more accurate perhaps to say that one individual is honest over a wider range of settings and circumstances than some other individual (i.e., *more* or *less* honest than the other person). It is probably not appropriate to believe that this first person is always honest or cannot be dishonest (i.e., intrapsychic forces will not let the person be dishonest).

The result of this controversy has been a reanalysis of our previous practices and a shift in emphasis. Many organizations have dropped personality tests from their screening devices as selection tests. This change was brought about partly

---

[12]W. Mischel. Toward a cognitive social learning reconceptualization of personality. *Psychological Review*, 1973, **80**, 252–283.

[13]I. G. Sarason, R. E. Smith, & E. Diener. Personality research: Components of variance attributable to the person and the situation. *Journal of Personality and Social Psychology*, 1975, **32**, 199–204.

because they discovered that these traits were not in fact good, consistent predictors of behavior in other settings and later in one's career. The emphasis has shifted to a more situation-specific type of analysis: given this particular setting, what type of person is most likely to succeed? With this approach both an investigation of the situation and the personality are important.

From this discussion it is clear that personality does not hold as dominating a position today as it did previously. It is, however, still an important and useful concept, and the following sections will review the formation of personality, the measurement of personality, and its use as a predictor of organizational behavior.

Determinants of personality

The interplay of three major determinants affects the formation and development of personality. They are the individual's physiological inheritance, the groups with which one is affiliated, and the culture in which one participates.

Physiological determinants. Heredity supplies the individual with the basic equipment for survival and growth. This includes such constitutional factors as body type, muscular and nervous systems, and the glandular apparatus. But the ways in which these factors manifest themselves in later life are more a function of environment.

Other physiological determinants of personality include reduction of organic drives such as hunger, thirst, and sex. These drives and others like them, while basic to the species, may be satisfied in many ways which are determined more by the culture than by the primitive urge itself.

The group. The family and the school are the most influential institutions in shaping the emerging personality. Later in life so-called anchorage groups or primary affiliations at work or in social or recreational activities mold the personality. These associations are labeled anchorage or reference groups because they give the individual points of reference; they define the role played by the individual along with his or her position in a social matrix.

The culture. This determinant is closely associated with the anchorage groups above. The individual is a participant in a generalized or prevailing culture which defines social roles and sanctions their performance. Certain broad cultural expectations with respect to major roles, such as parent, husband, wife, minister, or teacher, act on the individual. Also, being a member of many anchorage groups within a society, the individual participates in a number of subcultures which modify behavior.

Measurement of personality

There appear to be four major methods of measuring personality characteristics. In some cases, *experimental procedures* are established which help in the assessment of some characteristic. The military, for example, has certain simulations through which they purport to measure leadership skills. A second method uses *rating scales*. In this situation peers or friends make judgments about an individual's traits. These types of ratings are frequently used in recommendation forms. A third approach requires the subject to fill out a *questionnaire*. These questionnaires typically present a set of structured questions to the individual, and he or she responds by checking the correct answer or with a true-false or choice response. The Minnesota Multiphasic Personality Inventory is perhaps the most well-known and frequently used test of this variety. The test employs over 400 questions and provides information about a variety of personality characteristics. A final approach to the measurement problem utilizes *projective tests*. These tests have the subject respond to a picture, an inkblot, or an uncompleted sentence by writing a story about the stimulus information. The responses are then scored on a set of dimensions supposedly related to personality traits.

In all four methods there are strong and weak points and excellent and poor tests. It is suggested that the reliability and validity of the test be thoroughly checked before instituting such a device. Recent Supreme Court decisions and congressional hearings have also stressed limitations with which the personnel director should be acquainted.

Use of personality tests

Almost all organizations use some kind of selection devices to gain information about possible employees. We will discuss the empirical findings that relate personality characteristics to organizational behavior and performance throughout the book. In general it appears as if these techniques have been incorrectly used in many cases. Even in cases where they have been applied with extreme caution, the results are not terribly impressive. Both the uniqueness of the individual and the complexity of the situation have forced us to realize that there are no simple formulas for selecting people for organizational positions. In the following section we discuss some specific personality measures and their relationship to important aspects of the organizational environment.

Personality and behavior

The utility of personality measures depends upon their accuracy in predicting those behaviors that may be important for organizational effectiveness or adjustment to organizational life. Jobs are different in so many ways that often the best we can do is simply to examine the relationship between some personality characteristic and a broad occupational category or status level. Since much of the research emphasizes the use of personality inventories within a specific firm, the literature is filled with studies that report, let us say, a correlation between nine different factors of a specific personality inventory and one's position or job type in a specific company. So, an initial question would simply ask whether personality measures are in general related to what occupation a person selects.

A review of a series of studies by numerous researchers shows a number of differences. The data suggest that in fact certain personality measures do show rather consistent relationships for certain occupational groups. The strength of these relationships, however, is weak. Most of these results make sense in terms of our general beliefs of what certain groups are like. Salesclerks, for example, tend to be high in measures of empathy, which tap an individual's ability to put oneself in another's position. If we believe that people generally seek out jobs in which they will feel comfortable, then we would expect at least some relationship between their personality and type of occupation chosen.

But besides the general question of occupational differences one might want to know how well personality measures predicted specific behavior or performance within an organizational setting. In this instance personality measures serve as selection devices. We have already mentioned that the indiscriminate use of these tests typically provides at best moderate predictions for later success. For example, one research project followed up the success of three Stanford M.B.A. classes.[14] After 5 years the groups were divided into thirds according to their income, and the top third was compared with the bottom third on 55 personality measures gathered when the M.B.A.'s were still at Stanford. Only 13 or the 55 measures showed reliable differences, and these traits were as we would expect. High earners tended to have a lot of energy, self-confidence, and boldness and to have less apprehension about making decisions. These findings are fairly typical in terms of the effectiveness of personality inventories in predicting later success.

A much more frequent research strategy is to examine a small set of personality measures for given groups or situations in attempts to predict specific behaviors. Thus, our theoretical development has become more refined. And when one examines the research findings of this type, some consistency appears. A review of these relationships is presented below.

Interpersonal style and group behavior. Some personality measures attempt to assess the particular ways in which people respond to others and how this general interpersonal style is reflected in their social behavior. Some studies, for example, have found that socially distant leaders tend to be more directive in their behavioral style and tend to be most effective in situations calling for such a style. A prominent personality measure that fits in this category is an individual's authoritarian orientation. People who score high on this scale believe it is correct that there should be status and power differences among people and that the use of power and hierarchical decision making is proper in organizational settings. In general, the research shows that these types of people use directive behavior, are more inclined to conform to rules and regulations, and tend to emerge as leaders in situations requiring a more autocratic and demanding style. Another set of interpersonal style measures assess the general tendency to like or trust other people or to avoid and distrust them. People high on the trust dimensions enjoy group situations, contribute positively to group cohesiveness, enhance social interaction, and avoid competitiveness.

[14]T. W. Harrell. The personality of high-earning MBA's in big business. *Personnel Psychology,* 1969, **22,** 457–463.

Social sensitivity. A second set of traits can be described as those dealing with the individual's sensitivity to other people. There are a number of tests available that measure empathy, sociability, and insight. As one would expect, people high on these dimensions tend to do well in social settings, are warmly accepted in the group, and interact more with others.

Ascendant tendencies. One would expect that individuals differ in their attempts and desires to be prominent and dominating in organizational settings. Numerous tests attempt to measure such traits as assertiveness, dominance, or prominence. The machiavellian scale described at the end of this chapter is an example of a measure which supposedly taps the degree to which one uses people to gain their ends.

The results using these types of tests are somewhat mixed. It is fairly well accepted that these types of individuals are more assertive in their behavior and make more leadership attempts. They also seem to have a substantial impact on group decisions. The data are unclear, however, as to whether such people actually make good leaders or are accepted and well liked. In most cases it seems as if this type of style is accepted only where the group is highly task-oriented or under stress.

Dependability and social stability. People who are consistent, responsible, and generally predictable seem to behave in some consistent ways that are important for group effectiveness. People who are seen as dependable and stable will probably be desirable as group members. Unconventional or unexpected behavior is likely to be disruptive.

The research on these traits supports these predictions. Unconventional people are frequently disliked and rejected by the group. People who are anxious or show emotional instability are likely to be found in groups that are low in cohesiveness or morale. The anxious individual is frequently unable to pursue the group task, tends to vacillate on important judgments, and has lower aspirations for the group.

Locus of control. There are also a number of personality measures that tap an individual's cognitive style. These traits are related to the ways in which the individual processes information and the judgments he or she makes, based on these observations. Locus of control (as well as the next three traits discussed) refers to such a characteristic.

People who see what happens to them in the world as being caused by their own behavior are classified as having an *internal* locus of control. Those who believe that what happens to them occurs because of luck or chance are said to have an *external* locus of control. One recent review paper summarizes most of the results found for organizational participants.[15]

In general, internals tend to be more satisfied with their work and are more satisfied on the job when they are working under a participative management system. Externals, on the other hand, appear to prefer a directive style more than

[15]T. R. Mitchell, C. M. Smyser, & S. E. Weed. Locus of control: Supervision and work satisfaction. *Academy of Management Journal*, 1975, **18**, 623–630.

internals do. It was also found that internals were more likely to hold managerial positions than lower-level jobs. This implies either that internals are more likely to rise to managerial positions or that people become more internal as they increase in status.

In examining the power bases and behaviors used by internal and external managers, we find a fairly consistent picture. The internal manager tends to use more considerate behavior and relies on expertise, rewards, and attractiveness as sources of influence. Externals emphasize more coercive power bases and use more structuring behaviors. This trait may be of potential importance for predicting individual effectiveness in the more open and flexible organizational settings that are being forecast for the future.

Risk taking. There has recently been a major research effort aimed at assessing an individual's tendency to take risks either individually or within the group setting. There is some agreement that there are individual differences on this dimension and that this characteristic can be systematically related to various aspects of the group interaction and decision process.

In general, high-risk takers seem to spend less time making decisions and use less information making these decisions. A recent study substantiated these findings with 79 line managers of a large manufacturing firm.[16] These managers worked on some simulated personnel decisions involving the choice of which

[16]R. N. Taylor & M. D. Dunnette. Influence of dogmatism, risk taking propensity, and intelligence on decision-making strategies for a sample of industrial managers. *Journal of Applied Psychology,* 1974, **59,** 420–423.

Some people like to take chances and take risks more than others. (*By permission of University of Washington* Daily.)

individual to hire. High-risk takers took a shorter time to make their choice and used fewer bits of information than did low risk takers. The decision accuracy, however, was the same for both groups.

Dogmatism. A cognitive style that refers to people being close-minded and inflexible is frequently described as dogmatic. Scales developed which purport to measure this trait have been used in a number of studies investigating leadership, group process, and interpersonal adjustment.

In decision-making tasks we find that these types of individuals take little time to make their decisions but are highly confident of their accuracy. There are also results that suggest that dogmatism is associated with limited search for information as well and poor managerial achievement. They are poor perceivers of how they spend their time on the job.

There is also some evidence on the proper match between a leader's behavioral style and the degree to which subordinates are dogmatic types. One study found that a structuring leadership style was preferred by subordinates high on the dogmatism dimension, while a considerate style was preferred by people low on the dimension.[17] Across four different types of tasks it was found that performance was highest when low dogmatic subjects worked with a leader who was high on both considerate and structuring behavioral dimensions.

Cognitive complexity. One final cognitive dimension refers to the individual's ability to differentiate and integrate various aspects of a cognitive domain. That is, to what extent is the individual able, let us say, to break a task down into its component parts, see the underlying similarities and differences with other tasks, and generally view the situation in a complex fashion. There are currently numerous tests that tap cognitive complexity, and reviews of this research are available.

Two major areas of research are relevant for organizational settings. First, there are a number of well-documented findings in the decision-making area. People who are high in complexity process more information, search for more information, entertain more alternative solutions, and use more complex decision strategies than people who are low in complexity. Data from both laboratory and field settings substantiate these general findings.

A second area of research has tied complexity to leadership style and effectiveness. There is some evidence that highly complex leaders are more interpersonal in their behavioral style and that they tend to use more resources in problem solving. There is also some support for the idea that situations high in variability of the environment are handled better by leaders high in cognitive complexity.

In summary, then, we can see how personality measures may have an important impact on how people behave in a group or organizational context. Obviously the goal of the organization is to try to match an employee's personality with the job and the people with whom he or she works. As we suggested

[17]S. E. Weed, T. R. Mitchell, & W. Moffitt. Leadership style, subordinate personality, and task type as predictors of performance and satisfaction with supervision. *Journal of Applied Psychology,* 1976, **61,** 58–66.

earlier, using one test or one inventory has historically turned out to generate poor predictions of long-run success. However, a more recent approach being used by many companies is the assessment center. In this type of situation the prospective employees take a series of personality, cognitive, and ability tests and also engage in a number of simulations that reflect the work setting for which they may be selected. The emphasis is on the use of multiple predictors for rather specific situations and jobs. Thus, the particular emphasis on any given trait may differ from job to job. We will discuss these centers more thoroughly at a later point in the book.

Summary

The following points summarize the major issues discussed in the chapter.

1 People vary widely in their needs, intentions, and behavior. Two reasons for these individual differences are the perceptual process and the development of a distinctive personality.

2 Perception entails the selection and organization of sensory inputs. What we actually experience is influenced by internal factors such as our past frequency of exposure to the input, the positive or negative reinforcing properties of the input, and contemporary aspects of the situation such as our current needs or expectations. External factors influencing what we perceive include the intensity, motion, and size of the input.

3 Perceiving people includes more complex inferences about internal states. First impressions are dominated by the physical or biographical characteristics of the person perceived, the personality of the perceiver, and the situational constraints.

4 More intense interactions produce attributions about the observed person's personality. Decisions about the internal or external causes of behavior are based upon the criteria of behavioral distinctiveness, consensus, and consistency.

5 The perceptual process in general results in a number of systematic errors of judgment in interpersonal interactions. People use stereotypes, generalize their impressions (halo), project their feelings onto others, and selectively screen out what they do not want to see or hear.

6 Personality traits represent the individual's general pattern of responding to various situations. Such traits are seen as consistent over situations and persistent over time. Our biological makeup, social affiliations, and culture all help to shape these characteristics.

7 In recent years researchers have realized that personality traits are somewhat less permanent than originally believed. Both personal characteristics and the environment jointly cause behavior, with the latter being increasingly recognized as relatively more important.

8 Personality traits have not been particularly good predictors of broad or long-range criteria such as career success. On the other hand, some personality traits predict fairly well certain types of behavior in relatively specific settings.

Implications for practice

The description of the perceptual process pointed out two major issues with relevant implications. First, people vary widely in their needs, characteristics, and skills. Each individual is unique, based upon physiological, psychological, and social development. The logical inference that follows from this fact is that organizations must in some sense be prepared both to deal with and to utilize this individualism.

What we are saying is that greater *flexibility* in organizational design, interpersonal interactions, and individual evaluations is necessary for organizational effectiveness. This point will reappear elsewhere in the book (e.g., in Chapter 7, "Motivation," and Chapter 14, "Employee performance"). We will elaborate on some specific mechanisms to encourage flexibility. It is sufficient at this point to simply emphasize the fact that in order to gain the maximum commitment and motivation from an organization's human resources, we must systematically recognize and capitalize on the individual's unique capabilities.

The second point that stands out is the number and kind of perceptual errors we make, especially in our interpersonal judgments. We tend to use simple classification mechanisms, make attributions which are too broad in scope, use our own personality as a basis for inferring the causes of other people's behavior, and systematically select information (in or out) based upon our own particular needs, wants, and biases.

Correcting these errors probably involves at least two activities. The first would involve an explicit recognition of the problems. Training courses, for example, are available that help managers remove rating errors (such as halo or "similar to me") from their evaluation judgments. But besides recognition we can also encourage the use of more factual and reliable information on which our judgments can be made. Past performance records can be easily stored and retrieved by computers. New performance appraisal instruments tend to include a greater emphasis on observable behavior rather than inferred traits. Through active recognition of the problems and the systematic implementation of training and "checking" mechanisms, the impact of these perceptual biases can be reduced.

The sections on the definition of personality seem to be particularly relevant for current organizational practices. We used to believe that people carried around these deeply ingrained, stable predispositions to behave in one way or another. Now it appears that these predispositions are (1) not so deeply ingrained—they can be changed—and (2) not so stable—changes in the environment produce changes in the behavior.

This new definition of personality as more flexible, changeable, and adaptable to the situation causes problems for a couple of reasons. First, from attribution theory we have learned that it is our natural inclination to attribute traits to people based upon their behavior. It makes our interpersonal functioning much simpler to be able to say that an individual has a certain set of characteristics. The labels help us to deal with that person interpersonally and psychologically. Thus, this new definition of personality seems to run counter to our natural predilections to make personality attributions.

A second problem is one with more practical implications. The traditional definition of personality and our preconceived attributional tendencies both placed a heavy emphasis on the use of personality tests and measures for the selection, placement, and evaluation or organizational participants. For many years the battery of personality tests was the major screening device used by most personnel departments.

The new conceptualization of personality has caused changes in numerous personnel practices. We must be sure that stereotypes and attributions do not lead to discrimination. Personality tests need to show clear relationships to performance on the job or they can be legally challenged as discriminatory selection or evaluation devices. Performance evaluations have shifted their emphasis from traits to observable and countable behavior. And in general there is recognition of the idea that maximum effectiveness comes from the proper match of people (personality) with the environment (job). The increased understanding of the important causal role of the situation has produced better techniques of job analysis and research on situational characteristics. Combining the implications from the perception and personality sections suggests that organizations are both recognizing and trying to cope with the problems produced by individual differences.

Discussion questions

1 Are stereotypes a good or a bad thing? What is their effect on various organizational decision processes?
2 How can attributions lead you to make inaccurate judgments about others? Are there remedies for these problems?
3 How stable and persistent are personality traits? What are the implications of the new way of looking at personality for organizational behavior?

Case: The main manipulator

One of the important characteristics of any management position is that things have to get done through people. The manager cannot do it all. Delegation and the use of power and influence are central aspects of effective managerial performance.

Hundreds of years ago Niccolo Machiavelli wrote his book, *The Prince,* which describes the personal characteristics that are necessary to be a good prince. Some selected quotes should give you the flavor of the writing.

"Therefore it is necessary for a prince, who wishes to maintain himself, to learn how not to do good, and to use this knowledge and not use it, according to the necessity of the case."

"A prince, therefore, must not mind incurring the charge of cruelty for the purpose of keeping his subjects united and faithful; for, with a very few examples, he will be more merciful than those who, from excess of tenderness, allow disorders to arise, from whence spring bloodshed and rapine—for these as a rule injure the whole community, while the executions carried out by the prince injure only individuals."

"I conclude, therefore, with regard to being feared and loved, that men love at their own free will, but fear at the will of the prince, and that a wise prince must rely on what is in his power and not on what is in the power of others, and he must only continue to avoid incurred hatred, as has been explained."

Based upon these writings, the term *machiavellian* has come to take on a common meaning in our language. It is defined in the dictionary as "the view that politics is amoral and that any means however unscrupulous can justifiably be used in achieving political power." It portrays an individual who is manipulative and highly rational. Other people are used as means to achieve the goals of the leader.

Using this type of background, Richard Christie at Columbia University set out to see if there was such a thing as a "machiavellian" personality—were there types of people who seemed to fit into this general category described in the prince. † Christie looked for four main characteristics—people who are amoral, are cool interpersonally, derive pleasure from manipulating others, and are highly rational. Using these definitional premises he developed what is called the Mach V Scale—a paper and pencil personality test which is designed to identify those individuals who have machiavellian tendencies.

Using this personality measure to pick out people with high and low Mach V scores, Christie did some empirical research. He wanted to see if people with high scores on the scale would demonstrate the kinds of behavior he predicted. In a number of studies he found that people with high Mach V scores attempted more interpersonal manipulations, were inventive in the process, had a wide variety of manipulations in their repertoire, and derived more satisfaction from successful manipulations than people with low scores. This type of research has led us to conclude that (1) people do differ systematically in their desire to manipulate others, their success at such manipulations, and the satisfaction derived from the manipulations, and (2) we can measure these differences scientifically.

Questions about the case

1 Do you think the prince is an accurate description of some people?
2 Is it desirable to have such people as our leaders? Why or why not?
3 What do you think leads to the development of such personality characteristics?

Additional readings

** Bonner, H. *Psychology of personality*. New York: Ronald Press, 1961.
   Gemmell, G. R., & Heisler, W. J. Machiavellianism as a factor in managerial job strain, job satisfaction, and upward mobility. *Academy of Management Journal*, 1972, **15**, 51–62.
 * Ghiselli, E. E., & Barthol, R. P. Role perceptions of successful and unsuccessful supervisors. *Journal of Applied Psychology*, 1956, **40**, 241–244.
   Gormly, J., & Edelberg, W. Validity in personality trait attribution. *American Psychologist*, 1974, **29**, 189–193.
 * Jacobson, M. B., & Effertz, J. Sex roles and leadership: Perceptions of the leaders and the led. *Organizational Behavior and Human Performance*, 1974, **12**, 383–396.
 * Kartol, K. M., & Butterfield, D. A. Sex effects in evaluating leaders. *Journal of Applied Psychology*, 1976, **61**, 446–454.

†R. Christie & F. Geis. *Studies in machiavellianism*. New York: Academic, 1970.

** Kogan, N., & Wallach, M. A. *Risk taking: A study in cognition and personality.* New York: Holt, 1964.

 * Lazarus, R. S. *Personality and adjustment.* Englewood Cliffs, N.J.: Prentice-Hall, 1963. See short excerpt reprinted in W. R. Nord (Ed.), *Concepts and controversy in organizational behavior.* Pacific Palisades, Calif.: Goodyear, 1977, 126–134.

Nisbett, R. E., & Borgida, E. Attribution and the psychology of prediction. *Journal of Personality and Social Psychology,* 1975, **32,** 932–943.

** Rokeach, M. *The open and closed mind.* New York: Basic Books, 1960.

 * Rosen, B., & Jerdee, T. H. Influence of sex role stereotypes on personnel decisions. *Journal of Applied Psychology,* 1974, **59,** 9–14.

Scharde, K. W., & Parham, I. A. Stability of adult personality traits: Fact or fable? *Journal of Personality and Social Psychology,* 1976, **34,** 146–158.

** Secord, P. F., & Backman, C. W. *Social psychology.* New York: McGraw-Hill, 1974.

** Shaw, M. E. *Group dynamics.* New York: McGraw-Hill, 1971.

 * Zalkind, S. S., & Costello, T. W. Perception: Some recent research and implications for administration. *Administrative Science Quarterly,* 1962, **7,** 218–235.

6

Attitudes

Significant numbers of American workers are dissatisfied with the quality of their working lives. Dull, repetitive, seemingly meaningless tasks offering little challenge or autonomy, are causing discontent among workers at all occupational levels.

Work in America: Report of a Special Task Force
to the Secretary of Health, Education, and Welfare, 1973

In a 1935 article which reviewed the research on attitudes, Gordon Allport stated that "the concept of attitude is probably the most distinctive and indispensable concept in contemporary American social psychology."[1] In the organizational setting, attitudes are thought to be tied to one's personality and motivation. An employee is said to have a good "attitude" about work, or we seek out our supervisor's opinion or attitude about some topic. The purpose of this chapter is to clarify what we mean by the word "attitude" and to discover how it can be useful in understanding organizational behavior.

Definition

Although Allport uncovered over 100 different definitions in his review, he did find some consistencies. Social scientists from a variety of fields seemed to agree that attitude could be seen as a *predisposition to respond in a favorable or unfavorable way* to objects, persons, concepts, or whatever. Underlying this definition are some important assumptions. First, *attitude is related to behavior*. Based upon one's attitude toward something, an individual is predisposed to behave in a particular way. One could argue that one's attitude about the job is related to the attendance record. People who like the job come to work, and those who do not stay home. Second, *attitude is an unidimensional variable*, and

[1]G. W. Allport. Attitudes. In C. Murchinson (Ed.), *A handbook of social psychology.* Worcester, Mass.: Clark University Press, 1935, 798.

that dimension is tied to one's feelings about an object. The particular feeling is one of favorability or affect or attraction—that is, the degree to which something is liked (a pleasant feeling) or disliked (an unpleasant feeling). Third, *attitude is a hypothetical construct*. It is something which one carries around inside. Its consequences may be observed, but the attitude itself cannot.

Background

To help us understand what an attitude is, we must distinguish it from other well-known but different concepts. First, an attitude is not a *fact*. An attitude is an evaluative statement; it is how one feels about something. Facts, on the other hand, are meant to be statements about the existing state of nature. Telling someone that you like the UCLA basketball team is an expression of your attitude. Telling someone that the UCLA team has won more college basketball championships from 1965 to 1975 than any other team is a fact. The facts may be related to the attitude, but they are different things.

Second, attitudes are different from *beliefs*. Beliefs are typically defined as statements about the relationships between objects, concepts, and events. "I like my job" is an attitude. "My job gives good pay" or "I have a smart supervisor on my job" are beliefs. These beliefs describe the relationship between one's job and other aspects of the work setting. Sometimes a belief may be a fact, but in other cases it may not. For example, the belief that "I will get promoted if I stay on this job for another year" is a belief but not necessarily a fact. We will find that most attitude theorists see the attitude concept as a summary of beliefs. One can think of all the beliefs that one has about a job (e.g., it is interesting/boring; well paid/poorly paid; varied/routine; etc.) and infer their attitude from these beliefs. Many of the attitude measurement techniques follow this procedure.

Finally, attitudes are different from *values*. Values are broader, more encompassing concepts. Some people see values as a summary of many attitudes. Our attitudes toward many different minority groups may provide a good representation of the degree to which we value equality. Besides being broader, values carry with them an "oughtness" component. They are frequently defined as ideas about how everyone *should* feel or behave. Most of us value freedom, equality, and peace, and we feel that everyone should feel the same way.

What we are saying is that an attitude is a fairly specific evaluative feeling. It is not factual although it is probably formed by our beliefs. Figure 6-1 shows the relationship between attitudes and these other concepts. One can see that attitudes are firmly embedded in our psychological framework. It is an important predictor of action, it summarizes many of our beliefs, and it gives us an indication of deeper, broader values. We will elaborate on the attitude-intention-behavior relationship later in the chapter.

Importance

Attitudes serve a number of purposes and are important for a variety of reasons. From a personal perspective, attitudes provide a knowledge base for our interaction with others and with the world around us. Your attitudes about various

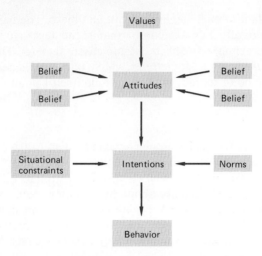

Figure 6-1. Attitudes and related concepts.

social issues (e.g., abortion, gun control) should help you to form your attitudes about political candidates. Also, as you come into contact with other people, you quickly learn whether their attitudes are similar or different from your own. In many cases this mutual assessment of attitude similarity determines the extent to which future interaction will occur.

Attitudes are also used as social indicators. Throughout the 1976 presidential campaign we were engulfed with attitude surveys about the two major candidates, Gerald Ford and Jimmy Carter. While at the end these surveys said the race was "too close to call," for many other races they have served as good predictors. The marketing departments of most large companies are constantly monitoring and trying to influence your attitude toward their product. National surveys of job dissatisfaction provide information about the general well-being of the work force. "How do you feel about this?" or "How do you feel about that?" have become common questions in almost every aspect of our personal and organizational lives.

Formation and development

In Chapter 3, "Understanding Human Behavior," we discussed how people learn to behave the way they do. Answers to this question were in part related to early childhood behavior. A child has a variety of physiological drives which are satisfied in various ways. The satisfaction of these drives becomes linked to the circumstances that surround the satisfaction. If the child finds food satisfying, he or she will begin to associate that good feeling with the surrounding circumstances of the event such as mother or a time of day. After a while very complex patterns of behavior may become associated with need satisfaction, and just how specific attitudes are formed will be determined by an individual's personal history.

The central idea running through the process of attitude formation is that these feelings are *learned*. An individual acquires these feelings through experience with the world around him or her. An implication of this idea is that *all objects acquire an attitude*. One has feelings that may run from positive to negative about everything. Attitude is a basic component of how we ascribe meaning to our interpersonal and physical environment.

Another important implication is that people develop attitudes about things or objects based upon what the things or objects are related to. Food is related to a feeling of satisfaction, mother is related to food, and so on. One's attitudes about an object are formed through the relationship of that object to other things or objects. If those related objects are liked, so is the new object; if they are disliked, the reverse would be true. We may like a supervisor because he or she is friendly, sincere, and honest, or we may dislike our job because it is boring or tiring. In either case, the evaluations are formed according to the association between the attitude object and other related states, concepts, or objects.

Measurement

The most common and frequently used attitude measures are questionnaires which ask the respondent to rate or evaluate the attitude object directly or to respond positively or negatively to some beliefs about the attitude object. If, for example, you wanted to know how favorable your employees were toward a union, you might use some bipolar scales (opposite adjectives) to assess their attitudes. The questionnaire might look like this:

				Unions				
Pleasant								Unpleasant
	+3	+2	+1	0	−1	−2	−3	
Good								Bad
Beneficial								Harmful

Alternatively, you could generate a number of belief statements and have your people indicate whether or not they agreed with them and how much. Some possible statements are listed below:

Unions protect the rights of workers.
Unions will result in better wages.
Unions increase the conflict and tension in the workplace.
Unions suppress individual freedom.

People's responses to these statements should give you a fairly good assessment of where they stand on this issue. We should hasten to point out that there are rigorous procedures for the development and scoring of such instruments. One should either use a standard questionnaire or consult an expert to obtain a valid estimate of attitude.[2] But from a practical standpoint what we are saying is obvious: Attitudes are typically measured by looking at one's beliefs, and this can be a fairly simple procedure.

---

[2]M. Fishbein & I. Ajzen. *Belief, attitude, intention, and behavior: An introduction to theory and research*. Reading, Mass.: Addison-Wesley, 1975.

Job attitudes: Measurement of morale

There are numerous attitudes related to job activity which have interested social scientists. There is a large body of literature dealing with interpersonal attraction (our attitudes toward other people, for example). The most frequently researched attitudes, however, are those dealing with one's overall feeling toward his or her

Think of your present work. What is it like most of the time? In the blank beside each word given below, write

__Y__ for "Yes" if it describes your work

__N__ for "No" if it does NOT describe it

__?__ if you cannot decide

Work on present job

_____ routine

_____ satisfying

_____ good

_____ on your feet

Think of the pay you get now. How well does each of the following words describe your present pay? In the blank beside each word, put

__Y__ if it describes your pay

__N__ if it does NOT describe it

__?__ if you cannot decide

Present pay

_____ income adequate for normal expenses

_____ insecure

_____ less than I deserve

_____ highly paid

Think of the opportunities for promotion that you have now. How well does each of the following words describe these? In the blank beside each word put

__Y__ for "Yes" if it describes your opportunities for promotion

__N__ for "No" if it does NOT describe them

__?__ if you cannot decide

Opportunities for promotion

_____ promotion on ability

_____ dead-end job

_____ unfair promotion policy

_____ regular promotions

Think of the kind of supervision that you can get on your job. How well does each of the following words describe this supervision? In the blank beside each word below, put

__Y__ if it describes the supervision you get on your job

__N__ if it does NOT describe it

__?__ if you cannot decide

Supervision on present job

_____ impolite

_____ praises good work

_____ influential

_____ doesn't supervise enough

Think of the majority of the people that you work with now or the people you meet in connection with your work. How well does each of the following words describe these people? In the blank beside each word below, put

__Y__ if it describes the people you work with

__N__ if it does NOT describe them

__?__ if you cannot decide

People on your present job

_____ boring

_____ responsible

_____ intelligent

_____ talk too much

Figure 6-2. Sample items from the Job Descriptive Index. Each of the five scales was presented on a separate page. The instructions for each scale asked the subject to put "Y" beside an item if the item described the particular aspect of his or her job (e.g., work, wages, etc.), "N" if the item did not describe that aspect, or "?" if he or she could not decide. *(The JDI is copyrighted by Bowling Green State University. The complete forms, scoring key, instructions, and norms can be obtained from Dr. Patricia C. Smith, Department of Psychology, Bowling Green State University; Bowling Green, Ohio 43403.)*

job. This attitude is typically called morale or job satisfaction, and specific methods have been developed to measure it.

The technique which is most well known is the Job Descriptive Index (JDI) developed by Pat Smith and her coworkers.[3] This scale presents the worker with a series of adjectives as possible descriptions of five aspects of the job (work conditions, pay, promotions, supervision, coworkers). The employee places a "Y," "N," or "?" for a "yes," "no," or "don't know" response next to each adjective. A copy of this scale is presented in Figure 6-2.

The favorable points about the JDI are worth mentioning. First, the technique generates a satisfaction score for five job areas as well as an overall score. This information helps the investigator in using the tool as a diagnostic device. He or she can determine with what areas people are more or less satisfied. Another strong point is the scale's ease of administration. It is not necessary to develop a new scale for each job. There is also extensive normative data available for the JDI. Thousands of employees have filled out this scale in many different types of organizations across the country. It is possible, therefore, not only to make comparisons between job aspects in the same organization but also in some cases to compare different organizations on the same job aspect. For example, if data has been gathered in a similar organization, then one could compare the satisfaction with pay at that firm with the other firm.

A second technique which is frequently used was developed and used by Porter and Lawler.[4] Their method also gathers information about different job aspects. Employees are asked to what degree they think a certain job characteristic exists in their present position (e.g., pay) and how much they think there should be. They also rate the importance of that characteristic. A difference score between what there is now and what there should be is weighted by the importance score. Two or three questions may be included for each job aspect which again provides an overall score as well as a score for each aspect.

The JDI is typically employed for lower-level, routine-type jobs, while the Porter and Lawler technique is frequently used for managers. Both measures assume that the respondent can read. For illiterate or marginally literate workers there is a scale called the Faces Scale, which presents five faces similar to those pictured below.[5] The employee is asked to circle the face which best represents

his or her feelings about their job.

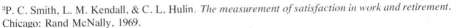

[3]P. C. Smith, L. M. Kendall, & C. L. Hulin. *The measurement of satisfaction in work and retirement.* Chicago: Rand McNally, 1969.

[4]L. W. Porter & E. E. Lawler, III. *Managerial attitudes and performance.* Homewood, Ill.: Irwin, 1968.

[5]T. Kunin. The construction of a new type of attitude measure. *Personnel Psychology,* 1955, **8,** 65–78.

While there are a number of other good attitude measures available, these three techniques are probably the most frequently used today. Similar to our discussion of the measurement of attitudes in general, the measures of job attitudes are direct, paper-and-pencil techniques. Also, note that both the JDI and Porter and Lawler techniques assess one's attitude by measuring the extent to which the job is associated with other favorable or unfavorable aspects. This assumption forms the foundation for most of the literature on attitude measurement and theory.

Attitudes and behavior

The question that is frequently asked after surveying all this busywork on the definition and understanding of the attitude concept is: "So what? Is it related to what people actually do? Can I use it to predict behavior?" The answer is a qualified yes.

Perhaps the most famous research on this topic was conducted by Richard La Piere.[6] From 1930 to 1932, La Piere and a Chinese couple traveled around the United States by car. Of the 251 establishments which they approached for services, food, or lodging, only one refused to serve them. La Piere later sent out a questionnaire to these establishments to discover their attitudes toward Orientals and their willingness to serve them. Of the returned questionnaires, 95 percent of the people said *they would refuse service to Chinese*. Clearly there was a discrepancy between reported attitude and actual behavior.

The results caused an uproar among social psychologists, and numerous explanations were cited for La Piere's findings. New theories were proposed, attitude was redefined, and rigorous measurement procedures developed. Out of all this activity came some general conclusions with which most investigators are comfortable.

First, the more specific the attitude measured, the more likely it is to be related to behavior. The measure La Piere used simply asked about Chinese people in general—not the well-dressed, highly educated, young couple which actually appeared at the desk. If you want to know whether an individual is going to join a particular union, your prediction will be better if you measure the attitude toward that specific union rather than toward unions in general.

Second, as we pointed out in Figure 6-1, situational variables and norms often intervene between our attitude and our behavior. For example, an innkeeper might be opposed to serving a minority group member based on attitudes but be compelled by the legal constraints to provide service. In terms of social norms we can easily think of a situation where an employee wants to join a union but coworkers do not. In this case, even though the person's attitude favors joining a union, the social pressure or norm against unions may deter action.

In summary, attitudes are in fact related to behavior. They indicate a personal predisposition to respond in a particular way. They put pressure on the individual. However, other forces can outweigh or counteract this pressure. Sometimes the situation or social norms prohibit us from behaving the way we would like. But the important point is that if these other *external* forces did not exist, the

[6]R. T. La Piere. Attitudes versus action. *Social Forces*, 1934, **13**, 230–237.

individual would probably behave in line with his or her attitude. Therefore, if we can help to form or change a person's attitude, we can usually influence their behavior.

Attitude organization and dynamics

Isn't it because you're free to choose the one that you love
That you love the one you choose like you do?   Cashman and West

A recognition of the importance and the complexity of the attitude-behavior relationship is necessary for practical reasons. In most cases, from a practical perspective, what we want to do is *change* people's attitudes and consequently change their behavior. We may be trying to convince friends that a particular candidate is outstanding so that they will vote Democratic, or the human resources department of a large corporation may try to increase morale and thereby reduce turnover and absenteeism.

But we have already pointed out that attitudes are firmly developed in a complex structure of beliefs, values, and other attitudes. In order to create change in this structure, we must understand how it is organized. We must know what methods of change are likely to occur and how they take place. All these ideas are tied to the ideas of attitude organization and dynamics.

Consistency theories

Fritz Heider was one of the first investigators to suggest a general theory of attitude organization (called balance theory).[7] Heider's model was very simple. He looked at a person's attitude toward one other person and how both of them felt about one attitude object or topic. He was interested only in whether their feelings were positive or negative toward one another and the attitude object. His specific interests were in the area of interpersonal attraction and he suggested that we like people who like the same things we like. When this situation does not exist (e.g., when we perceive that a friend likes something we dislike, or someone we do not like is attracted to something we do like), we feel uncomfortable and are motivated to change one of our attitudes.

This type of consistency model has been developed for *other issues* besides interpersonal attraction. *Complex* attitude structures have been analyzed that contain links between more than just one other person and a single attitude object. The links have also been *quantified* as opposed to just a simple positive or negative feeling. The *degree* of change is predictable from some of these models. So, as a basic model, Heider's theory was very helpful. The central point was that we tend to hold consistent attitudes, and when they are inconsistent, we are motivated to change them.

[7]F. Heider. Attitudes and cognitive organization. *Journal of Psychology,* 1946, **21**, 107–112.

Bust open the door, yell "Morris for Senator! Power to the people," then barge in, tell them Morris is cool, ask for a handout, then split.

When an attitude object is linked to things you do not like, it is probable that you will change your attitude in a negative direction.

Dissonance theory

Two major criticisms of consistency theories were that they were too simple and that they failed to look at behavior. Their major focus was the interrelationships among attitudes. In an attempt to deal with these two problems, Leon Festinger developed the theory of cognitive dissonance.[8] According to Festinger, two cognitive elements are dissonant if the opposite of one follows from the other. These cognitive elements, however, can be more than just attitudes; they can be beliefs or observations about one's own behavior. Thus a belief, such as smoking causes cancer, coupled with the act of smoking, would be expected to arouse feelings of discomfort (dissonance) and motivate the individual to change his or her behavior or beliefs.

A number of qualifications should be discussed. First, Festinger argues that we must look at the proportion of dissonant elements to consonant elements in order to predict changes in behavior or attitudes. We must examine the overall cognitive structure to see how much dissonance exists. Thus, one dissonant belief in the midst of many consonant ones will probably not produce enough discomfort to produce change. As a related issue, Festinger argues that these cognitions must be weighted by their importance. Therefore, in some cases when

---

[8]L. Festinger. *A theory of cognitive dissonance*. Evanston, Ill.: Row, Peterson, 1957.

only a few elements are dissonant, if they are important enough, the individual will be uncomfortable and motivated to change.

How does one reduce dissonance? Festinger suggests three major strategies. First, one can reduce the importance of the dissonant elements. Second, one can add more consonant elements. Third, one can change the dissonant elements. Let us say, for example, that you are in an advertising firm that accepts the account of a pharmaceutical product which you believe might be harmful to people's health (including your own, perhaps). You must help market the product (behavior) but you feel uncomfortable doing so (you have a negative attitude toward the product). One strategy to reduce the dissonance would be to simply say something to yourself such as, ''Well, any drug that we take probably

I've never heard the Alphas play before, but they must be great to attract such a crowd. I'm really looking forward to seeing them.

Cognitive dissonance shows how we justify our actions (standing in line) by bringing our attitudes in line with our behavior.

does a little harm,'' and thereby reduce the importance of the dissonant element. You might, on the other hand, try to find out more about the positive effects of the product in an attempt to heavily outweigh the dissonant element. Finally, you might initiate some research to perhaps reduce the negative effects of the drug. A number of similar practical applications of dissonance theory are especially related to decision-making issues, and three of these are discussed below.

Postdecisional dissonance. One particular situation that almost always produces dissonance is decision making. Whenever we are forced to choose one alternative from among a set of possible courses of action, we must usually forgo the good aspects of the unchosen alternatives and live with the bad aspects of our choice. If, for example, you must choose between investing in firm A or B, and both seem attractive for a variety of reasons, then once the choice is made, certain cognitive processes occur. First, there may be a brief stage of regret where the unchosen alternative (let us say firm B) becomes more attractive. This period lasts only a brief time, during which dissonance begins to operate (i.e., you chose A and you must justify this behavior). Dissonance theory predicts that you will increase your positive attraction toward firm A and become more negative toward firm B.

The research results confirm these types of predictions. A typical study involves people evaluating consumer products, before a choice is made and after a choice is made (but before the product is actually used). What tends to happen is that people become more positive toward the chosen product than the unchosen one even though they have no new information. In order to justify our action and reduce dissonance, we change our attitudes.

A number of points should be emphasized. First, note that we are talking about attitude change that occurs after the behavior. Choice is determining attitudes rather than the reverse. One of the major contributions of dissonance theory was its emphasis on this fact. A second related point is that the theory predicts that we shift our attitudes in line with our behavior which will then, in turn, influence later choices. To the degree that choices are repetitive, and between two fairly competitive alternatives, we will tend to bias our judgments because of dissonance reduction. In some objective sense, an alternative which was passed over may become the action that would maximize payoffs for the organization at some later point in time, but because of dissonance processes this alternative will have been devalued further and will be overlooked.

Disconfirmed expectancies. Another situation that occurs frequently in organizations is the situation where some sort of expectation is disconfirmed or turns out to be incorrect. You decide that the route to success for your company is to buy out a number of small competitors. You spend many months and lots of money to reach your objective only to find that you were wrong, and company performance is down. Again we have dissonance directly related to some sort of decision activity.

The individual may attempt to reduce discomfort in a variety of ways. One might argue that things are not so bad, and besides, the cause of the slump appears to be something other than the purchase of the small firms. A person may believe that the basic idea was all right even though the expectation was incorrect. Different positive outcomes may be substituted, such as, "Well, we're not making more money, but we're reaching a wider audience and we're better known." Rather than recognize and admit that a poor choice was made, the individual may become more committed to the mistake.

An excellent study by Staw recently appeared which illustrated this point (it was appropriately entitled "Knee Deep in the Big Muddy").[9] A simulation was run where business students played the role of corporate executives of a company in financial trouble. The executive was asked to make a decision about the allocation of $10 million in additional R&D funds to one of two of the corporations largest divisions: consumer products or industrial products. The events supposedly took place in 1967. After the decision the students were presented with a financial report dated 1972—a 5-year update. For half of the students their expectancies were confirmed (the company did well as a result of their decision), and for half of the students the expectancies were disconfirmed (the company did poorly as a result of their decisions). They were then asked to make a further allocation of funds to the two divisions for which there would be high or low personal responsibility. The design is shown below:

| | Expectancies | |
Responsibility	Confirmed	Disconfirmed
High	1	2
Low	3	4

One might rationally expect that people who had been wrong in the past (disconfirmed expectancies) would change their mind and redistribute the funds to the other corporate division (cells 2 and 4 of the design). On the other hand, those with confirmed expectancies should follow the same course as chosen previously (cells 1 and 3 in the design). These predictions should be especially true when the personal responsibility for the decision was high. Dissonance theory, on the other hand, might suggest the opposite; people who were wrong will try to justify their prior choice by making the same choice again. This is exactly what Staw found! More money was allotted to a choice that had been disconfirmed than to the one that had been confirmed, and this difference was greatest when the responsibility was high.

The ramifications of this idea are important. It appears as if people change their attitudes and values to justify their behavior. For the decision-making process, it means that time and effort is spent in justifying a choice already made rather than trying to find out if a better choice could be made. Instead of learning from our mistakes and correcting our errors, we may compound our errors and make more serious mistakes.

[9]B. M. Staw. Knee deep in the big muddy: A study of escalating commitment to a chosen course of action. *Organizational Behavior and Human Performance*, 1976, **16**, 27–44.

Attitude-discrepant behavior. This third area of application is perhaps the most interesting, as well as the most controversial, topic of dissonance theory. Frequently we are pressured or asked to do something we find unpleasant. Decisions must be made about allocating resources, hiring and firing, etc. When we behave in a way which is discrepant with our underlying attitudes, we experience dissonance. The critical questions are, of course, how much pressure is needed to produce the discrepant behavior, and what are the implications for attitude change.

One set of predictions comes from Festinger's model of forced compliance, presented in Figure 6-3. This model attempts to predict an individual's attitude when pressured to do something against his or her wishes. If, for example, one wished to have a subordinate do an unpleasant job (such as handle a customer's complaint), the theory predicts that just enough pressure to induce the person to comply should be used (position 3). At this point the subordinate has done something he or she finds unpleasant and should be experiencing dissonance. That is, the person's behavior is not consistent with his or her attitude. The person should, therefore, become more favorable toward the act just done in order to reduce the dissonance and to justify the behavior. If too much pressure is administered (a threat of dismissal perhaps), the employee would probably comply with the supervisor's wishes but still detest the task (position 4). People have little trouble justifying their behavior under this condition. If too little pressure is applied, the employee may refuse to do the job and may even become more unfavorable toward this type of work (position 2). This prediction is made due to the fact that the individual has said no to the supervisor and must justify this behavior in order to avoid feeling uncomfortable. The person, therefore, becomes even more negative about the job involved. Clearly, in position 1 there is little need for change. The employee says no to a passing suggestion to do

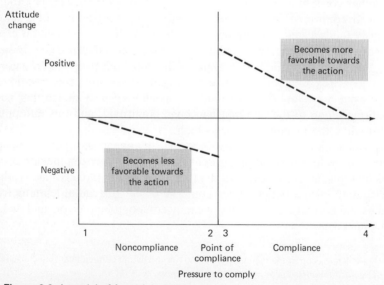

Figure 6-3. A model of forced compliance.

some unpleasant task. This behavior is consistent with the person's attitude, and the individual has not been made to feel uncomfortable in the refusal (as is the case for position 2).

The research results tend to confirm this model. This is especially true when the individual is *free to choose to comply or not to comply*. The greater the amount of freedom, the more powerful the effect of the dissonance. As the poet Milton once said, "He who overcome by force hath overcome but half his foe." If someone has no choice but to comply, the underlying attitude will remain unchanged.

These latter findings are of crucial importance for the execution of decisions and leadership. Obviously a manager does not want to have to constantly increase the pressure on subordinates in order to obtain their compliance. It is unpleasant to have to push and threaten. The manager would prefer situations in which the subordinates came to enjoy what they were doing. The implications are that it is perhaps better to start out with a little too much pressure and work back to less pressure than to do the reverse. If too little pressure is exerted, the individual will not comply and will come to dislike the task even more (which will then require more pressure the next time to obtain compliance).

Attitude change

At this point we arrive at the central issue: How can we change attitudes? We know what attitudes are, how they develop, and how they fit into a fairly complex psychological network of beliefs and values and other attitudes. We also know that from a motivational perspective people try to maintain a fairly consistent and harmonious pattern of beliefs and attitudes. To change all of that requires that we successfully change part of the cognitive structure, or in the case of dissonance-theory predictions, we can try to change the person's behavior. But whichever strategy we select, the desired result is the same: a change in attitude and a change in behavior.

Before we proceed to cover this complex topic, an initial distinction between job satisfaction and other attitudes should be made. First, job satisfaction is so important and such a central topic in the organizational literature that it requires separate attention. Over 3000 articles have been written on the subject. Second, as you will recall from our section on attitude measurement, job satisfaction is typically seen as an attitude composed of numerous components (beliefs about pay, supervision, the physical environment at work, etc.). To change that attitude you would obviously change a whole variety of *situational* and informational aspects of the job, with a heavy emphasis on the former. On the other hand, most of the attitude-change research from social psychology deals with people's attitudes about issues (e.g., labor unions), products (e.g., toothpaste), or people (e.g., political candidates). The technique to induce change is typically conceived of as an *interpersonal exchange of information:* how can individual A get B to change his or her attitude. So for reasons of emphasis and conceptual clarity the section on job satisfaction will follow our section on attitude change in general.

Figure 6-4. A model of attitude change.

A model of change

When one person is trying to change another person's attitude, a number of factors are involved. Figure 6-4 presents a model of the attitude-change process. First, as we would expect, the personal characteristics of the communicator may influence how much change occurs: Is the person believable? Second, the way in which the message is presented may make a difference: Is the message biased or poorly organized? Third, the characteristics of the target person may affect the amount of change: Is the target paying attention? And finally, some situational variables may help to increase change: Is there a supporting audience surrounding the target? The research on all these factors is extensive, and the findings are summarized below.

Communicator characteristics. There are a number of factors about the communicator which will influence the target's amount of attitude change *independent* of the message. The first, and perhaps most important, is the expertise or prestige of the communicator. If the person is seen as well qualified in the area, then more change will occur. The typical study has two people reading the same message with one communicator having high prestige and one having low prestige. The high-prestige communicator produces the greatest amount of attitude change.

A second characteristic of the communicator that is important to the target is whether the communicator is perceived as biased or not. The target is likely to question whether the communicator has something to gain or lose in the issue. The more bias thought to exist, the less attitude change. All the advertisements on TV that refer to an "independent study" done by a "team of experts" are trying to make you believe you are hearing an unbiased report from a very prestigious source.

Finally, as we would suspect, people that we like and identify with are more persuasive than those we dislike or are unfamiliar with. Obviously the reason that football players or movie stars advertise spark plugs or beef stew is not because they are expert mechanics or cooks. It is because these people are attractive and liked. This sort of prediction is easily made using the very simple balance model suggested by Heider. We like products that are liked by people for whom we have positive feelings.

The communication. There are some ways in which the message itself can be constructed that increase the chances of change. One initial question would be the degree to which an extreme stand should be taken. Should we try the hard sell or the soft sell? The research results seem to suggest that if the topic is fairly unimportant to the target, an extreme position taken by the communicator can produce large amounts of change. However, if the issue is of great importance

(Sample--Warning card to be placed in R. R. Trains, &

Beware! Young and
All Walks of

This [ ] may be handed

by the friendly stranger. It contai

na"-- a powerful narcot

Murder!   Insar

WARNING!

Dope peddlers are sh

put some of this druo

A message has to be credible before it will have an effect on attitudes. It is unlikely that a poster proclaiming that marijuana causes murder and insanity will change many peoples' behavior. (*By permission of the University of Washington* Daily.)

(e.g., politics, religion, sex), an extreme position will be rejected and very little, if any, change will occur. In this type of situation a more moderate appeal is likely to be successful.

Think about our discussion of this attitude embedded in a complex framework of other beliefs, attitudes, and values. If the topic is unimportant, it is likely not to be bolstered by many beliefs and important values. It should be relatively easy to create change without producing discomfort. However, if the attitude is firmly supported by many important and basic beliefs and values, trying to change it means that many deeply held values may also need to be changed. The person is far more likely to reject an extreme communication under these circumstances.

A second issue is whether the communicator should present a one-sided or two-sided argument. Should you recognize the strong points of your competitor? Most of the research says yes. A two-sided argument seems to be seen as less biased and is therefore more persuasive.

A third and highly controversial issue is the use of fear appeals. Does it help to tell people of all the terrible consequences that may occur if they do not change

Mark Waters was a chain smoker. Wonder who'll get his office?

Too bad about Mark. Kept hearing the same thing everyone does about lung cancer. But, like so many people, he kept right on smoking cigarettes. Must have thought, "been smoking all my life... what good'll it do to stop now?" Fact is, once you've stopped smoking, no matter how long you've smoked, the body begins to reverse the damage done by cigarettes, provided cancer or emphysema have not developed. Next time you reach for a cigarette, think of Mark. Then think of your office—and your home.

American Cancer Society

THIS SPACE CONTRIBUTED BY THE PUBLISHER AS A PUBLIC SERVICE/PHOTO: MONTE CASSACA

Sometimes fear arousal is used as a technique to change attitudes. *(By permission of the American Cancer Society.)*

their attitudes and behavior? Think of the antismoking ads that appeared in the news and on television a few years ago. Which do you think was more effective: one that mentioned all the details about lung cancer or one that depicted the smoker as socially rather inept (bad breath, nervous, etc.)? The research results seem to show that fear appeals can be effective, especially when the target can do something to reduce the fear immediately. Studies on automobile safety, atom-bomb testing, fallout shelters, and tooth decay all show that fear appeals can change attitudes and behavior.

Characteristics of the target. Perhaps the most important characteristic of the target is commitment to his or her initial attitude. Has the person taken any action or made any public statements about where he or she stands? If so, the person's attitude is less likely to change. Also, the more central the attitude is to other attitudes and values, the less change is possible. Firmly held attitudes to which we are verbally and behaviorally committed are hard to change.

It also appears as if people who are generally more self-confident and have high self-esteem are less susceptible to change. Apparently, people with high self-esteem believe their attitudes are more correct and justified than those with low self-esteem. People with high self-esteem may be more likely not to care about what attractive stars or athletes have to say.

Situational factors. There are a number of situational variables, separate from the communicator-message-target links, that may affect how much attitude change occurs. One homily that seems to be true is that "forewarned is forearmed." If people know that someone else is going to try to change their attitudes on a subject, they are better able to resist the persuasion attempt. One plausible reason why this should be is that the people have the opportunity to think through their position beforehand. They can construct counterarguments and strengthen the defense of their own position. All this activity tends to reduce the amount of change that occurs.

Another situational factor concerns the support of people around you. Is everyone in favor of what the communicator says? Are they nodding their heads in agreement and smiling? Are they paying attention? If the target believes that the group is favorable toward the communicator, more change should occur, especially if these people are important to the target.

In summary, there are many ways to change people's attitudes. A liked or respected communicator should help. Two-sided, unbiased arguments are probably most effective. The uncommitted, low-confidence people are most likely to change. And social support for the communicator's position is likely to result in high levels of attitude change. At first blush it sounds quite easy—we ought to be able to change people's attitudes whenever we want. Our everyday experience, however, tells us that this is not true, and the following section briefly documents why.

Resistance to change

If all these techniques exist to change attitudes, why are companies unable to easily sell their products or political candidates to easily get elected to office? Partly it is because of competition—other people and products offer conflicting arguments or in some cases, the same arguments. Most studies of national political or advertising campaigns show that very few people actually change their attitudes as a result of these attempts.

Research on how people resist such attempts show that both personal and situational factors are involved. In terms of personal variables, the target frequently rejects either the expertise or attractiveness of the source. President Ford, in the closing days of the 1976 campaign, had Joe Garagiola (a baseball player) travel around with him, and in fact Garagiola introduced the President when he made his last-minute appeal to the voters on election eve. If you were a Jimmy Carter supporter, an easy way to reject this appeal was to say, "What does Joe Garagiola know about politics? Nothing!" The rest of the arguments then have little impact.

People also will occasionally distort a message; they will hear what they want to hear (remember selective perception). The target may not think you are advocating as much change as you think you are.

The situational variables are also important. Most attitude-change appeals of a political or advertising nature occur in social settings. The typical situation is an ad on TV which the targets may watch while surrounded by friends and family. What happens in this case? First, they may be distracted. Advertisements are often used as a time to get a snack or to talk with friends. Second, most people watch what they want to watch: they selectively expose themselves to information. If you know that there is a show on that discusses the negative effects of smoking and you smoke, you are less likely to turn it on than if you do not smoke.

Finally, most people are sitting around or interacting with people who are similar to them in terms of attitudes. Therefore, there is likely to be social support for arguments that refute the communicator's position if you are initially against that stand.

All of this supports much of what we know—it is frequently very hard to change people's attitudes and behavior, especially on important topics. It is hard to determine which beliefs are central and therefore most important to change. It is difficult to make people listen to you and pay attention to you. It is hard to always have a one-on-one discussion. However, we have come a long way toward understanding how this change takes place. In the case of job satisfaction this knowledge has been very helpful in suggesting ways that the quality of one's working life can be increased.

Attitudes and the world of work

When we consider our attitudes toward work, we are involved in a complex, ever-changing phenomena. Most work is done in large, organizational settings where policy is set by infrequently seen professionals. Most people work directly in some capacity with machines, and production and profits are of central importance. Most of this activity is carried out during set hours and in urban settings. Work also serves many different purposes for people. It is obviously a source of economic security—a way in which needed goods and services can be provided and obtained. It is a source of social interaction. Most people's social lives center around people they know from work. Finally, work is a source of self-esteem. We evaluate ourselves partially according to our work performance. However, for any one of these descriptive dimensions or functions there is great personal variety. Thus we have some difficulty in finding a commonality of meaning for the term "work."

Whatever the task, however, people have evaluative feelings about it. They like or dislike certain aspects of their work and they have an overall assessment of favorability about what they do. Job satisfaction, as an evaluative appraisal of one's job, is a good reflection of these feelings and has been an important aspect of organizational research for 50 years. Over 3000 studies are available on the topic.

The Hawthorne studies first highlighted the importance of worker attitudes. As a result of the attention given to small groups of employees who were being observed, the workers reported a freer attitude about what they did on the job. They felt the organization was interested in them, and they liked it. Their social and work activities changed, and performance increased as well. These initial studies prompted the researchers to investigate further the attitudes of all the employees, and an extensive program of interviewing was commenced. From these data management gained an insight into the employees' attitudes about work conditions, rate-busters, supervisors, and many other issues which affected their behavior on the job and their overall satisfaction with that job.

The situation today

After 50 years of investigating job attitudes, many authors feel we are facing a crisis of major proportions. A special task force of the U.S. Department of Health, Education, and Welfare recently published a review of current trends and suggested that significant numbers of American workers are dissatisfied with the quality of their working lives.[10] This same report lists the following signs of problems in the workplace:

The growth in the number of communes

Numerous adolescents panhandling in such meccas as Georgetown, North Beach, and the Sunset Strip

Various enterprises shifting to four-day workweeks

Welfare case loads increasing

Retirement occurring at ever earlier ages

There are reported increases in absenteeism, sabotage, and turnover in many industries. Productivity may be decreasing, and there is a great increase in the days per year lost from work through strikes.

An economist or technologist viewing these symptoms may point out the numerous favorable changes that have occurred in the workplace. Working conditions are generally better. Industrial safety is important, and the possibility of severe injuries has decreased. Women and children are seldom engaged in backbreaking labor, and arbitrary dismissals and pay cuts are rare.

The economic conditions are better for most employees. Real income, standard of living, health status, and life expectancy are all greater. Pensions, while still far from perfect, are available for many employees. The *Work in America* report presents us with a paradox: Things seem better by almost any standard, yet people are not satisfied with their jobs.

The response to this paradox has been twofold. First, many writers point out

---

[10]*Work in America: Report of a special task force to the secretary of HEW.* Cambridge, Mass.: M.I.T., 1973.

that the needs of employees have shifted. Instead of placing their major emphasis on the economic aspects of the job, they are concerned with the meaning of the job in some broader context. A recent survey conducted by the Survey Research Center at the University of Michigan with a representative sample of 1533 workers from all occupational levels found the following ranking of job aspects in terms of their importance.

1 Interesting work
2 Enough help and equipment to get the job done
3 Enough information to get the job done
4 Enough authority to get the job done
5 Good pay
6 Opportunity to develop special abilities
7 Job security
8 Seeing the results of one's work

Thus, while working conditions have become better, employees' expectations about organizational life have changed as well.

A second suggestion that explains the paradox argues that researchers have been investigating the wrong types of job attitudes all these years. Some authors argue that we have focused too much attention on jobs themselves. From the time of Frederick Taylor's scientific management we have seen jobs as activities to be done and have attended to what makes these activities easier to accomplish. Attention has been placed on the specific work activities rather than the setting surrounding the job.

This primary focus with the job has omitted a larger view: the structure and content of jobs in a broader social, political, and organizational setting. Rather than treating the individual as the operating unit, we should move to a more global analysis. Rather than seeing the individual as being primarily motivated by comfort and money, we should stress a more involved and personal accomplishment frame of reference. Finally, rather than seeing employees as a labor commodity, we must view them as integral members of the organization. What these authors are suggesting is that we are moving into a postindustrial era and that people want different things from organizational life. Our new interest in attitudes about job autonomy and involvement has influenced our ideas about what makes a job satisfying and how work itself should be defined. Organizational strategies for analysis and change are beginning to reflect these changes.

The research results

The empirical findings on job satisfaction in general and on specific aspects of the job that lead to satisfaction seem to reflect some of these concerns. A recent monograph on job satisfaction was prepared for the Manpower Administration (U.S. Department of Labor) by the Survey Research Center (SRC) at the University of Michigan.[11] These researchers reviewed a large number of national

---

[11] United States Department of Labor. *Job satisfaction: Is there a trend?* Manpower Research Monograph No. 30, 1974.

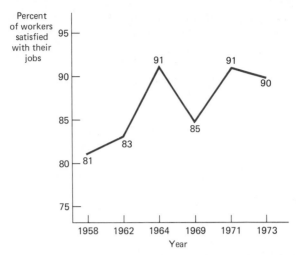

Figure 6-5. Percentage of "satisfied" workers, 1958 to 1973, based on six national surveys.

surveys on job satisfaction carried out by Gallup and by SRC since 1958. A summary of the SRC survey data is presented in Figure 6-5 because the Gallup data is very similar. One can see that anywhere from 9 to 19 percent of the people surveyed reported they were dissatisfied with their job. It is likely that unemployed people (5 to 10 percent) are also dissatisfied with their opportunities to attain a meaningful job. Thus, up to one quarter of the people seeking work or current employees may have negative attitudes about the workplace. A number of interesting findings were discussed in more detail in the SRC report. First, there seems to have been very little change in the last 10 years. According to their report, things have been at the same level of satisfaction (or dissatisfaction) for the last 15 years. Second, as we would expect, the most dissatisfied people are young, poorly educated, members of minorities, or in low-status occupations.

These data present additional reasons for our general feeling that people are dissatisfied with their work even in the face of greater economic and physical security. First, it is only in the last 10 years that we have systematically attempted to listen to minorities, the young, and the worker in marginal jobs. Thus, while these people have probably had low job morale for many years, it is only recently that we are attending to their concerns. Also, as we listed earlier, people want interesting jobs that provide them with information and responsibility. Since researchers and practitioners have only recently shifted their focus to these factors, it will probably take some time before any appreciable increase in job satisfaction will appear nationwide.

Causes of favorable job attitudes

If we want to know how to increase satisfaction, we have to know what causes it or is associated with it. As one can guess from the section on the measurement of satisfaction, many factors are involved. There is a considerable body of research that deals with both the causes of satisfaction and the consequences of satisfaction.[12] We will briefly summarize this literature in the following two sections.

Supervision. In general, considerate supervisory behavior seems to correlate positively with job satisfaction. A number of studies show first that changes in supervision lead to changes in satisfaction, and second, that a considerate style of behavior is also positively related to satisfaction. Two precautionary comments are worth making. First, most of the evidence for the above relationships and for many that follow is correlational and therefore does not imply causal relationships. It is just as plausible that having satisfied workers causes a supervisor to be considerate rather than the reverse. Second, since the relationships are generally moderate (correlations of 0.20 to 0.40), there are numerous cases where the reverse may be true; that is, there are most certainly situations where close supervision is appreciated. There just happen to be more cases where it does not (at least for the situations that have been empirically investigated).

Another important aspect of supervision is the degree to which subordinates may participate in decisions that affect their work. In general, it appears that some participation is related to positive feelings about the job. However, there are some limiting conditions. The decisions should be about topics with which the employees are familiar and have some expertise (for example, the work pace). The participation should be real—that is, the information offered by the employees should actually be part of the decision process. And finally, too much participation may be related to negative attitudes. To some extent employees want to be supervised, or at least they do not want to be inundated with all of the organization's problems.

Job challenge. A number of factors that are positively related to job satisfaction can be placed under the label of job challenge. Included here are such things as variety on the job, creativity, difficult goals, and the use of one's own personal skills. People seem to be more satisfied with their job when it demands something from them. Such challenge may have other benefits as well. It appears as if people are more committed to the job and are more involved with their work when they are challenged by what they do.

The opposite of challenge is boredom. Numerous studies show that boredom can lead to high levels of dissatisfaction and may eventually result in absenteeism and turnover. Challenge, or the lack of it, can have both attitudinal and economic impacts.

Job clarity. Another set of factors that seem to be important for job satisfaction refer to the degree to which the job is clear versus ambiguous. Up to a point it appears as if people like to have a clear, unambiguous work environment. Studies of factors like job clarity and specificity show positive relationships with job satisfaction.

[12]E. A. Locke. The nature and causes of job satisfaction. In M. D. Dunnette (Ed.), *Handbook of industrial and organizational psychology*. Chicago: Rand McNally, 1976, 1297–1349.

Two related factors are role clarity and feedback. When one's relationships with others are fairly clear (role clarity), job satisfaction seems to be higher than when these relationships are ambiguous. People also like to know how they are doing (feedback). Giving accurate and frequent feedback can increase job satisfaction. In general, what all of these variables suggest is that reducing uncertainty and ambiguity seems to increase job satisfaction.

Job content. Both the standardization and specialization of work tasks have tremendously increased productivity throughout the world. The relationship with satisfaction appears to be curvilinear. A moderate amount of these variables appears to be most highly related to satisfaction. Figure 6-6 shows this relationship.

When the job is neither specialized nor standardized, an employee would have difficulty knowing what or how to do the job. At the other extreme are situations which are highly repetitive and boring. Although these points may differ for different types of people or jobs, it is clear that the extreme ends of these continuums are related to low morale.

Two possible corrections for the problems of too much specialization are job rotation and job-enlargement programs. The employees are able to either expand the number of tasks they are doing or to rotate to different tasks. We will discuss these strategies more fully later on in the book. The important point to make is that one must first ascertain the current location of employees on the curve.

Traditional incentives. Promotional opportunities and wages have traditionally been cited as variables which are related to job satisfaction. In the case of promotions it does appear that employees are more satisfied with situations where this opportunity is likely than when it is not. The relationship is weak, however, and this is probably due to the fact that promotions are a relatively infrequent experience. There are numerous other things that happen every day (supervision, the job content, and so on) that are more highly related to job attitudes.

The research on the effect of wages on satisfaction and productivity is vast, and no attempt will be made here to immerse ourselves in this morass. It does appear that people are more satisfied with high wages than low wages. The

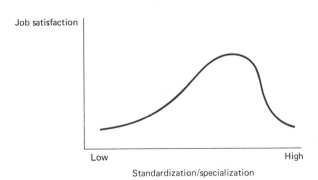

Figure 6-6. Graph of the relationship between job satisfaction and job content.

strength of the relationship is questionable as is the causality question. An important factor seems to be one's reference group. People seem to be satisfied when their wages are higher than those received by others who are doing a similar job. When one compares favorably, he or she is satisfied, and the reverse seems to be true when the comparison is unfavorable. Satisfaction related to wages, therefore, seems to be a joint function of the absolute amount and a comparison with others. Just what this function looks like is as yet unknown.

Consequences of favorable job attitudes

The question here is simply, "In what ways do satisfied employees behave differently from dissatisfied ones?" Four main topics will be reviewed: turnover, absences, health, and productivity.

Turnover. One would expect the relationship between job satisfaction and turnover to be negative. The greater the satisfaction, the lower the turnover. In general, the results support this hypothesis. It appears, however, that the strength of this relationship is partly dependent on the degree of full employment that exists. There are always going to be some people who leave because of dissatisfaction and some who leave because they have to (the individual moves, a family crisis, and so on). In times of full employment when numerous job opportunities are available, we would expect the percentage of those who leave because of low satisfaction to be greater than when times are hard. Accordingly, the relationship between turnover and satisfaction should be stronger during full employment, and indeed this is what is reported in the literature.

Absences. The relationship between absenteeism and satisfaction is also predicted to be negative. The higher the satisfaction, the fewer the absences. Although generally supportive, the results are far from conclusive (correlations from -0.14 to -0.38). Again, the issue is clearer if one considers a third variable. Many long-term periods of absence are experienced by old faithful members of the organization, and these people are probably not dissatisfied. One study in a metal-fabrication factory pointed out this problem.[13] Job satisfaction was correlated 0.51 with total absenteeism for twenty-nine departments. This figure suggests that satisfied departments had greater absenteeism. However, when *unexcused* absences were correlated with satisfaction, the coefficient was -0.44; that is, high satisfaction was related to low absenteeism. As we would expect, people who choose to stay at home and lose their pay are less satisfied than those who have good attendance. Also, recent reviews of the research in the last 20 years have provided substantial support for the relationship between dissatisfaction and turnover and absenteeism.

Health. While the studies in this area are fewer in number and poorer in methodological rigor, the findings are consistent and significant. They overwhelmingly suggest that both physical and mental health is increased by working

[13]W. A. Kerr, G. Koppelmeier, & J. J. Sullivan. Absenteeism, turnover, and morale in a metals fabrication factory. *Occupational Psychology*, 1951, **25**, 50–55.

on a satisfying job. Reports of fatigue, headaches, and ill health are lower, as are measures of cholesterol and heart disease for satisfied employees. In fact, a number of studies suggest that life expectancy is higher for satisfied workers! The same is true for studies of mental health: less anxiety and tension are found in satisfied employees. The data clearly suggest a causal relationship between job satisfaction and other psychological and physical factors related to one's health.

Productivity. For many years it was assumed that a happy ship was a productive ship. The way to obtain higher levels of efficiency was through morale. A number of thorough and rather devastating reviews have shown little support for this hypothesis. The average correlation between job satisfaction and productivity is about 0.15. Satisfaction and productivity are not related to one another in any consistent manner. Some authors have even argued that what little relationship does exist could be attributed to the reverse relationship: productivity causes satisfaction.

When one considers the models of motivation and attitudes which have been discussed, this relationship is no longer so puzzling. If attitudes or behavior are related to the degree to which they are tied to favorable or unfavorable related objects, then there is no reason to believe that liking the job will prompt one to high levels of effort. People are attracted to jobs for various reasons (the work conditions, the friendships, the supervision, and so on). They may find that all these things can be obtained without extra effort, and indeed, this is the case in many organizations. It is true that some rewards may be lost, such as a bonus or a promotion, but in many cases these incentives are not of utmost importance. Other incentives (e.g., salaries, days off) are typically not related to effort, and it should not be surprising, therefore, that overall job satisfaction is only slightly related to output.

To summarize, there are a variety of things that lead to high satisfaction. Some of the variables are related to the people with whom you work (supervisor, coworkers), some are related to the job itself (challenge, clarity), and some are related to the payoffs that occur (pay, promotions). An increase in satisfaction can have positive benefits for both the individual and the organization. Better physical and mental health as well as lower absenteeism and turnover seem to be the result. While individual productivity may not be increased, these other factors are important for a smooth-running organization which is also a pleasant place to work.

Summary

This was a fairly long chapter with much information in it. The summary below highlights the major points.

1 Attitudes are a predisposition to respond in a favorable or an unfavorable way. They are learned, evaluative feelings about the people, objects, and concepts that exist in the world around us.

2 Attitudes are firmly embedded in our psychological makeup. They are related to more basic values and they reflect a summary of our beliefs about a topic. If measured with enough specificity and if other factors such as

social norms are taken into account, attitudes can be powerful predictors of our behavior.

3 Most measures of attitudes use our reactions to a set of beliefs as a reflection of our underlying attitude. For attitudes about the job, the important beliefs seem to be factors related to supervision, the work environment, and traditional incentives such as pay and promotions.

4 Most people try to maintain a consistent and unified pattern of beliefs, values, and attitudes. When elements of this structure are contradictory, the individual is motivated to reduce the dissonance caused by this inconsistency. Thus, by changing one's attitude, other attitudes and eventually one's behavior can be modified.

5 Dissonance theory also pointed out that by changing one's behavior, their attitude could be changed. This principle has been used to explain why we often stick with bad decisions or come to like tasks that we initially felt were unpleasant.

6 In order to be effective in changing attitudes about people, issues, or products, one needs (1) a high-status, expert, or well-liked communicator, (2) a fair, unbiased message, and (3) a receptive and attentive audience that is (4) not pressured or bothered by outside forces.

7 Job satisfaction is the most important and frequently studied job attitude. The causes of high job satisfaction are considerate supervision and coworkers; a challenging and unambiguous job; and adequate pay and traditional incentives.

8 The consequences of having satisfied employees are better physical and mental health, lower absenteeism, and lower turnover. However, high satisfaction does not necessarily result in high productivity.

Implications for practice

Probably the first thing that should be recognized is the pervasiveness of our attitudes and their importance. We have attitudes about lots of topics that are related to our behavior in organizations. We have attitudes about safety programs, minority groups, unions, and of course, our overall job satisfaction. These attitudes are firmly embedded in a complex psychological structure of beliefs, other attitudes, and values. Since these attitudes are related to our behavior (e.g., do we wear a safety helmet, do we discriminate against women, do we participate in a slowdown?), the crucial question becomes the method and means by which these attitudes can be influenced and changed.

Two major conclusions can be drawn from our review. First, since attitudes are a summary of beliefs, they reflect a very complex overall evaluation. What this means is that you may hold the same attitude as someone else, *but for very different reasons*. Two people may dislike a safety program with equal intensity, but one may feel that way because he or she believes the program is a bother and takes up time, while another may believe that the program will not work. These individuals' belief structures are a product of their own learning experience.

Therefore, to be effective in changing attitudes you first should have some idea what people think. If you want to change attitudes by changing beliefs, that requires that you identify the important beliefs before trying to change things. If, for example, there is a high level of absenteeism, do not automatically assume that low pay or lazy employees are the causes. It might be poor supervision or a boring job. Find out the problem first, then try to change the appropriate beliefs and attitudes.

A second conclusion, generated by dissonance theory, is that in some situations the best way to change attitudes is to work directly on behavior. For many years there were people who said that forced racial integration in the areas of housing, jobs, school, and services would not work. They contended that people's attitudes had to be changed first. However, legislation was passed and enforced, and all indications are that attitudes, in fact, came into line with behavior. It is never pleasant to pressure people into doing something they originally don't want to do, but if this pressure is (1) not too extreme, (2) maintains the individual's freedom of choice, and (3) is explained in a reasonable, rational manner, it can be an effective way to change both attitudes and behavior.

Finally, our review of the job-satisfaction literature pointed out a very important fact: Job satisfaction does not necessarily lead to high productivity. A happy ship is not necessarily a productive one. This should not be too surprising. Job satisfaction is caused by multiple factors, only some of which should logically increase effort.

But while job satisfaction may not directly affect productivity, it does have indirect effects. People are healthier, are present more often, and stay with the company longer if they are satisfied. These outcomes can have a substantial effect on other costs such as health benefits, selection and training costs, and retirement costs. Changing this attitude in a positive direction can benefit any organization.

And it *can* be changed. Obviously, where physical discomforts are at issue, they can be removed, or where ambiguity or misperceptions seem the problem, more accurate or detailed information can be provided. Participation and involvement in meaningful decisions seems to increase satisfaction, and various group exercises can facilitate this working arrangement. Job previews also seem to clarify expectations and facilitate adjustment to new jobs. Other techniques involve role playing where employees attempt to see organizational life from the point of view of someone else (e.g., their supervisor, an upper-level manager). Many types of job redesign have been shown to change attitudes. But these topics carry us beyond the central concern of this chapter and will be dealt with later. Attitudes clearly affect our feelings about organizational life and our job-related behavior.

Discussion questions

1 How are attitudes different from other familiar concepts such as facts, beliefs, and values?
2 How are attitudes related to each other and to behavior? Do changes in attitude cause changes in behavior? Is the reverse true?
3 It has been reported to you (as personnel manager) that morale is low. It is your job to correct the situation. What would you do?

Case: Morale and malaise

Gerry Buckland heard the alarm but he didn't move. He didn't even turn it off. The thought of facing another day on the line was just too much. "Maybe I'll call in sick," he thought. But then he dismissed that idea—he'd skipped two days last week. If he was absent any more, he might lose the job.

Just then Janet, his wife, walked in. "Come on Gerry, its a lovely day, get up and have some breakfast before you leave for work. I hate to see you miss breakfast."

Gerry exploded: "What the hell difference does breakfast make?" he asked. "Breakfast has nothing to do with it. I just don't want to go to work. I hate it down there. Every day it's the same thing. You get there, change your clothes, say hi to your buddies, and then the bell rings. For most of the day I stand at the same spot using the same drill doing the same thing—attaching doors to the cab of a truck—big deal. I feel like a robot."

"Oh come on, Gerry, let's not get into that again," replied Janet. "I know you don't like it sometimes, but think of the positive things. The pay is good and you've got some seniority after 13 years. Pretty soon you might get a shot at the foreman job. Besides, you got plenty of friends there as well."

"The friends and the money don't count a thing," responded Gerry. "It's the work itself. It's so boring and repetitious—the same thing day after day. It's noisy, dirty, and you can't talk to anybody except at break time. I'm spending one-third of my life sleeping and one-third doing something I despise. That doesn't leave much, does it? I've had it. I'm going to look for another job."

"Well," Janet mused, "I'm certainly not going to tell you what to do. It's your life and your job. If you hate it so much, you probably ought to look around for something else. But don't forget that Christmas is next month and we'll need some money for the kids. Also, Danny has to have braces put on his teeth—why don't you wait until the new year?"

Janet left the room as Gerry sat up. "She is probably right," he thought. "We do need the money and now is a particularly bad time to be short. I guess I'll just have to put up with it a little while longer."

Questions about the case

1 What do you think was the major cause of Gerry's dissatisfaction?
2 Could the job be improved in such a way that his attitude would change? What would you suggest?
3 Do you think Gerry will ever leave the job? What sorts of pressures besides the economic ones would keep him where he is?

Additional readings

* Davis, L. E. Job satisfaction research: The post-industrial view. *Industrial Relations,* 1971, **10,** 176–193.

Festinger, L., & Carlsmith, J. M. Cognitive consequences of forced compliance. *Journal of Abnormal and Social Psychology,* 1959, **58,** 203–210.

** Fishbein, M. *Readings in attitude theory and measurement.* New York: Wiley, 1967.

** Freedman, J. L., Carlsmith, J. M., & Sears, D. O. *Social psychology*. Englewood Cliffs, N.J.: Prentice-Hall, 1974, Chapters 8, 9, 10, and 11.

 * Garson, Barbara. Luddites in Lordstown. *Harpers,* June 1972, 73ff.

** Himmelfarb, S., & Eagly, A. H. *Readings in attitude change*. New York: Wiley, 1974.

 * Hovland, C. I. Reconciling conflicting results derived from experimental and survey studies of attitude change. *American Psychologist,* 1959, **14**, 8–17.

 * McQuade, Walter. What stress can do to you. *Fortune,* January 1972, 102–107ff.

Miles, R. H., & Petty, M. M. Relationships between role clarity, need for clarity, and job tension and satisfaction for supervisory and nonsupervisory roles. *Academy of Management Journal,* 1975, **18**, 877–883.

Rogers, R. W., & Mewborn, C. R. Fear appeals and attitude change: Effects of a threat, noxiousness, probability of occurrence, and the efficacy of coping responses. *Journal of Personality and Social Psychology,* 1976, **34**, 54–61.

 * Schwab, D. P., & Cummings, L. L. Theories of performance and satisfaction: A review. *Industrial Relations,* 1970, **7**, 408–430.

Sheridan, J. E., & Slocum, J. W. The direction of the causal relationship between job satisfaction and work performance. *Organizational Behavior and Human Performance,* 1975, **14**, 159–172.

Steers, R. M. Factors affecting job attitudes in a goal setting environment. *Academy of Management Journal,* 1976, **19**, 6–16.

** Triandis, H. C. *Attitude and attitude change*. New York: Wiley, 1971.

** Vroom, V. *Work and motivation*. New York: Wiley, 1964, Chapter 5.

 * Waters, L. K., & Roach, D. Job attitudes as predictors of termination and absenteeism: Consistency over time and across organizational units. *Journal of Applied Psychology,* 1973, **57**, 341–342.

 * Wool, Harold. What's wrong with work in America. *Monthly Labor Review,* March 1973, 38–44.

*Possible reading for students

**Review of literature or comprehensive source material

7

Motivation

Learn thou, whate'er the motive they may call,
that pleasure is the aim, and self the spring of all.   Robert Southey

When we observe a group of employees on the job, we may be struck by their differences in performance. Some people do an excellent job, while others are marginal in their output. Some employees come early, put in a hard day, and stay late, while others are always talking, taking a coffee break, and are never around when needed. In some cases the best worker may produce 2 or 3 times as much as the poorest worker.

How do we explain these differences? Well, obviously we attribute certain traits and abilities to the productive employee. The person may be intelligent, aggressive, and extroverted. But there is more than just ability. There is something willful about the differences between the employees. Somehow the productive worker seems to want to do well while the marginal employee appears disinterested. It is at this point that we refer to motivation. The productive employee is described as more motivated or driven than the other person.

Motivation, as we are describing it, implies a willful or volitional act on the part of the individual. The employee may choose to try hard and to exert a lot of effort or may choose to just get by. To understand motivation, then, we must understand those inner forces which energize and move the individual to behave the way he or she does. While the external environment may be the same (e.g., reward systems, leadership, the task) for all employees in a group, it is how these external events are interpreted and evaluated internally which causes different people to behave in different ways. The remainder of this chapter will be concerned with describing these inner forces, the way they combine to produce motivated behavior, and techniques that can be used by the organization to increase the motivation of its employees.

Basic background

The focus of most motivational research is to understand two psychological processes: arousal and choice. When we speak of arousal, we are dealing with the question of why we do anything at all. What gets us going? Why do we initiate action? The second process, choice, occurs after we are aroused. Given that we are active and seeking some goal, why do we attempt to do one thing rather than another? What are the determinants of our choice of action? So, we are concerned with what activates people, and after they are active why they choose the particular behaviors that they do.

The earliest ideas about what motivates people dealt with *choice* behavior. The writings of Greek philosophers and later the work of the British philosophers John Stuart Mill and Jeremy Bentham were focused on this issue. The underlying idea, called hedonism, was that people behave in a fashion that will maximize their pleasure. We do what we do because we believe that what we do will give us more pleasure than anything else we might do. However, since these authors never attempted to assess just what people anticipated to be the consequences of their acts, the theory was of little use empirically. That is, it did little to further our understanding of how these choices came to be more or less favorable.

Further developments in the choice area began to shed some light on the answers to this question. First, it was argued that of several responses that an individual makes to a situation, those which result in satisfying or pleasurable consequences are strengthened. Those that lead to uncomfortable or unpleasant outcomes are weakened. Those that are strengthened become more probable, those that are weakened become less probable, in response to the same situation. Our present choices were explained in terms of past consequences. We choose a given alternative today because in the past this alternative led to more favorable consequences than any other alternative. However, this "law of effect," as it was called, still did little to explain *why* the consequences were pleasurable or not pleasurable.

The explanation of why the individual behaves at all (arousal), and consequently why responses are more or less pleasurable, was tied to the idea of physiological needs. The individual was seen as having hunger, thirst, and other drives, and pleasure resulted from reduction of these drives. At this point the law of effect or reinforcement would become important.

A simple example might help. A child is aroused by the drive of hunger. There are physiological cues and internal cues which trigger the arousal (such as a rumbling stomach). At first, perhaps, the child reacted to these cues by randomly moving around, crying, and generally trying out a whole set of behaviors. Magically, after one set of these actions, some food appears. Those activities that immediately preceded the presentation of the food (and the reduction of the need) would become strengthened. That is, they would be more likely to occur the next time the child was hungry since they had been positively reinforced. Over time rather strong links between behavior and anticipated outcomes are created and what we call "habits" are established. The list following shows a simple representation of these relationships.

BASIC MOTIVATIONAL QUESTIONS

1 *Question of arousal.*

Physiological or social *needs* and *drives* cause arousal.

2 *Question of choice.*

Behavior likely to lead to most positive *reinforcement* is chosen.

In an analysis of most psychological theories of motivation we find that they can be easily categorized into two approaches. Those theories that attempt to specify and codify the drives that motivate people are concerned with content. Those that try to describe people's choice behavior will be designated as process theories. Although this distinction is not clear for every theory, it points out quite nicely the differences we have stressed so far.

Psychological theories: Process and content

Perhaps the most well-known classical theory of motivation (content and process) was developed by C. L. Hull.[1] This theory suggests that behavior can be predicted from two major classes of variables: drive and habit strength. Drive is composed of variables representing the amount of deprivation of some need and the incentive value of the consequences of an act. Drive was originally concerned with just physiological needs but was later broadened to include the reduction of any strong internal stimulus. Specifying these needs falls into the area of content theories. Habit strength refers to the frequency of previous stimulus-response connections in similar circumstances. After a particular drive was activated, the choice of behavior would be determined by those habits which had been previously developed. So, Hull's theory can be viewed as one early approach that attempted to answer both the question of arousal (through the concept of drive) and the question of choice (through the concept of habit strength).

Other theories dealing with human needs have produced an extensive list of items that arouse an individual. The idea is that an unsatisfied need produces tension (sometimes called motives) and that tension reduction is satisfying. Reviewing these lists produces three general categories of needs or drives.

Basic drives. The biological drive, already mentioned, requires the satisfaction of those basic needs essential to maintain physiological integrity—organic survival. The nature of satisfaction for this drive is specifiable. The need for food, water, rest, air, and elimination is necessary for the survival of the human organism, even though the level of satisfaction of these biological requirements differs from person to person.

Primary motives. There are two primary motives—psychological and social. The psychological motive results in a quest by an individual to maintain mental integrity or balance. The social motive stems from the natural gregariousness of humans and their need to associate with other humans.

[1] C. L. Hull. *Principles of behavior.* New York: Appleton-Century-Crofts, 1943.

Derived motives. This last category provides the richest source of motives underlying human behavior. These motives are derived from the basic social and psychological motives. Examples might include the individual's need for security, recognition, or power. It is these motives which are highly variable in the sense that they change in their importance both between and within individuals. An example of such a theory is presented by H. A. Murray. Throughout his career he postulated about twenty different needs that he believed humans attempted to satisfy, and this list included needs from all three of the categories above.[2]

Motivation in organizations

The above theories only help us to understand the motivational process in general. They do little to tell us about what happens in organizations. What needs are operating? What sorts of choices face us? To proceed further we must analyze motivation in the organizational context.

Almost all of us will spend a good deal of our lives in organizational settings. We may have full-time or part-time jobs. We may be volunteer workers or only work a part of each year. No matter what our particular situation will be, it is true that more than 80 percent of our population works in some sort of organization during their lifetime. Thus, one important reason for the study of motivation in organizations is that working is an experience which is common to most of us.

But a second and perhaps equally important reason is that our society is highly dependent on the effective and efficient performance of our organizations. We are highly interdependent, and the failure of one economic sector, function, or large organization can have serious consequences for the rest of the country. It becomes imperative therefore to have a highly motivated work force.

Besides these practical reasons there are some more scientific reasons that make organizations an excellent milieu for the study of motivation. Even though organizations come with many different sizes, locations, and objectives, there are some common elements as well. First, the organizational participants are bound together by some sort of objective or common goals. Goals and objectives are a major part of organizational life. Second, there is a fairly small but agreed-upon set of rewards (reinforcers) that are used to motivate people. These rewards include monetary incentives (pay, bonuses), developmental incentives (training, promotion), security benefits (retirement pensions, health insurance, tenured jobs), recreational rewards (vacations), and more personal rewards such as recognition, status, increased autonomy, and the chance to participate in decision-making activities. A third element that most organizations have in common is their hierarchical structure. Some people have higher status positions than others. Some people are leaders, some are followers. Finally, most organizations assign people to jobs. They have an agreed-upon task that more or less defines the boundaries of their work-related activities.

All these common elements help us describe the environmental setting (e.g.,

[2]See H. A. Murray. *Explorations in personality*. New York: Oxford, 1938.

the hierarchical structure and the task descriptions), the initial incentives (goals and objectives), as well as the existing reward contingencies (compensation plans, etc.). Thus an analysis of both the needs and the choice of behavior approaches can be easily conducted in the organizational setting.

Early motivation research

The early research in this area focused on what made a worker productive. The emphasis was on performance. One basic distinction which we have already mentioned was between ability and motivation. Good performers seemed to have both the skill and the motivation to do well.

In response to this distinction one set of researchers focused on the assessment of job-related skills and abilities. Tests have been developed to measure these abilities, and they are frequently used in the selection and placement process. However, skill without desire or motivation was useless. Just because employees could do the job did not mean that they would.

So most theorists suggested that ability and motivation combine to produce performance. One common approach was as follows:

Performance = ability × motivation

The suggested relationship is multiplicative, which means that both factors must be present to obtain high performance. When either ability or motivation are low or absent, performance will be low as well. For example, baseball players who hustle but cannot field or hit will not make it very far. Conversely, players who have great skill in the field and at bat will not be successful if they loaf. Both skill and motivation are necessary. Since researchers were beginning to do fairly well

Recognition for excellence or a job well done is a reward frequently used to motivate organizational participants. (*By permission of University of Washington* Daily.)

It's that rabbit's motivation that worries me, not his ability.

Performance equals ability times motivation.

in the description and measurement of ability factors, the emphasis began to shift to the motivational factor.

Theories of motivational arousal

Most motivational theorists can be categorized as working on one of three major problems: individual needs or motives, classification systems of needs and motives, and an analysis of the motivational process. The individual needs and classification systems basically deal with the arousal question, while the process theories are concerned with the behavioral-choice question. Table 7-1 lists these categories and the theories which we will describe.

Table 7-1. Theories of Motivation

Content		Process
Individual Motives	**Need-Classification Systems**	**Behavioral Choice**
1 Competence	1 Hierarchy of needs	1 Expectancy theory
2 Curiosity	2 ERG theory	2 Equity theory
3 Achievement	3 Theory X and theory Y	3 Goal setting
4 Affiliation	4 Dual factor theory	4 Operant conditioning

Individual motives

Competence and curiosity. Some basic motivational characteristics that are related to work behavior are described as competence and curiosity motives. Early animal research seemed to show that animals were active and exploring even in the absence of any noticeable external reward. Research with humans seemed to show the same results. There appeared to be some sort of drive to master the environment for its own sake; being competent was pleasant by itself. The motive could be activated by the presentation of new, challenging situations and tended to dissipate when the task or situation became mastered. The implications for organizational settings are obvious: some degree of variety and challenge should be maintained in order to sustain the motivating force of competence needs.

A related area of research seemed to show that animals and people were curious about their environment. There seemed to be a need for knowledge independent of its usefulness or reward possibilities. Some of our commonsense notions as well as our empirical research substantiates this idea. People engaging in highly repetitive and simple tasks often report being bored and fatigued. They may increase their work breaks or engage in disruptive activities or sabotage— anything to add something new or different.

A number of theoretical explanations suggest that we become used to or adapted to certain levels of stimulation, variety, and challenge. Once this adaptation level is established, small increases from it are perceived as pleasurable, interesting, and exciting. However, large discrepancies in either direction are noxious and likely to produce the opposite reaction. In this case, people are likely to leave their jobs occasionally or perhaps for good. Somehow we must fit the degree of need for variety and challenge with the external characteristics of the task.

The achievement motive. Perhaps the most thoroughly researched individual motive is the achievement motive. David McClelland is most closely connected with this work and has developed a rather comprehensive theory around the need for achievement (nAch). He suggests, first of all, that people differ in their need for achievement and that this need is illustrated in their writing and behavior. His technique for assessing nAch is the Thematic Apperception Test (TAT), which presents the subject with an ambiguous picture and asks for an interpretation of what is happening in the picture. Achievement-related themes are counted, and the subject's score supposedly reflects the individual's desire for high achievement.[3]

The behavioral characteristics of high achievers have also been investigated. First of all, they tend to prefer moderate risks to situations where there is no risk or where the risk is very high. Situations where outcomes are left to chance like slot machines are avoided. A second major characteristic of high achievers is that they like immediate feedback. They like to know how they are doing and will tend to gravitate to jobs where there is frequent assessment on fairly specific performance criteria (e.g., sales or certain management positions). Finally, high

[3]D. C. McClelland. *The achieving society.* Princeton, N.J.: Van Nostrand, 1961.

achievers seem to enjoy doing a task just for the sake of accomplishment. Task completion provides intrinsic rewards, and money is desired only as a measure of excellence, not as a provider of material wealth. Because of this interest in accomplishment, the high achiever is frequently involved with the task and may be seen as *task-oriented*.

An obvious question is, "How does one become a high achiever?" McClelland suggests that child-rearing practices are most important. Children who are fairly independent but have parents who provide clear expectations and feedback (preferably physical rewards such as hugging) develop into high achievers. But McClelland also believes that adults are changeable and can acquire greater nAch. He has developed a comprehensive training program designed to increase achievement motivation and has tested it in numerous settings.

The theory has also been developed on a broader scope than individual behavior. McClelland feels that the productivity of whole cultures and societies can be predicted from the degree to which the population illustrates a need for achievement. He cites historical examples of analyzing the major written works of a culture for nAch. He reports that societies that exhibit high nAch will later experience economic growth and prosperity. Countries low on nAch will face economic decline.

Thus, we have two major propositions: first, the productivity of a firm or country can be tied to the nAch of its members, and, second, people can increase their nAch through training. The empirical support for these hypotheses is fairly convincing. There are research reports that company growth rates of a number of technically based firms were predictable from nAch scores, and the same thing has been found for small firms in India as well. McClelland has also attempted to increase nAch through various training procedures. In a number of cases, those who were trained experienced subsequent entrepreneurial success and were more active in stimulating business growth and in new economic ventures. So nAch can be learned both early and later in life.

Affiliation motive. In contrast to nAch, not much research has been conducted on the motive to affiliate with others. Early research with monkeys suggested that we have some sort of innate need for personal contact. Harlow provided two surrogate mothers one of wire and the other of cloth.[4] Even though half of the monkeys were fed from the wire mother (by means of a bottle inserted in the wire), almost all of the monkeys preferred to cling to the terry-cloth mother. If we believe in physiological drive reduction as the explanation of behavior, then either mother should have been equally attractive. It appears from Harlow's research, however, that monkeys develop attachment to their mother based partly on contact comfort.

Another well-known study which illustrates the affiliation motive was conducted by Schachter.[5] Undergraduate females were subjects in the experiment and were introduced to a rather sinister-looking Dr. Zilstein who stood in front of machines that were littered with wires, knobs, and switches. The women were told that they were going to participate in an experiment on the effects of electric

[4]H. F. Harlow. The nature of love. *American Psychologist,* 1958, **13,** 673–685.

[5]S. Schachter. *The psychology of affiliation.* Stanford, Calif.: Stanford, 1959.

shock and that while the equipment was being set up there would be a short delay. Each subject had the opportunity to wait alone or with another subject (who was a stranger). The results showed overwhelmingly that they preferred someone else's company.

A more refined version of the study gave women the same initial story but then divided the subjects into two groups. One group was given the same choice as above. They could wait alone or with someone else who was a participant in the experiment. The second group was given a choice of being alone or with someone else who was just waiting out in the hall to talk to an adviser. In the latter case, most of the women preferred to be alone. Thus, people may prefer to affiliate with others, but these other people are more desirable when they are similar in some important ways.

The more general implications are interesting. There is some sociological literature about how people tend to congregate together during a crisis. Reports from combat situations indicate that soldiers frequently bunch up during a battle, which may be exactly what the enemy wants. There are also a number of organizational case studies which discuss similar problems. The classic example is the systems expert who rearranges all the desks in the office in such a way that productivity should be greatly increased. However, in the process the systems expert also severely restricts the employees' ability to communicate with one another. And rather than increases, decreases in performance are observed.

To date, however, very little research has been specifically conducted on this motive. McClelland has developed a measure of need for affiliation, but the nAch results are far more substantial. Part of the problem is that affiliation is so complex, and it is hard to separate out the factors. We are not sure if someone seeks out the comfort of another for stimulation, status, love, or just to be with someone else. While affiliation is obviously important, it is hard to isolate.

Other motives. While the motives listed above are the ones most frequently investigated, there are other topics of interest. Some people have argued that there is a basic need for power or security. Recent anthropological literature suggests an innate need for status. Some of these topics will be discussed more fully in other chapters, but right now we will turn to those theorists who have attempted to integrate individual needs into overall classification systems.

Motive classification systems

Maslow's hierarchy of needs. The first major attempt to classify needs relevant to organizational behavior was produced by Abraham Maslow.[6] His formulation suggested that we have a prepotency of needs: some needs were more important than others, and those that were initially most important had to be satisfied before the other needs could serve as motivators. He postulated that there were five need categories, and they are ordered below in terms of their prepotency or importance.

1 *Physiological needs.* Fulfillment of thirst, hunger, and sex drives.

[6]A. H. Maslow. *Motivation and Personality*. New York: Harper, 1954.

2 *Safety needs*. The freedom from fear of external harm, climatic extremes, or criminal activity.

3 *Belonging needs*. The desire for affection and caring relationships: the personal liking and support from others.

4 *Esteem needs*. The respect and positive evaluation of one's peers and associates. Status and recognition are major factors.

5 *Self-actualization*. The opportunity to fulfill one's basic potential—to become more like one's natural self.

There are a number of specific elements of this theory that need elaboration. First, Maslow argues that this category system holds for most normal, healthy people. It is not necessarily applicable to everyone. Second, while the idea of prepotency is important, it is not entirely rigid. More specifically, while Maslow would argue that love needs must be fulfilled before esteem needs begin to operate as motivators, he would probably not argue that the love needs had to be 100 percent fulfilled. The general idea is that the greater the fulfillment of a particular need, the less it serves as a motivator.

A final point is that in our society the physiological and safety needs play a relatively minor role for most people. Only the severely deprived and handicapped are dominated by these lower-order needs. The obvious implication for organization theorists is that higher-order needs should be better motivators than lower-order ones. This fact seems to be supported by surveys which ask employees about what motivates them on the job.

Unfortunately, the empirical research which specifically tests Maslow's theory has shown only limited support for some aspects of his theory.[7] The ordering suggested by Maslow is perhaps more flexible and less specific than he originally suggested. Employees seem to be able to readily distinguish between rather broad categories of higher- and lower-order needs. Managers, for example, seem to prefer self-actualization and esteem motivators to love and safety rewards. But there is very little evidence to support the specific five-category system.

The prepotency idea has also been criticized. It is not clear that fulfillment of one need automatically means that the next-higher-order need is activated as a motivator. It has also not been shown that deficient needs are necessarily important ones. Thus, some of the specific dynamics of the theory are still in question.

But the impact of this approach should not be dismissed. Maslow's hierarchy was the first clear statement that management should recognize the importance of higher-order needs. The emphasis began to shift the attention of organization theorists from the more traditional lower-order motivators (pay, promotion, hours of work) to higher-order motivators (autonomy, responsibility, challenge). This was an important contribution to management thought.

A second implication is that people will be at different levels of the hierarchy at different times. Managers must be aware of individual differences in reward preferences. What will motivate one subordinate will not work with another individual. Different people want different things, and managers must be sensitive to these needs if they want to motivate their subordinates.

[7]M. A. Wahba & L. G. Bridwell. Maslow reconsidered: A review of research on the need hierarchy theory. *Proceedings of the Academy of Management*, 1973, 514–520.

Aldefer's ERG theory. One recent modification of Maslow's ideas has been presented by Aldefer.[8] He postulates that there are three main categories of needs: existence, relatedness, and growth. The parallel with Maslow's theory is shown in Table 7-2. Aldefer's approach, while keeping the basic higher-order and lower-order need distinction, does not include any reference to prepotency of needs or to the idea that deprivation leads to activation. Both higher-order and lower-order needs can serve as motivators. In some cases, once a higher-order need is satisfied, people may be motivated by lower-order needs. Also, all the needs may be active to given degrees at any specific time. A need may never cease to be a motivator, and in fact, Aldefer suggests that growth needs may increase in intensity the more they are satisfied.

While the empirical data seems to fit Aldefer's ideas a little more closely than Maslow's, there has been little research designed to specifically test it. However, the basic higher order and lower order need classification is still apparent, and it is this idea which should be emphasized.

Table 7-2. Maslow and Aldefer Classification Systems

	Lower-Level Needs		Higher-Level Needs		
Maslow	Physiological	Safety	Love	Esteem	Actualization
Aldefer	Existence		Relatedness		Growth

Related approaches. While not specifically designed as need classification approaches, there are two other major motivational theories which fit nicely with the higher- and lower-order-needs idea. An early statement on the topic of management was made by McGregor.[9] His argument is that there seem to be two distinct and different approaches to management and motivation. The first, called theory X, assumes that people are motivated by lower-order needs, while the second, theory Y, advocates the use of higher-order needs. Table 7-3 summarizes some of McGregor's points.

It is easy to see the similarities between Maslow's hierarchy and McGregor's

[8]C. P. Aldefer. *Existence, relatedness and growth: Human needs in organizational settings.* New York: Free Press, 1972.

[9]D. McGregor. The human side of enterprise. New York: McGraw-Hill, 1960.

Table 7-3. McGregor's Approach

	Theory X	Theory Y
Management's role	Organizing, directing. Emphasis on control, coercion, and punishment.	Organizing, directing. Emphasis on growth, autonomy, and reward.
View of human nature	People are lazy, lack ambition, like to be led, and are motivated strictly by personal economic concerns.	People by nature enjoy work, want to do well, and are motivated by self-control and self-development.

analysis. Both researchers place a strong emphasis on the higher-order needs and argue that we have been remiss in our frequent dependence upon theory X or lower-order-need incentives.

The last approach that can be seen partly as a need classification system was developed by Herzberg.[10] The emphasis of this approach was on those rewards in the organization that were related to job satisfaction and job dissatisfaction. Herzberg suggested that organizational rewards could be broken down into two categories, the motivators and the hygienes, which are listed below:

HYGIENES
1 Monetary rewards
2 Competent supervision
3 Policy and administration
4 Working conditions
5 Security

MOTIVATORS
1 Achievement
2 Recognition
3 Responsibility
4 Advancement

Herzberg argued that the hygienes were related to job dissatisfaction, while the motivators were related to satisfaction. More specifically, the theory suggests that having all the hygienes present at an acceptable level would produce a neutral feeling about the job—it was almost as if they were expected. Of course, if hygienes were at an unacceptable level, dissatisfaction would occur. On the other hand, if management really wanted motivated and turned-on employees, they should use the motivators. It was this factor that would produce high job satisfaction. The relationships are shown below.

$$\text{Dissatisfied} \xrightarrow{\text{hygienes}} \text{Neutral} \xrightarrow{\text{motivators}} \text{Satisfied}$$

Since much of the job-satisfaction research defines satisfaction as the extent to which job-related *needs* are fulfilled, the inclusion of Herzberg's model in this section becomes easy to understand. Essentially Herzberg is saying that hygiene rewards or outcomes satisfy what we would call lower-order needs. The motivators, on the other hand, satisfy higher-order needs. It is these latter types of needs which Herzberg argues are frequently unfulfilled in today's organizations.

Because of the rather loose theoretical formulations present in most of the need classification approaches, they have been extremely difficult to test. Most of the empirical-research reviews are critical of the Maslow and Herzberg approaches, while Aldefer and McGregor have been infrequently tested (but frequently cited). Some of these debates revolve around rather minor points and are not really important for our purpose.

What is important is the clear and agreed-upon emphasis on higher-order needs. All these theorists argue that these needs should receive greater attention. Herzberg's work in the area of job enrichment is a good example of an attempt to apply these principles, and we will discuss this topic at a later point in the book. In summary, while the hierarchical concept fell short of some of the original goals of suggesting exactly how one proceeds through life in terms of specific motiva-

[10]F. Herzberg. *Work and the nature of man.* Cleveland, Ohio: World Publishing, 1966.

tions, it did provide a valuable insight into a whole new set of organizational rewards.

Theories of motivated choice

There are a number of theories that suggest why people choose to behave the way they do. In organizations there are some obvious critical choices that are made. Why work hard? Why come to work? Why should one choose to join a particular organization? The four approaches which will be discussed represent the major attempts to explain these choices.

Expectancy theory

> The hope and not the fact of advancement,
> is the spur to industry.
>
> Sir Henry Taylor

One approach to the motivational process suggests simply that people try to maximize their payoffs. More specifically, expectancy theory states that people

I think of myself as an expert in motivation research.
Every morning I try to figure out why I get up and go to work.
People make motivated decisions all the time.

look at their various alternatives (e.g., coming to work versus not coming to work) and choose that alternative which they believe is most likely to lead to those rewards which they want most. If they believe that staying home is likely to lead to more good things than going to work, they are likely to stay home.

There are a number of important elements in this type of analysis. First, it is the anticipation (expectation) of what will occur that influences choice. It is our estimate of the future that is important. A second point is that the theory includes two major factors: the expectation that some outcome will occur and the value (anticipated satisfaction) of that outcome. These two factors are formally called *expectancies* and *valences*.

The earliest statement of this approach was made by Victor Vroom.[11] He presented two models: one to predict certain choices such as what occupation an individual will choose or how much effort the person will exert on the job and the second to predict an employee's attitudes about the job. Figure 7-1 presents an example of the choice model.

The researcher can assess the expectancies and valences shown in the figure. Each expectancy is multiplied by its valence, and these products are summed for a particular behavioral alternative. This process provides a sum of the expectancies times valences for each alternative, ΣEV. This ΣEV roughly represents an "expected value" or an expected return. The theory predicts that the individual will choose the alternative that has the highest payoff or expected return.

In our situation described in Figure 7-1, one individual might value a pay raise and advancement more highly than socializing or reading, *and if* the person thinks that working hard is likely to lead to the attainment of those outcomes, he or she will probably choose to exert a lot of effort on the job. If, on the other hand, socializing and reading are more highly valued than a raise or a promotion and the individual is more likely to attain those outcomes by just getting by, the person will probably choose not to work very hard.

[11]Victor H. Vroom. *Work and motivation.* New York: Wiley, 1964.

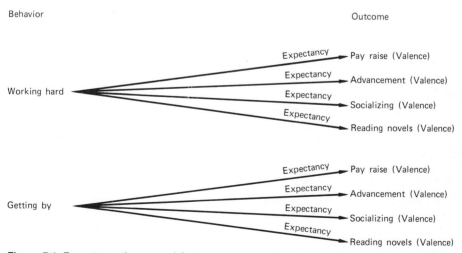

Figure 7-1. Expectancy-theory models

Note that it is a combination of both expectancy and value that determines what one will choose. If some choice leads to something you value highly but is unlikely (a long shot) or something you do not care about but is very likely (a sure thing), you probably will not choose it if it is compared to an alternative that is likely to lead to something you value highly.

This is a fairly simple model and it has been used in a number of research investigations. Reviews of the literature are fairly encouraging.[12] While people obviously do not make these explicit calculations, they do appear to behave as if they were attending to these factors in the manner described. It appears as if expectancy models can do an excellent job of predicting occupational choice and job satisfaction and a moderately good job for predicting job effort. For example, a recent review article on occupational choice reported on sixteen different studies using expectancy or expected-value-like models.[13] Every single study provided strong, significant support for the theory. In some cases the model was able to predict actual job choice with 80 to 90 percent accuracy. This is very impressive.

The implications for management practice are threefold. First, it is the anticipation of reward that is important. People make choices based upon what they think they will get, not what they got in the past. Second, rewards need to be closely and clearly tied to those behaviors that are seen as desirable by the organization. If attendance, punctuality, or working hard are important, then they should be rewarded explicitly, publicly, and frequently. Finally, since different people value different rewards, there should be some attempt at matching organizational outcomes or rewards with the particular desires of the individual employee. These techniques should increase the degree to which employees are described as highly motivated.

Equity theory

Take gifts with a sigh:
most men give to be paid.   John Boyle O'Reilly

There is a large body of literature that suggests a more exchangelike relationship as the underlying dynamic of motivated behavior. Somehow individuals have an internal balance sheet which they use to figure out what to do. The theory predicts that the individual will choose that alternative for which a fair exchange exists. The major components of this exchange theory are somewhat different from expectancy theory. A description of these components and how they combine is presented below:

Reward. Any outcome that contributes to need gratification.

[12]For a review, see T. R. Mitchell. Expectancy models of job satisfaction, occupational preference and effort: A theoretical, methodological and empirical appraisal. *Psychological Bulletin*, 1974, **82**, 1053–1077.

[13]T. R. Mitchell & L. R. Beach. A review of occupational preference and choice research using expectancy theory and decision theory. *Journal of Occupational Psychology*, 1976, **49**, 231–248.

Cost. Activity as part of process required to attain the outcome (e.g., fatigue, anxiety).

Outcome. Refers to rewards minus costs. One has a profit if it is positive and a loss if it is negative.

Comparison level. One compares outcomes across alternatives and chooses the outcome that represents a "fair" exchange.

The idea of rewards and comparison levels is similar to expectancy theory. However, the idea of subjective probability is not included in the exchange analysis, while the idea of cost or input invested is made more explicit than in the expectancy approach.

The interesting application of this theory to the organizational setting is called equity theory.[14] The comparison-level component is in many cases defined as one's coworkers. The idea is that we look at how hard we are working and the payoff we receive and we compare that to other people doing a similar job or to what we got when we worked on similar jobs at some other time. If a state of equity exists—that is, if there is little difference between these comparisons— then the individual is comfortable with the situation and no change is predicted to occur.

However, when inputs are seen as too great in comparison with outcomes and with this internal standard, then a state of *underreward* inequity is experienced. Obviously employees can (1) reduce their inputs, (2) increase their outcomes, or (3) change their internal standard. If outcomes are too great when compared to inputs, a state of *overreward* inequity exists, and people can relieve this tension by (1) increasing their inputs (e.g., working harder), (2) decreasing their outcomes (e.g., accept less pay), or (3) changing their internal standard.

Let us take an example. Suppose you are working on a construction project and you are hauling wood around so that the carpenters can do their job. You have lunch every day with a person who is working on a similar project across the street. This person does the same job you do but makes $3.40 an hour while you only make $3.20. What can you do? Well, you could talk to your foreman about a $0.20 raise (increase your outcome), or you could start taking it easy on the job (decrease your inputs). Or you might stop having lunch with the person and start eating with some of your fellow workers who make the same amount you do (change your comparison standard). The point is that as long as the discrepancy exists and is salient to the employee, the employee will continue to feel that he or she is being treated unfairly.

The empirical research in this area has produced some interesting results under salaried conditions.[15] When people experience underreward, they generally decrease their effort. When they experience overreward (they are getting paid more than others for doing the same job), they increase their effort. On a straight incentive plan (piece rate), the results are somewhat different. People experienc-

[14]J. S. Adams. Inequity in social exchange. In L. Berkowitz (Ed.), *Advances in experimental social psychology*. Vol. 2. New York: Academic, 1965, 267–299.

[15]John P. Campbell, Marvin D. Dunnette, Edward E. Lawler III, & Karl E. Weick. *Managerial behavior, performance, and effectiveness*. New York: McGraw-Hill, 1970, 347.

ing underreward are likely to decrease the *quality* of the output, and if they perceive overreward they attempt to increase the quality. Obviously, to increase or decrease the *quantity* of output under a piece-rate system would simply increase or decrease the inequity. Thus, both changes in quality and quantity of output can be predicted from the equity-theory approach.

Other research-related topics should be mentioned as well. For example, one study found that feelings of inequity were positively related to turnover in a large aerospace firm.[16] Also, a number of studies have shown that underpayment has greater motivating effects than overpayment. People are less likely to change their behavior when they are being overpaid. However, the profit should not be too large or it may lead to hostility on the part of one's peers.

The emphasis, then, is a little different from expectancy theory. Equity theory suggests that people choose a level of effort on the job that they somehow think is fair or equitable. There is not the same emphasis on maximizing rewards as there is for the expectancy theorist. Thus an expectancy model might predict that an individual will choose that work level that brings the highest payoff, while an equity theorist would predict the choice of that level of effort which produced the fairest level of reward.

Two major implications seem important. First, organizations must strive to reward people equitably. When people feel they are not getting a fair shake, they may be dissatisfied, reduce their effort, and/or leave the job. But an equally important implication is that employees see rewards in a relative rather than an absolute fashion. It is not how much one is getting that is important, it is how much one is getting compared to other people who have the same type of job. It is the social or interpersonal comparison that is important, not the absolute amount. An employee may be getting $25,000 a year for driving a delivery truck, but if the person down the street gets $26,000 for the same type work for another company, unhappiness, dissatisfaction, and reduced performance may be the result.

Goal setting

> When a man does not know what harbor
> he is making for, no wind is the right wind.   Seneca

Another major contribution to our understanding of motivation has been made by Edwin Locke.[17] He argues that employees have certain goals they set for themselves and that one can have a strong influence on work behavior by influencing the employees' goals. The following list presents definitions of the major theoretical components of goal-setting theory. Figure 7-2 is a graphic representation of the theory.

[16]C. S. Telly, W. L. French, & W. G. Scott. The relationship of inequity to turnover among hourly workers. *Administrative Science Quarterly*, 1971, **16**, 164–172.

[17]E. A. Locke. Toward a theory of task motivation and incentives. *Organizational Behavior and Human Performance*, 1968, **3**, 157–189.

Figure 7-2. Goal-setting theory

Intentions or conscious goals. The target the individuals report they are shooting for.

Task goals. Some sort of performance standard. The conscious goal and task goal may or may not be the same.

Goal acceptance. The degree to which the task goal becomes the conscious goal or intention.

Goal commitment. The amount of effort expended to achieve the goal.

Incentive. An outcome that has positive or negative properties.

The theoretical generalizations have suggested that hard goals are better than easy ones as long as they are accepted. One would also expect that participation in the goal-setting process would be more effective than assigning goals. Participation should increase commitment and acceptance. It appears as if individual goal setting is more powerful than group goals. It is the impact of the goals on individual intentions that is important. Finally, the more specific and well defined the goal, the greater the impact on motivation. Supposedly, a general goal such as "do your best" is ineffective.

Locke's argument is somewhat different from expectancy and equity notions. While incentives or rewards may affect goal acceptance and commitment, they are not the crucial factor; the goal is. Locke argues that we are constantly engaged in the goal-setting process and that the major antecedent to task-relevant behavior is our intention to reach some goal. Comparisons with others and our expectations of rewards are only important in so far as they affect our goals. It is the goal that causes motivation, not the reward.

A recent review of the empirical studies carried out in organizational settings is fairly supportive of these propositions.[18] Latham and his colleagues have carried out a number of field applications of goal setting with Weyerhaeuser employees. For example, one report shows that a group of pulpwood producers and their logging crews who engaged in a training program on goal setting produced significantly more cords of wood than a control group. Another study found that logging truck drivers increased their productivity 50 percent (resulting in a savings of hundreds of thousands of dollars) when specific hard goals were set and accepted. No financial rewards were specifically contingent on goal attainment, and Locke and Latham both suggest that it was the goal itself that motivated the employees.

Organizations may increase the motivation of their employees through the goal-setting process. Incentives can be tied to goal attainment, and every effort

[18]G. P. Latham & G. A. Yukl. A review of research on the application of goal setting in organizations. *Academy of Management Journal,* 1975, **18,** 824–845.

Logging trucks with drivers who were given specific difficult goals carried significantly more wood than those with drivers without goals. *(By permission of Weyerhaeuser Company.)*

should be made to explicitly define goals, gain commitment to them, and set them at a level which is difficult but reachable. Increased effort and performance should be the result.

Operant conditioning

One of the dominant influences in the field of psychology has been the work of B. F. Skinner on behaviorism.[19] His contribution to our understanding of human behavior is immense. Recently he has applied his ideas to the field of organizational behavior, and his approach is quickly becoming one of the more controversial topics in our field.

The two major components of the theory are the ideas of reinforcement and environmental determinism. To define these concepts we must understand that the two types of behavior attributed to humans are operant and respondent.

[19]B. F. Skinner. *Beyond freedom and dignity.* New York: Knopf, 1971.

Respondents are controlled by instinctual and direct stimulation such as sneezes. *Operants,* on the other hand, are emitted in the absence of any apparent external stimulation and are the major focus of analysis.

Whenever an operant behavior is followed by an environmental event (consequence) that changes the likelihood that the behavior will occur again, that event or consequence is called a *reinforcer.* If the consequence increases the frequency of behavior, it is called a positive reinforcer. If it decreases the frequency of the behavior, it is a negative reinforcer. Skinner's argument is that once we discover what consequences serve as positive or negative reinforcers for a particular behavior (e.g., coming to work), we can manipulate the frequency of the behavior by manipulating the reinforcers.

Notice that there are no references to any internal cognitive processes. Reinforcers do not feel good or bad, they simply change the frequency of the behavior. The true behaviorist believes that operant behavior is caused by environmental events. This philosophy is called *environmental determinism.* It is our past history of reinforcement that causes our current behavior.

Besides these underlying ideas there are some practical principles that have been developed that are relevant for our discussion. One major research emphasis has been to develop schedules of reinforcement which describe the optimal frequency with which rewards should be administered. Rewards could be given every time a certain behavior occurred (continuous rewards) or they could be given on some sort of intermittent or variable schedule.

A study by Latham with tree planters illustrates the technique.[20] The individuals in one group received a $2.00 bonus for each bag of trees planted; in a second group they received a $4.00 bonus for planting a bag of trees and correctly guessing the toss of a coin (called variable-ratio-2 schedule); in a third group they received $8.00 for planting a bag of trees and correctly guessing two coin tosses (a variable-ratio-4 schedule); and a fourth group which continued receiving their regular wage served as a control group. The three experimental groups in the long run will theoretically receive the same amount of money; $2.00 every time or $4.00 half of the time or $8.00 a fourth of the time. The results were interesting. The three experimental groups showed an average increase in productivity of around 14 percent, while there was no change for the control group. From both a cost-benefit analysis and a productivity-increase perspective the continuous schedule did best (a 33 percent increase in productivity and a savings of $4.14 per bag of trees). Reinforcement in this case seemed to be very beneficial.

A review of all the empirical research in this area shows that in some cases variable schedules are better and in some cases continuous schedules work best. Probably the best schedule depends on the type of job, the employees, and the particular behavior in question. However, the results show one more thing: Reinforcement has a powerful effect on behavior. Almost all the studies show that reinforcement procedures, properly administered, can significantly change employees' behavior in the desired direction.

---

[20]G. P. Latham. The effect of various schedules of reinforcement on the productivity of tree planters. Paper presented at the annual meeting of the American Psychological Association, New Orleans, September 1974.

To implement such a system in an ongoing organization requires a number of steps. The behavior to be changed must be clearly measurable, observable, and countable. We must initially have some idea of its frequency (called a base rate). We can then administer various outcomes contingent upon the behavior and observe changes in frequency. Eventually we should be able to determine what works best in terms of the type of reward and the particular type of schedule.

There are a number of similarities between operant and expectancy techniques. Both theories argue that the contingency between the behavior and the reward is important. Both of them include the positive or negative aspects of the reward itself. However, the major contribution of the operant technique is the emphasis on schedules of reinforcement. Knowing when, how frequently, and how much to reward is an important addition to our understanding of organizational behavior.

A number of criticisms have also been leveled at the operant technique. First, many people argue that just because behaviorists only look at the relationship between environmental contingencies and behavior, there is no convincing evidence that these environmental events are necessarily the only cause of that behavior. One's cognitive assessment of the environment—for example, the expectancies of receiving a reward—and evaluation of the reward may also be

Tree planters in Latham's study increased their performance when a reward was directly contingent on the number of trees planted. *(By permission of Weyerhaeuser Company, Tacoma, Wash.)*

the cause. Many cognitive theorists (e.g., those who believe in goal setting) would certainly see reinforcement as a powerful determinant of cognitions and behavior. But they would argue that environmental events are not all that cause behavior. There are also some who fear the application of operant ideas as a technology. They argue that individual consent (e.g., goal acceptance) is an integral part of the motivational process and any attempt to omit it smacks of manipulation and control. To the degree that behaviorism is based on the underlying principle of environmental determinism there may be room for concern. Clearly, under operant techniques there is no reason why personal inputs are necessary. If you can manipulate the contingencies, you can change the behavior. Some people find this an unacceptable alternative, and debates are published and available on the topic.[21]

Summary

We have reviewed much important material in this chapter, and there are some principles which should be emphasized:

1 Performance can be seen as a combination of both ability and motivation. Both aspects are probably necessary for good performance to occur.
2 Motivation is important in terms of two major questions: What gets us started or aroused? What process determines the direction in which we choose to go?
3 Theories of individual needs and classification systems of needs focus on the question of arousal. One major conclusion is that different people want different rewards from their job.
4 The need classification systems brought recognition of the importance of higher-level needs. Most employees today are more concerned with belonging, esteem, and actualizing needs than physiological or safety needs.
5 The process theories of motivation are attempts to explain the choice of behavior. Most of them suggest some sort of underlying rational system that determines what people will do.
6 Both expectancy theory and operant conditioning place their emphasis on contingency relationships. The most important factors for motivation are the direct link between appropriate behavior and rewards and the value of the reward itself. Operant techniques can be used to suggest when, how much, and how frequently rewards should be administered.
7 Equity theory calls our attention to the fairness of the reward system. People are often motivated by a comparison with their coworkers. One must conclude that fair, equitable rewards are a necessity.
8 Finally, goals are an important motivator. Having clear, specific, agreed-upon objectives increases effort on the job.

[21]T. R. Mitchell. Cognitions and Skinner: Some questions about behavioral determinism. Paper presented at the thirty-fourth annual meeting of the Academy of Management, Seattle, Wash., 1974. Also available in *Organization and Administrative Sciences*, Summer 1976, 63–72.

Thus, motivation is an individual process. Different people want different things, and a number of processes are operating at any given time. The more flexible the organization is in terms of reward administration, the more likely individuals are to receive valued rewards as a function of what they do. These reward contingencies should be made explicit and administered with extreme attention to fairness. Finally, through the process of goal setting, it is possible to bring together more easily the joint interests of management and nonmanagement employees. It is hoped that these techniques when properly administered will lead to a more productive and satisfied work force.

Implications for practice

Some of these points have been covered already but they bear repeating. As background we must reemphasize that performance is a *joint* function of ability and motivation. Since the organization can select and change abilities *and* since it can motivate people through the type of organizational environment that it presents, motivation should be seen as a *central concern and responsibility* of management. All too frequently, attempts at increasing motivation are seen as being softheaded or impossible to do ("if they don't have it they just don't have it"). What we are suggesting is that selection procedures, training programs, performance appraisal, and reward systems can have a powerful impact on performance. We will discuss these topics in more detail later in the book.

A second point is that people have different needs and different desires. A reward system that is flexible and provides people with some choice of rewards will probably be more effective than one that is more rigid in nature. Both hierarchical need approaches and expectancy approaches would support such a prediction. People will work harder for something they value.

Another important principle is that contingencies should be made explicit and open. People are more likely to feel they are being equitably treated if they have a good idea of why people receive the rewards or punishments that they do. People may not like it, but at least they will understand it, which is better than what currently happens all too frequently. Again expectancy theory would also make similar predictions. The higher the perceived relationship between a particular behavior (e.g., working hard) and a desired reward (e.g., a promotion), the greater the chance the behavior will be performed. The message is clear: Be explicit and open about what leads to what.

Finally, lay out some targets. People like to have something to shoot for. Any job is routine and boring some of the time. Goals provide incentives. They can give a sense of accomplishment. They can be used as a reliable, agreed-upon system of evaluation. Motivation increases when task goals are present.

Discussion questions

1 What are the two basic psychological questions that motivation theories seek to answer? Why are they important for organizations?
2 Do you think the content theories of people such as Maslow, Herzberg, and Aldefer are

good descriptions of how people behave? How would you use their principles to increase motivation in an organization?

3 Expectancy and operant approaches seem to suggest that people are primarily motivated by personal rewards, while goal-setting and equity approaches suggest that less self-serving concepts such as accomplishment and fairness are the major motivators. How do you feel about this question? Why?

Case: Pushing papers can be fun

A large metropolitan city government was putting on a number of seminars for some of their managers in various departments throughout the city. At one of these sessions the topic to be discussed was motivation—how we can get public servants to be motivated to do a good job. The plight of a police captain became the central focus of the discussion.

"I've got a real problem with my men. They come on the force as young inexperienced rookies and we send them out on the street, either in cars or on a beat. They seem to like the contact they have with the public and the action involved in crime prevention or the apprehension of criminals. They also like helping people out at fires, accidents, or other emergencies.

The problem occurs when they get back to the station. They hate to do the paperwork, and because they dislike it the job is frequently put off or done inadequately. This lack of attention hurts us later on when we get to court. We need clear, factual reports. They must be highly detailed and unambiguous. As soon as part of a report is shown to be inadequate or incorrect, the rest of this report is suspect. Poor reporting probably causes us to lose more cases than any other factor.

I just don't know how to motivate them to do a better job. We're in a budget crunch and I have absolutely no financial rewards at my disposal. In fact, we'll probably have to lay some people off in the near future. It's hard for me to make the job interesting and challenging because it isn't—it's boring, routine paperwork, and there isn't much you can do about it.

Finally, I can't say to them that their promotion will hinge on the excellence of their paperwork. First of all, they know it's not true. If their performance is adequate, most guys are more likely to get promoted just by staying on the force a certain number of years than for some specific outstanding act. Second, they were trained to do the job they do out in the streets, not to fill out forms. All through their career it is the arrests and interventions that get noticed.

Some people have suggested a number of things like using conviction records as a performance criterion. However, we know that's not fair—too many other things are involved. Bad paperwork increases the chance that you lose in court but good paperwork doesn't necessarily mean you'll win. We tried setting up team competitions based upon the excellence of the reports, but the guys caught on to that pretty quickly. No one was getting any other type of reward for winning the competition, and they figured why should they bust a gut when there was no payoff.

I just don't know what to do."

Questions about the case

1 What is the behavior that the captain wants to motivate?

2 Do you think he has tried everything he can do?

3 What would you suggest he do? Think of some specific strategies that might help.

Additional readings

** Campbell, J. P., & Pritchard, R. D. Motivation theory in industrial and organizational psychology. In M. D. Dunnette (Ed.), *Handbook of industrial and organizational psychology*. Chicago: Rand McNally, 1976, 63–130.

** Cofer, C. N., & Appley, M. H. *Motivation: Theory and research*. New York: Wiley, 1964.

* Hackman, J. R., & Porter, L. W. Expectancy theory predictions of work effectiveness. *Organizational Behavior and Human Performance,* 1968, **3,** 417–426.

Jaques, E. *Equitable payment*. New York: Wiley, 1961.

* Latham, G. P., & Kinne, S. B. Improving job performance through training in goal setting. *Journal of Applied Psychology,* 1974, **59,** 187–191.

* Lawler, E. E. *Motivation in work organizations*. Belmont, Calif.: Brooks/Cole, 1973.

* Paul, W. J., Jr., Robertson, K. B., and Herzberg, F. Job enrichment pays off. *Harvard Business Review,* March–April 1969, 61–78.

* Pertrock, F., & Gamboa, V. Expectancy theory and operant conditioning: A conceptual comparison. In W. R. Nord (Ed.), *Concepts and controversy in organizational behavior*. Pacific Palisades, Calif.: Goodyear, 1972, 175–187.

** Pritchard, R. D. Equity theory: A review and critique. *Organizational behavior and human performance,* 1969, **4,** 176–211.

** Skinner, B. F. *Walden II*. New York: Macmillan, 1948.

** Weiner, B. *Theories of motivation: From mechanism to cognition*. Chicago: Markham Press, 1972.

* Wiard, H. Why manage behavior? A case for positive reinforcement. *Human Resource Management,* Summer 1972, 15–20.

*Possible reading for students
**Review of literature or comprehensive source material

THREE
SOCIAL
PROCESSES

Given that we know what people perceive, how they feel about it, and what motivates them, the rest should be easy. Alas, it is not the case. The individual's needs and actions operate in a social setting. They may perceive that working hard will get them more money and money may be a very important reward to them, but it does not necessarily mean they will work hard or perform well. There may be social pressure to keep production down, or the coordinating and communicating aspects of interpersonal interaction may misdirect or spoil their efforts. Social processes can dramatically affect their behavior.

Chapter 8, "Group Dynamics," provides an overview of the group literature. A definition of the small group and how it develops is provided. We discuss, in some detail, how people behave differently in a group setting than they would if they were alone. We present a model of group interaction which suggests that behavior in the group is caused by three major factors: (1) personal characteristics (attitudes, personality, etc.), (2) situational characteristics (space, type of task, group size, etc.), and (3) group structure (the influence or communication patterns that have developed in the group).

Since much of the literature on personal characteristics has been discussed in Part 2, these topics receive little attention here. The major focus is on how the situational and group-structure characteristics affect the group process and eventually affect satisfaction and productivity. The conclusion one is forced to reach is that the behavior of people in groups is very difficult but not impossible to predict.

The topic of Chapter 9 is communication. A model of the communication process is presented which includes the sender, the message, the recipient, and the surrounding situation. Each factor is discussed in terms of how more effective communication—agreement about the meaning of a message—can be attained.

Chapter 10 discusses the social processes that clarify the organizational environment for the individual. Roles are seen as the total set of expectations that others have about how someone in a particular organizational position should behave. These external expectations often dominate what we do—even when they run counter to our own desires.

Norms deal with a slightly different topic. They are defined as expectations about how everyone within a group should behave (as opposed to roles which focus on a specific position). There are norms about how you should dress, where you should eat, whom you should talk to, and so on. There are ways in which groups enforce these norms, and to violate them often causes the individual to experience considerable stress.

Status differences are also discussed in Chapter 10. The existence of status hierarchies clarifies one's position with respect to others. Also, a recognition of who has high or low status gives the individual a good idea of what the group values and scorns.

In short, while Part 2 focused on the individual, Part 3 focuses on the social setting. A knowledge of both is essential to understand people's behavior.

8

Group Dynamics

When many are got together, you can be
guided by him whose counsel is wisest.
If a man is alone he is less full of
resource and his wit is weaker.   Homer

Our everyday experience as well as research findings indicate that people in organizations spend a large percentage of time in interpersonal interaction. Many of these exchanges take place in small groups. The purpose of the following chapter is to describe what goes on in these groups and to suggest some ways that what they do can be done better. More specifically, we will describe (1) how people working in groups behave differently than if they were alone, (2) why people join groups, (3) how groups develop, and (4) the factors that influence the manner in which a group actually carries out its task. The understanding and utilization of this knowledge can help both individuals and organizations to function more effectively.

What is the small group?

Numerous formal definitions of the small group are available in the literature. The common elements of these definitions suggest that the small group is composed of a restricted number of people, usually fewer than ten, who enjoy personal interaction over a fairly long span of time. People in this relationship show a degree of commonality of interest often expressed as a goal upon which there is mutual agreement. To facilitate the actual process of goal accomplishment, a differentiation of role and function usually exists in the small group. Additionally, the group itself has some amount of self-sufficiency to enable it to adapt to changing conditions in its environment.

Let us elaborate briefly on the important aspects of this definition. First, there is some sort of size constraint on the small group. It is more than one but probably less than ten. The reason for this constraint is that the other factors of the definition infrequently occur in larger-sized collections of people. The members of a small group have a common goal or interest. There is something that binds them together. The members often speak of the group as an entity: "We did this" or "We think that." The group usually has some history and meets or works in a specific place; it is an enduring set although individual members may come or go. The people interact with one another frequently and most of the time in face-to-face exchange. There is some recognition of the different roles that people play in the group. One person might be the leader, another the comic, and a third the organizer.

Given this definition, we can describe some collections that do not qualify as a small group. The people riding on a bus, waiting in line for football tickets, or attending a play fail to include some elements of this definition. Either they lack a common goal, they do not interact, they are too numerous, or they show no differentiation of roles. The same would be true for all the employees of General Motors, the students in a large introductory class (but not a small seminar), or people taking a civil service exam.

Types of groups

Within organizations the most important distinction is whether the group is *formal* or *informal*. Formal groups are usually prescribed by the organization. People are assigned positions in these groups such as supervisor or chairperson. They often appear as part of the organizational chart. The most common formal groups are task or command groups and committees. A task group might be a supervisor and his or her subordinates. Examples are a research team, a commando unit, a highway crew, or the sales force for a small company. Committees usually are formed for some specific purpose and usually, but not always, include upper-level employees. As anyone working in an organization knows, there can be committees for just about everything.

Informal groups also exist. You will recall that the Hawthorne studies first pointed out their importance for organizational effectiveness. People join together because of common interests, friendship, or social needs. They may not formally appear anywhere on the organization chart, yet they do exist, The people may eat together, go to and from work together, play cards or golf together, and take their coffee breaks together. They have their unwritten rules and norms about appropriate behavior and responsibilities. They know who belongs and who is an outsider. The effective functioning of both formal and informal groups is important for the organization.

Individuals and groups

An initial area of interest was to point out how people working together in groups behaved differently than when they were alone. At the heart of such inquiry was the desire to know whether groups were *more effective* than individuals. The answer to this question has important policy implications: Should we appoint a committee or leave a task up to an individual? Is an assembly line more effective than a team approach?

The results of this research pointed out a number of ways in which groups *differed* from individuals working by themselves, rather than concluding which process was best. It appeared that the most effective process depended upon a number of situational factors. However, to predict which one would be most effective, one first had to understand how the processes differed.

Social facilitation

The study of social facilitation concerns the effects of the mere presence of others on individual behavior. Early research showed that people's perceptions, judgments, attention, and motivation were changed in a social as opposed to an isolated context. One's motivation appears to be heightened in the group context, and more dominant (well-practiced) behavior tends to appear. We go with what we know. One's attention may be raised, but so may one's tendency for distraction. The appropriateness of the behavior is dependent on both one's past experience and the present situational demands.

The current explanation for these phenomena is that having people around increases one's attention and concern about the evaluation of others. In the group context, our behavior, to some extent, is meant to please others. We are aroused by their presence and it affects what we do. The well-practiced or dominant behavior is used because it is easier and we are less likely to make mistakes or look different or foolish. So being in a group causes arousal, and in some cases this arousal can be helpful.

Weighting

Another area where groups differ from individuals is the weighting given to individual contributors. If five people are working alone on some problem and we aggregate their work, then each person's contribution would be roughly 20 percent. If we observe a group, however, a very different picture emerges.

No matter what size the small group may be (two to ten), the interaction is usually dominated by a small percentage of the group. For example, in groups of four or five, two people usually speak 70 to 80 percent of the time. This results in differential rather than equal contributions being made by group members. Obviously, if the heavy contributors are bright competent members, then effectiveness will be the result. However, talkative people are not always the most effective, and this differential weighting can cause problems in group functioning.

Brainstorming

A somewhat different question is whether a group can generate more and better ideas than can the same number of individuals acting alone. We have already mentioned that not everyone in the group is heard and that certain people often dominate the discussion. Also, there is a tendency for group members to evaluate

suggestions as they appear, and this process may inhibit a free flow of suggestions. Groups may settle for a solution too early in the life of the problem-solving
process. It was Osborn who first suggested some techniques for facilitating the
generation of ideas in a group, and he called this process *brainstorming*.[1] The
general procedure for a brainstorming group is to consider some problem, such
as a brand name for a new product, under the following conditions: (1) ideas are
generated without reference to quality, (2) evaluation of ideas takes place only
after all the ideas have been produced, and (3) people are encouraged to
elaborate on the ideas of others. Under these conditions, it was hoped that more
new and creative ideas could be elicited. Not only would the group have access
to all the individual ideas that might be thought of alone, but they would also
have ideas that were triggered off by other group members, ideas that an
individual might not have thought of alone.

Research on this issue at first seemed supportive. Initial studies found that a
greater number of ideas were produced by groups working under brainstorming
instructions than individuals under nonbrainstorming instructions. Studies in
which both groups and individuals working alone received brainstorming instructions found little difference between the two conditions. Apparently it was the
fact that the early studies provided brainstorming instructions to the group but
not to the individuals working alone which caused the initial findings. When one
adds the fact that more work hours are spent in the group context to generate the
same number of ideas as people working alone, it appears as if brainstorming is
not necessarily a good method for increasing group effectiveness.

Risky shift

One facet of choice behavior that is affected by the group setting is the individual's propensity for taking risks. A large volume of research has resulted in a *risky
shift* hypothesis which suggests that an individual, confronted with a specific
problem, will make a more risky decision after participating in a group discussion
than he or she will make alone. Somehow being in a group makes the individual
take greater chances or incur greater risks than when a decision is made in private
and alone.

There are a number of competing explanations for this phenomenon. Some
researchers believe that since the weighting process is different, more confident
people will dominate the group and be willing to take risks. Others believe that
there is a cultural norm supporting risk taking which people feel obliged to support
in front of others. Finally, some authors suggest that more relevant and risky
arguments are brought out by the group process. While there is still disagreement
about why this riskiness occurs, there is little disagreement about the fact that it
does occur. This increased risk taking could have a significant impact on organizational decision making.

[1]A. F. Osborn, *Applied imagination: Principles and procedures of creative thinking.* New York:
Scribner, 1941.

Groupness

One final characteristic of people working in a group is that they develop a sense of unity or cohesion—they see the group as an existing entity and they identify themselves with this collective. No such identification exists for individuals working alone.

This "we-ness" or "groupness" can serve important political as well as social functions. If a group is formed of people from different departments or subgroups, communication and political representation functions may be served. More specifically, the group setting can provide a situation where people from different organizational units exchange information. Also, the fact that they have representation serves a political purpose in that people are more supportive and accepting of decisions in which they have a part. A much more thorough discussion of the effects of participation and the use of group decision making will appear later in the book.

In summary, groups are distinctly different from individuals working alone. People are aroused in groups, they contribute different things to the final product, and they seem to be more willing to take risks. Groups also provide a forum for an exchange of information across organizational units and can serve a variety of political purposes as well. One must conclude that we cannot just generalize our research on what makes individuals effective to the group setting. In order to understand group effectiveness we must study the group composition, structure, and process.

People working in groups behave differently than they do when they are alone. (*By permission of University of Washington* Daily.)

An overview of group variables

A frame of reference for the study of the small group is presented in Figure 8-1. The variables presented in the diagram do not represent all the possible dimensions that are operating in small groups. The figure merely lists most of the major variables which have been studied extensively by social scientists. There is one aspect of this diagram on which we should elaborate. It presents rather dramatically the complexity of the situation. For many years social scientists have been studying the relationships between two or perhaps three variables. For example, an industrial psychologist might examine the correlation between the leader's intelligence and group performance. Given that there are so many factors influencing performance, it is not surprising that the results generated have produced few consistently high relationships.

A research example

We recently completed some research which highlights this complexity rather well.[2] We were interested in whether the following three variables had a positive effect on an individual's job performance:

1 Does having a specific and fairly difficult goal result in higher performance than a goal of "do your best"?
2 If people believe their performance will be evaluated and compared with others, do they work harder than if they believe their performance cannot be traced to them personally?
3 Will individuals work harder if they have a coworker who clearly likes the task and works hard than if they have a coworker who is neutral or negative about the task?

[2]S. E. White, T. R. Mitchell, & C. H. Bell. Goal setting, evaluation apprehension, and social cues as predictors of job performance and job satisfaction. *Journal of Applied Psychology*, **62**, 1977.

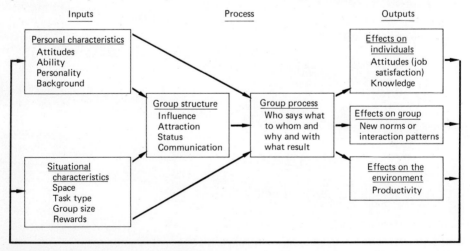

Figure 8-1. Overview of group variables.

These three hypotheses were based on research from the motivation area (e.g., goal setting), from the social-facilitation research (e.g., evaluation apprehension), and from the group-dynamics literature (e.g., social influence).

We hired people to work on a part-time clerical task, and we set up the different work conditions described above. The task involved the correct coding of some computer cards, and we were able to keep exact records of how many cards were correctly coded by each employee. Everyone worked under an hourly pay structure, so there were no differences due to the money received.

Our results showed that all three hypotheses were supported. People with specific goals produced more than those without specific goals; people who were to be evaluated produced more than those who believed they were not to be evaluated; and people with a coworker giving off positive social cues produced more than those working with a coworker giving off negative cues. Taken alone, any one of the variables (goals, evaluation, or social cues) only accounted for a small amount of the variation in performance (e.g., 3 to 4 percent), but taken together the three variables accounted for almost 20 percent of the variation in performance. Also, the evaluation-apprehension variable was about twice as important as the goal-setting or social-cues variables.

This research study supports two points we are trying to make about the whole area of group dynamics and performance. First, the area is complex—performance is caused by many different variables. Second, we must begin to analyze these factors together and in combination so we can tell which factors are more or less important.

A systems view

A second characteristic of Figure 8-1 is that it may be viewed as an input-process-output system. There are people working together who have abilities, traits, attitudes, and other individual characteristics. These people are interrelated in various ways according to the structure of the group and the situational constraints. These three sets of variables (personal, group, and situational characteristics) might be viewed as inputs. The group process covers who says what to whom and deals mainly with the actual behavior that occurs in the group. The final three sets of dimensions cover the major outputs or consequences of the group's behavior: changes in the group (group development), changes in the environment or task (task performance), and changes in the people (effects on group members). These outputs in turn become inputs.

The purpose of this chapter is to review the empirical findings that relate input characteristics to group process or output. We will not attempt to cover all the possible relationships that could be generated from the figure. Certain findings are presented elsewhere in the book (for example, the relationships between job attitudes and performance) and others have been infrequently examined. The results reported represent what we consider to be the most important and most reliable findings generated to date on small-group dynamics. Before we begin the survey of results, however, we wish to briefly describe how groups form and develop.

Group formation

Why do people join groups? What makes groups attractive? There are many reasons people join groups, some of which we have already described (e.g., task assignment, friendship, etc.). A summary of the research in the area would include the following reasons.

First, people join groups because of the need to affiliate with others. Just being with other people can fulfill a desire for social interaction. Second, groups can provide a source of information about oneself and about the outside world. Other people can serve as a source of comparison. Also the experience of others is different from your own, so new information is available. Third, groups serve as a source of rewards. Being on the job, on the bowling team, a member of a special task force, or a member of a committee can bring rewards of friendship, recognition, status, and financial benefit. Fourth, being in a group may allow the individual to accomplish some goals it would be difficult to accomplish alone. It is hard to play bridge by yourself or run a business without any employees. It is often necessary for people to join together and jointly contribute their resources in order to accomplish their goals. One should recognize that this final reason is similar to the general reason that organizations form in the first place—a point discussed in Chapter 2.

Group development

Most of the research and interest in group processes has focused on what happens after the group is an ongoing entity. This approach makes sense because obviously the early development stage of most groups is short in duration compared to the overall group existence. However, some researchers have investigated the preliminary phases of group development and have uncovered some consistencies about this process.

The initial development phases of any group consist mainly of individuals finding out and clarifying their place in the group. This place or position may vary on a number of dimensions—all of which need to be sorted out. People soon find out who are the high-status or powerful members of the group. They learn who demands deference and who must defer to them. They quickly learn who they like. These personal-attraction bonds will greatly influence later group interaction. The communication patterns also get clarified. To some extent, this may get determined by situational variables such as the group size or the physical location of group members. Attraction and status differences will also affect who talks to whom.

In other words, the early life of a group is characterized by a great flux. However, after a while things begin to settle down. People begin to know where they fit and what is expected. Later interactions will be more stable and predictable.

This development stage, therefore, can be of great importance to later group performance for two major reasons. First, it establishes the pattern of interaction for subsequent group meetings. As we shall see, the communication, attraction, and status structures of a group greatly influence the group process and the problem-solving abilities. Second, this early development process makes later meetings easier in some sense. Little time will be wasted on the developmental phases later on. Occasional reaffirmations of one's position will occur, but in general the group will be able to devote most of its resources to the task at hand. This is especially true if the development process has gone well—people are relatively satisfied with their positions and responsibilities in the group.

Once the development stage is over and a stable group exists, we can ask somewhat different questions. We can look at how different types of group structures (e.g., communication or influence patterns) and settings (e.g., group sizes) that have become established result in different types of interaction processes and eventually result in different outputs. The next few sections cover these topics.

Group inputs: Personal characteristics

Based upon our Figure 8-1, we will discuss the major inputs to group process and output. These inputs include the characteristics of individual members, the existing situational or environmental characteristics, and the structure of the group.

Most of the literature on personal characteristics we have already discussed. The chapter on personality pointed out that most personality measures are relatively poor predictors of overall performance across time and settings. The same is true for attitudes. However, when specific attitudes or traits are used in combination with situational variables, somewhat better predictions result. A review of the specific relationships can be found in Chapters 5 and 6.

Perhaps the only other personal characteristics that should be mentioned are interest and ability measures. The empirical results on job performance show that specific-ability indexes are the best predictor, followed by vocational-interest inventories, with personality measures holding up the rear. What this suggests is that the more specific we can be about what actual behaviors (observable and measurable abilities) are needed for specific jobs, the better our prediction will be. A later section of the book discusses how this can be done.

Group inputs: Situational variables

Some of the characteristics that affect the group's behavior and output can be fairly well controlled by the organization. That is, there are certain given conditions under which the group works. For example, the type of task, the size of the group, and the conditions of reward are all part of the "work environment." As shown in Figure 8-1, these variables may be related to both the group structure and to the group process and output measures.

Territorial variables

One of the most interesting areas of relatively recent research has been on the topic of the relationship among individuals and their environment in terms of territoriality and physical space. Think of the classes where there are no assigned seats but where you usually sit in the same place every day. How would you feel if you came in and someone was in the seat you typically occupy? You would probably resent the intrusion and you might even ask the person to move from "your" seat. Also recall the different seating arrangements in classrooms. In some cases, you may sit in a horseshoe-type arrangement which allows you to see the professor and your classmates. In other situations there are rows of seats and the professor stands up in front. This latter arrangement only allows you to see the professor. It is a much more impersonal setting. As we shall see, these factors can have a significant effect on the group interaction.

Territoriality. It is a common observation that individuals and groups often come to feel that they own or have rights to certain objects or space. These objects may be chairs, desks, offices, buildings, or neighborhoods. This feeling is distinguished from ownership in that the people involved have no legal right to these objects or territory. The territory is simply used or occupied by them and they act as if they own it.

This orientation can affect group functioning. If for some reason, people are not allowed to maintain their territorial integrity, conflict often occurs. If a group member takes your favorite seat or makes it clear that he or she covets your office, bad feelings will be the result. There is often resentment of an "intruder" or "newcomer" who comes into the office. Other similar areas where territoriality occurs would include clubhouses, bars, park benches, and so forth. The important point is that people resent the intrusion and will frequently act in such a way to regain their territory.

Personal space. Personal space differs from territoriality in that it refers to our bodies. We carry our personal space around with us—it is that area around the individual which is felt to be private—a space that others should not enter. It does not have as firm physical referents as territoriality. The boundaries of our personal space may vary according to the situation.

People resent intrusion into their personal space. Negative feelings are the result, and people will seek to reestablish the distance at which they feel comfortable. If this alternative is not available, conflict and poor interpersonal relationships often occur.

The interesting point is that there seem to be appropriate and inappropriate distances for interpersonal interactions. Close friends stand nearer than acquaintances or strangers. People of similar ages or status interact more closely with one another than with people who are older or of higher status. In summary, people establish a comfortable distance for each interpersonal exchange. When this distance is violated, discomfort and anxiety are often produced.

Spatial arrangements. The effect of these feelings of territoriality and personal space is that the spatial arrangements for any group interaction can influence the quality of that interaction. Where we sit, who we sit next to, the closeness of the seats, and their orientation all affect the group process.

Look at the different arrangements diagrammed in Figure 8-2. People who want to cooperate tend to prefer a side-by-side arrangement, and people who are

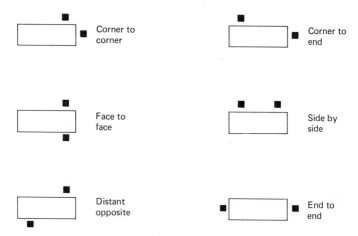

Figure 8-2. Possible seating arrangements around a rectangular table.

working fairly independently prefer a distant opposite or end-to-end arrangement. Competing people prefer a face-to-face or corner-to-corner arrangement. Empirical research tends to show that arrangements which either place a physical object like a desk or table between individuals or where individuals are physically far apart result in less interaction and more formal interaction and are characterized by less friendly exchanges. A relevant example for students was recently published.[3] The study found that faculty members who had placed their desk between them and a visiting student were older, were of higher status (academic rank), and were rated as more formal (less positively overall) than teachers who utilized a less formal interaction arrangement.

The results suggest strongly that the quantity, quality, and pattern of interpersonal interactions can be manipulated simply by controlling the environment in which the exchange takes place. The manager who wishes to maintain distance and reassert his or her status can use props and seating arrangements to do so. If a more informal exchange is desired, he can move around to the other side of the desk or perhaps sit corner to corner. A leader's position in the group can be accentuated or played down according to where the person sits at the table. Also, people who sit at the head of a table are more likely to emerge as a leader of a group that starts without one. All these findings suggest that the group interaction can be influenced by changing the physical arrangements which dictate the amount of space and orientation among the group participants.

The task

A review of the literature in the small-group area reveals an uneven distribution of scientific effort in several substantive and methodological areas. One area which has received insufficient attention is the area of the group task. What generally happens is that more often than not, a researcher, interested in testing certain choice predictions from a pet theory, designs a neat study and devises a

---

[3]R. L. Zweigenhaft. Personal space in the faculty office: Desk placement and the student-faculty interaction. *Journal of Applied Psychology,* 1976, **61,** 529–532.

clever task or finds groups that are working on such a task, which is uniquely suited for the particular subject population, variables, and conditions under investigation. Furthermore, not only do different investigators use different tasks, but the same investigator quite often will use different tasks for different studies in the same research program.

Two major problems occur because of this lack of comparability. First, to the degree that the type of task influences group interaction and output, the use of noncomparable tasks will result in systematic variation across studies. For example, it has been found that more interaction resulted from discussion of human-relations problems than mathematical problems. Generalizability of results is therefore limited.

The second problem is that different success criteria are used as assessments of group performance. Typical performance measures are correctness of the solution, how much time it took, quantity, creativity, etc. These are not all the same thing, and to the degree that they differ it is again difficult to generalize. The overall problem, then, is that small-group researchers have often used tasks to study groups, but not groups to study tasks.

The major thrust of research trying to solve these problems has concentrated on the development of a description of the components of different tasks. A number of important distinctions seem to come out of these descriptions. First, it is important to know how much interaction is required among group members. How much communication is needed? Second, are the task activities themselves interdependent? Does one individual need the work of another group member before proceeding? Third, does the task have just one way to be done as opposed to numerous solutions? And a fourth, but similar distinction, has to do with the degree to which the task is highly structured and laid out as opposed to unclear and ambiguous.

What we tend to find is that the task serves as a "moderator" for our research findings. For example, certain types of leadership styles will be effective on one task, but not on another. We will discuss later a number of studies which suggest that a directive leadership style is more effective with an unstructured task and a more interpersonal style is most appropriate when the task is structured. Likewise, we find that strong group pressure inhibits generation of alternative ways for accomplishing a task which is unstructured and thus results in poor performance. On the other hand, conformity can be helpful where there is only one way to do the task and it is well laid out for the group what path they should follow.

What this means is that our understanding of the task and its effects on group interaction has led to more sophisticated approaches to predicting group performance. As we have mentioned throughout the text, the type of leadership, group process, or reward system that is most effective partly depends upon the type of problem (task) on which people are working.

Group size

Managers are often faced with the job of setting up a group to carry out some function. Some decision about the size of the group must be made. Numerous researchers have studied the impact of group size on group interaction, satisfaction, and productivity.

Size and interaction. Perhaps the most well-known research on small-group interaction processes has been done by Bales. His interaction process analysis is one of the best-known and most-reliable observation systems that have been developed. Observations are made about who says what to whom, and each act is placed in one of twelve categories (e.g., gives information or shows tension). One study investigated the interaction of groups ranging in size from two to seven.[4] The experiment was carried out in a laboratory with subjects working on a human-relations case problem.

The findings reported by Bales and replicated by others seem to indicate that very small groups show more tension, agreement, and asking for opinion, whereas larger groups show more tension release and giving of suggestions and information. The authors argue that in very small groups it is more important that everyone get along well together and people have more time to develop their ideas and arguments. In larger groups one can be more direct because of the greater number of people and also because any given individual's talking time is reduced.

It is also reported that groups with an even number of members behave differently from groups with an odd number of members. The even-numbered groups have a greater difficulty in obtaining a majority, and therefore there is more tension and less antagonism or disagreement.

Size and satisfaction. A study by Slater replicated the above findings and extended the research to cover the area of member satisfaction.[5] Subjects were placed in groups of sizes two to seven and worked on a human-relations case. Their interaction was recorded, and afterward the participants filled out a questionnaire which included questions about the subjects' feelings toward the size of the group and the reasons for these feelings.

Besides replicating Bales' results, Slater also found interesting relationships between group size and satisfaction. For this type of task it appeared that participants were most satisfied when working in a group of size five. This result is probably task-specific and one should be careful in the generalizations of the findings. The reasons that subjects gave for choosing size five do seem to be more general. Slater reports that smaller groups were tense and nondirect and larger groups failed to provide enough time for everyone. He summarizes the results by implying that small groups provide physical freedom with psychological restrictions, while large groups are physically restricting but psychologically less tense.

Size and productivity. The relationship between group size and output seems to depend mostly upon the type of task upon which people are working. Let us take

---

[4]R. F. Bales & E. F. Borgatta. Size of group as a factor in the interaction profile. In A. P. Hare, E. F. Borgatta, and R. F. Bales (Eds.), *Small groups.* New York: Knopf, 1956.

[5]Slater, P. E. Contrasting correlates of group size. *Sociometry,* 1958, **21,** 129–139.

some examples. Think of a task where each new member adds a new independent amount of productivity (certain piece-rate jobs might fit here). If we add more people, we will add more productivity. We may suffer some lowering of motivation and coordination, but still, adding new people should help. On the other hand, there are tasks where everyone works together and pools their resources. With each new person the added increment of new skills or knowledge decreases. After a while increases in size will fail to add much to the group except coordination and motivation problems. Large groups will perform less well than small groups. The relationship between group size and productivity will therefore depend on the type of task that needs to be done.

Research in organizational settings on group size has typically investigated groups ranging from size four or five and up. Since very small units (two or three members) are typically not part of the analyses, we would expect a negative relationship between size and satisfaction: the smaller the group, the greater the satisfaction. Since most organizations have people working on many different types of tasks, we would expect the relationship between group size and productivity to average around zero (some positive and some negative). The research data supports these hypotheses. Group size is in fact negatively related to indexes of job attitudes such as absenteeism, turnover, and grievances. Large groups are less satisfied. However, no consistent relationship between group size and productivity is apparent. These empirical findings in organizations seem to support the small-group data and lend strength to our overall conclusions about the effects of group size.

Reward structure

The purpose of this section is not to discuss the relationship between amounts of reward and satisfaction or productivity (see Chapters 5 and 6) but rather to look at the way in which the rewards are distributed. In some organizations one's reward is tied explicitly to the output (piece-rate systems, for example), while in others salaries or bonuses may be partially tied to group efforts (athletic teams). Still other organizations establish systems where a fixed amount of money must be divided up among employees so that what one person stands to gain another may lose (academic salaries and raises are often from a "fixed pot"). These different reward structures have frequently been classified along a cooperation-competition dimension, and it is this literature with which we will now deal.

The best summary to date on the literature covering this area was presented by Miller and Hamblin.[6] These authors reviewed twenty-four studies that compared cooperative with competitive groups and found that fourteen of the research projects supported the contention that competitive groups were more productive while ten projects found the reverse—hardly conclusive support for either hypothesis.

In rethinking the concepts of cooperation and competition, these authors

[6]L. Miller & R. Hamblin. Interdependence, differential rewarding and productivity. *American Sociological Review*, 1963, **28**, 768–778.

suggested that these two concepts were not pure types anchoring down the opposite ends of a single dimension. They pointed out that these concepts could be most usefully broken down on two dimensions rather than one, and the dimensions they suggested were (1) interdependence and (2) differential reward. By interdependence they meant the degree to which the group members need each other to complete the task. By differential reward they meant the degree to which individual effort received compensation. A high differential reward situation would be one where, for instance, the most efficient member received twice as much as the least efficient member from a somewhat fixed amount of resources. A low differential reward situation would be one where everyone in the group received the same compensation. Dividing these variables into highs and lows, one can produce the accompanying two-by-two table with four possible situations (see Table 8-1). Miller and Hamblin believed that productivity would be lower in situations 1 and 4 than in 2 and 3. In situation 1 people are highly dependent upon each other, and yet, to the extent that one person does well, another group member stands to lose. In situation 4, group members do not need each other to complete the job, yet everyone receives the same compensation. In both cases, there appears to be a mismatch between how success is achieved and how the rewards are distributed. Situations 2 and 3, on the other hand, show a consistent relationship between effort and reward. In situation 2, where everyone is highly interdependent, rewards are distributed equally. In situation 3, where people work independently, rewards are given based upon one's individual contribution.

Table 8-1. An Analysis of Cooperation and Competition in Terms of Differential Reward and Interdependence

Differential Reward	Interdependence	
	High	Low
High	1	3
Low	2	4

This theoretical conceptualization was tested by Miller and Hamblin and was generally supported. Also, in a reanalysis of the twenty-four studies on the topic, they found the results of twenty-three of them could be predicted from their formulation. Recent research has generally supported and broadened this conceptualization.

The implications of these findings are important. Organizations should be careful to match their reward structure with the degree of interdependence inherent in the task. To introduce what is traditionally called a competitive system (high-differential reward) when employees are dependent upon each other may very well decrease performance instead of increasing it. To make sure that everyone gets the same compensation on a task where employees work and contribute independently may hinder effectiveness. These variables are also important for determining certain structural characterisitcs of the group which we will discuss next.

Group inputs: Group structure

After the development stage, certain patterns or structures exist within the group. These patterns may reflect who talks to whom (communication), who likes whom (attraction), or who influences whom (power, conformity). There are also some clear expectations about appropriate behavior (norms) which develop to regulate and guide our behavior. All these factors have an impact on the group process and output. Because of their significance and importance, communication and norms, status, and roles are discussed separately in Chapters 9 and 10. We will cover the effects of social influence and interpersonal attraction below.

Social influence and conformity

One way in which a group is able to regulate the behavior of its members is through the process of social influence. This process is concerned with the ways in which the situation, and especially the group norms or expectations, control how one behaves. Conformity is seen as "giving in to the group"; most social scientists define conformity as a situation where individuals do something they would not have done ordinarily except for the group pressure.

We discuss it as a structural variable because, as mentioned earlier, the developmental stage of a group results in a situation where people know the influence pattern within the group. That is, people know who has the formal power and how much pressure the group can bring to bear on a dissident member. This existing pattern or structure of influence relationships can have an impact on how one behaves in the group setting.

Before we turn to the research data on this topic we should mention a couple of points. First, conformity has a negative connotation for most people. People who are conformists are somehow seen as slaves or individuals who cannot think for themselves. Heinous crimes such as the massacre at My Lai during the Vietnam war and the extermination of Jews during World War II are blamed on conformity—people bowing to the pressures of their group. The same is true for many of the defendants in the Watergate trials. Over and over again there was the theme that "I knew it was wrong but I went along with the group."

We should point out that conformity can have positive effects as well. It can bind a group together, increase solidarity, and present a united front. It can increase a person's commitment to a behavior if it brings that person's attitudes into line with their actions (remember cognitive-dissonance theory). It is also true that people who do not conform are frequently labeled as deviates or nonconformists. That is, in some people's eyes it is bad to conform and bad not to conform. What we would like to point out is that conformity is not good *or* bad, in and of itself. What is good or bad is whether the behavior required is viewed as good or bad by the society. Conformity can both increase and decrease the effectiveness of group performance.

Perhaps the most well-known empirical research in this area was first conducted by Solomon Asch.[7] In a series of classical experiments, Asch demonstrated the profound effect group pressure has on individual judgment. Asch

[7] S. E. Asch. Studies of independence and conformity: A minority of one against a unanimous majority. *Psychological Monographs*, 1955, **20** (Whole No. 416).

Photo by Menken/Seltzer

Your girlfriends can get you pregnant faster than your husband.

Sometimes it looks like there's a conspiracy to get you to have children.

You're married and it's great being alone with your husband, discovering each other and feeling free to do whatever you want.

But already your girlfriends are telling you how wonderful children are and how selfish it is to wait and anything else they can think of to make you feel guilty.

Actually the girls are only part of it.

Let us not forget the future grand-parents, bless their impatient hearts.

There's an awful lot of pressure on you. It becomes hard to resist.

But if you want to, you have to know the facts of birth planning. (Lots of people who think they know, don't. Research statistics show that more than half the pregnancies each year are accidental.)

As for the pressure from relatives and friends, just remember that if you're going to have a baby it should be because you really want one.

Not because you were talked into it.

Planned Parenthood
Children by choice. Not chance.

For further information, write Planned Parenthood, Box 431, Radio City Station, New York, N.Y. 10019.

Planned Parenthood is a national, non-profit organization dedicated to providing information and effective means of family planning to all who want and need it. advertising contributed for the public good

POPULATION CAMPAIGN
NEWSPAPER AD MAT NO. PC-101-72——600 LINES (4 columns x 150 lines)

Social influence can have a major impact on our behavior. *(By permission of Planned Parenthood.)*

rigged an experimental situation in which each member of a group except one was preinstructed to state wrong judgments when asked to match the length of a given line with one of three unequal lines (see Figure 8-3). In a substantial number of cases, the uninstructed (naïve) subject who perceived the correct relationship between the lines denied the evidence of his other senses when subjected to group pressure. One-third of the time the naïve subject went along with the group. The independent subjects did not know they were being plotted against. Furthermore, each was so placed in the group as to be the last to state his or her judgment. The research using this setting has been extensive and is included in the following discussion.

The major causes of social influence can be broken down into four categories: task demands, group characteristics, individual characteristics, and combina-

Conformity often produces similarities in looks, dress, and behavior. (*By permission of University of Washington* Daily.)

tions of these three. We will review these causes and then briefly discuss the results or outcomes that occur in groups with high or low amounts of influence.

Task demands. The first variable of interest is the degree of ambiguity of the answer and whether there is an answer at all. In situations which are ambiguous and for which there is no answer, there appears to be more conformity than where either of these two conditions do not hold. That is, there is less conformity when the situation is not ambiguous and has no answer (opinions about politics, for example) or where it is not ambiguous and there is an answer (Asch's study). The more that people are unsure about handling the task correctly, the more they will use the information given to them by others.

A second dimension of task demands has to do with the conditions under which one must respond to pressures or influences. It has been found, for example, that the earlier in time one commits oneself to an issue the more

Figure 8-3. Stimulus objects used in Asch experiment. Confederates are instructed in advance to make the false statement that line C was closest in length to line X.

difficult it is to change later. Coupled with this is the idea of public commitment. Individuals who declare their position on an issue publicly are more likely to conform to group pressure than those who can make a private declaration.

The reward structure of the task has also been studied. In conditions where the group is interdependent (they need to work together to accomplish the task), there seems to be greater conformity. It appears that if we feel that both ourselves and others stand to suffer as a consequence of our behavior, we will deviate less from what the group thinks is the correct thing to do than if only we would suffer.

Characteristics of the group. One result found in studies by both Asch and others indicated that the unanimity of group pressure was strongly related to how frequently an individual conformed to the group. More specifically, individuals tend to conform less to the group consensus when this consensus is not held by all the members. All it takes is one other person to disagree with the group and conformity drops significantly.

The number of people in the group also affects conformity. Asch presented results showing that the effects of unanimous pressure on conformity changes very little after the group reaches four or five members. In the experimental setting described earlier where the naïve subject responds after hearing the responses of a number of confederates, Asch found that the amount of conformity ceases to increase by utilizing more than four confederates. Apparently, additional members do not add additional pressure.

Finally, some studies have indicated that the closeness of supervision affects the conformity. In situations where the group can use surveillance (close to the idea of public commitment) to check the responses of the pressured individual, there is more conformity than when the individual is left alone.

It is probably important to point out that the investigations cited here deal with behavioral conformity, not necessarily attitude change. There is a difference between *compliance* and *private acceptance*. In both cases the individual conforms, but in the former case only the public behavior is changed, not the underlying resentment or opposition to the act. In the case of private acceptance the individual comes to believe that what he or she did was in fact the correct course of action. Both the behavior and the attitudes are modified. Most groups would probably prefer acceptance but may settle for compliance.

Personality characteristics. The research on the kinds of people who are likely to conform is limited. One well-known study by Crutchfield correlated a variety of personality test scores with the amount of conformity displayed in an Asch-type experimental setting.[8] Negative correlations between intelligence, tolerance, and ego-strength scores and conformity were reported. Brighter, more tolerant people with a strong self-concept or ego tend to conform less than those who are low on these dimensions. Also reported was a positive relationship between a measure of authoritarianism, or rigidity, and conformity. However, no consistent relationships between conformity and a set of other personal and physical characteristics were found.

---

[8]R. S. Crutchfield. Conformity and character. *American Psychologist*, 1955, **10**, 191–198.

Combinations of the task, the group, and the people. There appears to be ample evidence that people who work together and like each other have greater influence over each other than when this attraction is absent. Cohesive groups have both more communication and more influence with group members than groups that are low in cohesiveness.

Also, the degree to which one can deviate from group norms appears to be tied to his or her past record of performance and conformity. One study provides evidence that shows that individuals who have displayed competence in the past and have conformed to group norms can deviate from these norms in order to initiate change or move the group in a new direction.[9] It is argued that the competent, conforming individual builds up "idiosyncrasy credits" with his or her fellow group members. They come to trust that person's judgments and believe that he or she has the group's interests at heart. When this situation is reached, the individual may initiate change without great fear of rejection or refusal.

In summary, there appear to be a number of strategies available to the organization that would facilitate conformity. They may choose certain types of people, encourage discussions of important issues, initiate reward systems that demand interdependence, keep a close watch on what is done, and so forth. Whether the outcomes are beneficial or not depends upon the organization's goals.

Conformity outcomes. Very little research has studied the differences in performance or satisfaction as a function of the degree of conformity present in the group. Some inferences, however, do seem to be justified. To start with, the relationship between conformity and effectiveness should be moderated by the task and the motivational inclinations of the employees. For tasks where diversity of opinion is needed, a group with everyone conforming to one opinion would probably have a detrimental effect on performance. Also, the employees may not be motivated to use their influence to further productivity. There are, in fact, cases where group pressure has been used to hinder effectiveness. The binging of rate-busters by group members (rate-busters were hit on the arm) in the Hawthorne studies is a good example.

Lastly, it would appear that an individual's satisfaction or morale vis-à-vis the group's ability to pressure one to conform would depend on the similarity of the opinions of the individual and the group. For those who concur with the group this pressure might increase morale. For those who disagree it should be a very unpleasant situation in which to work.

Interpersonal attraction

Birds of a feather flock together.   Aristotle

The second structural characteristic of groups is the pattern and the amounts of attraction that exist among group participants. We will proceed with the same

[9]E. P. Hollander. Competence and conformity in the acceptance of influence. *Journal of Abnormal and Social Psychology*, 1960, **61**, 365–369.

format by describing the variables that lead to attraction and then turn to the relationship between attraction, group process, and various organizational outcomes.

Antecedents of attraction. Once again, the trilogy of the task, group, and individual is an excellent frame of reference for studying the variables that contribute to interpersonal attraction. The one aspect of the task which has been frequently studied is the physical closeness of the participants. Investigations in numerous organizational settings have shown that the closer people are, the more likely it is that they will become friends. People who live or work next to one another are likely to communicate with each other and are more likely to form friendships than they are with people who are more remote. Also, it is usually true that people who are physically close to us in an organizational setting will continue in the future to be close to us. Therefore, both the frequency of interaction and the expectation of future interaction increases the likelihood that we will come to like those who are near by.

A second finding related to the task is that groups that have a successful history with a task seem to like each other more than if they have been unsuccessful. In attempts to discover the causal nature of this relationship it appears that success does cause attraction (we will discuss the reverse relationship later). When success is manipulated in experimental settings, the groups with high success have greater liking for their fellow members than do the members of unsuccessful groups.

Some characteristics of the group also lead to member attraction. As we would expect when groups have a common goal, there is higher attraction than when the group members have different goals. The common goal provides a common bond around which friendships can develop. Similar findings are available for groups that engage in participative decision making. Being able to influence the decision process of the group seems to increase attraction to the group.

The greatest contributions to interpersonal attraction, however, appear to come from the personal characteristics of the participants. In our elaboration of

We'll never make it Betsy; you're a Capricorn and I'm an Aries.

People who are similar tend to be attracted to one another.

attitude theories one of the ideas that frequently reappeared was that people like people who like the same things they do; that is, people are attracted to those who are similar to them. Empirical results supporting this contention have been summarized elsewhere, but in general it appears that similarities in race, background, education, attitudes, and values all lead to attraction. Other studies have seemed to show that people who are similar in personality characteristics *before* they meet have a better probability of becoming good friends than those who have different personalities. The "opposites-attract" theory has minimal empirical support.

To summarize, people seem to like other people because they have common goals, because the other person can be rewarding in a variety of ways, or because they are similar on a number of important dimensions. This increased attraction will in turn influence the group process and output.

Consequences of attraction. Two of the most important results of high levels of interpersonal attraction are communication and influence. People who like one another tend to talk to one another. This exchange also tends to be more free and unrestrained than for people who are neutral or hostile toward one another. So both the quantity and quality of the interaction is increased by attraction.

The social-influence process also operates more smoothly when people like one another. In general, the greater the attraction the greater the influence. Only in those cases where the individual feels that it is very important to maintain freedom over the required behavior does the expected compliance not occur.

The effects of attraction on two important group outputs—job satisfaction and group performance—should also be discussed. The results for job satisfaction are fairly clear: increased attraction leads to increased satisfaction. This makes sense. Remember that most definitions of satisfaction include a component that refers to one's relationships with coworkers. If the other factors are held constant, greater attraction to group members will result in greater job satisfaction.

However, the major output of interest—performance—has not been positively related to the level of attraction. In some cases it was helpful; in others this was not the case. A brief summary of what has been covered so far should explain why this has occurred. Given that group members are highly attracted to one another, it follows that they will have influence over one another, that they probably think and believe similar things, and that they will frequently communicate these feelings. All these tendencies should lead to greater productivity only when the employees are motivated to work hard. When this motivation is lacking, these characteristics should lead to the lowest level of output. One classic experimental study tested these assumptions.[10] Groups of three were set up to perform an assembly-line type of task, and the attraction and motivation of the participants was manipulated. Half the groups were told that they were similar and would like one another, while half were told the opposite (this has been shown to be a fairly good way to manipulate attraction). During the task the

[10]S. Schachter, N. Ellertson, D. McBride, & P. Gregory. An experimental study of cohesiveness and productivity. *Human Relations*, 1951, **4**, 229–238.

participants were allowed to communicate with one another by notes. These messages were controlled by the experimenter, and half the subjects received notes urging them to work hard (high motivation) and half received messages suggesting that they slow down or "take it easy." These manipulations produced four types of groups which are shown in Table 8-2. Groups that had high attraction and high motivation (cell 1) had the highest productivity, whereas groups that had high attraction with low motivation had the lowest productivity (cell 3). These results support the idea that attraction can increase or decrease output depending upon employee motivation.

Table 8-2. The Relationship between Interpersonal Attraction and Group Productivity

	Motivation	
Attraction	**High**	**Low**
High	1	3
Low	2	4

Productivity: 1 > 2, 4 > 3

Groupthink. We have suggested various ways in which both interpersonal influence and attraction can be increased. An organization can put people together who are similar, provide a common goal and reward, place them in an isolated setting, reward them for group success, and so on. These factors should produce a tightly knit, highly cohesive group. Is this good? Do we want groups like this? At first blush we might respond positively.

Irving Janis has written a highly provocative book about just such groups.[11] He analyzes the foreign-policy decisions made by the Kennedy and Johnson administrations and comes to the conclusion that these groups were similar to what were described above: highly cohesive, close-knit groups. He labels their decision-making process as groupthink and characterizes it in the following manner.

First, there was an illusion of invulnerability. The group members felt they were invincible. For example, Robert Kennedy on the eve of the Bay of Pigs fiasco (an attempt to invade Cuba in April of 1961 which resulted in total disaster) reported that he felt that with such talent, "bold new ideas," and "common sense and hard work" they would overcome whatever challenged them. John Dean, in discussing his role in the Watergate cover-up, mentioned that Nixon's personal staff (also characterized by groupthink) felt that "nothing can go wrong in this institution while we're here." Second, there was a general tendency to moralize, to see the United States as the leader of the free world and to portray the opposition as evil, weak, and stupid. Our continuing commitment to the war in Vietnam again and again represented this type of atmosphere. A third characteristic was the feeling of unanimity. The reports from inside the Executive Committee were that everyone was unanimously in support of the President's

[11]I. L. Janis. *Victims of groupthink: A psychological study of foreign policy decisions and fiascos.* Boston: Houghton Mifflin, 1972.

decisions. It was only later that doubts were expressed. For example, both Arthur Schlesinger and Theodore Sorenson reported that they had doubts about the decisions being made and the policies being developed with regard to Southeast Asia during the Kennedy years. Each felt, however, that everyone else was in agreement and that he was the only one with divergent views. Rather than appear "soft" or "compromising" they kept their feelings to themselves. Both men regretted their hesitancy later.

A fourth and crucial factor was the pressure toward conformity. When discussions were held on a topic, President Kennedy would occasionally call in an "expert" and have him respond to the critical questions which might appear. Instead of actively inquiring about the extent of dissent or seeking divergent views, Kennedy would simply let the expert silence the critic. Also, in many cases informal pressure was placed on members of the President's staff or cabinet officers. Schlesinger reports, for example, that Robert Kennedy took him aside and mentioned that while he could see there might be some problems with the President's decision on some topic, the President needed unanimous support on the issues. There was an appeal for group solidarity.

Finally, because of the similarity of attitudes of the group members, their liking for one another, and the pressure for conformity, outside criticism or relevant arguments were often dismissed prematurely. It is reported that there was a lot of evidence available that suggested that the Bay of Pigs invasion would fail.

And now, Russell, I understand you wish to present some silly minority opinion as to how this case should be judged.

The pressure from our peers to conform can be very intense.

However, due to the factors mentioned above, this evidence was never given proper consideration.

In summary, the decision-making process of the group was severely hindered in effectiveness by the cohesiveness and conformity structure of the group. They closed themselves off from others. They rejected both internal and external dissent. They failed to recognize valuable criticism when it appeared. They overlooked important details. They felt they could do no wrong.

Obviously, this can be an ineffective and sometimes dangerous state for a group to be in. This is especially true when it is vitally important that different viewpoints be expressed and multiple alternatives considered. Janis mentions a number of factors that may decrease groupthink. He suggests that a leader should try to stay neutral and should encourage criticism and new ideas. Small subgroups or outside consultants may come up with a different viewpoint. People sympathetic to an alternative view should be encouraged to present their views.

As we have said before, whether cohesiveness and influence help or hinder group effectiveness depends upon a number of factors relating to the problem at hand. What is important to recognize is that the typical view that cohesiveness is good and conformity bad is just not true. Both processes can play important positive *and* negative roles in the effectiveness of the organization.

Overall perspective

The purpose of this chapter, as stated earlier, was to acquaint the reader with the research conducted in the area of group dynamics. A systems framework was used, and a review of the various inputs and their effects on organizational behavior and outputs was presented. By now, the complexity of the area is surely appreciated. There are numerous dimensions of the people, their jobs, and the structure of their groups which are related to how they behave toward one another, how much they like one another, and how much they produce.

In a recent review of this area Hackman and Morris suggest a number of ways that organizations can change or modify these inputs in order to improve performance and effectiveness.[12] Their argument is as follows. In order for a group to be effective, three things are necessary: (1) hard work or effort, (2) the proper abilities or skills, and (3) the appropriate task strategy or group process.

The organization can influence the motivation or effort of the employee through its reward system by the proper administration of appropriate rewards. It can also influence the group norms with regard to motivation. Hackman and Morris state that "whether a group develops a norm of high or low effort depends substantially on the quality of the experiences members have as they work on the task—that these experiences in turn are largely determined by the task itself." In general, people will be more motivated on jobs which have some variety, closure, importance, feedback, and a chance for individual input.

The major ways to increase the abilities and talents of individual group

---

[12]J. R. Hackman & C. G. Morris. Group tasks, group interaction process, and group performance effectiveness. In L. Berkowitz (Ed.), *Advances in experimental social psychology*. Vol. 7. New York: Academic, 1975.

members is through the proper use of selection and training processes. But the group can also influence this use of talent by making sure that the correct distribution of talent to tasks takes place. A well-known example of such a process occurred when Babe Ruth was switched from a pitcher to an outfielder. Even though his talents as a pitcher were great (he was a twenty-game winner), his ability with a bat was needed every day.

Finally, groups can learn about task strategies and task redesign. As Hackman and Morris point out, there are ways both to study what your group is actually doing and to change it. A group can often choose the way it wishes to perform its task. They can increase or decrease representation; they can work more or less independently; they can increase or decrease checking or summary points; they can reduce evaluative comments or change existing norms. The important point is that groups should become aware of the facts that (1) they have an existing strategy of problem solving which can be described, (2) there are different strategies available besides the one they are using, and (3) they can usually change their strategy if they want to. It is hoped that an increased understanding of these group processes will lead to a better match among group members, the group interaction process, and the task at hand.

Summary

The major points from the chapter that should be emphasized are listed below:

1 The small group consists of a few people (two to ten) who interact over a fairly long period of time. They have common goals and a division of roles and responsibilities.
2 The group interaction and outputs are different from what is produced by individuals working alone. Group members are aroused by the presence of others, they may make more risky decisions, they contribute unequally to the final product, and they engage in communication and political functions.
3 An overall systems analysis of groups shows that there are some inputs in the form of personal characteristics, situational characteristics, and group structure. These inputs affect the group interaction process and the group outputs in the form of job satisfaction and productivity.
4 People join groups for a variety of reasons: as a way to fulfill affiliative needs, as a source of information, as a source of rewards, and as a means for accomplishing a goal.
5 Groups go through a distinct development phase. This stage clarifies the friendship, influence, and communication patterns that later determine the group process and output.
6 Situational characteristics play an important role in structuring group interaction and performance. The physical spacing and placement of chairs and desks, the type of task, the size of the group, and the reward system all affect process and output.
7 The interpersonal influence and attraction structure that develops is also important. Similar, interdependent, successful group members with com-

mon goals tend to have high levels of attraction and influence. Whether these processes increase or decrease group effectiveness depends on the demands of the task.

8 In general, an effective group must have (1) hard working members, (2) the proper assignment of people to tasks, and (3) a group process that is appropriate for the people involved and the job to be done. All these factors can be measured and changed.

Implications for practice

Some of the major implications of this chapter are simply informational issues. Many people in organizations believe that groups can do a better job than people working alone. For example, the brainstorming idea is still very popular in many quarters. The research simply does not support this contention. Groups may be riskier than individuals, they may take a longer time to solve a problem, and they may be less effective. On the other hand, communication and political goals can be better served through group interaction. What is important to recognize is that groups work *differently* than people alone. To maximize their effectiveness demands a complex match of people, the situation, and the job to be done. This is not an impossible match and many of the following chapters will explicitly point out these contingencies.

A second important implication comes from our discussion of input-process-output relationships. One of the striking conclusions than can be drawn is that organizations can have a significant impact on how a group carries out its task. The physical environment (tables, chairs, etc.) can be manipulated as can the size of the group or the way in which rewards are distributed. These variables can increase or decrease the formality, cooperativeness, and freedom of information exchange that results. The organization can also construct a group with similar or dissimilar people, with independent or interdependent activities, with public or private recognition or evaluation; with structured or unstructured regulations; and so on. These variables would increase or decrease the amount of influence or attraction among group members. Thus, to a much greater extent than typically is recognized, the organization can construct and change the ways in which a group will go about doing its job.

A third point which needs elaboration is the fact that highly cohesive groups, where everyone likes one another and is committed to the group goal and where high levels of attraction and influence exist, are not necessarily a good thing. Some of the propositions generated from the human-relations approach and its current proponents have been oversimplified. Many managers may believe that having highly cohesive groups will be the answer to increased performance and productivity: if everyone likes one another and communicates openly and is committed to the goal, then we are bound to be effective. Well, it just is not necessarily so. Who gets into the group, the match between their skills and the task, and the problem-solving process are equally important factors in group performance.

In summary, groups in organizations provide both positive and negative outcomes. They may be inefficient information generators, and various elements of individual initiative or responsibility may suffer. On the other hand, they are often part of the "participation" process, and because of our technologies people frequently must interact in groups in order to successfully understand and deal with broad problems. The question is not groups versus no groups, but rather a set of questions related to when groups are most effective and how they can be more effective. The implication is that social scientists must begin to handle this complex situation with more complex theories. Studies should be conducted to examine the relative contribution of these variables to outputs. New computer facilities and statistical techniques that can handle highly complex information should facilitate the development of this type of research.

A related implication is that organizations must first decide upon their goals before introducing various programs or selection procedures designed to increase effectiveness. Attraction and influence can be legitimate goals but they should not be equated with productivity. Competition may hurt you rather than help you. Selecting an exceptionally bright manager (differing from subordinates) may do the same. In sum, there are no simple formulas for assuring high morale and productivity.

Discussion questions

1 What are the differences in an individual's behavior when working as a member of a group and when working alone? When does it seem particularly useful to form groups?
2 Discuss the various territorial variables that seem to affect group process. How could you manipulate these variables to increase or decrease intimacy?
3 What makes a group highly cohesive with high levels of influence? When is this type of group desirable and undesirable?

Case: The holdout

Kelly was angry with himself as he slipped into the car next to his wife. "Well, the trial's over and so is my jury duty obligation," he told her. "I'm glad that it's finished, but it sure didn't turn out the way I thought it should."

"I heard on the radio that you brought out a verdict of guilty," commented Marcia. "I'm sort of surprised. I didn't think he was guilty."

"I didn't either. That's what makes me so mad. We sat up there for three days discussing all the details—on and on. It started out with me and a guy named Roberts being for acquittal and the other ten people thought the guy was guilty. I guess they had some good points, but somehow it all didn't fit together."

"Did they ever find any of the stolen stuff—the jewelry or the stamps?"

"No, they never did. I don't think he had the stuff. I think the poor slob got framed. I know that a couple of witnesses said it was him, but I just don't believe it. His alibi was pretty good and they never did find the stolen property. I think he was just plain unlucky."

"What did you tell the rest of the jury?"

"Just that. I told them that I thought he was just at the wrong place at the wrong time.

Just because a guy looks like someone else isn't enough evidence to put him in jail. But I couldn't convince anyone. They were all out for blood."

"How did they convince you to go along with them?"

"Well on the first day we mostly went over the facts in the case—what we knew and what we didn't know. We clarified things and tried to get all the details straight. It was the second day when things got tough. The foreman, a woman named Phillips, really thought she knew it all. She put a lot of pressure on Roberts first. Everyone started to ask him why he felt the way he did, and every time he would mention anything, three or four people would chime in with their reasons that he was wrong. Finally he gave in and said he thought they were probably right.

"Then everybody got all over me and gave me the treatment. But nothing they said changed my mind. I didn't think there was sufficient evidence to send the guy to jail and I told them so. Well, they talked to me all day and nothing happened.

"Today they used a somewhat different strategy than yesterday. They went back over the facts, talked to one another, and sort of left me out. Then finally this Phillips woman turned to me and says, 'Well, what are you going to do, Mr. Kelly? The rest of us think the man is guilty. We've spent three days in here trying to decide. All of that will be wasted if we leave here without agreement. Besides that, the judge told me if we didn't agree he'd send us back here for three more days. Its eleven to one for a guilty verdict. Is there not a reasonable doubt in your mind about this man's innocence?'

"Well, I gave in. I couldn't see spending three more days at it, and I figured the guy might be guilty. So, I said, 'Okay, let's take in a verdict and go home.'"

Questions about the case

1 What were the factors that made Kelly change his mind? Why was he angry with himself?
2 What were the factors that made Roberts change his mind?
3 Do you think Kelly would have maintained his position if Roberts had not switched? Why?
4 Try to describe the group process and pressures that went on in this group.

Additional readings

Bouchard, T. J., & Hare, M. Size, performance and potential in brainstorming groups. *Journal of Applied Psychology*, 1970, **54**, 51–55.

Brehm, J. W., & Mann, M. Effect of importance of freedom and attraction to group members on influence produced by group pressure. *Journal of Personality and Social Psychology*, 1975, **31**, 816–824.

* Cecil, E. A., Cummings, L. L., & Chertkoff, J. M. Group composition and choice shift: Implications for administration. *Academy of Management Journal*, 1973, **16**, 412–422.

** Cottrell, N. B. Social facilitation. In C. G. McClintock (Ed.), *Experimental social psychology*. New York: Holt, 1972.

* Cummings, L. L., Huber, G. P., & Arendt, E. Effects of size and spatial arrangements on group decision making. *Academy of Management Journal*, 1974, **17**, 460–475.

** Kogan, N., & Wallach, M. A. *Risk taking: A study in cognition and personality*. New York: Holt, 1964.

** Lott, A. J., & Lott, B. E. Group cohesiveness as interpersonal attraction: A review of relationships with antecedent and consequent variables. *Psychological Bulletin*, 1965, **14**, 259–309.

* Manners, G. E. Another look at group size, group problem solving, and member consensus. *Academy of Management Journal*, 1975, **18**, 715–724.

Okun, M. A., & DiVesta, F. J. Cooperation and competition in coacting groups. *Journal of Personality and Social Psychology*, 1975, **31**, 615–620.

** Porter, L. W., & Lawler, E. E., III. Properties of organization structure in relation to job attitudes and job behavior. *Psychological Bulletin*, 1965, **64**, 23–51.

Seta, J. J., Paulus, P. B., & Schkade, J. T. Effects of group size and proximity under cooperative and competitive conditions. *Journal of Personality and Social Psychology*, 1976, **34**, 47–53.

** Shaw, M. E. *Group dynamics*. New York: McGraw-Hill, 1976.

** Sommer, R. *Personal space: The behavioral basis of design*. Englewood Cliffs, N.J.: Prentice-Hall, 1969.

Steiner, I., & Rajaratnam, N. A model for the comparison of individual and group performance scores. *Behavioral Science*, 1961, **6**, 142–148.

* Stores, A. W. Conformity behavior of managers and their wives. *Academy of Management Journal*, 1973, **16**, 433–441.

Weinstein, A. G., & Holzbach, R. L., Jr. Impact of individual differences, reward distribution and task structure on productivity in a simulated work environment. *Journal of Applied Psychology*, 1973, **58**, 296–301.

*Possible reading for students

**Review of the literature or comprehensive source material

9

Communication

It takes two to speak truth—
one to speak and another to hear.   Henry David Thoreau

If we could enter an organization as an unobtrusive observer, what would we see? There would be people sitting at desks, standing at machines, taking breaks, talking on the phone, dictating letters, reading reports, and so on. A large percentage of the activity would concern the transmission of information between people. This process is defined as interpersonal communication. It includes face-to-face discussions, memos, telephone calls, reports, letters, and any other form by which information is passed along or exchanged.

This process is the heart of effective organization. Estimates of the amount of time devoted to communication in organizations range from 50 to 90%. Most organizational participants are engaged in the communication process most of the time. We are constantly involved in the absorption, evaluation, and distribution of information.

Obviously, the organization wants to have "effective communication." It is a term frequently cited as the cause of major triumphs. Ineffective communication, on the other hand, is often used as the explanation for failure. For example, Ray Scott, the Coach of the Year in the National Basketball Association in 1974, was fired in 1976. The reason given to the media by management was "a breakdown in communications." Also, in recent years analyses of governmental events has blamed faulty communication for (1) much of the Watergate affair, (2) the escalation of the Vietnam war, (3) the Bay of Pigs fiasco, (4) the intervention of the Chinese into the Korean conflict, and (5) the "surprise" attack at Pearl Harbor. In many cases the information that would have led to accurate assessment of these events was available. However, it was either evaluated incorrectly or not brought to the attention of the right people.

So, communication involves more than just having the right information: the information must be believed, weighted correctly, reach the right decision makers, and result in the appropriate action. It is a highly complex process. We will spend the rest of this chapter examining this complexity and the research on how communication can be done effectively.

A communication model

Interpersonal communication involves an individual or a group attempting to transmit information to another individual or group. Effective communication implies that the message has similar meaning to both the sender and receiver. Figure 9-1 presents a diagram which represents the complexity of this process.

Our initial concern will be the *motivation* to communicate in the first place. Personality traits, current needs, and perceptual cues all contribute to this motivation. Our gregariousness, our need for information, or our perception of uncertainty may prompt us to seek or transmit information. It is also important to analyze *what is being sent*. Verbal communication is more than just words: it is the tone of voice, the emphasis on various phrases, the smile or gesture that accompanies these words. For written communication there is the type of letterhead, the form of the message, the formality implied. Thus, the actual message sent encompasses a number of verbal and nonverbal cues.

The next issue which we will discuss is the *mode or medium* of the message. Is it written or verbal? Why choose one or the other? Is one more effective than the other? We will briefly describe some research on this topic. The *flow of the message* is also of importance. Is it a one-way or two-way message? Is feedback involved? Another aspect of the flow is whether the message is being sent up, down, or laterally in the organization. The same words said to one's boss or one's subordinate (e.g., I think you made a mistake on this last report) may be said in very different ways and for different reasons, and have a very different meaning. We will discuss these differences in some detail.

The final stage of the communication process involves the *reception of the message and its decoding*. Here we are concerned with the meaning ascribed to the message by its recipient. There are many reasons why this meaning may be very different from the one intended. The message may be distorted, the recipi-

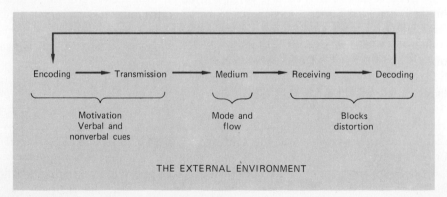

Figure 9-1. The communication process.

ent may be hassled by other things, the message itself may get changed through the transmission process. Each of these problems will be discussed.

Surrounding the whole interaction is an ongoing organizational environment. A dyadic interaction infrequently occurs in isolation. There are other people involved, and numerous researchers have attempted to describe these complex interaction networks. As we shall see, where one resides in these networks is important for the effectiveness of the communication process.

Motivation to communicate

People communicate with others for a large number of reasons. Sometimes we want to reduce ambiguities or justify our opinions. In other cases we are seeking information that supports our position. And sometimes we communicate just because we think it's about time we said or did something. There have been research studies on all these motives, and we will try to summarize the findings below.

Reducing uncertainty. We are frequently faced with situations that we do not understand. Something happens and we want more information. For example, within 90 minutes after the first news release about the death of President Kennedy, over 95% of a random sample of people in a large city in the United States knew of the event. The phone lines were clogged; the television and newspaper coverage was extensive. People wanted to know more information: what happened, how did it happen, when and where did it happen?

This type of thing occurs in organizational settings as well. We go away for 2 days from the university and when we return we discover that the course schedule for the coming term has been changed. Or a business client calls us up and unexpectedly cancels the order for some product. A patient arrives at a hospital with an unusual set of symptoms. When we are faced with unusual and unexpected events, we frequently seek out additional information. This information, in turn, serves to reduce our anxiety and uncertainty about the situation at hand.

The more important, uncertain, and unexpected the event is, the more we tend to communicate with others. Some theories have suggested that in general the underlying mechanism is the conflict or anxiety which is produced by the uncertainty, importance, or novelty of the event. For example, a number of research studies show that the more conflicting items of information we have, the more we seek additional information. So, one obvious motivating mechanism for communication is the need for more information to help us accurately assess what is happening around us.

Problem solving. A second and somewhat related topic is problem solving and decision making. An event may occur with which we are familiar and which we are expecting, yet it requires communication. The President knows, for example, that every year some sort of budget needs to be prepared and submitted to Congress. He requests initial estimates of expenditure from the various governmental departments and agencies; this information is evaluated and discussed, and finally some sort of budget is prepared. Most of this communication activity is prompted by the desire to solve this particular problem.

Much of the decision-making literature emphasizes a similar type of process. Some sort of problem occurs and the manager has to make a decision to remedy the problem. The resolution of the problem typically involves at least two major stages that require communication. First, there is the information-search stage where large amounts of data are accumulated which help to define the problem and the possible alternative solutions. A manager may ask his or her subordinates to generate a list of options or to report back on some historical events that led up to the current situation.

The second stage involves the evaluation of alternatives and frequently entails gathering information about the likely consequences of particular alternatives. Once information is accumulated about what is likely to happen as a result of the different options, one can make a more rational choice in that the choice should reflect what the decision maker believes will result in the best solution. Thus, much of the communication in organizations is prompted by a desire to gather information to solve particular problems.

Belief confirmation. There are a number of situations where we are (1) publicly or privately committed to a position or belief and (2) we are not very sure we are right. In this case we often communicate with others in an attempt to obtain support for our position. We like how a particular subordinate has been performing and we think he or she should be promoted. But before we make a formal recommendation, we say to some of our collegues, "Johnson's been doing pretty well, don't you think?" We're not really looking for new information and we are usually not looking for conflicting information. The motivation is for consensus and some justification of our action.

It is interesting to note the interaction of committees with regard to this issue. Numerous research studies show that the people holding the majority opinion in a group frequently communicate with the minority in an attempt to gain consensus. The majority are confident of their position and they want the support of others. After a while, however, if support fails to materialize, the majority members may start to communicate among themselves, as will the minority members. It is at this point that effective communication often breaks down.

Control of the situation. In many cases we communicate simply because it is expected of us because of our position or because we want to influence what is going on. We are not seeking more information or attempting to reduce our internal uncertainty. Rather, we wish to contribute to and have a part in the ongoing activity.

How many times have you been in a group and found yourself talking not because you wanted information but simply because you figured you better get your two cents in. It is somehow expected that everyone contribute in a group discussion. Also, if you hold a certain organizational position which has typically dealt with or influenced some particular organizational action, you are likely to want to influence the outcome of the decision process.

So many times we communicate with others because we desire to influence them or control the situation. Clearly, the degree to which it is "expected" that we will have some control effects our frequency of communication. For example, studies of the interaction of juries has shown that high-status people (e.g., executives and professionals) talk twice as much as people with lower status (e.g., laborers). Through this process of influencing others we receive feelings of importance, power, and effectiveness—a feeling that we can deal with and control our interpersonal environment.

Feedback. Finally, much of our communication is simply prompted by a need to respond to someone else's communication. When we are asked a question or information is sought by others which we have or are expected to have, we usually reply. Most communication situations are two-way interactions, and this fact is represented by the feedback loop in Figure 9-1. While the four topics discussed above describe the major motivations to initiate communication, much of what is described as communication is actually a response to someone else's communication.

Verbal and nonverbal cues

There's a language in her eye, her cheek, her lip,
Nay her foot speaks.
Her Wanton spirits look out
At every joint and motive of her body.   William Shakespeare

After one has decided to communicate, some sort of verbal or written message is actually sent. This message is usually composed of words. But far more information is conveyed than just the textbook definitions of the words. For example, the particular choice of words and the way in which they are put together is an important source of information. We may know, for example, that our boss only uses certain terms when he really wanted something done yesterday. Thus, the phrase "I really need this as soon as possible" may really mean "I should have had this last week and you better get it to me pronto or there will be trouble."

A number of vocal cues are also important. The speed, accent, loudness, and number of errors or breaks in the message provide us with information. People who are anxious tend to speak quickly and make a number of errors, while a more dominant, confident person will speak more slowly and loudly. Some researchers had people listen to messages on tape which had the exact same words but were read in different ways (they varied on dimensions such as breathiness, flatness, or loudness). The ratings of the communicator and the communications varied widely as a function of the qualities of delivery.[1]

Recently, a whole area of research interest has evolved around the study of nonverbal communications. The thrust of the research is to determine what information is sent by the communicator that is independent and different from the verbal information. Three main categories are usually discussed: physical

[1]D. W. Addington. The relationship of selected vocal characteristics to personality perception. *Speech Monographs,* 1965, **35,** 492–503.

cues, symbolic cues, and signs. The physical cues are all those characteristics of the individual's physical presentation (e.g., movements, facial expressions, etc.) which might convey information. The symbolic cues are things such as a St. Christopher medallion or a Key Club pin. These types of symbols tell the recipient something about the communicator that may strongly influence the interpretation of the message. There are also some signs which communicate messages, such as blowing the horn in your car. However, the physical cues have been most frequently studied, and we will elaborate on them below.

Physical nonverbal communication serves at least three main functions. First, there are a variety of physical cues that help to structure the exchange between people—that is, they tell the recipient some additional information about some specific attitudes of the communicator. If people wish to convey a superior attitude, they may stand very erect, unsmiling, and stare directly at the recipient. Second, many nonverbal cues are good indications of the communicator's emotional state. Anger, anxiety, fear, despair, or joy are readily interpreted from facial expressions, movements, and tone of voice. Finally, nonverbal information is also part of what is called self-presentation. Sex, age, dress, grooming, and the general style of interaction all present a picture to the recipient. These cues can have a major impact on how a particular message is interpreted.

While numerous researchers have been investigating these issues, one group that is readily identified with this area is Michael Argyle and his colleagues. In a number of articles, he has reviewed what has been found, and the list below summarizes these findings.[2]

A REVIEW OF FACTORS THAT PROVIDE NONVERBAL INFORMATION
1 Static features
   a Distance. The distance one stands from another frequently conveys nonverbal messages. In some cultures it is a sign of attraction, while in others it may reflect status or the intensity of the exchange.
   b Orientation. People may present themselves in various ways. Face-to-face or side-to-side or even back-to-back presentations may reflect specific information. For example, cooperating people are likely to sit side by side while competitors frequently prefer to face one another.
   c Posture. Obviously one can be lying down, seated, or standing. But other elements of posture convey messages. Are we slouched or erect? Are our legs crossed or our arms folded? Postures can convey messages of the degree of formality and the degree of relaxation in the exchange.
   d Physical contact. We can be touching, holding, pushing, or embracing. Shaking hands, kissing, or patting on the back all convey messages. In most cases they reflect an element of intimacy or feelings of attraction (or lack of attraction).
2 Dynamic features
   a Facial expressions. The smile, frown, raised eyebrow, yawn, puckered lips, and sneer all convey information. These features are continually changing during interaction and are constantly monitored by the recipi-

[2]M. Argyle. Nonverbal communication in human social interaction. In R. Hinde (Ed.), *Non-verbal communication.* New York: Cambridge, 1972.

What are the nonverbal messages conveyed in this picture? Does he look like a man you would trust? (*By permission of University of Washington* Daily.)

ent. There is also some evidence that the meaning of these expressions is similar across cultures.

b *Gestures.* One of the most frequently observed, but least understood, cues are hand movements. Most people have certain hand movements they regularly use when talking. While some gestures (e.g., a clenched fist) have universal meanings, most others seem to be individually learned and idiosyncratic.

c *Looking.* A major feature of social interaction is eye contact. It can convey emotions, as well as signals about when to talk or when to finish, sexual interest, or aversion. The frequency of contact suggests interest or boredom. The lowering of the gaze can have sexual implications.

This list shows that both static features such as one's posture or distance and dynamic features such as facial expression convey important information.

Some of the research has developed a general theory of how information is actually conveyed through nonverbal cues.[3] Apparently many of the "display rules" are learned quite early in life. Some people have argued that the cues conveyed by facial expressions and eye contact may even be instinctual. In general, the facial expressions, eye contact, and orientation convey information about the type of emotion, while the posture, gestures, and distance cues are more related to the intensity of the emotion or feeling. Specific meanings may

[3]P. Ekman & W. V. Friesen. The repertoire of nonverbal behavior: categories, origins, usage and coding. *Semiotica,* 1969, **1,** 49–98.

differ in different cultures, but the conclusions to be drawn are still very similar. Whenever we communicate with someone we are obviously sending more information than is contained in the words. In order to understand communication fully and make changes to increase its effectiveness, we must analyze both the verbal and nonverbal content of the message.

The medium and the flow of the message

Once we have decided to communicate some information within an organizational setting, we have to decide how we want to send the message and to whom. Should we write a memo, pick up the phone, or schedule a meeting? Should we include our boss or just our subordinates? How about that manager over in marketing—should she be included as well? The answers to these questions are often important in determining both the effectiveness and acceptance of the communication.

One initial problem is whether we wish to have a one-way or two-way communication process. We must decide if we want any feedback or questions of clarification about the message. Since using the phone or calling a meeting would usually result in a two-way exchange of information, the most frequent medium chosen for one-way communication is the written message. Using this technique has some advantages and some disadvantages, and Harold Leavitt, who has

The telephone is an important mode of communication. (*By permission of University of Washington Daily.*)

done considerable research in this area, has summarized these points.[4] They are presented in the following list.

ONE-WAY VERSUS TWO-WAY COMMUNICATION

1 *Formality.* A one-way message can be phrased and presented more formally. It looks more official and businesslike and it does not have to be written.For example, military officers often come in to a room, brief their subordinates, and leave. An official memo, on official stationery, can have a similar effect. It makes the message appear important.

2 *Speed.* One-way messages take less time. There are numerous times when managers have to endure long meetings when a simple two-page document could have accomplished the same goal.

3 *Simplification.* When two-way communications occur, the process becomes by definition more complex. The recipient not only has to understand the sender, but the reverse is true as well. People's needs, feelings, and attitudes become involved. One-way messages avoid these complexities.

4 *Organization.* In many cases a formal, written document is more carefully planned than the things that are said in a meeting or in a personal exchange. One has to be more thorough, orderly, and systematic with the written message. It takes planning.

5 *Effectiveness.* If we define effective communication as the agreement between the sender and the recipient on the meaning of the message, then a two-way process usually does better. Points can be clarified and corrections made. Sharing and discussing information may take more time, but it will probably result in more agreement about what was said.

This list suggests that two-way interaction may result in greater complexity, slower decision making, and a less formal, orderly process, but it also may result in a more accurate assessment of what needs to be done.

The choice of the medium

The palest ink is clearer than the best memory.

Chinese proverb

Whether one wants a one-way or two-way communication process still does not determine the medium by which the message is sent. It can be oral or written, and within these two groups there are some further distinctions. Oral messages can be face-to-face, in a meeting, on the phone, and so on. Written messages can take the form of formal memos, personal letters, or statements tacked up on a bulletin board. And combinations of these media often occur. For example, a manager may send out a memo and then schedule a meeting to talk about it. Or the process may be reversed—the minutes of a meeting may be written up, summarized, typed, and circulated.

While not much research is available that specifically addresses this topic,

[4]H. Leavitt. *Managerial psychology*. Chicago: University of Chicago Press, 1964.

there is some.[5] For example, a number of experiments have compared the following media in terms of their effectiveness: (1) oral only, (2) written only, (3) use of a bulletin board, (4) the grapevine (no formal message sent), and (5) oral *and* written. The general procedure has been to have a message distributed by different media for different groups in an organization. Then after a couple of days the recipients of the message are tested to see how much content they can accurately remember. The results are usually the same: The written plus oral message results in the greatest retention. The oral exchange is second in effectiveness, followed by a written message, the bulletin board, and the grapevine.

However, one should have some caution with respect to the acceptance of these results. They refer specifically to the transmission of factual information rather than issues about which there is a difference of opinion or intense feelings. One should also add that in many ways effectiveness is expensive. Using both written and oral media requires more time, and time costs money. As we said earlier, an oral exchange is frequently slower than a written one. The bulletin board and grapevine are obviously the cheapest strategies. So, the individual supervisor or the organizational unit must weigh the importance of the message before they decide what to do. They may wish to spend more time and money to increase the effectiveness of important communications.

It also appears as if the type of communication is important in terms of which medium is likely to be effective.[6] One study, for example, asked business supervisors to rate the effectiveness of (1) written, (2) oral, (3) written and then oral, or (4) oral and then written communication for different types of situations. In general, the oral-followed-by-written technique came out best. Supervisors saw it as most effective for situations which (1) required immediate action, (2) passed along a company directive or order, (3) communicated an important policy change, (4) reviewed work progress, (5) called for praising a noteworthy employee, and (6) promoted a safety campaign. The written-only technique was judged best for passing along information that (1) required action in the future or (2) was of a general nature. An oral-only message was suggested for reprimands or to settle a dispute among employees. A summary of all this work would suggest that the oral-combined-with-written message is likely to lead to the most effective communication in most settings.

The direction of the communication. Part of the description of the flow of information has to do with the direction in which it is going. Is the message to one's boss, subordinate, or peer? Some work has been done to record what managers actually do.[7] Whom do they talk to? To whom do they write their memos? Are the messages sent horizontally, vertically, or diagonally?

Over a large set of types of information and people it appears as if the frequency of communication is fairly equally distributed into the horizontal,

[5]T. L. Dahle. An objective and comparative study of five methods of transmitting information to business and industrial employees. *Speech Monographs,* 1954, **21,** 21–28.

[6]D. A. Level. Communication effectiveness: method and situation. *Journal of Business Communication,* Fall 1972, 19–25.

[7]A. K. Wickesberg. Communication networks in the business organization structure. *Academy of Management Journal,* 1968, **11,** 253–262.

vertical, and diagonal categories. This varies, of course, according to the type of message and job. For example, managers are more likely to pass scuttlebutt along to their friends and peers (horizontal), while they typically look for approval from their boss or subordinates (vertically). The striking finding, however, is that both managers and nonmanagers communicate so frequently in the diagonal direction—either up or down, but in another unit or department. There is hardly any research on this type of communication, and we can say little about it except that it seems to be important.

The greatest emphasis has been placed on the upward versus downward versus sideways directions of communication. Most of us are highly familiar with the downward technique of communication, whether it comes from our boss, the central university administration, or the President of the United States. These types of messages frequently come through the chain of command or by memos, handbooks, posters, or group meetings. They may also come via the telephone, loudspeaker systems, annual reports, or inserts in our pay envelopes. Massive amounts of information flow in this direction, and lots of attention has focused on its inadequacies. It frequently tends to be one-way, and a number of studies have shown that the further down the line a message is sent (the further away it is from the source), the more information that is lost. If information has to travel through four or five levels of management, it may lose up to 80% of its informational content. We will discuss this problem again in the section on blocks to effective communication.

The motivation, desire, and techniques for sending information upward may

Come in, Zimmerman, I've been anxious to communicate downard to you.
Most communication travels from upper levels to lower levels of the organization.

be somewhat different. First, while the primary motivation for a downward flow might be simply informative, there are a number of other factors influencing the upward transmission of information. Subordinates who have upward mobility aspirations tend to send messages upward. Also, if subordinates trust their boss and feel that he or she has influence in the organization, they are more likely to communicate upward.[8]

The technique for communicating upward can be formal or informal. There are questionnaires, grievance procedures, and interviews in the former category. The face-to-face exchange, group meetings, and open-door policies are less formal. Perhaps the most popular technique currently involves the issue of participation in decision making. That is, to what extent should managers encourage and utilize information communicated upward by their subordinates? We will evaluate and elaborate on this issue in our discussion of new techniques designed to change organizations (Chapter 16).

The focus on horizontal communication increased dramatically as a result of the findings from the Hawthorne studies discussed earlier. Vertical communication was part of the formal organization structure while horizontal links were not. Yet, clearly many horizontal links existed. Managers and nonmanagers get a lot of information and pass along a lot of scuttlebutt to their peers. It is an informal way for nonmanagers and staff people to find out what is going on.

The amount of horizontal communication varies partly as a function of the situation and partly as a function of the type of organization. Some organizations now formally include committees and linking positions for the purpose of distributing information across the organization rather than up or down. These types of channels are especially encouraged in organizations faced with a rapidly changing situation. In this way new information can quickly be transmitted throughout the organization.

Blocks to effective communication

Now that we understand the communication process better, we can ask why we do not do it very well. What factors prevent us from having individual A send a message to individual B and have both of them agree about its meaning and importance? What are the blocks to effective communication?

The importance of this problem should be emphasized. We have mentioned that anywhere from 50 to 90% of an individual's time may be spent in communication. Yet some studies show that up to 50% of the information transmitted is interpreted incorrectly. Individuals A and B disagree about what was sent or what was received. The boss thinks that he gave a formal order and the subordinate sees it as a friendly suggestion. Or a manager institutes a new safety plan and circulates a memo describing its implementation. Two weeks later the manager notices that the employees are not wearing safety gear and inquires why they are not following the new regulations. "What new regulations?" is the response.

[8]L. Porter and K. H. Roberts. Organizational communications. In M. Dunnette (Ed.), *Handbook of industrial and organizational psychology*. Chicago: Rand McNally, 1975, 1553–1589.

Understanding the reasons for poor communication is the first step toward more effective communication. If we know the problems, we can suggest some remedies. Discussed below are four sets of problems: (1) situations where the information never gets from A to B, (2) situations where the message is actually distorted by the sender or by someone transmitting the information, (3) situations where the recipient distorts what is received, and (4) situations where environmental factors external to the recipient produce misinterpretations.

A break in the communication link

One factor that frequently causes a breakdown in the communication process is the sheer size and complexity of large organizations. To get a message to another person can be terribly frustrating. The mail might get lost, the phone message might get thrown away, the person might be out of town. There are numerous times when individuals play what is called "telephone tag" with someone whom they are trying to reach or someone who is trying to get hold of them. There are plenty of messages at both ends, but somehow they can never link up. In some cases the individuals resort to the use of a letter—a much slower but sometimes more reliable way to send a message.

The number of status levels in the hierarchy may increase the chance of a breakdown. When a message has to pass through many levels, especially upward, it often gets changed, misinterpreted, or lost. Our discussion of the upward and downward flow of information covered some of these points.

Another block to communication is the increasing specialization of the work force. Everyone has a special job, and it becomes increasingly more difficult to see and talk to people outside one's specialty. It is the classic case of the right hand not knowing what the left hand is doing.

Finally, we have situations where information is not sent to B because somehow A feels that B is not entitled to the information or that B is not interested in the information. In the former case, having information is synonymous with having power, and not everyone is willing to share their power. People who need to know certain things are often left in the dark simply because someone else wanted them excluded from the information exchange. In the latter situation people often make erroneous assumptions about what other people want to know. If you are in doubt, you should probably inform the other person.

Distortion by a sender

Now let us discuss those cases where B actually receives a message from A. It may have traveled through a number of people to get there, but it eventually arrives. In what ways will it be different from what was intended to be sent?

One frequently noticed distortion is described as condensation. When messages are passed along, they are often reduced in length. For example, when the Department of Labor contracts to have a large evaluation study of some manpower program such as Job Corps, the submitted document may be 200 to 400 pages long. Attached as well is a 20-page summary. This summary is typically reduced to 2 to 3 pages and passed on to the deputy assistant of Policy, Evaluation, and Research. Three years' work and 400 pages of results are ultimately condensed to 2 pages of summary which require 10 minutes of the decision maker's time. This is an extreme example, but it accurately reflects what frequently occurs in organizations.

A second and often-noted distortion may be described as premature closure or uncertainty absorption. Besides reducing the length of a message, one frequently makes the message sound more certain and specific when it is passed along. Karl Weick sees this process as a major factor inherent in the organizational process itself. He states that "information results when uncertainty is removed. It is more or less ambiguous and is subject to a variety of interpretations. If action is to be taken the possibilities must be narrowed and the equivocal properties of the message made more unequivocal. Organizing is concerned with removing equivocality from information and structuring processes so that removal is possible."[9] In this way, what was uncertain becomes more certain.

Distortion by the recipient

What sorts of things make us misinterpret the information we receive? That is, given that the message sent by A actually gets through to B (even though it may have been changed along the way), what sorts of further distortions are going to occur?

The first point to discuss is an obvious one—semantics. People mean different things even when they are using the same word. The president of a company states that times are hard and we must be constantly aware of ways to increase efficiency. The manager of the R&D department sees this statement as needed recognition for his work group. The production manager believes that finally the new machine that was needed will be delivered, and the personnel manager starts

[9]K. Weick. *The social psychology of organizing.* Menlo Park, Calif.: Addison-Wesley, 1969, 29.

What seems to be a clear communication to the sender may be confusing for the receiver.

looking around for people to lay off. All three people interpret the demand for efficiency differently.

Closely related to the above process are the ideas of denial and selective perception. As Simon and Garfunkel have aptly put it, "A man hears what he wants to hear and disregards the rest." We have preconceived notions or expectations about what is going to be said to us. Just think about your reactions when you pick up your mail. Usually you look at the source of the letter, and if the source is easily determined, you probably have a good idea about the content. Is it an advertisement, a bill, or a note from a family member? These expectations that you have before you even look at the content of the message can distort your interpretation of this content.

Outside factors that hinder effective communication

There are some external events or situations which may also disrupt the communication process. One of the most frequently researched is the concept of overload. In many cases an individual may receive a message but misinterpret it simply because there are so many other issues currently impinging on the person. Somehow when you recieve the fifth phone call within an hour, you tend to pay less attention to what is being said. Your mind is on other things. Therefore, one of the problems caused by information overload is a lack of attention. A related problem is a lack of reflection. When one is faced with numerous important inputs, the sheer time to ponder about any given one is severely reduced. Thus, overload limits the emphasis on and time to think about any one item of information.

A second factor that is weighed by the recipient is the credibility of the communicator. How many times has this person been right in the past? Even though a communicator may be correct 50 percent of the time, the recipient of the message tends to see the situation as more extreme. That is, the recipient typically treats the communicator as credible or not credible. If the communicator is seen as credible, then frequently too much weight is put on the information. The reverse is true if the person is seen as not credible.

Finally, there is what is described as the communication climate. Do people trust one another. Is it all right to tell your boss how you really feel? This prevailing atmosphere effects how you interpret incoming messages and in many cases leads to distortion.

So, we have lots of ways to go wrong. Messages are frequently lost, people change a message as it is passed along, the recipient has a particular set of needs and motives that influence what is heard, and the current environmental situation may influence the meaning of what is communicated. There have been attempts to remedy the situation, and the rest of the chapter discusses these strategies in more detail.

The external environment

The communication process exists within some surrounding environment. Some of the characteristics of this environment are important in terms of both the content of the communication (what gets sent) and its effectiveness (the agreement about its meaning). The two approaches to understanding these situational factors have been experimental and descriptive. The experimental approach involves setting up some communication structure and asking people to work on some problem using the communication channels established by the researcher. In this way different types of communication patterns can be compared.

The descriptive approach is somewhat different. In this research strategy the investigator tries to find out who talks to whom, about what, and how much in some ongoing group or organization. In this manner a picture or description of the process can be developed and certain problems uncovered. We will discuss both of these approaches.

The experimental approach

Organization planners and designers would like to know how to set up communication channels such that group members can transmit information with maximum efficiency. One way to do that is to try out different patterns of communication and compare their effectiveness. The research work in the area of communication networks has done just that.[10]

In most investigations the subjects have been placed in adjacent cubicles and communicate with written messages passed through slots in the walls. The tasks vary from simple mathematics or identification problems (e.g., identifying a missing symbol out of a whole set) to more complex discussion problems. Performance is typically measured by assessing the time to solve the problem, the number of errors, or the number of messages sent. Clearly, if the type of structure is related to the amount of information exchanged, its speed of exchange, and its degree of error, then these data could have major implications for structuring organizational decision units to obtain efficiency in handling various decision problems. Figure 9-2 presents some of the networks that have been studied extensively.

The research over the years has produced a number of interesting findings. First, the person in the middle of the pattern, who has more channels, tends to receive more messages, be chosen more frequently as the leader, and have more social influence. Further, the type of structure greatly determines the pattern of interaction. For example, in patterns such as the wheel or the Y, it is much more likely that a central structure, in which one member is responsible for processing a large amount of information, will develop. A more decentralized structure will tend to arise in patterns such as the circle or the slash.

The effectiveness of particular networks seems to depend upon the difficulty of the task. For very complex problems a decentralized structure seems to produce a quicker solution time, fewer errors, and greater member satisfaction than a centralized structure. For rather simple problems, a centralized structure seems to be quicker, and fewer errors occur than in a decentralized structure.

[10]A. Bavalas. Communication patterns in task-oriented groups. *Journal of the Acoustical Society of America,* 1950, **22,** 725–730; and M. E. Shaw. *Group dynamics: The psychology of small group behavior.* New York: McGraw Hill, 1971.

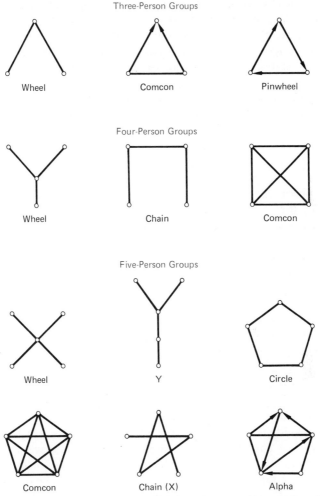

Figure 9-2. Some communication networks which have been used in experimental research investigations. Note that arrows indicate one-way channels and lines represent two-way channels.

The results point out a very crucial problem. They suggest that when a complex problem needs to be solved, a centralized communication structure has some serious drawbacks. First, the leader or person in the middle becomes overloaded. They have too much information to be able to function effectively. Secondly, the centralized structure does not allow the other members to have as substantial an input as a decentralized structure. Specific members are often isolated from the exchange, and satisfaction with the group seems to decrease. Thus, an additional criterion of the effectiveness of one's communication is whether it eventually results in the correct action or decision. Whether one accomplishes this objective is partly dependent upon the channels of communication that are available. To understand is not enough—the message must get to the right people as well.

Some experimental work has focused on situational factors other than communication channels. Numerous studies, for example, report that the closer together people are physically, the more likely they are to communicate with one another. If it is important that two people keep in touch, they should have their offices or work stations close together. Accessibility increases the likelihood of communication.

Another factor that has been frequently researched is the size of the group. It appears as if increases in group size increase the chance that a small number of people or even one individual will dominate a group discussion. For example, one might find that in a three-person group one person talked 45 percent of the time, another person 35 percent, and a third person 20 percent. If this were a five-person group, the figures would likely be 40, 30, 15, 10, and 5 percent. The input of one or two people, while decreasing slightly, does not decrease as much as the input made by the other group members.

In summary, the experimental approach helped to point out some important situational factors that influence communication. The number of channels, the flow of the information, the size of the group, and the physical location of the participants are all important. The research highlighted the facts that centralized structures often produce overload and isolated, dissatisfied members, especially on complex tasks. Also, the closer together two people are the more likely they are to communicate. These findings, coupled with the descriptive results discussed below, can help organizational designers to construct more effective communication systems.

The descriptive approach

A second research process focusing on the surrounding communication environment for an individual simply attempts to describe the actual ongoing communication patterns that currently exist in the whole group or the whole organization. This can be done by having an observer record what goes on, by using a tape recorder, or by having people respond to a questionnaire. The use of a questionnaire requires that people can indicate and accurately report about the people with whom they interact.

Using this type of information one can get a picture of who communicates with whom, where they do it, when they do it, how much they do it, and what it is about. These data provide the "big picture." They indicate the overall structure of communication in the organization. Along with this descriptive information, a number of criteria can be gathered related to the effectiveness of decisions and the satisfaction of group members. These criteria can be related to the descriptive picture in an attempt to find out what communication variables are related to job effectiveness and satisfaction.

Take for example some work we recently did in a large organization that was undergoing some major changes in the formal organizational structure. New departments were set up, new managerial positions were established, and a whole new committee structure was instituted. Part of our task was to note what changes occurred in the communication structure and whether people were more effective and satisfied under this structure. We gathered masses of data from a descriptive questionnaire for every organizational member and generated a number of summary indexes of the communication process.[11] One index was generated from the number (and names) of people with whom one frequently interacted (called a role set). Since we had this data for everyone, we could tell how many times a person was described by other people as being in their role set. We could compare these two measures (who is in my role set versus whose role sets I am in) to get a feel for the individual's "accuracy" of description. By looking at everyone's choices we could get a measure of "connectedness" for an individual or for a group. This measure specified the ease with which one could communicate with everyone in the organization. Some people only had to talk to one or two people and they could be fairly sure that almost everyone would get the word, while other people were so isolated that much of what they communicated never got beyond a few immediate recipients.

As expected, the formal organizational changes produced major changes in the communication structure. In general, people became more connected, and connectedness was positively related to satisfaction. People with higher status were more central in the structure and were seen as highly influential. While not everyone became more satisfied and productive, those who somehow became more integrated into the communication flow were more pleased with their jobs.

The above example is only one of many similar research projects.[12] The favorable aspects of such research are that we are better able (1) to describe what actually goes on in an organization and (2) to understand how communication is related to effective job performance and high job satisfaction. We can identify isolates in the communication structure, and we can determine who seems to be overloaded with information. Blocks in the process can be located, and key central people, identified. These data are becoming increasingly useful as aids for helping establish better communication.

Some remedies for poor communication

There are some things we can do to increase the effectiveness of communication in organizations. There are some simple rules that individuals can follow which are helpful, and there are some programs, courses, and training techniques that the organization can sponsor which should help.

As a sender of information one should always attempt to use language that is clear, concise, *and* appropriate to the situation. Think twice, go over the message one more time, and try to imagine the audience. Will the information be appropriate? This is an important factor.

A sender must also establish credibility. The message should be both understood and believed. One rule of thumb is to make sure that what is said can be factually validated or acted upon. The old homily that "actions speak louder than words" has some truth to it. Information has to be believed to have any impact.

[11]L. E. Rice & T. R. Mitchell. Structural determinates of individual behavior in organizations. *Administrative Science Quarterly,* 1973, **18,** 56–70.

[12]Porter and Roberts, op cit.

Try to avoid the use of labels and unnecessary classifications and let the recipient receive as much factual information as possible. If an employee has failed to meet three deadlines in a row it is better to describe that situation accurately than to describe the person as a shirker or as irresponsible. This does not mean that attitudes, opinions, and feelings should be omitted, but simply that they should be labeled as such.

The organization can introduce systems of feedback which should increase the effectiveness of the communication. One can gain knowledge about what was received, who received it, and what sort of action was taken. Various training programs can also be helpful in increasing the communication skills of employees. For example, role playing can teach an individual to take the position of the "other" person in an interpersonal exchange. This process should help the recipient of a message to fully understand the sender's meaning.

Finally, there are a number of courses and programs available that are specifically constructed to help people communicate better. There are Dale Carnegie courses which are designed to help one's verbal skills, and various letter-writing and speech-writing courses to help with written communication. Evelyn Wood's Speed Reading course may increase people's comprehension and the amount of material they can consume. There are also "listening" courses (e.g., Xerox) that are intended to help people assess the true meaning of a communication. While I am not aware of much data supporting the claims made by such courses, it is true that they are designed to increase the effectiveness of communication. Any organization seriously interested in supporting such activities should obviously evaluate their usefulness for its employees.

Summary

We have attempted to define and describe the communication process. The blocks to effective communication have been discussed and a number of remedies suggested. The following summary statements seem appropriate:

1 Communication is important. It takes up much of our time and is often the cause of major organizational failures.
2 The communication process involves a sender, a message, a channel or method of communication, a recipient, and a surrounding environment.
3 The motivation to communicate is complex. It includes needs to reduce uncertainty, gather information, confirm beliefs, and exercise power.
4 The message itself is composed of both verbal and nonverbal cues. The latter are in many cases as important as the written or spoken words.
5 There are many different ways and combinations of ways to send information. An oral combined with a written presentation seems to be very effective.
6 There are a number of ways in which effective communication is disrupted or blocked. A message may not be recieved, may be distorted somewhere along the line, or misinterpreted by the recipient.
7 Communication goes on in a context. A number of situational factors such

as group size, accessibility of key people, and general patterns of interaction influence the effectiveness of the communication process.

8 A number of personal and organizational aids are available to help people communicate more effectively.

Implications for practice

We have already listed a number of ways in which poor communication can be made more effective. Using clear, appropriate language, establishing credibility and avoiding labels, and using role playing, training programs, and communication courses can all increase the effectiveness of an individual's communication. But there are some additional issues which should be mentioned.

First, organizations seem to take communication for granted. People tend to *assume* that what they have said or written is received and understood. It is only when blunders occur that poor communication is brought out as the cause of the failure. These circumstances can be reversed. The organization can and should analyze its communication patterns. Isolated positions can be made less isolated. Overloaded positions can be relieved. Messages that have to travel through many levels or units can be checked on. Upward communication can be solicited. An analysis of the communication structure can remedy old problems *and* establish more effective patterns for the future.

The second implication is that individuals should be made aware of both the complexity of the communication process and the alternatives that are available. There are a variety of ways that ambiguity can be decreased, labels avoided, definitions or clarifications used where possible, and nonverbal cues kept to a minimum. But besides methods for increasing the agreement about the meaning of a message there are things we can do to make sure that the message is received by those who need to know or should know. Think about who should receive a message—err in favor of keeping others informed. You can make decisions about what channels to use and the direction of the message. The more important the issue, the better it is to use multiple communication messages and modes (e.g., written and oral). Build in feedback loops if you must. For example, you can have people check off their names on a memo once they have read it.

The important point to realize is that good communication is not just speaking or writing clearly or unambiguously. It is a matter of understanding the whole process. Effective communication includes not only an understanding of your input but also an understanding of how the message will be received and the situational factors that influence the exchange.

Discussion questions

1 Why do we communicate with others? What is meant by effective communication?
2 What are some nonverbal cues that you pay attention to when interacting with others? Do you think these cues are more or less important than the substance of the message?

3 In your experience, what are the major blocks to effective communication? How would you remedy the situation?

Case: On being informed and being well informed

Atlantic Aircraft produces small pleasure and business airplanes. They are situated in the Northeast and have recently been plagued by problems of turnover, absenteeism, and suspected sabotage. The president of the company, Craig Kaplan, calls in his Vice Presidents and asks them what they think is the problem. After much discussion they decide that the employees feel they are being overworked and underpaid and it is agreed that some sort of bonus system should be tried. Peg Randolph, the Director of Personnel, is asked to develop and implement such a system.

It becomes obvious to Peg that to have a good bonus system one must first develop a good performance appraisal device. With this goal in mind she interviews a number of managers about how high and low performers actually behaved on the job, and a behavioral checklist was evolved that described the actions of good performers and poor performers. A bonus system was then aligned with scores on the checklist so that people who behaved appropriately would recieve a bonus and those that did not would get nothing.

Before implementing the system, Peg called two meetings. First, she sat down with the Vice Presidents and explained what she had done. Copies of the appraisal form were distributed, reviewed, and discussed. The VP's seemed preoccupied with other problems but in general the group was supportive. While not terribly enthusiastic or excited, the group told Peg to proceed with the program. The second meeting involved the management team including the lower levels of supervision. They were the people who would be asked to actually use the form. There was some grumbling and whispers, but not many overt objections. Some people suggested that one form didn't cover all the types of jobs people did, but this point was not pressed. Since Peg had mentioned that the VP's were behind the idea, there seemed to be a good deal of support. Again, she was given the green light to proceed.

A brief memo describing the bonus system was distributed to all employees and the new system was implemented. Rating forms went out to all supervisory and managerial personnel asking that they rate each of their subordinates twice during the next three months and return the forms to her. She would handle the processing of the data and the distribution of the bonuses.

Well, it was not long before Peg began to sense that something was wrong. Instead of getting positive reports about employee attitudes, the reverse was true. They were angry that they were being watched and evaluated. They didn't like the idea of their behavior being rated, especially on a form that they had never seen before and had had little help in developing. The use of only one form seemed silly and oversimplified.

The data themselves also presented problems. Only a small percentage of the rating scales were actually being turned in. And on those submitted, almost everyone was rated high. At this rate, everyone would end up getting a bonus. Peg was convinced that scientifically, the rating instrument was sound. If used properly, people would get rewarded for doing a good job. However, somehow the process of implementation had been bungled. The support and enthusiasm she expected were not there. The whole system had to be scrubbed.

Questions about the case

1 Do you think that Peg acted too hastily? What cues were there that should have alerted her to some possible difficulties?
2 Were the employees properly informed? Do you think the descriptive memo was sufficient information?
3 How could the program have been implemented in such a way that it would have been accepted?

Additional readings

* Allen, T. J., & Cohen, S. I. Information flow in research and development laboratories. *Administrative Science Quarterly*, 1969, **14**, 12–20.
** Burgess, R. L. Communication networks and behavioral consequences. *Human Relations*, 1969, **22**, 137–160.
* Chapanis, A. Prelude to 2001: Explorations in human communication. *American Psychologist*, 1967, **1** (26), 949–961.
Cohen, A. R. Upward communication in experimentally created hierarchies. *Human Relations*, 1958, **11**, 41–53.
* Davis, K. Management communication and the grapevine. *Harvard Business Review*, 1953, **31**, 43–49.
** Guetzkow, H. Communication in organizations. In J. G. March (Ed.), *Handbook of organizations*. Chicago: Rand McNally, 1965.
Hage, J., Aiken, M., & Marrett, C. Organization structure and communication. *American Sociological Review*, 1971, **36**, 860–871.
* Howell, W. S. A model as an approach to interpersonal communications. *Pacific Speech Quarterly*, December 1967, 11–19.
* Porter, G. W. Nonverbal communications. *Training and Development Journal*, June 1969, 3–8.
* Read, W. Upward communication in industrial hierarchies. *Human Relations*, 1962, **15**, 3–16.
* Rosenberg, M. S. Words can be windows or walls. In W. R. Nord (Ed.), *Concepts and controversy on organizational behavior*. Pacific Palisades, Calif.: Goodyear, 1972, 485–490.
Triandis, H. Cognitive similarity and interpersonal communication in industry. *Journal of Applied Psychology*, 1959, **43**, 321–326.
* Wickesberg, A. V. Communications networks in the business organization structure. *Academy of Management Journal*, 1968, **11**, 253–262.

*Possible reading for students

**Review of literature or comprehensive source material

10
Roles, norms, and status

All the world's a stage,
And all the men and women merely players.
They have their exits and their entrances;
And one man in his time plays many parts, . . .

William Shakespeare

We have already elaborated on the point that much of the behavior that we observe in an organizational setting is learned behavior. Through interaction with the organizational environment the individual learns what is appropriate and what is not. We learn the ropes if you like.

Therefore, to understand how this behavior is learned we must be able to analyze the interaction that occurs between the individual and the organization. Perhaps the best way to do that is to present a brief story about a typical employee's first experiences with a new job. This type of analysis should point out the crucial aspects of the learning process.

Jim Hanson, who has recently received his B.A. from a big Midwestern school of business, has interviewed for a number of jobs. He is interested in the field of marketing and luckily he receives a job offer from a large corporation which produces computer software. He eagerly accepts the job and reports for work July 1.

The first day on the job is rather routine. Jim, along with some other new employees and some summer help, is given a brief 2-hour orientation. They learn some history about the company, its size, and its locations throughout the world and hear some general statements about how they hope that everyone will be one big happy family. Along with this orientation probably come a number of forms and pamphlets. These materials provide or ask for important information about insurance, benefits, health care, recreational opportunities, and general organizational policies. These latter regulations usually appear in the form of an organiza-

tion handbook or manual.

After this brief meeting everyone goes their separate ways, and Jim is off to meet the people in the marketing department. Usually one or two people are responsible for Jim during this time. He will probably be introduced to everyone (e.g., ten to fifteen people), shown his desk, and given some materials to read or look over. This latter information is meant to help Jim understand what is currently going on in the department and the kind of work that he will probably be doing. He is encouraged to ask questions and get acquainted with everyone on a leisurely basis.

Over the next few weeks Jim is basically fairly cautious. He observes what goes on and he listens to what is said. He makes mistakes, and he gets corrected. He asks questions about things he does not understand, and he begins to feel like part of the group.

What exactly did Jim observe? Let us make a list of things that were probably important factors in what was learned about the job.

1 He learned what types of work he was expected to do and his areas of responsibility.
2 He learned information about both the quantity and quality of the work that was expected of him.
3 He observed how people in positions similar to his own behaved.
4 He noticed the degree to which people obeyed the rules and regulations of the organization (e.g., did people come to work on time?).
5 He took note of the dress worn by others—its formality or informality.
6 He observed how hard people worked.
7 He noticed who talked to whom—who talked and who listened.
8 He was very sensitive to the relationship with his boss: What did he want? How was he treated by others?

The list is not inclusive. There would be other things that would undoubtedly be noticed. However, the important point is that we can systematically classify the above list as a function of what is being learned.

First, items 1 through 3 deal with specific things Jim learned about his job. They clarify the expectations about how someone in his *particular position* should behave. He learns what to do, how to do it, who to talk to, how much to do, and the general responsibilities that accompany his position. This set of expectations, rules, and regulations for a particular position are typically described as one's *role* in the organization.

Second, items 4 through 6 helped Jim to understand what was going on within his subgroup or unit. The focus was on the appropriate or expected behavior for the group not for a specific position. Jim learned the "informal" rules and expectations of his peers, and these expectations are frequently labeled group *norms*. Their focus is on the lateral or horizontal interactions within a group.

Finally, items 7 and 8 refer to the expected behaviors that occur with respect to people above or below one in the formal or informal organizational hierarchy. Jim learned to whom he should defer and how to interact with people who were his immediate superiors or subordinates. These expectations in terms of vertical relationships are often discussed under the heading of *status* differences.

In summary, Jim learned a lot in those first few days. He began to understand

Table 10-1. A Summary of Role, Norm, and Status Concepts

Behavioral Focus	Relationships	Concept
Job	Horizontal and vertical	Role
Subgroup: same level	Horizontal	Norm
Subgroup: all levels	Vertical	Status

the scope of his job—his role. He began to understand the generally accepted behavior in his group—the norms. And he began to figure out the complex vertical relationships inherent in any organization—the status hierarchy. Table 10-1 summarizes these relationships. The rest of this chapter will discuss roles, norms, and status in more detail.

Role relationships

> I was sitting in the classroom
> Trying to look intelligent
> In case the teacher looked at me.
>
> Elton John

We have suggested that the expected behaviors for a particular position can be defined as one's role. In our example above, Jim's knowledge about how to do the job, whom he should work with, and the kinds of social interactions that were expected were all part of this role. These expectations came with the *position* not because of Jim's personal characteristics. The role expectations would have been the same for anyone filling that position.

But let us pursue the situation a little further. After work, Jim leaves to catch a bus to get home. There are a number of women who get on the bus at the same time as Jim and there are only a limited number of seats on the bus. Jim decides to stand. When he gets home his wife is fixing dinner and the children are outside playing. Since there are a few hours of daylight left, Jim quickly mows the backyard before eating. After playing with the children for a while and talking to his wife, Jim leaves with a couple of his buddies to go bowling. Jim belongs to a bowling league and is the captain of the team. This means that he really has to be there every week, and he feels responsible for choosing who will bowl in what positions and for motivating his teammates. He loves it. After a few laughs, a few beers, and some good sport Jim returns home and goes to bed.

The point of the above example is that we all fill numerous roles. There are certain expectations that come along with the position of male, husband, father, and bowling-team leader. Generally, males are expected to let females sit down on the bus. In some families, husbands are expected to mow the lawn and wives to cook dinner. Leaders are expected to organize and motivate team efforts. While sex-role sterotypes are increasingly breaking down, and in some cases reversing, this does not negate the existence of roles. It simply means that the expected behaviors that accompany the position are changing.

So, we all have many roles which we fill. Our primary concern here, however, is with roles as they affect our behavior on the job. There are certain characteris-

How would you like me to answer that question? As a minority
group member, a college graduate, a housewife, or a Catholic?

We often belong to many different groups which have certain beliefs and expectations about appropriate behaviour.

tics of these roles that should be emphasized. First, they are impersonal. It is the position that determines the expectations, not the individual. Second, they are related to task behavior. An organizational role is that set of expected behaviors for a particular position vis-à-vis a particular job. If you like, it is a formal and informal behavioral job description. Third, roles can be fairly difficult to pin down exactly. The problem is to define who determines what is expected. Is it the role occupant's perceptions of what others expect? Or should we ask group members what they expect of someone in a particular job and use some sort of average set of expectations to define the role? What one actually does—that is, how one behaves—could also be used. What we perceive as our role, what others perceive as our role, and what we actually do may be very different, and, therefore, defining what is the "real" role is often difficult to do. Fourth, roles are learned quickly and can result in major changes in behavior. Much of what we do is determined by our roles.

One classic example of how quickly and dramatically we learn organizational roles was provided by Lieberman.[1] He gathered data from 2000 workers in a factory and determined their attitudes toward management. After a year he

[1]S. Lieberman. The effects of changes in roles on the attitudes of role occupants. *Human Relations*, 1956, **9**, 385–402.

returned and discovered that 23 men had been promoted to foremen and 35 had been elected as union stewards. He readministered the questionnaires to these people who had changed jobs and to a matched sample of workers who were similar in many respects but had not changed jobs. Before the promotions, all the men had similar attitudes. After the promotions, the foremen were pro management, the stewards were pro union, and the people who had not changed jobs had not changed their attitudes. The change in position had caused quite extreme changes in attitudes. For both groups, 41 percent of the men were favorable toward management before the change. After 2 to 3 years, 76 percent of the foremen were favorable while only 14 percent of the stewards were favorable. These data strongly suggest that these men learned their roles quickly and believed them strongly.

Roles and group process

The research work using the concept of role is vast. A large portion of the sociological and small-group research concerns itself with the ways in which roles are learned, changed, and affect group behavior and performance. Three of the major issues are discussed below.

First, we would want to know how people learn their roles. The most frequently used concept to aid one in this area is called the *role episode*. Figure 10-1 presents the components of the episode. The group members have some expectations which are communicated. The role occupant perceives and interprets these expectations and then behaves according to what he or she believes is appropriate. All these stages represent an ongoing cyclical process. If the actual behavior (stage 4) differs widely from the group's expectations (stage 1), then the feedback mechanisms will point out this discrepancy. This process should result in changes in the communication or sent expectations and, it is hoped, result in more appropriate behavior.

One can see some other interesting aspects of the model. Stages 1 and 3 are essentially cognitive or perceptual evaluations. They have to do with what people think should be done. On the other hand, stages 2 and 4 are observable behavior—what is communicated and what is actually done. Data can be gathered about all four stages, and the comparisons between and among the stages has led to some important insights about job stress and morale. We will return to these points in the next section.

A major concept that has evolved from an analysis of how we learn our roles is called the *role set*. In the process of trying to determine who the people were in stage 1 of the role episode (the group members who determine the role expecta-

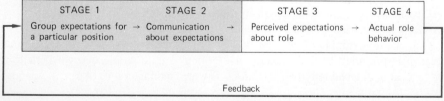

Figure 10-1. The role episode.

tions), researchers had to come up with a term that described the relationship between the role of interest and other organizational members. In most cases those people who interact frequently and discuss important matters with the focal person are defined as that person's role set. These are the people that communicate what is expected in that particular role.

The role-set idea has been used in numerous ways. The size and diversity of this group can tell us much about the communication process. We discussed in the previous chapter, for example, how an analysis of role sets could tell us how quickly and extensively people could communicate with one another. If role sets are small, we may have clearer expectations but more small cliques and isolated groups. Large role sets may lead to greater ambiguity and confusion.

The third way that role theory has been used to look at group interaction is to analyze the degree to which distinctly different types of roles are performed by people within the same subgroup. This process is described as *role differentiation*. In Chapter 8, "Group Dynamics," we pointed out that the development stage and the structure of a group provides people with certain types of roles that need to be filled in order for a group to be effective. One person might be primarily concerned with providing emotional or interpersonal support. Such a person would be concerned with the maintenance of good group relations. Another person might take a more procedural role and be concerned with schedules, the agenda, and deadlines. A third might simply be concerned with the substantive information necessary to solve the task or problem. This role would consist of initiating ideas, giving information, or clarifying problems.

The point to be made here is that an understanding of roles tells us much more than just how people learn what they are supposed to do in their particular position. It also helps us describe the ongoing interaction and communication process—who people talk to and about what. And finally, it helps us to see how one role is differentiated from other roles in the same group and how all these roles may fit together like a complex puzzle to produce a smooth-running, effective group.

Role problems

An analysis of how roles are learned has helped organization theorists to understand many of the problems that exist in organizations. Three concepts generated from this research are described below.

Role conflict. As we mentioned before, people hold numerous roles at one time. Some of these are on the job and some are off the job. We may be a member of our church choir, on the bowling team, a Little League coach, a parent, a spouse, a supervisor, a union representative, and head of the Heart Fund drive. All these positions carry along a set of expectations—a role.

One problem occurs when these expectations are simultaneously incompatible. Roles may conflict with another by advocating conflicting modes of behavior. These types of conflicts are typically broken down into four categories. The first is described as *intrasender* conflict. This occurs when the same person sends you conflicting demands such as, "I don't care how you get it done, just do it.

But don't break any rules in the process." Sometimes different people see your role differently. The classic example is the shop supervisor who may have risen through the ranks to get the job. Is this person part of the management or is the supervisor's allegiance with the workers on the shop floor? This job is described as being high on *intrarole* conflict; the role itself is composed of conflicting expectations.

A third type of conflict occurs when two or more roles being held by the same individual are in conflict. The head of the marketing department must meet with the heads of the other departments to discuss how certain monies will be distributed. As a member of the management team the person wants to do what is best for the whole organization but as the head of marketing the person wants that department to receive an increase in emphasis. This type of conflict is called *interrole* conflict, and with the increasing complexities and interdependencies within today's organizations it seems to be on the rise.

Finally, there is what we call a *person-role* conflict, where our personal attitudes or values differ from the role requirements. You see a fellow student cheat on an exam. Your personal values tell you to report the incident, but your role as a student may inhibit you. Students somehow are expected to be bound together, a cohesive group that in some cases must outwit their teachers. The Watergate affair was filled with examples of person-role conflicts, and it was interesting to note how different people resolved the problems: some left the government, some looked the other way, some joined actively in the cover-up, some pleaded ignorance, and some went to the prosecutor.

In summary, there are many ways in which our roles can conflict. The important question is what happens when the problem occurs. That is, what are the consequences of role conflict?

The research results are clear on this point. Role conflict results in negative consequences for both the individual and the organization. Numerous studies have shown that conflict produces greater levels of tension, anxiety, and turnover and lower levels of satisfaction and productivity.[2] People are extremely stressed by conflicting expectations, and it affects numerous aspects of their work-related behavior. They may resign, they will undoubtedly show signs of anxiety, and it will take their minds off of the tasks at hand. Role conflict can be seen as a serious problem in organizations.

Role ambiguity. A different type of problem, but one of equal or perhaps greater importance than role conflict, has to do with the amount of ambiguity in the role. There are a number of facets to this problem that have to be explored. One is simply to examine the discrepancy between what people expect us to do and what we think we ought to do. Does the individual understand and accurately perceive what is expected? A second issue is whether one knows clearly how to meet the expectations inherent in the role. It's one thing to know you are expected to sell so many thousands of dollars of insurance a month; it is another thing to know exactly how to do that. Finally, ambiguity can be created when the

[2]J. R. Rizzo, R. J. House, & S. I. Lirtzman. Role conflict and ambiguity in complex organizations. *Administrative Science Quarterly*, 1970, **15,** 150–163.

job incumbents' perception of what the job ought to be differs from what they perceive they are expected to do.

All these examples describe elements of *role ambiguity*. If we're not really sure about what is expected of us or how to do it, we are in an ambiguous situation. This type of problem may cause major personal and professional problems.

The research literature is again fairly extensive and in agreement. The attitudinal data show greater stress and tension with ambiguity and lower satisfaction and self-esteem. Some data from medical research shows that ambiguity increases the heart rate and may lead to anxiety and depression. Finally, some studies with more "hard" data suggest that turnover is greater and productivity lower when role ambiguity exists.

There are also some interesting results that compare role conflict and role ambiguity.[3] It appears as if role conflict is a more serious problem at lower levels of the organization, while role ambiguity causes more difficulties at higher levels. The rationale is that at higher levels managers can use their power and influence to reduce conflict by changing rules, regulations, structural variables, or responsibilities. These upper-level jobs may continue, however, to be ambiguous or hard to define.

At lower levels the jobs may be better defined and less ambiguous but role conflict may be more extreme. Moreover, the lower-level employee may not have the resources to remove the conflict.

The overall picture is that ambiguity makes it harder for us to do our jobs. We strive for certainty, and based on our learning-theory principles it should be obvious that in ambiguous situations the contingencies about what leads to what are unclear. This is a very uncomfortable situation for most employees.

Role overload. There is one additional role concept that deserves our attention— *role overload*. It occurs when the expectations and demands of the job exceed the ability of the role occupant to respond. Overload frequently appears in situations which are also ambiguous. Because of the lack of clarity of expectations, more and more demands are made of the individual.

The human-resources director within a personnel department might serve as a good example. This individual is seen as an expert on human problems and is often asked to serve as an organizational troubleshooter. There are few explicit demands except to help people out when they have difficulties. What frequently happens is that everybody thinks they have access to this person's time and expertise. They have no idea who else is demanding the director's time, so they go to him or her and say, "We have a managerial problem with our group in Peoria," or "How can we keep the union out of our Albany plant?" or "The turnover is high for our production groups—what do you think is the problem?" The number of projects with which the director may get involved can get quickly out of hand, yet it is hard to say no, simply because few clear regulations exist as to how the person's time should be spent. It can be a very frustrating experience.

---

[3]R. S. Shuler. Role perceptions, satisfaction and performance: A partial reconciliation. *Journal of Applied Psychology*, 1975, **60,** 683–687.

The research on role overload has produced similar findings to role conflict and ambiguity, though much less research has been done. In general, overload creates dissatisfaction, fatigue, and tension. Little information is available on the medical or "hard-data" consequences of overload.

The problems created by role ambiguity, conflict, and overload are serious. The loss in benefits to individuals and organizations is immense. Remedies to the problem are sorely needed, and some work has been done to do just that.

Remedies for role problems

Essentially, we are faced with three alternatives: (1) change the job, (2) change the people, or (3) select the "right" type of person in the first place. We will discuss each of these options.

Change the job. The suggestions here are to reduce ambiguity, conflict, or overload through structural techniques. Interdependencies can be reduced or the use of authority can be modified. More explicit job descriptions can be supplied. A number of studies have shown that these techniques can successfully reduce ambiguity and conflict.

The real problem with this alternative is that many jobs have ambiguity or conflict inherently built into them. For example, a portion of the role-theory literature focuses on what are described as boundary-spanning positions. These are jobs in organizations that require the people to deal with organizations and institutions outside of the one in which they are employed. The procurement of resources, public relations, and marketing are activities that may demand such positions.

One would expect that boundary-spanning positions would have large degrees of both conflict and ambiguity, and in general the research results support this hypothesis. However, these types of positions are important and necessary for the functioning of the organization. It is hard to conceive of getting rid of them as a viable option.

The same type of argument could be made for other types of positions. Most roles that demand creativity are often unstructured. The university professor is one example, as are positions in marketing or research and development in business organizations. If we cannot change the job, we must explore other means of resolving the problem.

Change the people. A second alternative is to use training techniques to help people adjust to their roles. The most obvious technique is called *role playing*. Essentially, role playing contains the following steps: (1) people read a script or case about some situation, (2) they then are assigned the role of one of the persons in the case, (3) the case is actually played out, and (4) the participants in the exercise along with the trainer discuss and evaluate how they behaved in the play.

The purpose of role-playing techniques in terms of role problems is twofold. First, it acquaints the individuals with a role or situation that they may actually face in an organizational setting. If they have just been hired or promoted, it can serve as a useful job preview. Having knowledge about areas of conflict and ambiguity before they occur can help people to adjust to and deal with the problems. Second, it gives people practice in developing skills to cope with ambiguity and conflict. One can become more proficient at playing the role.

Other training techniques are available which emphasize planning skills or interpersonal skills that might be helpful in teaching people how to cope with role ambiguity and role conflict. However, these techniques are more general in nature and are less concerned with role-related problems than the role-playing technique. We will elaborate on these techniques in Chapter 15, "Training and Development."

Selection. Finally, there is much evidence that certain types of people are just better able to deal with conflict and ambiguity than other types of people. Some people have a higher tolerance for stress and ambiguity. People who are high on the need to achieve have difficulty in ambiguous situations, while extroverts seem to be able to adjust to such situations. There are personality measures available to assess all these characteristics. If people know that the job has built-in conflicts and ambiguities, they should try to select someone who can adjust favorably to such a job.

There are two summary conclusions that should be stated. First, organizations should be aware of role ambiguity, conflict, and overload as possible problems or reasons for low morale and productivity. These negative outcomes are frequently attributed to the personality characteristics of the person or the technical nature of the job. What role theory says is that the way in which the job is defined is also a crucial determinant of effectiveness. The second conclusion is that organizations can assess these problems, and methods are available to remedy them. Through proper job analysis, job design, training and selection, problems such as role ambiguity, conflict, and overload can become recognizable and manageable issues.

Norms

If we observe work groups over a period of time, we begin to notice certain regularities in the behavior of the group. They may begin work at a certain time (after they have been there a while), they take some coffee breaks, they produce a certain amount, and they may quit working at some seemingly prearranged time (before they actually leave). There are patterns of dress, style, and interaction that are consistent. If we ask people why they behave the way they do, they say, "That's the way things are done around here," or "All of us expect to leave a little early."

These regularities in group behavior are defined as *social norms*. They represent shared group expectations about appropriate behavior. So, just as roles define what is appropriate for a particular job, norms define acceptable group behavior. Roles differentiate one position from another, while norms tend to integrate positions in the sense that norms typically refer to behavior that is expected of everyone within the subgroup. We will spend some time describing

The first thing to learn around here,   kid, is don't try to break any records.

Learning the norms on a new job is very important for success. *(By permission of the Penton Publishing Company.)*

the characteristics of norms as well as the important function they serve in group interaction.

Properties and characteristics

The first thing to do is to analyze our definition of norms in a little more detail. There are essentially three criteria that we use to judge whether a social expectation may be described as a norm. First, is it a clear statement or belief about what is appropriate? Second, is there some agreement among group members about this belief? And third, is the group aware of and able to actively acknowledge that the norm exists? If all three conditions are met, then we can call this expectation a norm.

There is a set of properties that accompanies norms. That is, there are certain characteristics that most norms have in common. First, they have an "ought-ness" about them. They are descriptions of how one "should" behave. Second, they are usually more obvious and recognized for issues or behaviors that are important to the group. Your group members may not care if your skirt is white or light blue but they do think it is important that a skirt, blouse, and jacket are worn each day. Third, norms are enforced by the group. This is important because many of the behaviors expected of you are monitored or enforced by the organization in the form of rules, procedures, and handbooks. For norms, it is the group members that must regulate the behavior. Fourth, there is variability in both the degree to which norms are shared and the degree to which behavior that deviates from the norm is acceptable.

An example might help. During college I worked in the summer for the department of motor vehicles in a big city. We painted the lines on the streets. There were a number of crews, and each crew consisted of three or four men. We came to work at 8:15 (punched a time clock) and left at 4:45. Like a good, eager new employee I was there the first day at 8:00 and I was ready to paint lines at 8:15. Well, it turned out we had to spend a little time loading up the truck, getting our work orders, changing our clothes, and generally fooling around until about 9:00 when it was appropriate for the trucks to leave the yard. Few left before. Once we were in the truck I was asked if I would like to stop and get some coffee. I declared, "No, I don't drink the stuff." We stopped anyway, at a local drug store, and by the time we actually started painting it was usually 10:00. Lunch (formally 30 minutes) usually lasted from 12:00 to 1:00, and we began to pick up our cones and clear the streets by 3:00 to 3:30. We were always back in the yard by 4:00. The next 45 minutes were spent "reporting," changing clothes, and cleaning up. My overall estimate was that on the average we worked about a 4-hour day.

One could cite numerous examples of social norms in this story. But let us take just two: the amount of time on the street painting lines and the time the crew left the yard. If members of the different crews were presented with a questionnaire (which they were sure would never be seen by management) and asked about what was appropriate, you might see something like what is presented in Figure 10-2.

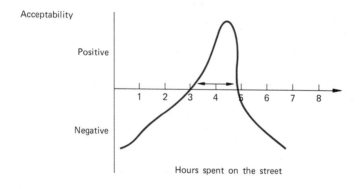

Hours spent on the street

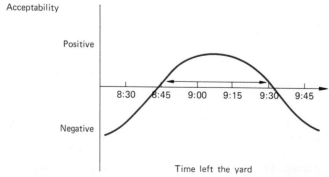

Time left the yard

Figure 10-2. A diagram of social norms.

A couple of points are worthy of note. First, there is variability about the most desirable behavior. While 4 hours' work and a 9:00 A.M. departure time are most desirable, other behaviors are still acceptable. You could be on the street anywhere from 3 to 4½ hours without much comment. You could also leave the yard 20 minutes early or late. Beyond these limits people began to talk to you about it; "Leaving a little early these days aren't you?" or "What's your big hurry to get out on the street?"

The second point is the relative importance of different norms as illustrated by the different heights of the curves. How many total hours were spent on the street was more important than when the truck left the yard. If you left early *and* came back early, it was usually all right. However, if you left early and came back late, you were in for social criticism: "Trying to make us look bad?" or "What did you do, paint all of the northeast part of the city?"

In summary, an analysis of this type of data can tell you (1) what is most appropriate, (2) what are the acceptable ranges, (3) how important is the issue, and (4) the amount of consensus among group members. In the following section we describe how these aspects of social norms are important for understanding what goes on in groups.

Norms and group behavior

Now that we understand what a norm is and its various characteristics, we can describe more specifically how they develop and operate in group situations. According to most researchers, norms develop in situations where group members either do not know what is expected or where some other competing expectation in the form of a rule or regulation might determine their behavior. The norm is able to provide both a structure about what to do, and the group can bring to bear enough pressure to enforce it.

Learning the norm. The process by which norms are developed and communicated includes three major steps. First, the norm must be defined and expressed. In other words, the focal person must either be told or must be able to unambiguously observe the behavior in question. Second, the group must be able to monitor the relevant behavior. We have to be able to tell whether the norm is being followed. And finally, the group must be able to reward the individual for conformity and punish for nonconformity. Reinforcement is a necessary element in the learning process.

Norms are, of course, sent in very different ways. Sometimes the group may be very explicit about it. As the picture shows, a new employee may be told not to break any records. But there are less direct ways to send norms. People use models and they learn by example. So, while your boss may not tell you that you are expected to work evenings and weekends, it may soon become clear that (1) everyone else does, (2) the amount of work you have is too much to do in 8 hours, and (3) your boss becomes angry when people miss deadlines. You learn the norm pretty quickly.

Norm enforcement. This brings us to the next issue which is the way in which norms are enforced. As mentioned earlier, reinforcement, both positive and negative, is the key. Groups have a variety of ways they can reward and punish their fellow members. First, they can praise you—tell you that you are doing a good job. Second, they can include you in various social activities and functions. Third, they can pass the word along to others about how well you're performing. Not only can group acceptance be a powerful personal reward, but it can also help with respect to areas such as who gets a bonus or who gets promoted.

However, in most cases, it is the negative rewards or sanctions that are frequently cited. Negative feedback can be expressed by a look, a snide comment, an angry denunciation, or even more physical ways. An individual can be ostracized or left alone by the group. A person can be made a social outcast. In some settings the individual may actually be subject to physical abuse (remember the Hawthorne studies where workers binged the rate-buster).

Research on the enforcement of group norms has mostly focused on the consequences of deviating from the group. The pressure to go along with the group is intense, and most people do (otherwise there wouldn't be the norm). But what about the individuals who do not go along? What happens to them?

The first thing that happens is that the group will try to convince the deviant of the error in behavior. They will try to change the person's opinion about the issue through increased communications. The interaction will be more frequent and more direct and more explicit as time goes on. The clearer the norm, the more important the norm, the more cohesive the group—the greater the pressure. Eventually the deviant must either change behavior or be rejected by the group.

If rejection occurs, a number of interesting things may take place. The deviant becomes isolated interpersonally from the other group members. However, since most group members are somewhat interdependent, the rest of the group may still need the deviant in order to successfully complete its task. Usually the individual is either replaced or some sort of agreed-upon truce develops where the deviant is tolerated but excluded from most group activity and interpersonal interactions. All that stops is the harassment.

Coch and French describe a classic examples of a new employee's reaction to group norms about productivity.[4] The woman was working as a presser during the 40 days following a change in jobs. Table 10-2 shows her productivity level over the 40-day period. For the first few days she approached and then passed the standard production output of about 50 units per hour (the norm). She then became a scapegoat and social pressure was brought to bear to make her slow down, which she did. However, after 20 days the rest of the group was split up, and the woman worked alone for the remaining 20 days. During this time her efficiency rating almost doubled. So, in this case, the norms were responsible for a substantial decrease in the amount of productivity that was possible.

Resistence to the norm. What prompts an individual to resist a group? It is important to understand why the employees subject themselves to this type of pressure and abuse. It seems so much easier to go along. One answer to this question comes from the fact that norms exist both inside and outside the organizational context. We have other groups we may belong to such as a church, a political party, or a country club. The norms of this outside group may

---

[4]L. Coch and J. R. P. French. Overcoming resistance to change. *Human Relations*, 1948, **1**, 512–532.

Table 10-2. The Focal Employee's Production Record

Days	Phase	Efficiency Rating
1–3	Starts work with the group	46
4–6		52
7–9		53
10–12		56
13–16	Scapegoating begins	55
17–20		48
21–24	Becomes a single worker	83
25–28		92
29–32		92
33–36		91
37–40		92

SOURCE: L. Coch & J. P. R. French. Overcoming resistance to change. *Human Relations*, 1948, **1**, 512–532.

conflict with the norms of the work group. An individual strongly identifying with this outside group will be better able to resist the work-group pressure.

These outside groups are typically described in the literature as *reference groups*. The important feature of a reference group is that it is a group whose norms and standards the individual accepts. It is these norms and standards to which the individual refers when in need of defining what type of behavior is appropriate. The distinction then is based upon our psychological and behavioral commitment to a group. Those groups whose norms we believe in and adhere to are called reference groups. Groups to which we belong where we are deviates or isolates are called *membership groups*. So, just as for roles, norms may be conflicting for the individual.

The general issue here is why we have regularity in group behavior. Why do most groups' members seem to behave in fairly similar and predictable ways? The research seems to suggest that norms are one method of reducing uncertainty. They provide social rules that help the individual adjust to and cope with a job. They make it easier to predict what people are going to do.

To some extent this is a good thing. If we can avoid norms designed to keep down production, and try to introduce norms that will increase morale and efficiency, people should generally feel more comfortable in a nonambiguous, clear situation. Chapter 8, "Group Dynamics," discussed a number of ways in which comformity can actually be increased through selection, reward administration, and task design. But the crucial issue is the content of these norms—the prevailing "climate" if you like. We will return to a discussion of organizational climates in Chapter 16, "Organizational Change."

Status

The social animal does not merely seek to dominate his fellows; he succeeds. And succeeding, he achieves a status in the eyes of the other. That status will be permanent; and oddly enough satisfying as a rule to all parties.

Robert Ardrey

The final facet of group structure which provides expectations about appropriate behavior is called *status*. This term usually reflects an individual's rank or worth within some group, organizational, or social setting. It is determined by the group itself. If a person has those attributes, characteristics, or possessions that are valued by the group, he or she will have high status. Those people without the attributes have low status.

Note some things about this definition. First, status is determined by the criteria set by a group. The characteristics are generally agreed upon by a group of people as being valued. Second, it is an aggregate or overall estimate of worth. Status typically includes more than just one dimension. Third, and most important, status serves as a device for ranking people, for putting them in some order to one another.

It is this latter point which needs major emphasis. Status helps us to know what behaviors are appropriate in our interactions with people at *different levels* within a hierarchical structure. It is easily observable that almost every social group or organization has some sort of informal or formal ordering of people. Once we discover this ordering we know to whom we must defer and who should in turn defer to us. It is a process of vertical differentiation. Just as roles differentiate jobs, status provides differentiations up and down the hierarchy. It is one more way to reduce ambiguity and clarify what is expected of us.

The characteristics of status

We mentioned that roles and norms could occur both inside and outside the organizational context. So can status. At perhaps the broadest level of analysis is what we call *social status*. This term describes our rank as determined by our society as a whole. Numerous variables would be used to determine this rank such as age, wisdom, wealth, family relationships, occupation, and personality. It is a composite of all those attributes valued by a society.

While differences exist as to how "class" is defined in the sociological literature, it often refers to this general social-status idea. It is a conglomerate of education, salary, occupation, and background. People in the "upper" class are expected to be higher on all these dimensions than people in the "lower" class. We find that very distinct differences in expected and actual behavior exist for these groups in areas such as child rearing, social relationships, and on-the-job behavior. There are also some informal rules about how people from one class should behave toward people from another class. In a fairly mobile society such as the United States where social-status levels can be changed relatively easily and are not so clearly recognized by attributes such as titles or dress, these rules are not too specific. However, in societies where social status is more obvious and clear, as in India, there are very specific behavioral expectations across status levels. This is true for many of the societies in Asia.

We are more interested in organizational issues, however, so we should look for the effect of status differences there. The major distinctions that are made are either between organizations or within organizations. The former is called *occupational prestige* while the latter is frequently labeled *organizational status*.

Occupational prestige differs somewhat from our definition of status because it is usually based on only one characteristic: an individual's occupation. However,

Table 10-3. Distributions of Prestige Ratings, United States, 1947 and 1963

Occupation	1947 Rank	1963 Rank
U.S. supreme court justice	1.0	1.0
Physician	2.5	2.0
Nuclear physicist	18.0	3.5
Scientist	8.0	3.5
Government scientist	10.5	5.5
State governor	2.5	5.5
Cabinet member in the federal government	4.5	8.0
College professor	8.0	8.0
U.S. representative in Congress	8.0	8.0
Chemist	18.0	11.0
Lawyer	18.0	11.0
Diplomat in the U.S. foreign service	4.5	11.0
Dentist	18.0	14.0
Architect	18.0	14.0
County judge	13.0	14.0
Psychologist	22.0	17.5
Minister	13.0	17.5
Member of the board of directors of a large corporation	18.0	17.5
Mayor of a large city	6.0	17.5
Priest	18.0	21.5
Head of a department in a state government	13.0	21.5
Civil engineer	23.0	21.5
Airline pilot	24.5	21.5
Banker	10.5	24.5
Biologist	29.0	24.5
Sociologist	26.5	26.0
Instructor in public schools	34.0	27.5
Captain in the regular army	31.5	27.5
Accountant for a large business	29.0	29.5
Public school teacher	36.0	29.5

this dimension is used as a very powerful determinant of differentiation and expected behavior. There is, for example, within the United States some agreement about what occupations are high in prestige and which ones are low. Table 10-3 provides a listing of the top thirty based on national samples taken in 1947 and 1963.

It is interesting to note that during this space-exploration era more value is placed on educationally and scientifically related occupations (such as scientist or physicist), while business- or government-related occupations (e.g., diplomat, governor, banker) have slipped somewhat. At the top, of course, are occupations such as Supreme Court Justice or physician. All you have to do is think about your interactions with physicians to realize the degree to which these status differences influence your behavior. Medical doctors are often reported to talk in "speeches." It is all formal, impersonal, aloof, and in many cases demeaning. The doctor is "expected to know," and the patient is "expected to listen." Interactions with senators and Supreme Court Justices can be similar in many respects. You are expected to address them by their title and be very deferential. You do not treat the local gas-station attendant like that.

Organizational status is the differentiation that occurs within an organization. It includes more characteristics than occupational prestige but fewer than social status. It is more than just one's position in the organization; it includes some personal attributes, tenure, and effectiveness judgments. In the university, for example, there may be five full professors in the physics department. They all have the same rank but not the same status. The professor who has outside grant support, gets excellent teaching ratings, and gets along well with the dean is more likely to have higher status than a professor who is lacking these characteristics. As we shall discuss, these differences in status have important implications for a number of aspects of group interaction and organizational effectiveness.

But let us summarize. Status refers to one's rank as determined by a group. One has a status level in every organizational setting. This status helps to clarify how one should behave toward others and what they should expect in return. It is based on the attainment of socially valued attributes such as birth, personality, achievements, possessions, or authority. People defer to people with higher status because they respect them, fear them, idolize them, want favors from them, or want to be like them. Whatever the reason, it helps to structure interpersonal interactions.

A couple of inferences can be made. First, status can be attained many different ways. Distinctions are made between the status you are born with (your family name and possessions) and the status you achieve on your own (your education or job success), and between the status that comes along with your job (e.g., supervisor or vice-president) and the status accorded you because of your personal qualities (e.g., pleasant, friendly, aggressive). So, many characteristics contribute to status. Second, status can be quite different for the same individual

The judge's robe and elevated seat suggest status differences. (*By permission of University of Washington* Daily.)

across groups or organizational settings. This distinction is described as *active* versus *latent* status. A janitor (low status) may be the deacon of a church (high status). When on the job the person's low status is active and the high status is latent. The reverse is true at church. The next section explores how these status differences are important for group interaction.

Status and group process

Within the group setting, status is both quickly and easily recognized. A number of research studies show that people can quickly identify status differences within groups. Some studies have used films, others have used photographs or actual observations of group interactions. Even with very short exposure times, people are able to reliably identify status differences.

How do they do it? Well, all the topics discussed in Chapter 9, "Communication," about verbal and nonverbal messages (independent of the content of some statement) offer possible explanations. One's air, composure, dress, and style convey status.

Status symbols. But there is also a class of readily observable, more formal things which we refer to as status symbols. Certain objects of apparel imply positions, such as a judge's robe, a nun's habit, a doctor's white coat, or a monarch's crown. Some organizations such as the military have formal identification patches as visible marks of status.

There are titles such as doctor, senator, professor, captain, and vice-president. These are very formal and usually easily ascertained. We should note, however, that both dress and title can be absent in some situation that is separate from the organization in which the symbol is used. At that point we must refer to more subtle cues.

In many cases, physical possessions convey status—the type of car we drive, the quality of our clothes, our house, or our attaché case. In a large business organization one looks for the size of the office, the view, the rug on the floor, and the name on the door. At the university a student may look for glasses without rims, a sorority pin, a calculator hanging from the belt, or ski-lift tickets punched onto one's coat. Status is usually easy to recognize and quickly conveyed. As such it greatly influences the behavior of group members.

Status and group interaction. In the research on status differences, a number of results consistently appear. People with higher status tend to initiate more interaction. They start the conversation or the exchange. These same people will frequently make policy statements or generalizations without providing data or information to back them up. They usually talk more, represent "the group" in many situations, and have the greatest number of connections within the group. They have more influence and power. One can see that numerous aspects of the group interaction are influenced by status.

However, the major problem with this line of research is inherent in the definition of status itself. Because status is composed of a number of dimensions, it is often difficult to determine what actually *causes* these differences in

Being a doctor is really a trip. Around home, I'm all thumbs and constantly in the way—but I come to work, put on this white coat and name tag, and God I'm it.

We often defer to people who have high-status jobs as illustrated by their dress or title.

behavior. Is it the position, the personality, or the expertise of the person? Also, the behaviors that are examined reflect more than just power or influence. They are broader in nature; they reflect a general disposition of deference. So, we know that status has an impact on a wide variety of activities, but it is hard to identify exactly what aspects of status are related to specific behaviors. Two other areas of status research have not been quite so restricted by this problem.

Status change. Throughout our lives we may change our status numerous times: we get a college degree, or we get a promotion, or we win some award, or we retire. This type of change can cause a number of serious problems. A person is expected to behave in new ways; there are new things to learn. The old norms and reference group are left behind. We are faced with a new, ambiguous stituation.

In many societies major changes in status (e.g., puberty, marriage) are accompanied by rites or religious ceremonies. These activities serve to mark the event and also to provide some information about the expected behavior in the new position. These rites are meant to make the status transition easier and to clarify expectations.

Similar sorts of procedures are often found in large organizations or occupations. There are certain expected career steps and a general timetable for taking these steps. In many cases the change is highlighted by some sort of training, recognition, raise in salary, and change in physical location. As one would expect, the more clearly defined the transition is, the easier it is to make.

Situations that do not have explicit passage events are often anxiety-producing. For example, in graduate school students are often treated as students yet told they are colleagues. When do they become professionals? Is it after their "general" exam or after they get their Ph.D? Since many students take their first job before they finish their Ph.D., they are often filling an assistant-professor position before they are "officially" in the club. Their colleagues and students at the new job may treat them appropriately, but every time they return to work on their Ph.D., the relationships are unclear. For these reasons, many academics report that getting their Ph.D. was anticlimactic and that the transition was difficult to make.

The implication of all this research is that there are ways to reduce the stress of status passage. Previews of what is to come, training in new skills, and ceremonies to mark the occasion all help the transition. They reduce uncertainty and ease adjustment.

Status incongruence

> Nothing is more annoying than a low man
> raised to a high position.   Claudian

The other area of research deals with what is called *status incongruence*. This state exists when someone seems to be high on a few valued dimensions but low on others or where one's characteristics seem inappropriate for the particular position the person is in. One of the best illustrations is the college student who works as a laborer during the summer. Most of the student's fellow employees will be older and have more experience but less formal education. In some cases this can be a very uncomfortable situation for the college student. Unless able to play down the educational attributes, the student is likely to be labeled a smart guy or the "college kid." It will be difficult to gain full acceptance.

This type of problem often occurs with respect to decisions about selection, placement, and promotions in organizations. If almost everyone in a particular management area has a certain degree (e.g., M.B.A.), could you hire someone to be the department head who only had a B.A.? What kinds of problems would it create?

The research on the issue relies heavily on equity theory and balance theory to explain what happens. People feel first of all that it's not fair somehow that someone should have a high-status position if they don't have all the other qualifications. It's not equitable. A second explanation is that somehow status incongruence is like cognitive-balance theory: When there are incongruent characteristics for an individual it creates psychological tension, and this state is unpleasant and dissatisfying.

All of this suggests that status incongruence is uncomfortable and may lead to motivational and behavioral problems. However, the solution to the problem suggests either that we (1) only select or promote those people whose characteristics are all congruent with the job or (2) change the group's values about what leads to high status. The first solution is not acceptable to many people because it would seriously limit mobility, while the second solution is hard to accomplish. It is not easy to change people's values. Probably the best we can do is make people aware of when they are entering incongrous situations and the types of problems they are likely to face.

Summary

There are a number of specific points which are probably worth repeating, and they are listed below:

1 Roles deal specifically with the appropriate behavior for a particular job. They are behavioral job descriptions.
2 Roles suffer from incidents of conflict, ambiguity, and overload. All three problems are related to negative organizational outcomes.
3 Norms serve as general behavioral expectations for all group members. There are both pressure and sanctions to enforce the norm.
4 Violation of norms can lead to breakdowns in communication and isolated group members.
5 Status refers to an individual's rank based upon these attributes valued by the group. It is concerned with clarifying vertical relationships.
6 Status is quickly and easily recognized. There are many cues and symbols.
7 Status change and incongruence can cause uncertainty and ambiguity. Low morale, high tension, and high anxiety may be the result.

But besides these particular points there are some common themes that should be emphasized. Roles, norms, and status all share some similar characteristics. First, and probably most important, they all serve to reduce ambiguity in social settings. In general, people like to live in a fairly predictable world, and we have developed social mechanisms that help us to do that. Roles, norms, and status are useful both for learning (e.g., contingencies and expectations are clear) and for reducing uncertainty and ambiguity, which results in lower tension and anxiety.

Another common element about roles, norms, and status is that they are all *socially* determined. It is group consensus or agreement that characterizes all three concepts. The implication of this similarity is that it again shows the impact of external sources on an individual's behavior. What we often define as a person problem may be a group problem.

The final theme is one that suggests the generality of the role, norm, and status concepts. Throughout the chapter we mentioned that all three concepts were not limited to one's particular job. They exist in our social groups, our family, our church, recreational groups, and political groups. Almost every organizational context can be viewed in terms of roles, norms, and status.

Implications for practice

There are really two main implications for organizational practice. First, understanding these concepts provides us with an excellent way to analyze group process and interaction. A description of particular group roles, norms, and status differences can be a helpful diagnostic device. If we can begin to see problems in terms of their social or interpersonal causes, it should help us to have more effective organizations.

The second implication is partly dependent upon the first. Once we understand that much of a group's activity is spent clarifying roles, norms, and status, we can begin to devise organizationally sponsored mechanisms that will facilitate the process. Various types of structured changes can be made that will clarify roles, norms, and status. Job previews and simulations can help relieve the pressure and anxiety of role or status change. Training programs can be devised to both mark the event of change and clarify future expectations. Selection systems can be developed which can provide a better match between an individual's personal characteristics and the amount of ambiguity on the job. Part 5 of this book deals with these techniques in more detail.

Discussion questions

1 Describe your first time in a college class. How did you learn what was expected of you? Did roles, norms, and status differences influence your behavior?
2 Describe the various types of role conflict and ambiguity that can occur. How do these factors help or hinder effectiveness?
3 What people do you think have high status? What attributes or characteristics do you use to make these judgments?

Case: From the diaries and letters of President Truman*

April 13, 1945: Signed Proclamation for President Roosevelt's funeral and holiday. First official act.

Lunch with the Senate and House Leaders. Saw *all* the Senators.

Most overcome by treatment.

Feb. 15, 1950: To the Attorney Generals' Conference on Law Enforcement: "This postwar increase in crime has been accompanied by a resurgence of underworld forces—forces which thrive on vice and greed. This is a problem that in one degree or another affects every community in the country."

June 13, 1945: Had breakfast with Hopkins, Davies and Leahy to discuss the Russian-British-Polish situation. Propaganda seems to be our greatest foreign relations enemy. Russians distribute lies about us.

Aug. 28, 1951: A letter to a former state senator from Missouri: "Dear George: I have just received two booklets called 'Old Trails Area of Missouri' and 'Old Settlement Playgrounds of Missouri.' They are excellent and I hope you will keep published booklets such as these. I am very glad to see Missourians let the world know what a grand old state it really is."

*Hillman, W. *Mr. President,* New York: Farrar, Straus and Young, 1952.

Aug. 10, 1945:   Had a Cabinet meeting after lunch, which was a very satisfactory one. Getting a team together. Took them into my confidence and told them all about the Japanese situation. They kept the confidence—an unprecedented thing in the immediate past.

Feb. 2, 1948:   I am sending the Congress a Civil Rights message. They, no doubt, will receive it as coldly as they did the State of the Union Message. But it needs to be said.

Sept. 17, 1951:   *To the National Association of Postmasters:* "It seems to be open season, these days, on government employees. There are a lot of people who are trying to make political capital by slurring the loyalty and efficiency of government employees, and trying to bring the public service into disrepute. I think that is a contemptible way to try to get votes. We have the greatest government in the world, and the most loyal and efficient government servants. I am *proud* to be a part of it. I think you are proud to be a part of it too."

Aug. 5, 1945:   Had lunch with Britain's King George VI. He is a very pleasant and surprising person. He showed me a sword which had been presented to Sir Francis Drake by Queen Elizabeth. It was a powerful weapon but the King said it was not properly balanced. We had a nice and appetizing lunch—soup, fish, lamb chops, peas, potatoes and ice cream with chocolate sauce. The King, myself, Lord Halifax, a British Admiral, Admiral Leahy, Lascelles, the Secretary of State in that order around the table.

1946:   The desk at which I sit has been the President's desk since the time of Theodore Roosevelt. Every President since has used it and I shall continue to use it.

1948:   The President of the United States has to be very careful not to be emotional or to forget that he is working for one hundred and forty-five millions of people primarily, and for peace in the world as his next objective.

1949:   I am not and never have been in favor of absentee Landlordism in our farm program. One of the difficulties with which we are faced in this machine age is to keep the farms in the hands of owners and occupiers of the land.

Questions about these quotes

1 Try to list all the *different* types of problems with which the President was concerned.
2 To what extent is the job of President essentially defined by outside expectations, pressures, and traditions?
3 Are many of the problems of Truman's time still problems today?
4 To what extent do you think people defer to the President because of who he is or because of the position he holds?

Additional readings

Bales, R. F. *Interaction process analysis, A method for the study of groups.* Reading, Mass.: Addison-Wesley, 1950.

** Bendix, R., & Lipset, S. (Eds.). *Class, status and power.* New York: Free Press, 1966.

* Berger, J., Cohen, B. P., & Zelditch, M., Jr. Status characteristics and social interaction. *American Sociological Review,* 1972, **37,** 241–255.

** Biddle, B. J., & Thomas, E. J. (Eds.). *Role theory: Concepts and research.* New York: Wiley, 1966.

* Bonham, T. W. The foreman in an ambiguous environment. *Personnel Journal,* 1971, 841–845.

** Graen, G. Role-making processes within complex organizations. In M. D. Dunnette (Ed.), *Handbook of industrial and organizational psychology.* Chicago: Rand McNally, 1976, 1201–1246.

* Feshbach, N. D. Nonconformity to experimentally induced group norms of high-status versus low-status members. *Journal of Personality and Social Psychology,* 1967, **6,** 55–63.

* Gouldner, A. W. The norm of reciprocity: A preliminary statement. *American Sociological Review,* 1960, **25,** 161–178.

Hare, A. P. *Handbook of small group research.* New York: Free Press, 1962.

** Katz, D., & Kahn, R. L. *The social psychology of organizations.* New York: Wiley, 1966.

Linton, R. *The cultural background of personality.* New York: Appleton-Century-Crofts, 1945.

* Sales, S. M. Organizational role as a risk factor in coronary disease. *Administrative Science Quarterly,* 1969, **14,** 325–336.

* Sussman, G. I. The concept of status congruence as a basis to predict task allocation in autonomous work groups. *Administrative Science Quarterly,* 1970, **15,** 164–175.

*Possible reading for students

**Review of literature or comprehensive source material

FOUR
ACCOMPLISHING ORGANIZATIONAL OBJECTIVES

Much of what we do in organizations involves getting things done. In order to accomplish our goals and objectives, various means or steps to the goal must be completed. But the particular way in which we do things is dependent on both (1) the goals we choose to set and the means we choose to use (decision making) and (2) the extent to which we can get others to join cooperatively in this effort (power and control) and the manner in which we carry out these demands (leadership). Part 4 deals with these topics.

Decision making is the subject of Chapter 11. We discuss how people perceive a problem, evaluate information, generate alternative solutions, and finally make a decision. The type of decision strategy used seems to depend on the type of problem and the circumstances surrounding the choice. We then turn to a discussion of how decisions are made in groups. A central question that is evaluated is the degree to which joint or participative decision making should be employed in organizations.

The thrust of Chapter 12 is how to get people to do things they do not want to do. By definition, we relinquish some freedom just by joining an organization. Implicit in the agreement is that we will be asked to do things some of which may be unpleasant. Social power is seen in this context as the pressure that individual A can bring to bear on individual B to get B to do something he or she would not ordinarily do. Control, on the other hand, focuses on the social and institutional mechanisms that get people to behave in the appropriate manner. The actual techniques used to exert power and control in organizations are discussed and evaluated.

Leadership is discussed in Chapter 13. We review the literature on how people gain leadership positions and how they can be effective in those positions. Early approaches to the effectiveness question suggested that personality traits were the answer. All we had to do was find out what personal traits great lead-

ers had in common and then select those sorts of people for our leadership positions. Unfortunately, this explanation was too simplistic. Different situations demand different types of people and behavior.

The last half of the chapter reviews a couple of contingency models of leadership. These models attempt to specify what sort of person is likely to be a good leader in a specific situation. Included here is a discussion of what happens when the situation changes. More specifically, if we originally choose the right type of person for a particular situation, what can we do if this situation changes? The answer to this question has important implications for personnel policies of selection, placement, and promotion.

To summarize, Part 4 discusses how people in organizations get things done. Someone has to decide what needs to be done. Ideally, we would all comply— however, that is not usually the case. Power, control, and effective leadership are all processes that help to direct and focus our behavior on those activities deemed to be important.

11
Decision making

Most of our waking hours are spent making decisions: Should we go to work? What should we wear? What do we want to eat? and so on. We are constantly choosing courses of action to guide our behavior. It is a central part of human existence.

Decision making in organizations is central to the effectiveness of any group or institution. It is often seen as the heart of administrative action! Some authors have even based their entire approach to management on an analysis of how and where decisions are made.

Because of the breadth of behavior described by the term *decision making,* we must try to limit and clarify our focus for this particular chapter. Our concern will be decision making in the organizational context. It encompasses the process that leads up to and includes the choice of a course of action from among two or more alternatives. These courses of action are seen as organizationally relevant. That is, they are actions that are meant to help achieve organizational goals. Thus, organizational decision making is the process of choosing actions that are directed toward the resolution of organizational problems.

Finally, this process can be carried out by individuals acting alone or by groups. This distinction is an important one. The processes involved and the decision-making theories and models that have been developed are different for individual and group decisions. The rest of the chapter will describe these processes, theories, and models with an emphasis on how the decision-making process can increase organizational effectiveness.

The decision-making process

As we mentioned before, decision making is more than just making a choice. It is also the actions and activities that precede the choice. It is a process—a series of

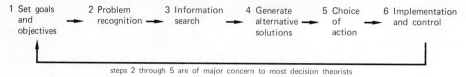

steps 2 through 5 are of major concern to most decision theorists

Figure 11-1. The decision-making process.

distinct steps that lead up to and beyond the actual choice. Figure 11-1 presents a diagram of the process.

Decision phases

Every organization has some *goals* and *objectives*. It is part of the reason for organizing in the first place. These goals and objectives tell us where we are going and why. They are a general blueprint for organizational design and action and they form the first phase in the decision process.

In many cases, however, our goals and objectives are not realized. Individuals, subgroups, units, and whole organizations often fall short of their targets. It is this discrepancy between what is observed and what is expected that provides the bases for the *problem-recognition* stage of decision making. Somehow things are not as they should be, and the person in charge must find out why and resolve the problem.

Problem recognition really involves two things. First, the manager or decision maker must be scanning and keeping track of what is going on. He or she must be alert to recognize discrepancies when they exist. Second, the decision makers have to be able to evaluate the discrepancy. Only if the problem is deemed to be an important one will the next phase of the process be included.

If the problem is serious, then the decision maker must try to find out why the problem occurred. This is described as the *information-search* phase. The decision maker must gather information about both the causes of the problem and some possible ways to proceed to solve the problem. Past records can be used, interviews may be held, and opinions can be solicited. This phase takes time and ingenuity. It is often the phase that is handled least well.

Once the information is gathered, it must be integrated, and alternative choices or courses of action can be explored. Typically, a large set of alternatives is narrowed down to a smaller set. This stage is known as the alternative-generation phase. To generate plausible solutions requires experience, creativity, and the ability to integrate complex information and make judgments about the future. It is very demanding intellectually.

Finally, there is the evaluation of alternatives—the *choice* phase. At this point the possible courses of action are have been presented. They must be compared to one another, and some decision about what is best must be made. In most cases, there are good and bad points about any alternative, and one must weigh these aspects carefully. There is uncertainty and ambiguity about the consequence of most actions. Values enter the picture in terms of what are judged as good or bad aspects of each alternative. But a decision must be made, and it usually is. Somehow, one alternative is selected.

The last part of the process involves the *implementation and evaluation* of the decision. Did the discrepancy between expectation and observation disappear? Did we solve the problem? If not, it is back to the drawing board. We cycle back to phase 2 and try again.

As indicated in Figure 11-1, the goals and objectives phase and the implementation and control phase are not frequently studied by theorists interested in the decision process. We will, therefore, discuss these topics separately in Chapter 12, "Power and Control." Most writers tend to focus on stages 2 through 5—how we recognize a problem and act to correct it. And in fact, most of the studies on these four phases seem to center on stages 4 and 5—how we integrate information, evaluate alternatives, and finally make a choice. While problem identification and information search are important, they are less frequently studied. Our review of the literature below will reflect this uneven distribution of effort.

A decision example

You are the personnel manager for a small hospital in the Southwest. You are in charge of all personnel activities, such as training, selection, placement, performance appraisal, handling grievances, and public relations. Over the last year it has come to your attention that there is some sort of problem in the pharmacy. There is a head pharmacist and two other employees in charge of filling prescriptions. A number of patients have complained about the long waits to get their drugs, and the employees themselves have griped about being overworked. You note that the absenteeism in that group has been higher than expected lately. You also find out from one of your colleagues in accounting that the 20 percent projected increase in prescription drug sales for the year has not materialized. The demand should be there; the number of patients has increased, as has the number of prescriptions given by the physicians. Somewhere, something is wrong.

So you attempt to find out the cause of the problem. You interview some patients as well as the employees. You look at the past sales records. A number of causes are possible. Your people could be poorly trained or lazy. Perhaps new federal regulations which have increased the paperwork and record-keeping responsibilities of these people is taking up their time. Perhaps certain crucial ingredients are in short supply or prescriptions are becoming more complex to make up.

After searching around for all this information, it becomes fairly obvious that the cause of the problem is that the staff is overworked. The employees are well qualified. However, due to the complexity of their job and increased demand, they need more help; an additional person is needed. You put an advertisement in the newspaper requesting applicants for the job.

In 2 weeks you have four people who want the job. You have five alternatives: hire one of the four people or hire no one. Each person is a complex aggregate of skills, training, experience, and personal characteristics. After a while the choice is narrowed down to two people. Both have excellent training. One of the persons seems more friendly, more outgoing, and it is your estimate that this characteristic will help in the group as well as with public relations. The other person, however, has more experience, having worked at another pharmacy for 5 years. This experience should help in dealing with the pressures of the job and with difficult problems that might arise.

Finally, you decide on the person with more experience. You inform both candidates of your decision, and the hired employee starts to work the following month. After a 6-month period you note that sales are up, complaints are down, and absenteeism has decreased. You recognized the problem, discovered its cause, evaluated some alternatives, and made a choice which you followed up. It looks as if you made a good decision.

Individual decision making

We mentioned at the start of the chapter that the distinction between individual and group decision making is an important one. Figure 11-2 describes some different types of settings in which decisions can be made. At the one end of the continuum we have the situation where the individual works alone. The decision maker works independently of others. He or she discovers the problem, gets information, evaluates alternatives, and makes a choice. Other people may be involved in that they provide solicited information, but the decision maker is essentially alone. Our pharmacy example illustrates this cycle. On the other extreme is the situation where a group such as a committee discusses a problem, evaluates some alternative actions, and makes a choice based upon some sort of group-decision rule (e.g., majority rule, consensus). In consensus, the group as a whole makes the choice.

Over the years, these two types of decision processes have often been researched separately; some writers have been concerned with individual decisions and others have focused on groups. Different theories and models have been developed for both types of decisions. We will first discuss individual decision making and then turn our attention to decisions made in groups.

Beliefs and values

Probabilities direct the conduct of the wise man.   Cicero

The basic concepts that form the cornerstone of most decision making are *beliefs* and *values*. Any item of information that is gathered is evaluated in light of two criteria: Is it true? Is it important? The truth of the statement typically is probabilistic—that is, we have more or less confidence in its truth. This estimate of truth is described as our strength of *belief*. But given a whole set of beliefs or items of information, we find that some are more relevant than others and some are more important than others. These are questions of *value*.

Let us return to our example in the hospital pharmacy. First our decision maker had to evaluate a number of possible causes of the problem at hand. Numerous alternatives (beliefs) were suggested (e.g., employees were over-

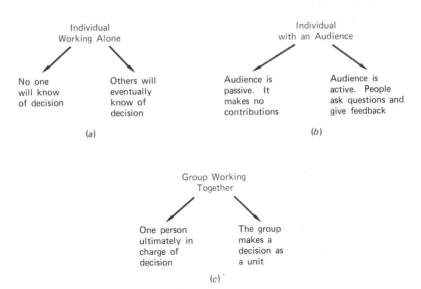

Figure 11-2. Decisions made by (*a*) an individual working alone, (*b*) an individual with an audience, and (*c*) a group working together.

worked, lazy, poorly trained), but the one deemed to be *most probable* was the overwork hypothesis. The remedy to the problem was to hire someone else.

The decision problem focused on the choice of this new employee. Each person had a number of attributes such as experience, training, and personal traits. Each attribute-person combination served as a belief for the decision maker. For example, "Person A is well trained" indicates a belief about person A. Somehow all these beliefs had to be combined to gain an overall impression of each person.

Two factors in this combination process are important to mention. First, the decision maker will be more or less certain about various attributes. That is, the degree of confidence in each belief will vary. For example, one may feel absolutely certain that person A has had 4 years' experience but be only moderately confident in the belief that person A is rather shy and withdrawn.

The second point is that these beliefs will vary in their importance. Perhaps the past history of this manager has suggested that experience is a more important determinant of good performance than the employee's personality. In this sense, experience is a more *valuable* characteristic than a pleasant personality (which is possessed by candidate B). Both the beliefs and their values were important for making the final choice.

The research on individual decision making has focused on two major questions: (1) How do people actually form and combine their beliefs and values? and (2) How should they combine them? The first question is a *descriptive* one. It attempts to find out what people *actually do*. The second question is *normative* in nature. It seeks to show how people *should* make decisions. Both descriptive and normative models exist for the generation and evaluation phase of decision making as well as the choice phase. We will briefly review the most important of these models.

Processing models

After we have searched for information, we begin the process of generating and evaluating alternatives. This activity requires us to integrate and combine many of our beliefs and our values. Decision theorists have developed a number of models to describe and help us be more effective in this information-processing activity.

Say, for example, that a small Midwestern college has recently decided to include a master's of business administration (M.B.A.) program in its curriculum. The admissions office is swamped with applications. Fifty people want to get in, and there are only twenty positions. Each applicant has a large amount of information in his or her folder, but the three most important items are (1) college grade point average (GPA), (2) the score on the business entrance examination (BE), and (3) a rating of the excellence of the applicant's undergraduate institution (UI).

Somehow the admissions officer must combine this information, rank-order the candidates, and then choose the top twenty. From a descriptive point of view we want to know how it is actually done. From a normative point of view we want to know how it ought to be done.

We can gather much of the descriptive information by watching what choices are made by the decision maker. After twenty people are ranked and then selected, we can examine the dossiers of the chosen and compare them to those that were not chosen. Various mathematical procedures can provide us with what is called the decision maker's "policy." This policy reflects the underlying rules of combination of information that were used.

Perhaps in looking over the decisions made we find that *everyone* chosen had a high score on the business entrance exam, while those not chosen had a low score. *Almost all* the people chosen had high GPAs in college and almost all of those rejected had low GPAs. *Most* of those chosen went to an excellent undergraduate institution, while most of those rejected did not. These decisions suggest that the admissions officer weighed the BE score most heavily, the GPA score next, the UI last. The mathematical models available can provide actual numerical weights that reflect the magnitude of importance of each of these factors. One might find, for example, that the BE was twice as important as GPA, which was in turn twice as important as the UI. This policy might best be represented by the formula

$$PS = 4BE + 2GPA + UI$$

where PS = predicted success.

This information is descriptive in that it tells us how the admissions officer made the decisions. It is often very useful for feedback purposes. People are often unaware of how they weigh information, and these procedures provide them with a mathematical model that reflects their decision process. They can then formalize the procedure by just using the model instead of agonizing over each dossier. Or they can systematically change their decision procedure so that some new set of weights is used which they feel is more appropriate.

But often the decision maker wants more than just descriptive information. He or she may want to know how to make better decisions. The question of concern is how the three predictors (the BE, GPA, and UI) *should* be combined to get the *best* twenty students. Fortunately, models exist to do this as well.

Let us say that the school admitted twenty students because they knew that some would fail or drop out for various reasons. After two quarters in the M.B.A. program, each of the twenty students has a GPA which reflects how well he or she is doing. These scores can then be mathematically compared to the scores on the three predictors, and a model can be generated which indicates how the three predictors ought to be weighed. Perhaps college GPA turns out to be the best predictor followed by the BE and UI. The formula would be

$$GPA_m = 4GPA_c + 2BE + UI$$

where GPA_m reflects the grades in the master's program and GPA_c is for the college GPA.

If the admissions officer feels that the GPA from two quarters in the M.B.A. program is a good criterion of excellence, then this new policy model can be used to select the next class of incoming students.

Use of processing models. The types of models described above are being used with increasing frequency in organizations. The research conducted has included studies of people engaged in admissions tasks such as the one above and studies of investment counselors, bank loan officers, physicians making diagnoses, clinical psychologists, court judges setting bail, personnel staff in charge of selection and promotion, and many others. The characteristics of the task are very much the same: some stimulus (e.g., a person or a stock) has some characteristics (e.g., grades, symptoms, growth potential), and these characteristics must be combined to form an overall evaluation. This evaluation is then compared to simular stimulus objects, and some sort of rank order of alternatives is generated.[1]

The descriptive or normative policies that are used can be helpful in a number of ways. They can tell us how we actually combine information and how we should combine it. The research has also pointed out some limitations in both the models and in humans. These limitations are briefly discussed below.

Criticisms of models. One major controversy which is still to be resolved concerns the basic psychological processes that people seem to use. Some researchers argue that a weighed sum is the best representation while others argue that a weighed average is more accurate. Do we add or average information is the question, and there is support for both sides of the issue.[2] So, while the models do indicate that people can and do combine complex information to make overall assessments, just exactly how they do it is as of yet unknown.

[1]For a review see R. J. Ebert & T. R. Mitchell. *Organizational decision processes*. New York: Crane, Russak, 1975, pp. 99–132.

[2]See N. H. Anderson. Functional measurement and psychophysical theory. *Psychological Review*, 1970, **77**, 153–170. Also see R. Slovic & S. Lichtenstein. Comparison of Bayesian and regression approaches to the study of human judgment. *Organizational Behavior and Human Performance*, 1971, **6**, 649–744.

A second problem is that the models always fall short of either exact description or exact prediction. No matter how sophisticated the model, it never completely describes what the decision maker has done or should do. This is partly because humans are not computers—they make mistakes, change their mind, get tired, and forget things. But it also has to do with the mathematical characteristics of the models themselves. If it is possible to exactly describe what the decision maker does, we have not figured out how.

Finally, most models are static. That is, they represent a decision maker's policy for only one specific time. As we all know, people and situations change over time. Perhaps a new entrance exam for business students is developed, or perhaps everyone's college GPA rises so high (due to a general easing up on the part of the professors) that the GPA is no longer an effective predictor. The old model is obsolete. A new model is needed. This problem has prompted some attempt to model *revisions* of evaluations, and a whole body of literature is now developing on that topic.[3]

Criticisms of people. The shortcomings of the models are important, but so are the contributions that the models have made to our understanding of human information processing. Perhaps the most important findings have been the sources of human error. There are some ways in which people are just poor judges, and the models have helped us to identify these areas.

First, people are inconsistent. While the policy generated from the mathematical formula may generally represent the overall process by which information is combined, it does not represent any specific instance very well. People change around their weights and are influenced by extraneous factors. Second, people use irrelevant information. A number of studies have shown, for example, that evaluations are higher if the applicants (e.g., for a loan or promotion) have similar attitudes to the decision maker. Third, human policies are hard to change. People get set in their ways and tend to modify their weights less than new information would suggest. And finally, people are not unlimited information processers. They tend to use only a few cues or factors to make their judgments. Complex information is handled poorly, and the greater the distractions or time pressures, the simpler the policy that is used.[4]

What this suggests is that, in spite of their faults, the models can be helpful. They can provide an excellent feedback mechanism and they can increase fairness and consistency. More complex information can be handled. Decision makers who have been trained in the use of such techniques can use the models as helpful tools to increase the effectiveness of their decisions.

Choice models

Other decision models have focused on the end point of the decision process: the actual choice between alternatives. The early literature on decision theory

[3]B. H. Beach. Expert judgment about uncertainty: Bayesian decision making in realistic settings. *Organizational Behavior and Human Performance,* 1975, **14,** 10–59.

[4]P. Wright. The harassed decision maker: Time pressures, distractions and the use of evidence. *Journal of Applied Psychology,* 1974, **59,** 555–561.

focused almost exclusively on this issue. The questions again were both descriptive and normative in nature: How is the choice made? and How should it be made?

One normative model that served as the foundation for much of the work that followed was called the *expected-value model*. It is one of the most pervasive theoretical explanations of human behavior available today. It appears in one form or another in our discussions of attitudes, motivation, social power, and decision making. The basic idea is simple. The model suggests that people in a choice situation will select the alternative that promises to bring the highest

If you give up Cigarettes, you might gain a few pounds.

(And also a few years.)

The plain, unfiltered fact is that people who smoke cigarettes get lung cancer a lot more frequently than nonsmokers.

And lung cancer can finish you. Before your time.

We'd rather have you stay alive and in good health. Because even if you do gain a few pounds, you'll have the time to take them off.

American Cancer Society

We make decisions mainly as a function of what we believe to be the likely consequences. *(By permission of the American Cancer Society.)*

payoff (or highest expected value.) This expected value is determined by two factors: (1) the probability that a particular action will lead to various outcomes and (2) the value or importance of the outcomes. We are predicted to choose the alternative which is most likely to lead to outcomes we value or desire.

Notice that these two components are a direct representation of beliefs and values. The probabilities reflect our belief about the action-outcome relationship (does action X really lead to outcome Y), and the values reflect our evaluations of the outcomes. These two components are said to combine in the following way.

$$EV = \sum_{i=1}^{N} \psi_i V_i$$

where EV is the expected value of a specific alternative, ψ is the probability that a particular outcome will occur, V is the value of the particular outcome, and N is the number of outcomes. You multiply the probability times the value for each outcome and sum up the products. This overall EV is then compared to the EV for other alternatives, and the model predicts that the one with the highest EV will be chosen.

Suppose, for example, that you have to decide whether to insure your company car against theft. You are told by your insurance agent that an automobile policy is available which will pay you 75 percent of the value of your $4000 car if it is stolen. The cost of the insurance is only $25 a year. However, you know the chances are only about one in a hundred that someone will steal your car. Should you buy the insurance? The payoff matrix is presented below:

	Stolen	Not stolen
Buy	−1025	−25
Do not buy	−4000	0

If the car is stolen and you have the insurance, you lose $4000 plus your $25 premium, but you are paid $3000 by the insurance company (a net loss of $1025). If you buy the insurance and nothing happens, you have lost $25. If you do not buy the insurance and the car is stolen, you lose $4000. And, of course, if you do not buy it and nothing happens, you neither gain nor lose. These figures represent the values of the four possible outcomes.

The choice of the two alternatives is obviously dependent upon the chance that the car will be stolen. If it is very likely to be stolen, you should buy the insurance; if it is unlikely, you might not. But we already know these probabilities, so we can use them in our equation to determine the proper choice.

$$EV_{buy} = (\psi_1)(V_1) + (\psi_2)(V_2)$$
$$= (.01)(-1025) + (.99)(-25)$$
$$= -\$35.00$$
$$EV_{do\ not\ buy} = (\psi_1)(V_1) + (\psi_2)(V_2)$$
$$= (.01)(-4000) + (.99)(0)$$
$$= -\$40.00$$

In this particular case you should buy the insurance. Your expected loss is less if you purchase than if you do not.

Note that from a normative point of view this model tells you how you ought to behave in the *long run*. Thus, over a period of years (which may be occasioned by the pilfering of your automobile), you would be wise to buy the insurance. You will come out ahead.

From a descriptive point of view the model is fairly demanding. It suggests that people have certain information about actual probabilities and values and that they combine them in particular ways (multiplying and then adding.) There is also an assumption that people will choose to maximize their gains or payoff. Just as for the information-processing models, the expected-value model in its original form proved inadequate as an exact explanation of how we make decisions but useful in understanding more about the decision process.

Criticisms of expected value. One of the most critical problems with the expected-value model was its use of objective probabilities and values. The decision maker had to know what the probabilities were and be able to place some objective monetary value on the outcomes. This requirement proved to be too demanding and not very realistic.

Research tended to indicate that subjective estimates of probability and subjective feelings of value (called *utility*) could replace the objective measures. In fact, in many cases, the subjective measures proved to be better predictors of behavior than the objective ones. People made decisions based more on what they thought was likely to happen and what they felt was important than on some objective (external) estimate of probability or monetary estimate of value. The model switched from expected value to subjective expected utility (SEU). It is this SEU model which is most frequently used today.

Simon's model. Even with the switch to subjective components, the SEU model was criticized. There was little doubt that as a normative model it made sense. If, in fact, people behaved the way that SEU prescribed, they would maximize their gain over the long run. It was the descriptive implications that were most bothersome. The SEU model did not appear to be a very good description of what people actually did.

SEU is a very rational and demanding model. It requires that we have complete knowledge about what will happen as a consequence of various actions. We must know all the outcomes. It requires that we have subjective utilities about these outcomes—where some of these outcomes may never have been experienced before. It assumes that we are aware of all the possible behavioral alternatives. We have to have thought of all possible courses of action. SEU demands that we take all this information and combine it in some fairly complex mathematical ways to come up with an overall evaluation of each alternative. Finally, the model demands that we maximize—that is, we keep searching until we find the *very best* alternative. The picture of the decision maker is that of a highly rational, all-knowing, speedy computer who continually maximizes payoff.

It was in response to this model that Herbert Simon and his associates developed the "bounded-rationality" model.[5] Simon described two main areas where real decision makers seemed to differ from the highly rational individual described by SEU. The first of these areas dealt with human information-processing abilities and the second concerned the maximization assumption.

[5]See H. A. Simon. *Models of man*. New York: Wiley, 1957, and H. A. Simon & A. Newell. Human problem solving: The state of the theory in 1970. *American Psychologist*, 1971, **26**, 145–159.

Simon suggested that people are not capable of being truly informed about anything. Instead of searching for all possible alternatives, they quickly focus on just a few. Not all possible outcomes are considered. Estimates of future utility are often vague. In other words, choice activities involve a much more simplified and personally biased view of the decision problem than SEU suggests.

The second and related point is that Simon argued that people tend to "satisfice" rather than maximize. By satisfice Simon meant that the decision maker would often choose the first minimally acceptable alternative that came along rather than the optimal alternative.

The picture described is quite different from SEU. It suggests that people *sequentially* evaluate alternatives; that this evaluation takes place with a *limited* and *personally biased* set of outcomes, probability, and utility estimates; and that the first *minimally satisfactory* alternative will be selected. People are less than optimal, and the research seems to support the description suggested by Simon.[6]

Uses of SEU. Just because the model is not an accurate description of what people actually do does not mean it cannot be useful. As a *normative* guide the SEU model can be quite helpful. That is, if we can teach people to think in terms of probabilities and utilities, and to search for alternatives, and to combine the information in the proper way, we can teach them to make better decisions.

Perhaps the most obvious example of the use of such models is the decision tree. This technique requires the decision maker to graphically represent the available alternatives, the outcomes, the probabilities, and utilities. Figure 11-3 presents a decision tree for the decision problem we discussed earlier.

Using this technique forces people to think about the components of the decision problem. They uncover things they had not thought of and they use probabilities in a manner that is much more systematic. A number of recent research papers have shown that the use of such models and the use of probabilities to estimate outcomes can be helpful in decisions about military matters, predicting the weather, choosing an occupation, making medical diagnoses, and for various investment and financial problems.[7]

So, as a model to shoot for, SEU can be helpful. As a normative model it is very powerful. With proper training we can approximate the requirements of the model. The research evidence suggests that we are capable of much of what is demanded and that, when used properly, the model can improve our decision-making abilities.

Contingency models of individual decisions

One thing that we learned from all our busywork on processing models and choice models was that no one model was a very good description of what different decision makers did across settings and problems. Different people use different decision styles, and different decision problems demand different approaches. The problem was to try to match up the styles with the problems.

---

[6]For a recent review see A. C. Filley, R. V. House, & S. Kerr. *Managerial process and organizational behavior*. Glenview, Ill.: Scott, Foresman, 1976, 110–129.

[7]Beach. Op. cit.

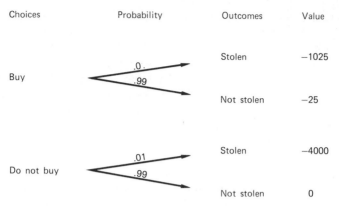

Choices	Probability	Outcomes	Value

Buy — .0 → Stolen — −1025
     — .99 → Not stolen — −25

Do not buy — .01 → Stolen — −4000
          — .99 → Not stolen — 0

Figure 11-3. A decision tree for the purchase of car insurance.

One fairly recent paper has attempted to present such a contingency model.[8] The authors argue that the decision maker uses one of three decision strategies: aided analytic, unaided analytic, and nonanalytic. The aided analytic strategy employs some sort of a model or formula or aid such as a checklist. Making a decision tree is also an example of an aided analytic strategy. An unaided analytic strategy is one where the decision maker is very systematic about the problem and perhaps follows some sort of model but does it all in his or her head. Thinking of all the pros and cons for each alternative or trying to imagine the consequences of each action would fall in this category. Finally, there is the category of nonanalytic strategies. Here the decision maker chooses by habit or uses some simple rule of thumb ("nothing ventured, nothing gained," or "better safe than sorry") to make the choice.

Which particular strategy is selected depends on the personal characteristics of the decision maker and the demands of the task. The list which follows presents some variables that might be important.

THE VARIETY OF DECISION STRATEGIES	TASK CHARACTERISTICS	DECISION-MAKER CHARACTERISTICS
1 Aided analytic	1 Decision-problem characteristics	1 Knowledge
2 Unaided analytic	*a* Unfamiliarity	2 Ability
3 Nonanalytic	*b* Ambiguity	3 Motivation
	c Complexity	
	d Instability	
	2 Decision-environment characteristics	
	a Irreversibility	
	b Significance	
	c Accountability	
	d Time and/or money constraints	

[8]L. R. Beach & T. R. Mitchell. A contingency model for the selection of decision strategies. Technical Report No. 76-6, Decision-Making Research. Seattle, Wash.: University of Washington, December 1976.

The underlying assumption is that the person will choose that strategy which takes the least amount of time and effort expended to reach a satisfactory decision. The more analytic, the more time and effort are required.

Since aided analytic techniques take more effort and analysis, to use such techniques requires (1) that the individual have the personal characteristics necessary to employ such techniques (e.g., knowledge, ability, and motivation) and (2) that such techniques are demanded by the characteristics of the problem. Both the person and the task are involved.

For example, if (1) the decision maker cannot reverse the decision, (2) it is significant, (3) he or she is accountable, and (4) there are no constraints of time and money, then the decision maker is likely to use a more thorough analytic technique to increase the chances of a high-quality decision. Also, analytic techniques can aid the decision maker when he or she is overloaded by the ambiguity, unfamiliarity, complexity, and instability of the problem.

The point is that different strategies are used depending upon the decision problem and the person involved. The research available seems to support these ideas. The implications are that we must train people to recognize what type of problem they are facing and what sort of strategy would be most appropriate for them under these circumstances. This may be a difficult task, but it is the way in which much of the future research in decision making seems to be heading.

Decision making in groups

Group decision making (GDM) is often criticized as frustrating and wasteful. Popular sayings are that "a camel is a horse designed by a committee" or that "the possibility of avoiding a decision increases in proportion to the square of the number of members on the committee." In this next section we examine how GDM is different from individual decision making (IDM), when it is preferable to IDM, and some ways in which we can increase the effectiveness of GDM.

The foundations for GDM are similar in some ways to IDM. We still are dealing with beliefs and values. However, now we must figure out ways to combine the beliefs and values of group members. Thus, *both the gathering of the information and the agreement about its contents* are important. We are also still dealing with the same decision process. That is, we still have problem identification, information search, alternative generation, and choice stages. However, for GDM we have more than one individual participating in some or all these stages. So, while the major elements of the decision-making process are similar for groups and individuals, the way in which these elements are handled in GDM may vary dramatically from their use in IDM.

Review of the literature

If you will recall, in Chapter 8, "Group Dynamics," we listed a number of ways in which groups were different from individuals working alone. At that point we mentioned that people are aroused in groups, the weighting of contributions to the group is uneven, and groups often tend to make risky decisions. All these factors can have an influence on whose beliefs and values dominate, whether the decisions are risky, and the process by which an actual choice is made.

Decision making is often performed in groups. (*By permission of University of Washington Daily.*)

Reviews of the empirical research seem to suggest that groups can have both beneficial and harmful characteristics with respect to the decision process. In perhaps the most well-known summary of this area Maier describes the advantages and drawbacks of GDM. The list below presents this summary.[9]

ASSETS	LIABILITIES
1 Groups can accumulate more knowledge and facts.	1 Groups tend to work more slowly. They take up more time to reach a decision, and time costs money.
2 Groups may have a broader perspective and consider more approaches and alternative solutions.	2 Group effort frequently results in compromises which are not always the optimal decision from an effectiveness perspective.
3 Individuals who participate in the decision process are more likely to be satisfied with the decision and support the decision.	3 Groups can and frequently are dominated by one individual or a small clique.
4 The group decision process serves as an important communication device and political device.	4 Too much dependence on group decisions can limit management's ability to act quickly and decisively when necessary.

[9]N. R. F. Maier. Assets and liabilities in group problem solving: the need for an integrative function. *Psychological Review,* 1967, **47,** 239–249.

So, groups can help or hurt. The question is how the manager decides that participation will be beneficial, and given that a group is used, how the assets can be maximized and the liabilities minimized.

Participation in decision making

In essence the decision whether to engage in GDM or IDM is a decision about participation. If groups are used, then by definition others are participating in the process. The literature on when to encourage participation and its effects is vast. However, there is some agreement about the issues, and the findings are mentioned below.

First, in many cases executives and managers often resent the idea of participation and believe it is unjustified. For example, a recent survey of business executives showed that most managers (79 percent) feel that top management people know best and have the right to make organizational decisions as they see fit.[10] In many cases, participation is seen as an imposition on managerial prerogatives.

Second, there is substantial literature available showing that subordinates enjoy participating in the decision process (given some limits mentioned below). People like to have a say in the decisions that are important to them, and this participation often increases commitment to and acceptance of the group's decision. Thus, motivation and satisfaction can be positively affected.

Third, the positive impact of participation has limits. The decisions must be important and relevant to the participants, their contributions must be actually considered, and the decisions must be about areas in which the participants are knowledgeable. Most people do not want to be involved in every decision, especially those which they do not care or know anything about. But when they do contribute, they want the contribution to be taken seriously.

Vroom and Yetton's model. Perhaps the most detailed attempt at describing when participation should be used has been developed by Vroom and Yetton. Based on the above research findings, these authors developed a model which helps managers to diagnose decision problems and encourage participation at the appropriate times.[11]

The first point the authors make is that there are five degrees or amounts of participation that are possible. Table 11-1 presents these choices. As you can see they range from no participation at all, to consultation, to full participation in which the group makes the decision.

Vroom and Yetton argue that the correct choice from these alternatives depends on the decision problem itself. More specifically, they list seven diagnostic questions that the manager should ask about the problem before the

[10]R. Krishnan. Democratic participation in decision making by employees in American corporations. *Academy of Management Journal,* 1974, **17,** 339–347.

[11]V. H. Vroom & P. W. Yetton. *Leadership and decision making.* Pittsburgh: University of Pittsburgh Press, 1973.

Table 11-1. Different Degrees of Participation Possible

A I	Manager makes the decision alone.
A II	Manager asks for information from subordinates but makes the decision alone. Subordinates may or may not be informed about what the problem is.
C I	Manager shares the problem with subordinates and asks for information and evaluations from them. Meetings take place as dyads, not as a group. and the manager then goes off and makes the decision.
C II	Manager and subordinates meet as a group to discuss the problem, but the manager makes the decision.
G II	Manager and subordinates meet as a group to discuss the problem, and the group as a whole makes the decision.

NOTE: A = alone; C = consultation; G = group.

degree of participation is chosen. Table 11-2 shows these questions and the appropriate degree of participation dependent upon the answer.

Obviously, if subordinates have useful information, if their acceptance is critical, if they share the organizational goals, and conflict is unlikely, then having participation is helpful. If these conditions do not exist, then less participation will be more effective. The point is that the use of participation as a decision-making strategy is a decision in itself. It should be thoroughly studied and rationally considered. There are times when it will help and times when it will not. The Vroom and Yetton model helps to describe these conditions.

The research using the model has been quite supportive. Vroom and Yetton first gathered hundreds of actual decision problems from a wide variety of managers. These problems were then categorized into one of the fourteen problem types described in Table 11-4. Then the most interesting relevant and important problems were used as training materials to help other managers increase their effectiveness in diagnosing decision problems and deciding when to increase participation.

The results show that managers who have been trained as to what diagnostic questions to ask are better able to classify decision problems and choose appropriate participation levels than those without such training. Also, there is some evidence that this type of training increases the overall effectiveness of the managers as well. The training increases diagnostic skills, and the correct participation level increases effectiveness. The model is a major step forward in our understanding of when participative decision making is helpful.

Contingency models of group decision making

Given that we have decided to utilize a group decision-making process, the next question is how to do it effectively. We know from our discussion on group dynamics (Chapter 8) that groups can vary in their structure and process. We can have high or low levels of influence, attraction, and communications. We can impose various decision rules such as unanimous agreement, or a majority can be enough. Over the years a number of researchers have attempted to deal with this

Table 11-2. Summary of Vroom and Yetton Model

Types of Problems	1 Is there a criterion which will show that one solution is better than another?	2 Do I have enough information?	3 Is the problem structured?	4 Do I need subordinate acceptance?	5 Will I get acceptance if I decide alone?	6 Do subordinates share the organizational goals?	7 Is conflict among subordinates likely?	Amount of Participation
1	No			No				A I
2	No			Yes	Yes			A I
3	No			Yes	No			G II
4	Yes	Yes		No				A I
5	Yes	Yes		Yes	Yes			A I
6	Yes	Yes		Yes	No	Yes		G II
7	Yes	Yes		Yes	No	No	Yes	C II
8	Yes	Yes		Yes	No	No	No	C I
9	Yes	No	Yes	Yes	Yes			A II
10	Yes	No	Yes	No				A II
11	Yes	No	No	Yes	Yes			C II
12	Yes	No	No	Yes	No	Yes		G II
13	Yes	No	No	Yes	No	No		C II
14	Yes	No	No	No				C II

NOTE: Blanks in the table simply mean that the information is irrelevant due to the response to some other question.

issue. Their main interest was to describe how different conditions affected the decision process and to suggest ways in which this match could be most effectively done—that is, given different types of decisions and decision environments, how should the group be structured so that the best decision will be made.

Group decision rules. One line of research has focused on the particular decision rule that evolves in a group.[12] If a number of alternative solutions are suggested, how does the group make a decision about which one to accept. Is a plurality needed, a majority, two-thirds consent, or unanimity?

The research at a descriptive level tends to indicate that different strategies develop depending upon the amount of certainty or uncertainty about the occurrence of various outcomes or consequences. In the classical decision literature, when we know an outcome will occur with a probability of 1.00, we call that decision making under conditions of *certainty*. When we are sure an outcome will occur with a probability of less than 1.00 (e.g., when flipping a coin we know the probability of heads or tails is 0.50), we call that decision making under conditions of *risk*. When we are unsure of the probabilities, it is described as decision making under conditions of *uncertainty*. Under conditions of *risk* it appears that majority or plurality decision rules seem to evolve, while conditions of uncertainty tend to result in less formal and more disorganized decision rules. In these latter cases alternatives are often chosen with a minimum of support (only one or two members).

At this point few normative data exist in this area. We have little idea about which strategies lead to better decisions for given problem types. While it is obvious that different decision rules can evolve, we have not yet been able to describe which rule should evolve. Some research on specific types of groups and problems has been done (e.g., juries), but its generalizability is questionable. Work is sorely needed on this problem.

Group structure and process. A much more global and broader approach to the problems has focused on how the organizational and decision environment can influence the group structure and interactions process. The types of models suggested are extensions of the classical contingency ideas discussed in Chapter 2. These earlier theories tried to describe the appropriate organizational structure and managerial approach, given a certain type of organizational environment. The more recent decision models focus on the decision environment and how the parameters of the decision problem should match up with the structure and process of the decision-making group.

A number of these types of models are available, but we will not attempt to discuss all of them.[13] There is some agreement, however, about the general

[12]See J. H. Davis. Group decision and social interaction: A theory of social decision schemes. *Psychological Review*, 1973, **80**, 97–125, and J. H. Davis, N. Kerr, M. Sussmann, & A. K. Rissman. Social decision schemes under risk. *Journal of Personality and Social Psychology*, 1974, **30**, 248–271.

[13]See P. C. Nutt. Models for decision making in organizations and some contextual variables which stipulate optimal use. *Academy of Management Review*, 1976, **1**, 84–98. Also see H. Simon. *The new science of management decisions*. New York: Harper & Row, 1960, Chapters 2 and 3, and J. Thompson & A. Tuden. Strategies, structures, and processes of organizational decisions. In J. Thompson and A. Tuden (Eds.), *Comparative studies in administration*. Pittsburgh: University of Pittsburgh Press, 1959.

environmental aspects that are important and the proper group response. For example, almost all the theories in this area suggest that when a group is faced by an uncertain, nonpredictable, changing situation, it should use a highly flexible group structure. Every effort should be used to increase creativity by using different types of people, exploring fully all ideas, having full participation by all members, and encouraging a relaxed atmosphere and a nondirective style of management. When the decision problems are routine and predictable, a different type of group is appropriate. Specialists can be used; much independent effort can be encouraged, with the leader taking a coordinating role; and clear, concise objectives can be set up. When decision problems arise because of competing or conflicting organizational interests and responsibilities, then every effort should be made to have the group represent different views, with individuals clearly advocating different positions, with formalized procedures to ensure equal treatment, and with formalized voting procedures: disagreement can be encouraged, as can frankness.[14]

What little research exists on these topics tends to support the above interpretations. A more flexible group structure is certainly needed for complex, uncertain, and ambiguous problems, while a more structured and formalized procedure can often be effective for routine decisions or problems of conflicting interests. The problem for organizational participants is how to recognize different types of decision problems and to ensure that the appropriate group structure evolves.

Techniques for creative decision making

In most cases it is the uncertain, ambiguous problems that are most difficult for groups to handle. Most organizations have rather structured and formal group processes. It is the unstructured, nonevaluative, supportive types of groups which are hard to establish. Because of these difficulties a number of specific techniques have been developed that are designed to increase the creativity and effectiveness of groups trying to deal with problems of this nature.

While there has been a variety of strategies suggested, by far the most well known are the nominal group technique (NGT) and the delphi technique.[15] Both techniques are used when creative, independent, and equally treated ideas or judgements are needed. NGT is designed for a group meeting and includes the following format: (1) individuals silently and independently generate their ideas about a task or problem; (2) then each member, in turn, presents one idea to the group, and the ideas are recorded on a blackboard or flipchart; (3) after all ideas are presented, they are discussed for clarification and evaluation; (4) the meeting ends with a silent independent vote on the ideas presented. The group decision is

[14]See F. A. Shull, A. L. Delbecq, & L. L. Cummings. *Organizational decision making.* New York: McGraw-Hill, 1970, pp. 155–163.

[15]A review of many different strategies is presented in T. Summers & D. E. White. Creativity and the decision process. *Academy of Management Review,* 1976, **1**, 99–108, and a detailed description of NGT and delphi is available in A. L. Delbecq, A. H. Van de Ven, & D. H. Gustafson. *Group techniques for program planning.* Glenview, Ill.: Scott, Foresman, 1975.

determined by various mathematical procedures using the input from the final votes.

The delphi technique is similar in many ways, but it does not require the physical presence of group members. Usually the procedure is as follows: (1) a questionnaire is designed to solicit opinions and ideas on an issue and is sent to a group of people who are anonymous to one another; (2) the responses are tabulated and summarized, and a report of this information is returned to the respondents along with a second questionnaire designed to probe any issues that need further clarification or consideration; (3) the feedback report is evaluated, and respondents vote or rate the various ideas presented; (4) these data are tabulated, a decision is made, and a summary of these data and the decision are returned to the respondents.

There are many similarities between the two techniques. They both utilize independent work for idea generation and evaluation. All individuals' judgments are treated equally and are pooled to give an overall response. Both techniques separate the idea generation and evaluation stages and both use mathematical procedures to arrive at a group decision. In short, they are designed to get maximum idea generation, equal treatment, separate evaluation, and a decision based upon pooled responses.

The differences are relatively minor. NGT members know one another, they meet face-to-face in a group, and much of their communication is direct and verbal. Delphi members are anonymous, they are physically dispersed, and they communicate only by written messages. The choice of one or the other technique is partly dependent upon how easy it is to assemble people and whether the issue is so sensitive that anonymity is required.

The research using such techniques has been very supportive. Comparisons with regular interacting groups or committees shows that NGT and delphi processes are superior. More ideas are generated and people are more satisfied with the decision process in NGT and delphi groups. Interacting groups seem to waste too much time on interpersonal relationships, ideas are evaluated prematurely, a few individuals tend to dominate the group, too much time is spent on tangential discussions, conformity often inhibits idea generation, and felt accomplishment is low.

NGT and delphi, on the other hand, seem to ensure that everyone is heard, that the focus of the group remains on the task, that each idea gets evaluated, and that everyone has an equal vote in the final decision. The implications are rather clear; when confronted with decision problems where pooled ideas are needed of a creative nature, some sort of NGT or delphi technique should increase effectiveness.

Summary

Decison making is a complex and important organizational activity. The major points discussed in the chapter are as follows:

1 Organizational decision making is the process of choosing actions that are directed toward the resolution of organizational problems. It includes the

phases of problem identification, information search, the generation and evaluation of alternatives, and choice.

2 Beliefs and values are the major components of the last two decision phases, and models are available to describe how they are combined and how they should be combined. The EV and SEU models, based on a highly rational, maximization view of humans, are the most well known.

3 Human beings, however, are only adequate in their decision making. Their search techniques are not thorough, their processing of information is prone to error, and they often choose satisfactory alternatives rather than optimal ones. In response to these problems, a "bounded-rationality" model was developed which is a more accurate description of how decisions are actually made.

4 It does not appear as if any one decision model is used all the time. People use more or less analytic strategies, depending upon their personal characteristics and the characteristics of the decision environment.

5 Group decision making includes all the above but also has the problem of soliciting, evaluating, and combining individual judgments. People also behave differently in groups: they are aroused, their opinions are weighted differently, and problems of coordination and interpersonal relations are apparent.

6 Whether to engage in GDM is a conscious decision which can be made by the group, a manager, or organizational policy. Based on research it appears that participation is more effective when the members have important information, their support is needed, their goals are similar to the organization's, and group conflict is unlikely.

7 Different types of group structures, process, and decision rules should be used for different types of decision problems and organizational environments. Some techniques such as the nominal group and delphi can increase the effectiveness of groups requiring creative decision processes.

Implications for practice

There are some important areas of the decision-making process that can be handled more effectively than they are currently. One point which needs to be strongly emphasized is that decision making is a long process involving many steps. It is not just the choice phase or the action phase. All too often managers confuse action with decision making. They evaluate problems too quickly, they generate only available and well-practiced solutions, and they confuse symptoms with problems.

This behavior is understandable. There is immense pressure to act and to act quickly. However, every person making an important decision should ask himself or herself whether the preliminary phases of the decision process have been handled well—have all information sources been tapped? Do we know the real cause of the problem? All the evidence seems to indicate that better decisions are made when these preliminary decision phases are dealt with thoroughly and comprehensively.

The machine stores the commands and uses a complex formula to solve the problem in seconds, and the answer comes out on a printed sheet over there. Then Ms. Harris files them God-knows-where and we can never find them again.

The use of computers and decision aids is only as effective as the people who program the machine and interpret the information.

But there are other types of human problems that are not so easily changed. In some cases our information-processing capabilities are just not up to the complex mathematical processes required. We also make certain systematic judgment errors in combining and evaluating information.

There are two ways to help remedy these problems. First, people can be trained to recognize their fallibilities and the places where errors are most likely to occur. This training can be coupled with instruction on the use of various models, formulas, and decision aids. If people know the problem and can use an aid such as the expected-value formula or decision tree, they can compensate for their natural inaccuracies.

Another remedy is the use of computers. Many human errors are made either in the recollection of past events or the anticipation of future ones. Computers can store and accurately retrieve vast amounts of data. They can use complex formulas to estimate future events. They can help combine and process information of a complex nature. In short, training, decision aids, and computers can all help us overcome our human limitations and increase the effectiveness of our decision making.

The major implication about group decision making is that groups can change their structure, process, and decision rules if they want to. These factors are not given; they are not static. Participative processes can be used on some problems and not on others. Or, given that groups are to be used, one can have a highly structured, formal interaction or an unstructured informal one. Where creative decisions are needed, the NGT and delphi techniques can be used. Again, the most important point is that the process of the group is under the group's control. It can be changed and often should be changed to reach more effective decisions.

Discussion questions

1 Who did you vote for (or would you have voted for if you had voted) in the last Presidential election? What did you believe would be the consequences of each candidate being President? Were these important and highly valued consequences? Does this sort of process explain your choice?
2 Think about your own strategies for making decisions. Do they vary as a function of the problem and the situation? What are the important factors that make you use one strategy rather than another?
3 Have you ever been in a group that just could not seem to make a decision and much time was wasted? If you could have controlled the structure and process of the group, what would you have done?

Case: To go or to stay—that is the question

Julie graduated from college in 1971 and took a job with a small consulting firm in San Francisco. The company is opening a branch office in Chicago, and Julie's boss has asked her to move to the Midwest to manage the new office. Her quandary is whether to remain in San Francisco and stay in the same job or move to Chicago.

One of the major factors that is influencing Julie is her reaction to the location of the job. Living in a pleasant environment is a moderately positive aspect about any job Julie would take. She likes to live in pleasant surroundings. She likes the climate and she likes being near the sea. Julie feels that if she moves there is a 50–50 chance she will not like Chicago, but she is certain that she likes San Francisco. If that were the only factor involved, it is clear what she would do.

Another issue, however, is what her boss will do if she chooses to go or stay. She is almost certain that if she moves she will get a raise, and this is extremely important to her. She needs the money. On the other hand, if she stays in San Francisco she is far less likely to get the raise.

It is also fairly likely that if she turns down the offer she will have some friction with her boss. He obviously expects her to take the job and he is counting on her. This would be a slightly negative consequence of remaining on the job in San Francisco. On the other hand, if she goes to Chicago she will see less of her boss, and the relationship is bound to be more harmonious.

Finally, she was just getting used to the work in San Francisco. It took her 3 years to get to the point where she knew her colleagues, clients, and the ins and outs of the consulting business well enough to do an outstanding job. She is apprehensive about moving to a new position and learning everything all over again. It is a tough decision, but it has to be made.

Questions about the case

1 What would you do if you were Julie and felt as she did?
2 What were the factors that influenced your choice?
3 Did you use any sort of cognitive balance sheet (e.g., weighing the pros and cons) to arrive at your decision?

Additional readings

** Cyert, R. M., & March, J. G. *A behavioral theory of the firm.* Englewood Cliffs, N.J.: Prentice-Hall, 1963.

** Elbing, A. O. *Behavioral decision in organizations.* Glenview, Ill.: Scott, Foresman, 1970.

* Hall, J. Decisions. *Psychology Today,* November 1971.

** MacCrimmon, K. R., & Taylor, R. N. Decision making and problem solving. In M. D. Dunnette (Ed.), *Handbook of industrial and organizational psychology.* Chicago: Rand McNally, 1976.

Peterson, C. R., & Beach, L. R. Man as an intuitive statistician. *Psychological Bulletin,* 1967, **68,** 29–46.

* Rowe, A. J. The myth of the rational decision maker. *International Management,* 1974, 38–40.

* Scheibe, K. E. *Beliefs and values.* New York: Holt, 1970.

Simon, H. A. *Administrative behavior.* New York: Macmillan, 1965.

Soelberg, P. O. Unprogrammed decision making. *Industrial Management Review,* 1967, **8,** 19–29.

Sung, Y. H. Effects of attitude similarity and favorableness of information on Bayesian decision making in a realistic setting. *Journal of Applied Psychology,* 1975, **60,** 616–620.

* Van de Ven, H., & Delbecq, A. L. The effectiveness of nominal, delphi and interacting group decision making processes. *Academy of Management Journal,* 1974, **17,** 605–621.

** Wood, M. T. Power relationships and group decision making in organizations. *Psychological Bulletin,* 1973, **79,** 280–293.

*Possible reading for students
**Review of literature or comprehensive source material

12

Power and control

In our initial discussions of organizations, we mentioned that part of the informal contract of joining an organization was that the individual gave up some freedom. In order for a group to meet its goals, compromises must be made. Not everyone can do exactly what they want to do. However, reaching a compromise, channeling effort in a given direction, and getting people to do activities they would not elect to do are difficult tasks. At the individual interpersonal level they often involve the use of power—one person trying to get another person to do something he or she does not want to do. At the organizational level they involve the setting of goals, standards, and objectives along with systems of control to evaluate how well these objectives and standards are being reached.

Systems of both power and control, therefore, serve as regulators of behavior. They are meant to clarify expectations, direct behavior, reduce ambiguity, and provide feedback. The rest of this chapter will discuss these two systems in more detail.

There are two major areas of ambiguity that surround the topics of power and control which we hope to clarify in this chapter. First there is the theoretical ambiguity. Nobody seems to agree about what power and control actually are. Every author has a different definition of these concepts. So, one of our goals will be to simply clear up this confusion by showing what these definitions have in common and where the major areas of disagreement lie. Hopefully this exercise will provide answers to such questions as: How is power different from influence or leadership? Does control mean using a budget system or using a system of participation in decision making?

The second area of ambiguity concerns practice. People in organizations are unsure just how much freedom they have or should relinquish. The agreement made between the individual and the organization is informal, implicit, and unclear. Because of this ambiguity the greatest stress and controversy often revolves around the use of power and control. Yet every manager knows that power and control are necessary. Therefore, we will attempt not only to describe these processes and their effects but also to evaluate them. We will indicate how power can be used constructively or destructively. We will suggest ways in which control systems are more or less likely to be successful. This focus on the negative and positive aspects of power and control should help us to understand how these systems can both be accepted and increase organizational effectiveness.

Social power

The topic of social power has interested and intrigued numerous social scientists and social philosophers throughout history. "That some people have more power than others is one of the most palpable facts of human existence," wrote Robert Dahl in his discussion of social power.[1] "Because of this," he continued, "the concept of power is as ancient and ubiquitous as any that social theory can boast." In fact, many writers have seen power as a concept occupying the central position in the social sciences. The philosopher Bertrand Russell once wrote, "I shall be concerned to prove that the fundamental concept in social science is Power, in the same sense in which Energy is the fundamental concept in physics."[2]

Despite this level of interest and suggested importance, the concept of power has failed to occupy the central position suggested above. Two of the major reasons for this failure are the lack of theoretical clarity in what we mean by power and a paucity of empirical results supporting one position or another. Only recently has some clarification and support been produced.

Definition of power

There are some points of agreement among most theorists discussing the topic of power. It is usually seen as an interpersonal relationship where one individual (A) tries to get another individual (B) to do something. Thus, power involves individuals trying to change the behavior of other individuals. Even this basic level of agreement can be helpful in differentiating power from other similar concepts.

In Table 12-1 we present a diagram which classifies the various ways that people can try to change the behavior of others. At the top we distinguish between an individual or a group as the initiator of behavioral change and on the side we distinguish between an individual or a group as the recipient of the change attempt. Where a group brings pressure to bear on the individual, we describe that process as social influence, a topic discussed in Chapter 8. Where one individual tries to affect the behavior of a group, we typically talk about

[1] R. A. Dahl. The concept of power. *Behavioral Science,* 1957, **2**, 201.

[2] B. Russell. *Power.* New York: Barnes & Noble, 1962, p. 9.

Table 12-1. A Classification of Social Power and Related Concepts

Recipient of Change Attempt	Initiator of Change Attempt	
	An Individual	**A Group**
An Individual	Social power	Social influence
A Group	Leadership	Bargaining

leadership—a topic discussed in the following chapter. When one group tries to change another group, the process is often described under the heading of bargaining. Since both parties concern groups and not individuals (the focus of this book), there is little coverage of this topic in the text. Finally, we come to social power—the situation where one individual tries to change the behavior of another individual.

Aside from this initial agreement among theorists, there is mostly disagreement about the questions that logically follow. Does individual A actually have to ask B to do something, or can the request be anticipated? Does individual B actually have to comply for A to have power? What if B would have behaved in the desired fashion anyway? Does power only go in one direction? Different theories have taken different positions on these questions, and a brief review of these positions is presented below.

Theories of social power

Field theory. The work of Kurt Lewin and some of his followers saw power as the *force* that individual A could bring to bear on B to engage in some behavior.[3] This force is generally seen to be a function of the resources (rewards, punishments, etc.) that A can use as well as B's "motive bases" (evaluation of the rewards). The force is *felt* and *perceived* by B. Thus, to know how much power A has, one must ask B. Note also that force is defined in terms of the felt pressure of A on B, not in terms of actual behavioral compliance. Under field theory, A could have great power even when B does not comply.

Exchange theory. The exchange theories provide a more economic-like analysis of the interaction between A and B.[4] The general assumption is that individuals behave so as to maximize the difference between the rewards and the costs they experience. These theorists say that A has power over B and can change B's behavior to the extent that A can determine or control the rewards and costs that B experiences. The major emphasis of this approach is the *actual* rewards that A controls, not their *perception* by B. Also note that there is explicit recognition of the fact that while A controls some rewards and costs for B, it is also true that B can control some costs and rewards of A. Power is a reciprocal process.

[3]K. Lewin. *Field theory in social science.* New York: Harper, 1951.

[4]J. W. Thibaut & H. H. Kelley. *The social psychology of groups.* New York: Wiley, 1959.

Political-science decision-making theory. The work of March and others in this political-science tradition defines power in terms of actual changes in behavior.[5] Thus, the power of A over B is defined as the extent to which A can get B to do something B would not otherwise do. A cannot have power unless B complies with A's request. The focus is on the actual result of the exchange, not on the perception or feeling of B. Also, the theory explicitly concerns behaviors that B would not have done without A's intervention.

Decision-theory analysis. Finally, we have an approach based on the expectancy and expected-value formulations discussed in Chapters 7 and 11. Individual B is seen as making a decision between alternatives X (compliance) and Y (noncompliance). B should choose that alternative which has the highest expected value—the one that has the *highest probability* of leading to outcomes B *values*. Individual A has power over B to the extent that A can increase the expected value of compliance and decrease the expected value of noncompliance.[6]

This last approach is rather recent in its development but is felt by many to include most of the facets of the other approaches. First, the power of A is defined in terms of what *B* values and feels is likely to happen as a result of his or her behavior. A's feelings or actual behavior are not relevant for this analysis. Second, B can be responding both to an anticipated request as well as an actual one. It is B's *feeling* that A wants something that is important. Third, B does not have to comply for A to have power. The power of A is defined in terms of the pressure B feels as a result of how much B values the outcomes he or she believes A may use and as a result of a belief about the likelihood of their use. Also, whether B would have performed the act regardless of A is not critical. Power is defined in terms of the *pressure* A brings to bear on B to comply. So even if the expected value of X exceeded Y before A said something, if the EV of X increases and Y decreases after the request, then A has power. Finally, power can be a two-way exchange. B can influence the outcomes that A values as well as the reverse.

Some examples of social power

To get a thorough understanding of this concept, a few examples might help. For instance, imagine that you are at home on Saturday morning thinking about whether you should finish up some work or play handball. You decide the work can wait; so you get ready to go over to a nearby gym. Just as you are about to leave, the phone rings. It is your boss, inquiring about the status of the report which you know needs to be finished. The boss mentions that the report is due on Monday. What do you do?

Well, if you decide to forgo the handball and go to the office, this is a clear-cut

---

[5]J. G. March. An introduction to the theory and measurement of influence. *American Political Science Review,* 1955, **49,** 431–451.

[6]W. E. Pollard & T. R. Mitchell. Decision theory analysis of social power. *Psychological Bulletin,* 1972, **78,** 433–446.

case of power. Individual A (your boss) brought pressure to bear on individual B (you), and you (B) changed your behavior.

But what if the handball match was a crucial one? You belong to a team and you have a shot at the city championship. If you are not there, you forfeit, and the team has lost. The alternative of going to work was made more attractive by your boss's call (due to the potential rewards for compliance and punishments for not complying), but the handball match is very important. Instead of an easy decision (one with a large difference between compliance and noncompliance), you have a very difficult decision (the expected value of both alternatives is about equal).

You decide to play handball. Now the question is: "Did A have power over B in this situation even though B did not comply?" According to our decision-theory analysis, the answer is yes. And according to common sense, the answer is yes. Research has shown if you ask B whether A had power in such situations, B will respond affirmatively. The pressure was felt; it just was not enough to ensure compliance.

The same would be true if you had decided to go to work before your boss called. Perhaps before the call the decision was a tough one, but the work still had a higher expected value than handball. However, after the call, there is little dilemma. You are still going to go to work, but now it is an easy choice; the increased pressure brought to bear by A on B increased the expected value of compliance. Again, theory, common sense, and research suggest that A has power in such situations.

One final point: Let us say part of the reason you decide to go to work is because you think your boss will put in a good word with the vice president of your division and perhaps you will get that raise you want. In the past your boss has implied that they are on good terms and that they see each other frequently. In fact, your boss sees the vice president infrequently, and when they do meet, your boss seldom discusses the work of subordinates. However, the *reality* of the situation is not what influences you. It is what *you think* the boss *can* do, not what the boss actually can do or does that influences your decision.

To summarize, power is seen as the force that A can bring to bear on B to act in accordance with A's wishes. This force is determined by asking B about his or her perceptions of what A wants and is likely to do if B complies or does not comply and how important those consequences are to B. If A's perceived or actual request in some way increases B's desire to comply or decreases B's desire to not comply, then A has power over B. Thus, someone has power over you to the extent that (1) you think they will control and will use outcomes to back up their request, (2) you value highly the outcomes that may result, and (3) you have few alternatives—that is, little way to change or decrease this pressure that A can exert.

Power in use

Given that we understand what power is, we can proceed to a discussion of how it is used in organizations. With the above definition we can see that some of the important components of the power relationship are the resources at A's disposal, B's dependency on those resources, and B's alternatives. The next three sections discuss these factors.

Power resources

What are some of the resources that B might perceive A had that would be important for B's decision? French and Raven's classic analysis of this issue and some later works have produced the following six categories of resources.[7]

1. *Rewards.* Reward power is seen as the number of positive incentives which B thinks A has to offer. Can A promote B? To what extent can A determine how much B earns or when B takes a vacation? To some extent A's reward power is a function of the formal responsibilities inherent in his or her position.

2. *Punishment.* Coercive power or punishment has to do with the negative things that B believes A can do. Can A fire me, dock my pay, give me miserable assignments, or reprimand me? These factors are again often organizationally and formally determined as part of A's position.

3. *Information.* Information is often controlled by individuals within organizations. They can decide who should know what. To the extent that B thinks A controls information B wants and perhaps needs, then A has power. This information can be both formally *and* informally gathered and distributed.

4. *Legitimacy.* Legitimate power as a resource stems from B's feeling that A has a right to make a given request. Legitimate power is sometimes described as authority. The norms and expectations prevalent in the social situation help to determine A's legitimate power: Has A done this before? Have others complied? What are the social consequences of noncompliance?

5. *Expertise.* A is often an expert on some topic or issue. B will often comply with A's wishes because B believes that A "knows best" what should be done in this situation. Expertise and ability are almost entirely a function of A's personal characteristics rather than A's formal sanctions.

6. *Referent power.* In some cases B looks up to and admires A as a person. B may want to be similar to A and be liked by A. In this situation, B may comply with A's demands because of what we call referent power. Note again that this resource is mostly a function of A's personal qualities.

Research on the bases of power

Looking over the six categories, we can see that there are some factors which are organizationally determined (rewards and punishments), some which have to do with the person's position (information power and legitimacy), and some which have to do with personal characteristics (referent power and expertise). The

[7]J. R. P. French & B. Raven. The bases of social power. In D. Cartwright and A. F. Zander (Eds.), *Group dynamics.* (2d ed.) Evanston, Ill.: Row, Peterson, 1960, pp. 607–623.

One's formal power may be more important than one's expertise.

empirical research on these topics shows that all the power bases are used but that the particular mix employed in any given situation seems to depend upon the circumstances and the people involved.

For example, it appears that legitimate, expert, and referent power are more often cited as reasons for compliance than reward and coercive power. Coercive power seems to be used mostly when a manager is faced with problems of discipline or an unwilling subordinate. (This is the old fist-in-the-glove technique—if persuasion and kindness do not work, use a threat.)

Some individuals and organizations differ in their use of power. For example, managers who are less authoritarian and more participative in their style tend to rely on expertise and referent power (social pressure) to get things done, while more authoritarian and less participative managers tend to use more formal resources such as rewards and punishments. Besides individual differences there are organizational differences. Some research shows that enlisted people in the navy see their superiors as relying heavily on authority, threat, and punishment even though they report a preference for expertise, trust, and respect. On the other hand, when power is exercised in academic settings, it is almost entirely based upon expertise and information.

Dependencies

So far we have simply focused on what B thinks are the reasons for A's request and the possible outcomes that may occur as a function of compliance or noncompliance. An equally important question has to do with B's dependence upon A. That is, to what extent does it matter to B what A does? There are a number of factors that contribute to this dependency, including B's values, the nature of the relationship, and B's ability to alter the pressure being exerted.

B's values. If the outcomes that A can influence are important to B, then obviously the pressure will be greater than if the outcomes are irrelevant to B. In most organizational settings, if A is B's boss, then A should be able to control some important outcomes for B. It may be a raise, being in the know, a promotion, or social rejection that is the key. One of the real criteria of an excellent manager is the degree to which that person can understand and utilize the proper resources with the proper people. It is not an easy task but it is a feasible one. A manager can observe what seems to work and keep records. This information should be helpful in the long run.

The relationship. Another factor in the dependency category is the type of relationship that A and B are in. Are they peers, or a boss and a subordinate? Is this a job or a volunteer group? Is this summer work or one's first professional position? The question here is how important is the relationship itself. Short-term jobs are less important than long-term ones. A volunteer group may be less important than a position that provides economic support. It may be less damaging to refuse a peer than a superior.

The point is that part of B's considerations are often about the relationship itself. If B decides that it is not very important or that it is short term, then B will be less likely to comply.

Counterpower. The final component of dependency resides in B's ability to change the pressure being brought to bear by A. In many cases this is described as counterpower. That is, B may control some resources that are important to A. The classic example is the secretary who has great power over his or her boss. The power does not reside in the secretary's formal resources but in informational resources. The secretary often knows where things are filed, how to get through the administrative maze, who to call to get things done, and so on. Thus B may be able to change A's request by asking for favors in return or by putting subtle pressure on A to ease up.

The empirical research on these topics is quite supportive. The more B values A's resources, the greater A's power. The more important the relationship is to B, the greater A's power. The fewer resources B can muster against A, the greater A's power.

One fairly recent study looked at a number of these variables.[8] A number of stories in which one individual was trying to get another individual to do something were rated by students. The stories included a salesman and the regional manager, a newspaper editor and a local judge, and two members of congress. The authors were interested in four factors: (1) A's resources, (2) A's probability of using the resources, (3) B's ability to block the use of A's resources, and (4) B's ability to bring countermeasures to bear. As we would expect, A's power was rated highest when A had many resources and was likely to use them, when B could do little to block his efforts, and when B had little ability to bring countermeasures to bear. This research is representative of most of the research in this area. Power is seen as a function of A's resources, the nature of the relationship, and B's ability to change or counter A's request. Table 12-2 summarizes these factors.

Power strategies

While the discussion so far has focused on a better understanding of power and how it works, there is also some research which has looked at how people actually use their power. The topic of interest switches to what A actually does to get B to do something. There are a number of strategies that are used, and they seem to parallel quite nicely the resources mentioned above.

The first of these strategies might be called the *invoking of norms*. This strategy appears when A pairs a request with other information about what is expected of B. For example, a boss might start a request by saying, "I think it is only fair" or "in all fairness." Besides the norm of fairness, there are the norms of altruism and reciprocity. One can invoke the altruism norm, by seeming to be in great need, or the reciprocity norm, by reminding someone of a recent favor.

[8]H. A. Michener, E. J. Lawler, & S. B. Bacharach. Perception of power in conflict situations. *Journal of Personality and Social Psychology,* 1973, **28,** 155–162.

Table 12-2. A Summary of the Power Relationship

A	has power over	B
Resources		Dependencies
Rewards		Values
Punishments		Importance of relationship
Information		Counterpower
Legitimacy		
Expertise		
Reference		

A has power over B to the extent that B believes:
1 A has resources and will use them,
2 B values those resources,
3 B values the relationship, and
4 B has little counterpower or other options that can reduce the impact of A's actual or perceived request.

In these situations A is depending on social norms and expectations to induce B's compliance.

A second strategy involves the *management of information*. In these situations A might illustrate his or her expertise on some topic by providing background or inside information. The idea is to get B to comply to a request because A knows what he or she is talking about. Both informational and expert power resources can be used in this strategy.

The third and perhaps most obvious strategy is the use of *threats and promises*. In most cases this strategy is not explicit or frequently used. But it is always there—always implied—that if norms or expertise, information, or legitimacy do not work, then the rewards and punishment are the next resource to be tried. Usually, the promises precede the punishments—probably because coercive power is seen by most people as the last resort. Most of us do not like to use force or be forced.

The final strategy that we shall discuss involves the *actual use of resources*. A salesperson wants you to buy the new Buick at $6000, which is $400 under the sticker price. Your offer is $5700. The salesperson takes it to the boss (in the back room) and then returns after 15 minutes: "No way will the boss accept that. The best we can do is $5900." This type of process goes on until finally the salesperson says: "Okay. We'll sell it to you for $5800. But I want you to know that this last $100 came out of my commission." In this situation A is relinquishing his or her own financial resources to induce your compliance.

The most obvious term for this process is *compromise*. You have to give a little to get a little. When all the other strategies fail or are inappropriate, compromise is often used.

Reactions to power attainment and use

The final two questions to consider in this topic are people's reactions to power and its use. How do people act when they attain power? How do you feel when power is used on you?

One base of power throughout history has been the threat of force and physical harm. (*By permission of University of Washington* Daily.)

Power attainment. Over the years there has been a heated debate about whether power is corrupting or ennobling. Some people have argued that power brings with it responsibilities and that the powerful may be more compassionate and understanding. On the other side are those that argue that power is corrupting, that power induces people to act in an inequitable and exploitative manner.

The research seems to favor the latter interpretation. A number of studies have observed the behavior of people who have attained power or of people who have more power than others in certain positions. The data suggest that power holders use the power, devalue and exploit the less powerful, and decrease interpersonal associations with the less powerful.

Perhaps the best of these studies was done by Kipnis in 1972.[9] He had twenty-eight undergraduate business school students act as managers in an industrial simulation. Each manager was in charge of four workers who were performing a coding task in another room. Each worker's output was known to the manager (every 3 minutes), and while the manager could not see the workers, he could communicate with them (and they with the manager) by written message. The manager's job was to operate the company at a profitable level by maintaining the efficiency of the workers. The managers received $2 per hour, the workers $1.

All the managers had the same job. However, fourteen of the managers were delegated a range of institutional powers. They could promise or reward pay increases, transfer workers, give additional instructions, deduct pay, and terminate employment. The other fourteen managers could use only their powers of persuasion and expertise; they had no formal power.

In fact, the workers in the other room were fictitious. In this way the experimenter could bring in exactly the same performance data and messages from the workers. The only difference between the two groups of managers was their power.

The data were clear and unambigous. The managers with power (1) sent more messages, (2) rated their workers less highly on an overall appraisal, (3) indicated a lower willingness to meet socially with the workers, and (4) were more likely to attribute the workers' performance to managerial expertise than were their less powerful counterparts. What this suggests is that powerful people use their power, that power may inhibit social relationships, that powerful people devalue the efforts of less powerful people and reevaluate their own efforts in a more positive light.

Power use. The reverse of the coin is also clear. People do not like power to be used on them. Any attempt by someone to alter their behavior produces initially at least a small amount of resistance. The research seems to show that when strategies are used based on legitimate, expert, or normative resources, this resistance is low. However, the more that coercion and punishments are used, the greater the resistance. There is also some evidence that the direct use of rewards may make the task of compliance somewhat less pleasant. It seems to be nicer to do something for someone else because we want to—not because we think we have to.

To summarize, power is used in organizations all the time. It is a necessary way to get things done. However, there are ways and there are ways. Power strategies based on coercion may bring compliance, but it is less satisfactory to both parties, especially the less powerful. Strategies based on expertise, legitimacy, and normative pressures are more readily used and accepted. One way in which an organization can formalize and emphasize these strategies is through the use of rules, regulations, agreed-upon objectives, guidelines, and procedures.

[9]D. Kipnis. Does power corrupt? *Journal of Personality and Social Psychology,* 1972, **24,** 33–41.

All these factors are typically described under the heading of organizational control, a topic to which we now turn.

Control systems

The word "control," just like "power," has been used loosely in the last few years. It has many different meanings. We will attempt to clarify some of these ambiguities in the definition and then evaluate control as it is used in the organizational sense as an influence on individual behavior.

Definition

Probably the most important distinction to make initially is between *personal* control and *organizational* control. We will be interested primarily in the latter type of control in this chapter.

Personal control. One of the hottest topics in the current social-psychological literature is the issue of individuals' control over the outcomes that happen to them. To what extent do individuals control, that is cause, something to happen to them? The research issues revolve around what types of people have control, whether people naturally seek control, what happens when control is gained or lost, and whether the illusion of control is just as effective as real control. The basic proposition is that having control reduces uncertainty and anxiety while at the same time increasing confidence and competence.

This usage of the word "control" is employed in much of the participative-management literature. The discussion focuses on the extent to which subordinates should have greater control over their destinies and work situation (i.e., outcomes that happen to them) by participating in the decision-making process. For example, all the famous work done by Tannenbaum and his associates use the word "control" in this sense.[10] While this is certainly a legitimate way to define control, we have saved our discussion of this topic for other chapters in the book, such as Chapter 11, "Decision Making," and Chapter 17, "Political Support," where participative decision making is discussed in more detail. For the moment we will concentrate on organizational control.

Organizational control. The concept of organizational control has in some cases been very narrowly defined as systems of performance appraisal or budgets or cost-effectiveness systems. More recently, however, the definition has broadened and become more inclusive. Most writers now see organizational control as a process that includes planning—the setting of goals, objectives, and standards; establishing procedures designed to meet the goals and objectives; data gathering and feedback systems to indicate when standards and objectives are being met; and systems of action to reduce any deviations from the charted course.

This is a fairly encompassing definition. It includes the setting of long- and

---

[10]A. S. Tannenbaum. *Control in organizations.* New York: McGraw-Hill, 1968.

short-term goals with regard to production, manpower, community relations, marketing, research, and numerous other areas. It includes the steps and procedures and standards that are used to get there. What kind of information do we need, what sorts of people should we have, how should we evaluate them? And finally it includes ways in which all of this can be monitored, corrected, and kept on track.

It is a monumental task and it is the heart of an effective organization. But before we describe this process in more detail, we should emphasize its relationship to how people behave in organizations. The major function of control systems from an individual perspective is to clarify expectations about what should be done. We have discussed in previous chapters how roles and norms help to regulate behavior and clarify expectations. But these were interpersonal concepts, as was social power. They had to do with people interacting together in pairs or in groups.

Control, however, is meant to be a more impersonal process. It usually involves organization-wide rules, regulations, and procedures. It tells people how the job should be done, what we are shooting for, what is expected of the individual, how he or she will be evaluated, and what is expected of the unit or organization as a whole. The major focus of a control system, however, is on *organizational effectiveness,* not individual effectiveness (although the aggregate of individual effectiveness is obviously a part). Thus, most control systems involve the total organization—its planning, selection, training, budgets, performance appraisal, and cost effectiveness. While control systems obviously influence individual behavior, they do so with a focus on the whole, not on the individual parts. Table 12-3 summarizes this definition and outlines the topics we will discuss.

Planning

As we define it, planning is part of the overall process of organizational control. It is the initial step without which effective control systems are not possible. We will discuss the planning process in more detail, covering the research on planning and some current trends in the area.

Description. First of all, a plan is a path to a goal. It is a step-by-step description of the manner in which an organization will meet its goals and objectives. Obviously, the first step in the process must be the setting of these goals and objectives. We have to know where we are going before we can plan how to get there.

Most organizations serve many interests. There are stockholders and the board of directors, who want a good return on their investment; consumers, who want high-quality goods; employees, who want interesting and high-paying jobs; and "the public," who wants the environment and social concerns to be the organization's concerns. In order to meet the needs of these groups every organization must clarify its purpose, rank-order its goals and objectives, and attempt to draw up plans that will best reach these goals.

While many different classification systems exist for types of goals, there is

Table 12-3. Description of Planning and Control

Process Involved	Planning		Control	
Basic Question	What are we doing?		How are we doing?	
Secondary Question	Where are we going?	How do we get there?	How do we know?	How can we improve?
Operation	Set goals and objectives	Allocate resources and draw up plans	Measure the criteria of quantity, quality, cost, and time	Utilize feedback, response time, and change

some agreement about three major categories: societal, output, and system goals. The societal or environmental goals have to do with the basic purpose of the organization's existence. The organization has to provide some goods or service, probably at some regular intervals, in accord with the laws of the land and with some semblance of order. The output goals are more specific. They suggest the amounts of various goods and services that are to be produced per unit of time. These goals may be for individuals, units, or the organization as a whole. The system goals refer to the methods of design and operation: does the organization believe in rapid or slow growth, much or little research, product innovation, or more cautious imitation.

The point to recognize is that this goal-setting process is often difficult and involved. It takes time, information, and difficult negotiations. Figure 12-1 diagrams the process. First there has to be some general concensus about the

Figure 12-1. The goal-setting process.

societal or broad goals and about some of the alternative options that are available. Next comes a thorough and intensive stage of gathering information. Forecasts must be made as well as an assessment of the current environment. Then comes a period of evaluating the information and the alternative options that are available. This often involves conflict and compromise. Finally, some actions or decisions are made, and the plans for implementation can be drawn up.

The actual planning stage involves the drawing up of ways in which resources (human, material, financial) can be allocated so that objectives can be reached. This may require that certain performance standards be set and time limits established. It may demand new structural relationships, lines of command, and communication links. In short, the plans are the nuts and bolts—they are the specifics of how the organization will attempt to meet its goals.

Since goals are often stated for both the short term and the long term, the same distinction is made for planning. *Tactical planning* is described as plans dealing with the current operations and current allocation of resources. The annual budget is always a good reflection of the plans for that year. *Strategic planning,* however, is more concerned with long-term issues: Where do we want to be in a few years? How big? What kinds of people will we be hiring? Who will be our competition?

Both tactical and strategic plans are important, but in most cases the tactical plans reflect the strategic plans. Current plans are part of the long-term plans. Because of this relationship, strategic planning has become a critical part of most large organizational planning efforts.

One excellent example of strategic planning has occurred at Sears, Roebuck.[11] Over the years a number of critical decisions were made with regard to long-term plans. In the 1920s Sears decided to add retail stores to its catalog business (anticipating the movement to cities). The company centralized merchandizing and controlled the cost, quantity, and quality of its merchandise. After World War II Sears expanded rapidly and aggressively, quickly snatching up choice locations in the suburbs. In the 1950s it broadened its product lines to become a full-line department store. Sears also modernized its image and sold fashionable products. It set up its own service organization to ensure the quality of its products. And most recently Sears has diversified into insurance and other financial services (through Allstate) and invested heavily in its personnel (through large-scale programs of training and policies of promotion from within). The result has been that Sears has been a highly successful firm with an image of inexpensive, reliable goods.

In short, the planning process involves the setting of goals and the drawing up of plans. Both processes include long- and short-term concerns. Combined, they determine where an organization wants to go and how it plans to get there.

Research evidence. The research on planning is not extensive, but what there is seems supportive of what we have said. First, most organizations are involved in planning of both a short- and long-term nature. Some studies report that as many as 95 percent of the firms surveyed had planning periods of 1 to 10 years.

A second issue is whether planning is helpful for the organization. That is, do managers or organizations that systematically plan do better than those who do not. The answer here seems to be an unqualified yes. Studies in educational institutions, the aircraft industry, and in drug and chemical companies all showed that managers who planned were seen as more effective than those who did not.[12]

The same seems to be true at the organizational level as well. In comparative studies, organizations that engage in planning seem to do better than those who do not or who do it informally rather than formally. For example, one study compared the performance of seventeen firms that engaged in formal plans with the performance of nineteen firms that engaged in the planning process only informally.[13] The firms were placed in the formal planning category if they set goals and corporate strategy for at least 3 years in advance and developed specific action plans to meet the goals. The performance criteria included sales, stock prices, earnings per common share, return on common equity, and return on total capital employed. The thirty-six firms represented six industries: drugs, chemicals, food, steel, oil, and machinery.

The data supported the hypothesis. The formal planners outperformed the informal planners on three of the five criteria and were equal on the other two. Also, just taking the formal planning group, the data showed that, after planning,

[11]J. McDonald. Sears makes it look easy. *Fortune*, 1964, **69**, 120–123.

[12]A. C. Filley, R. J. House, & S. Kerr. *Managerial process and organizational behavior*. Glenview, Ill.: Scott, Foresman, 1976.

[13]S. S. Thune & R. J. House. Where long-range planning pays off. *Business Horizons*, 1970, **13**, 81–87.

The wood-harvesting industry is involved in long-range planning concerned with reseeding as well as harvesting trees. *(By permission of the Weyerhaeuser Company.)*

performance was greater than that for a similar time period preceding the implementation of planning.

The final research issue focuses on how the planning process is conducted. One important element seems to be the search process. The more "idea getting" and substantive information that is gathered, the more accurate the forecasts and the better the plans. The implication is that search takes time—one should not close off alternatives too early. The second point is that people are more committed to and involved in goal attainment when they participate in the planning process. Thus, input should be gathered from all those who (1) have substantive information to offer and (2) will be concerned with the implementation of these plans.

In short, planning involves attempts to organize the present and clarify the future. Organizations that do it and do it well seem to be more effective than those that do not. However, planning is only half the picture. The control mechanisms are equally important if plans are to be implemented and objectives attained.

Control

Control consists in verifying whether everything occurs in conformity with the plan adopted, the instructions issued and the principles established.

Henri Fayol

As we said at the outset, control includes what is typically described as planning as well as control. Once the plans are made, the next steps are to measure and evaluate how well the organization is attaining its goals. If discrepancies exist between what is expected and what is actually happening, then some sort of corrective mechanisms are put into action. In the next few sections we will discuss the criteria that are used to assess goal attainment and ways in which the organization can apply these criteria to ongoing operations.

But before we elaborate on the control system, one point should be made clear. The research data indicate strongly that control systems are necessary for effective organizations. Plans are needed (we have already reviewed these data) as one means of assessing progress and correcting mistakes. Organizations that do not have these systems or have inadequate systems developed are likely to fail. The question for us then becomes not whether to have a control system but what type of control system is most effective. The latter question will be the focus of our discussion.

Criteria of control. There are three major criteria of organizational effectiveness. These are (1) quantity and quality, (2) cost, and (3) time.

The quantity and quality of output—whether they be students graduated, mental-health patients cured, legislative bills passed, or cars produced—is one of the most frequently used indexes of effectiveness. In most cases quantity is easier to determine than quality. Quantity simply requires that we count.

Quality, on the other hand, involves some subjective judgement. It involves a decision about what is good. It is easy to count the number of students graduated, but it is harder to know how well they were educated. Attempts in this direction might include measures of starting salary or Graduate Record Examination scores. Another example easily comes to mind in the auto industry. The number of recalls in recent years could be used as an assessment of the excellence of workmanship and engineering.

Cost is another frequently employed criteria. Organizational inputs and outputs can usually be translated into dollar terms. However, in many cases the "human" elements are harder to assess, and much disagreement exists about the use of cost statistics for activities such as training and development. We will discuss this topic more fully later.

Finally, the criterion of time is important. Time, like materials, is a resource. Deadlines have to be set and met. The difference of a month for project completions can often cost millions of dollars. Besides the cost factor there are quantity factors. If each student takes 5 years rather than 4 to get a Ph.D., it will cost more to educate him or her and fewer students will graduate per year (given the same input).

So, quantity, quality, cost, and time are the major criteria used to assess effectiveness. Some combination of all of them generally is used. Some of them are more appropriate than others, given certain situations. Which criterion is used depends on the area or strategy of control.

Strategies of control. Part of the control function is to specify appropriate behavior, structure the task to be done, and clarify expectations. This clarification and specification process can take place in many ways. That is, there are many different strategies for controlling behavior. The six most important are described below.

1 *Policies and rules.* Both policies and rules are used to prescribe acceptable action. In most cases policies are seen as more flexible than rules. They are more conditional. Rules, on the other hand, are meant to be binding on everyone. Also, policy is usually made only at upper organizational levels, while rules may be made at all levels.

2 *Formal organizational design.* The structure of the organization also serves as a mechanism of control. Decisions about who has formal authority (and the rewards and punishments that go along with this authority) and who communicates to whom (the use of an organization chart) regulate behavior. By specifying responsibilities, paths of communications, the number of subordinates, and the relationship among organizational subunits, control is exercised.

3 *Human-resource functions.* The functions of selection, placement, and training may also serve as mechanisms of control. The selection process can serve as a screen through which the organization lets pass only those individuals who illustrate the desired and appropriate behavior. Proper placement and training can also be used to provide new experiences and modify behavior.

4 *Appraisal and compenstion.* The systems of performance appraisal and financial reward serve as major mechanisms of control. The appraisal system should tell people what is expected and provide feedback about their performance. Rewards should be administered for appropriate action and punishments for inappropriate action.

5 *Budgets.* The allocation of financial resources to organizational units, projects, and plans is a powerful way to regulate behavior. Budgets establish targets and they delimit action. They serve as a reflection of the ranked importance of organizational goals and in this way they can be used as guides as to how one should allocate his or her time.

6 *Technology.* One final method of control is through technology. The most obvious example of technological control is automation and closed-loop feedback control. Many manufacturing operations have machines which check the quality of products automatically. This frees the employee's time for other activities. The use of computers and communication systems has also served to regulate behavior through the use of specified forms and procedures for recording, filing, and passing along information.

So, there are many different mechanisms of control. Some deal with individual behavior (e.g., rules and structures), and others are impersonal in their nature (e.g., budgets and technology). Any overall system of control will include a mix of these strategies: some will have a more personal, behavioral flavor, while others will show a more impersonal, technical quality. As we will see in the final section of this chapter, there are very different reactions to different types of control systems.

Control systems in use

As we mentioned earlier, the major criteria of organizational effectiveness are quantity and quality of production, time, and cost. In most organizations the traditional method of assessing these criteria has been the budget. A budget can be designed to include both financial and behavioral terms, although the former are more common. The monetary emphasis is usually represented in some type of balance-sheet format. Physical and behavioral factors such as labor, machine hours, and material aspects can be included. The advantage of the system is that many diverse activities are reduced to one criterion—money. Since making a profit is an important goal for most business organizations, the financial budget is an excellent method for ensuring planning, control, evaluation, and change.

However, over the years the inadequacies of the traditional budget have been recognized. First, many aspects of the organization's effectiveness were not usually seen as quantifiable in financial terms. For example, only recently has there been an attempt to estimate in financial terms the worth of employees to the firm over their entire career. Described as human-resource accounting, these data are meant to provide information not covered in the traditional budgeting process. It has met with only moderate success due to the difficulty inherent in estimating the "worth" of human beings.

Another problem is that organizations have many different goals now—of which profit is just one. Also, many organizations are government run or regulated or are explicitly nonprofit. The traditional budget has some difficulty, for example, in assigning dollar amounts to the well-being produced by good medical care. The patient leaves the hospital perhaps never to return—is the "well-being" a credit or financial resource? The same problem occurs in schools, governments, churches, and other similar organizations.

The response to these problems is that new systems of control have developed over the years to reflect these new concerns. Some of these new control systems are described briefly below.

Cost criteria. Probably the two most well-known innovations using cost-related criteria are the planning-programming-budgeting system (PPBS) and cost/benefit analysis. PPBS was meant to provide long-term integration of plans, programs, and budgets. It was introduced into the Defense Department in 1965 partly as a response to problems of program overlap, cost overruns, and waste. Cost/benefit analysis is being used elsewhere in the government, especially as a system designed to evaluate government social programs. The cost of training people in a Job Corps program, for example, is compared to the benefit the program provides to the individuals and society. These benefits are measured by factors such as how many people get jobs, how long they keep them, how much they earn, how the salary compares with what they made previously, and so on. Both PPBS and cost/benefit systems have met with only moderate success. However, they serve as good examples of how traditional budgeting ideas and techniques are being modified to address other important questions.

Time criteria. Perhaps the most well-known control system that emphasizes the use of time is the program evaluation and review technique (PERT). This system places major emphasis on scheduling. All the necessary tasks needed for project accomplishment are listed and arranged in a sequential network reflecting which activity must be completed before another begins. In this way, the overall project can be monitored and kept on course.

Behavioral criteria. The most highly publicized system of behavioral control is the system of management by objectives (MBO), which will be discussed more fully later in the book. Suffice it to say that MBO places its major emphasis on goal accomplishment rather than cost. A good system of MBO includes goal setting, action plans, and performance review. The criterion of success is the result—did we accomplish what we set out to do.

It is beyond the scope of this book to cover control systems in more detail. This topic is discussed in courses on policy, personnel, and management. The important point to realize is that systems of control are one of the major factors that shape people's behavior in organizations.

Reactions to control

The literature abounds with examples of employees' negative reactions to control systems.[14] Control increases anxiety and pressure. Deadlines are introduced, cost limits imposed, performance standards are set. People report feeling threatened and pushed.

These reactions can be seen as normal responses to the imposition of control. By definition, control systems are designed to regulate behavior, and the regula-

[14]For an excellent review of this area, see E. E. Lawler. Control systems in organizations. In M. D. Dunnette (Ed.), *Handbook of industrial and organizational psychology*. Chicago: Rand McNally, 1976, pp. 1247–1292.

tion of behavior implies loss of freedom. People react negatively to this loss of freedom, and the resultant behavior can be damaging for the organization.

There are numerous research examples available. Rules and procedures often limit flexibility and creativity. Deadlines become the criteria rather than the quality of work. Budgets often produce inflated estimates so that cost overruns will not occur. Subjective performance appraisals often cause employees to spend more time buttering up the boss than doing the job.

But these responses do not have to occur. Like anything else, the way in which control systems are introduced seems to make a difference in terms of their acceptance. The research seems to suggest the following five factors:

1 *Understanding.* Employees seem to be less offended by policies, rules, budgets, and appraisal systems if they understand why they were introduced and the input that led up to the decisions that were made. A little explanation helps.

2 *Participation.* People seem to be less threatened by and more committed to the control system if they contribute to it in those areas where they can help. Their help should be solicited.

3 *Flexibility.* Control systems, including budgets, can be more or less flexible. There are often good reasons why overruns occur, deadlines are not met, or performance is substandard. The system should be flexible enough to adjust to these problems.

4 *Feedback.* Most control systems include feedback about how units or individuals are performing. This feedback, if relayed properly, can help correct mistakes, increase learning, and be used for developmental purposes.

5 *Fairness.* A control system has to be perceived as fair to be accepted. Preferential treatment is sure to create hostility and rejection. Evaluation should be openly discussed and procedures uniformly applied.

If these principles are adhered to, there is a good chance the control system can serve both as an indicator of organizational effectiveness and also as a source of motivation and development. Handled well, a control system can reduce ambiguity, provide rewards, increase involvement, and stimulate development. We will discuss some of these issues in more detail in our chapter on performance appraisal (Chapter 14).

Summary

Listed below are the major points presented in the chapter:

1 Power is seen as the force that A can bring to bear on B to modify B's behavior. It is based on B's perception. If B thinks A will use outcomes B values as a result of compliance or noncompliance, then A has power over B.

2 The outcomes that A controls are based on A's resources. These resources include rewards, punishments, information, expertise, legitimacy, and

attractiveness (referent power). If B values these outcomes, values the relationship, and has few other options or counterpower, B is likely to comply.

3 Specific behavioral strategies are often used by A to indicate to B what power resources are operating. Norms may be invoked (e.g., fairness, reciprocity), information manipulated, expertise illustrated, threats or promises uttered, or compromises suggested. The particular strategy used depends on the person and the setting.

4 The use of power is frequently not very pleasant for the recipient or ennobling for the user. The user of power often devalues the efforts of the less powerful, attributes their success to his or her own skills, and inhibits good interpersonal relationships—not a very pleasant picture.

5 Control systems refer to the organization's attempts to assess, regulate, and modify effectiveness. At the individual level these systems clarify expectations, structure tasks, evaluate action, and provide feedback.

6 Planning is the first component in the control system. It includes the setting of objectives and goals along with specific plans to meet these goals. Both short-term tactical goals and long-term strategic goals are important.

7 The control component focuses on evaluation and feedback. The criteria for effectiveness are based on quantity, quality, cost, and time data. The strategies for controling behavior and thus effecting these criteria are policies and rules, the organizational design, personnel activities, performance appraisal and compensation, budgets, and the technology.

8 Systems of control which are thoroughly understood, are jointly established, provide feedback, and are flexible and fair are more likely to be accepted and serve positive functions than systems without these properties.

Implications for practice

We should be clear about one point: Both power and control are used to get things done. In that respect they are organizational necessities. An effective organization invariably has effective systems of control and uses of power.

There are some issues that were raised in the discussion of power that should be repeated and emphasized. First, power is not just what you see. A powerful manager may frequently not gain compliance while a less powerful one will. Power lies in the pressure felt by the recipient, not in the recipient's behavior. One manager may be saddled with a group of malcontents while another is blessed with acquiescing subordinates. To evaluate a manager's power (or leadership ability) based on compliance alone would be a mistake. Much more is involved.

Besides the knowledge of who has power, there is the question of its use. The research is clear on this topic. People prefer to use and have used on them the resources of expert, referent, and legitimate power. Both the powerful and the powerless generally find the reward and punishment resources to be distasteful. We like to feel that we have some choice in the matter—not that we are being manipulated or forced into action.

We are not saying that rewards and punishments are not needed. They serve a very important function as the resource of last resort and as feedback mechanisms. However, we should recognize that when promises and threats are used as inducements, negative consequences are likely to occur. Rarely will B come to like what he or she is doing, and the relationship between A and B is likely to be strained and uncomfortable. The prognosis for long-term effectiveness is poor when these resources form the major use of power.

Similar types of analogies can be drawn for control systems. Although the focus shifts to organizational effectiveness from individual effectiveness, the implications are the same. Systems in which the employees participate in establishing the control mechanisms, understand it, and see it as flexible and fair are likely to be accepted and can serve as positive systems of motivation and development. To use the power-resource analogy, such systems would be based upon legitimate, referent, expert, information, and reward power rather than punishment power. People would do things because they wanted to, not because they had to.

As a final point, we should mention that control systems serve another very important function: they reduce ambiguity and uncertainty. We all like to know what is expected of us as individuals, as groups, and as an organization in a larger social framework. Such knowledge provides meaning for our actions. For this reason, it seems imperative that systems of control should be explained. The rationale behind the systems, the goals accepted and those rejected, and the plan to reach those goals should be made available whenever possible. Such frank and open disclosures should enhance individual commitment to both the immediate task and the long-range organizational goals.

Discussion questions

1 Think of some people who have power over you. What power bases do they use? Which ones are most effective?
2 Do you think power corrupts? Does it ruin effective interpersonal communication? Can we get things done without it?
3 Describe the various control strategies used in organizations. What factors make control systems more acceptable?

Case: Obedient Betty

Mr. Musgrave was having one of his tantrums. He had been harassed all day with petty details and he had not gotten anything done. He was ready to snap at anyone.

Just then his secretary buzzed him on the intercom. "Yeah, what do you want?" growled Musgrave. "It's Casey Templeton on the phone, sir," replied the secretary, Betty Odland. "He says he's not happy with the last shipment we sent him and he's ready to cancel his contract. He sounds angry."

"Tell that SOB to jump in the lake. I can't be bothered with his moaning and groaning. And don't interrupt me again until after lunch," yelled Musgrave.

Ms. Odland was fed up. She did not like being treated that way. So, with the intercom still on, she calmly picked up the phone and said, ''Mr. Templeton? Mr. Musgrave said you should go jump in the lake. He can't be bothered with your moaning and groaning.''

Questions about the case

1 Should Betty have done what she did?
2 Who is responsible in this situation? How literally should we follow instructions or orders?
3 Is there a point where we can and should refuse to obey? What is that point?

Additional readings

Bass, B. M., & Leavitt, H. J. Some experiences in planning and operating. *Management Science,* 1963, **10,** 574–585.

* Block, E. B. Accomplishment/cost: Better project control. *Harvard Business Review,* May–June 1971, 110–124.

** Boulanger, D. C. Program evaluation and review technique. *Advanced Management,* 1961, **26,** 8–12.

** Emery, J. C. *Organizational planning and control systems.* London: Macmillan, 1969.

Fodor, E. M. Group stress, authoritarian style of control and use of power. *Journal of Applied Psychology,* 1976, **61,** 313–318.

** Giglioni, G. B., & Bedeian, A. G. A conspectus of management control theory: 1900–1972. *Academy of Management Journal,* 1974, **17,** 292–305.

Hall, W. K. Corporate strategic planning—some perspectives for the future. *Michigan Business Review,* 1972, **24,** 16–21.

Ivancevich, J. M. An analysis of control, bases of control and satisfaction in an organizational setting. *Academy of Management Journal,* 1970, **13,** 427–436.

** Lefcourt, H. M. The function of the illusions of control and freedom. *American Psychologist,* 1973, **28,** 417–425.

* Martin, N. H., & Sims, J. H. Power tactics. *Harvard Business Review,* November–December 1956, 25–29.

Mechanic, D. Sources of power of lower participants in complex organizations. *Administrative Science Quarterly,* 1962, **7,** 349–364.

Nealey, S. M. Organizational influence: Interpersonal power in military organizations. *Final Report ONR N00014-73-0259.* Seattle, Wash.: Battelle Human Affairs Research Centers, 1976.

Pettigrew, A. M. Information as a power resource. *Sociology,* 1972, **6,** 187–204.

Reimnitz, C. A. Testing a planning and control model in nonprofit organizations. *Academy of Management Journal,* 1972, **15,** 77–90.

* Thompson, P. H., & Dalton, G. W. Performance appraisal: Manager beware. *Harvard Business Review,* January–February 1970, pp. 149–157.

*Possible reading for students

**Review of literature or comprehensive source material

13
Leadership

Better to reign in hell than serve in heav'n.   John Milton

Leadership is a key process in any organization. We attribute the success or failure of an organization to its leadership. When a business venture, a university, or an athletic team is successful, it is the president or coach that often receives the credit. When failure occurs, it is usually the same individual at the top that is replaced. Thus, one of the key elements of concern in any organization is how to attract, train, and keep people who will be effective leaders.

This concern seems to be justified by the research data. Numerous studies show that variations in the behavior of the leader are related to variations in group morale or group productivity. What we need to know, however, is how to select the people with the right approach, how to train them, and where to place them. To do this well demands that we define clearly and precisely what we mean by leadership.

Definitions of leadership

Suppose you were asked to go into an organization, select a work group, and find out who was the leader. What would you do? You might refer to the formal organization chart or you might simply ask some of the group members to point out their leader. Some people might observe the group to see who talks the most, who gives orders, who has the expertise, who is most liked, who has "charisma," or who has the greatest impact on productivity. All these alternatives are possible and have been tried at one time or another.

But any one of these definitions might cause some problems. What if the formal leader was not the person chosen by the group? Is a person a leader only if the group members recognize the person as fulfilling that role? What if two
306 people were equally liked or if one person was the most influential but another

individual had the greatest impact on productivity? Is it possible to have more than one leader in a group? Also, some of the criteria for leadership listed above describe personality traits while others refer to observable behavior. Does leadership have to do with who a person is (i.e., personality) or what he or she does (i.e., behavior)?

All these questions are meant to illustrate an important point. Researchers could not agree on what was meant by leadership. Different investigators defined it in different ways. There was some consensus on general statements such as ''Leaders have followers'' and ''Effective leaders somehow get others to do things that are helpful for group performance.'' But how and why performance increased was unclear. More recently, however, some consensus is being reached on how we should handle this problem.

One suggestion was to break down the question of ''What is leadership?'' into two questions: (1) What characteristics or behaviors make it more likely that an individual will become a leader? and (2) Once someone holds a formal position as a leader, what characteristics make it more or less likely that he or she will be effective? The first question is one of *leader emergence*—who is likely to assume and hold the position of leader.

The second question sees *leadership* as those characteristics or behaviors that make an individual effective in a given position. Leadership is seen not as some set of universally agreed-upon traits (e.g., charismatic, influential, well liked) but as those things which are positively related to group productivity in a given situation. In some cases being liked may be a help, in others it may be a hinderance. In some jobs, being aggressive and manipulative may get one promoted, while in other jobs the same traits may lead to dismissal. The critical idea is that there is no one best style of leadership. What will work best depends on the proper combination of personal characteristics and the specific situation in which one works. To understand this position more fully, we must examine how researchers came to these conclusions.

Leadership emergence

Interestingly enough, one of the reasons that leadership emergence has become a topic of interest is based on political traditions. Most Western nations with some sort of democratic political process allow all sorts of people to rise to positions of responsibility. One does not need great wealth, personal friends, or family tradition to gain access to power. As far back as Weber's early statements of the classical approach to organization theory comes the idea that the position of leader is awarded on the basis of merit. Therefore, the study of how people obtain these positions has been of major importance.

Two issues seem to be worthy of discussion. The first centers on why someone would want to become a leader and the second identifies what one must do to attain such a position.

It is fairly obvious that a leadership position can provide important economic benefits. In some organizations, top management may receive 10 to 50 times the salary of the lowest-level employees. But there are other rewards of holding such a position. Typically, a leader is respected. Also, the job itself may be challenging, and the higher up one goes in an organization, the more individual input or impact one may have on organizational policies. Thus, a greater sense of achievement and accomplishment may be possible.

But just wanting to be a leader is not enough. There are some traits and characteristics which do make it a little more likely that one will rise to a position of leadership. In the most comprehensive review of this literature, Stogdill reports:

1 The following conclusions are supported by uniformly positive evidence from 15 or more of the studies surveyed:
   (*a*) The average person who occupies a position of leadership exceeds the average member of his group in the following respects: (1) intelligence, (2) scholarship, (3) dependability in exercising responsibilities, (4) activity and social participation, and (5) socioeconomic status.
   (*b*) The qualities, characteristics, and skills required in a leader are determined to a large extent by the demands of the situation in which he is to function as a leader.
2 The following conclusions are supported by uniformly positive evidence from 10 or more of the studies surveyed:
   (*a*) The average person who occupies a position of leadership exceeds the average member of his group to some degree in the following respects: (1) sociability, (2) initiative, (3) persistence, (4) knowing how to get things done, (5) self-confidence, (6) alertness to, and insight into, situations, (7) cooperativeness, (8) popularity, (9) adaptability, and (10) verbal facility.[1]

Two points are worthy of note. First, these traits or characteristics are essentially what one would expect. People who rise to leadership positions have certain personal and behavioral characteristics which help them to get along with people yet get things done. But the second point, and perhaps the most important one, is that while some skills or abilities generally may be helpful, in most cases it is the situation which partially determines what traits will be most likely to lead to leadership status. For example, physical prowess may be important on athletic teams while intellectual skills may be important for academic roles.

Some group characteristics which are important have also been identified. We find, for instance, that as the group size increases, the number of acceptable leaders decreases. Apparently, the larger the group, the greater the demand for greater skill and competence in the leadership position. This makes sense when you consider the fact that as a group grows larger, the impact of any one follower is proportionally less. Probably as one feels that one's own impact decreases, it becomes more important that the leader be effective.

There are research studies which suggest that one's physical location in the group is important. The more central the individual in terms of access to people and information, the more likely the person is to emerge as the leader. Also, individuals who take leadership positions (e.g., the chair at the head of the table) in group discussions are also likely to be chosen as leader. Thus, a number of

[1] R. M. Stogdill, *Handbook of leadership*. New York: Free Press, 1974, p. 62.

The leader frequently sits at the head of the table and has various leadership props, such as the gavel in the above photograph. (*By permission of University of Washington* Daily.)

personal, interpersonal, and situational characteristics all influence who will become a leader.

But given that a group has a leader, how can we tell which leaders will be most effective? This is our second question, and a number of major approaches have been suggested through the years.

Trait approach

Young men are fitter to invent than to judge. fitter for execution than for counsel and fitter for new projects than for settled business. Francis Bacon

The earliest work in the area of leadership effectiveness shared a common bias—most behavior was attributed to the underlying personality of the actor. If observations were made of a particular leader, the causes of that person's behavior were seen as personality traits, such as aggressiveness, extroversion, or enthusiasm, or personal qualities, such as age or experience. It was not the situation or the environment that was important but the enduring personal characteristics of the leader. The man made the times rather than the reverse.

This approach was sometimes called the "great man" theory of leadership. The idea was that if we could somehow observe large numbers of effective leaders, we could determine a small set of common traits which could be used to identify future great leaders. The job of selection would become an easy one: simply administer the right tests and select people with the appropriate personality profiles or scores. This was an intuitively appealing idea.

It also led to hundreds of research studies designed to determine what personal

Blonk cannot say any words, but he sure is good at the snort, grunt, and howl.

Leadership is partly related to the traits of the leader.

characteristics were related to leadership effectiveness. Physical traits such as age, height, weight, and energy were investigated along with social background (e.g., education, social status), intelligence, and a long list of personality measures (e.g., assertiveness, dominance, independence, self-confidence, and objectivity) and social characteristics (e.g., attractiveness, popularity, tact).

The reviews of this literature that appeared in the late 1940s and early 1950s were rather devastating. They indicated that there was very little consistency in the results. In most cases a particular trait might be positively related to performance in one setting but negatively related to performance in some other situation. The most recent review by Stogdill (mentioned previously) is somewhat more encouraging. While he most certainly recognizes the fact that some situations require one sort of person while other situations may require a different type of person, there are some general characteristics that seem to be present in most effective leaders in most situations. He suggests that effective leaders can be seen as having " . . . a strong drive for responsibility and task completion, vigor and persistence in pursuit of goals, venturesomeness and originality in problem solving, drive to exercise initiative in social situations, self-confidence and sense of personal identity, willingness to accept consequences of decision and action, readiness to absorb interpersonal stress, willingness to tolerate frustration and delay, ability to influence other persons' behavior, and capacity to structure social interaction systems to the purpose at hand'' (p. 81).

To summarize, the trait approach, while helpful in some ways, fell short of its goal. To understand effective leadership, one had to look at more than just personality traits. Critics of the trait approach focused on two main issues. First, they felt that personality measures typically were unreliable and that our efforts should concentrate more on actual observations of leader behavior. The question should be not "Who is he?" but "What does he *do*?" The second issue concerned the situation. What elements of the environment were important for determining who would be an effective leader? Obviously some traits worked in one place but not in others. What was it about these different situations that demanded different traits?

Behavior approach

Dissatisfaction with the trait approach to leadership led to a new tactic which focused on leadership behavior. The methodological and theoretical emphasis was on reliable observations rather than on internal states or traits. Leadership was viewed as the performance of those acts which helped the group achieve its preferred outcomes (e.g., improved the quality of interaction, built cohesiveness, made resources available to the group, or increased effectiveness).

One well-known theoretical statement about general leadership philosophies has been made by McGregor.[2] He suggested that there were two main management styles which he called theory X and theory Y. The former approach was seen as highly directive and authoritarian and is based on the premise that employees need to be controlled and guided by their superior. Theory Y was more permissive. Employees were seen as self-motivated and striving for goals of excellence and accomplishment (see Chapter 7 for a full discussion of McGregor's work). While the theory X versus theory Y distinction was an important theoretical contribution, it did little to tell us how leaders actually behaved.

Three major behavioral approaches which attempt to measure what the leader actually does in a group can be identified. Table 13-1 summarizes what the researchers found. The conclusions that can be drawn from this table are worth

[2]D. McGregor. *The human side of enterprise*. New York: McGraw-Hill, 1960.

Table 13-1. Leadership Styles

School	Researchers	Setting	Respondents	Styles
Harvard	Bales Slater	Laboratory	Observers	Activity Task ability Likability
Ohio State	Shartle Stogdill Fleishman	Field	Members	Consideration Intiation of structure
Michigan	Katz Kahn Likert	Field	Leaders	Job centered Employee centered

Table 13-2. Summary of the Number of Research Studies Relating Leadership Styles to Productivity and Satisfaction*

	Direction of Relationship		
	Positive	Zero	Negative
Productivity and interpersonally oriented styles	47	32	14
Productivity and task-oriented styles	47	26	7
Satisfaction and interpersonally oriented styles	48	9	7
Satisfaction and task-oriented styles	14	8	11

*Adapted from R. M. Stogdill. *Handbook of leadership.* New York: Free Press, 1974.

emphasizing. First, the different schools did their research in different ways. Some of the work was in the laboratory (Harvard) while some was in the field (Ohio State and Michigan); some used ratings made by observers (Harvard), some used questionnaires filled in by group members (Ohio State), and some used questionnaires filled out by the leaders themselves (Michigan). Yet, the major findings were the same for all three groups.[3] There was general agreement that at least two distinct leadership styles could be identified. One was task-oriented (task ability, initiation of structure, job centered) and the other was more interpersonally oriented (likability, consideration, employee centered). These findings fit well conceptually with McGregor's work and are accepted by most researchers as valid.

But the empirical results were somewhat puzzling. It was far from clear that one or the other of these styles was most effective. In some cases task orientation was best, in other cases an interpersonal style was best. Stogdill's recent review of all the research in this area documents this problem.[4] Table 13-2 tabulates these results.

Looking at the productivity results suggests that there are almost as many cases where either style is unrelated or negatively related to productivity as there

---

[3]R. Bales & P. Slater. Role differentiation in small decision-making groups. In T. Parsons et al. (Eds.), *Family socialization and interaction process.* Glencoe, Ill.: Free Press, 1955, pp. 259–306; C. L. Shartle. *Executive performance and leadership.* Columbus: Ohio State University Research Foundation, 1952; R. M. Stogdill. *Manual for the leader behavior description questionnaire—Form XII.* Columbus: Ohio State University. Bureau of Business Research, 1963; R. Likert. An emerging theory of organization, leadership and management. In L. Petrullo and B. Bass (Eds.), *Leadership and interpersonal behavior.* New York: Holt, 1961, pp. 290–309; R. L. Kahn & D. Katz. Leadership practices in relation to productivity and morale. In D. Cartwright and A. Zander (Eds.), *Group dynamics: Research and theory.* New York: Harper & Row, 1953, pp. 612–628.
[4]Stogdill. Op. cit.

are situations where it is positively related. This can hardly be seen as strong support that one style is better than another or that one style is good across a variety of settings.

The satisfaction results, on the other hand, are quite clear: an interpersonal style is positively related to satisfaction, while task-oriented styles are not very effective in this regard. In short, then, it seems as if a leader's show of consideration was likely to lead to higher job satisfaction on the part of subordinates. To predict who would be most effective, however, required more information. Some researchers felt we needed additional ways to classify leaders, and some more complex behavioral style assessment and identification procedures have been developed. Other researchers, however, thought that we needed to know more about the situation in which the leader worked. Some of this research had been going on since the demise of the trait approach (simultaneously but independently of the behavior approach) and had emphasized the functions that groups had to fulfill.

Functional approach

One way to analyze situations was to look at the things that needed to get done in a group. Different researchers came up with different typologies. Variables such as defining objectives, maintaining goal direction, maintaining group structure, facilitating interaction, facilitating group performance, and maintaining morale were frequently listed. A summary of these functions was made, and it is presented in the following list.

1 Functions which are largely *procedural:*
    a Encouraging, permitting, selectively restricting participation
    b Problem proposing—stating and restating the problem, what remains to be solved, diagnosing the situation, interpreting (synthesizing) the contributions of others
    c Information seeking—asking for facts, ideas, etc.
    d Summarizing, maintaining orientation to the agenda
2 Functions which are largely *substantive:*
    a Substantive contributions, fact giving, etc.
    b Stating agreement, disagreement, voting, etc.
    c Obtaining facts through investigation, and so forth as in case of much committee action
3 Functions which are largely *maintenance* functions:
    a Producing behaviors which encourage tension release
    b Encouraging, complementing, joking, creating situations in which some self-oriented needs may be satisfied

This type of analysis suggested that the three group characteristics that were most important for leadership had to do with how well people get along with one another (maintenance), how well the task was specified or structured (procedural), and how well the group was able to move toward task accomplishment (substantive).

An important part of the leadership function is to provide structure and expertise in order that subordinates have a clear idea of what they are supposed to do. (*By permission of University of Washington* Daily.)

However, it was also fairly obvious that it would be hard to find leaders that could fulfill all these functions. Maintenance functions required neutrality and interpersonal skill. Procedural functions required neutrality with a task orientation, and substantive contributions required nonneutrality and a task orientation. It would be hard for one individual to handle all functions at the same time.

What was needed was some way to analyze situations in terms of what was needed and then to match that situation with a leader that had the appropriate behavioral style. Since we now had some agreement about the major behavioral styles and the major situational characteristics, the next logical step was to develop a theory which combined both leader characteristics and situational demands to predict group effectiveness.

Contingency approaches

It had become clear that effective leadership was contingent upon the right person being in the right place at the right time. Previous research had given us some ways to classify people and some ways to classify situations (see Figure 13-1). At this point a number of rather broad contingency type approaches were suggested.

The contingency model

An extensive research program by Fiedler has resulted in the development of the "contingency model of leadership effectiveness." This model suggests that to be

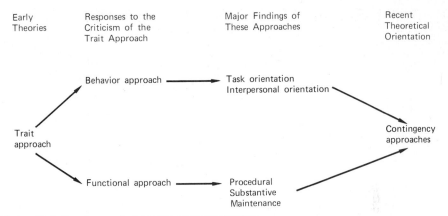

| Early
Theories | Responses to the
Criticism of the
Trait Approach | Major Findings of
These Approaches | Recent
Theoretical
Orientation |

Figure 13-1. Development of contingency approaches.

effective a leader's "style" must be matched with the demands of the situation. To understand this model it is necessary to define effectiveness, leadership style, and the situational demands. The next sections of this chapter will describe the model, the data on which it is based, validation evidence, and the implications of using such a model.[5]

Effectiveness. By *effective* leadership, Fiedler means that the leader's group has performed well, or that it has succeeded in comparison with other groups. In other words, leadership effectiveness, as the term is defined here, is based on group performance.

Leadership orientation. Relationship-oriented versus task-oriented leadership is assessed by means of the least-preferred-coworker scale (LPC). The individual thinks of all the people with whom he or she has ever worked and then describes the least preferred coworker on seventeen bipolar-scale adjectives (e.g., efficient——inefficient). A favorable description of the least preferred coworker suggests a relationship-oriented or motivational leader; an unfavorable description indicates a task-oriented leader.

Factors determining situational favorableness. Fiedler defines the basic component of leadership as influence. That is, leadership is seen as a relationship in which one person tries to influence others in the performance of a common task. Therefore, Fiedler's attempt to describe the situation consists of one underlying dimension: the degree to which the leader can influence group members.

Fiedler argues that this influence dimension is composed of three major factors. The first and most important variable which contributes to the leader's influence is defined as the leader-member relationships. In situations where these relationships are positive, the leader is believed to have greater influence than where they are negative. The second factor is defined as the degree to which the task is structured or unstructured. The greater the structure, the easier it is for the leader to tell group members what to do. The last factor is the leader's formal

[5]F. E. Fiedler. *A theory of leadership effectiveness.* New York: McGraw-Hill, 1967.

Table 13-3. Classification of Situations According to Fiedler

	Leader-Member Relationships	Task Structure	Position Power
1	Good	Structured	High
2	Good	Structured	Low
3	Good	Unstructured	High
4	Good	Unstructured	Low
5	Poor	Structured	High
6	Poor	Structured	Low
7	Poor	Unstructured	High
8	Poor	Unstructured	Low

position power. The more positive and negative rewards that the leader can use, the more influence the leader will have. Dichotomizing these three dimensions leads to the classification system of group situations shown in Table 13-3. Note that this system says nothing about how intrinsically difficult the task itself may be. A structured task—say, building an electronic computer—may be much more difficult than a more unstructured job such as preparing an entertainment program. But the leader's problem of influencing the group should be greater in a volunteer entertainment committee than in the task of building a computer. It will obviously be easier to lead if you are the liked and trusted captain of a rifle squad (cell 1) than if you are the informal leader of a recreational baseball team (cell 2), and it will be very difficult indeed to be the disliked and distrusted leader of a volunteer group which is asked to plan the program of an annual meeting (cell 8). In other words, the cells can be ordered on the basis of how favorable or unfavorable the situation will be for the leader in terms of the leader's influence.

Empirical results. Given that you have a measure of leadership orientation and a situational classification system, the next step is to combine the two. The combination should allow the researcher to predict what sort of style is best for a particular situation. Fiedler's results with over 800 groups have provided fairly consistent results. Using basketball teams, tank crews, surveying parties, boards of directors, and many other types of groups produced the findings presented in Figure 13-2.

The correlation between LPC scores and performance is positive in situations of moderate favorability (situations 4, 5, and 6). The more interpersonally oriented the leader (i.e., the higher the LPC score), the better the group performance. Moreover, the correlation between LPC scores and performance in highly favorable situations (i.e., 1, 2, and 3) or highly unfavorable situations (i.e., 8) is negative. In these situations the more task-oriented the leader (i.e., the lower the LPC score), the better the performance.

Taken as a whole, the figure shows that the task-oriented leaders are more effective in situations in which the leader has very little or very much influence. The relationship-oriented person is most effective in situations which are only moderately favorable for the leader. Fiedler argues that in the very easy or very difficult situations, strong task-oriented leadership is needed to be effective. Someone needs to keep things going. In situations of moderate favorability, the leader who spends time being concerned about the interpersonal relationships in the group will be most effective. Thus, the model gives us some idea of what type of person should be best for a particular setting.

The contingency model, however, has its critics as well as its proponents. The use of the LPC scale has been questioned by many researchers. They argue that better, more reliable measures of actual leader behavior are available. A second criticism is that the classification system of situations is seen as too simplistic. Other factors besides the three suggested by Fiedler are obviously important. But the criticisms nonwithstanding, the contingency model is an important contribution to understanding leadership. It was the first major attempt to combine estimates of the leader's style with estimates of the situation. This was a major step forward.

Fiedler has recently attempted to extend the findings of the contingency model to organizational processes designed to train or rotate leaders to improve their performance.[6] The contingency model predicts that any general training or rotation experience that was similar for all the trainees would increase the effectiveness of some leaders and decrease the effectiveness of others. For example, if all the upper-level managers of a particular organization gain interpersonal skills through sensitivity training, this will in some cases make a better match between leaders and their situation and produce an equally poor match for other leaders. A person-oriented leader in an unfavorable situation may be able to make the leader-member relationship better with such training. The leader would then be in a situation of moderate favorability where a good match occurs (a move from situation 8 to 4 for a high-LPC leader). However, the same training with the same change in situational favorability will result in relatively worse performance for a low-LPC, task-oriented leader (who does not perform well in situation 4.)

[6]F. E. Fiedler & M. M. Chemers. *Leadership and effective management.* Glenview, Ill.: Scott, Foresman, 1974.

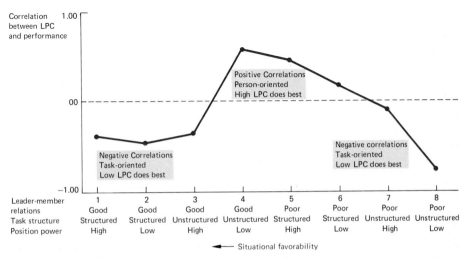

Figure 13-2. Results from the contingency-model research.

Yes, she is definitely taking over the leadership role—
looks like the right bee in the right place at the right time.

A contingency theory of leadership in action.

The crucial point is that Fiedler argues that the contingency model can help to predict what type of training will be most effective for different types of leaders in different situations. Fiedler has recently presented data from a number of research studies which suggest success in making such differential predictions. Potentially, the theory may be very useful in dealing with some areas of leadership, such as training, which have been confusing to date.

The path-goal approach

Another major theory that attempts to match the leader's style with certain interpersonal and situational variables is called the path-goal approach. The major concern of the theory is how the leader's behavior is motivating or satisfying because of its impact on a subordinate's perception of his or her goals and the paths to those goals. A leader through the use of positive and negative task and interpersonal rewards can have a major impact on these perceptions. The leader can specify goals that are more or less attractive to a subordinate and can make it easy or difficult to attain the goals. Thus, a leader can influence both the type of outcomes experienced by the subordinate as well as clarify the behavior-outcome relationship.

House and Mitchell have recently provided a review of the work on this approach,[7] and a diagram of the main relationships is presented in Table 13-4. As

[7]R. J. House & T. R. Mitchell. Path goal theory of leadership. *Journal of Contemporary Business,* 1974. **3,** 81–99.

Table 13-4. Summary of Path-Goal Relationship

Leader Behavior	and	Contingency Factors	Cause	Subordinate Attitudes and Behavior
Directive		Subordinate characteristics	Personal perceptions	Job satisfaction
		Authoritarianism		Job → Rewards
Supportive		Locus of control		Acceptance of leader
		Ability		Leader → Rewards
Achievement-oriented		Environmental factors	Motivational stimuli	Motivational behavior
		The task		Effort → Performance
Participative		Formal authority system	Constraints	Performance → Rewards
		Primary work group	Rewards	

one can see, there is a somewhat more complex classification system of both leaders and situational variables than that suggested by the contingency model. Four leadership styles are identified: directive, supportive, achievement-oriented, and participative. The situational variables important to the leader are of two types: (1) the environmental factors such as task structure, power, and interpersonal relations in the work group and (2) subordinate personality characteristics such as authoritarianism or internal-external locus of control. Taking into account both the leadership style and contingency factors allows the researcher to make predictions about who will perform best.

Let us take an example for each class of contingency factors. One set of research studies has shown that employees with an internal locus of control (people who believe that what happens to them occurs as a function of their behavior) are more satisfied with a participative leader than employees with an external locus of control (people who believe that what happens to them occurs because of chance or luck). Externals, on the other hand, are more satisfied with a directive leader than are internals. Intuitively these findings make sense. A more independent, internal-type person prefers more autonomy and say in decisions, while a more dependent, external person prefers a leader who structures the environment. The best match is dependent upon both the leadership style and the subordinate's personality.[8]

Using one of the environmental factors has produced similar findings. For example, House has shown that a more structuring, directive leadership style is generally more effective when the group is working on an unstructured task. Assume you are given a number of blueprints which depict the construction of some new mobile homes. You are asked for an estimate of needed raw materials. But suppose you do not know how to read blueprints, or how to make the computations, or what types of materials were available, etc. Comments that helped structure and direct your efforts would be greatly appreciated.

On the other hand, when the task is more structured, a more supportive leadership style seems to be best.[9] If you had much experience working with blueprints and the needed steps were all part of the job order, what you do not need is a supervisor standing over your shoulder telling you things you already know. Support and encouragement are more likely to be helpful than redundant reminders. Again, the proper match of style and situation is needed.

While the path-goal approach is recent in its development, it too has provided important insights into the leadership-effectiveness question. First, it has based its theoretical assumptions squarely on the expectancy theory of motivation discussed earlier. More specifically, the way to motivate subordinates is to link hard work frequently and consistently to goals that are highly valued by the subordinate. Second, the theory has attempted to include some factors such as subordinate personality into the overall contingency framework. While the specification

[8]T. R. Mitchell, C. M. Smyser, & S. E. Weed. Locus of control: Supervision and work satisfaction. *Academy of Management Journal,* September 1975, **18**, 623–630.

[9]R. J. House & G. A. Dessler. Path-goal theory of leadership: Some post hoc and a priori tests. In J. G. Hunt and L. L. Larson (Eds.), *Contingency approaches to leadership.* Carbondale, Ill. Southern Illinois University Press, 1974, pp. 29–59.

of situations does not have an underlying classification dimension (such as Fiedler's situational favorability), it has suggested a number of areas for further research.

Other approaches

There are some other contingency-type approaches which, while not as highly developed and tested as the two mentioned above, have helped us to understand what makes a leader effective. The role-theory approach of Katz and Kahn saw leadership from an open systems perspective.[10] Organizations and levels within organizations differ in terms of their complexity, pressure for change, and flexibility. Different types of leaders are suggested for different jobs, such as a structuring leader for lower-level routine jobs but a leader with more consideration for upper-level positions. The theory is rather broad in its perspective, however, and few specifics as to the important leadership styles or situational variables are provided.

Some other approaches by Yukl, Bass and Valenzi, and Graen are available.[11] While the particulars are different, the general thrust is similar. Different types of leaders are needed for different types of situations and people. This conclusion has some important implications for practice.

Summary

A few points which bear repeating are listed below:

1 Leaders have a substantial impact on group performance. It is important, therefore, to understand how this occurs.
2 Some personal characteristics are available which will distinguish leaders from followers and effective leaders from ineffective ones. But in general, the situation is a more important determinant of what behavior is most appropriate.
3 Two main behavioral styles are easily identified, and these are a task orientation and an interpersonal orientation. More refined distinctions are available, but these two seem most important.
4 Some theories are now available based on contingency notions. They suggest the particular leadership style that is most effective in a specific situation.
5 These contingency ideas have some important implications for organizational practice. In general, they question the idea that excellence as defined

---

[10]D. Katz & R. L. Kahn. *The social psychology of organizations.* New York: Wiley, 1966.

[11]G. A. Yukl. Toward a behavioral theory of leadership. *Organizational behavior and human performance,* 1971, **6,** 404–440; B. M. Bass & E. R. Valenzi. Contingent aspects of effective management styles. In J. G. Hunt and L. L. Larson (Eds.), *Contingency approaches to leadership.* Carbondale, Ill.: Southern Illinois University Press, 1974, pp. 130–152; G. Graen, F. Dansereau, & T. Minami. Dysfunctional leadership styles. *Organizational behavior and human performance,* 1972, **7,** 216–236.

by some global set of traits or past performance in a different job is really the best criteria to be used for selection or promotion.

Implications for practice

What we have suggested has some major relevance for the ongoing processes of selection, promotion, and training that regularly occur in most organizations. First, the best leader to select is not just the person with the highest score on some general set of traits (e.g., intelligence). It is far more important to know the specifics about the particular job for which the individual is being selected. With this information, one can select an individual with a style or set of skills and traits that match the actual behavioral requirements of the job.

A similar type of analysis is true for questions of promotion or transfer. Just to take someone who has done well in the past (especially if it is a very different type of job) does not ensure that this high level of performance will be sustained. So, past performance is not necessarily a good predictor of how an individual will do on a new job, especially if the job differs widely from the previous job. Again, it is important to match the job demands with the behavioral style of the prospective incumbent.

Finally, the same generalization is applicable for training programs. To send all top-level managers to the same type of training disregards the fact that different types of managers work in different types of settings with different types of subordinates. Giving everyone the same training may help some and hinder others. Fiedler has argued that one way to solve this problem is to use a new type of training: teach the manager how to diagnose his or her own style and the situation and then teach how to change the situation, so that the manager will be able to create a better style-situation match.

This idea is diametrically opposite of the underlying philosophy inherent in most training. Fiedler suggests that rather than attempting to change the person, we should show leaders how to change the situation. While little hard data currently exists to support this new perspective, Fiedler and others are currently researching the proposition. The results should be interesting.

Discussion questions

1 What do we mean by effective leadership? How would you select the effective leaders from a group of leaders?
2 Are leaders made by their times or do they make their times? Which is most important, the person or the situation?
3 Should we use training programs to change people or to teach people how to change the situation? What are the implications of your answer for other processes such as selection, placement, and promotion?

Case: Will the leader please stand up

The following is a transcript from a university faculty committee meeting.

Alan: Oh, here comes Connie. I guess we're all here now.

Glenn: Does anyone have an extra agenda? I lost mine.

Sheila: Sure, here have a couple. . . . Say, Glenn, I see that your department wants to offer a new course in accounting.

Glenn: Yeah, they're concerned that the students don't have any knowledge about taxes. They want . . .

Connie: Excuse me, but I think its getting late and we ought to get started.

Alan: Good, I agree. Let's get on with it. The first item on the agenda is the use of graduate students as teaching assistants. What's the problem here?

Jeffrey: Well, we're getting a lot of complaints from the undergraduates. They seem to think that some of the graduate TAs are unprepared and not very well supervised.

Alan: Well, how many classes do we staff with graduate students?

Jeffrey: In our department it is about 50 percent.

Sheila: That's about right for management as well.

Alan: What about accounting, Glenn?

Glenn: We're up to about 60 percent. Most of our introductory classes are taught by doctoral students. Our feedback has been really good. We don't get any complaints at all.

Sheila: Are you saying that somehow accounting graduate students are better teachers than those in finance and economics?

Glenn: No, I'm just saying we don't have any problems.

Connie: Do you supervise them in any way?

Glenn: Yes, we have a pretty well agreed-upon list of topics, books, and exercises that are to be used in these courses.

Connie: We have a similar thing in marketing. We gave the students some outlines and a list of possible texts and suggest strongly that they stay within those boundaries.

Jeffrey: That's a good point. I'll have to tell the rest of our department about it. Besides these lists do you provide any other feedback?

Alan: We do. We have a faculty course coordinator in charge of each undergraduate course for which we have multiple sections. The course coordinator meets with all students and helps them prepare materials. He also gives them teaching aids and tips if they are needed. We like the system . . . it seems to be working fairly well.

Jeffrey: Do you think it would be good for this committee to pass a resolution suggesting that all the departments use similar procedures?

Connie: I do. Why don't you put it in the form of a motion.

Jeffrey: I so move.

Sheila: Second.

Alan: Can anybody think of any reason why we shouldn't have such a system?

Glenn: Wait a minute, what exactly does the motion include?

Jeffrey: It suggests that each of the five departments do three things: First they have a faculty course coordinator for each undergraduate course taught by graduate students. Second, they generate an agreed-upon list of topics, texts, and exercises for each course, and, third, they provide systematic and periodic feedback to the TAs.

Glenn: I call the question.

Connie: All in favor?

The vote was unanimous in favor of the motion.

Questions about the case

1 Was there a leader of this group? Who do you think it was?
2 What sorts of dimensions distinguish the leader from the followers?
3 Do you think the type of leadership that was effective in this kind of situation would be effective in a military setting?

Additional readings

** Bass, B. M. *Leadership, psychology and organizational behavior.* New York: Harper, 1960.
   Fleishman, E. A. Twenty years of consideration and structure. In E. A. Fleishman and J. G. Hunt (Eds.), *Current developments in the study of leadership.* Carbondale, Ill.: Southern Illinois University Press, 1973, pp. 1–37.
   Gibb, C. A. *Leadership: Selected readings.* Baltimore: Penguin, 1969.
   Hemphill, J. K. Why people attempt to lead. In L. Petrullo and B. M. Bass (Eds.), *Leadership and interpersonal behavior.* New York: Holt, 1961.
   Hollander, E. P. *Leaders, groups and influence.* New York: Oxford University Press, 1964.
 * Hollander, E. P., & Julian, J. W. Contemporary trends in the analysis of leadership processes. *Psychological Bulletin,* 1969, **71**, 387–397.
** Hunt, J. G., & Larson, L. L. (Eds.). *Leadership frontiers.* Carbondale, Ill.: Southern Illinois University Press, 1975.
 * Korman, A. K. Consideration, initiating structure and organizational criteria. *Personnel Psychology,* 1966, **19**, 349–363.
** Likert, R. *The human organization.* New York: McGraw-Hill, 1967.
   Maier, N. R. F. *Problem-solving discussions and conferences: Leadership methods and skills.* New York: McGraw-Hill, 1963.
 * Raven, B. H., & Reitsema, J. The effects of varied clarity of group goal and group path upon the individual and his relation to his group. *Human Relations,* 1957, **10**, 29–45.
 * Sales, S. M. Supervisory style and productivity: Review and theory. *Personnel Psychology,* 1966, **19**, 275–286.

*Possible reading for students

**Review of literature or comprehensive source material

FIVE
INDIVIDUAL AND ORGANIZATIONAL EFFECTIVENESS

We come now to a section which represents the application of much of the preceding material. By now one should have a fairly firm understanding of individual and group behavior. Part 5 is designed to apply these principles so that individual and organizational effectiveness is enhanced.

Chapter 14 focuses on individual performance. The first problem discussed is one of selection—how we get the right person into the organization in the first place. Probably the most promising techniques are those that try to assess the degree to which a job applicant actually possesses the behavior necessary to perform effectively in a particular position. The closer the match between job requirements and behavioral skills, the higher the performance and satisfaction.

Two other topics discussed in Chapter 14 are performance appraisal and reward systems. Appraisal can be used both as an evaluation mechanism and for counseling purposes. An emphasis is placed on having a fair and continuing process of feedback. Reward systems also are a means of providing such feedback. Different sorts of compensation systems are discussed and evaluated. The most important point is that the particular reward system should match the requirements of the job.

Chapter 15 discusses training and development. Some of our principles of learning discussed earlier serve as the theoretical foundation for this chapter. Given the proper preliminary work, a thorough understanding of the learning process, and a sound empirical evaluation of the training, most programs can do what they are designed to do. All too frequently, however, one or more of these critical steps is omitted. A large portion of the chapter discusses current training programs, their shortcomings, and some possible solutions.

The final chapter in this section (Chapter 16) moves the level of analysis from the individual to the group. Much of the current work in the area of organizational behavior is concerned with organization development as contrasted with individual development. The goal is to discover ways in which groups can interact more effectively with other groups and within their own group. It is also an attempt to make the climate of the workplace more enriching and personally satisfying. The emphasis is on open, adaptive organizations that value personal development and enriching jobs.

To summarize, Part 5 concerns itself with what organizations can actually do to increase their effectiveness. The traditional personnel activities of selection, evaluation, development, and change, if properly employed, can have a major impact on the future success of any organization.

14

Employee performance

We are being whipsawed by both inflation and recession and pressured by powerful foreign economic forces . . . at the heart of our problem is the need to improve productivity.

Gerald Ford, 1975

In 1972 a Gallup poll reported that over 50 percent of the adult population of the United States thought that American workers were not producing as much as they should. People seem to feel that we are not working up to our capacity and that there is still room for significant improvement in productivity.

This issue is of central importance to the citizens of any society, because it bears directly on our standard of living. If we are more productive, we can increase the profits that a company makes and increase the salaries that the employees earn. However, increases in wages without increases in productivity usually lead to increased prices, inflation, and therefore a decreased standard of living. It is probably in everyone's best interest to increase our level of productivity.

Determinants of performance

The chapter on motivation pointed out that we often observe wide variations in performance for employees working on the same job. Some people may produce twice as much as their coworkers. In our earlier discussion we suggested that both personal abilities or skills *and* one's motivation contribute to their effectiveness, and we elaborated on a variety of ways in which social scientists had investigated motivation on the job. At that time we presented the equation

Performance = ability × motivation

This formula specifically incorporates the idea that the two factors are important 327 for good performance and that *both* must be present for good performance to occur. Ability without motivation or motivation without ability is not likely to lead to a high level of output. In the first case, the worker knows what to do but does not care, and in the second case the person works hard but does not have the skill.

Many examples occur in the sports world. Every year there are cases of individuals who have great skill but loaf. There are also individuals who go far on hustle without much ability. But eventually they either learn new skills or abilities, get excited and motivated by the game, or they leave. Rarely do they become the true stars of the sport. The focus of the present chapter is the actual policies and procedures that an organization can establish to ensure that it has highly qualified *and* motivated employees, and how these policies are seen and reacted to by the employees themselves.

Dated points of view

But before we proceed further, we should point out that our assumption about ability and motivation as joint contributors to performance is a fairly recent idea. Through the years there have been numerous other theories about how to ensure high employee performance. Some of these positions are reviewed below.

The great-man theory. For many years it was assumed that motivation was primarily economic (e.g., classical theory) and that most employees wanted the same things from their jobs. Differences in performance were attributed to differences in personal traits, abilities, and skills. The great-man approach suggested that all we had to do was identify the personal characteristics of our effective employees. Once an agreed-upon set was established, we could select people who fit these requirements and we would have an organization staffed with super performers.

The problems occurred when the theory was put to practice. First, the research results seemed to show that different characteristics were important for different jobs. To find a small agreed-upon list for all jobs was next to impossible. Second, some characteristics that clearly led to good performance on some jobs seemed to produce poor performance on others. Even a trait such as intelligence was occasionally a drawback for effectiveness. And finally, even when some agreed-upon list *for a particular job* was generated, selection of these types of people did not invariably mean they would all be successful. We began to recognize that motivation was an equally important factor in the performance equation.

Satisfaction produces effectiveness. From the human-relations movement came a new perspective on motivation. The employee was seen as being concerned about social and interpersonal aspects of the job. The physical and social environment should be pleasant in order to have highly motivated employees. For example, some theorists with this view stated in 1951 that "management has

Davis is a lousy ballplayer, but he sure gets along well with the fans.

People who are happy and satisifed are not necessarily productive.

at long last discovered that there is greater production, and hence greater profit, when workers are satisfied with their jobs. Improve the morale of a company and you improve production."[1]

This theory proposes that satisfaction causes productivity: a happy worker is a productive worker. The role of management is to design an environment that is physically and socially satisfying. Unfortunately, the research results over the years have not supported this position. It is just too simple an explanation. Numerous reviews of the literature show that performance and satisfaction are only weakly related and that very little evidence exists that satisfaction causes increased productivity.

These findings are not really surprising. The satisfaction causes productivity thesis omitted almost all concern for our ability or personal traits. Many people can be happy with a high-paying, interpersonally pleasant job but not have the skill to perform well. Also, the motivational explanation was inadequate. There was no emphasis on goals, equity, reinforcement, and other major factors that motivate individuals. The focus on satisfaction was just too narrow.

[1]Willard E. Parker & Robert W. Kleemeier. *Human relations in supervision: Leadership in management.* New York: McGraw-Hill, 1951, p. 10.

Past performance predicts future performance. The final dated proposition that we will discuss focused on the selection and placement of employees. The argument was that if people had performed well on other jobs they should do well on any new job. This approach is still used today as the major factor in personnel decisions in many organizations. We look at the employee's dossier and vita and letters of recommendation, and we base our prediction of future performance on their past performance. To be effective, all we have to do is select people who were previously effective.

This idea has some merit. As it turns out, this is a very good strategy under a restricted set of conditions. When the prospective employee is being asked to do a job that is *highly similar* to one where he or she has previously been effective, then past performance may be a good predictor of future performance.

In many cases, however, the jobs will differ a modest amount or perhaps even dramatically. As we mentioned under the great-man discussion, there is no reason to believe that the traits and skills that are effective in one job will necessarily be effective in another. Also, what motivated the individual was specific to the first job: a new and different job may present very different conditions that will affect the employee's effort.

The Peter principle, an amusing theory developed by Peter and Hull, described the logical extension of this proposition. Peter and Hull argue that since we continually use past performance to predict future performance, eventually we select or promote someone to a job where they are not effective. At this point, they no longer receive further promotions, because they are no longer effective. In the long run, Peter and Hull suggest that everyone is promoted to a level of incompetence, and the effectiveness of organizations suffers accordingly.[2]

The Peter principle is overly pessimistic. Past performance is not the only factor in the selection or promotion decision. However, their work did call attention to the problem that arises when past performance is used to predict future performance for different types of jobs.

New ideas

Rejection of the classical and human-relations approaches led to what we have described as contingency approaches. At the heart of the contingency idea is the proposition that performance is contingent upon the proper match between the individual and the job. The ability or skill factor in our earlier performance equation is essentially the assessment of the individual. The motivation factor is the social and environmental conditions that make up the job. The contingency idea forms the theoretical basis for our performance equation.

The aim of the organization using this approach is to maximize the fit between the individual and his or her job. To ensure that the employees have the proper skills and abilities, the processes of selection and training can be used. To ensure that the environment is motivating for these people requires that performance is properly rewarded and the job properly designed. To obtain effectiveness we

[2]Lawrence J. Peter & Raymond Hull. *The Peter principle: Why things go wrong.* New York: Morrow, 1969.

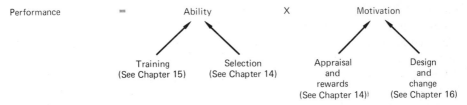

Figure 14-1. A general equation that summarizes the factors that contribute to employee performance.

must be sure that the right people are working on the right job under the right conditions.

The rest of this chapter and the two that follow are devoted to a discussion of how an organization can select and train people to have the proper skills and how rewards can be administered and jobs designed in order to maximize motivation. Figure 14-1 represents these topics and how they will be covered.

Selection

Suppose that you are an entrepreneur with a new product (e.g., a collapsible bicycle). You and some friends have developed a couple of prototypes, and it turns out that a large sporting goods company has decided to finance the production of your product. You know it will take thirty or forty people to produce a fair number of the bicycles, and these people will have to work on a variety of jobs. Some engineers will be needed, as well as some managers, a financial expert, some skilled workers for the actual construction process, and so on. You need to attract, select, and keep people who will do a good job.

How do you do it? How do you get the right people matched up with the right job? Probably the first thing you do is to imagine what sorts of tasks actually are to be performed. That is, you try to analyze the jobs themselves in terms of their requirements. This process is called *job analysis,* and it should provide a rough idea of the kinds of characteristics your employees will need.

The next step is to actually *select* people. This process requires that you find out something about the job applicants. Somehow you must discover whether the potential employees possess the characteristics that are important for successful performance. Should you use an interview, psychological tests, or some on-the-job simulation to gather this information? There are strengths and weaknesses for all these techniques.

Finally, after you have described the job and selected the people, you want to be able to check on how good a job of selection you did. Some people will not work out, while others will. The crucial question is whether you could have predicted these differences from your job analysis and the information you had about the applicants. It is important that you *validate* your selection procedures; you must find out whether your selection devices actually predict performance on the job. If they do not, you should change them until they do.

The ideal situation is one where we are able to place people in positions where they use their skills and are highly effective. The people will feel that their potential is being realized, and the organization will have high levels of effectiveness. The personal and economic benefits to both the individual and the company and society in general will be maximized.

This is the ideal. Unfortunately, we fall short of that goal. The processes of job analysis, selection, and validation are far from exact sciences. People and jobs change over time. What is a good match today is a poor one tomorrow. However, most of the failure to reach this goal is not due to the inadequacy of the scientific information; it is due to the fact that most personnel managers are poorly informed about this information and how to use it. A thorough understanding of job analysis, selection, and validation is a necessity for successful personnel planning.

Individual differences

> It is the common wonder of all men, how among so
> many millions of faces, there should be none alike.   Sir Thomas Browne

At the heart of the selection process is the idea of individual differences. Human beings vary on every dimension we can measure: their physical, psychological, biological, emotional, and behavioral characteristics. Any individual that applies for a job is a *unique* combination of characteristics; there is no one else that is exactly the same. Thus, the job of the personnel manager is to (1) accurately assess what characteristics the individual does possess and (2) determine whether those characteristics are important for some particular position.

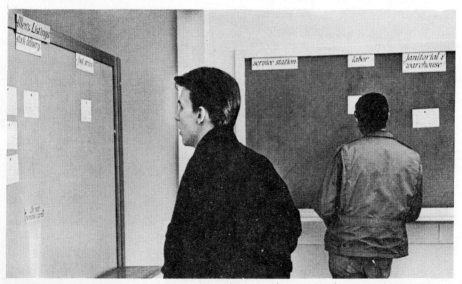

People look for jobs they think will be a good match with their skills, interests, and aspirations.
(*By permission of University of Washington* Daily.)

The implications of this principle of individual variation are important for managers and the company as a whole. First, supervisors and subordinates must realize that there will always be some people who perform better than others. Not everyone can perform at the level of the best employee. By firing the worst performer you simply make another individual the worst performer in the group.

Similarly, if everyone is producing exactly the same amount, a supervisor should check for informal norms. The lack of variability is probably due to enforced norms concerning how much work should be done. Left to their own initiative or motivation, the individuals in the group would show some variability.

Individual differences are an important element for planning at the company-wide level as well. Different productivity rates result in different labor costs per unit and different overhead costs per unit. Also, the costs for selecting and training people for different jobs vary widely. It may be relatively easy and inexpensive to find and train a shipping-room packer, while an electronics engineer may cost 100 times as much to recruit and train.

Finally, from society's point of view, individual differences make up the human resources that keep the country going. People differ in their skills, potential, and actual performance. We have much talent and many different types of jobs, and the optimal match should be the mutual goal of both employees and management. People are happier and more productive when they are using their skills and talents.

Job analysis

Our first step in a successful selection procedure is to have an accurate description of the jobs we wish to fill. Before we can select people, we must have a good idea about what we want them to be able to do. The process of developing detailed descriptions of jobs is called *job analysis*.

Sources and methods. The process of job analysis demands that we gather data about particular jobs and the kinds of things that people do to be successful in those jobs. The methods used to gather such data include a variety of techniques. We can *observe* individuals while they are actually performing their jobs. From these observations we could generate a description of the types of tasks performed by people in these positions. A *film* could provide us with similar information. Another frequently used source of data is the *interview*. One or more job incumbents can be asked to describe what they do on the job. A *questionnaire* is a somewhat more impersonal way to collect similar information. Finally, training manuals, reports, records, and other sources of available information may be appropriate.

Some of these methods of data gathering have been combined to develop specific techniques for analyzing jobs. The most frequently used procedure has been to combine observations and interviews to produce a *narrative description* of the job. This description will provide some feeling for the kinds of activities actually performed on the job. However, this technique often suffers from the fact that it has insufficient detail, and while it may describe what is generally done on the job, it provides little information about those areas of behavior that separate good performers from poor performers.

Responses to these criticisms led to more thorough procedures which might be labeled *activity analysis* and *time and motion studies*. These techniques involve a very detailed description of the actual behaviors performed on the job. Where tasks are highly standardized and specialized, these procedures can be especially useful. They can tell where people should stand, how they should orient themselves, and the types of movements required for good performance.

For positions that are less standardized, the *critical-incident* procedure is frequently used. Employees are asked to describe actual behavior that led to success or failure on the job. After a large number of these incidents are collected, they can be sorted and categorized to produce a behavioral description of the good performer and the poor performer. A good job analysis should be able to tell us not only the general behavioral requirements of the job but also what types of behaviors distinguish high performers from low performers. A well-done time and motion study or critical-incident checklist can meet these criteria.

Suppose you wanted to do a job analysis for teachers. You might start by taking the best criteria of excellence you can find (e.g., a combination of student ratings, faculty opinions, demand for classes, etc.) and divide your faculty into three groups: outstanding, average, and poor teachers. Through interviews, observations, and the gathering of critical incidents, you might find that the good teacher (1) came to class on time, (2) put an outline on the board, (3) was well organized, (4) used different teaching media, such as films, exercises, and visual aids, (5) used language that was understood by the students, (6) responded helpfully to questions, and (7) finished on time. The poor performer might be characterized as disorganized, tardy, reads from notes, talks down to students, uses technical language, and keeps everyone late. Once you have determined those characteristics that are related to effective performance, you will have a better idea about what sorts of skills and abilities you will look for the next time a teacher is to be hired.

But besides the simple *job description* mentioned above, you might also find that certain personal traits and abilities differentiate your good performers and poor performers. From personnel files you discover that the good teachers are higher on measures of need for achievement, tolerance for ambiguity, and sociability than poor teachers. The combination of the job description plus these personal characteristics and any other legal or corporate policies may be joined together to form the job specification—what a prospective employee should have or be able to do in order to get the job and be a success at it.

Points for consideration. Some summary comments about job analysis seem appropriate. First, the most useful analyses are specific and tied to behavior. They provide a detailed description of what people actually do, and they generate behavioral dimensions that will distinguish good performance from poor performance. Second, they are multipurposed. As we shall see in our discussions of performance appraisal and training, a good job analysis can be used for many things. It can be helpful for selecting employees, for generating a performance-appraisal instrument, and for pinpointing individual needs for counseling and training. And finally, from the prospective employee's point of view, a job specification can be very helpful. It gives a description of what will be required and it can reduce uncertainty. It is a very powerful and important tool.

Finally, a word of caution. People and jobs change over time. Some of this change is systematic and planned, and some is not. The point is that a job analysis, especially one that describes very specific behaviors, may become obsolete with the introduction of new technology or other factors. The process of analyzing jobs must be seen as an ongoing activity rather than something that is performed once and then used without modification for the next 20 years. Periodic checks are needed to ensure that the job description and job specifications are still accurate predictors of good performance.

Candidate assessment

Once we have developed our job specifications, we have to establish a selection procedure that will generate the information we need to make personnel decisions. Job candidates provide some of this information with biographical data, work histories, and letters of recommendation. But most companies actively pursue additional information through the use of interviews, psychological tests, work simulations, and other procedures. These techniques are designed to tell us whether a particular candidate fits the job specifications and is therefore a good bet to succeed. Some of the more important strategies for gathering such information are reviewed below.

Interviews. Perhaps the most widely used selection technique is the interview. Job candidates sit down and talk with a company representative about a variety of topics which are usually chosen by the interviewer. It is meant to provide both the prospective employee and the employer with a more personal feel for each other. It may also be used by the interviewer to gather some information that was not available from other sources. After the interview is over, the interviewer typically makes some judgments from his or her notes, and this information is entered into the candidate's file and becomes part of the decision-making process.

But besides providing information of a substantive nature, the interview serves some other purposes as well. In many cases, the interview is used to sell the company. By presenting the company's "best side," the interview may be part of the recruiting process. The candidate is not the only one who is being evaluated. Prospective employees will be interested in the terms of employment, work conditions, and other factors that may influence their decision. Thus, the interview should be seen as a two-way exchange.

The type of interview that most frequently occurs is called the patterned or structured interview. The interviewer has a fairly well-established format or outline of questions to pursue. The questions are usually direct and unambiguous and may require a fairly short answer (e.g., what courses in your business school education did you enjoy most?). As we shall see, the more direct, structured, and unambiguous the exchange, the more reliable and useful the information turns out to be.

In some cases a different type of interview process will be used. Occasionally a

The job interview is often an important source of data for both the organization and the job candidate. (*By permission of University of Washington* Daily.)

stress interview is employed which is designed to see how the candidate responds to a difficult or stressful situation. Or a group interview or a panel interview might be used where there are either multiple candidates or multiple interviewers. These types of procedures are used less frequently and typically in response to some particular demands of the type of job. For example, stress interviews were used to look at possible candidates for espionage operations during World War II.

Our knowledge about the problems with the interview process is fairly extensive. The most prevalent source of error is due to the fact that the interviewer must interpret the meaning of what the candidate says. To the extent that any interview requires much judgment, interpretation, and subjective assessment, it will produce less reliable data than an objective, factual summary.

This source of error shows up in a variety of ways. The more subjective or nonstructured the interview, (1) the less agreement among raters, (2) the greater the distortion of facts, and (3) the more the interviewer's personal biases enter into the decision. We know from a number of research studies that interviewers make mistakes, have biases, and are influenced by some factors more than others. For example, negative information is weighed more heavily than positive information. The candidate's dress and appearance may influence the decision. The pressure to hire someone may bias the interviewer. And finally, most interviewers tend to make an evaluative judgment about the candidate early in the exchange, and this "premature" decision often colors subsequent judgments.

What can be done to increase the reliability of the interview? Well, a number of procedures have been suggested. The construction of a structured, agreed-upon interview format is the most important consideration. At least under this strategy, the same questions will be asked of all the candidates, and the responses should be accurately recorded. There is also some evidence that interviewers can be trained to be more accurate and avoid some of the errors described earlier. Also the person being interviewed will feel the situation is more fair if everyone is asked the same questions and evaluated on the same criteria. Finally, the interview should be seen as only one part of an overall selection process and therefore should be designed to obtain specific information. This information can fill in gaps that were not covered by other sources. In this perspective the interview can make a unique contribution, but it is not the only contribution.

Tests. A second source of information about the job candidate can be provided by psychological tests. In many cases a whole battery of tests may be used to assess characteristics of the individual in four main areas: (1) mental abilities, (2) muscular or motor coordination, (3) personality traits, and (4) physical and sensory capacities. The scores on these tests are then used to supplement the interview, biographical, and job-history data already gathered.

The number of psychological tests is vast. There are just too many to even begin any sort of review here. But we can mention some typical examples that are frequently used. The most obvious measures of mental abilities are the intelligence tests. While there is great controversy over just what the term "intelligence" means, there is some agreement that these types of tests are closely associated with success in school and academic-related activities. Tests of motor coordination might assess such functions as muscular control, manual dexterity, or other manipulative activities. These tests are highly specific (while intelligence tests are more general) and usually involve rather complex equipment. The personality tests are designed to measure the types of personal characteristics that we have discussed earlier, such as sociability, dominance, extroversion, or dogmatism. Finally, tests designed to measure sensory capacities might test for judgments of distance, night vision, color differentiation, hearing acuity, or sense of smell (e.g., for wine tasters).

The critical questions that one must ask about tests are concerned with their reliability and validity. You will recall we mentioned these terms in Chapter 4, "Research Foundations." Essentially, the reliability refers to the reproducibility of the test score. If I take an intelligence tests today and I get a high score, will I get the same high score if I take the test tomorrow? A reliable test is one that we can count on. It is one that is subject to little error in measurement, and therefore we can feel fairly comfortable that the score is not due to some set of chance circumstances.

The validity of the measure refers to its substantive content. Are we really measuring what we think we are measuring? If the test is invalid, it will be of little use in predicting on the job behavior or performance. A valid test of extroversion, for instance, should in fact be predictive of various behavioral measures (observations) of on-the-job activity.

A more-detailed description of psychological tests is available in most industrial psychology textbooks.[3] The important points to emphasize here are that there are numerous tests and that they vary in quality. A personnel manager must use tests like any other tool. They are not a panacea or cure-all. For some jobs, some tests will be fairly good predictors of job performance. For other jobs, tests may not be relevant. Again, tests are only one means of predicting future job behavior.

Work samples. One relatively recent strategy for selection is described as work sampling.[4] The basic idea is to simulate as closely as possible the actual conditions of the job. Job candidates participate in the simulation or exercise, and measures of their behavior are gathered. The underlying premise is that samples of actual behavior for a specific job will be the best predictor of later behavior on that job.

For some types of positions, such as typing, work samples have been routine elements of the selection process for a long time. However, more recently we have seen this technique employed to assess the behavior of people applying for other types of jobs. One of the most popular techniques is described as the "in-basket" test. From a thorough job analysis a set of "action items" can be put together that reflects the types of problems and issues with which a manager in a particular company at a particular level might have to deal (e.g., letters, memos, routine forms, etc.). These items are placed in an in-basket, and the job candidate is asked to play the role of the manager and make decisions about each item. The way in which these items are handled provides a quantitative score which can be used to predict later performance on the job.

In some research, this type of procedure has been shown to be a more effective predictor of performance than other procedures such as psychological tests. For example, Campion reports on a study using work samples to predict the performance of maintenance mechanics employed by a food-processing company. By means of a job analysis some tasks were selected, such as repairing a gearbox or installing and aligning a motor, that were deemed to be representative of actual on-the-job behavior. Measures of proficiency on these work samples turned out to be better predictors of performance on the job than more traditional testing techniques designed to assess mental abilities and mechanical comprehension.

Obviously, such techniques are most useful when there are specific, agreed-upon, observable behaviors that are necessary for good performance. Some positions are more difficult to define or to simulate. In these jobs one must rely on some of the other techniques discussed above.

Assessment centers. The newest development in selection techniques is called the assessment center. It is an attempt to combine interviews, pscyhological tests, and work samples into an integrated evaluation process. The data generated can

---

[3]See, for example, N. R. F. Maier. *Psychology in industrial organizations.* Boston: Houghton-Mifflin, 1973.

[4]James E. Campion. Work sampling for personnel selection. *Journal of Applied Psychology,* 1972, **56,** 40–44.

then be used for selection, promotion, training, and development. While few conclusive research studies have been done on assessment centers, it has become an increasingly popular technique. Companies such as American Telephone and Telegraph, IBM, Standard Oil of Ohio, Sears, and Caterpillar Tractor have such programs.

The typical center involves a 1- to 5-day session. There are usually four to six professionals in charge of the assessment process who have been trained to administer and score the various assessment tools. In most cases the participants are candidates for management jobs either from within the company or from outside, and the ratio of candidates to assessors is usually small (e.g., 3 : 1). The candidates participate in a number of group exercises, simulations, and management games. They take a battery of tests and they are interviewed by a number of assessors. Their performance is rated by themselves, their peers, and the assessors. All this information is then used to make judgments about successful managerial performance.

The research results to date are rather encouraging. Reviews of this literature suggest that assessment centers can in fact predict later managerial success, although one must qualify these findings somewhat.[5] Most of the results are not very strong. While the assessment center does provide some predictability, there is still much error in the system. The assessment center can do better than flipping a coin or using some psychological tests or interview information by itself, but not too much better.

The problems created by the technique have also been fully discussed. Assessment centers are expensive to run and may create great anxiety for the participant. The candidates not only are being thoroughly tested, but also know they are competing with others. Moreover, when candidates are selected from within the company, the nomination and assessment process itself may cause problems. The person who is not nominated may become labeled as someone who does not have management potential. The candidate who does well in the center may carry a positive stereotype throughout his or her career, while the candidate who does poorly may never be considered again.

In short, there are many different procedures for generating information about job candidates. Interviews, tests, work samples, and assessment centers can all provide valuable data. Given a thorough job analysis and a thorough assessment strategy, the personnel manager should be in a fairly good position to place the right people in the right jobs.

Validation

Ultimately one's selection strategy must be evaluated. A company will want to know how well it is actually able to predict on-the-job performance. This is an important part of the overall development of a selection procedure, for both cost effectiveness and human-resources reasons. If many people are placed on jobs where they do not succeed or if people are rejected who could have succeeded,

---

[5]Ann Howard. An assessment of assessment centers. *Academy of Management Journal,* 1975, **17,** 115–134.

the financial costs of evaluation and training are increased. There is also the human element. People are being asked to do things for which they are not qualified or prepared. Turnover, absenteeism, and job dissatisfaction will be high.

The two most common procedures used to check the accuracy of our prediction are described as concurrent and predictive validity. For concurrent validity the steps are as follows: (1) we do a thorough job analysis and develop job specifications, (2) a list of predictors for effectiveness is put together, (3) we assess employees *currently* in the job for their scores on these predictors, and (4) we determine whether the predictors discriminate between the high and low performers. If the predictors do discriminate between effective and ineffective individuals, we can feel fairly comfortable trying them out with new candidates.

The predictive-validity procedure is simply a check on how well our predictors actually do in picking out successful and unsuccessful job candidates. We assess their scores, hire them for the job, and track their performance over time. Again, the scores should distinguish the good performers from the poor performers.

Unfortunately, most American companies have not developed rigorous evaluation of their selection processes. In many cases the job interview is the only procedure used. This lack of evaluation has in the past proven to be expensive. But today it is frequently *illegal*. Given the recent legal decisions pertaining to equal employment and nondiscriminatory hiring, it becomes the responsibility of the organization to show that its selection devices are in fact related to performance on the job. Support for the concurrent and predictive validity of specific selection procedures is the minimum standard that should be used to evaluate the selection process.

Performance appraisal

An ounce of image is worth a pound of performance
Lawrence J. Peter and Raymond Hull

We mentioned at the beginning of the chapter that performance was dependent jointly on the ability and the motivation of the employee. Once we have selected our people and have them on board, we can switch our attention to the motivational aspects of the job. Two factors that are important for successfully motivating employees are the ease with which correct behavior can be learned and the rewards which are contingent upon that behavior. The employee wants to know how he or she is doing. Only through the process of feedback and learning can employees ascertain what they are doing poorly or well. But there is more than just learning. We also want to be recognized and rewarded for a job well done. The process of evaluating employee performance can serve both of these goals; it can provide feedback for counseling and learning and it can provide evaluative information upon which rewards can be based. This next section describes the performance-appraisal system in some detail.

Purposes

Using a rather broad perspective, the two main purposes of performance appraisal are counseling and evaluation. The counseling information can be used as feedback, as recommendations for training, or as a general periodic review for self-improvement. The evaluation uses include promotions, dismissals, wage and salary administration, and bonuses. In most cases the performance appraisal will serve multiple functions from both the evaluation and counseling areas. In this manner, both the individual and the organization are kept formally advised of the individual's progress.

Appraisal techniques

The possibilities for evaluating performance are fairly large. Some suggestions are: (1) measures of volume or quantity of output, such as items produced or words typed, (2) measures of quality, such as spoilage or items rejected, (3) measures of lost time, such as absenteeism or tardiness, (4) measures involving training or promotion time, such as time in a particular position or (5) measures of performance based on personal characteristics or behavior.

In those jobs where clear, unambiguous measures of the quantity or quality of output are available, they are frequently used. In most cases, however, these measures are not as clear as we would like. The employee may be part of a team, and each person's output may be partially dependent upon the output of others. It is also possible that the employee is dependent upon the whims of the customer or the reliability of machinery. Under these circumstances some sort of behavioral assessment can be used.

The criteria for these behavioral types of ratings fall into two main categories: other people and absolute standards. When other people are used as the criteria, the assessor is essentially asked to compare the employee with other employees and rate the person on a number of traits or behavioral dimensions. Figure 14-2 presents an example of such a form. The problem with such a technique is that there is a tendency for the rater to give everyone high ratings. To avoid this problem, one can make comparisons in a number of ways other than the system shown in the table. Sometimes the rater may be asked to rank-order all the employees on an overall performance estimate. Or a paired comparison procedure can be used, where each employee is specifically compared to each of the other employees in the group that does the same job. Finally, some sort of forced distribution system is possible. With this technique the rater is asked to pick the employees falling in the top 10 percent, the next 20 percent, 40 percent, 20 percent, and the bottom 10 percent. All these techniques will clearly point out who is seen as doing well and who is not. They force the rater to spread out the ratings.

The criticism that is often leveled at comparison evaluation techniques is that the basis for judgment is often ambiguous and subjective. Some of the research shows that different raters may produce somewhat different rank orders or

NAME OF EMPLOYEE _____

Personal Trait	Rating				
	1 Exceptional	2 Above Average	3 Average	4 Below Average	5 Poor
1 Aggressiveness					
2 Tolerance of stress					
3 Physical energy					
4 Creativity					
5 Self-confidence					
6 Adaptability					
7 Leadership					
8 Personal integrity					
8 Emotional balance					
10 Enthusiasm					

Figure 14-2. A personal-trait rating form.

forced distributions. To remedy the problem, many personnel experts would suggest ratings based upon absolute standards.

Most appraisal instruments that employ absolute standards are based upon a preliminary job analysis. As we discussed earlier, this type of analysis can provide a more detailed description of the actual behavior necessary for effective performance. So, the criterion becomes the actual illustration of behavior rather than a comparison with other employees.

The most common technique of this type is some sort of checklist. The behaviors necessary for effective performance in a number of areas are described, and the rating is made. Table 14-1 presents a somewhat amusing example of how Superman might be evaluated on such a scale. More elaborate procedures such as weighted checklists, behaviorally anchored rating scales, and the critical-incident techniques are also available. These strategies usually demand a job analysis which generates a large number of actual behaviors that occur on the job, some sort of weighting as to their importance for good performance, and some sort of categorization process which places similar behaviors into dimensional groupings.

Let me give you an example. Gary Latham and I recently developed a performance appraisal instrument for the members of a research and development department of a large business organization.[6] We asked each employee in an interview to give us five specific examples of behavior that led to good performance and five that led to poor performance. All these behavioral incidents (around 750) were classified by judges (R&D employees) into similar categories.

[6]G. Latham & T. R. Mitchell. Behavioral criteria and potential reinforcers for the engineer/scientist in an industrial setting. *JSAS Catalogue of Selected Documents in Psychology,* 1976, **6,** 316.

Table 14-1. Guide to Employee Performance Appraisal

Area of Performance	Far in Excess of Job Requirements	Exceeds Job Requirements	Meets Job Requirements	Needs Improvement	Does Not Meet Minimum Requirements
Quality of work	Leaps tall buildings in a single bound	Leaps tall buildings with a running start	Can leap short buildings if prodded	Bumps into buildings	Cannot recognize buildings
Promptness	Is faster than a speeding bullet	Is as fast as a speeding bullet	Would you believe a slow bullet?	Misfires frequently	Wounds self when handling guns
Initiative	Is stronger than a locomotive	Is as strong as a bull elephant	Almost as strong as a bull	Shoots the bull	Smells like a bull
Capability	Walks on water	Keeps head above water	Washes with water	Drinks water	Passes water in emergencies
Communication	Talks with God	Talks with the angels	Talks with himself	Argues with himself	Loses arguments with himself

Redundant and irrelevant items were discarded, and the sorting procedure was performed again by different judges to make sure that there was a high level of agreement. After a number of other validation checks, an appraisal instrument was developed composed of eight dimensions with about five behaviors in each category. For example, one dimension was planning and scheduling, which was composed of the following behaviors: (1) develops a project plan prior to conducting the project, (2) prepares for meetings, and (3) can work on two or more projects effectively at the same time.

The advantages of such a technique are numerous. First, it refers to actual behavior rather than some subjective estimate of excellence. Second, it can be reliably constructed, with definite criteria available for when a satisfactory instrument has been produced. Third, it usually involves the actual input of the employees who are going to be evaluated. They are more likley to be favorably committed to such an evaluation procedure. Fourth, the behaviors that are evaluated are directly tied to performance. This aspect of the procedure rules out the use of behaviors that are irrelevant for job performance. Finally, in the evaluation process it can provide the employee with specific feedback about where improvement is needed. It may be difficult for an employee to know how to become more aggressive (as rated on a personal-trait form), but it is fairly obvious what needs to be done about a low rating on preparation for meetings and developing a project plan.

To summarize, then, there are evaluation procedures that demand a global rating and some that use multiple dimensions. Some use employee comparisons as the criterion while others utilize an absolute standard. In general, a thoroughly constructed technique that includes multiple dimensions and is based upon actual behavior will prove to be the most useful tool for both evaluation and feedback purposes.

Other considerations

There are some additional issues about the appraisal process that should be briefly discussed. The first topic concerns who is doing the evaluation. In the overwhelming majority of cases the immediate supervisor has been the person in charge of the ratings. From a legitimacy point of view this makes sense; we expect and more readily accept evaluative feedback from our boss.

However, recent research on the evaluation process has suggested that in some cases peer reviews, self-ratings, or outsider assessment may be appropriate. When individuals rate themselves and this rating is used as part of the evaluation, there is frequently an increased sense of commitment and feelings of fairness on the part of the employees. Outside raters are often seen as unbiased and perhaps fairer than one's own supervisor. Peer ratings can also be important, especially where the supervisor is frequently separated from the group and group members trust one another. Perhaps the best strategy is to gather different types of ratings (e.g., superior, peer, and self) and use each rating as a source of valuable information. Ultimately, however, decisions have to be made and made by people with the appropriate responsibility. In most cases this responsibility resides in the position immediately above the one being rated.

A second consideration is the frequency of evaluation. Since both people and jobs change over time, some sort of annual review is probably the minimal requirement. In some cases a quarterly or semiannual assessment will make the most sense. Somehow, a balance has to be struck between being evaluated too frequently (where the employee feels constantly threatened) and being evaluated too infrequently (where the employee feels that evaluation fails to provide feedback and recognize improvement).

Finally, there is the question of feedback. Should the employee have access to the evaluation? The answer to this question partly rests on the reasons for the assessment. If counseling, development, and training are the major concerns (e.g., in jobs where tenure is assured and raises are based on seniority), feedback can obviously be helpful. When evaluation is used for promotion and financial rewards, the use of feedback creates problems. There is much data showing that supervisors give higher ratings when they know that the employee will see the ratings, and this is especially true when global ratings are used. The military is a good example of an organization that has had such problems in the past.

Again, the best remedy seems to be the type of procedure used. If observable behaviors are rated and if the employees participate in the development of the instrument, it may be possible to use the technique for both counseling and evaluation purposes. Evaluation is never easy and it is usually not very pleasant, but it can be fair.

Problems and remedies

Throughout the discussion of performance appraisal, we have touched on a number of problem areas. A list of these potential problems and some possible remedies are presented below.

Rater bias. People who evaluate others either in selection interviews or performance appraisals tend to make some systematic errors. Individuals who are seen as being similar to the rater receive higher scores. This is not surprising; we generally like people who are like ourselves. Another type of error is called a halo error. Raters may use some outstanding single characteristic (either good or bad) and generalize this evaluation to every other dimension. For example, nonjob related qualities (sports activities) may be used to make judgments about job-related topics. A third type of error is the contrast effect. A pretty good employee may look good or bad depending upon whether the person who was rated immediately beforehand was excellent or average. Finally, there are first-impression errors. Some information that comes out early in an interview or appraisal may bias later judgments.

These errors in rating can be avoided. Where hard behavioral or productivity data are available (e.g., absences or quantity of output), there is less room for subjective judgment. Also, even on those jobs where behavioral ratings are

Well, yes, Mr. Roberts. I think you would fit in very well in our organization.
We tend to evaluate favorably people who are similar to ourselves.

gathered, the errors can be avoided or minimized by the proper training of those people making the judgments.[7] Not only can the errors be reduced, but also it appears as if this type of training may have lasting effects.

Single criteria. The performance on most jobs cannot be adequately described by the use of just one criterion measure. There are numerous examples in the literature citing the dysfunctional consequences of such an approach. For example, it may seem as if a simple output measure is appropriate (e.g., number of court cases reviewed or number of bushels of corn produced). But what often happens is that the employee focuses on that single criteria to the detriment of other important aspects of the position. A judge who simply counts the number of cases completed each month may tend to choose easy cases near the end of the month to meet some quota or standard. The farmer may disregard crucial maintenance requirements on machinery in order to have high output during a period of evaluation.

Most researchers agree that multiple criteria measures should be employed. It is usually a more accurate reflection of what really leads to good performance. In many cases, these separate measures can then be combined in some fashion to produce an overall rating as well. This composite and the separate criteria can then be used for both evaluative and counseling purposes.

[7]G. P. Latham, K. N. Wexley, & E. D. Pursell. Training managers to minimize rating errors in the observation of behavior. *Journal of Applied Psychology,* 1975, **60,** 550–555.

Differences in jobs and raters. What can you do when one supervisor seems to consistently rate people higher than another supervisor? Or how about the situation where the same evaluation form is used for slightly different types of positions.

The question is one of standardization. The employee should not be subject to the whims of a "tough judge" or the bias of doing something a little different from the rest of the group.

One way to handle these problems is through statistical techniques. If over a number of evaluation sessions it becomes clear that there are easy and tough raters or jobs, you can use outside raters or make some mathematical adjustment. For example, where it is clear that there is no difference between jobs, but there are differences in ratings (attributable to the rater and not supervision or other factors), then a constant can be added or subtracted from your score. In this way employees are less likely to feel they are the victims of circumstances beyond their control.

General resistance. The last problem may be the most difficult to deal with. People are threatened by evaluation. Few people are truly outstanding at what they do, so there is usually room for improvement. Also, due to individual differences, there will always be some people who are better than others at a particular task. The rater will typically be faced with some people who are not doing as well as others.

This is a very trying time for both the supervisor and the subordinate. In many instances, it is seen as the most unpleasant aspect of the job. Teachers, for example, often report that giving grades is the least favorable part of the teaching process. No one likes to be the conveyer of bad news.

The remedies in this area have been discussed before. The more objective and observable the criteria, the easier it is to give and discuss evaluative data. There is less chance for disagreement. Also, if people can participate in the construction of the appraisal instrument, they feel more committed to its use. An objective device jointly constructed may not be warmly embraced, but at least it should be perceived as fair and equitable, which is probably the best we can do.

So, performance appraisal can serve as an important device for feedback and the learning process. It will also determine partially how rewards are distributed. Motivation should be high in those settings where (1) it is clear what leads to good performance and (2) the rewards contingent upon that performance are highly valued. Performance appraisal should have an impact on the clarity of what leads to good performance. The determination and administration of rewards is important for linking valued rewards to performance, and it is this topic which completes the chapter.

Systems of rewards

After performance evaluation comes the administration of rewards. Somehow the organization must develop a system which provides compensation to its employees that is considered sufficient in some absolute sense and fair as well. Compensation is the basis of the original contract between the individual and the organization. It is the agreement as to what the organization gives in exchange for the employees' services. If the system of rewards is poorly designed, other factors such as selecting the right people, placing them in the right jobs, and fairly evaluating their performance may be irrelevant. Unless rewards are perceived as being attractive and linked to what we do, motivation is likely to be comparatively low.

The compensation system from the organization's point of view serves a number of functions. First, it can be used to attract and keep high-quality employees. If everything else is equal, people will want to go where the rewards are greatest. Second, it is used as a reward for services rendered. It is a means of recognizing past performance. Finally, it can be used as a motivator for future performance. Rewards can be used as goals or targets to shoot for.

From the individual's perspective, the reward structure also serves a number of functions. First, it provides a sense of security. Pay, pensions, sick leave, and other parts of the compensation package ease the psychological burdens of trying to make a living for oneself and one's dependents. Second, rewards are a source of recognition. They let individuals know how well they are doing. In this light they are also seen as a feedback mechanism. Finally, rewards serve as goals to attain. A certain level of pay or promotion may be a crucial lifelong ambition.

Types of rewards

There are really two main types of rewards that an individual receives on the job. Those rewards which are part of doing the job itself are frequently described as *intrinsic rewards*. We discussed these types of rewards in our chapters on learning and motivation, and they include more intangible types of things such as feelings of competence, completion, or self-actualization. While the organization can have some control over the intrinsic aspects of one's job, they are infrequently discussed as part of the reward or compensation system.

The second type of rewards are described as being *extrinsic;* they are tangible external factors that are controlled by the organization. In terms of compensation systems these rewards fall into two subcategories: pay (and promotions) and "other benefits." The latter includes (1) legally required benefits, such as unemployment compensation, disability insurance, or Medicare hospital benefits, (2) private health and security benefits, such as a retirement plan and life insurance, (3) employee services, such as discounts, meals, or transportation, and (4) compensation for time not worked, such as vacations, sick leave, jury duty, or lunchtime.

The interesting point about most "other" benefits is that they usually are the same for all employees that fall in specific classifications. There is little attempt to differentially distribute these rewards as a function of past performance or to use them as motivators for better performance. Instead, they serve to meet legal requirements, attract people initially to the organization, and provide security for them once they are on the job.

It is pay and promotions that typically are used as the device to differentially

This one is for keeping a clean desk, and this one is for wearing the company colors, and this one is for not calling my friends on company time.

The organization can use different types of incentives to reward any number of behaviors.

recognize excellence and to encourage greater effort. They are distributed in a number of different ways with differing requirements and impact. Promotions often involve a change in job plus a change in pay, and it is therefore difficult to tease out which factor serves as a motivator. The effects of financial payments, on the other hand, are easily specifiable and, in some cases, measurable. The next section briefly describes the major types of pay systems used in organizations today.

Systems of pay

Most managers, professionals, and upper-level employees receive a salary or some sort of time-based pay. The amount they earn is dependent upon the amount of time they work, either by the hour, day, week, or month. Note that money in these cases is not tied to performance. It is not how much you produce that matters but how long you work.

Organizations with time-based pay systems are usually forced to find other rewards to motivate their employees. Promotions, recognition, and more intrinsic rewards, such as the assignment of challenging tasks, may be used. But more frequently, some sort of bonus or incentive system is installed to provide additional pay based on merit.

These incentive or bonus systems tie money as directly as possible to productivity. The idea is to reward past excellence and encourage future excellence. Obviously, in those settings where good performance is easily defined, these types of systems will be easier to establish than where good performance is a more elusive concept.

Individual plans. The simplest and most direct individual incentive plan is a piece-rate system. Here the employee is paid for the number of items or pieces completed or produced regardless of the time or effort expended. Those who produce a lot get a lot, those who do not produce much are not paid much.

While this system may be intuitively appealing, it has some drawbacks. In most cases employees are not entirely independent of other workers or machines. Their output may not always be a direct reflection of their effort. Also, unless there is substantial agreement and trust about how the rate per piece is determined, there may be dissatisfaction. Employees may establish informal norms to hold down production. There are numerous reports of such tactics in the literature. The workers feel that if they produce a large amount, management will lower the piece rate, so they hold down output.

The response to these problems has been to provide some sort of guaranteed time rate for each employee, and the piece rate is then added to this hourly wage. This protects employees somewhat from circumstances beyond their control reducing their income.

Other individual incentive plans (where piece rates are not applicable) base the incentive on some behavioral estimate of performance. It is in these settings where a reliable and valid performance-appraisal system is most important. The employees must feel that the incentive is in fact based on what they do and that it is attainable. The system usually includes both a time-based wage as well as the incentive, and the incentive may be distributed daily, weekly, or monthly. In some cases it even takes the form of an annual Christmas or end-of-the-year bonus.

Group plans. However, in many organizations people work together as teams or groups. Everyone is highly dependent upon each other. In order to perform well everybody must contribute. If you will recall our discussion of competition and cooperation in Chapter 8, "Group Dynamics," we mentioned that in highly interdependent groups rewards should not be highly differentiated. For motivation to be high, we would want rewards distributed to the group members fairly equally.

There are available a number of compensation systems which are specifically designed to reward individuals according to their group's or the total organization's productivity. At the extreme end of this continuum are companywide profit sharing plans where a percentage of the profits are distributed to the employees as a function of their position (level) within the organization. Some well-known systems such as the Scanlon Plan or the Lincoln Electric Group Incentive Plan use variants of this idea. The basic point of this type of system is to instill in employees a sense of organizational commitment. If they see their own pay as tied to the overall success of the company, they are more likely to help in increasing the overall effectiveness of the organization.

Evaluation. An evaluation of the research that has studied these different types of reward programs emphasizes one major point: Pay can be—and is—an effective method for motivating organizational participants. The performance appraisal must be properly constructed and the reward must be distributed to the appropriate unit, be that the individual or the group. Trust in, and commitment to, the system are needed. But if it is thoroughly and thoughtfully developed and administered, an incentive system can have a powerful impact on individual performance.

This conclusion needs to be emphasized. For many years a number of theorists (mostly associated with the followers of the human-relations movement) have downplayed the effects of money. They have argued that the interpersonal aspects of the job are the most important factors for motivation and that pay plays a minor role. The research results simply do not support these conclusions. Pay is an important determinant of job satisfaction as well as productivity.

In terms of our earlier discussions about linking rewards to behavior, this makes sense. It also suggests that where they are appropriate (i.e., where workers are somewhat independent), individual incentive plans will be more effective than group plans. Both incentive and group plans should also be more motivating than a 100 percent time-based plan where pay is not linked to performance at all. The research generally supports these conclusions as well.[8] One review summarized the findings by saying: "Overall, it appears that the charge leveled by the human relationists of fifty years ago—that managers overemphasize the importance of money as a motivator—is incorrect today. It appears that managers fail to recognize the full potential of money, properly used, as a way of improving individual employee performance."[9]

Summary

This has been a long and information-packed chapter. There are numerous points which could be repeated, but the ones below appear to be the most important:

1 An individual's performance on the job is a joint function of his or her individual personal characteristics and his or her motivation to do a good job. Both factors are needed for good performance.

2 The organization can help to determine the abilities and characteristics of its employees through selection, feedback, and training. The motivational fac-

[8]See H. G. Heneman, III, and D. P. Schwab. Work and rewards theory. In D. Yoder and H. G. Heneman, Jr. (Eds.), *Motivation and commitment.* Washington, D.C.: American Society for Personnel Administration, 1975, pp. 1–21. Also see E. E. Lawler, III. *Pay and organizational effectiveness.* New York: McGraw-Hill, 1971.

[9]O. Behling & C. Schriesheim, *Organizational behavior: Theory research and application.* Boston: Allyn and Bacon, 1976, p. 250.

tor can be influenced through evaluation, reward administration, and job design.

3 The underlying principle for effective performance is job fit—the right person working on the right job under the right conditions.

4 A good selection system involves a thorough job analysis, comprehensive assessment, and empirical validation.

5 Performance appraisal serves a dual function: it is both an evaluation mechanism on which rewards may be based and a counseling tool for feedback and personnel development.

6 Appraisal is typically made by comparisons with others or by comparison to some absolute standard. If a behavioral criterion is thoughtfully and scientifically developed, it can be reliable, valid, and accepted.

7 Pay is an important source of motivation and satisfaction. Properly administered rewards will increase output.

Implications for practice

At a more general level, there are two points that have important practical implications. First, people are different. The real task of the employer is to ascertain how each individual can give full expression to his or her own particular needs, skills, and abilities. The better the fit, the greater the benefits to both the individual and the organization.

A second point is that people can change their behavior. Productivity and satisfaction can be favorably influenced by the system of rewards. It should be explicit as to the contingencies and perceived as equitable by the employees. The idea is that an organization motivates those behaviors it rewards. To attain good performance you must reward it.

Discussion questions

1 What are the two major factors that contribute to performance? Which do you think is most important in the academic setting and why?

2 What is the problem with the job interview and how can it be more effective? Why do you suppose it is used so extensively?

3 How should students in a classroom setting be evaluated? Should progress or absolute amount learned be the criteria? Could group rewards or bonuses be helpful?

Case: Affirmative action in action

The undergraduate curriculum committee at a large Midwestern university is in charge of setting policy and guidelines for all aspects of the undergraduate program in the school of business. Over the last few years the demand to get in the business school has increased dramatically. In fact, it has gotten so intense that 50 percent of the applicants are being turned away. There are 1400 possible slots, and more than 3000 people tried to get in for the current year.

The result of this pressure has been twofold. First, since entrance is competitively determined, the grade point average required for entrance is now over 3.0 in the first 2 years of college. People with 2.8s and 2.9s who would have been received with open arms a few years ago are now being turned away. The second result is that it is hard to decide on a clear policy for selection of students, especially with respect to affirmative action.

Here is the rub: Many applications from women and minorities are being received, but a large percentage of them do not meet the 3.0 cutoff. In many cases there are obvious hardship reasons for the lower grades. But how does one justify turning away a student with a higher average in order to accept one with a lower GPA? The task of the committee is to develop legally and morally sound policies with which they can live.

Everyone on the committee is aware of the DeFunis case of a few years ago. In that situation, a law school rejected a white student who had a better academic record than a number of minority students who were accepted. Several lower state courts supported DeFunis and ordered the university to accept him, which they did. By the time the case reached the Supreme Court, however, DeFunis was about to graduate. The Court refused to hear the case.

But the question raised by the case is still unanswered. How can the number of women and minorities be increased? How can affirmative action take place without "reverse discrimination"? Arbitrary quotas are unsatisfactory to almost everyone.

One of the women on the committee is a student, and she feels very strongly about the situation. There is a rumor about that women are being accepted with lower GPAs than men, and she is angry about it. "The men look down their noses at you," she says. "They think you got in the easy way. I don't think anyone should be accepted below the cutoff—hardship or not. We either make it or we don't, just like anybody else."

Another committee member disagrees. She feels that the grade point average is a poor criterion for selection. She thinks that many people, and especially minorities and women, frequently undergo some sort of hardship economically. They are forced to go to school and work at the same time. They may also have a family to whom they are responsible. Therefore a low GPA may not be a good reflection either of potential performance in school or success on the job.

Questions about the case

1 What sort of selection program would you suggest? How can you justify your policy?
2 What is "reverse discrimination"? How do you feel about it?
3 Was the woman student right? Should there be any special treatment of women and minorities? If so, how do you deal with rumor and innuendo? What is a fair selection procedure?
4 Can people be accepted on an "overload" basis—that is, fill the first 1400 spots competitively and then accept a few petitions based on some set of agreed-upon criteria?

Additional readings

* Byham, W. C. The assessment center as an aid in management development. *Training and Development Journal,* 1971.
* Carlson, R. E., Thayer, P. W., Mayfield, E. C., & Paterson, D. A. Improvements in the selection interview. *Personnel Journal,* April 1971, 268–275.
  Cummings, L. L., and Schwab, D. P. *Performance in organizations.* Glenview, Ill.: Scott, Foresman, 1973.
** Dunnette, M. D. A modified model for test validation and selection research. *Journal of Applied Psychology,* 1963, **47,** 317–323.
** Dunnette, M. D. (Ed.). *Handbook of industrial and organizational psychology.* Chicago: Rand McNally, 1976. See McCormick, E. J. Job and task analysis, pp. 651–696; Guion, R. M. Recruiting, selection and job placement, pp. 777–828; and Finkle, R. B. Managerial assessment centers, pp. 861–888.
  Hamner, W. C., & Schmidt, F. L. (Eds.). *Contemporary problems in personnel.* Chicago: St. Clair Press, 1974.
  Harare, O., & Zedeck, S. Development of behaviorally anchored scales for the evaluation of faculty teaching. *Journal of Applied Psychology,* 1973, **58,** 261–265.
** Korman, A. K. *Industrial and organizational psychology.* Englewood Cliffs, N.J.: Prentice-Hall, 1971.
** Lawler, E. E., III. *Pay and organizational effectiveness.* New York: McGraw-Hill, 1971.
* Lawler, E. E., III, & L. W. Porter. The effect of performance on job satisfaction. *Industrial Relations,* October 1967, **7,** 20–28.
  Meyer, H. H., Kay, E., & French, J. R. P., Jr. Split roles in performance appraisal. *Harvard Business Review,* January–February 1965, 123–129.
* Miner, J. B. Management appraisal: A capsule review and current references. *Business Horizons,* October 1968, 83–96.
* Ridgeway, V. F. Dysfunctional consequences of performance appraisal. *Administrative Science Quarterly,* 1956, **1,** 24–27.

*Possible reading for students

**Review of literature or comprehensive source material

15
Training and development

The Federal manpower program is a vital part of our national effort to conserve and develop our human resources and to help individuals adjust productively to changing economic conditions.

Richard M. Nixon

The selection and performance appraisal techniques described in the previous chapter can help an organization to match people to jobs and motivate them on the job. These are two of the most important factors that contribute to good performance. But people and jobs change over time. Individuals are promoted to new positions. New employees need information about their specific jobs. Technological advances require retooling of people and machines. The function of organizational training and development is to *initially create* and to *maintain* the proper people-job match and high levels of motivation.

The importance of training can be viewed in terms of sheer numbers. In the last 40 years we have progressed from 3 percent of the major U.S. companies having executive training programs to over 90 percent having such programs. The cost of these programs is immense. Peat, Marwick, Mitchell and Co. estimate its training and development costs at $10 million a year. First National Chicago spends $2 million a year on its first scholar program designed to develop new managers. Similar increases are apparent for lower-level jobs. The federal government estimates that almost 2 million jobs are replaced by machines every year. In response to such human obsolescence, the Manpower Training and Development Act was passed in 1962. Since that time, the Department of Labor has provided training for over 2 million people in occupations such as architecture, engineering, clerical work, sales, farming, work in fisheries, service occupations (food, barbering, etc.), machine trades, and structural work (welding, electrical assembly, painting, construction, etc.). Taxpayers have supported billions of dollars worth of training. Private industry has incurred comparable costs. The aircraft *industry*, for example, used to spend around $30 million per year for training; now a single *company* spends that much.

Besides the financial or numerical emphasis, there is a human emphasis. We are beginning to understand that investment in training and development is an investment in human resources. Human assets grow and increase in value. Maintaining and upgrading employees' skills not only increases productivity but also is likely to increase commitment and motivation. Most employees appreciate learning new tasks and being able to work up to their full potential.

Organizations have begun to think in terms of careers rather than jobs. There is an increased awareness and understanding that there are various stages involved in career development. One author, for example, cites pre-entry, entry, training, first position, other positions, tenure, and exit as different stages and positions through which an employee may pass.[1] The executive development coordinator at Exxon recently stated, ''The life blood of our management development system is the rate at which we can move talent through the ranks, always providing a greater challenge.'' Training and development, to be successful, must not only emphasize specific positions and specific people but also a long-term career orientation.

Unfortunately, the research evaluating training has been minimal, and the attempts at applying what we do know have not always been successful. A recent review of this literature cited the following problems:[2]

1 Practitioners rather than psychologists dominate the field of training in organizations.
2 Training ''programs'' are emphasized over training content or evaluation.
3 Fads tend to dominate the field.
4 There is little emphasis on or concern about using or building theory to produce better training.

These facts leave us with an unsettling conclusion. Training is obviously an important activity related to both financial and productivity criteria of organizational effectiveness. Yet it is seldom done well and infrequently evaluated. The rest of this chapter will attempt to provide (1) a sound theoretical basis for training, (2) some how-to-do-it steps important for effective implementation, (3) a review of current training programs, and (4) an evaluation of the circumstances under which specific programs are most likely to work best. Our first step is to more clearly define just what training is.

Training defined

Training is basically *learning*. The organization attempts to provide experiences which will help the individual perform more effectively on the job. A training program is meant to structure these experiences in such a way that the appropriate attitudes or skills are acquired and developed. Thus, training can be seen as

---

[1]E. H. Schein. The individual, the organization, and the career: A conceptual scheme. *Journal of Applied Behavioral Science*, 1971, **7**, 400–426.

[2]J. R. Heinrichs. Personnel training. In M. Dunnette (Ed.), *Handbook of organizational and industrial psychology*. Chicago: Rand McNally, 1976, pp. 829–860.

an attempt by the organization to change the behavior of its members through the learning process in order to increase effectiveness.

Kinds of change induced by training

The two major factors of the above definition are the ideas of *change in behavior* and *learning*. We must describe what it is we want to change and know how to change it. The term "change in behavior" encompasses a wide variety of activities. It could include learning how to walk, drive a car, paint a house, or add up a column of numbers. It could also include changes in how we interact with our peers. Because of the diversity of this list, researchers have developed some broad categories which help to describe the kinds of changes typically found in organizational training.

Transmitting information. A substantial portion of many training programs is simply the learning of factual information. People are shown where they work, what their job is, and whom to contact about different issues and are briefed about the rules and regulations. This information provides the trainee with the factual material which is essential for effective adjustment and performance.

Development of attitudes. Closely linked to the imparting of knowledge is the development of attitudes. Actually, it is probably more accurate to say "changing the attitudes" of trainees. People enter training programs with many preconceived evaluations of the training, their job, their boss, and the informal norms of the organization. It is important to change these attitudes if the program is to be successful.

Therefore, many experts in the training field feel that it is not sufficient just to impart knowledge about a particular job or field. It is also necessary to work on changing the attitudes and evaluations of the participants. This aspect of training is often difficult to execute successfully, and it is hard to evaluate its success.

Development of skills. Assume that in a given training program a considerable amount of information has been transmitted to participants and that in the progress of training their attitudes have been changed. In other words, the first two aspects of training were accomplished well. Is the program then a success? The answer probably is no, because the trainees have not yet had an opportunity to develop "human skills" in the application of the material imparted to them. Consequently, another important aspect of training is skill development.

Some argue that the development of skills derived from training must come from on-the-job experience. Classroom simulation of human problems through case studies and role playing, it is claimed, is inadequate even when conducted under the supervision of a training expert. As a consequence, many of the training programs designed to develop specific skills are carried out on the job. However, people in the training field are constantly working on new devices and techniques which endeavor to fill the need for realistic forms of classroom experiences where skills can be developed.

Conceptual changes. Perhaps the most difficult and most complex type of changes are those designed to teach people general principles of human behavior. Behavioral science has developed a number of conclusions about human personality, motivation, communication, group processes, leadership, and so on. The learning and application of these general rules involves learning of new information, attitudes, and skills.

In an example that we used earlier in the text, a manager had a problem with an employee who failed to meet deadlines. We mentioned that a typical reaction to such a problem was for the manager to think that the employee was lazy or disorganized and that the appropriate response was a warning or reprimand. Training this manager to analyze the problems in terms of external causes (e.g., work load, role conflict, etc.) rather than internal causes (e.g., personal characteristics) involves a number of changes. The trainer must provide information about how to analyze the problem—what to look for, what information should be gathered. Basic beliefs and attitudes about what causes behavior need to be changed, and the actual problem-solving skills need to be modified. The manager needs to *behave* differently in response to the problem.

It can be seen that different aspects of training are emphasized at different organizational levels. Managerial development may concentrate on changing attitudes, concepts, and interpersonal skills, whereas the training of front-line supervisors might emphasize the transmission of knowledge and the development of certain motor skills. The important point is that the trainees change their behavior in some way.

Principles of learning

What we have to learn to do, we learn by doing.   Aristotle

Our discussion of learning principles in Chapter 3 was rather broad and general in its coverage. Many of these ideas can and have been directly applied to the field of training. More specifically, there are a number of ways in which training can be made more effective by utilizing specific learning principles. The five most important principles are described below.

Motivation. Perhaps the best starting point is to state that the trainees should want to learn. This is not to say that participation in a training program without motivation would result in no learning. Up to a certain point, however, wanting and trying to learn (paying attention, and so on) will increase the amount learned. Certain types of programs may be interesting and motivating by themselves, or external rewards can be provided. One principle used to make training intrinsically interesting is to assure the active participation of the trainee. Rather than read a case study, a trainer could have the trainees play the roles of the characters mentioned in the case. Some authors even suggest that the trainee participate in the planning and formulation of the training program itself.

For external motivation, a variety of financial or social rewards could be used. Some researchers argue that the competitive nature of training can serve as a good motivator for managers. In any case, the desire to do well is an important determinant of how much one receives out of a training program.

Reinforcement and feedback. One of the most powerful principles of learning says that when one receives positive rewards, information, or feelings for doing something, then it becomes more likely that one will do the same thing in the same or similar situations. On the other side there is the fact that punishment for a particular response will decrease the probability of its occurrence in similar settings. The trainer should thus be able to increase the frequency of desirable behavior through the correct use of various rewards (praise, money, status, and so on). The major problem, however, is to determine what will serve as reinforcers. Different people want different things, and the use of rewards which an individual does not desire will not affect learning in the manner anticipated.

Coupled with the idea of reinforcement is the very similar idea of giving individuals feedback or knowledge of when they are correct or incorrect. Providing this information in an explicit manner lets the trainees correct their mistakes and often makes the task more rewarding or stimulating. Research studies have frequently cited situations where individuals show greater performance on a variety of tasks when they have feedback than when it is absent. One study, for example, reports on a management training course where those receiving feedback showed greater changes in their behavior than those without feedback.[3] The two principles together suggest that trainers should tell trainees when they are doing poorly or well, why that is the case, and provide attractive or unattractive consequences as a result of the trainees' behavior.

Practice and repetition. The greater the opportunity to repeat or practice something we learn, the better it is learned. With practice, individuals may become more familiar and at ease with what they are supposed to do. Also, by the judicious use of various ways to teach similar things, the trainer may illustrate the generality of the information to be learned. For certain managerial training courses, there could be multiple chances to play roles or practice behavioral skills. For other types of supervisory training involving motor skills, the trainee should be allowed to repeat the correct responses over and over. These behaviors become overlearned, which results in a minimum of forgetting at a later date.

Meaningfulness of material. There are at least three ways that the organization and presentation of the material is important. First, the material should be meaningful in the sense that it is understandable and interpretable by those participating in the training. There are certain techniques available to trainers, such as putting together meaningful units, creating association with familiar terms, and providing a logical reason for the material.

A second related topic is the amount of information presented at one time to the trainee. The question here is whether to split the information into smaller parts or present it as a whole. Surveys of the literature suggest that the trainer

---

[3]A. W. Ayers. Effects of knowledge of results on supervisors' post-training test scores. *Personnel Psychology,* 1955, **32**, 152–155.

should use as large a unit of information as can be handled and meaningfully presented. Too much information or too broad a scope may confuse the trainee. The major problem with this principle involves the determination of the "correct" unit.

Finally, it has been argued that training should space out the learning periods rather than present them all together. When all the information is presented together, it seems to couple the problems of not breaking the information down into smaller units and probably presents limitations on practice time. By spacing out the sessions, the material is easier to assimilate and practice. One study of managerial training procedures indicated that managers who received their training over a 2-week period made fewer mistakes than those who received their training in 3 successive days.

Transfer of training. Clearly, the purpose of training employees is to prepare them for some position in the organization. One important aspect of any training program, therefore, is the degree to which the material to be learned can be transferred to the job. The goal is to make the training experience maximally similar to the job experience. There are at least two possible strategies for obtaining transferability. The first is to make the training situation similar to the actual job in terms of the physical characteristics of the situation. Simulations that attempt to physically represent the situation in which one will work would display this similarity as well as most on-the-job programs. However, most management and leadership training takes place off the job and requires a somewhat different approach.

The second strategy is the teaching of *principles* that may be applied on the job. One may learn about the interdependence of organizational parts or the complexity of individual decisions through a series of case studies, role-playing sessions, or simulations. It is hoped that the trainee will carry these principles onto the job. However, as we shall see, this hope is often not fulfilled.

Understanding training needs

To produce the desired changes, one must be familiar with the needs of the organization, the kinds of changes possible, and the ways in which one brings about these changes. Before an organization chooses a training program for any of its employees, there are some preliminary questions which should be asked. A thorough analysis of the organization, the jobs involved, and the employees affected should be conducted in order to discover what is needed in the way of training.

Organizational goals. A general consideration of both the long- and short-term goals of the organization is important for developing a broad perspective of one's training philosophy. How does the organization feel it will grow? How will both the social and physical environment be related to this growth? In general, what sort of "climate" and "image" is being sought?

If the organization wishes to hire minority-group members living in the neighborhood, this may affect the selection of a training program. Or perhaps management wants to emphasize the relationship between the organization and the physical environment. What sorts of waste products are there? How does the firm handle these issues? Since organizations are constantly being forced to plan their production or services years in advance, the same emphasis should be placed on their goals and training philosophy. Otherwise, they will fail to correspond to one another, and the training will be of limited value.

Job analysis. In the consideration of training procedures, management must also keep in mind the jobs for which people are being trained. An analysis of these jobs requires knowledge of the kinds of skills, attitudes, behaviors, and personality characteristics that are most effective for those positions. These data would spell out rather clearly the tasks that constitute the job.

It should be pointed out that in some cases this may be a very difficult task because of the flexible nature of some managerial positions. But it is just this difficulty that makes it crucial. We know that different kinds of situations require different types of people with different attitudes, behaviors, and skills. There are three possible consequences of training: greater effectiveness, no change, and less effectiveness. Since two of these are costly, it pays for the organization to know what is needed.

Work-force analysis. The final assessment of the functioning of the organization involves the employees currently filling the positions of interest. Some attempt should be made to find out if performance is substandard to begin with. Second, it may be true that the problems with performance are due to nontrainable factors. More specifically, technological or mechanical changes may be needed—not changes in the employees. It would also be important to determine if the employees currently in the positions are capable of improvement through training or whether new personnel are needed. In short, a thorough look at the goals, jobs, and job occupants is needed before one decides what and how to train.

Training programs

The research on actual training programs is rather diverse. More specifically, some studies have looked at all forms of training while others have gathered information only on managerial development. However, there are three broad trends that seem to be evident. First, training is increasing. Firms are spending more money on developing and maintaining the effectiveness of their employees. We have already documented some examples of these increases.

A second trend is that training is now taking place to an increasing extent outside the organization. Many training programs are run by an outside agency or institute that provides the service for a fee. The implications of this trend are that specialists in training now exist and that providing this service has become a big business in itself.

The third point is tied to the first two: training is currently broader in scope than it used to be. Numerous training programs today emphasize the learning of

The military is well known for the extensive training of its members, who learn specific skills as well as the general behavioral norms of being in the service. *(By permission of University of Washington Daily.)*

complex emotional and behavioral skills. Sensitivity training is one of these. Other programs emphasize attitudinal and informational issues. Training is no longer used just to teach motor skills to assembly-line employees. There are feasible programs for employees at all levels in the organization.

There are numerous ways we could classify this variety of training programs. We could separate them according to the audience (manager versus nonmanager), the task (motor versus interpersonal), what is learned (information, attitudes, skills), or the setting where the training takes place (on the job versus off the job). We have decided to use the on-the-job/off-the-job distinction for two major reasons. First, it is historically the way that these programs are frequently reviewed, both in the research literature and in organizations. And second, it encompasses most of the other distinctions mentioned above. Most on-the-job training programs are for lower-level employees, dealing with specific motor tasks and imparting information or skill. Off-the-job programs, on the other hand, usually are geared toward managers, attitudes, and interpersonal skills. While there are exceptions to these classifications, in general they seem to hold up fairly well.

Because of the multiplicity of programs developed, we will only describe some of the more representative types of programs both for on-the-job and off-the-job training. The programs will generally be evaluated in terms of the utilization of learning principles discussed earlier.

On-the-job training

One of the most common procedures over the years has been to train a person while on the job. A practical reason for this approach is that the individual is producing while being trained. No special space or equipment need be used. There are, however, some shortcomings associated with these approaches. A competent trainer or coach must be provided from within the organization. If the trainee must work at a reduced pace, then certain equipment or facilities may be tied up. The trainee must experience some of the stress and pressure of the job while trying to learn. In short, the use of such training should be carefully evaluated in terms of needs, costs, and effectiveness.

Job instruction. Most firms have some means of introducing the employee to the work environment. Traditional programs would include a general survey of the firm, personal introductions to the people with whom the trainee will work, and some instruction about the job. During World War II, the War Manpower Board formalized some of the procedures involved for introducing the new trainee to a variety of technical jobs. In general, the trainee receives some introductory information about the task to be learned. The trainer then presents a step-by-step review *and demonstration* of how to do the job. At this point, the trainee is asked to perform the operations alone and, as he or she goes through these operations, explain what is being done and why. During this phase the trainer asks a number of questions and corrects any mistakes the trainee might make. The trainee continues to practice the task until a satisfactory level of performance is reached, at which point close supervision is removed. The trainer periodically checks back to see if the level of performance is being maintained and if more help or instruction is needed.

Notice that repetition, feedback, active participation, and easily transferable experiences are built into this type of training. However, no matter how well the materials or jobs are organized, the skills of the trainer are potential problems. The trainer must be highly skilled at the task in order to train others effectively. It should also be pointed out that this type of training is suited best for jobs that have fairly specific content. It also requires close supervision, which means that the trainer's time and potential productivity are being used for this task.

Coaching. A less formalized procedure than the one described above is often called *coaching*. In this type of program, the trainee may have one person who is the tutor or "big brother" in the organization. The coach will attempt to help the trainee by providing feedback, setting goals, and discussing any problems that may occur. Training of this kind may be used for positions at many different levels within the organization.

One study of certain coaching practices used by General Electric indicated that coaches (who had been trained how to coach) increased their ability to set performance standards, provide feedback, and assistance for trainees.[4] The major problem with the coaching approach is that it is dependent upon the skills of the coach. The amount and kinds of feedback and reinforcement, as well as the way the material is presented, could present difficulties. And again, to the degree that the coach spends time coaching, he or she is not doing other things.

Job rotation. When the trainee is required to work in a number of assignments before assuming a permanent position, he or she is involved in a job-rotation program. Many law firms and the medical profession require this sort of training. In large organizations, the trainee may become familiar with the existing divisions or departments. The program may not only provide scope but also allow the trainee to work at different levels within the organization. This variety of experience is designed to give the trainee an overall view of the organization and the interrelationships of its parts.

There are a variety of problems with this approach. The supervision or feedback that the trainee receives is often spotty or inconsistent. It is also worth arguing that some of the experiences are nontransferable—that is, not useful for the permanent position. Finally, it is one of the more long-term and expensive procedures for training.

To be effective, a trainee should be able to have a flexible job-rotation program. Different positions in the organization should require different training, and the job-rotation program for an individual should reflect these needs. The organization should also provide consistent feedback, reinforcement, and goal-setting procedures through the use of competent managers, coaches, or advisers.

Junior boards. A shorter and less-involved strategy than job rotation is to assign the trainee to a committee or junior board which deals with programs concerning the whole organization. In this way the trainee is able to gain information about the different departments or subunits of the organization and how they operate. In some cases this board may be set up for the explicit purpose of serving as a training device. These assignments are often used as supplements to the programs already described. Their effectiveness depends upon the degree to which the task is related to activities that the trainee will have to perform later and the degree to which the trainee learns the correct information.

Assistantship or apprenticeship. In these types of programs the trainee is often assigned as an assistant or apprentice to an individual in the organization. In most cases, this trainer holds a position similar to the one the trainee hopes eventually to hold. So, for example, a trainee (in graduate school) may be a teaching or research assistant, or in occupations such as plumbing or carpentry an individual may serve an apprenticeship before assuming the position.

These programs have some rather distinct features. The trainee is usually assigned to one person and for a given length of time. Before assuming the position, there are typically a number of tests or competencies that the trainee must display. It is precisely these features which may weaken this type of

[4]D. M. Goodacre. Simulating improved management. *Personnel Psychology*, 1963, **16**, 133–143.

Sometimes training is clearly related to the technical aspects of the job. *(By permission of the Boeing Company.)*

training. First, the dependence on one coach or trainer demands that he or she be good in providing feedback and reinforcement. Second, the rigidity of the program often restricts the individual from moving along faster than the program allows. It is just this problem that is being contested by many minority groups. They argue that the apprenticeship programs can be completed sooner than some trade unions may allow. A third and related point is that the competencies or tests may not reflect what the individual needs to know for the position to be assumed. More specifically, the wrong material may be emphasized.

To summarize, most on-the-job techniques have the advantages of being similar to what the trainee will actually be doing (transfer of training), and they allow the organization to obtain some benefit from the trainee who is working while being trained. The degree to which the materials are effectively organized and feedback is provided are generally matters which require attention, as does the motivation of the trainee. In some cases, organizations have decided that this function is handled more effectively by outside trainers. But before we turn to a review of off-the-job training, we should briefly discuss the success of on-the-job programs as training programs for the "hard to employ."

Training the hard to employ

Besides the large group of people who need training because of changes in job requirements or their entrance into a new job, there are a substantial number of people described as hard to employ. These individuals have little or no prolonged work experience, education, or skill development. According to the Department of Labor, the hard to employ are usually members of a minority group who have had little work experience, have less than a high school education, often are young, and are living at or below the poverty level.

In recent years, many organizations have attempted to develop training programs for these people. In most cases, these programs are designed to teach specific job-related skills, although in many instances the training itself may occur off the job. So, while the intent and content of the training may be similar to the on-the-job programs, its actual physical location may be elsewhere.

The research on the success of these programs is increasing significantly. One review of this literature found almost 200 articles related to training the hard to employ.[5] A summary of this review suggested that retention was higher (1) for females, (2) for married people, (3) for people from the rural South, (4) in situations where the supervisor was supportive, and (5) where training included a comprehensive program of counseling, training, transportation, and other support facilities.

A more recent report by the same researchers examined the training issues in more detail.[6] They selected 114 companies in the Chicago area that had made a pledge to the National Alliance of Businessmen to employ disadvantaged workers. The employment, training, and retention figures were compiled from these companies over an 18-month period, and the following results were found:

1 Length of training was unrelated to retention.
2 The percentage of job-skills activities in the training program was positively related to retention. The greater the emphasis on specific job skills, the greater the retention.
3 The percentage of attitude training was unrelated to retention.
4 The use of role-playing techniques was negatively related to retention. The more that role playing was used, the lower the retention.
5 The greater the attempt to discover the causes of absenteeism and attempts to solve these problems, the greater the retention.
6 The more personal counseling that was available, the greater the retention.

The overall picture suggests that the content of training should be skill-oriented rather than attitudinal and that other support services such as counseling will increase retention. The data on the type of *trainer* that is most successful in these types of programs fits the same picture. The trainer should provide counseling, be flexible, provide *relevant* material, and use *practical* illustrations.[7] The more clearly related the training is to actual job experiences, the more likely it is to be successful.

Off-the-job training: Informational techniques

In many cases the organization wishes to provide training that would supplement its on-the-job efforts or facilities. In these situations, off-the-job techniques are used. The advantages of this approach are numerous. The trainee is not obliged

[5]P. S. Goodman, P. Salipante, & H. Parensky. Hiring, training and retaining the hard-core unemployed: A selected review. *Journal of Applied Psychology,* 1973, **58,** 23–33.

[6]P. Salipante, Jr., & P. S. Goodman. Training, counseling and retention of the hard-core unemployed. *Journal of Applied Psychology,* 1976, **61,** 1–11.

[7]I. Gray & T. B. Borecki. Training programs for the hard core unemployed: What the trainer has to learn. *Personnel,* 1970, **47,** 23–29.

to perform under the stress or anxiety of the actual work setting. Removal from the setting may provide opportunities for the trainee to practice various skills and test acquired knowledge without the possibility of dire consequences.

The organization is, of course, obliged to pay for these services. This cost, however, may be lower in the long run than the cost of using the organization's existing personnel and perhaps risking major mistakes while the trainee is learning on the job. Finally, it is an opportunity for the organization to utilize the skills of specialists in the field of training. These resources can help when the organization does not have the skills or facilities to conduct the training itself.

The major problem with most off-the-job training is just that: it is off the job. When the training is not similar to the actual work requirements, it becomes questionable as to how much of the training is actually transferable. The trainee may learn a great deal, but is he or she learning the right thing?

In recent years there has been an increase in these supplementary programs. Changing needs, widened interests, and technological advances have all influenced this increase. We will break these programs down into two categories: those that deal with the dissemination of information and those that attempt to change behavior. Although this distinction is not applicable for all the programs, it is useful in terms of identifying the major emphasis and actual applications of most training techniques.

Lectures. This technique typically involves a trainer reading and organizing some material which is presented orally to a group of trainees. It is probably the most widely used method of training, and this is because it is an inexpensive way to distribute information to a large number of people. In fact, in its economy lies its chief positive point.

It has been suggested, however, that lectures became obsolete with the invention of type. It is argued that the trainee could read the material. While this may be true, it still does not account for the difference in work hours expended when each member of a class reads some information versus one individual reading it and passing along only the most important information. The trainer should have expertise in the area and therefore ought to be able to organize and synthesize the material in the most meaningful fashion.

Other problems with the lecture focus on its one-way communication process. Essentially the instructor passes on information to a passive audience. There is little opportunity to clarify the meaning of ambiguous material, and except for formal examination procedures, it is hard to know what and how much is being learned. Also, the lecture provides little flexibility for individual needs, interests, or abilities. Everyone hears the same thing. Thus, there is little opportunity for practice, reinforcement, or involvement. In short, the advantages of providing a large amount of information to a large audience can be offset by the inadequate emphasis on principles of learning inherent in the lecture process.

Discussion or conference. This type of training typically involves trainees discussing preselected topics that are related to the work setting. It is very often used to teach principles of communication, problem solving, and decision making, and it is perhaps the most frequently used method of training for managers.

The advantages over a lecture are numerous. The trainer may provide feedback, and the trainees can be actively involved in the learning process. The communication is two-way. Also important is the fact that trainees may learn from others or their own errors by receiving positive or negative reinforcement that corresponds to the way in which they have behaved.

This technique requires a highly skilled trainer. It is difficult to control a discussion without hindering the desired freedom. The trainer must know what to say to different people and must be ready for unanticipated events. The major problems with this method occur when trainers are not able to properly carry out their functions. In these situations, the discussion may get off the topic or may dwell on one point too long. When the material is poorly organized or poorly covered, it reduces the chance of transfer from the session to the work setting.

Films and TV. Both television and films are examples of technological advances that are used in training. The use of a videotape or actual film is usually skillfully done and has some distinct advantages. First, the tape can be used again. Thus, the organization of training material is not dependent upon which lecturer or discussion leader is available on a given day. Second, certain scenes or visual effects may be used to maximum advantage. For example, pictures of actual accidents in industry are used in safety films. Third, films often heighten the motivation and interest of the trainee.

The major problem with the material presented in this form is that there is no two-way communication. It is effective in the distribution of information but seldom provides for the active participation of the trainee. Feedback and reinforcement processes are also absent. One way to circumvent some of these problems is to couple discussions with films or TV presentations, and in fact, this is often done.

Special study. Some training programs consist of a special format of study that the individual pursues off the job. These special study courses may be given by universities under the label of "continuing education," or they may be tailor-made for a given set of managers or executives. Usually, there are specific reading lists and lectures provided as well as discussion groups. The readings and discussions are topic-oriented and focus on a wide variety of issues. Probably the most important consideration for this type of program is its organization. If it is poorly organized or the material is poorly selected, there may be very little transfer of information to the real organizational setting.

Off-the-job training: Behavioral programs

In recent years, a number of new types of training programs have been developed for off-the-job use. Although in certain cases the differences between these methods and some of those already described may be slight, the basic underlying goal of the new programs is to change behavior through active involvement and experiential learning. One of the major problems with the traditional techniques that involved lectures or films was that the communication was one-way, the trainee was not involved, and the applicability of the material was not always apparent. The programs that evolved addressed themselves specifically to the use of one or more of these principles in an attempt to improve the training.

Case study/role playing. The typical case study used for business purposes is a thorough description of some events that actually occurred in an organization. Cases have been included in training programs because it is believed that leadership effectiveness can be achieved through the study of situations with which managers have been actually confronted.

The application of the technique is flexible, with a few basic processes seen as standard procedures. The trainee or trainees read the case and present some alternative solutions or lines of action. These suggestions may then be discussed in a class session where the individual is able to obtain information about how others viewed the case. The trainee is therefore actively involved and is working in a setting which is supposedly similar to a setting he or she might encounter.

In discussions of the case method, many authors point out that there is no one correct solution to the case. The trainee is encouraged to consider a variety of alternatives and to explore different points of view. Trainees should project themselves into the case to some extent by asking, "What would I do if I were in this situation?" The emphasis on flexibility however, creates some problems. To the degree that there are no definitive answers, it is difficult to use effective reinforcement techniques and to judge objectively whether the trainee has done a good job. Hopefully, the trainee is learning to come up with both numerous and constructive plans of action.

In an attempt to increase the participation and involvement in case studies, trainees are sometimes asked to play the roles of the case participants. That is, they act out a case as if it were a play. This technique is known as role playing and differs from the case-study technique in a number of ways. As one can see, compared to case studies, the role-playing technique is more lifelike, involving behavior and emotions and allowing for the practice of interpersonal skills. There is continual feedback, and the trainee actually experiences the ongoing process. By switching roles, one may gain insight into how the other person feels. Although the content is not necessarily tied to cases, the emphasis seems to be similar in that both techniques are designed to provide practice in the development of one's interpersonal insights and skills.

There are some shortcomings, however, with the procedure. The trainer must be careful in the way in which the group plays out the roles. Some individuals may become too involved in the "acting" and lose sight of the purpose of the exercise. The trainer must also be careful that the trainees receive correct feedback and reinforcement: more to the point, the trainer must be sure that trainees are not reinforced for doing the wrong thing. Finally, some sort of supplemental discussion period is probably necessary to discuss the feelings and insights experienced by the trainee. Without this supplement the trainer will not be able to provide necessary information about an individual's reactions during the training.

Simulations. Simulations attempt not only to involve the individual but also to duplicate the environmental setting in which the trainee will eventually work. The major features of a typical simulation are (1) the actual experience of working in lifelike situations, (2) the chance for trainees to be themselves (rather than to act, as in role playing), (3) a telescoping of time and events, (4) a continual feedback and reevaluation process, and (5) a critical review session at the end of the simulation. A well-developed simulation would, therefore, utilize many of the learning principles which we have described.

Examples of simulations for business fall under two major headings, those that deal with games of some sort and those that attempt to duplicate a task setting. In the case of business games, an environment is designed to replicate the economic and administrative functioning of an actual organization. This duplication is based on various principles linking inputs with processes and then with eventual outcomes or output, which in turn change the inputs. The trainees make decisions (as individuals or in teams) about the market, the budget, personnel policy, or so on; these decisions modify the situation; and more decisions are required. The games are typically conducted over a series of sessions or trials where the trainees are given some information and some general statements about how to use the information (e.g., economic principles, probability estimates). The trainees must then make a variety of decisions, and a given session will end when this is done. The trainer must then figure out the implications of the decisions that were made according to the preestablished relationships underlying the game. The trainer then gives this information back to the trainees, and another trial begins. It should be mentioned that the sophistication of these games is highly variable. Some use computers to provide rapid and continual feedback, while some use the discrete steps described above.

There are a few drawbacks associated with these games. Under certain circumstances trainees may discover some gimmick or principle which allows them to win or to perform successfully. This gimmick, however, may not be a good strategy to employ in an actual organizational setting. A similar problem occurs when trainees become so involved in winning the game that they fail to learn the major principles that are being taught. Finally, where the simulation is inaccurate in its representation of the environment, the trainee may actually learn the wrong thing.

The type of simulation designed to represent a more specific task setting is best illustrated by the in-basket technique.[8] The trainee is presented with a situation where he or she must take over for a manager who is absent. The trainee is provided with an in-basket full of materials which must be dealt with. These materials may be phone calls, meetings to set up, complaints to handle, orders to make, and other demands, which supposedly duplicate the tasks to be faced if the person held such a position. These materials typically are gathered by assessing what a manager of a certain type of firm actually does during a day. The trainee must go through the material and deal with it as skillfully as possible. This may require a list of priorities and, in fact, may result in some demands to which the trainee will not attend. After the session is completed, the trainer and trainee should meet to discuss and evaluate the trainee's performance. Similar techniques may have people working together as a management group or may supplement the task with films. Again, the same strong and weak points that were applicable for business games are applicable here. The trainer must be sure that the trainee is learning the correct material.

[8]N. Fredericksen, D. R. Saunders, & B. Ward. The in-basket test. *Psychological Monographs,* 1957, 71(9, Whole No. 438).

Programmed instruction. A relatively new approach to training has emphasized a technique known as *programmed learning*. The characteristics of this type of instruction are:

1 The material to be learned is broken down into small units called *frames* which are presented to the trainee one at a time (in a book or on a screen).
2 The trainee is required to respond to each frame as to a multiple-choice question—that is, read the frame and then respond to a question about it.
3 The trainee then receives immediate feedback and reinforcement. If the answer is incorrect, the trainee usually must reread the frame and choose again.
4 Material is sequenced according to its complexity, with more difficult items dependent upon knowledge acquired in the earlier stages of the program.

These principles emphasize the organization of the material, feedback, reinforcement, and the active participation of the trainee. Modification of the basic format, called *linear programming,* has allowed the trainee to progress at his or her own speed. That is, if trainees show that they know certain material by their responses on a set of separate frames, they may be "branched" to more complex material. Trainees who have trouble may be given an extra set of frames to help them master a given topic.

Although the technique seems to be most applicable for the teaching of factual material, there are a number of situations where it has been used for training behavioral skills. For example, over the last 10 years we have developed a programmed instructional text for people working in specific foreign countries. This device, called the *culture assimilator,* presents frames consisting of intercultural encounters between Americans and the people from the culture of interest. Figure 15-1 presents one frame from the Greek assimilator. (The correct answer is marked with an X.) The trainee reads a large number of these stories (from 150 to 300), makes responses to each one, and receives feedback about what is the correct behavior and why. Research on the use of this device conducted in Greece, Iran, Honduras, and Thailand shows that this technique produces better interpersonal relations, adjustment, and in certain cases productivity than that produced by other training techniques.[9]

There are a number of considerations, however, which limit the use of this type of program. First, it can be very expensive, both to develop and to maintain. If the programs are to be placed on computers and presented on teaching machines (small consoles with a screen and a variety of buttons on which one can respond), the cost may be prohibitive. It is also important to note that the transfer of the training may be questionable. Just because some information is learned does not necessarily mean that one will behave in the fashion desired.

Laboratory training. Sensitivity or laboratory training is a fairly recent innovation in executive development. It has grown out of the work of applied group

[9]F. E. Fiedler, T. R. Mitchell, & H. C. Triandis. The culture assimilator: An approach to cross-cultural training. *Journal of Applied Psychology,* 1971, **55,** 95–103. Also see T. R. Mitchell, D. L. Dossett, F. E. Fiedler, & H. C. Triandis. Culture training: Validation evidence for the culture assimilator. *International Journal of Psychology,* 1972, **7,** 97–104.

Rob Johnson and his wife had been in Greece for about 4 weeks and were having a wonderful time. Rob was a visiting Fulbright scholar at Athens College and had met a number of Greeks during his first few weeks there. Rob and his wife decided to have a dinner party for all their new Greek friends. They asked about what time the Greeks eat in the evening, and they were told 9:00 P.M. The invitations were made for everyone to come at 9:00 P.M. for cocktails and dinner. Mrs. Johnson figured everyone could have a drink or two and that dinner would be served at 9:45. However, by 9:45 only half of the guests had arrived and the dinner got cold. By 10:30 when everyone had arrived, both Rob and his wife were very upset and angry and the atmosphere was very strained.

How would you account for the tardiness of the Greek guests?

X 1. The Greek conception of time is different from the American conception of time.

Go to page 2-3

2. The guests were outgroup members; consequently, they had no desire to be prompt.

Go to page 2-4

3. Such behavior is rare in Greece. Most Greeks are quite prompt.

Go to page 2-5

4. In Greece it is impolite to require all guests to arrive at the same time. The guests resented this requirement and they expressed their resentment by arriving late.

Go to page 2-6

2-3

You selected 1: The Greek conception of time is different from the American conception of time.

Correct: Greeks do not emphasize promptness nearly so much as Americans. For a Greek a social invitation for 9:00 P.M. means "around 9:00" rather than "exactly at 9:00." However, not all Greeks use "Greek time." Many nontraditional and urban Greeks use American criteria. As a result half of those invited may arrive promptly and the other half 1 1/2 hours later. Be prepared for this much variety.   **Go to page 3-1**

Figure 15-1. A frame from the Greek assimilator, a programmed instructional text for Americans working in Greece.

dynamics and has been used in a variety of ways. The objectives of all types of sensitivity training, however, are basically the same.

It has been repeatedly observed in this chapter that the purpose of training is to change behavior. In the realm of human interrelationships, attitudes are fairly rigid and loaded with emotional content. The aim of most human-relations or sensitivity training is to accomplish organizational goals through the efforts of people. The assumption is that managers are effective or ineffective because of their attitudes about people. Therefore, human-relations training attempts to change attitudes so that, ultimately, behavior itself will change.

Sensitivity training attempts to accomplish this goal of behavioral change through a philosophy and technique of training which is best described as a concern with the "how" of things—how trainees appraise themselves, how a group behaves, how another would react in a given situation. In short, sensitivity training has as its purpose the development of executives' *awareness* of themselves, of others, of group processes, and of group culture.

The core of a laboratory program is the T group. From the standpoint of those who design and sponsor the program, the T group's purpose is to help people (1) explore their values and how they affect others, (2) determine if they want to modify their values, and (3) develop awareness of how groups can limit as well as facilitate human growth and interpersonal effectiveness.

To the trainees the T group, or the small group into which they are put, appears objectiveless and structureless at the start. There are few rules or regulations. People are free to talk about whatever they want. But as they interact, structure and objectives emerge. In viewing this process, the trainees can get an understanding of small-group behavior and their impact on it. At the same time, through communication with and feedback from other members of the group, the trainees learn about themselves as seen through the eyes of others. By being told frankly how their behavior and attitudes are "read," they have opened alternatives for change.

From this experience, it is hoped that individuals will see behavioral shortcomings in themselves and others which impair interpersonal relationships. If people experience failure in relating with other members of the group, and are told why by the group, they then may change their attitudes and, ultimately, their behavior in order to interact more successfully. Obviously these kinds of laboratory experiences can generate a high degree of individual involvement, because people's basic assumptions about their own behavior and the behavior of others are directly challenged.

The goal of laboratory training is to enhance *authenticity* in human relationships. This can only be accomplished in a setting where there is a high degree of individual awareness and acceptance of other people. Thus authenticity comes from the *relationship* between aware and sensitive individuals who have reached maturity in interpersonal transactions.

Laboratory programs differ widely in design. They may incorporate varying amounts of lecture, conference, case studies, and role playing. They may vary also in the degree of structure. But to repeat, the central feature of these programs is the T group, which exists to accomplish the purposes mentioned above. The trainee is actively involved and receives feedback about this action. However, due to the lack of structure in the situation, the degree of organization of the material and its transferability to the job is questionable.

Evaluation

In the beginning of this chapter it was suggested that an organization should make a thorough analysis of its goals, people, and positions *before* choosing a training program. It is equally important that the program itself be evaluated both before and after it has been introduced. It is silly to choose a training program when one is not sure of one's needs; it is wasteful and sheer folly not to evaluate it. One useful area of information would include knowledge of how well a particular program attends to the learning principles discussed earlier. After a brief discussion of these principles, we will present a summary of some of the empirical findings on the effectiveness of management training programs.

Table 15-1. Utilization of Learning Principles in On-the-Job and Off-the-Job Training Programs

	Active Partici- pation	Feed back	Organi- zation	Practice	Transfer
On-the-job programs					
Job instruction	+	?	+	+	+
Coaching	+	+	?	?	+
Job rotation	+	−	−	?	+
Junior boards	+	?	?	?	+
Assistantships or apprenticeships	+	+	?	+	+
Off-the-job programs: information					
Lectures	−	−	+	−	−
Discussions or conferences	+	?	?	?	−
Films and TV	−	−	+	−	−
Special study	+	?	+	−	−
Off-the-job programs: behavioral					
Case studies/role playing	+	+	?	+	?
Simulations	+	+	+	+	?
Programmed instruction	+	+	+	+	?
Sensitivity training	+	+	−	+	?

This table is a modification of one presented by B. M. Bass & J. A. Vaughn. *Training in industry: The management of learning.* Belmont, Calif.: Wadsworth, 1966, p. 131.

Theoretical evaluation

One way to evaluate the potential effectiveness of any training program is to assess the degree to which the activities incorporate motivation, feedback, practice, reinforcement, sensible organization, and transferable experiences. Table 15-1 represents the strengths and weaknesses of most of the programs we have discussed. As you can see, most on-the-job techniques can be successful if the material is well organized and the coach is well prepared and committed to the task at hand. But as we have mentioned before, these types of techniques are usually better suited for lower-level jobs concerned with the learning of information or skills.

For most managerial training, some type of off-the-job program is frequently selected. The major difficulties with these programs are their expense and the fact that the training conditions are often inadequate with respect to the transfer of learned material to the actual job setting. The strengths of such programs can be their use of well-organized materials prepared by knowledgeable professionals.

Empirical evaluation

The evaluation of most on-the-job programs for lower-level employees is encouraging. In almost every case, people with training do better than people without training. But a second question is whether such programs are cost effective— that is, does the cost of the training exceed the financial benefits produced by the increased performance of the trainee? The Department of Labor, for example, in evaluating its programs attempts to assess the total hours spent in the program

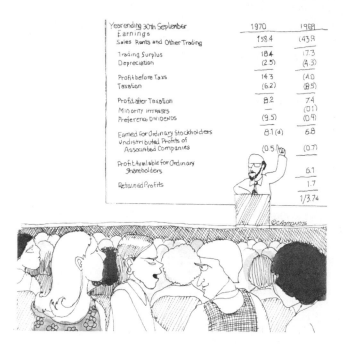

Year ending 30th September	1970	1969
Earnings		
Sales Rents and Other Trading	158.4	(43.8
Trading Surplus	18.4	17.3
Depreciation	(2.5)	(4.3)
Profit before Taxs	14.3	(A.0
Taxation	(6.2)	(8.5)
Profit after Taxation	8.2	7.4
Minority interests	—	(0.1)
Preference DIVIDENDS	(9.5)	(0.4)
Earned for Ordinary Stockholders	8.1 (d)	6.8
Undistributed Profits of Associated Companies	(0.5) (m)	(0.7)
Profit Available for Ordinary Shareholders		6.1
Retained Profits		1.7
		1/3.74

*All this theoretical accounting leaves me cold. I just
want to know how to balance my checkbook.*

One criterion for evaluating training programs is the extent to which the training is concerned
with actual problems an employee will face.

and the cost of each hour for enrollees, completers, and noncompleters. These
figures can then be compared to estimates of financial gain realized by the
company hiring the trainees. The results here are less encouraging. In many
cases the dropout rate is high (e.g., Job Corps), and the number of people who
actually obtain employment using the skills acquired in the training is low.
Similar but less severe problems occur in privately supported programs. So,
while it is clear that trained people perform better than untrained ones, it is not
clear that this increase in effectiveness always covers the cost of the training.

The evaluation of management programs is even more confusing. In a recent
review of this research literature, the various types of programs were divided
into five groups: general management; general human relations; problem solving
and decision making; sensitivity training; and specialty training.[10] It should be
pointed out that these categories reflect the goals of the programs and not
necessarily their content. For example, both human-relations and T-group training might include conferences or role-playing techniques.

Seventy-three different studies were reviewed according to their goals and two

[10]J. P. Campbell, M. D. Dunnette, E. E. Lawler, & K. E. Weick. *Managerial behavior, performance
and effectiveness.* New York: McGraw-Hill, 1970, pp. 525–535.

other factors: criterion measures and amount of control. Those studies that provided information about changes in the trainee as a function of the training (learning, attitudes, opinion, and so on) are said to have internal criteria. Those that assess changes in actual job behavior (absences, effectiveness, reported grievances, and so forth) are classified as having external criteria. Those studies defined as having some experimental controls used a control group, while those with only a pretest-posttest comparison (no control group) are classified as having few controls. A breakdown of the seventy-three studies reviewed is presented in Table 15-2.

Table 15-2. Summary of Research Findings on Training

	General Management Programs	General Human-Relations Programs	Problem Solving and Decision Making	T Group and Laboratory Education Programs	Specialty Programs	
External criteria						
Some controls	2	—	—	6	5	
Few controls	1	3	1	3	—	
	3	3	1	9	5	21
Internal criteria						
Some controls	8	10	3	8	3	
Few controls	5	6	—	9	—	
	13	16	3	17	3	52

SOURCE: John P. Campbell, Marvin D. Dunnette, Edward E. Lawler, III, & Karl E. Weick, Jr. *Managerial behavior, performance, and effectiveness.* New York: McGraw-Hill, 1970, p. 322.

One can see from the figure that a majority of the studies used internal criteria and have some control over the evaluation process. It is also clear that human-relations and T-group training programs have been evaluated more extensively than the other types of training.

A review of the experimental results prompted the following general statements:

1 Approximately 80 percent of the human-relations and general management programs produced significant changes in the anticipated direction. Most of the studies, however, used internal criteria which focused on attitudinal information, and it is therefore hard to tell if the training produced actual behavioral changes back on the job.

2 The results for T-group training, although generally supportive, are not as one-sided as those above. Most of the studies that show support are of the internal-criteria, few-controls type. The most well-known and thorough reviews of this literature are also cautious in their overall evaluations of T groups. Millions of dollars are being spent on this type of training every year, and yet the evidence for its effectiveness is minimal. At best one might

say with confidence that certain types of T groups are helpful for certain types of people working in certain types of settings.[11]

3 Very few studies have been designed to test problem solving or specialty programs, and, in general, the results are inconclusive or not supportive of those programs that have been studied. Either the programs are ineffective or their changes have not been accurately assessed. Both alternatives require further evaluation.

In summarizing the literature, we should note some further issues. First, most of the programs evaluated contained combinations of lectures, cases, role playing, conferences, or T groups. The implications are twofold. Numerous kinds of training techniques discussed earlier, such as business simulations, programmed learning, and on-the-job techniques, have been assessed infrequently. A related implication is that since many programs combine techniques, perhaps we should assess particular *combinations* of training rather than gloss over these combinations by classifying them by their goals. Both the specific techniques and particular combinations may be useful in certain situations.

Finally, as mentioned earlier, most of the studies evaluated the training with either internal criteria or few controls, and of the thirteen that had external criteria and some control, only three or four were considered to be experimentally sound. We must conclude that, to date, our assessment of training programs has been inadequate and that we still have much to learn about what works and when it works.

Ethical evaluation

Two questions of ethical importance should be mentioned. First, how much pressure can and should be put on individuals to participate in these programs? Can managers refuse to participate in a T group if they wish, without fear of losing their job or damaging their career? The current situation in most organizations provides the employee with little choice but to attend. This is an issue for further discussion.

A second question has to do with advertising claims. Management training is big business, and there is much fame and fortune for people with programs that get widespread adoption. To some extent the best programs will survive, and the natural process of competition will weed out those programs that are ineffective. But this can be an expensive process and perhaps is wasteful of both human and financial resources.

The real question is whether the profession should be held to certain truth-in-advertising principles rather than the buyer-beware principle which is currently operating. These are not idle concerns. Consider the manager who gets an advertisement in the mail from well-known professionals that suggests that T-

[11]R. J. House. T-Group education and leadership effectiveness: A review of the empirical literature and a critical evaluation. *Personnel Psychology,* 1967, **20.** 1–32. Also J. P. Campbell & M. D. Dunnette. Effectiveness of T-Group experiences in managerial training and development. *Psychological Bulletin,* 1968, **70,** 73–104.

group training can increase an industry's effectiveness by improving the cost ratio, increasing performance, and enriching interpersonal relationships. The empirical support for these claims is just not there. Two large surveys of the industrial success of T groups suggest that these programs can successfully change attitudes, but there is little evidence that cost ratios and performance are improved.[12] Dunnette and Campbell concluded their review of this research by saying: "Thus there is little to support a claim that T-group or laboratory education effects any substantial behavioral change back on the job for any large proportion of trainees. Whatever change does occur seems quite limited in scope and may not contribute in any important way to changes in overall job effectiveness."[13]

This is only one example of a more general problem. How is the manager to select wisely from the alternatives that are available? The answer lies in two practical steps for the manager and one for the academic community. First, the manager should make sure that the type of program selected fits the needs of the particular setting. If better interpersonal relations are the goal, then T groups may be the best option. If problem-solving or decision-making activities are the focus, then some other type of program may be most effective (e.g., simulations, role playing). A thorough goal, manpower, and job analysis should accomplish this step. Second, the manager should *evaluate* the effectiveness of the program, using accepted measurement and research procedures. In this manner the manager can ascertain exactly what the program did or did not do. This information will be helpful for subsequent choices among training alternatives.

The academic and professional people involved in the administration and implementation of training programs should be urged to be candid and specific about the strengths and weaknesses of particular programs. If self-restraint proves inadequate, then the profession itself should monitor the claims of its practitioners. If social scientists are to avoid being accused of selling "snake oil," they should demand thorough and accurate evaluations and representations of their peddled product.

Summary

Training and development should be an integral part of any organization's plan for successfully coping with the future. Our review of this topic emphasized the following points:

1 Training and development is increasing in importance. More money is being spent on these activities because of both the increased rate of change in

[12]S. J. Carroll, F. T. Paine, & J. J. Ivancevich. The relative effectiveness of training methods—expert opinion and research. *Personnel Psychology*, 1972, **25**, 495–509. And C. P. Wagoner & V. H. Ingersoll. A survey of organizational utilization of T-Groups. Paper presented at the Western Academy of Management meetings, Reno, Nevada, 1973.

[13]M. D. Dunnette & J. P. Campbell. Laboratory education: Impact on people and organizations. *Industrial Relations*, 1968, **8**, 19.

technology (e.g., inventions, mechanization) and people (e.g., career changes).

2 Training can be defined as the learning of new information, attitudes, and behavior.

3 The principles of learning that are most important for successful training programs are active participation, reinforcement, well-organized materials, practice, and transferable experiences.

4 Most on-the-job programs are designed for lower-level employees and specific skills. A good coach and well-organized materials are needed for success.

5 Most off-the-job programs are designed for upper-level employees and they emphasize attitudes and interpersonal behavior. Their major drawback is the lack of transferable experiences.

6 Research shows that on-the-job programs can increase the skill level of trainees. Off-the-job programs seem to be better at changing attitudes than increasing productivity.

Implications for practice

There are a few generalizations about training that can help the practitioner. The first implication of our discussion is that training should be seen as a long-term investment in human resources. Recall our earlier equation

Performance = ability × motivation

Training can have an impact on both these factors. It can increase the skills and abilities of the employees and it can increase their motivation by increasing their sense of commitment and by encouraging people to develop and use new skills. It is a powerful tool that can have a major impact on both productivity and morale if properly used.

The second point is that one can choose a training program with confidence, given that the proper background preparation has been carried out. It is not necessary to be subject to current fads or managerial whim. A personnel director should assess what sorts of skills are needed by using a thorough job analysis. He or she can ascertain the skills and deficiencies of current employees to find out where training could help. Combining this information with an idea of the short- and long-term organizational goals will provide a fairly good picture of *what is needed*. This type of analysis will automatically rule out a substantial number of possible training approaches.

After the choice has been limited to a smaller set of programs, the director can analyze each option in terms of its recognition and inclusion of our major principles of learning. Is there feedback? Will the employees be actively or passively involved? Can they practice what they learn? Is what they learn *really relevant?* The answers to these questions should narrow the field even further.

Finally, given that a program eventually is chosen, it should be evaluated. This evaluation should probably assess (1) whether trainees did better than an untrained group and (2) whether financial benefits realized as a result of the training were greater or less than the cost of the training. The former evaluation is easier to do than the latter, simply because the long-term benefits (commitment, advancement) of training are hard to quantify. But the important point is that evaluation should be included as part of any training process. It is the minimum requirement necessary if both practitioners and academics are going to increase their knowledge about what works and why it works.

Discussion questions

1 What are the basic principles of learning that should be built into any training system?
2 What are the general differences between on-the-job and off-the-job training? When should you use one or the other?
3 What steps can an organization take both before and after training to increase the likelihood that a good program is being used? In your experience, are these steps taken very often?

Case: The popular panacea

You have been appointed manager of a large graphic and printing plant. You are aware that there have been serious problems with respect to productivity, accidents, and machine failures. Your job is to find out why people cannot do the job right.

The particular plant you are running has a number of separate operations. There are machines and people involved in collating, setting type, drawing, binding, folding, stapling, padding, and cutting. Your main product is postcards and business cards although your promotional advertising brings in substantial revenue as well.

To do all this work requires about forty employees doing about twenty different jobs. These people are generally selected from the surrounding population, a city of about 20,000 people. Normally there are plenty of people looking for jobs, so filling positions is not the problem. The problem is how to ensure they can do the job correctly.

You decide that the main thing to concentrate on is training. If you can just figure out what to do and how to do it, you will be all right. So you call in an outside consultant—a self-proclaimed expert on organizational effectiveness.

The first thing the consultant tells you is that you have a people problem. "Morale is the issue here. People don't like the work. That's why productivity is down. What you need is a little team building and some increased interpersonal awareness. After all, a happy ship is a productive ship."

This does not sound exactly right to you, but what do you know? This person is the expert and is supposed to know. Besides which, you have heard the consultant has done marvelous things over at that machine shop down the street. You decide you might as well pay an expert to do the job.

Six months and $5000 later you are still dissatisfied. The training has not helped a bit. Productivity is still low, and machine downtime is still increasing. Rather than spend good money after bad, you decide to tackle the problem yourself.

Questions about the case

1 What would you do? What sorts of information do you need?
2 Why do you think the outside consultant failed?
3 Who was to blame for the failure? Was the manager partly responsible?

Additional readings

Anshen, M. Executive development: In company vs. university programs. *Harvard Business Review*, 1954, **32**, 83–91.

* Barrett, J. E. The case for evaluation of training expenses. *Business Horizons*, 1969, **12**, 67–72.

** Bass, B. M., & Vaughn, J. A. *Training in industry: The management of learning.* Belmont, Calif.: Wadsworth, 1966.

* Bolda, R. A., & Lawshe, C. H. Evaluation of role playing. *Personnel Administration*, 1962, **25**, 40–42.

* Buckley, J. W. Programmed instruction in industrial training. *California Management Review*, 1967, **10**, 71–79.

** Campbell, J. P. Personnel training and development. *Annual Review of Psychology*, 1971, **22**, 565–602.

Fox, W. M. A measure of the effectiveness of the case method in teaching human relations. *Personnel Administration*, 1963, **26**, 53–57.

** Gagne, R. M. (Ed.). *Learning and individual differences.* Columbus, Ohio: Merrill, 1967.

** Gagne, R. M. (Ed.). *Psychological principles in system development.* New York: Holt, 1965.

* Gunderson, M. Employer role in hard-core trainee success. *Industrial Relations*, 1974, **13**, 94–97.

* Klaw, S. Two weeks in a T-group. *Fortune*, 1961, **64**, 114–117.

Maier, N. R. F., Solem, A., & Maier, A. *Supervisory and executive development.* New York: Wiley, 1957.

** McGehee, W., & Thayer, P. W. *Training in business and industry.* New York: Wiley, 1961.

Raia, A. P. A study of the educational value of management games. *The Journal of Business*, 1966, **39**, 339–352.

* Utgaard, S. B., & Bawis, R. V. The most frequently used training techniques. *Training and Development Journal*, 1970, **24**, 40–43.

*Possible reading for students

**Review of literature or comprehensive source material

16
Organizational change

There is nothing permanent except change.　　　　Heraclitus

The press, other media, and social science literature are filled with stories about alienation, the "blue-collar blues," white-collar crime, sabotage at work, and other examples of malaise in the workplace. The explanations for these problems are numerous: people are different today—they want different things; organizations are too big—they are less human; society is changing too rapidly—we cannot adjust.

There is some truth in most of these explanations. People are different. Education levels—and correspondingly, expectations and abilities—have risen. People are generally more affluent and have greater security in this country. The role of the church and the family has decreased, and there is some evidence that obedience to authority has declined as well. Society has begun to emphasize cooperation and self-actualization over competition and hard work directed toward organizational goals. All these changes suggest that people come into the work setting with different values and expectations than in the past.

But what do they face at work? One author has suggested the following discrepancies between work expectations and organizational realities.

1 Employees want challenge and personal growth, but work tends to be simplified, and specialties tend to be used repeatedly in work assignments. This pattern exploits the narrow skills of a worker, while limiting his or her opportunities to broaden or develop.
2 Employees want to be included in patterns of mutual influence; they want egalitarian treatment. But organizations are characterized by tall hierarchies, status differentials, and chains of command.
3 Employee commitment to an organization is increasingly influenced by the intrinsic interest of the work itself, the human dignity afforded by management, and social responsibility reflected in the organization's products. Yet

organizational practices still emphasize material rewards and employment security and neglect other employee concerns.

4 What employees want from careers, they are apt to want right now. But when organizations design job hierarchies and career paths, they continue to assume that today's workers are as willing to postpone gratifications as were yesterday's workers.

5 Employees want more attention to the emotional aspects of organization life, such as individual self-esteem, openness between people, and expressions of warmth. Yet organizations emphasize rationality and seldom legitimize the emotional part of the organizational experience.

6 Employees are becoming less driven by competitive urges, less likely to identify competition as the American way. Nevertheless, managers continue to plan career patterns, organize work, and design reward systems as if employees valued competition as highly as they used to.[1]

Besides these changes in employee expectations and needs, there are changes in our organizational environments. The world around us is changing at an increasing speed, and people have difficulty adjusting to this pace of life. We are also highly interdependent on other cultures, economies, regional groups, and small segments of the work force. A strike by people in one occupation (e.g., garbage collectors, police officers, truck drivers) can seriously alter our lives as can the whim of a Middle East political leader. Communication media bring us instant reporting with films transmitted by satellite. Our changes and everyone else's changes are exposed immediately. And through communication individual differences in life-styles, norms, and habits are more apparent and acceptable. One consequence is that organizations are finding it more difficult to reconcile individual or group differences through a powerful "efficiency imperative." What is good for General Motors is not necessarily good for the country.

Somehow organizations have to adapt to these different environments and to the different types of demands made by their participants. Over the last 20 years, numerous change strategies have evolved and been tested, implemented, and evaluated. The rest of this chapter will deal with these strategies and the current "state of the art."

Perspectives on change

The demand for a better working life has resulted in a proliferation of change technologies. These technologies are designed to make people more satisfied and productive in the work setting. Some of them deal with issues of job status, job content, relationships with peers and supervisors, reward systems, working conditions, and numerous other aspects of one's job.

In an attempt to deal with this great variety of strategies, a crude system of

---

[1]R. E. Walton. How to counter alienation in the plant. *Harvard Business Review,* November–December 1972, 72.

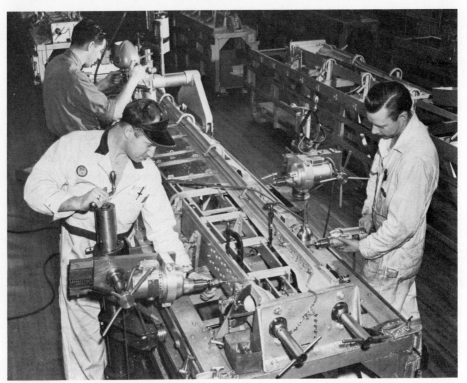

The traditional assembly line has often been the source of turnover and absenteeism on the job. *(By permission of the Boeing Company.)*

categorization has been imposed. In general, there are two major distinctions that need to be made. First, one needs to know whether structure or process is the primary focus of the change attempt. Second, where the change takes place (i.e., individual jobs, groups, or the whole organization) is also important. An elaboration of these distinctions is presented below.

Structure and procedures versus process and content

One way to approach organizational change is to modify either structural or procedural factors. These changes might include technological innovations (e.g., new machines, changing the design of a task), social-structure changes (e.g., lines of authority or communications), or procedural changes (e.g., rules, regulations). In other words, some formal aspect of the organization is modified in an attempt to bring about greater effectiveness, satisfaction, and adaptability.

The process approach tends to focus more on how things are done. It is concerned with interpersonal interactions and personal attitudes and feelings. It is a more humanistic approach to change. Instead of introducing a new machine (a structural suggestion), a process approach might attempt to make a job more interesting and challenging. Instead of firing or transferring quarreling people (a structural technique), a process approach might suggest some sensitivity training.

While the distinctions between these two approaches are frequently muddled on a practical level, they are much clearer on a philosophical and theoretical level. The structural approach has its historical roots in classical theory. Its emphasis is on effectiveness and efficiency. The primary question is not whether employees will like some change but whether it will work.

The process approach, on the other hand, reflects the position staked out by the human-relations approach. There is an interest in and concern about personal and interpersonal attitudes. The emphasis is on personal satisfaction and accomplishment. The focus is the content of the work experience. The underlying rationale is that people who enjoy their work and their coworkers will be more productive in the long run. As we shall see, both the structural and process approaches have suggested a number of important organizational-change strategies. But the historical progress has generally been from structural to process, reflecting the impact of the human relationists.

What do we change: Jobs, relationships, organizational policy

Besides the structural/process distinction there are some distinctions that should be made about what gets changed. The focus can be on specific jobs and the way they get done or the focus can be on relationships within and between groups. Job changes may emphasize new machinery or increased responsibility. Group changes might include increased task interdependence or more open communication. Finally, there may be changes that are designed to modify organizational policies. These latter strategies are wider in scope and impact. They are meant to affect all the organizational members. Examples might be a new control system (e.g., performance appraisal) or increased decentralization (e.g., participation in decision making).

When we put these distinctions together we can generate the classification system shown in Figure 16-1. We will find in our review of current change

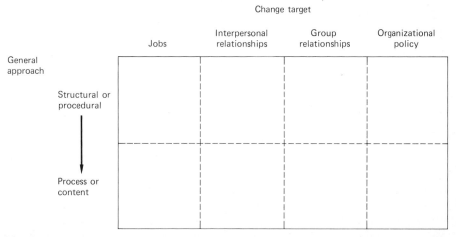

Figure 16-1. A classification of change strategies. *Note:* The dotted lines reflect the fact that the boundaries presented are not clear and distinct. Some change strategies change both structure and process, and others deal with jobs, interpersonal relations, and organizational policy.

strategies that most fit nicely into this system. However, before we turn to a discussion of specific change techniques, we should first discuss the concept of change at a more general level.

The change process

Introducing organizational change is similar in many ways to the decision-making process in that a number of different steps are involved. There is a problem-recognition phase, an attempt is made to discover the cause of the problem, some sort of change is introduced, and an evaluation of the change takes place. Each of these phases is discussed below.

Problem recognition

Probably the most common signs of organizational problems appear in the routine organizational data gathering process. The statistics on turnover, absenteeism, grievances, union disputes, and productivity all reflect the general health of an organization. These measures are usually part of any inclusive control system. When people are leaving the organization, not coming to work, breaking regulations, and generally slacking off, you can be fairly sure that (1) something is wrong and (2) something needs to be done about it.

Besides these obvious signs of malaise, there are some more subtle ones as well. Are there more arguments among coworkers? Do people seem tense? Does there seem to be less commitment and enthusiasm? While less objective and countable, these latter signs also reflect problems. They are in some cases as important or more important than the objective factors.

Identify causes: Diagnostic devices

Once the problem is recognized, the next step is to discover its cause. The most common technique is to ask people to tell you why they are unhappy, upset, or dissatisfied. This quest for information may take the form of informal chats, formal interviews, questionnaires, or personal observation. Most of the literature on change strategies shows that questionnaires are used most often. However, the focus and purpose of the questions may vary dramatically, depending upon the problem or the inclinations of the investigator.

Jobs. When the job itself is suspected to be the problem, some sort of descriptive device may be used. For example, there are now available questionnaires that are designed to assess a whole range of job components for both lower-level and upper-level jobs. For example, the position-analysis questionnaire designed by McCormick and his colleagues measures such things as (1) the amount of information input (e.g., visual, perceptual, information), (2) the mediation processes involved (e.g., decision making, information processing), (3) the factors involved in work output (e.g., machine or manual control, body activity, dexterity and handling skills required), (4) the interpersonal activities involved (e.g., communication, contact with others), and (5) the job context or setting (e.g., unpleasant or hazardous settings, noise.) The assessment of the degree to which particular jobs include these factors can help pinpoint problems.[2] Perhaps too much or too little information is being processed, or maybe the job is not technologically well designed. Perhaps it is perceived as a dangerous and unpleasant job to do.

A similar type of device has been developed for management-type positions. However, the focus is on the degree to which the manager has to engage in various activities such as planning, coordination, control, customer relations, consulting, approval of financial commitments, direct supervision, and so on.[3] It is hoped that the investigator can determine from such descriptive devices what sorts of aspects of the job itself may be causing the problem.

Note that the two approaches mentioned above are mainly concerned with the structural and procedural aspects of the job. They measure what is required on the job in terms of time, skill, and effort and activities as well as some description of the setting in which the activity takes place. There are also some more evaluative or process-oriented approaches available.

Probably the most obvious techniques are job-satisfaction questionnaires. You will recall that most of these measures used descriptive and evaluative items. For example, the Job-Descriptive Index asked people to describe their job in terms of five factors: the work itself, pay, promotions, coworkers, and supervision. While some of these factors reflect concerns other than the job itself, the scale can obviously be used to investigate the causes of job problems.

Recently, a questionnaire labeled the Job Diagnostic Survey has been developed by Hackman and Oldham.[4] The instrument assesses five key job dimensions: (1) the variety of activities performed and skills needed, (2) the amount of personal identity with the task, (3) the significance or importance of the task, (4) the amount of job autonomy, and (5) the amount of feedback about performance. The more of each dimension the better. Also assessed are a number of psychological states having to do with the meaningfulness of the job and one's responsibilities, along with some assessment of the affective reactions to the job overall and its subparts.

The authors argue that the questionnaire can be used first as a diagnostic device and then as an instrument for evaluation. In the latter case one can monitor the impact of various organizational changes that have been implemented. Since a well-developed theory of job enrichment underlies the construction of the instrument, we will discuss the Hackman and Oldham research more fully in connection with job enrichment.

[2]E. J. McCormick, P. R. Jeanneret, & R. C. Mecham. A study of job characteristics and job dimensions as based on the Position Analysis Questionnaires (PAQ). *Journal of Applied Psychology,* 1972, **56**, 347–360.

[3]W. W. Tornow & P. R. Pinto. The development of a managerial job taxonomy: A system for describing, classifying and evaluating executive positions. *Journal of Applied Psychology,* 1976, **61**, 410–418.

[4]J. R. Hackman & G. R. Oldham. The Job Diagnostic Survey: An instrument for the diagnosis of jobs and the evaluation of job redesign projects. *Journal of Applied Psychology,* 1975, **60**, 159–170.

Interpersonal relations. There are a number of devices which focus on the interpersonal aspects of the job or the relations between and within units or groups. Some descriptive (and more structural) devices simply attempt to assess communication or friendship patterns. For example, the sociometric devices discussed in Chapter 9, "Communication," describe who talks to whom about what or who likes whom. This information can uncover serious problems in the distribution and flow of information or in personal relationships.

The job-satisfaction questionnaires can also be used to assess interpersonal aspects of the job. Most of the measures include some questions on how well the individual gets along with peers and the boss. In some cases these factors can be isolated as the cause of high or low satisfaction.

But perhaps the greatest source of data on these relationships comes from a general strategy of information gathering described as survey feedback. As the title implies, it is both a diagnostic technique (survey) as well as a problem-solving approach (feedback). Many of the practitioners involved in organizational change utilize this technique. In general, some sort of individually developed questionnaire or group discussion is used to generate data to explore, clarify, and identify problem areas. These sessions actively involve the employees in the data-generation process. The next step is to engage employees in the problem-solving process. This is done through a survey-feedback technique. The data that has been collected is tabulated and organized by the consultant but not interpreted or evaluated. Instead, these data are fed back to the client groups for the purpose of problem solving. The decisions about implementing change are based upon these data.

The whole organization. Some of the questionnaire devices often assess both interpersonal issues and organization-wide issues as well. One factor which fits in both of these categories is the general style of management used throughout the organization. A leader's style is in some sense an interpersonal and small-group issue as well as a reflection of a more pervasive policy.

One set of well-known measurement tools has been developed by Rensis Likert to assess the type of leadership pattern typically being employed by management. Managers are asked to describe the highest- and lowest-producing departments about which they have had some knowledge. Likert finds that these descriptions generally fit into four distinct patterns: (1) exploitative-autocratic, typified by low trust and no participation, (2) benevolent-autocratic, typified by condescension and token participation, (3) participative, typified by substantial trust and participation—but control and decision-making power still reside with the manager, and (4) democratic, typified by complete confidence and democratic decision making.[5]

From reading the descriptions of the styles it is clear that system 4 is loaded with positive words and system 1 with negative ones. Likert and his colleagues, while recognizing that system-4 leadership may not be the most efficient in all situations, believe this style is way ahead of whatever is in second place. Based upon the data generated, a consultant can recognize areas where the leadership pattern may be inadequate and suggest possible remedies.

[5] R. Likert. *The human organization.* New York: McGraw-Hill, 1967.

A somewhat broader concept revolves around the *climate* of the organization. Climate is seen as those factors that describe the way in which the organization deals with its members and the environment. It is a reflection of the pervasive atmosphere. It is oriented toward the way people treat one another. The underlying assumption is that some consistent organizational style exists and that people agree about what it is. While some researchers have questioned these assumptions, measures of climate have proliferated and are being employed in a substantial number of organizations.[6]

Implementing change: A taxonomy of strategies

Once we have identified the problem, the next step is to suggest some remedies. Invariably, these solutions involve change of one sort or another. In some cases we will want to focus on the jobs themselves. Strategies typically included here are sometimes structural in nature, such as job design or the 4-day workweek. The emphasis is on changing some physical aspect of the activity. Process approaches to changing the job often involve enlarging the job (adding more activities) or enriching it (making it a more meaningful or satisfying task). We will discuss these techniques (and the ones briefly mentioned below) in more detail later in the chapter.

The interpersonal strategies that use structural techniques usually involve either personnel changes or procedural changes. If people are not getting along with one another, then change the mix of the group or rearrange who reports to whom. A process approach would try to improve the interaction through such techniques as sensitivity training. When the group itself seems to be the source of the difficulty, various team-building and conflict-resolution or mediation strategies are available.

Finally, when there seem to be pervasive problems with organizational policies, rather large and sweeping changes are often utilized. New incentive systems or performance-appraisal techniques would reflect a structural approach. Management by objectives (MBO) is often described as such a device. This technique focuses on the goals of the organization—how they are set and evaluated. The management grid, on the other hand, is a technique designed to change the management style. It is aimed at the interpersonal process and general organizational climate.

What we are saying is that there are both measures and change technologies to fit into all of the cells which we presented in Figure 16-1. Putting all of this information together and filling in the cells results in Figure 16-2. Much of the rest of this chapter is devoted to a more detailed discussion of the change techniques that we have mentioned above. Before we turn to that analysis, however, we should briefly discuss two more issues: the evaluation of change and the general philosophy of organization development, which has helped in the development of these change strategies.

---

[6]See David Hellriegel & J. W. Slocum, Jr. Organizational climate: Measures, research and contingencies. *Academy of Management Journal,* 1974, **17,** 255–280, for a review. For an example of a comprehensive climate measure, see J. Taylor & D. Bowers. *Survey of organizations: A machine scored standarized questionnaire instrument.* Ann Arbor: University of Michigan, Institute for Social Research, 1972.

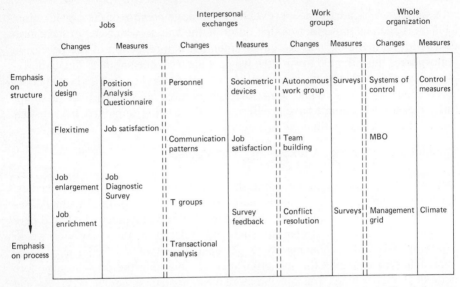

Figure 16-2. Diagnostic measures and problem-solving strategies for organizational change.

Evaluating change

The final step in any change process should be to evaluate its effectiveness. The question is whether what was changed did indeed result in increases in satisfaction, interpersonal harmony, and more effective employees. In some sense this is the bottom line—the ultimate criterion of the effectiveness of any change strategy. Unfortunately, however, we are woefully remiss in this area. Most of our time has been spent figuring out how to diagnose problems and suggesting solutions for particular situations. Very little systematic effort has been expended on trying to find out how well a strategy has actually worked or the circumstances under which some strategy such as MBO or sensitivity training was most or least effective. As we go through the chapter, we will discuss the evidence that is available for each technique. At the end of the chapter, we will try to summarize these results both in terms of their substantive content and methodological excellence. The important thing to recognize at this point is that a good program of organizational change should include some attempt to systematically and objectively evaluate the change.

Organization development

Over the last 10 years, the study of organizational change has become a separate field of academic inquiry. It is called *organization development,* or OD. There are researchers and practitioners who specialize in this area, and there are courses and textbooks devoted exclusively to the topic. It is often difficult, however, to differentiate OD from everything else. It is a wide, encompassing field and difficult to define. Some changes might be called OD by one investigator but not by another. With these problems in mind, we will try to define OD, give some indication of its philosophical roots, discuss briefly the empirical findings on the topic, and evaluate its usefullness.

Definition

Organization development is usually seen as a long-term attempt to bring about greater levels of personal and interpersonal effectiveness (with special emphasis on the work group) in an organization. In most cases some sort of outside consultant (or "change agent" as he or she is often called) participates in the initial phases of the change process. The long-run goal is to help the organization learn to change itself, without outside help, in response to new problems and difficulties it encounters.

Notice the key parts of this definition. There is an emphasis on the "long-range" effort. OD is more than a one-shot intervention. The main target of the effort is usually interpersonal relationships and communications. There is a distinct "humanistic" flavor to OD. The way to increase organizational effectiveness is through the work-team climate. Finally, note that the use of a change agent is part of the process. Both the content and the process of intervening are important for determining what constitutes an OD effort.

Philosophical foundations

Two main historical trends contributed to the development of OD: laboratory training and action research. Laboratory training or sensitivity training (T groups) focus on the interpersonal relationships that exist in the small work group. Through group interaction participants learn about how they are perceived by others as well as the impact they have on their peers. We discussed this topic in Chapter 15. The action-research contribution is the survey-feedback, data-gathering process which we discussed earlier. There is a preliminary diagnosis, some gathering of data, some feedback and discussion, some action plans, and implemented change. These two technologies were joined to form the broader organizational-development strategy.

The general characteristics of the OD approach have been specified in a number of places. One author suggests that OD includes the following factors:

1 Focus on the total system of interdependent suborganizational groupings (work units, teams, management levels) rather than upon individual employees as the object of training. Team development is frequently a major component of the change process.
2 The approach to change is "organic." It seeks to establish a climate in which growth, development, and renewal are brought about as a natural part of the organization's daily operation, rather than superimposed unilaterally.
3 Experiential learning techniques (role playing, problem-solving exercises, T groups) in addition to traditional lecture methods are utilized. Subject matter includes real problems and events that exist in the organization and often in the training groups, as well as hypothetical cases or examples. Often there is gathering and analysis of organization data—either formally or informally.

4 Emphasis is placed upon competence in interpersonal relationships rather than upon task skills. Much of the content and method is based on the behavioral sciences rather than upon management theory, operations research, or personnel techniques, although these may be included as part of the program.
5 Goals frequently have to do with developing behavioral competence in areas such as communication, decision making, and problem solving, in addition to understanding the retention of principles and theories. The trainer often sees himself more as a consultant or change agent than expert-teacher.
6 The value system is humanistic. It is committed to integrating individual needs and management goals, maximizing opportunity for human growth and development, and encouraging more open, authentic human relationships.
7 There is less intention to refute the traditional structural-functional conception of the organization than to augment this conception with newer data and help remedy some of its major dysfunctions.[7]

Again, one can see the emphasis on long-term changes in the interpersonal climate as the goal.

The initial work on OD focused almost entirely on process changes. However, as often happens in more applied areas, people began to include in OD any strategy that seemed to work. Thus, techniques which were originally more structural or procedural in nature (e.g., MBO) have become part of the OD repertoire. In fact, OD has become so encompassing that there are few change strategies that would be omitted today.

Change techniques

While many of the techniques for change that are listed in our summary figure (16-2), would fall under the heading of OD, there are also many OD techniques that are not listed there. The same categories from that figure, however, can be used. That is, there are OD techniques for individuals, for relationships within groups and between groups, and for the total organization. A brief description of some of these techniques is given below.

The individual techniques tend to focus on self-awareness. For example, life- and career-planning exercises ask the individual to indicate what he or she would like to be doing at different points in their career. One's goals, successes, and failures are explored in an attempt to help the individual accurately evaluate strengths, weaknesses, and potential. T groups or sensitivity training also focus on the individual and his or her interpersonal competence.

Some of the group activities include approaches such as the role-analysis technique. The role-analysis technique requires the group to choose a role (say, the role of group leader or supervisor) and analyze how that role should be carried out in the most efficient manner. The person who actually fills that role may or may not be present, depending upon the group relations. However, the role occupant can use the data to analyze those areas which need the most improvement.

---

[7]W. W. Eddy. From training to organization change. *Personnel Administrator*, January–February 1971, 37–43.

An intervention for intergroup relations is called *organizational mirroring*. This technique requires that each group indicate how it views its own behavior and the behavior of the other groups involved, and how it thinks the other groups view their behavior. These data are then exchanged, and a given group can see two main discrepancies: the difference between how it sees other groups and how those other groups see themselves, and the difference between how it sees itself and how the other groups see it. Again, action plans can be designed to remedy the problems that emerge.

Finally, some techniques are designed to deal with total organizational problems. For example, strategic planning and survey feedback involve getting together the different segments of an organization and making explicit the various needs, demands, and resources required for effective functioning. To summarize, the OD interventions are highly heterogeneous in nature. There are different kinds of remedies for different types of problems. In this sense, it is somewhat of a clinical approach in that data gathering, diagnosis, feedback, interventions, and follow-up are designed around a specific problem or set of problems. Its "humanistic" orientation is reflected both in the goals of interpersonal improvement and its techniques for change. Process and content have traditionally been emphasized over structure or procedure, but this is changing somewhat today.

Empirical evaluation

The problem with any sort of empirical evaluation of OD resides in its heterogeneous nature and its interpersonal orientation. The heterogeneity makes it difficult to draw any broad or sweeping conclusions. Each OD study is different from every other one. A different set of problems exists and a different set of remedies is used in each study. To throw together the evaluation of T groups, MBO, and job design makes little sense.

The interpersonal and applied orientation has also led to a deemphasis on good research. Few OD efforts are adequately evaluated. In most cases the gathering of data is for diagnostic or problem-solving use, not for evaluation. Because of these two problems, we will spend considerable time in the following sections attempting to evaluate the research on particular strategies rather than OD as a whole.

But before we leave this broad focus, we should mention that a number of current reviews of the OD literature are available.[8] The conclusions that are drawn from these papers are fairly similar. First, most of the research that gets published does show positive effects for OD interventions. This figure ranges from 80 to 90 percent. But the second point about which the authors are generally in agreement is that the research which generated the findings is usually not very

[8]See C. P. Aldefer. Organization development. *Annual Review of Psychology,* **28,** 1977, 197–233, and S. E. White & T. R. Mitchell. Organization development: A review of research content and research design. *Academy of Management Review,* 1976, **1,** 57–73. Also see T. G. Cummings & P. F. Salipante. Research based strategies for improving work life. In P. Warr (Ed.), *Personal goals and work design.* New York: Wiley, 1976, pp. 31–42.

good. Few studies use control groups or comparison groups. The treatment is seldom assigned to a group on a random basis. Little is known about the reliability or validity of many of the measures used. Thus, even though the support is strong in terms of the results that do exist, one can have little confidence in these results due to their methodological inadequacies. We will discuss some of these issues in more detail at the end of the chapter.

A critique of OD

Besides the methodological problems, there are some other areas where OD has been criticized. Probably the two most frequently cited are OD's humanistic philosophy and its faddish nature. The humanistic philosophy that formed the foundations for the approach has often led to an overemphasis on interpersonal processes and an underemphasis on structural or procedural methods of task accomplishments. There is also some indication that when new change techniques are developed, they become a fad among OD practitioners. Sensitivity training, transactional analysis, and other examples are available. A technique is frequently used not because of any sound empirical rationale but because it is new and popular.

The review by Aldefer of the OD literature seemed to show some promising changes with regard to these problems. There seems to be a greater breadth in the OD field in terms of the techniques being used. Structural and procedural strategies are being included more frequently. There is also a greater emphasis on evaluation and research. The data being gathered is more reliable and of better quality. Finally, OD is broadening its concerns. Besides business organizations which dominated the early focus of OD, there are now a number of studies on churches, schools, hospitals, governments, correctional institutions, and the military. Thus, the field of OD, which was initially interested in interpersonal processes and action rather than research, is now becoming a more inclusive area of study.

Organizational change techniques

> Everyone accepts the obvious notion that new technology
> can and must eliminate dumb-dumb jobs.   R. N. Ford

This portion of the chapter is devoted to a detailed description and evaluation of a number of change techniques currently being used in organizations. The discussion is not inclusive. Only the most important strategies are discussed. The review is also uneven in its distribution of emphasis. This is mostly because some topics such as sensitivity training or participation in decision making appear elsewhere in the book. Finally, the format used is the categorization system presented in Figure 16-2. We will look at structural and process strategies designed to change jobs, interpersonal interactions, group and intergroup activities, and the total organization.

Job changes

The first systematic attempt to discover the principles of matching the individual to the job in some optimal fashion was carried out by Frederick W. Taylor. His "scientific-management" approach suggested that through scientific methods we could design jobs and train people to attain maximum output. While Taylor's ideas included a rather broad ideal of management and workers involved in a cooperative effort to increase productivity, his followers were more restrictive in their approach. They concentrated on two main aspects of Taylor's ideas: determining the one best way to do a job and the use of incentive pay to ensure compliance with the prescribed work methods.

This emphasis on the one "best way" led to what is referred to as *time and motion* studies. This research was designed to do the following:

1 Find the best way for people to move, stand, and generally physically deal with a task.
2 Break jobs down into easily repeatable, learnable tasks.
3 Arrange tools and equipment in a manner that minimizes effort and lost time.
4 Construct the plant environment in such a way that noise, ventilation, and other support facilities do not reduce effectiveness.
5 Design special tools for specific jobs such as conveyors, and other machines to reduce unnecessary actions.
6 Eliminate all activities that are fatigue-producing which are unrelated to the task at hand.

The underlying idea is clear: The worker and the job are to be treated as machines. The time and motion studies markedly increased our knowledge about how people fit with machines. Certain aspects of an individual's physical endowment were emphasized, such as the amount of work space that was easily accessible, the fact that symmetrical movements were easiest to carry out, and that a sequence or rhythm to physical movements is best. Circular movements were found to be easier than back and forth movements; picking things up is harder than moving them.

All this activity had a number of profound implications. Jobs were timed, and there was a "best way." Jobs became simpler and more repetitive. The assembly line in many modern organizations is an excellent example of how these techniques were used. But probably most important was the fact that many of the benefits originally hoped for went unrealized. Training became more expensive because of higher turnover; high wages were needed to keep people on the job; and people were bored with the repetitive work.

In short, people disliked the work. They had greater education and higher expectations. They spent a large part of their lives working at dull, repetitive tasks. Technology had been used in a rather limited fashion with a narrow perspective, and people began to realize that there was a new and more important function for technology.

In the late 1950s and 1960s, there was a change in the emphasis of job design.

Louis Davis stated quite early that "the assembly line has designed out of the job virtually everything that might be of personal value or meaning to the workers."[9] There was an increased interest in the human problems associated with work. It was at this point that the industrial humanists and those people who participated in the human-relations movement brought their knowledge to bear on the job-design problem. The approaches fall into two main categories: job enlargement and job enrichment. Under the heading of job enlargement we usually include those changes designed at horizontal job enlargement (widening the scope of the job) and some other job aspects such as the hours of work. Job enlargement usually maintains the basic task with minor modifications. Job enrichment, on the other hand, is an attempt to introduce major modifications in the job.

The name most readily paired with the job enlargement and later enrichment ideas is Frederick Herzberg. While there is some disagreement in academic circles about the validity of a number of aspects of his theory (discussed in Chapter 7, "Motivation"), there is little doubt about his impact on the general idea of job enlargement. Four major ways to enlarge jobs have generally been discussed:

1 *Challenging the employee.* The emphasis is on asking employees to work up to their potential. Obviously, this will work only if other aspects of the job are changed as well.
2 *Replacing difficult, repetitive, and boring tasks by machines where possible.* This would leave the employee the more interesting aspects of the job.
3 *Assigning more tasks or more operations to the job.* There is less monotony and more variety.
4 *Using job rotation.* This allows the employee to learn new skills and to engage in a variety of tasks.

In general, the available evidence seems to support the use of such techniques.

A more recent set of change techniques which is sometimes placed into this category deals with the employees' hours of work. One fairly popular idea has been the *4-day workweek.* Rather than change anything basic about the job or the relationships involved, the 4-day workweek simply provides longer weekends and, therefore, larger blocks of leisure time for employees. A modification of this idea is called *flexitime.* Using this procedure, the employee decides upon the hours he or she will work, given some limitations. Usually there is an agreed-upon total of hours (e.g., 40) and some "core" hours (e.g., 10 A.M. to 2 P.M.) when everyone must be there. How the other hours are put in is up to the individual employee.

The empirical results on these approaches are not entirely clear. Reports about the 4-day workweek suggest that people like it and that productivity may initially increase. However, these changes may disappear over time. In some cases people report fatigue at the end of 10-hour days, and it appears that the productivity of older workers may decrease. The flexitime results are fewer in number but seem more supportive. The research seems to indicate that people on a

---

[9]L. E. Davis. Job design and productivity: A new approach. *Personnel,* 1957, **33**, 413–418.

flexitime schedule are more satisfied in their work, and absenteeism is reduced. It seems to have been a helpful intervention where it was tried.[10]

Thus, the research results for many of these enlargement strategies are generally supportive. In most cases, there is a more recognizable impact on satisfaction than on productivity. While increased satisfaction should reduce turnover and absenteeism, many people felt that more inclusive changes were needed. They felt that enlargement did not go far enough.

Job enrichment was the response. The concept of enrichment entails both horizontal and vertical restructuring of jobs in an effort to increase the meaningfulness and satisfaction of work. It is more than just an expanded job, it is a new job. New skills and abilities can be used, and the job is upgraded. Below are listed some principles of vertical job loading.

[10]For reports on the 4-day workweek, see J. G. Goodale, & A. K. Aagaard. Factors relating to varying reactions to the 4-day workweek. *Journal of Applied Psychology*, 1975, **60**, 33–88, and J. M. Ivancevich. Effects of the shorter workweek on selected satisfaction and performance measures. *Journal of Applied Psychology*, 1974, **59**, 717–721. A good flexitime study is reported by R. T. Golembiewski, R. Hilles, & M. S. Kaguo. A longitudinal study of flexitime effects; some consequences of an OD structural intervention. *Journal of Applied Behavioral Science*, 1974, **10**, 503–532.

A new hammer and chain is hardly my idea of job enrichment.
Job enrichment must involve meaningful changes in the job or it will be rejected.

1 There is less direct control of the employee, with an emphasis on results.
2 Personal accountability is increased. The individual is responsible for his or her activities.
3 Whenever possible, complete units are assigned. The individual performs a whole task.
4 One has greater freedom on the job and access to information. The employee understands why activities are being done.
5 Upgrading the skills and development of each employee is emphasized. New and challenging tasks are frequently assigned.

Job enrichment is more comprehensive than job enlargement. The employee has more responsibility and discretion. There is feedback about performance, communication is two-way, and there is some attempt at having an individual do a whole job. That is, there is an attempt at closure. Through these practices, motivation, performance, and satisfaction are hoped to increase.

A fairly specific theory of job enrichment has recently been developed by Hackman and Oldham.[11] They suggest that certain core job dimensions have an impact on a number of psychological states, which in turn relate to attitudes and behavior on the job. Figure 16-3 presents their theory.

There are some important implications of this theory. First, changing only one job dimension may have only a minor impact on eventual behavior. Second, changing the job will change behavior only by changing the critical psychological states. Third, the theory will vary in effectiveness, depending upon individual needs. It would be expected to work better for people who highly value autonomy, growth, and responsibility. There is currently an increasing amount of data being presented on job-enrichment projects. Robert Ford has published the results of enrichment projects conducted at AT&T; Herzberg has introduced enrichment at a number of large corporations; and Lawler has done similar work

[11]J. R. Hackman & G. R. Oldham. Op. cit.

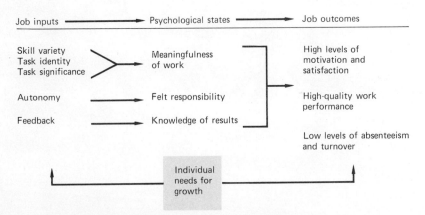

Figure 16-3. Hackman and Oldham's theory of job enrichment.

in a variety of settings.[12] The summary of data presented in the OD section of this chapter was also generally supportive of these attempts to redesign jobs, although the results are stronger for the satisfaction and attitudinal outcomes than for productivity. It is not surprising, therefore, that many theorists and practitioners are enthusiastic about the possibility of job enrichment.

Perhaps an actual example would be a good way to give you the flavor of job enrichment. We recently did some research where we hired some people for a week to do clerical work.[13] The specific task involved coding some sections of a map so that separate plats of land and acreage could be easily identified. Everyone performed the same task, but for half the people the job was enriched and for the other half it was not enriched.

In order to induce enrichment, we used the theoretical foundation provided by Hackman and Oldham. Enrichment was manipulated by the procedures described in Table 16-1. Using the Job Diagnostic Survey, we found out that people in the enriched condition indeed felt that they had more variety, task identity, task significance, autonomy, and feedback than those in the unenriched condition. Our criterion measures were job satisfaction and job performance. The latter was assessed by quantity of output (number of areas coded.) The data were clear on two points. First, the people in the enriched condition were more satisfied with their job than those in the unenriched condition. Second, the productivity data showed no appreciable difference between the two groups.

These data are fairly typical of job enrichment results. The effects on satisfaction tend to be stronger than the effects on productivity, although some studies have shown productivity increases. In some cases where enrichment is combined with a technique such as goal setting, both high satisfaction and productivity can be attained.

Changes in interpersonal activities

The response to many interpersonal problems is to use traditional personnel techniques. These may include the time-honored strategies of termination or transfer. Rather than trying to increase the interpersonal effectiveness of the parties involved, the problem is resolved by moving or getting rid of "problem" people.

In many cases the problem is seen to reside not in the personalities of the individuals involved but in the communication process. Information was not distributed to the proper people, or someone failed to pay attention or recognize the importance of some occurrence. Again, the structural response may include various technical ways to increase the effectiveness of these communications

---

[12]R. N. Ford. Job enrichment lessons from AT&T. *Harvard Business Review*, January–February 1973, 96–106. F. Herzberg. *Work and the nature of man*. Cleveland, Ohio: World Publishing, 1966, and E. E. Lawler, III. Motivation and the design of jobs. *ASTME Vectors*, 1968, 14–25.

[13]D. D. Umstot, C. H. Bell, & T. R. Mitchell. Effects of job enrichment and task goals on satisfaction and productivity: implications for job design. *Journal of Applied Psychology*, 1976, **61**, 379–394.

Table 16-1. Summary of the Manipulations Used to Induce the Independent Variables

Independent Variable	High Condition	Low Condition
Job enrichment: Skill variety	1 Worked on one map until done	1 Worked sequentially; plats first, then acreage
	2 Obtained own supplies	2 Supervisor provided all supplies
	3 Selected different communities (e.g., rural or city)	3 Area assigned by supervisor
Task identity	1 Selected a community of their "own"	1 No community; areas randomly assigned by supervisor
	2 Wrote names on wall chart indicating "ownership"	2 No wall chart
Task significance	1 Importance and uses of task outcomes stressed	1 No information on importance given
	2 Complete description of zoning codes on cards	2 No description on cards; only the number
Autonomy	1 Freedom to determine methods, breaks	1 Methods predetermined; breaks rigidly controlled
	2 Unlimited mobility	2 Restricted mobility
	3 Obtained own supplies	3 Supervisor obtained supplies
Feedback from the job	1 Completed areas on maps crossed off	1 No maps for gauging progress
	2 Full day's production remained visible	2 Production removed hourly
	3 Completed boxes of cards stacked in same room	3 Completed cards merged with uncompleted in another room

(e.g., computers, routing slips, tape recorders, etc.). Most of the personnel activities are discussed more fully in Chapter 14 and the communication changes are covered in Chapter 9. Suffice it to say that in many cases the problem does reside in the people involved, and changes involving interpersonal processes are needed.

Probably the most widely used technique to increase the interpersonal skills of individual employees is sensitivity training and the T group. This technique was fully described and evaluated in the preceding chapter. You will recall that T groups are generally unstructured group meetings in which individuals explore and gain insight into their interpersonal behavior. The research seems to suggest that these activities can increase an individual's openness, listening ability, and consideration, but there is little evidence about the long-term effects on job performance.

A more recent approach to increasing interpersonal effectiveness is labeled *transactional analysis (TA)*. Developed by Eric Berne, TA is designed to get people to focus on the roles they play when interacting with others and the types of elements that influence the exchanges.[14] He suggests that we are capable of taking three different roles: that of a parent (giving advice, setting limits), that of an adult (gathering information, setting objectives, making decisions), and that of a child (earlier desires and needs). Once one understands these roles and the various factors influencing interpersonal relationships, such as the environment, our long-term goals, and game playing, we can better understand and therefore change our interpersonal behavior.

TA differs from sensitivity training in some important ways. It is less threatening, it is well based on a specific theory, it involves less personal risk taking (personal revelations, etc.), and it places the emphasis of individual change on individual examination. TA in one form or another has been used by some large corporations, such as Bank of America, Mountain Bell, and IBM. As of yet, however, little research data exists to evaluate its effectiveness.

Changes in work groups

In this section we shift the focus from the individual to the work group. A number of structural and technological change strategies have evolved over the years that are designed to increase group harmony, interdependence, and effectiveness. Perhaps the most well-known strategy is the *autonomous work group*. The historical foundations for the autonomous work group can be traced back to the early work of the Tavistock Institute in England on the British coal-mining industry. However, the most famous and current example of the idea has been the work being done in Sweden with Saab and Volvo.

The basic concept of the autonomous work group is to replace the traditional assembly line with work teams. Instead of each individual doing one or two separate tasks over and over again, the team is responsible for the whole unit. At

[14]E. Berne. *Transactional analysis in psychotherapy*. New York: Grove Press, 1961. Also see E. Berne. *What do you say after you say hello*. New York: Grove Press, 1972.

Bored people build bad cars.
That's why we're doing away with
the assembly line.

Working on an assembly line is monotonous. And boring. And after a while, some people begin not to care about their jobs anymore. So the quality of the product often suffers.

That's why, at Saab, we're replacing the assembly line with assembly teams. Groups

of just three or four people who are responsible for a particular assembly process from start to finish.

Each team makes its own decisions

about who does what and when. And each team member can even do the entire assembly singlehandedly. The result: people are more involved. They care more. So there's less absenteeism, less turnover. And we have more experienced people on the job.

We're building our new 2-liter engines this way. And the doors to our Saab 99. And we're planning to use this same system to build other parts of our car as well.

It's a slower, more costly system, but we realize that the best machines and materials in the world don't mean a thing, if the person building the car doesn't care.

Saab. It's what a car should be.

There are more than 300 Saab dealers nationwide. For the name and address of the one nearest you call 800-243-6000 toll free. In Connecticut, call 1-800-882-6500.

One form of job enrichment is to do away with the assembly line and have people work in teams. *(By permission of Saab.)*

Saab, for example, the automobile engine is assembled by a small group of five to ten workers. They all have related duties, and they decide among themselves how to assign tasks and distribute their effort. They rotate jobs—each team member learns how to do all the assembly tasks. The group has broadened responsibilities to include inspection, quality control, housekeeping, and maintenance. Each group puts together the cylinder block, heads, rods, and the crankshaft. They work at their own pace and they determine the time they will spend on breaks—so long as 470 engines are produced over a 10-day span.

The results of such changes are encouraging. There is evidence of higher satisfaction, lower turnover and absenteeism, and improved quality of work.[15] Job attitudes are more positive. Autonomous work groups, at least in this instance, seemed to be an excellent alternative to the traditional assembly line.

There are also strategies that attempt to change the interpersonal processes within the work group. One technique which focuses on change within group activities is labeled *team building,* and its objective is to improve the communication and interpersonal exchanges that occur within the group.

The team-building technique usually entails bringing the group together and

[15]See N. M. Tichy. Organizational innovations in Sweden. *Columbia Journal of World Business,* Summer 1974, 18–22, and Job redesign on the assembly line: Farewell to blue-collar blues. *Organizational Dynamics,* Autumn 1973, 55–60.

dealing with four major issues: problem diagnosis, task accomplishment, team relationships, and team processes. The diagnosis phase first attempts to identify problems (without evaluating or solving them). Problems are brought out and recorded. The problems can then be discussed and some solutions suggested. Usually the problem areas are either in the task or the interpersonal relationships. If task accomplishment is the major problem, than various procedures can be used to increase the work group's effectiveness. If relationships are the problem, then techniques are available to increase trust and openness, such as sensitivity training, role analysis, and TA. Finally, the group can analyze the process of the group itself: the flexibility, formality, feedback, and participation that characterizes the unit as a whole. In many cases, an outside objective observer can be used to help assess these aspects of the group.

A slightly different group process occurs when there are problems between groups. Conflicts should be identified and recognized. Open confrontation is often encouraged in some group-change strategies. Groups may be called together and asked to (1) indicate their perception, of the other group, (2) have representatives meet to discuss these perceptions, (3) have each group separate and discuss these perceptions (e.g., how each group sees itself, how it sees others, and how others see it), (4) analyze the discrepancies in perceptions and identify reasons for the discrepancies, and (5) attempt to resolve these discrepancies through representatives and finally in a combined group meeting. In this way, misunderstandings, stereotypes, defensive behavior, and general misconceptions can be identified and clarified. This type of activity often is reported to significantly increase the harmony between groups.

Changing the organization

In some cases change techniques are used to implement wide-ranging modifications in the structure, procedures, or interpersonal processes of the organization. The introduction of a new control systems (e.g., human-resource accounting) or a performance-appraisal system are examples of techniques that are focused more on structural and procedural changes. One technique that also had its historical foundation in the classical and scientific management literature is management by objectives.

MBO. In Chapter 7, "Motivation," we discussed goal setting as a major example of theory and practice. The process of setting goals is frequently included as an integral part of an overall change technology called management by objectives. MBO is both a general philosophy of management and a fairly well-defined process. It is a philosophy which is highly rational in nature and suggests a proactive rather than a reactive management climate. Overall goals for the organization and its interrelated parts are jointly developed and specified at different organization levels. There is an emphasis on the observable and quantifiable, and also on improvement, on doing better. It encourages participation and tries to anticipate change. It is an overall philosophy designed to deal with current organizational problems.

As a process, MBO is broader in scope than goal setting. It requires not only the setting of clear, concise objectives, but also the development of realistic action plans and the systematic measurement of performance and achievement. Finally, there are built-in corrective measures to deal with problems of goal changes or inattainability.

Historically, Peter Drucker is generally cited as the first person to clearly describe the MBO process.[16] Management's job is to provide goals, jointly set and monitored, in order to increase both motivation and effectiveness. As an overall system, MBO includes three major phases: performance appraisal, planning and control, and integrative management systems.

The actual objective and goal-setting process can occur at all levels. Top management should specify the overall mission and central purpose of the organization as well as some more short-run performance objectives for the organization as a whole. These objectives should include some statement of resource and time commitments. These broad objectives can then be translated into more specific objectives at the department level and further on down the hierarchy. Obviously, at the top level, there must be explicit statements about what resources can be committed, what are the priorities for the objectives, and what are the trade-offs for these decisions.

Specific job objectives are of a more individualistic nature. Behaviors that are important must be specified and deadlines should be made clear. However, throughout the process there must be an element of flexibility and negotiation. Interruptions occur, and unforessen events may disturb the timetable. Goals and objectives are flexible targets, not written in stone. They can and should be changed when the situation requires it.

Another integral part of the MBO process is the need for performance appraisal. In order to set goals, monitor them, and evaluate goal attainment, we must know what sorts of behaviors are important for good performance. The MBO system requires a fairly rigorous procedure for evaluation. Goals are written down, recorded, clearly specified, and they have time constraints. Thus, the performance-appraisal system can be built upon a well-established, goal-setting program.

Finally, reward systems must be designed around the performance-appraisal process. People who reach attainable goals should be recognized and rewarded for goal attainment. Bonus plans or other reward strategies can be tied to the MBO philosophy.

There are some problems with MBO which should be raised. All too frequently, goals are set which are not specific, such as "improving customer service." These types of goals lead to frustration on the part of the employee. They are too subjective. It also frequently occurs that goals are unilaterally rather than jointly set. This tactic may lead to resentment or rejection of the goals. The crucial factor seems to be that MBO usually does well in a climate which is generally supportive and trusting—that is, an environment that is fairly well off to begin with. When it is done well, MBO can be a powerful tool for increasing effectiveness on the job.

[16]P. F. Drucker. *The practice of management*. New York: Harper & Row, 1954.

Management style. Besides MBO, a somewhat more process-oriented approach is to try to change the general style of management that exists in the organization. One technique is simply to decentralize decision making, which results in increased participation in the decision process. This is a topic that is thoroughly discussed in Chapter 11, "Decision Making," and Chapter 17, "Political Support." A summary of those discussions would suggest that participation, if it is introduced in the appropriate way, can in fact increase both satisfaction and productivity on the job.

Perhaps the most well-known and popular strategy for changing the general style of management is called the *management grid*. Developed by Blake and Mouton, this technique has been widely used.[17] Some of the large corporations in the United States that have used the grid are Texas Instruments, Pillsbury, Union Carbide, and Honeywell.

The theoretical basis for the approach is apparent from the grid presented in Figure 16-4. On the one hand, the management style can vary from very little concern about people (position 1) to high concern about people (position 9). The same can be true for concern about production. Combining the two dimensions allows us to describe a large number of different management styles ranging from 1,1 (described as impoverished) to 5,5 (described as middle of the road) to 9,1 (called task management because of its lack of conern for people) to 1,9 (called

---

[17]R. Blake & J. Mouton. An overview of the grid. *Training and Development Journal,* 1976, **5**, 29–36.

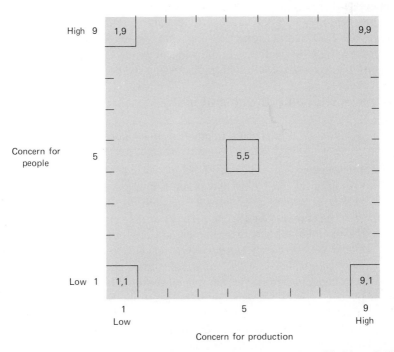

Figure 16-4. A representation of the management grid. Adapted and modified from R. Blake & J. Mouton. An overview of the grid. *Training and Development Journal,* 1975, **5**, 31.

country-club management because of its lack of concern with the job) and 9,9 (called team management and thought to be ideal.)

The objective of the management-grid process is to try to change the prevailing management style to the 9,9 approach, where there will be a high concern for people and for task accomplishment. This change is attempted through six stages of group interaction and training. Phase 1 entails the location of managers' current style on the grid and an understanding of its underlying theory. Phase 2 involves team-building procedures similar to those discussed earlier, while phase 3 works on intergroup processes. Phase 4 focuses on designing an ideal model of what the organization should become, and phase 5 entails attempts to implement the ideal organization. Phase 6 involves a critique and evaluation of the process so far, and if barriers still exist, opportunities for further development can be introduced.

As we mentioned, the grid has been employed in numerous organizations in this country and overseas as well. The research that has been reported is usually favorable. In many cases, attitudes and climate and general management style are reported to be more positive. The data on performance and productivity, while less strong, are still positive. The problem is that few of the reported studies were very well done. Few control groups are used, and the reliability and validity of the measures is questionable. Thus, like many of the other techniques we have described, the management grid is still rather an unproven tool.

A review of all of the techniques we have presented suggests that we have come a long way from the days of the time and motion studies. Techniques have been developed that focus on almost all aspects of the job, interpersonal relations, work groups, and the whole organization. Through the use of these techniques we have learned much about what seems promising. We have also discovered a number of problems in the ways in which we implement change and evaluate it. The chapter closes with a discussion of these topics.

Problems in changing organizations

The chief cause of problems is solutions.   Eric Severeid

Social scientists have obviously been hard at work attempting to develop technologies to remedy the problems of worker alienation and dissatisfaction. The attempts include a two-pronged attack on both the design of jobs and the interpersonal environment. And some reviews of the research literature, such as those cited at the beginning of this chapter, are obviously favorable.

But there are many researchers who advocate caution. They feel that there are reasons to doubt the validity of the empirical studies and that many problems in implementing change programs have not been thoroughly discussed. OD is being sold as a panacea for just about every business ill. Some people feel this is dangerous nonsense. Hackman has said that "what we have seen out there in the 'organizational heartland' is not very encouraging" and that "job enrichment is failing at least as often as it is succeeding."[18]

---

[18]J. R. Hackman. On the coming devise of job enrichment. *Technical Report No. 9*. New Haven, Conn: Yale University, Department of Administrative Sciences, 1974, p. 2.

What is the problem? Why do these differences of opinion exist? As a concluding section, we would like to catalog some of the problems that occur in changing organizations and perhaps suggest some remedies.

Characteristics of the setting

Two main problems concern the types of people involved in the change process. First, there is frequently some resistance to change. In some cases, employees are anxious or afraid that they will not be able to master the new skills required of an enlarged or changed job. They fear failure on the job. Finally, some employees are simply against changing the system. They prefer familiar habits to unfamiliar ones. Second, many workers may simply reject the value premise on which these change technologies are built. More specifically, for some employees, job content may be unrelated to job satisfaction. They may feel that social interaction is the primary source of job satisfaction and have no desire for more autonomy, responsibility, or enrichment.

Characteristics of the change process

We have described changes for both the job and the interpersonal relations and the problems which occur in both areas with regard to the implementation process. Hackman has listed a number of things that may go wrong in redesigning jobs.[19] First, in some cases, the work itself does not actually change. There is much motion but very little substance. Another issue is that job design requires attention to the whole system of interrelated units. Whenever a change occurs in one area, we should expect change in related areas as well. Also, in many cases, a systematic job diagnosis is rarely undertaken before the changes are implemented. Finally, in many situations, the line and staff people who are introducing change are poorly informed about how it should be conducted or evaluated. The feedback may be biased and unsystematic, and the management of the change may regress to more traditional bureaucratic practices.

The OD process also has problems. In many cases, too much emphasis is placed on individual problems in the "informal" organization. The total organization and its formal structure may be deemphasized, yet both should probably change together. On occasion certain steps in the OD process are omitted or underrepresented. For example, in many cases too little time is spent on diagnosis and task analysis, with an overemphasis on change interventions. Finally, OD practitioners sometimes assume that they know more about the organization's problems than the organization's participants.

The implications of these criticisms are rather explicit. To do a good job changing tasks or interpersonal processes takes a lot of time, effort, and commitment. It requires continual planning and evaluation. And most of all, it requires a slow, step-by-step feedback procedure. The consultant must really know the organization and be intimately involved with the planned change in order to assure effectiveness.

---

[19]Ibid.

In today's organizations it is often difficult for one to actually identify with the mission or product of the company.

Criticisms about the evidence

Throughout the chapter we have mentioned the fact that while most published research is supportive of various change strategies, the quality of much of this work is questionable. One recent review of the OD literature indicated that (1) over 50 percent of the studies were correlational in nature (causal references were not appropriate), (2) over 50 percent simply presented frequency or percentage data without any statistical comparison, and (3) almost 95 percent used questionnaire or recall data as opposed to "hard" data such as measures of productivity or absenteeism.[20] Few designs have random assignment of treatments, control groups, and reliable and valid measures. One is forced to conclude that while the reports are favorable, our confidence in those reports must be limited.

One particular problem has to do with the way in which much of this research is conducted. In most cases, the people involved in implementing the change have clear expectations about what should happen. They are far from naïve or

[20]S. E. White & T. R. Mitchell. Op. cit.

uninformed. Over 80 percent of the reported research involved a researcher who was affiliated in one way or another with the organization, and the people involved in the change were aware of the special arrangements being used.

As we know from the Hawthorne studies, these expectations and special arrangements can have a powerful effect on behavior. A recent study highlighted this point once more.[21] In this particular case, just the expectation that job enrichment would increase productivity created greater changes in performance than enrichment itself. Thus, the fact that the researcher and the management team is actually involved in the change process and hoping for success as well creates difficulties in any attempt at impartial evaluation.

Future directions are unclear. In general, there seems to be more correspondence between the more rational "scientific-management" people and the clinically oriented "industrial humanists." Attempts at job enrichment and organization development are more frequently including interventions from both schools of thought. However, we are still basically ignorant about what works, when it works, and why it works. We suspect that just as in other areas, there will develop a contingency approach to organizational change which will specify what kinds of interventions are best with what sorts of people dealing with certain types of problems. However, this goal will be realized only through more systematic evaluation of the implementation process and of the goals actually achieved.

Summary

By now you surely appreciate the complexity and heterogeneity of the literature on organizational change. The major points that you should remember from the chapter are as follows:

1 Organizational change involves attempts to modify the organization's structure and procedures or interpersonal processes. These changes may be focused on particular jobs, individuals, work groups, or the organization as a whole. These changes are designed to increase interpersonal and task effectiveness.

2 The change process involves a number of steps. The problem must be recognized, the cause of the problem properly diagnosed, a particular strategy implemented, and the change evaluated. Much work on diagnosis and implementation has been done, but evaluation procedures are still fairly simple and generally inadequate.

3 Organization development (OD) is a broad body of concepts, tools, and techniques designed to implement long-term change in the organization. The original focus of OD was on groups and interpersonal relations, but recently this humanistic orientation has broadened to include structural changes originating from a more "classical" position.

[21]A. S. King. Expectation effects in organizational change. *Administrative Science Quarterly*, 1974, **19**, 221–230.

4 The techniques for changing jobs have recently concentrated on techniques of job enlargement and job enrichment. Enlargement usually involves increasing the number of operations to be done (horizontal changes) while enrichment involves increased responsibility, autonomy, and input (vertical changes).

5 Some of the structural or procedural strategies for changing the interpersonal relationships are personnel actions or the creation of autonomous work groups. Those strategies with a focus on the group process might include sensitivity training, transactional analysis, or team building.

6 Organization-wide policy changes can take the form of new control systems, systems of planning and appraisal (e.g., MBO), or attempts to change leadership style (e.g., the management grid).

7 There are problems in introducing change. There is resistance and fear, and some people genuinely fail to benefit. There are also situations where the change is superficial or people are poorly informed.

8 The empirical results show strong support for most of the change strategies. However because of poor methodology in obtaining these results, one can have little confidence in them. Thus, we still need to know what works, where and when it works, but most of all, why it works.

Implications for practice

Organizations are constantly trying to increase their effectiveness. Rather than focus on technological or control-system changes, most of the strategies described in this chapter have centered on ways to (1) make people more motivated or (2) make interpersonal communications more effective. The primary ingredient for the changes we have discussed is people. Enriching jobs, changing the system by which goals are set, or changing the communication patterns are all meant to change the people involved in these activities. It is the changes in the people (i.e., their motivation or communication) that is supposed to result in increased effectiveness.

The problem is that people often resist change. Change is threatening. It causes uncertainty. People know how things are now, but how will it be tomorrow? Will their pay be decreased? Will they be separated from their friends? These are real concerns for employees, and in order to successfully implement change, they must be dealt with.

Some commonsense strategies are available which should facilitate change and make it more acceptable. One obvious idea is to get people's input throughout the change process. What do they think the problem is? How do they think things can be changed? Increasing participation in the planning of the change should increase acceptance of and commitment to the change itself. A second and related idea is to keep people informed. Let them know what is going on and why various techniques are being used. Information and participation should reduce uncertainty and anxiety about change. Finally, try not to make the changes coercive. It is hoped that people engage in change programs because they want to. In fact, in some firms employees have been given a choice between an autonomous work group or the traditional assembly line. Change programs should be flexible about who is included, the permanence of the change, and the rigidity of the change itself.

The final point is to recognize that implementing change successfully requires a number of steps, not just the change technique itself. Proper diagnosis is important as is evaluation. Both steps should be objective and unbiased. One way that is often suggested to ensure this objectivity is to employ an outside evaluator—someone who is not part of the organization or part of the change process.

Throughout the book we have emphasized a contingency type of approach to organizational effectiveness—different people want and respond favorably to different things. The same is true for change. MBO, T groups, job enrichment, and the management grid only work some of the time for some people. If you are going to engage in change, do it right: be thorough, avoid fads, be committed, keep people informed, and evaluate it.

Discussion questions

1 Suppose the university decided to change its grading system from the use of letter grades to numbers ranging from 0.00 to 4.00. How would you feel? How could such a plan be implemented successfully?
2 How is job enrichment different from job enlargement? Think of a job with which you are familiar. How would you enlarge it? How would you enrich it?
3 Do you think an organization has a prevailing climate? Do people agree about the climate? What are the important factors that you use to judge the climate?

Case: Implementing change

Recently the U.S. Navy decided to introduce management by objectives as a management tool in the Navy. Booklets were prepared describing the MBO process. Examples were given. Forms were provided. Numerous directives, instructions, and supplementary materials were sent out from Washington, D.C., to Navy personnel throughout the world.

One of the naval air stations in the Northeast part of the United States happened to be near a major urban university. At the school there were a number of organizational and industrial psychologists who had research contracts with the Office of Naval Research, and one of them, Dr. Colin Beard, was interested in the topic of motivation. Dr. Beard contacted the naval air station to see if he could help implement and evaluate the MBO program.

A couple of the squadron commanders were initially enthusiastic, so Dr. Beard arranged to meet with them the next day. He gathered together some materials on the subject and convinced one of his graduate students to accompany him.

The meetings were very cordial. Dr. Beard laid out what he wanted to do. He suggested that they gather data which would describe the current level of motivation, satisfaction, and performance of two squadrons. Then one of the squadrons would set up the MBO program while the other would serve as a comparison group. Then in 3 months they would reassess performance, satisfaction, and motivation. If MBO worked, it would then be implemented in the control squadron.

Well, this just would not do. Both squadrons were due to go on cruise in 3 months and they both wanted the program. Neither commander wanted to serve as a control. They were also hesitant about the measurement procedures and how their people would respond to a questionnaire. Dr. Beard explained that giving both squadrons the MBO program would prohibit them from any sort of useful evaluation—but the commanders would not budge. Finally, Dr. Beard said that he just could not justify the type of effort involved without the kind of research design he had suggested, so he recommended that they talk about it again after the ships came back from their tour in 18 months.

The commanders agreed to this proposal but they asked one last favor: could Dr. Beard come and lead a couple of lecture discussion sessions for the officers? "Sure," said Beard, "I'd be glad to. How about next Tuesday afternoon?"

"Good, that's a good time for us," replied the commanders. The attendance was high at the Tuesday session. Both commanders were there along with thirty other officers. Dr. Beard ran through the steps that were important in MBO. He particularly emphasized that differences in priorities should be discussed and *worked out jointly* so that the rank order of objectives was clear to everyone. One of the commanders interrupted at this point to say: "We don't have any problems in priorities here. Everyone knows our first priority is to have our planes and pilots prepared for battle." Everyone in the audience directly behind the commander nodded their heads up and down.

Dr. Beard was slightly uncomfortable but he went on. He described how individual goals should be *jointly* set between the commanding officer and the immediate subordinates. This process should be a participative exchange and a flexible one. Finally, Dr. Beard illustrated how records of goal attainment could be used to show individual progress and performance.

At the end of the session, one of the commanders stood up and thanked Dr. Beard and turned to the rest of the men and said: "I know everyone here found this session helpful and informative. I'm sure each of us has some goals we want to set for our men. Let's get to it."

Questions about the case

1 Do you think the commanders had the right idea about MBO? Where were they mistaken?
2 Should Dr. Beard have run the study without the research design he wanted?
3 Do you think some organizations are better suited for change then others? How would you have implemented a goal-setting program in the Navy?

Additional readings

Carroll, S. J., & Tosi, H. L., Jr. *Management by objectives: Applications and research.* New York: Macmillan, 1973.
* Fein, M. Job enrichment: A reevaluation. *Sloan Management Review,* 1974, **15,** 69–88.
French, W. L., & Bell, C. H. *Organization development: Behavioral science interventions for organization improvement.* Englewood Cliffs, N.J.: Prentice-Hall, 1973.
* French, W. L., & Hollman, R. W. Management by objectives: the team approach. *California Management Review,* 1975, **16,** 13–22.

* Greiner, L. E. Red flags in organization development: Six trends obstructing change. *Business Horizons,* June 1972, 19–24.

Hackman, J. R., & Oldham, G. R. Motivation through the design of work: Test of a theory. *Organizational Behavior and Human Performance,* 1976, **16,** 250–279.

* Herzberg, F. One more time: How do you motivate employees. *Harvard Business Review,* January–February 1968, **46,** 53–62.

** Huse, E. F. *Organization development and change.* New York: West, 1975.

** Latham, G. P., & Yukl, G. S. A review of the reasearch on the application of goal setting in organizations. *Academy of Management Journal,* 1975, **18,** 824–845.

Locke, E. A., Sirota, D., & Wolfson, A. D. An experimental case study of the successes and failures of job enrichment in a government agency. *Journal of Applied Psychology,* 1976, **61,** 701–711.

Payne, R. L., Fineman, S., & Wall, T. D. Organizational climate and job satisfaction: A conceptual synthesis. *Organizational Behavior and Human Performance,* 1976, **16,** 45–62.

* Sandler, B. E. Eclecticism at work: Approaches to job design. *American Psychologist,* 1974, **29,** 767–773.

* Short, L. E. Planned organizational change. *MSU Business Topics,* Autumn 1973, 55–61. Also in Herbert, T. T. *Organizational behavior: readings and cases.* New York: Macmillan, 1976, pp. 348–360.

* Warr, P. (Ed.). *Personal goals and work design.* New York: Wiley, 1976.

*Possible readings for students

**Review of literature or comprehensive source material

SIX
CURRENT TOPICS

This last part of the book is concerned with some current topics of relevance to organizations. Chapter 17 discusses political issues while Chapter 18 focuses on social issues. The two together provide a good view of what most organizations will face in the future.

A chapter on political processes is not included in most books on organizational behavior. For some reason the topic is usually avoided, probably because most people fail to see that organizations are political arenas just as governments are. Much of this chapter is designed to illustrate this similarity. We spend some time developing the idea that organizations are becoming increasingly concerned with the political support of their constituents. Systems of appeal are designed to combat managerial whim and capriciousness. Systems of participation tend to involve people in the legislative or decision-making processes of the organization. And finally, when one takes the broad view of managerial philosophy, systems of governance are evident that parallel or correspond to some classical systems with which we are familiar, such as democracy, totalitarianism, federalism, and autocracy.

What we are saying is that there has been a shift of emphasis in today's organizations. For many years simple efficiency was the accepted criteria of success. When organizations grew in size and complexity, there was increased concern about coordination and cooperation. Today, many decisions are made with political support as an important criterion along with efficiency and coordination. The implications of such shifts are discussed in some detail.

The final chapter (Chapter 18) provides a view into the crystal ball. Current problems of worker dissatisfaction, alienation, and turnover are projected into the future. The problems today and in the future related to employment of minorities and women are discussed. Alcoholism and drug abuse are also examined. Finally, we consider how the changing needs and values of the people in our society point to some problems for the future.

While the picture painted is not meant to be pessimistic, it is also not optimistic. Given more people who are better educated and want more meaningful jobs but are faced with diminishing resources, inflation, and high unemployment, the picture could hardly be glowing. On the other hand, if we intelligently use our resources and develop equitable and enriching organizational settings, progress can be made. The final chapter discusses some ways in which this progress may come about.

17
Political support

Throughout the book we have emphasized the fact that most of what goes on in organizations is based on rational decision making. There are various goals that need to be achieved, and people try to figure out *from their perspective* what the best way is to reach these goals. It is not necessarily objective, because people's perceptions are of course influenced by their own needs, desires, and experiences. But it is rational—it makes sense from a personal perspective and it is clearly a means-end type of analysis. How we can best reach our objectives is the central question that determines organizational processes and design.[1]

Rationality

Rationality as a general problem-solving strategy can be subdivided according to the type of problem which is facing the organizational members. In most cases, these have been technical problems. The question of paramount importance to most organizations is how to be more *efficient*. The goal is to increase our outputs relative to our inputs. For example, given labor and raw-material costs as inputs, how can a manufacturing firm increase its output? The answer may come in the form of a technological innovation or an invention which increases output and decreases production time (and perhaps labor costs), or it may come in the form of a new performance-appraisal system which increases motivation. In this

[1]The ideas that form the foundation of this chapter come from W. G. Scott, T. R. Mitchell, & N. S. Peery. Organizational governance. In W. Starbuck (Ed.), *The handbook of organizational design*. Elsevier, 1977. In Press. And from a chapter in W. G. Scott & T. R. Mitchell. *Organization theory: A structural and behavioral analysis*. Homewood, Ill.: Dorsey-Irwin, 1976, 427–458.

latter example, effort and thus productivity would increase, while labor costs would stay constant.

Technical rationality

Emphasis on efficiency is typically described as technical rationality. Historically, the evolution and success of large organizations has been dominated by technically rational decision-making strategies. In a highly competitive marketplace, either profit or nonprofit, the organization has to be efficient or it will perish. The organizational graveyard is filled with examples of inefficient management.

Organizational rationality

As organizations became larger, more complex, and more diverse, different sorts of problems arose. These problems focused on coordination. It was critical that different parts of an organization communicate and cooperate with one another. The right hand must know what the left hand is doing. As complexity increased, the focus of management shifted partly from technical rationality to what we might call organizational rationality—how we can structure and design the organization so that its members will exchange needed information and *cooperate* with one another.

For example, an organization which has many specialized units can divide into semiautonomous subunits or it may maintain its original structure but allocate certain decision responsibilities to lower levels of the management hierarchy. In this way the appropriate expert (the person with the proper knowledge) is responsible for what goes on. Once this is done, the organization must also figure out ways to maintain the interchange between subunits. Thus, the question of organizational rationality has to do with some issues of *differentiation* and *integration*—terms we discussed in Chapter 2 of the book. Because of the changing and highly specialized and complex society in which we live, decisions based on organizational rationality have increased in number and importance.

Political rationality

However, sharing information and allocating responsibility to lower levels of the organization has led us to a third type of rationality: political rationality. The goal is somewhat different from the other two types of rationality. In this case, management is concerned with how it can gain support for its decisions *and* the decision making process. Political rationality focuses on what we would describe as *regime maintenance*. Management essentially determines how information, power, decision making, and resources are distributed among organizational members. If management is to maintain a harmonious and committed work force, the organizational members must support to some extent this distribution process. Table 17-1 represents our three types of rationality and the goals on which they focus.

The suggestion that organizations are arenas for political activity is relatively

Table 17-1. Types of Rationality

Form of Rationality	Purpose Sought	Developmental Phase
Technical	Efficiency	Early growth of structurally simple organizations
Organizational	Cooperation	Moderate maturity of structurally complex organizations
Political	Regime maintenance	Full maturity of structurally complex organizations

recent. Most of the literature in political science has traditionally focused on how large organizations affect the national political process, such as the effects of big business or labor on the platforms and policies of political parties. Some literature, however, has mentioned that the basic process of politics is the control, regulation, and distribution of power and that one can study this process in any type of organization.[2]

Lyman Porter, who has served as the president of both the Academy of Management (1974) and the Division of Industrial and Organizational Psychology of the American Psychological Association (1976), has recently stressed the importance of organizational politics. In his presidential addresses to both professional associations, he cited the poor coverage that this topic has received in the traditional organizational-behavior literature. He charged that management has been "soft on organizational politics" and that it is a "fascinating but neglected problem area." He believes that unless we begin to tackle this issue, the impact of our field "will continue to be limited." The purpose of this chapter is to discuss what we do know about this topic.

The current emphasis on this issue has opened up a whole new area of academic inquiry. Investigators are interested in when and how management is concerned about its political climate. Obviously, management wants support for its activities and decisions on any particular issue. But it also wants and needs support for the prevailing political system. That is, it needs support for the way in which power is distributed throughout the organization. The way in which status (e.g., titles), privilege (e.g., use of the executive washroom), scarce resources (e.g., offices facing the park), and the ability of individuals to contribute to the goals of the organization are all part of this political environment. These allocation processes become accepted and routine. They become the political norms of the organization.

Summary

There are, then, three types of rationality which are important for understanding organizational processes and design. Technical rationality has a goal of effi-

[2]See W. G. Scott. *The management of conflict.* Homewood, Ill. Dorsey-Irwin, 1965.

The political processes found in organizations are often similar to those found in national or state governments. *(By permission of University of Washington Daily.)*

ciency, organizational rationality has a goal of cooperation, and political rationality has a goal of system support. All three of these goals probably are factors in most important decisions. For example, increasing the participation in decision making can be seen from a technically rational perspective (i.e., people will work harder), an organizationally rational perspective (i.e., cooperation is enhanced by sharing information and responsibility), and a politically rational view (i.e., people will be more committed to decisions which they have helped make).

What does differ, however, is the relative emphasis of each form of rationality in terms of importance in the decision-making process. Historically it appears as if we are increasing our emphasis on organizational and political rationality. For most large complex organizations, survival is no longer a question (Lockheed and the Penn Central Railroad notwithstanding). Efficiency, while still very important, has lost a little ground to the goals of cooperation and political support. While each individual organization may have its own particular blend of emphasis, the general trend does seem to be toward a concern for the support and commitment of organizational members.

From a developmental perspective we are saying that, as an organization increases in size and complexity, the goals of its members may shift from efficiency to cooperation and support. This argument would suggest that in the coming years political rationality will increase in importance. Every analysis of this process in the last 20 years has agreed on one central point: we are moving away from the tightly controlled, hierarchical, autocratic organizational structure. This trend should continue. However, this is not to say that all organizations will embrace a human-resources philosophy and institute widespread changes resulting in greater autonomy, participation, and satisfaction. We already know from our discussion of contingency approaches that these types of activities are only effective in certain settings. What we are saying is that the *relative* emphasis on and concern about political issues will increase.

In this chapter we will discuss several topics. First, we will attempt to describe the ways in which power traditionally has been distributed and controlled within organizations. Second, we will show how decisions initially concerned about organizationally rational objectives have had an impact on political outcomes as well. Finally, we will discuss how political norms develop and crystalize into what we will call governance models. These models represent governance systems that parallel to some extent the types of models used to govern nations and other political entities (such as cities or states) with which we are familiar. Figure 17-1 represents graphically an overview of our thinking.

The distribution of power

One purpose of a system of governance of any organization is to establish consensus among its participants about the norms of appropriate behavior. People have to accept the rules, regulations, and expectations if the organization

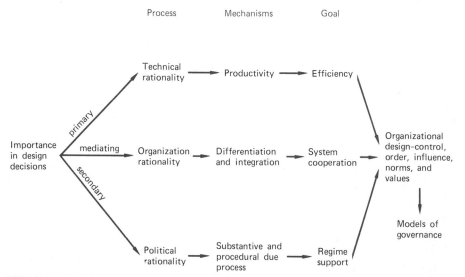

Figure 17-1. Summary of the impact of technical, organizational, and political rationality on organizational design.

wants to prosper. This idea has been a central theme throughout the history of management theory. Writers from both the scientific-management school and the human-relations school felt that consensus between management and employees was the best way to ensure increased effectiveness. A related concept espoused by Frederick Taylor was the "mutuality of interests," which argued that management should be equitable in the distribution of rewards so that employees would see their interests as similar to the interests of the ownership and management. The basic theme is that we should agree on our goals and work cooperatively toward them.

Political systems build this consensus in a variety of ways. Probably the two most easily described ways of building consensus are through what we would call legislative and judicial activities. The legislative process is concerned with who makes the rules and laws of the organization. The judicial process is concerned with a sense of equity and with the right to appeal or to question the normative order.

If we examine modern organizations, we can identify processes that are both legislative and judicial in intent. The legislative activities are concerned with the allocation of resources, information, and power. We call these activities *substantive due process*. The judicial activities are labeled *procedural due process*. Both these concepts are described below in more detail.

But before turning to these issues, we should clarify the boundaries of this discussion somewhat further. In many organizations there are unions that serve as bargaining agents and formal guardians against the arbitrary use of power. Frequently, the unions play an important role in prescribing how rewards and rules are formed and implemented. They may also have some sort of grievance procedure as part of their contract. Union workers, however, account for less than half of the people employed in the United States, and therefore much of our discussion will focus on settings where unions are not present or on issues about which unions have traditionally had little impact.

Substantive due process

Decisions have to be made allocating organizational resources to various individuals, interest groups, and economic sectors falling within an organization's domain. These decisions are *legislative* because they set the terms and establish the distribution rules for who gets what and how much of an organization's wealth. The substantive due process issue in organization governance is how such decisions are made—and the consequences that result from particular legislative decision-making forms. Allocation decisions can be made democratically, autocratically, constitutionally, or a number of other ways with various degrees of shading and overlapping.

At the University of Washington, for example, when the legislature decides to give money for raises (e.g., 5 percent of current salary costs), there is always the question of how it should be distributed. Should it be distributed on the basis of merit alone, or should everyone get an across-the-board increase? The decision on this issue may be made by the Dean with the consultation and advice of the faculty; or the Dean might decide alone; or the faculty might make a decision which was binding on the Dean. The point is that there are numerous ways in which this decision could be made, and they probably differ in terms of the amount of consensus that would result.

One of the most obvious modes of increasing consensus via the legislative process is through participation in organizational decision making. To date, participation seems to appear in two general forms. The first, which is representative of the American experience, is an attempt to have participation at the task level within particular organizations. In this frame of reference, participation is a technological innovation to increase productivity and effectiveness. The goal is efficiency, and the motive is technical rationality. The second form is participation at an organizational or occupational level. The power base is broader, the conflicts more general, and the underlying rationale is *political* rather than technical. This distinction is made by Hall and Clark when they discuss worker participation as an ideology "which can be political in the sense that there is a belief that workers ought to have more control over their lives and their work" or as a practical ideology concerned with the work environment.[3] Participation, therefore, can be seen as both a technically rational decision or a political decision concerned with the redistribution of power.

Participation as a technology. Participation at this level is founded in the concept of technical rationality. Management should and probably will use any technique which is likely to increase productivity. In their review of this literature, Heller and Rose argue that "in modern, large and progressive companies participation and power are seen to be anchored in the situation, particularly in the nature of the task." They label this a form of "sociotechnical analysis."[4] It is the technical demands of the situation that prompt the need for participation.

The impetus for this technique typically has come from psychologists doing field or laboratory experimentation. The usual experiment involves establishing participation of some form (e.g., representatives, group meetings) for some decisions about a specific job. This unit is compared to a "nonparticipative" unit (a control group), and appropriate inferences about the satisfaction and performance of participating employees are made. The early research was very supportive of participation, while later reports are more cautious.

This approach is essentially experimental in nature. The researchers are interested in where participation works best and why it works when it does. The underlying rationale for the research is not political. These researchers generally are more interested in the psychological processes operating in a participative environment than in the political implications. A number of areas where participation has been tried are mentioned below.

In some cases, workers have participated in the performance-appraisal sys-

[3]R. H. Hall & J. P. Clark. Participation and interorganizational relationships: Some suggestions and tentative findings. Proceedings of the First International Sociological Conference on Participation and Self-Management, Dubrovnik, Yugoslavia, 1972, **4**, 47–55, 97.

[4]R. A. Heller & J. S. Rose. Participation and decision making re-examined. Proceedings of the First International Sociological Conference on Participation and Self-Management, Dubrovnik, Yugoslavia, 1972, **4**, 123–133.

tem. The argument is that performance goals and appraisal should be carried out jointly so that the employees participate in setting the goal and evaluating their own progress. Why should this work better than the old system? Well, supposedly, by participating the individual will be less defensive in evaluating his or her work and will have higher motivation to reach the explicit, agreed-upon targets. Also, this system provides better data for training and development systems. These are all technically rational reasons for participation.

As an example of just such a process, we recently completed some research which evaluated participation in the performance-appraisal system.[5] We had developed an appraisal instrument using a behavioral checklist for engineers and scientists in a research and development department of a large industrial organization. Half these engineer/scientists met with their immediate supervisor and jointly evaluated the engineer/scientist's performance on the checklist. They then agreed jointly upon some specific goals for the next quarter. The other half of the engineer/scientists met with their supervisor, who evaluated them (unilaterally) and *assigned* (rather than jointly set) goals for the next quarter. One of the most interesting findings was that the goals set by the participative group were more difficult than those set by the assigned group. Thus the participative process seemed to affect both aspirations and motivation.

A second area where people advocate participation is in the organizational-change process. Many of the authors involved in organizational development suggest that participation is a fundamental necessity for effective organizational change. Employees will supposedly be more committed to the change and illustrate greater acceptance of new rules or norms if they have contributed to their formulation. There will be better coordination and less conflict about implementing change.

The third area concerns participation in decisions about the ongoing, day-to-day work practices. To participate here means increases in the accuracy and amount of information that workers have available. Thus, there is more certainty in the organizational environment, and group norms are likely to develop which support these practices. As group members have more control over work policies, it is more likely that they will support these policies through their informal group norms.

Most current reviews of participation, however, qualify their enthusiasm. They suggest that participation is only effective some of the time, in some places, and with some people. As we mentioned in Chapter 16, "Organizational Change Techniques," people have to (1) have some *expertise* about the issue, (2) have a *desire* to participate, and (3) feel as if they are actually making a *contribution* before participation seems to be effective. These reservations have led to contingency approaches to participation where a manager's decision style (i.e., degree of participation) is matched to the decision problems.

The most thorough analysis of this type has been developed by Vroom and Yetton, which we discussed in Chapter 17, "Decision Making."[6] You will recall

[5] G. Latham, D. Dossett, & T. Mitchell. The importance of participative goal setting and anticipated rewards on goal difficulty, goal acceptance, and job performance. *Journal of Applied Psychology,* In Press.

[6] V. H. Vroom & P. W. Yetton. *Leadership and decision making.* Pittsburgh: University of Pittsburgh Press, 1973.

that these authors attempted to outline the major decision parameters that management should use in determining the degree of participation that will generate effective decision making. These parameters include issues such as what sort of information is held by subordinates, whether the subordinates' acceptance is critical for implementation, the likelihood of conflict, and whether subordinates can be trusted to consider the organization's goals before their own. These issues should determine the level of participation necessary for making the right decision.

An overview of the emphasis on the technology of participation provides interesting insights. This strategy is being used essentially for technical rationality, not because of concerns about equity, equality, or rights. In most American organizations, participation is introduced because management believes it will increase the effort, motivation, and productivity of its employees. A vastly different emphasis is apparent in the European experience.

Participation as power redistribution. The other major perspective on participation comes from those people who view participation in terms of the political redistribution of power. Socialists such as Trotsky spoke of the justification of any end which increased the power of man over nature or abolished the power of man over man. Political scientists also have discussed the issue of "social equity" as contrasted with the more traditional technical or utilitarian points of view. Harmon, for example, states that: "for the sake of convenience, the two contemporary conceptions of organizational man will be labeled 'professional-technocratic' man, and 'politico-administrative' man, the former being an outgrowth of public administration's historical ties with management science, and the latter the result of the recognition that the public administrator's role was inherently political in nature."[7]

The power redistribution stance is couched in ethical and political terms, not in technically rational ones. The proponents of this approach do not usually talk about participation; they speak of workers' *control* as their means of avoiding arbitrary power in public or private organizations. Workers' self-management is seen as the goal of a socialist society.

The experimentation with these ideas has been extensive and varied throughout Europe. In some cases there is as much variability within a country as there is among different countries. In Sweden, for example, there are bodies such as the Development Council (trade-union members) and the Committee for Industrial Democracy. The latter is more concerned with power redistribution and has cited successful examples, such as an experiment with the Swedish Tobacco Company. Other groups, such as the Development Council, are sometimes viewed as supporting a more paternalistic consultation strategy. England has tended to follow the more consultative view. Joint councils are established containing management and worker representatives, and a review of 157 British enterprises shows that acceptance seems to vary according to the ability of a given group to manipulate the committee according to their interests. England has also developed the idea of the shop steward who is a union member paid by management but who promotes worker's demands.

[7]M. Harmon. Social equity and organization man: Motivation and organizational democracy. *Public Administration Review* , 1974, **34**, 12.

In Germany, there are workers' councils with elected representatives from management and workers. They jointly decide on issues dealing with topics such as the work schedule, social services, vocational training, and some personnel matters. A Works Council in Netherlands also has representatives from management and labor. Their purpose is to deal with general consultation and descriptions of tasks, jobs, and competences required. The success of this strategy seems to vary according to a number of variables, such as the size of the company, the age and length of service of the workers, and other factors.

The Eastern European countries have systems which provide the worker with more actual control. The Yugoslav case emphasizes assemblies of working people and the idea of "self-management." However, when one reviews the writings about this approach, it is obvious that many workers are dissatisfied and that the present experiment is far from drastically changing the traditional work patterns. Experiences in Poland have been somewhat similar. Here there is the Conference of Workers' Self-Government, and research has shown that in many cases there is minimal worker support for such systems. The "self-government" is seen more as a concern for discipline and production schedules than with the quality of the working life.

Limitations of power redistribution. There are a number of reasons why these attempts at self-management failed to yield the type of support and redistribution of power that was originally envisioned. In some cases, representatives became hard to control. And, in a problematic situation similar to one that occurs occasionally in the United States with union representatives, the European representatives have developed a separate professional role. That is, they are neither workers nor managers. Another problem has to do with the areas in which participation seems to be most effective. The major proponents have noted the better communication and more explicit exchanges between workers and management. Most reports, however, suggest that little action is really taken on issues which are of real concern to the worker.

Perhaps the most interesting paradox has been raised by Tannenbaum. He argues that participation in many cases will *increase* the power of managers over workers, and he suggests some reasons why this should be the case. First, worker representatives frequently become more sympathetic to management's point of view. By jointly working on the problem, they see the other side of the issue. Second, managers by and large have more technical expertise than workers and can, therefore, have a greater impact on decisions because of their "expert" power. Finally, workers feel more committed to the decisions made by councils simply because their representatives participated in the meetings. Research in Yugoslavia, England, Israel, Italy, Austria, and the United States by Tannenbaum and his colleagues has shown support for these ideas.[8] These researchers explain their findings by suggesting that workers generally trust management and that where they feel a sense of responsibility in the plant, they are likely to be responsive to management's influence attempts. Managers are

[8]A. S. Tannenbaum, B. Kavcic, M. Rosner, M. Vianello & G. Wieser. *Hierarchy in organizations: An international comparison.* San Francisco: Jossey-Bass, 1974.

therefore more likely to be influential under these conditions. The idea of increased worker power through participation may, in fact, lead to less power.

Thus, there are severe qualifications which one must make when evaluating the success of participation. From a psychological perspective (or technically rational view) it seems as if participation can increase commitment and consensus for certain types of activities. It may also increase motivation. From a political perspective, it may increase commitment to the normative order which is, of course, the aim of a politically rational decision-making process. It may not, however, increase the *actual* power of the participants. This is a controversial topic which will undoubtedly be researched further.

Participation, therefore, can be seen as a negotiated agreement (e.g., unions), as an experiment (e.g., participative managerial leadership styles), or as a right (e.g., workers' councils). Whatever the rationale, the outcome seems to be that participation does increase consensus and commitment when applied at the appropriate time and place. Since we suspect that a concern for political support

You remember how quickly the administration voted to give us a responsible voice in the management of the university? Well, now they want us to go out and help raise some money to stave off bankruptcy.

Participation in decision making carries with it some responsibility for the decisions made.

will increase in the near future, we also suspect that participation will play an increasing role in the legislative process of organizations.

Procedural due process

The argument often advanced in the participation literature is that when allocation decisions are unilaterally made by management, it is easy for a real or an imagined perception of injustice to creep into people's assessment of their rewards relative to others. Differential rewards are distributed to employees depending on a number of factors such as the type of work performed, level in the hierarchy, amount of bargaining power, and pure managerial whim. As we pointed out in Chapter 7, "Motivation," the way employees perceive fairness in distribution results in a perception of equity or inequity, and this feeling of equity is related to motivation, cooperation, and political support. In a more equitable situation, people are more likely to work hard, cooperate with others, and agree upon the norms established. Thus equity can affect technical, organizational, and political rationality.

Equity. Equity is perceptual and it is relative. A person feels justly or unjustly treated only in relation to how other people are being treated in the same situation. If a woman is paid less for doing the same work as a man, then it is appropriate that she feel that she has been done an injustice. However, most cases of inequitable treatment are not as clear cut as this example. People may feel unjustly treated, even if no objective discrimination exists. A sense of equity or inequity exists in individuals' minds, and it is arrived at through their perceptual apparatus regardless of how imperfectly or accurately it feeds data to them.

No matter how the norms of an organization originate, be it through participation or through unilateral acts of management, it follows that if people think they are being dealt with unfairly, they should have the right to appeal in order to obtain equity. The purpose of *procedural due process* is to provide a judicial function in organizations that limits and corrects arbitrariness and unfairness in the administration of allocation policies.

Examples of judicial procedures. There are many examples of such procedures—some formal, some informal. Formal *appeal* systems occasionally may arise from the benevolence of management—that is, they may be granted to employees as a unilateral act of management. Some others may be traced to a popular movement on the part of employees, such as unionization, to force management to give them channels for securing justice. Virtually every contract that management and unions sign contains a clause having a written grievance procedure. Still other appeal programs begin with public law. Most federal civil service employees have numerous avenues—guaranteed to them by civil service law and agency regulations—for appealing complaints of injustices. Thus, judicial procedures for implementing corrective justice in organizations are widespread.

Two principles underlie these procedures. The first principle is that appeal mechanisms must be available to all employees without prejudice. This is to say that people ought to be able to appeal for justice within the organization without fear of reprisal. The second principle is the separation of governance power, which simply means that those who make and execute the laws of the organization should not interpret these laws in the process of rendering judgments on disputes that arise from them. While these two principles are the minimum requirements necessary to assure that the adjudication of disputes is done fairly and dispassionately, they are frequently honored in the breach rather than in the observance of organizational governance.

The chief exception to this is found in collective-bargaining agreements between labor and management. Union contracts generally have a clause that provides union members with the opportunity to appeal alleged violations of their contract rights. Most negotiated grievance procedures have arbitration as a final step to which unresolved issues are submitted for impartial arbitration and for final and binding decisions.

For the most part, however, such separation of power is virtually unheard of in organizations. More often than not the level of corrective justice in organizations has not progressed beyond the feudal practice which allowed aggrieved people to approach the lord or the king to seek redress of an injustice. Likewise, in modern organizations, people may be directed *informally* to key executives who act in the role of a judge in resolving conflicts and correcting injustices. Thus, even where formal redress systems are absent, some sort of informal channel may be available.

As an example, what would you do if you did not like the grade you received on a paper you wrote for one of your courses? You could argue with the professor, you could agree to do additional work, or in some cases you might be able to convince the professor to get another evaluation. Beyond that, what could you do? Unless there was some final court of appeal, you would be stuck.

As it turns out, many universities have recently introduced such an appeal procedure. In these cases a board of students and faculty listens to both sides of the issue and makes a final binding decision. But this sort of procedure is relatively new and infrequently used. The prevailing norm is that professors have the right to determine the grade, and there are very few limitations on this power. Probably because of this lack of redress, students often see the grading procedure as arbitrary and capricious.

Informal versus formal procedures. The important point is that the procedural due-process function, whether formal or informal, must be performed in organizational governance. As with substantive due process, *how* it is performed determines the nature of the governance activity. The informal approach to corrective justice has the advantage of flexibility, but it does little to protect the employees' *right* to appeal and to prevent arbitrariness in the administration of justice. The formal approach, which depends upon written guarantees and specified legalistic procedures, offers the assurance that appeal privileges are available but has the danger that employee appeals will get bogged down in elaborate judicial machinery.

Another difficulty with informal due process is that the laws of the organization are seldom codified. It is frequently difficult for an employee to know what is appealable and what is not. The lack of codification results in clogging the judicial system with gripes and complaints. While such minor expressions of discontent are often important barometers of morale, they tend to create a lot of noise in the system that prevents major incidents of individual injustice from being heard and resolved.

In conclusion, substantive and procedural due-process guarantees are established as part of an evolution in organizational design. Both processes provide the individual employee with a feeling of equity and fairness. By participating in the decision process, people feel more committed to the actions taken and are more likely to support such positions. They are likely to say something such as, "Well, we all agreed this is what we would do, and even though it is not my first preference, I can support it." It is the process of contributing that causes these feelings of fairness. However, in many cases participation is not available. In these settings the basic minimum requirement for feelings of equity and fairness is some system of procedural due process. The employee has to feel that at least there is some control on the whims and capriciousness of management. Formal or informal systems of appeal provide some assurance against arbitrary action. The employee is likely to say, "I may not have much say around here, but I do know one thing—if they treat me wrong, the union will stand up for me." In the next section we will show how these different forms of due process are more or less likely in particular types of organizational environments—a contingency theory of political processes, if you like.

Some determinants of due process: Differentiation and integration

In our introduction we suggested that organizational rationality is the link between technical and political rationality. In this section we will attempt to describe this mediating role. Our argument is essentially that (1) organizations become more complex as they grow in size, technology, power, and functions, (2) with complexity come problems of organizing, problems of differentiation and integration, (3) decisions about how to handle these problems determine the structure of the organization, which in turn influences the ongoing political processes of substantive and procedural due process. The technical problems produce organizing problems whose solutions partly determine the nature of political activities in the organization.

The two basic processes used by organizational designers to structure organizations are differentiation and integration[9]. Differentiation simply refers to the amount of difference in the people and the structure of different organizational subunits. The greater these differences are, the greater the differentiation. Integration, on the other hand, refers to the ways in which organizations attempt to reduce differences by increasing collaboration, communication, and cooperation across these subunits. Thus, differentiation refers to differences, while integrations refers to attempts to overcome these differences.

[9]P. R. Lawrence & J. W. Lorsch. *Organization and environment.* Homewood, Ill. Irwin, 1969.

Differentiation

Differentiation can occur in a variety of ways. The major distinction is between what we could call perceptual and structural differences. Perceptual differences refer to the attitudes, goals, and information possessed by different people. Some organizational activities that tend to cause these differences are the selection, reward, and communication activities. If the people selected are very different in their skills, interests, and backgrounds, they are more likely to have different attitudes, goals, and beliefs. They are less likely to be good friends and to communicate with one another. Also, if very different reward structures exist for different groups (e.g., management versus nonmanagement; full time versus part time; salaried versus hourly), there are likely to be attitudinal and goal differences among the employees.

There are also some structural differences that may exist. Almost every large organization divides into departments. The division may take place along product lines (e.g., General Motors has separate divisions for its automobiles), along functional lines (e.g., finance, marketing, production), because of location in different areas, or because of different clientele. Whatever the reason, the greater the departmentalization, the greater the differences in rules, procedures, people, and so forth. Subdividing creates differences among the subgroups—otherwise you would not make the division.[10]

Of course, at the task level subdividing is called division of labor. It is a central reason for our great industrial expansion and growth. It is one of the major causes of our high standard of living. But it does cause differences. People specialize in their jobs and communicate with those that are similar to them. Dividing up the task creates distinctions and differences among people.

One structural distinction which clearly causes differentiation is the separation into line and staff. The staff people are typically professionals (e.g., engineers, lawyers, scientists) who serve in a sort of consulting role to the line managers. Because of their background differences and role differences, there is often conflict between the line and the staff personnel.

Problems of differentiating

The important point is that differentiation causes problems for the organization. These differences in the types of people, the jobs they do, and the groups to which they belong lead to conflict, lack of cooperation and coordination, and a loss of control. People with different interests and goals are more likely to disagree with one another, they are less likely to communicate with one another, and they are likely to think they are the best judge of what should happen in their own particular area of interest or expertise. This last issue is crucial. It suggests that with increased differentiation comes a decentralization of power and authority. The creation of subgroups by definition suggests that they are distinct in

[10]D. S. Pugh, D. J. Hickson, & C. R. Hinings. An empirical taxonomy of structures of work organizations. *Administrative Science Quarterly*, 1969, **14**, 115–126.

some way, and in most cases this distinction demands a certain amount of autonomy and authority. Control is being parceled out along with responsibility and authority.

If all these problems occur, then why do organizations do things that lead to differentiation? The answer is that it is *technically* rational to do so. Dividing and subdividing is done because management feels it will lead to greater efficiency. It makes sense from a production and from a management perspective to create these differences. Experts are needed, and different types of people with different skills are selected. Departments are established to allow people to concentrate on certain problems or functions. Staff people are brought in to provide expert advice. Tasks are subdivided because the engineering or industrial psychologist suggests that more could be produced with a greater division of labor.

Integration

The response to the problem is to provide mechanisms for integration. At this point the goal of *organizational* rationality is operating. In order to have people work together cooperatively and communicate with one another, some sort of integration is necessary. Some of the most common devices for integration are committees and "linking" positions designed to coordinate activities among subgroups and departments. In some cases, organizational rules demand that decisions be made in writing and circulated to various organizational positions. Rules and procedures are installed to ensure communication.

Political concerns

Both differentiation and integration have a political impact as well. As we have stated, the movement over the last 100 years has generally been to increased differentiation. Organization structures have become more and more complex. If the leaders of an organization attempt to solve this differentiation through rules, regulations, and formal communication channels, there is likely to be a greater emphasis on procedural due process than on substantive due process. Even though some authority is released through differentiation, it can be minimal if tight controls are still maintained. On the other hand, if greater autonomy is allowed *and* joint committees are established for communication and decision making, then some degree of substantive due process is likely to occur. People will perceive that they are playing a significant role in policy formation and the legislative process of the organization. Table 17-2 presents a summary of what we have said so far.

To summarize, organizations have been faced with increasing technology, the information explosion, and rapidly changing environments. They have become more and more complex in terms of both the types of people they employ and the types of organizational structures that evolve. To some extent, this increased differentiation and complexity has spread decision-making capacity and power throughout the organization, resulting in some increases in people's involvement in legislative activities. This has had a *minor* influence on due-process issues. The *major* influence on due process comes not from differentiation per se but

Table 17-2. Summary of the Effects of Differentiation and Integration on Governance Processes

	Definition	Basic Cause	Techniques	Result
Differentiation	Differences in people and structures	Technical rationality in response to task demands	Departmentalization Line and staff Division of labor Selection Reward system	Some changes in power distribution
Integration	Attempts to overcome differences caused by differentiation	Organizational rationality in response to problems of coordination and cooperation	Committees Linking positions Comunication channels Rules and procedures	Participative strategies lead to substantive due process Formalized strategies lead to procedural due process

from the way in which the organization deals with differentiation. It is the integration techniques which seem to matter most. If formal communication devices are used, such as routing slips or rules and procedures for reporting activities, then it is more likely that procedural due process (e.g., grievance systems) will be emphasized as a way to gather constituent support. If more participative techniques are used to increase cooperation and communication, then substantive due process is being affected. Through committees or participative decision-making activities, people will be engaging in the legislative process as well. Substantive due process will be encouraged.

The particular way in which organizational members choose to differentiate or integrate is caused by a number of factors. There are the particular demands of the task itself: some organizations need greater specialization than others. But there are also historical precedents and the particular management style or climate that exists. All these factors combine to produce different types of what we would call governance types or models. We turn now to a discussion of these models.

Governance models

> Democracy gives every man the right
> to be his own oppressor.
>
> James Russell Lowell

Throughout the text we have used the words "norms" and "climate" to refer to the general pattern of expected behavior within organizations. Within a particular organization, problems get solved and conflict is resolved in similar ways. An organization comes to have a history and a set of precedents for dealing with questions of power distribution and justice. This history and precedence forms what we could call the "constitution" of the organization. While this constitution does not exist as a written document, it does exist in people's heads, as part of the rules and procedures, and as part of the prevailing interpersonal atmosphere.

So far, we have used the terms "substantive" and "procedural" due process to refer to the way in which a sense of commitment and equity is established within an organization. Systems of participation and judicial guarantees have been used as primary examples of these processes. But the constitution of an organization includes more than just these strategies. It incorporates all the ways in which power and justice are handled. It is a broader, more encompassing concept.

In this last section we shall try to do two things. First, we will briefly describe a whole set of tactics or strategies that are used to gain power and ensure equity. This list will provide a richer description of what makes up an organizational constitution. Second, we will show how patterns of strategies—that is, how certain groups of strategies—tend to hang together to form general models of governance. As we shall see, these governance models for organizations are highly similar to those models currently employed to govern other political entities.

Dealing with conflict: The question of power distribution

If one wishes to gain a firm understanding of the political process in an organization, one should study the decision-making process in general and decision making in conflict situations in particular. Are decisions made by individuals or groups? Is information provided on request only or spontaneously? When conflict or differences of opinion exist, how are they resolved? Do people openly bargain or do they form coalitions or resort to rank and status as the ultimate criterion?

The answers to these questions give us an idea of how power is distributed. We will view these strategies as ranging from low equity and commitment to high equity and commitment. On the one end there are behaviors which seem to imply a low level of equity, trust, and justice. Thus we may find the following sorts of attitudes and behaviors used to resolve conflict.

Alliances with powerful people. The way to have input, get ahead, and win arguments is to know the powerful people in the organization. In many cases it is not what you know but who you know that dictates success on a particular issue or in an overall career.

Manipulation of information. In some organizations there are only a few people who really know what is going on. Access to these sources determines both one's amount of power and one's ability to persuade and convince others of one's position.

Co-optation. When new ideas or power sources or conflicting opinions appear, they are co-opted or incorporated into the strategy of the existing power elite. In other words, they take the sting out of the challenge by some partial and probably watered-down acceptance of the new people or positions.

Administrative fiat. Probably the process least likely to engender commitment and support is the statement "We do it that way because the boss says so." To be supportive of a position, people must, at the minimum, understand the reasons for it.

At the opposite end of this continuum would be strategies designed to increase support and equity. Some of them are:

Participation. Participation in the decision process is likely to encourage support and feelings of shared power and equity. We have discussed this point fully.

Objective performance appraisal. The more specific and objective the appraisal system, the greater the feeling of equity. With a good appraisal system, people will see that promotions (power distribution) and pay (reward distribution) are based on equitable procedures.

Access to information. The more open and public the decision process, the greater the acceptance of the decisions. People can weigh the information for themselves and feel free to voice their opinion on any subject. The better informed they are, the more likely they are to support the system.

Periodic review. Both people and policies should be regularly reviewed. People's input in this way can become an ongoing process.

Table 17-3. Strategies Used to Resolve Conflict and Distribute Power

Low Levels of Support and Equity	High Levels of Support and Equity
1 Alliances with powerful people	1 Objective performance appraisal
2 Manipulation of information	2 Access to information
3 Co-optation	3 Participation
4 Administrative fiat	4 Periodic review

Obviously, all these patterns of behavior do not always appear. Some organizations use them all or use some in certain situations and others when they seem more appropriate. But the important point is that consistent patterns do exist. Some organizations tend to lean more toward one side or the other (see Table 17-3). And it is this general pattern or most frequent response which has led to the development of governance models.

The models which we will describe are ideal types. They are extreme forms and they are pure forms. They are rigid in content and frozen in time. Obviously any given organization may have elements of different models. Also, governance styles and designs change, slowly or rapidly, depending on the demands of the environment. For these reasons, one must be careful in one's interpretation of our analysis. The analysis presented here is not meant to be descriptive.

The two factors that contribute to the classification of a governance system are (1) the strategies used to resolve conflict and distribute power (Table 17-3) and (2) the underlying assumptions about human nature. Table 17-4 summarizes the general outline for this section.

Autocracy and democracy. The two governance models that evolved from early organization theorists were autocracy and democracy. The earliest "classical" approach believed in the imperatives of centralized authority, control, and a rigid chain of command. The power of management was unilateral and unchallenged. This system in its extreme could be classified as an autocratic governance model. There was little or no participation or judicial redress, and punishment or threat of punishment was frequently used to motivate employees.

Table 17-4. Models of Governance

System	View of Human Nature	Strategies Used for Support	Strategies Used for Control
Autocracy	Negative	No participation	Punishment
Totalitarianism	Neutral	No participation	Punishment and rules and procedures
Federalism	Neutral	Some participation	Self-control and rules and procedures
Democracy	Positive	Full participation	Self-control

The autocratic system also had a rather negative view of human nature. It was assumed that most workers were basically lazy and primarily interested in money. Given such a view, it is easy to understand why the classicists preferred a system where an enlightened elite of managers could control effectively a mass of unenlightened workers. The autocratic structure gave administrators maximum control to maintain the rational decision process.

The democratic model was developed in response to the autocratic system. Based on the work of the human relationists, there developed a greater awareness of the individual employee and the work group. Their followers in the human-resources and related groups argued that the way to increase motivation was to provide interesting and stimulating jobs. Commitment and support for the organization would come through participation and involvement in company activities. Control came from within rather than being externally imposed.

The view of human nature was also different. Workers were seen as basically good, although they may have been corrupted by their environment. The role of the humanists was partly to restore people's sense of dignity and an awareness of their rights. Informed citizens govern themselves justly and effectively.

A large portion of the modern-day management literature still contrasts the democratic and autocratic systems. However, with the development of systems and contingency approaches along with our emphasis on technology, it has become clear that other alternatives are available. The two most frequently discussed are the totalitarian and federalist models.

Totalitarianism and federalism. A totalitarian system still maintains strict control. There is still a heavy emphasis on hierarchy, and a small elite makes the decisions.

There are two major differences between the autocratic system and the totalitarian system. First, the latter's view of human nature is more neutral in tone. The emphasis is on the flexibility and changeability of humans rather than their laziness. It is management's responsibility to design an organization that provides the appropriate contingencies. The focus on the cause of motivation shifted from an emphasis on internal flaws to the external environment.

The second difference is that totalitarian systems use modern technology to maintain control. Information content and access to information is controlled. The reward systems (and punishment systems) are planned in detail. In this way technology was applied to achieve higher levels of *structural* control, rather than self-control.

The federalist model is somewhere between the totalitarian and democratic systems. It suggests that organizations divide into teams or work groups based upon lines of expertise and knowledge. To some extent these groups are self-governing, but there is also a central hierarchy. Many large universities are run with a federalist-type system, as is our national government.

The federalist model is distinct from the totalitarian system in a number of ways. There is greater participation and self-governance in the federalist model, and the purpose of the central hierarchy is communication and coordination rather than control. The hierarchy would still be in charge of long-term goals and policy, but the emphasis on external control would diminish.

Well, yes, Harris, it is true that our country is run on democratic principles. However, in this company we operate under an autocratic regime.

Some organizations engage in participative democracy, and some do not.

The federalist approach, however, does not go as far as the democratic model. There is still need for some control and some hierarchy. The view of human nature is more neutral than positive, and there is still an emphasis on the use of technology. The federalist model recognizes the complexity of modern systems as well as the need for employee commitment and support.

To summarize, there are a number of different governance models available. Each model combines an underlying view of human nature with some strategy of control and distribution of power. Is there one best system? The answer to that question depends on the criterion used to assess "goodness." From a technically rational or efficiency perspective, the answer is probably that it depends on the situation. In some cases one system would be most effective, while in other cases a different system would be best. For example, it is hard to imagine an autocratic system working very well at a university, and it is hard to imagine a completely democratic military.

But there are other criteria besides efficiency. One might ask about the justness of the system or the support of its constituents. It is our contention that, since political rationality is increasing in importance, systems which produce such support (e.g., federalism or democracy) may become more prevalent. The crucial question is whether organizations will sacrifice some control and perhaps technical efficiency for political support. It is not clear whether people will agree that this needs to be done or should be done. Some people will argue that efficiency is more important than support, while others will argue the reverse. This controversy may be the major debate over the structure of future organization.

Summary

In general we have said that political processes play an important role in today's organizations. The development of that position included the following points:

1 Decision making is essentially a rational means-ends process. In organizations the goals fall into three categories: efficiency (technical rationality), cooperation (organizational rationality), and support (political rationality).
2 More complex and mature organizations are increasingly concerned with the support and commitment of their constituents.
3 The major techniques used to gain political support are substantive due process and procedural due process.
4 Substantive due process involves participation in the legislative or decision-making activities of the organization. Participation in the United States has historically been introduced for efficiency reasons, while a more political emphasis is prevalent in Europe.
5 Procedural due process involves judicial safeguards designed to provide the worker with a system of appeal and protection against the arbitrary use of power. In some cases these systems are informal and in others they are formal, such as union contracts.
6 In the process of dealing with problems of technical rationality and organizational rationality (problems of cooperation and communication), the organization has also influenced the political system. By differentiating, the organization may redistribute power, and the process of integration may either emphasize participative techniques (substantive due process) or emphasize formal reporting and communicating procedures (procedural due process).
7 Combining these general power-distribution strategies with the basic climate and assumptions about human nature leads to a typology of governance models. These models may be autocratic, democratic, totalitarian, or federalist.
8 An analysis of these issues suggests that our concern with the political processes within organizations will increase.

Implications for practice

The practical implications that can be generated from this chapter are not of the "how to do it" variety. Rather, they are more reflective in nature. We would suggest two major things. First, management should be more *aware* of the political impact of its decisions and of the organization structure in general. The process of how decisions are made can be analyzed. How many people contribute to the decisions? Are there important people who are left out? Are there unimportant people who have some expertise who are left out? To what extent does the legislative process attend to political rationality as well as to technical rationality?

Along a similar vein, the manager can be more aware of the mechanisms available for justice within the system. Where does one go with a gripe? Is there a system of appeal? Are there any checks on the arbitrary use of power? These are questions which are infrequently asked by most managers. We believe they should be asked more often.

The second suggestion has to do with *accountability*. Our society and our lives are increasingly controlled by the activities of large organizations. These institutions have the power to significantly alter our future for the better or for the worse. This projected impact suggests that organizations will be held responsible for their activities both by their employees and by the public at large. This increased accountability places the political activities within organizations in an even more important perspective. Management must be aware of the support it has not only from within but from without as well.

Discussion questions

1 Discuss the different types of rationality and their criteria for effectiveness. Do you think we are moving toward more politicized organizations?
2 How is power distributed in academic settings? Do students have legislative power? What can you do if you feel mistreated?
3 Are different governance models appropriate for different types of organizations? What would you recommend for a department store, a hospital, the Coast Guard, and a junior college? Why?

Case: The end of the line

You and four other accountants report to the vice president of finance. Over the last 6 months it has become increasingly obvious that the company is in deep financial trouble. Borrowed money is due, and the assets just are not there. Your company's reputation in the marketplace has slipped; it is hard to get money from anyone.

Because of these pressures, you and your four colleagues have been working 18-hour days, 6 days a week. Every possible avenue to raise cash is being explored. Budget cuts are necessary everywhere, but the question is how much and where exactly—who gets the axe, what programs get the axe? Your boss has been pushing everyone relentlessly.

After a particularly long Saturday your boss, Douglas Schauffer, comes in at 9:00 P.M. and tells you he is going to need a complete report on the firm's portfolio, including recommendations for changes in the selection criteria currently being used. And he needs it Monday morning.

After he leaves, you and your colleagues look at one another in disgust. Sunday is the only time you have for family and friends, and now that is being eaten up. Besides, you doubt that the request could be done well with twice as many people working twice as long.

Wayne, your best friend at work, says flatly that he will not do it. "I'm not coming in tomorrow. I am going to the ball game with my kids." Barbara, Dwight, and Bob agree. "We just can't do it. We've given enough and there is nothing more to give. My loyalty has just run out."

You are the senior accountant in the group, so it is your job to tell Mr. Schauffer the bad news.

Questions about the case

1 Did the group act wisely? What do you think will happen to them?
2 More importantly, what recourse do they have if Schauffer fires them? Who can they turn to?
3 How can an organization ensure the support of its members both in times of crisis and during routine functioning?
4 What sorts of checks exist in organizations to prevent the arbitrary abuse of power?

Additional readings

Adams, J. S. Toward an understanding of inequity. *Journal of Abnormal and Social Psychology,* 1963, **67,** 422–436.

* Child, J. Organizational structure and strategies of control. *Administrative Science Quarterly,* 1972, **17,** 163–177.

* Denhardt, R. B. The organization as a political system. *Western Political Quarterly,* 1971, **24,** 675–686.

French, J. R. P., Jr., Israel, J., and Aas, D. An experiment of participation in a Norwegian factory. *Human Relations,* 1960, **13,** 3–19.

* Hart, D. K. Social equity, justice and the equitable administrator. *Public Administration Review,* 1974, **34,** 3–11.

* Knowles, H. P., & Saxberg, B. O. Human relations and the nature of man. *Harvard Business Review,* 1963, **41,** 153–157.

Lehman, E. W. Toward a macrosociology of power. *American Sociological Review,* 1969, **34,** 453–465.

** Pateman, C. *Participation and democratic theory.* Cambridge: Cambridge University Press, 1970.

** Rawls, J. *A theory of justice.* Cambridge: The Belknap Press, Harvard University Press, 1971.

** Vollmer, H. M. *Employee rights and employee relations.* Berkeley: University of California Press, 1960.

Wildavsky, A. The political economy of efficiency. *Public Administration Review,* 1966, **26,** 292–310.

** Wolin, S. S. *Politics and vision.* Boston: Little, Brown, 1960.

*Possible reading for students

**Review of literature or comprehensive source material

18

Organizational outlook

The best prophet of the future is the past.   Lord Byron

We are constantly involved in the process of predicting the future. In most cases this is a personal activity: I wonder who will win the Super Bowl? Will my daughter get into the college of her choice? I wonder what we will have for dinner? We are justifiably concerned with what will happen to us and those around us for whom we care.

At a somewhat different level of analysis is an attempt to predict what will happen to our society in the future and especially the world of work and institutional activity. Will there be more jobs? Will machines replace people? Will government control of our lives increase? These are important questions about the evolution of work and organizational involvement.

The process of predicting our personal and societal futures is in many cases the same. We try to look at how things used to be and how they are today. From a review of these different times we infer trends and note certain changes. These trends and changes are then used to make projections into the future.

Of course, there is frequently some error in these predictions. Our knowledge of present and past circumstances may be inaccurate. But the more familiar we are with the topic, the more accurate our assessments are likely to be. Unanticipated future events may also upset our predictions (a key football player may get hurt warming up for the game or a new breakthrough in computer technology may occur). So, our estimates are really just calculated guesses, given the information at hand. Some people are better predictors than others, and some predictions are more likely than others. The key differences depend upon (1) our actual knowledge, (2) our experience with the topic, and (3) the stability of the environment in which the events are predicted to take place. If we have good facts, if we know the area, and if the environment is relatively stable and consistent, we should be able to make some fairly accurate predictions.

Given that introduction, we can proceed to the purpose of this chapter—the prediction of how organizations will look in the future, the problems they are likely to face, and some possible solutions to these problems. For some of these topics we have excellent information. We can document fairly clearly the changes in population size, age, education, and minority classifications. We can also describe with some accuracy the technological changes (e.g., computers) that have recently evolved, and some policy changes that have occurred in organizations (e.g., an international emphasis). On the other hand, changes in personal values and attitudes are a little more difficult to pin down. Much depends on whom you talk to and when you talk to them. In any case, we will try to project the present information about people, jobs, organizations, and values into the future.

We will also describe some current problems within organizations. Problems with drugs, labor unrest, turnover, theft, and discriminatory policies will be included. There are some fairly good data for a few of these topics and some pretty poor data for the rest. However, we will try to document the problems and their potential impact on future organizational life and to suggest remedies where they seem relevant.

Finally, we will attempt to place all these predictions within the framework with which the book began. There will be an analysis of our assumptions about the basic nature of human beings and the broad organization theories that support these assumptions. Some authors are very optimistic about the future. They see a time of growth, expansion, rising standards of living, and interpersonal harmony. Other writers predict the opposite: organizations will retrench, contract, and be characterized by conflict and competition. The position that one takes on these issues partially determines the recommendations that are made with respect to how we can prepare for the future. And, in the final analysis, it is today's recommendations that will determine how well we cope with tomorrow's problems.

Areas of change

Change doth unknit the tranquil strength of man.   Matthew Arnold

---

We are faced with a world in which changes are occurring at an increasingly accelerated pace. Medicine, physics, engineering, biology, and numerous other fields are engulfed in a knowledge explosion. Communications have become instantaneous (via satellite), and television allows us to view events live all over the world. We are constantly bombarded with new products, ideas, and innovations. We are a highly mobile society, in terms of jobs and places of residence.

What does all this change do to us? Well, the clinical evidence suggests it is not good. The greater the changes in our lives, the greater the stress and mental and physical illness. Coping with change has become a major component of our everyday existence.

The same thing is happening to organizations. They must assimilate new types of people and new knowledge, technology, and values. Having "well-informed" people requires attention to training and management-development programs.

Dealing fairly with minorities and women requires attention to programs of selection and appraisal. New technology also affects training and communication systems. In the next few sections we will try to document what sorts of changes are likely to occur in the people, jobs, organizations, and values of the future.

The labor force

The initial concept to point out is that the composition of the labor force is changing in two major ways. First, the mix of people looking for jobs will differ, and second, the characteristics of these people (age, education) will also differ. These changes will have a number of implications which we will discuss.

Types of people. Blacks and other nonwhites have traditionally encountered more obstacles than whites in entering the labor force and in attaining good jobs. Their salaries and status have been comparatively poor. Advancement has been slower, and there has been difficulty in gaining entrance to unions.

The data on changes in these inequities is only slightly encouraging. It is true that the number of nonwhites working has risen over the last 20 years by almost 3 million people. These are impressive gains. However, the percentage of nonwhite employees still lags behind the percentage of nonwhite people in the population (14.7 percent). Over the last 20 years the number of working minorities has risen from about 10.7 percent of the labor force to 11.3 percent. It is expected that this trend will continue and that the legal enforcement of equal opportunity guidelines will hasten this increase in minority members.

Women are also expected to increase their demands for employment and high-status jobs. The data show more dramatic changes for women than for minorities. In 1950, women were employed in only three jobs out of ten. In 1972, this figure rose to almost four jobs out of ten. These increases have occurred mostly for very young women (16 to 24) or older women (45 to 60). But again, these data are somewhat misleading. While there has been an increase in numbers of jobs going to women, the quality of these jobs is still relatively poor. Table 18-1 shows some figures taken from a survey reported by the Department of Labor. These data clearly show large discrepancies between the types of jobs held by men and women. The overall picture, therefore, is that there will be increases in the total number of women and minorities employed as well as in the status level of their jobs.

Table 18-1. Comparison of Jobs Held by Men and Women

Dimension	Men	Women
Percent of labor force	60.0%	40.0%
Income (full time)	$8,966	$5,323
Number of clerks	6.7%	33.9%
Professional jobs	13.7%	14.5%
Managers	14.6%	5.0%
Unemployed	4.2%	5.5%

SOURCE: United States Department of Labor. *Handbook of labor statistics,* 1975.

Table 18-2. Age Characteristics of the Labor Force Reported in Percentages

Year	16–19	20–24	25–34	35–44	45–54	55–64	65 and over	
				Age				
1960	7.3	10.6	20.9	23.1	20.7	13.0	4.4	= 100%
1973	9.7	15.0	22.7	18.4	18.7	12.3	3.3	= 100%

SOURCE: United States Department of Labor. *Handbook of labor statistics*, 1975.

Characteristics of the people. More than just the types of people will be different; there are some characteristics of all people employed that seem to be changing. In general, the work force will be younger, better educated, highly mobile, and live in urban areas. There is much data to support these inferences.

The figures on age are rather interesting. In the late 1940s and through most of the 1950s there was a great baby boom. Many children were born, and these young people are now entering the labor market in increasing numbers. The prediction for the near future, therefore, is that the average employee will become younger in age, since the percentage of youthful people will increase. Table 18-2 shows some labor statistics on these trends. However, in the late 1960s and 1970s we began to have a slowdown in the birthrate. This suggests that in 15 to 20 years the average age will begin to get higher rather than lower. Thus, in the near future we will have a more youthful labor composition, while in the more distant future the average age will increase.

The level of formal education also seems to be increasing. In 1960, only about 40 percent of the work force had a high school diploma or any college training. In 1973, this figure rose to almost 50 percent, and the prediction is that this trend will continue. People attempting to find jobs will have greater knowledge and skills than ever before. When one considers the types of problems with which these people will have to cope, it is somewhat comforting to realize that they should be as well prepared to face them as any previous group.

The type of education is also changing. There have been increases in the number of junior colleges and increases in the expenditures for private schools, home study, and adult education. There is a greater emphasis on the practical nature of education, and more types of educational activities are being recognized and developed.

All these trends are related to both occupational choice and success. The competition for higher-paying, higher-status jobs will be greater. For example, in 1950 there were 75 physicians for every 100,000 people in the country. This figure will almost double by 1980. And not only do better-educated people get better jobs, but they are also more successful in these jobs. If we use promotion as a criterion, we find that people with greater levels of formal education are more likely to attain higher-level jobs than those with less education.

Finally, we are still becoming an urban society. While this trend is not as pronounced as it used to be, it still exists. In 1950, 62.5 percent of the U.S. population lived in urban areas. This figure was 66.7 percent in 1960 and 68.6 percent in 1970. While there is some movement away from inner cities, we are still seeing more people living on smaller amounts of land. Some predictions suggest that by the year 2000 fully 90 percent of the people in this country will live on 2 percent of the land.

To summarize, we have projected current trends to suggest that (1) there will be more minorities and women wanting jobs, (2) they will want better jobs, (3) the average age will decline and then increase, (4) the education level will continue to rise, and (5) most people will live in urban areas. These changes will create a number of challenges with regard to the selection, training, appraisal, and reward administration of organizations.

Organizational characteristics

Not only are the people changing, but the organizations are changing as well. The pace of technological innovation has created new problems for systems of planning and control. Automation and computers have shifted the emphasis from human labor to humans interacting with and servicing machines. And finally, our great increases in travel and communication capacities have led to a great expansion of the activities with which organizations are concerned. All these topics require some further elaboration.

The pace of change. Many people describe the last 50 years as a knowledge explosion. Our universities and educational institutions have turned out an incredible number of highly trained people. In terms of sheer numbers, one has to realize that probably over 80 percent of all the social and physical scientists who have ever lived are living today. This great influx of human talent has had a major impact on our organizational life.

One consequence has been that knowledge in any field changes very quickly. Because of the vast resources allocated to education and technological innovation, any area of knowledge is both rapidly changing *and* increasing in size. A direct result of this expansion and accelerated change is that it is hard for any individual to grasp a whole area of knowledge. One is no longer an expert in physics or engineering, but rather in some specialty of physics or engineering. Instead of employing one person to do a particular job, it may be necessary to have two or three.

Another consequence of this knowledge explosion is the problem of human and material obsolescence. It has become increasingly difficult to keep abreast of the changes in one's field, be it structural engineering or personnel. The information that one learns in college may be out of date in 5 years. It is a terribly frustrating experience for many professionals to invest large amounts of time and money on an education that only helps them for a short time.

The same process occurs for the material or technological aspects of the organization. New machines or products are invented, are useful, and are then discarded. Something better comes along. In many cases companies (such as the large automobile manufacturers) actually plan for their product to be obsolete every few years in the hopes that people will purchase one of their new products.

Organizations have typically responded to these problems in a variety of ways. The research and development departments have, of course, grown in importance. New innovations in the marketplace can mean the difference between success and failure. There have also been technological devices developed to handle this expansion of knowledge, such as computers, which brings us to the second area of organizational change: the increased emphasis on technology.

Technological innovation. Mass production has been the foundation of American industry for 75 years. Our high standard of living has largely been based on our ability to produce large numbers of goods relatively inexpensively. The foundation for this productivity was originally the idea of mechanization, where machines were developed to do the work of a man or a woman. One hundred years ago the average employee worked about twice as long as employees today and produced about one-tenth as much per hour. Our increase in productivity has been substantial.

After mechanization came automation. We developed machines that run themselves. They can start, stop, correct, and repair themselves. The only human element required may be certain maintenance functions. While many people realized that these changes would increase available goods, few realized that jobs would increase rather than decrease. In the fields where technological innovation has occurred, there is still a strong demand for new technicians and for professional and managerial jobs as well as clerical jobs. Only the demand for farm workers and unskilled laborers has decreased in the last 10 years, and the latter by only 2 percent. New technology increases the demand for greater innovation; it seems to feed on itself.

Perhaps the most revolutionary technological change has been the development and use of computers. In the last 30 years the computer has become a dominating force in technological innovation; some people have argued that it ranks right up there with the wheel, the steam engine, the telephone, and canned beer.

The major difference between the computer and other forms of mechanization or automation is the fact that the computer is not just an extension of human physical capacities. It increases our ability to search for, process, organize, and manipulate information. And it does it with lightning speed.

It is truly an awesome machine. The computer can correct and control its output. Like the human mind, the computer can be taught to engage in very complex processes with a degree of flexibility and generality that is impossible for other machines. They can even play chess.

Given our discussion about the knowledge explosion, the emphasis on computer technology is likely to increase in the future. With increases in the size of the population, in the amount of change, and in the demand for planning, and with a shortage of people to handle these problems, the computer will play an increasingly important role in organizational decision making. The computer can store millions of items of information and yet find them and reproduce them in less than a second. Millions of simple mathematical operations can also be performed in seconds. Payrolls, business accounting, production control, and forecasting are simple tasks. Operations that took months take minutes. While resistance to these changes has in some cases been intense, it is beyond doubt that the computer is here to stay. We need it to cope successfully with the turbulent, changing environment which faces us.

Organizational expansion. The last major change in organizations that we will discuss is their propensity to expand their activities. In the last 30 years we have witnessed numerous companies diversifying their goals. The development of large-scale conglomerates is common. By penetrating different market segments, the company enjoys a number of benefits. The company's stability may be increased by the fact that while one product may do poorly, other products will do well. A conglomerate can also purchase equipment and services from its subsidiaries and diversify its selling and marketing capabilities.

This increased scope of interest has occurred in nonprofit and public organizations as well. Universities and hospitals for example now place an increasing emphasis on research, public service, and community involvement as well as teaching and helping sick people. Political entities at the local, state, and national level are concerned with pollution, crime, employment, health, food, drug rehabilitation, communication, energy, education, housing, and almost everything else. It is a far cry from the days when they collected taxes, paved the roads, picked up the garbage, and employed the cop on the beat.

One final area in which we have witnessed expansion has been the growth of multinational corporations. The prediction is that by the year 2000 more than half of the world's business will be done by international firms. This trend is already apparent. Since 1938, the United States has increased its imports from $2180 million (value in U.S. dollars) to over $35,000 million. And the exports have increased from $3064 million (value in U.S. dollars) to over $12,000 million. The investments have gone both ways. It is not just the United States that is investing abroad. Many foreign countries are setting up offices in the United States, especially the countries in the Middle East that have large cash reserves as a result of their income from oil sales.

So, not only does today's manager have to be able to function within an institution with multiple goals, it may also be necessary to understand and work within the boundaries of other cultures. With an increase in nationalistic fervor, we have found that international investments are a little more risky than we originally thought and perhaps a little more difficult to accomplish than previously was true. However, the prediction is that these activities will continue to increase and that we will have to adjust to this international atmosphere.

Changes in the nature of work and jobs

A number of changes will take place in the working conditions within organizations and the types of jobs which are available. The most obvious change over the last 100 years has been from an emphasis on farm products and produce to manufacturing and then from manufacturing to service-related jobs. Already the United States employs more than half of its people in jobs that are concerned with the production of services rather than goods, with state, local, and federal government agencies making a major contribution to this figure. By 1980, the agricultural sector of the economy should account for less than 5 percent of the jobs and manufacturing for less than 25 percent.

The implications of such changes are interesting. They suggest that large manufacturing companies will be a somewhat less potent force in our society.

Also, every company and organization will need to be increasingly aware of its political relationships. Government expansion may increase its regulation and control over business and nonbusiness organizations.

Besides the changes in the types of jobs, there will also be changes in the importance of work itself. These changes will be reflected in a variety of ways. First, the total number of hours or days worked is on the decline. In the last 30 years the average number of hours worked has decreased from about 42 hours a week to 38 hours a week. There are also estimates that anywhere from 2000 to 4000 companies are using some sort of modified workweek. This reduced working time means that individuals will have more free time and leisure time than ever before. These types of changes will continue to increase the emphasis on industries designed to deal with leisure (e.g., transportation, resorts, and communication media).

The decrease in the time allocated to work will come in conjunction with changes in career patterns and mobility. There is some evidence that people are changing career patterns more frequently and at a later age than they had previously. Because of social mobility and easy access to training or education, many people have changed their goals and aspirations after a number of years. The trend is away from step-by-step professional development or careers where one's future is planned from ages 18 to 65.

Changes in attitudes and values

> All their devices for cheapening labour simply
> resulted in increasing the burden of labour.   William Morris

A major part of the crisis which our future organizations will face is one of attitudes and values. Organizations in general and the business community in particular have evolved a set of values over the last 200 years which is now being seriously questioned. The underlying assumptions about why people join organizations and what they expect those institutions to provide are changing. This next section will attempt to describe the old value premises as well as the more recent attitudes about organizations and the world of work.

Traditional values. In the beginning of the book we discussed the fact that organizing was a process whereby people joined together in order to obtain their goals. The idea of *joint commitment* was part of organizing. In making a decision to enter an organization, an individual is relinquishing some of his or her own freedom in such a way that the group (the individual included) will be able to reach its objectives.

This idea of commitment is a central theme in the management literature.[1] It is one of the basic values on which organizing rests, and employees are frequently evaluated on a commitment criterion. Questions such as ''Will she work over-

---

[1]See L. E. Birdzell, Jr. The moral basis of the business system, *Journal of Contemporary Business,* Summer 1975, 75–87.

time?" "Does she come in on Saturdays?" "Does she come early and leave late?" "Will he drop what he's doing and help out?" "Will he entertain a prospective job candidate?" "Will he skip his lunch?" are often asked. Most managers believe that this commitment is crucial for organizational effectiveness.

A second value premise is the idea of a system of free exchange unfettered by government control. In fact, much of modern history can be described in terms of the constant conflict between the economically productive and the politically powerful. Because of this historical antagonsim, the business community in the United States has invariably resisted almost any form of legislation that restricted its activities.

An excellent record of these confrontations was presented by Theodore Levitt in 1968.[2] He documents how, over the years, the business community has opposed almost every intervention suggested by the federal government. These battles include the Sherman Antitrust Act, the Federal Reserve Act, the National Park Services Act, the Child Labor Acts, the Securities Exchange Act, the Fair Labor Standards Act, the Old Age and Survivors Insurance Benefits Act, the Federal Housing Acts, the Aid to Dependent Children Act, the Poverty Program, and many others. This list is so long that it seems as if the business community says no first and thinks about it later.

In some sense this behavioral reaction is the best illustration of the strength of the value system that opposes regulation. While most observers would agree in retrospect that business and organizations in general have really profited from much of this legislation, they still hold strongly to their value premise. They blame their failures and problems on politicians, bureaucrats, social do-gooders, and the mass media. It is always the imposition of external forces which hinders their effectiveness. They would succeed if they were only left alone.

A third value that operates quite strongly is one of equity. Business morality has always included an idea of fair exchange: one receives benefits commensurate with one's contribution. What is commensurate is partly determined by what the contribution (i.e., skills, training, effort) will bring on the market. But the idea behind the system is that one should receive tangible rewards as a function of performance.

Unfortunately, as we have discussed throughout the book, organizational participants seem to believe in this value more in principle than in practice. Performance-appraisal systems are often poorly developed, and there is some justified feeling that top-level executives to some extent set their own pay (which is often 10 to 20 times the salary made by lower-level employees). These facts frequently undermine the support for the equity value.

Finally, and perhaps most important, is the value of technical rationality. It is the goal of all organizations to minimize input and maximize output. For the business community it is the central focus of activity. People do not invest in concerns that they believe are going to lose money (unless they need some sort of tax break), nor do they continue to invest in companies that are currently losing money. The responsibility of management is to figure out the most efficient

[2]T. Levitt. Why business always loses, *Harvard Business Review*, March–April 1968, 81–89.

means to the most productive goal. It is rational, means-ends-oriented, and concerned with cost effectiveness. Rationality is the basic value upon which organizing is built.

Throughout the early history of our country the above set of values was widely held by most citizens, both at the upper and lower levels of organizational involvement. The Protestant ethic reigned supreme. In recent years, however, some broad social and cultural changes have occurred which have modified some values and created some new ones. People's attitudes toward organizations and jobs are different.

Attitudes toward organizations. One general change has been the decreasing role that all formal institutions are playing in our lives. Religion has decreased as a central force in determining values and has been replaced by what is frequently described as situation ethics. The calvinistic emphasis on hard work as a means of salvation and material success as an indication of righteous activity no longer dominates our religious beliefs.

Traditionally, religion, community, and family were all integrated and served as the foundation for the development of values. Today, most of us live in urban centers with nuclear families. Divorce has increased, as have new living arrangements between males and females. Church attendance is down.

What is taking the place of these institutions? Where are we learning our values? The answer seems to be that we get a little bit from everywhere. Certainly schools, the media (TV), and the government are playing a more important role. This process had led to a proliferation of values, a broadening of what is acceptable, and an increasing heterogeneity of life-styles.

The breaking down of the old values and the multiplicity of new ones has had an important impact on how people view organizations. The breaking down of old traditional attitudes is apparent in a number of surveys.[3] For example, in 1973, 1974, and 1975, random samples of Americans were surveyed, and the following responses were received:

1 56 percent said they did not get a fair shake from American business.
2 69 percent believed that "things have pretty seriously gotten off on the wrong track in this country."
3 65 percent agreed that business will ignore the public's needs in order to make a profit.
4 75 percent thought too much power was concentrated in the hands of a few large companies.

Not only are these absolute figures startling, but they also represent changes. When compared with similar questions asked in 1966 it is clear that people are becoming more pessimistic about the values of large organizations and business. Supporting this argument are some data which show that the percentage of people having confidence in business leaders has decreased from 55 percent in 1966 to 27 percent in 1973. The figures for financial leaders went from 57 to 39

[3]See R. B. Wirthlin. Public perceptions of the American business system: 1966–1975, *Journal of Contemporary Business*, Summer 1975, 1–14.

percent and for the executive branch of the government from 41 to 27 percent. There is a lack of confidence in and support for these powerful and public figures who have traditionally served as models for value development.

Combined with this general level of distrust is a challenge to the values of efficiency and rationality. Many people have argued that profits fail to reflect compassion and concern for human dignity. The central thrust of this position is that organizations should have a larger concern than their corporate balance sheet. The physical and social environment should be of equal importance. The responsibility of large organizations is not just to be effective, but also to serve the society in which they reside.

Perhaps the most readily apparent example of these changes in values is the interest in the preservation of our physical environment. The quality of the air, water, and land around us is a topic of increasing concern. The gas crisis

There is an increasing awareness and concern about the impact of of our society on our environment. *(By permission of Eastman Kodak Company.)*

probably more than any one event brought home the fact that the earth's resources are limited. The future promises to be one where there will be constant shortages of food, energy, and natural minerals and materials. In the past, organizations have been rather cavalier about what they have destroyed, discarded as waste, and polluted. Legal and social pressure has limited many of these activities and will continue to do so.

But, as some wise philosopher once said, "There ain't no free lunch." To maintain a social and physical environment of high quality takes work and costs money, and it is not always clear that people are willing to make the sacrifices that are necessary. If you want a car that does not pollute the air, you may have to drive less, simply because the attachments that process the exhaust make the car less efficient—that is, they use more gas. And gas is something we do not have a large amount of. If you want a source of energy that is abundant, such as nuclear energy or coal, you may have to live with the risks of pollution caused by the development and use of these resources.

These are not easy choices. Most people want to maintain their standard of living and have their jobs and the environment be pleasant as well. It is unlikely that both goals can be reached, and in fact, many people believe that we will need to sacrifice one for the other. Whatever the solution, one thing is clear: the pressure on large organizations to become more socially responsible will increase.

Attitudes about work. Combined with this general malaise and negative feeling about our organizations are some changes in the attitudes and values people hold about their work. The overall perspective is one of increasing expectations and a desire for challenging work in the face of what appears to be a depersonalizing, less meaningful work setting.

One must remember that the average worker will have had more education and be used to a higher standard of living than ever before. People are expecting to have more material goods than ever before. The mass media constantly exhorts us to buy, to have, to own, to spend; buy now, pay later, get ahead, keep up with your friends, credit available—all are common slogans. With the increase in leisure time already described, there will be an increased demand for high-paying jobs.

Coupled with this demand will be the expectation that jobs be meaningful, challenging, and interesting. A survey in 1972 of 1500 blue-collar workers reported that interesting work, an opportunity for personal development, and a chance for promotion were more important than job security or being asked to do extra work. Data from college students show that they value jobs that are challenging, compassionate, and helping over those that are just financially rewarding.

The problem for organizations is to discover how to respond to these demands in an environment where physical and financial resources will be more difficult to obtain and where size and technology have depersonalized rather than personalized many jobs. It is hard to give people more money when there is less of it to go around, and it is hard to make highly repetitive, standardized jobs interesting and exciting. This is one of the crucial challenges for our future.

*Don't worry about it, fellows. At least we won't have
to deal with this one when the recall letters go out.*

Some people report that many workers in today's complex organizations do not really care about the quality of their work.

Current problems

All the above changes are going to produce problems not only in the future, but also right now. The heterogeneity of the work force has resulted in heated debate over the issues of racial and sex discrimination in selection and promotion as well as the issue of quotas. The changing attitudes and general disaffection with our institutions has resulted in problems of theft, dishonesty, and white-collar crime. Some people believe the lack of a strong value orientation or moral code contributes to the increases in drug abuse and alcoholism. And, finally, the general lack of commitment to our organizational goals may have resulted in increased strikes, union militancy, and labor unrest. The following section will discuss these issues in more detail.

Employment

In March 1972, President Nixon signed into law the Equal Opportunity Act which finally provided the federal government with some effective means of enforcing equal employment opportunity. This act was in fact a series of amendments to the Civil Rights Act of 1964, and it allows the federal government to prohibit all forms of employment discrimination based on race, religion, color, sex, or national origin. The Equal Employment Opportunity Commission, which has the power to enforce this act, may now institute civil actions to eliminate discriminatory practices and has moved to do so. The act provided muscle to earlier legislation.

Perhaps the most fundamental concept of the act is that intent to discriminate or not to discriminate is irrelevant in terms of enforcement. What constitutes acceptable evidence is simply whether actions by the employer (e.g., hiring, promoting, firing) systematically excluded or discriminated against protected subgroups. If a selection device or procedure systematically screens out some minority group, it is the responsibility of the employer to prove that the device or procedure assesses characteristics that are in fact related to *actual performance on the job*. If that cannot be done, the employer is in violation of the law.

Besides the nondiscriminatory enforcement function of this legislation, there is an affirmative-action side. That is, the federal government not only wants organizations not to discriminate, it wants them to actively pursue women and minority employment. This position is taken partly for its moral correctness and partly because the data show rather convincingly that women and minorities are underrepresented in high-paying, high-status jobs. When minorities and women with the same training as white males are compared to the white males on criteria such as pay and status, the data are again clear: women and minorities fare poorly.

This legislation has caused quite an uproar in professional and business circles. Most organizations want to respond and have tried to respond in good faith. The problem is how to respond. There are at least four different positions that one could take: (1) *passive nondiscrimination,* where the organization simply hires the best-qualified candidate that applies for the job, (2) *pure affirmative action,* where the organization actively seeks out and encourages minority applications and then chooses the best candidates, (3) *affirmative action with preferential hiring,* where women and minorities are actually favored and hired because they are acceptable, even though they might not be the best-qualified applicant, and (4) *quotas,* where the organization tries to match the number of minorities employed with the percentage in the work force.[4]

While the federal government has said it would discourage the use of quotas, it has also seemed to discourage strategies 1 and 2. When it investigaes allegations of discriminatory practices, the evidence it seems to weigh most heavily is the number of women and minorities actually employed, not the selection process. The effect has been that many organizations are in fact employing strategies 3 and 4.

The controversy over this activity is still unresolved. It can and has been argued that both strategies 3 and 4 will result in lowered standards, that people with lower potential for good performance are being hired. Part of the legal interpretation made by the federal government is that minorities and women shall not be required to possess higher qualifications than those of the *least-qualified*

[4]D. Seligman. How "equal opportunity" turned into employment quotas, *Fortune,* March 1975.

Women are increasing their numbers in technical and managerial positions. *(By permission of the Boeing Company.)*

incumbent. What this suggests is that if we have made a mistake in hiring in the past (for example, have given tenure to an incompetent professor), women and minorities need not be more qualified than this person. Many minorities and nonminorities alike are uncomfortable with this position.

However, the problem will not go away. The question to be resolved is how we can correct the inequities that exist and do what is morally right: provide equal opportunity for employment and advancement for everyone. We will continue to wrestle with this problem in the future.

General lack of commitment

We mentioned that people in general seem to be less committed to organizational goals and institutional leaders. These negative attitudes are apparent in a number of ways. First, the United States between 1968 and 1974 lost 1500 days per 1000 workers because of strikes or lockouts. Only Italy and Canada have worse records. The data for countries such as Sweden (62 days per 1000 workers) and West Germany (74 days per 1000 workers) are startling. In 1972 alone there were 5010 work stoppages in the United States involving 1,714,000 employees. Over 27 million days of work were lost. Clearly, the workers were unhappy about their conditions of employment.

The public's reaction to unions has become increasingly more negative. For example, a survey published by the Opinion Research Corporation in 1972 found the following:

1 71 percent opposed the continual growth of unions.
2 68 percent think strikes hurt everybody too much. (Among union members 61 percent agree.)
3 68 percent blame higher prices and living costs on unions. (57 percent of the union members agree.)
4 62 percent believe there should be greater government control of unions.

But unions are not going to disappear. They are part of the American system, and they play an important role. The problem that faces us, however, is that projections for the future are not optimistic with respect to continued growth and economic expansion. If we are faced with a situation where everyone wants more but there is less to go around, we must learn how to distribute these rewards in an equitable fashion without the debilitating strikes and loss of productivity.

Some other signs of malaise are less formal and readily apparent than strikes, but may be equally expensive. There is some evidence that theft, dishonesty, and white-collar crime are on the increase. These acts may take the form of padding the expense account, pocketing some loose change, using office supplies for personal activities, reselling company property, and many others. Estimates of employee theft are as high as $10 billion annually, and these costs are passed along to the consumer of goods and services in the form of higher prices.

Coupled with the theft problem is the occasional act of actual sabotage. There are reports that in some cases dissatisfied employees have made mistakes on purpose which ruin machinery, cause defective products to be distributed, and endanger the lives of others. The most well-known of these cases has occurred in the automobile industry, where employees admitted (anonymously) to acts of sabotage.

The challenge for the future is to discover ways in which these negative attitudes can be reduced and commitment restored. At the minimum we must openly and actively discuss these problems, because they are bound to increase.

Social problems

The final set of problems has to do with the issues of alcoholism and drug abuse. Both activities are on the rise in organizational settings, and some managers see them as the major personnel problem in today's industrial setting. It is estimated that there are perhaps 9 million alcoholics in the United States, and that half of them are employed. Besides the alcoholic, who is defined as the chronic drinker

Alcoholism is a significant problem in today's organizations.
(By permission of University of Washington Daily.)

whose addiction is eventually incapacitating, there is the "problem drinker" who is not addicted but for whom alcohol produces disruptive behavior. Some estimates suggest that 5 percent of the labor force falls into one of these two categories.

The losses to American business are computed to be $10 billion annually.[5] Heavy drinkers have higher rates of absenteeism and turnover. They have more accidents. They work more slowly and their judgment is impaired. Morale is low and efficiency is reduced.

Similar figures and problems are cited for drug abuse. More companies are reporting that they have employees with drug problems. Drug abuse seems to be more recent than the concern about alcohol, partly because it is only within the last 15 years that drugs of all kinds (e.g., stimulants, tranquilizers, marijuana, barbiturates, and opiates) have become readily available to the interested buyer. Many of the young people entering the job market have used drugs, and some will continue to do so. Also, there is no longer the widely held assumption that all drugs are bad, addictive, and eventually self-destructive.

To summarize, the changing composition of the work force, the general dissatisfaction with organizational life, and the greater dependence on drugs have caused some serious problems for today's society. These problems are likely to increase, and somehow we must develop effective means to combat them. The next section covers some possible solutions.

[5]See The rising toll of alcoholism: New steps to combat it, *U.S. News and World Report,* October 29, 1973, **75,** 45–48.

Some possible solutions

One always feels hesitant about predicting the future. It is perhaps even more presumptuous to try to suggest solutions to future problems. However, as we mentioned above, some of the predicted changes in organizations are occurring right now, and some possible remedies have been implemented. Therefore, the foundation for our suggested solutions comes from today's experience. We have learned much about what can go wrong and about some corrective mechanisms. This section discusses some ways in which organizations may better deal with the problems of people, management, technology, and the formal structure of the organization.

Personnel

One major problem with which we must deal is the increasing heterogeneity of the characteristics and motivation of the work force. People of different ages, sex, and minority groups will be employed at all levels of the organization. Education levels will increase. People will pursue multiple careers.

One solution to the educational and aspirational changes will be increased attention to career development, adult education, and in-service education. Some form of continuing education may in fact become part of the job. In this way, employees can keep abreast of the changes in their fields as well as prepare themselves for new and perhaps different types of jobs.

The heterogeneity problem demands more flexible employment, placement, and reward procedures. Organizations should not be reactive with respect to discriminatory policies; they should be proactive. They should set up committees or subunits with the express purpose of vigorous affirmative action. Top management should be vocally and behaviorally committed to such activity. Where racist or sexist attitudes or behavior exist, training and education should be provided to change such attitudes. Every step must be taken to ensure that systems of selection, promotion, recognition, and reward are fair and equitable.

Another solution concerns the administration of rewards. Different types of people will want different types of rewards from their jobs. Management must be more creative and flexible in what rewards are used and how they are administered. Flexitime and cafeteria-style compensation plans are two examples we have already described. Some other suggestions are to allow people more flexibility in how they distribute their time to different tasks. Other suggestions are to let people participate in various bonus systems as a result of good performance and to let people try out other jobs to see how they like them and to allow them to assess their interest and expertise at a new task.

Management must also be prepared for the future. The pressure on the manager to be all things to all people will be immense. He or she will be expected to be an expert in his or her own field; this will require training and continuing education. The manager will need to be able to deal effectively with people from different parts of the organization; this will require knowledge of psychology, the social sciences, and interpersonal skills. He or she will have to understand technological innovations; this will necessitate further training and development. Finally, the manager will be faced with increasing change; this will demand an ability to tolerate ambiguity and successfully cope with change.

The problems with theft, dishonesty, and drugs will also require innovative solutions. While it is probably beyond the capability or responsibility of the organization to "cure" someone of alcoholism or to rehabilitate people with respect to theft, it is not beyond its capacity to recognize the problem and deal with it rationally and helpfully. Perhaps the first step is open recognition that the problems exist.

With respect to drug abuse (including alcoholism), organizations need to assess the extent of the problem and provide information to employees about how to recognize that they are in trouble. A program designed to help users should be established along with an active attempt to discourage the sale and distribution of drugs on company property. While preemployment screening seems to do little good (mostly because drug abuse rarely shows up on one's record or is talked about), it may be possible to have companies report abuses to the local health department, where subsequent employers could request this information. While there are some legal issues here that are still unresolved, it is clear that the responsibility of the company is divided: the company has concern for the employee who is using drugs; it has concern for organizational morale and efficiency; and it has a concern and responsibility to society when it terminates someone for drug abuse.

Managers should be briefed and trained to recognize and understand the alcoholic or drug user. Specific symptoms should be illustrated. The problem of absenteeism, lack of efficiency, and low morale should be highlighted. Finally, it should be recognized that dependence upon drugs or alcohol is a health problem. The person needs medical attention. If the person fails to participate in or respond to such treatment, the person should be terminated. The responsibility of the employer is not infinite, nor should it be.

Most solutions to the problems of theft and dishonesty are negative sanctions: reprimands, dismissal, and so on. However, thieves are infrequently caught, and the sanctions are seldom applied. Some monitoring devices such as televisions, frequent patrols, undercover agents, and thorough inventories may reduce the problem. Some more positive suggestions are to show employees how theft directly affects their lives (e.g., reduces profits and their benefits) and to have management set a good example. The latter is important and should not be underestimated. If people believe that top-level management is dishonest, they will have no difficulty rationalizing their own behavior. With this in mind, managers should be openly and obviously beyond suspicion and above board in their activities. It helps to establish a climate of honesty.

To summarize, new training and development techniques will be needed to deal with the changing composition of the work force. Managers will need to be flexible with respect to rewards and their personal interactions. Drug abuse and dishonesty must be curbed through recognition of the problem and positive steps taken to correct it. Some techniques which show promise are available, and organizations must implement them if they want to successfully respond to these issues in the future.

Technology

The increasing size, sophisticated technology, and turbulent environments of organizations will produce a number of technological solutions. First, as we have suggested before, computers will come to play an increasingly important role. Decision analyses previously made by humans will be made by computers. The manager will be required to feed in the data and to provide the appropriate weights, such as how important various items of information are, but the computer will analyze the information and generate optimal solutions (given some model and a set of assumptions).

In the past 15 years the computer has mostly been used for fairly routine tasks of data storage, analysis, and retrieval. In the future, however, the computer will play a greater role in the decision process as described above. One area that has been pursued with some success is computerized forecasts of future events. Simulations of possible futures and their impact can be run in seconds. For example, given past and present data, the computer can forecast what might happen if the company introduced a new product on the market or diversified into a new area. Different sales and packaging strategies can be programmed, as can projected personnel costs. Having better information about the impact of present decisions on possible futures will increase the effectiveness of our current choices.

One final technological change which will be evident in most organizations involves communications devices. Faster, more effective devices for exchanging information will be developed. Cable television and special closed-circuit transmitters and telephones will be commonplace. An organization will have immediate access to its regional or international offices. Communications systems will be tied into the computer system so that data, information, and analysis can be readily transmitted. Conference telephone calls are common today, and conference by television will be common in the future. These devices will aid organizations in adjusting to the increasing pace of change.

Organizational design

Throughout the book we have stressed a contingency analysis of organizational design: certain structures work best in certain situations. The same will be true in the future. Thus, it is very difficult to predict whether all organizations or their activities will be decentralized or centralized, or whether a fewer or greater number of organizational levels will be established. What is most likely is that some areas may be centralized (e.g., planning and forecasting) while others will be decentralized (e.g., operational decisions, reward administration).

However, one point is clear: We will experiment with and adopt those structures which best allow us to cope with the changing technological and personal demands. We have had much experience with rigid, hierarchical, traditional organizational design. Innovative designs such as the matrix organization are more recent and unfamiliar. The matrix design emphasizes the use of project teams responsible for a specific task. Horizontal communication is emphasized over vertical contacts, and the project leader is relatively independent. This type of structure seems particularly appropriate for research and development organizations or for aerospace firms, such as Boeing, which obtain much of their work through contracts of relatively short term.

The design of future organizations will therefore be concerned with the appropriate fit between the particular service or product produced and the environment within which it must function. This perspective will demand an overall or systems-type view of the organization. Management will be knowledgeable about the problems of differentiation and integration and the systems- and contingency-theory ideas. General solutions across the board (e.g., more power to the people) will be replaced by the question of what is appropriate under a particular set of circumstances. This type of design activity will require sophistication and flexibility, but it seems to be the only real solution in sight.

General reassessment

The introductory chapters of the book discussed some underlying assumptions that organization theorists have about the nature of human motivation (i.e., positive, neutral, and negative) and how these underlying assumptions were reflected in both classical and current theoretical statements. We mentioned that systems and contingency approaches presently dominate the field and that their view of human nature is essentially neutral: people are not inherently good or evil. Most behavior is learned, not inherited.

The major implication of such an orientation is to switch our focus from internal causes of behavior to external explanations. One's environment is seen as the dominant factor in personal development. This fact suggests that people are changeable and adaptable. It is therefore possible for organizations to have a significant impact on the motivation, behavioral skills, and satisfaction of its employees. By changing the work environment we can influence the efficiency and well-being of organizational members.

Much of the book has centered on just what sorts of changes can be made. We have described techniques for increasing (1) satisfaction, (2) interpersonal attraction, (3) social influence, (4) motivation, (5) decision-making effectiveness, (6) leadership skills, and (7) the clarity of communications. Strategies to achieve these changes, such as job design, training, job analysis, and performance appraisal, have been reviewed. There is some reason to believe that if these techniques are properly utilized, we can be optimistic about the future quality of life within organizations.

But there is a catch. To implement these techniques takes time and costs money. Substantial commitment of resources is required. To develop a behavioral yardstick for performance appraisal takes the equivalent of two professionals working full time for 2 to 4 months. The question that still remains unanswered is whether these resources will be available.

Some experts on management believe that things will continue to improve. Koontz and Fulmer, for example, project a time of "continued growth" and "increasing affluence" in the United States.[6] We will continue to grow, expand, and live in increased harmony.

Others are not so optimistic. William Scott is one well-known management theorist who strongly disagrees with these assumptions.[7] He suggests that we are headed for a time of decay, scarcity, and conflict. He argues that our natural and financial resources are on the decline and that the challenge for the future is how to adjust to a no-growth economy. The competition for any resources will be intense, and various priorities will have to be reevaluated and justified.

My own prognosis is somewhere in between. I think that our increased technical knowledge and sophistication in the social sciences will permit us to increase the quality of our working life even in the face of decreasing resources and increased competition. The important elements for successful attainment of these goals are knowledge and commitment. We must inform people of what can be done to change behavior and to increase effectiveness. Once the information is available, the commitment must follow. The implementation of these techniques must receive the highest priority if it is to be effective. The challenge for us all is to demand considerable attention for behavioral issues and to insist on an allocation of resources that will produce high-quality programs. It if is not worth doing well, it is not worth doing.

Summary

This chapter reviewed some general organizational trends that should continue into the future. We discussed some areas of change, some current problems, and some possible solutions. The most important points are emphasized below:

AREAS OF CHANGE

1 The work force will include a greater number of women, minorities, and better-educated people.
2 Organizations will increase their dependence on automation and technological advances, especially computers.
3 Jobs will, in general, take less time and be more service-oriented.
4 People will increasingly want high-paying, challenging jobs, even though confidence, trust, and commitment may decrease.

CURRENT PROBLEMS

1 Drug abuse of all forms is increasing.
2 A lack of commitment is apparent from the data on dishonesty, theft, and sabotage.

[6]H. Koontz, & R. M. Fulmer. *A practical introduction to business.* Homewood, Ill.: Dorsey-Irwin, 1975, p. 645.

[7]W. G. Scott, Organization theory: A reassessment, *Academy of Management Journal,* 1974, **17,** 242–254.

3 Discrimination still exists for women and minorities.
4 There is significant disagreement between unions and management (as
   indicated by strikes) about political and economic rights.

POSSIBLE SOLUTIONS

1 Implement programs to hire, train, and actively help minorities and women
   to work in good jobs.
2 Introduce more flexibility and support for employee education, development, and mobility.
3 Use computers and other technological devices to replace boring, repetitive,
   and unfulfilling work.
4 Utilize forecasting and communication devices to help deal with the increasing rate of change in knowledge and the environment.
5 Design organizations to be flexible and adaptable.
6 Instruct managers in those behavioral techniques which will help them to
   have motivated and satisfied employees.

In short, the future of organizational involvement will be both trying and
exciting. There will be room for achievement, advancement, and self-actualization, as well as for boredom, apathy, and alienation. We have some control over
how that future will develop. Our task is to ensure that we make decisions today
that increase the potential for a more fulfilling tomorrow.

Discussion questions

1 What do you want your first job to be like? How do your criteria of a good job differ
   from what your parents wanted?
2 We are faced with some real dilemmas. For example, how can we increase our standard
   of living yet decrease our use of natural resources? Is this possible? How?
3 Another problem has to do with the types of jobs that will be available. We have an
   expanding work force (women, minorities, different age groups—young and old—who
   want to work). Yet there seem to be fewer exciting jobs, due to technology. What do we
   do? Is there a solution?

Case: Knowledge as fuel[8]

''The rate at which man has been storing up useful knowledge about himself and the
universe has been spiraling upward for 10,000 years. The rate took a sharp upward leap
with the invention of writing, but even so it remained painfully slow over centuries of time.
The next great leap forward in knowledge-acquisition did not occur until the invention of

[8]Taken from Alvin Toffler. *Future shock,* New York: Random House, 1970, 30–31.

movable type in the fifteenth century by Gutenberg and others. Prior to 1500, by the most optimistic estimates, Europe was producing books at a rate of 1000 titles per year. This means, give or take a bit, that it would take a full century to produce a library of 100,000 titles. By 1950, four and a half centuries later, the rate had accelerated so sharply that Europe was producing 120,000 titles a year. What once took a century now took only ten months. By 1960, a single decade later, the rate had made another significant jump, so that a century's work could be completed in seven and a half months. And, by the mid-sixties, the output of books on a world scale, Europe included, approached the prodigious figure of 1000 titles per *day*.

One can hardly argue that every book is a net gain for the advancement of knowledge. Nevertheless, we find that the accelerative curve in book publication does, in fact, crudely parallel the rate at which man discovered new knowledge. For example, prior to Gutenberg only 11 chemical elements were known. Antimony, the 12th, was discovered at about the time he was working on his invention. It was fully 200 years since the 11th, arsenic, had been discovered. Had the same rate of discovery continued, we would by now have added only two or three elements to the periodic table since Gutenberg. Instead, in the 450 years after his time, some seventy additional elements were discovered. And since 1900 we have been isolating the remaining elements not at a rate of one every two centuries, but of one every three years.

Furthermore, there is reason to believe that the rate is still rising sharply. Today, for example, the number of scientific journals and articles is doubling, like industrial production in the advanced countries, about every fifteen years, and according to biochemist Philip Siekevitz, "what has been learned in the last three decades about the nature of living beings dwarfs in extent of knowledge any comparable period of scientific discovery in the history of mankind." Today the United States government alone generates 100,000 reports each year, plus 450,000 articles, books and papers. On a world wide basis, scientific and technical literature mounts at a rate of some 60,000,000 pages a year.

The computer burst upon the scene around 1950. With its unprecedented power for analysis and dissemination of extremely varied kinds of data in unbelievable quantities and at mind-staggering speeds, it has become a major force behind the latest acceleration in knowledge-acquisition. Combined with other increasingly powerful analytical tools for observing the invisible universe around us, it has raised the rate of knowledge-acquisition to dumbfounding speeds.

Francis Bacon told us that 'Knowledge. . . . is power.' This can now be translated into contemporary terms. In our social setting, 'Knowledge is change'—and accelerating knowledge-acquisition, fueling the great engine of technology, means accelerating change."

Questions about the case

1 Can you think of areas where you have been aware of rapid change? What did you do about it?
2 Is change good or bad?
3 What can individuals do to help themselves cope with change? What can organizations do?

Additional readings

** Appley, A., & Angrist, A. W. *Management 2000*. Hamilton, N.Y.: American Foundation for Management Research, 1968.

* Argyris, C. Today's problems with tomorrow's organizations. *Journal of Management Studies*, 1967, **4**, 31–55.

* Bass, B. Organizational life in the 70's and beyond. *Personnel Psychology*, 1972, **25**, 19–30.

Boldgett, T. B. Borderline black—revisited. *Harvard Business Review*, 1972, **50**, 132–139.

Boulding, K. E. The future of personal responsibility. *American Behavioral Scientist*, 1972, **15**, 329–359.

Drucker, P. F. *The age of discontinuity*. New York: Simon and Schuster, 1969.

** Dunnette, M. D. (Ed.). *Work and nonwork in the year 2001*. Monterey, Calif.: Brooks/Cole, 1973.

Galbraith, J. K. *The new industrial state*. Boston: Houghton Mifflin, 1967.

** Kahn, H., & Weiner, A. J. *The year 2000: A framework for speculation of the next 33 years*. New York: MacMillan, 1967.

Leavitt, H. J., & Whisler, T. L. Management in the 1980's. *Harvard Business Review*, 1958, **36**, 41–48.

Megginson, L. C., & Chung, K. H. Human ecology in the twenty-first century. *Personnel Administration*, May–June 1970, 46–56.

Michael, D. N. Some long-range implications of computer technology for human behavior in organizations. *American Behavioral Scientist*, 1966, **9**, 29–35.

The 1970's: A second look. *Business Week*, February 16, 1974, 51.

* Peterson, J. E. INSIGHT: A management program of help for troubled people. Proceedings of the 1972 Annual Meeting of the Industrial Relations Research Association, 1972, 422–495.

Toffler, A. *Future shock*. New York: Random House, 1970.

* Walton, R. E. How to counter alienation in the plant. *Harvard Business Review*, November–December 1972, 70–81.

Weisskoff, F. B. Women's place in the labor market. *American Economic Review*, 1972, **62**, 161–165.

* Women: Last in, first out in Detroit. *Business Week*, February 16, 1974, 51.

* Possible reading for students
** Review of literature or comprehensive source material

NAME INDEX

NAME INDEX

Aagaard, A. K., 397
Aas, D., 441
Adams, J. S., 163, 441
Addington, D. W., 209
Aiken, M., 227
Ajzen, I., 121
Aldefer, C. P., 158–159, 393
Allee, W. C., 57
Allen, T. J., 227
Allport, Gordon W., 118
Anderson, N. H., 261
Angrist, A. W., 466
Anshen, M., 381
Appley, A., 466
Appley, M. H., 172
Ardrey, Robert, 39–41, 57, 242
Arendt, E., 203
Argyle, Michael, 210
Argyris, C., 466
Arnold, Matthew, 443
Aronson, E., 58
Asch, Solomon E., 190, 193
Ayers, A. W., 359

Bacharach, S. B., 288
Backman, C. W., 117
Bacon, Francis, 309
Bales, R. F., 187, 252, 312

Bandura, A., 57
Barrett, J. E., 381
Barthol, R. P., 116
Bass, B. M., 305, 312, 321, 324, 374, 381, 466
Bates, F. L., 36
Bavalas, A., 229
Bawis, R. V., 381
Beach, Barbara H., 262
Beach, Lee Roy, 57, 162, 267, 279
Becker, S. W., 87
Bedeian, A. G., 305
Behling, O., 351
Bell, Cecil H., 180, 399, 412
Bendix, R., 252
Bennis, W. G., 36, 38
Bentham, Jeremy, 149
Berger, J., 252
Berger, S. M., 57
Berkowitz, L., 163, 199
Berkowitz, M. L., 57
Berne, Eric, 401
Biddle, B. J., 252
Birdzell, L. E., Jr., 449
Blake, R., 405
Block, E. B., 305
Bolda, R. A., 381
Boldgett, T. B., 466
Bonham, T. W., 252
Bonner, H., 116

Borecki, T. B., 366
Borgatta, E. F., 187
Borgida, E., 117
Bouchard, T. J., Jr., 87, 203
Boulanger, D. C., 305
Boulding, K. E., 466
Bourgeois, L. J., 35
Bower, G. H., 58
Bowers, D., 389
Brehm, J. W., 203
Bridwell, L. G., 157
Buckley, J. W., 381
Burgess, R. L., 227
Burns, T., 31
Butterfield, D. A., 116
Byham, W. C., 354

Campbell, D. T., 70, 81, 87, 94
Campbell, John P., 163, 172, 375–378, 381
Campion, James E., 338
Carlsmith, J. M., 146–147
Carlson, R. E., 354
Carroll, S. J., 378, 412
Cartwright, D., 312, 385
Carzo, R. J., 36
Case, P. B., 87
Cecil, E. A., 203
Chapanis, A., 227
Chemers, M. M., 317
Chertkoff, J. M., 203
Child, J., 441
Christie, Richard, 116
Chung, K. H., 466
Clark, J. M., 3
Clark, J. P., 423
Cleland, D. I., 36
Coch, L., 241–242
Cofer, C. N., 172
Coffman, T. L., 102
Cohen, A. R., 227
Cohen, B. P., 252
Cohen, S. I., 227
Cook, T. D., 87
Costello, T. W., 117
Cottrell, N. B., 203
Cronbach, L. J., 76, 87
Crutchfield, R. S., 193
Cummings, L. L., 147, 203, 274, 354
Cummings, T. G., 393
Cyert, R. M., 279

Dahl, R. A., 281
Dahle, T. L., 214
Dalton, G. W., 305

Dansereau, F., 321
Darwin, Charles, 14, 40
Davis, J. H., 273
Davis, K., 227
Davis, Louis E., 146, 396
Dean, L. R., 87
Dearborn, D. C., 104
Delbecq, A. L., 274, 279
Delprato, D. J., 82
Denhardt, R. B., 441
Dessler, G. A., 320
Dickson, W. V., 21
Diener, E., 106
Dill, W. R., 13
DiVesta, F. J., 204
Dossett, Dennis L., 371, 424
Drucker, Peter F., 404, 466
Dunnette, Marvin D., 87, 111, 140, 163, 172, 216, 252, 279, 301, 354, 356, 375–378, 466

Eagly, A. H., 147
Ebert, R. J., 261
Eddy, W. W., 392
Edelberg, W., 116
Effertz, J., 116
Einstein, Albert, 62
Ekman, P., 211
Elbing, A. O., 279
Ellertson, N., 196
Ellul, J., 36
Emery, J. C., 305
Eyring, H. B., 13

Fayol, Henri, 18, 36, 298
Fein, M., 412
Feshbach, N. D., 252
Festinger, L., 126–127, 130, 146
Fiedler, Fred E., 98, 314–319, 371
Filley, A. C., 266, 296
Fineman, S., 413
Finkle, R. B., 354
Fishbein, M., 121, 147
Fleishman, E. A., 324
Fodor, E. M., 305
Ford, Gerald R., 327
Ford, Robert N., 394, 398–399
Fox, W. M., 381
Fredericksen, N., 370
Freedman, J. L., 57, 147
Freize, I., 100
French, J. R. P., Jr., 241, 242, 285, 354, 441
French, W. L., 164, 412
Friesen, W. V., 211

Fromkin, H. L., 87
Fulmer, R. M., 463

Gagne, R. M., 58, 381
Galbraith, John Kenneth, 466
Gamboa, V., 172
Gardner, B. T., 58
Gardner, R. A., 58
Garson, Barbara, 147
Geis, F., 116
Gemmell, G. R., 116
Ghiselli, E. E., 116
Gibb, C. A., 324
Giglioni, G. B., 305
Golembiewski, R. T., 397
Goodacre, D. M., 364
Goodale, J. G., 397
Goodman, P. S., 366
Gormly, J., 116
Gouldner, A. W., 252
Graen, G., 252, 321
Gray, I., 366
Gregory, P., 196
Greiner, L. E., 413
Guetzkow, H., 227
Guion, R. M., 354
Gunderson, M., 381
Gustafson, D. H., 274

Hackman, J. R., 172, 199–200, 387, 398, 406, 413
Hage, J., 227
Hall, J., 279
Hall, R. H., 423
Hall, W. K., 305
Hamblin, R., 188
Hamner, W. C., 354
Harare, O., 354
Hare, A. P., 252
Hare, M., 203
Harlow, H. F., 155
Harmon, M., 425
Harrell, T. W., 109
Hart, D. K., 441
Hebb, D. O., 58
Heider, Fritz, 99, 125, 132
Heinrichs, J. R., 356
Heisler, W. J., 116
Heller, R. A., 423
Hellriegel, David, 389
Helmstadter, G. G., 87
Hemphill, J. K., 324
Heneman, H. G., Jr., 351
Heneman, H. G., III, 351
Herbert, T. T., 413

Herskovits, J. J., 94
Herzberg, Frederick, 90, 159, 172, 396, 398–399, 413
Hickson, D. J., 36, 431
Hilgard, E. R., 58
Hill, W. F., 58
Hilles, R., 397
Hilliman, W., 250
Himmelfard, S., 147
Hinings, C. R., 431
Hobbes, Thomas, 417
Hollander, E. P., 194, 324
Hollman, R. W., 412
Holzbach, R. L., Jr., 204
House, R. J., 234, 260, 296, 318–319, 377
Hovland, C. I., 87, 147
Howard, Ann, 339
Howell, W. S., 227
Huber, G. P., 203
Hulin, Charles L., 122–123
Hull, C. L., 150
Hull, Raymond, 330, 340
Hunt, J. G., 320
Hunt, R. G., 36
Huse, E. F., 413

Ilgen, D. R., 102
Ingersoll, V. H., 378
Israel, J., 441
Ivancevich, J. M., 305, 378, 397

Jacobson, M. B., 116
Janis, Irving L., 197
Jaques, E., 172
Jeanneret, P. R., 387
Jerdee, T. H., 102, 117
Julian, J. W., 324

Kaguo, M. S., 397
Kahn, H., 466
Kahn, R. L., 252, 312, 321
Kaplan, A., 87
Karlins, M., 102
Kartol, K. M., 116
Kast, F. E., 36
Katz, D., 252, 312, 321
Kavcic, B., 426
Kay, E., 354
Kelley, Harold H., 99–100, 282
Kelman, H. C., 87
Kendall, Lorne M., 122–123
Kerlinger, F. N., 87
Kerr, N., 273

Kerr, S., 266, 296
Kerr, W. A., 142
King, A. S., 409
Kinne, S. B., 172
Kintz, B. L., 82
Kipnis, D., 291
Klaw, S., 381
Kleemeier, Robert W., 329
Knowles, H. P., 441
Kogan, N., 117, 204
Koontz, H., 463
Koppelmeier, G., 142
Korman, A. K., 324, 354
Krishnan, R., 270
Kukla, A., 100
Kunin, T., 123

La Piere, Richard T., 124
Larson, L. L., 320, 321, 324
Latham, Gary P., 165, 167–168, 172, 342, 346, 413, 424
Lawler, E. J., 288
Lawler, Edward E., III, 27, 123, 163, 172, 204, 301, 351, 354, 375–376, 399
Lawrence, P. R., 31, 430
Lawshe, C. H., 381
Lazarus, R. S., 117
Leavitt, H. J., 13, 213, 305, 466
Lefcourt, H. M., 305
Lehman, E. W., 441
Level, D. A., 214
Levitt, T., 450
Lewin, Kurt, 282
Lichtenstein, S., 261
Lieberman, S., 231
Likert, R., 23, 38, 312, 324, 388
Lindzey, G., 58
Linton, R., 252
Lipset, S., 252
Lirtzman, S. I., 234
Locke, Edwin A., 140, 164–165, 413
Longenecker, J. G., 36
Longfellow, Henry Wadsworth, 59
Lorenz, Konrad, 40, 58
Lorsch, J. W., 31, 430
Lott, A. J., 204
Lott, B. E., 204
Lowell, James Russell, 49

McBride, D., 196
McCallister, D. W., 35
McClelland, David C., 154–156
McClintock, C. G., 203
McCormick, E. J., 354, 387

MacCrimmon, K. R., 279
McDonald, J., 296
McGehee, W., 381
McGrath, J. E., 87
McGregor, D., 23, 38, 90, 158–159, 311–312
McGuigan, F. J., 81
Machiavelli, Niccolo, 115–116
McQuade, Walter, 147
Magnusen, K. O., 30
Maier, A., 381
Maier, N. R. F., 269, 338, 381
Mann, M., 203
Manners, G. E., 204
March, J. G., 227, 279, 283
Marrett, C., 227
Martin, N. H., 305
Maslow, A. H., 90, 156–159
Mayfield, E. C., 354
Mayo, Elton, 16, 21, 79
Mead, Margaret, 38
Mecham, R. C., 387
Mechanic, D., 305
Megginson, L. C., 466
Merton, R. K., 37
Mettee, D. R., 82
Mewborn, C. R., 147
Meyer, H. H., 354
Michael, D. N., 466
Michener, H. A., 288
Miles, R. H., 147
Mill, John Stuart, 149
Miller, L., 188
Minami, T., 321
Miner, J. B., 354
Mischel, Walter, 106
Mitchell, Terence R., 12, 35, 110, 112, 162, 169, 180, 223, 261, 267, 283, 318–319, 342, 371, 393, 399, 408, 417, 424
Moffitt, W., 112
Montagu, M. F. A., 58
Morris, C. G., 199–200
Morris, Desmond, 40
Morris, William, 449
Mouton, J., 405
Murchinson, C., 118
Murdick, R. G., 36
Murray, H. A., 151

Nealey, S. M., 305
Newell, A., 265
Nimkoff, M. F., 57
Nisbett, R. E., 117
Nissen, H. W., 57
Nixon, Richard M., 355
Nord, W. R., 117, 172
Nutt, P. C., 273

Okun, M. A., 204
Oldham, G. R., 387, 398, 413
O'Reilly, John Boyle, 162
Orne, Martin T., 80
Osborn, A. F., 178

Pahl, B., 102
Paine, F. T., 378
Parensky, H., 366
Parham, I. A., 117
Parker, Willard E., 329
Pateman, C., 441
Paterson, D. A., 354
Paul, W. J., Jr., 172
Paulus, P. B., 204
Payne, R. L., 413
Peery, N. S., 417
Perrow, C., 29–31, 36
Persons, C. E., 82
Pertrock, F., 172
Peter, Lawrence J., 330, 340
Peterson, C. R., 279
Peterson, J. E., 466
Petrullo, L., 312, 324
Pettigrew, A. M., 305
Petty, M. M., 147
Pheysey, D. C., 36
Piaget, Jean, 45
Pinto, P. R., 387
Pollard, William E., 283
Porter, G. W., 227
Porter, Lyman W., 27, 123, 172, 204, 216, 223,
    354, 419
Pritchard, R. D., 172
Pugh, D. S., 36, 431
Pursell, E. D., 346

Raia, A. P., 381
Rajaratnam, N., 204
Raven, B. H., 285, 324
Rawls, J., 441
Read, W., 227
Reed, L., 100
Reimnitz, C. A., 305
Reitsema, J., 324
Rest, B., 100
Rice, L. E., 223
Ridgeway, V. F., 354
Rissman, A. K., 273
Rizzo, J. R., 234
Roach, D., 147
Roberts, K. H., 216, 223
Robertson, K. B., 172
Roethlisberger, F. J., 21
Rogers, R. W., 147

Rokeach, M., 117
Rose, J. S., 423
Rosen, B., 102, 117
Rosenbaum, R. M., 100
Rosenberg, M. S., 227
Rosenthal, Robert, 79, 82
Rosenzweig, J. E., 36
Rosner, M., 426
Ross, J. E., 36
Rowe, A. J., 279
Runkel, P. J., 87
Russell, Bertrand, 281

Sales, S. M., 252, 324
Salipante, P. F., 366, 393
Sandler, B. E., 413
Sarason, Irwin G., 106
Saunders, D. R., 370
Saxberg, B. O., 441
Schachter, S., 155, 196
Scharde, K. W., 117
Scheibe, K. E., 279
Schein, E. H., 356
Schkade, J. T., 204
Schmidt, F. L., 354
Schriesheim, C., 351
Schwab, D. P., 147, 351, 354
Schwartz, R., 81
Scott, W. G., 9, 12, 37, 164, 417, 419, 463
Seaman, J., 87
Sears, D. O., 57, 147
Sechrest, L., 81
Secord, P. F., 117
Segall, M. H., 94
Seligman, D., 455
Seta, J. J., 204
Severeid, Eric, 406
Shappe, R. H., 82
Shartle, C. L., 312
Shaw, M. E., 117, 204, 220
Sheridan, J. E., 147
Short, L. E., 413
Shuler, R. S., 235
Shull, F. A., 274
Simon, H. A., 104, 265, 273, 279
Sims, J. H., 305
Sirota, D., 413
Skinner, B. F., 167, 172
Slater, P. E., 187
Slocum, J. W., Jr., 147, 389
Slovic, R., 261
Smith, Adam, 14
Smith, Patricia C., 122–123
Smith, Ronald E., 106
Smyser, C. M., 110, 320
Soelberg, P. O., 279

Solem, A., 381
Sommer, R., 204
Southey, Robert, 148
Stalker, G. M., 31
Stanley, J. C., 70
Starbuck, W., 417
Staw, B. M., 129
Steers, R. M., 147
Steiner, I., 204
Stieglitz, H., 37
Stogdill, R. M., 308, 312
Stores, A. W., 204
Streufert, S., 87
Sullivan, J. J., 142
Summers, T., 274
Sung, Y. H., 279
Sussman, G. I., 252
Sussmann, M., 273

Tannenbaum, A. S., 292, 426
Taylor, F. V., 58
Taylor, Frederick W., 19, 138, 395
Taylor, J., 389
Taylor, R. N., 111, 279
Telly, C. S., 164
Terborg, J. R., 102
Thayer, P. W., 354, 381
Thibaut, J. W., 282
Thomas, E. J., 252
Thompson, J. D., 28–29, 37, 273
Thompson, P. H., 305
Thompson, W. R., 58
Thoreau, Henry David, 205
Thune, S. S., 296
Tichy, N. M., 402
Toffler, Alvin, 464, 466
Tornow, W. W., 387
Tosi, H. L., Jr., 412
Triandis, H. C., 96, 147, 227, 371
Triandis, L. M., 96
Tuden, A., 273

Umstot, D. D., 399
Utgaard, S. B., 381

Valenzi, E. R., 321
Van de Ven, A. H., 274, 279
Vaughn, J. A., 374, 381
Vianello, M., 426
Vollmer, H. M., 441

von Bertalanffy, Ludwig, 24
Vroom, Victor H., 102, 147, 161, 270–271, 424

Wagoner, C. P., 378
Wahba, M. A., 157
Wall, T. D., 413
Wallach, M. A., 117, 204
Walters, G., 102
Walton, R. E., 383, 466
Ward, B., 370
Warr, P., 393, 413
Waters, L. K., 147
Watson, G., 58
Watson, John, 45
Webb, E., 81
Weber, Max, 16–18, 37
Weed, Stan E., 110, 112, 320
Weick, Karl E., Jr., 163, 218, 375, 376
Weiner, A. J., 466
Weiner, B., 100, 172
Weinstein, A. G., 204
Weisskoff, F. B., 466
Wexley, K. N., 346
Whisler, T. L., 466
White, D. E., 274
White, S. E., 180, 393, 408
Whitehead, T. N., 21
Wiard, H., 172
Wickesberg, A., 214, 227
Wiener, Norbert, 16
Wieser, G., 426
Wildavsky, A., 441
Wirthlin, R. B., 451
Wolfson, A. D., 413
Wolin, S. S., 441
Wood, M. T., 279
Woodward, Joan, 30–31
Wool, Harold, 147
Wright, P., 262

Yanouzas, J. N., 36
Yetton, P. W., 270–271, 424
Yoder, D., 351
Yukl, G. A., 165, 321, 413

Zalkind, S. S., 117
Zander, A. F., 285, 312
Zedeck, S., 354
Zelditch, M., Jr., 252
Zweigenhaft, R. L., 185

SUBJECT INDEX

SUBJECT INDEX

Absences, 142
Achievement motive, 154–155
Administrative management principles, 18
Affiliation motive, 155–156
Applied research, 69–70
Arousal, motivational (*see* Motivational arousal)
Assessment of job candidates, 335–339
Assessment centers, 338–339
Attitude change, 131–136
   characteristics of target, 135
   communication, 132–134
   communicator characteristics, 132
   resistance to, 135–136
   situational factors, 135
Attitude organization and dynamics, 125–131
Attitudes, 118–125
   and behavior, 124–125
   definition of, 118–119
   formation and development of, 120–121
   job (*see* Job attitudes)
   measurement of, 121
   and world of work, 136–143
     causes of favorable job attitudes, 139–142
     consequences of favorable job attitudes, 142–143
Attributions, 98–101

Basic research, 69–70
Behaviorism, 45

Beliefs, 119
Blocks to effective communication, 216–219
   distortion by recipient, 218–219
   distortion by sender, 217–218
   outside factors, 265–266
Bounded-rationality, 265–266
Brainstorming, 177–178

Change, organizational (*see* Organizational change)
Changing organizations, problems in, 406–409
   characteristics of change process, 407
   characteristics of setting, 407
   criticisms about evidence, 408–409
Choice, motivated, 169
Classical theory, 16–20
   principles of, 17
Cognitive complexity, 112–113
Communication, effective (*see* Blocks to effective communication)
Communication model, 206–216
   choice of medium, 213–216
   medium and flow of message, 212–213
   motivation to communicate, 207–209
   verbal and nonverbal cues, 209–212
Communication networks, 220–222
Competence, 154
Computer simulations, 69
Conformity, 190–194

Consistency theories, 125
Contingency approaches, 27–33
  to leadership, 314–321
    contingency model, 314–318
    path-goal approach, 318–321
Contingency model, 314–318
Continuity of growth, 43–45
Control, 298–302
  control systems in use, 300–301
  criteria of, 298–299
  reactions to, 301–302
  strategies of, 299–300
  systems, 292–293
    definition of, 292
Correlational research, 66–68
Curiosity, 154
Current problems in organizations, 454–459
  employment, 454–456
  general lack of commitment, 456–457
  social problems, 457–458

Data gathering, 64–65
Deception, 84
Decision making:
  in groups, 268–275
    contingency models of, 271–274
    delphi technique, 274–275
    nominal group technique (NGT), 274–275
    participation in decision making, 270
    Vroom and Yetton's model, 270–271
  individual (*see* Individual decision making)
Decision-making process, 255–258
  decision phases, 256–257
Delphi technique, 274–275
Demand characteristics, 79–80
Determinants:
  of performance, 327–331
    dated points of view, 328–330
    new ideas, 330–331
  of personality, 107
Dissonance theory, 126–131
  attitude-discrepant behavior, 130
  disconfirmed expectancies, 128–129
  Festinger's model of forced compliance, 130–131
  postdecisional dissonance, 128
Distribution of power, 421–438
  equity, 428
  participation, 423–428
  procedural due process, 428
  tive due process, 422–423
    12
    y, 159

Due process, determinants of, 430–434
  differentiation, 431
    problems of, 431–432
  integration, 432
  political concerns, 432–434

Effective communication, blocks to (*see* Blocks
    to effective communication)
Environmental determinism, 167
Equity theory, 162–164
ERG theory, 158
Ethical considerations, 84
Ethology, 40
Evaluation of training programs, 373–378
  empirical, 374–377
  ethical, 377–378
  theoretical, 374
Expectancy theory, 160–162
Expected-value model, 263–265
Experimental research, 66–68
Experimenter bias, 81–82
Explanation, 65–66
External determinants of behavior versus
    internal determinants, 45–48
External validity, 70

Faces scale, 123
Factors influencing perception, 93–95
Field experiments, 68
Field studies, 68
Flexitime, 396
Forming impressions of others, 95–96

Goal setting, 164–166
Goals, 11
Governance models, 434–439
  dealing with conflict, the question of power
      distribution, 435–436
  systems of governance, 436–439
Group decision making (*see* Decision making, in
    groups)
Group dynamics, 175–183
  group development, 182–183
  group formation, 182
  overview of group variables, 180
  small group, definition of, 175–176
  systems view, 181
  types of groups, 176
Group inputs:
  group structure, 190–199
    interpersonal attraction, 194–199
    social influence and conformity, 190–194

Group inputs:
  personal characteristics, 183
  situational variables, 183–189
    group size, 186–187
    personal space, 184
    reward structure, 188–189
    spatial arrangements, 184–185
    task, 185–186
    territorial variables, 183–184
Groupthink, 197–199

Halo effects, 103
Hawthorne effect, 21–22
Health, 142
Hedonism, 149
Hierarchy of needs, 156–157
Human beings, uniqueness of, 39–43
Human limitations, 48–49
Human-relations approach, 20–24

Individual decision making, 258–268
  beliefs and values, 258–259
  bounded-rationality, 265–266
  contingency models of individual decisions,
    266–271
  expected-value model, 263–265
  processing models, 260–262
Individual differences, 332–333
Instrumental learning, 50–51
  punishment, 50–52
  reinforcement, 50–51
Internal determinants of behavior versus
    external determinants, 45–48
Internal validity, 70
Interpersonal attraction, 194–199

Job analysis, 333–335
Job attitudes, measurement of morale, 122–124
  faces scale, 123
  Job Descriptive Index (JDI), 123
Job challenge, 140
Job Descriptive Index (JDI), 123
Job enrichment, 496

Laboratory experiments, 68–69
"Law of effect," 149
Leadership:
  definition of, 306–307
  emergence, 307–309
  theories of, 309–321
    behavior approach, 311–313

Leadership:
  theories of: functional approach, 313–
    314
    trait approach, 309–311
Learning, 49–54
  definition of, 49–50
  instrumental, 50–51
  in social setting, 52–54
Limitations, human, 48–49
Locus of control, 110–111

Machiavellian personality, 116
Management, 11
Management grid, 405–406
Management principles, administrative, 18
MBO, 403–404
Measurement of personality, 107–108
Measures, unobstrusive, 81
Models, 64
Motivated choice, 160–169
  equity theory, 162–164
  expectancy theory, 160–162
  goal setting, 164–166
  operant conditioning, 166–169
Motivation:
  definition of, 148
  in organizations, 151–153
Motivational arousal, 153–156
  achievement motive, 154–155
  affiliation motive, 155–156
  competence and curiosity, 154
Motive classification systems, 156–160
  Aldefer's ERG theory, 158
  dual factor theory, 159
  Maslow's hierarchy of needs, 156–157
  Theory X and Theory Y, 158–159

Nominal group technique (NGT), 274–275
Norms, 44, 237–242
  and group behavior, 240–242
  properties and characteristics, 238–240
  reference groups, 242

Operant conditioning, 166–169
Organization, 10
Organization development, 390–394
  change techniques, 392–393
  critique of, 394
  definition of, 391
  empirical evaluation, 393–394
  philosophical foundations, 391–392
Organizational behavior, 3–4

Organizational change, 383–386, 443–454
  areas of, 443–454
    attitudes and values, 449–453
    labor force, 444–446
    nature of work and jobs, 448–449
    organizational characteristics, 446–448
    structure and procedures versus process and
      content, 384–385
    what do we change? 385–386
Organizational change process, 386–390
  evaluating change, 390
  identification of causes, diagnostic devices,
    386–389
  implementing change, taxonomy of strategies,
    389
  problem recognition, 386
Organizational change techniques, 394–406
  autonomous work group, 401
  flexitime, 396
  four-day workweek, 396
  job enlargement, 396
  job enrichment, 396
  management grid, 405–406
  MBO, 403–404
  sensitivity training, 401
  T group, 401
  team building, 402
  time and motion studies, 395
  transactional analysis (TA), 401
Organizational problems, possible solutions to,
    459–463
    organizational design, 461–462
    personnel, 459–460
    technology, 461

Path-goal approach, 318–321
Perception, 91–95
  factors influencing, 93–95
  person, 95–105
  selective, 104–105
Performance, determinants of, 327–331
Performance appraisal, 340–347
  appraisal techniques, 341–344
  problems and remedies, 345–347
  purposes, 341
Person perception, 95–105
Personal space, 184
Personality, 46, 105–108
  and behavior, 108–113
  determinants of, 107
  measurement of, 107–108
  __–298
  tion, remedies for, 223–224

Power:
  distribution of (*see* Distribution of power)
  social (*see* Social power)
  in use, 284–292
    dependencies, 287–288
    power resources, 285
    power strategies, 288–289
    reactions to, 289–292
Procedural due process, 428
Programmed instruction, 371
Projection, 104
Punishment, 50–52

Rationality, 9–10, 417–421
  organizational, 418
  political, 418
  principle of, 10
  technical, 418
Reactive effects, 76
Reference groups, 242
Reinforcement, 50–51, 167
Remedies for poor communication, 223–224
Research:
  applied, 69–70
  basic, 69–70
  correlational, 66–68
  design, 70–79
  experimental, 66–68
  types of, 66–70
Research design, 70–79
Response disposition, 93
Response salience, 93
Rewards, systems of (*see* Systems of rewards)
Risk taking, 111–112
Risky shift, 178
Role models, 53–54
Role relationships, 230–237
  remedies for role problems, 236–237
  role ambiguity, 234–235
  role conflict, 233–234
  role episode, 232
  role overload, 235–236
Roles, 44, 53

Scientific management, 19
Scientific method, 61–66
Selection, 331–340
  candidate assessment, 335–339
  individual differences, 332–333
  job analysis, 333–335
  validation, 339–340
Selective perception, 104–105
Sensitivity training, 371–373, 401

Simulations, computer, 69
Social facilitation, 177
Social influence and conformity, 190–194
Social power, 281–284
    definition of power, 281–282
    theories of, 282–283
Specialization, 141
Standardization, 19, 141
Status, 242–249
    characteristics of, 243–246
    incongruence, 248–249
    status change, 247–248
    status symbols, 246
Stereotyping, 101–103
Substantive due process, 422–423
Systems of rewards, 347–351
    systems of pay, 349–351
    types of rewards, 348–349
Systems approach, 25–27
    principles of, 25–26
Systems theory, 24–27

Team building, 402
Technologies, 28
Terms, 62–63
Testing, 84
Theories, 63–64
Theory X and Theory Y, 158–159
Time and motion studies, 19, 395
Traditional incentives, 141–142

Training, 356–361
    definition of, 356–357
    kinds of change induced by, 357–358
    principles of learning, 358–360
    understanding training needs, 360–361
Training programs, 361–373
    evaluation of (*see* Evaluation of training
        programs)
    off-the-job training: behavioral programs, 368–
        373
        informational techniques, 366–368
    on-the-job training, 363–365
    training the hard to employ, 365–366
Transactional analysis, 401
Turnover, 142
Types of research, 66–70
    applied, 69–70
    basic, 69–70
    correlational, 66–68
    experimental, 66–68

Unobstrusive measures, 81

Value orientation, 15–16
Values, 11–12, 119

Work samples, 338